Dr R.N. SWANSON teaches in the Department
of Medieval History at the University of
Birmingham.

Studies in Church History

35

CONTINUITY AND CHANGE IN CHRISTIAN WORSHIP

CONTINUITY AND CHANGE IN CHRISTIAN WORSHIP

PAPERS READ AT
THE 1997 SUMMER MEETING AND
THE 1998 WINTER MEETING OF
THE ECCLESIASTICAL HISTORY SOCIETY

EDITED BY

R. N. SWANSON

PUBLISHED FOR
THE ECCLESIASTICAL HISTORY SOCIETY
BY
THE BOYDELL PRESS
1999

First published 1999

A publication of the Ecclesiastical History Society
in association with The Boydell Press
an imprint of Boydell & Brewer Ltd
PO Box 9, Woodbridge, Suffolk IP12 3DF, UK
and of Boydell & Brewer Inc.
PO Box 41026, Rochester, NY 14604–4126, USA
website: http://www.boydell.co.uk

ISBN 0 9529733 4 0

ISSN 0424–2084

A catalogue record for this book is available
from the British Library

Library of Congress Cataloging-in-Publication Data
Ecclesiastical History Society. Summer Meeting (1997: St. Andrews
University)
    Continuity and change in Christian worship: papers read at the
1997 Summer Meeting and the 1998 Winter Meeting of the
Ecclesiastical History Society/edited by R. N. Swanson.
        p. cm. – (Studies in church history, ISSN 0424–2084; 35)
    Includes bibliographical references and index.
    ISBN 0–9529733-4-0 (alk. paper)
        1. Liturgics – History Congresses. I. Swanson, R. N. (Robert
Norman) II. Ecclesiastical History Society. Winter Meeting (1998:
King's College, London) III. Title. IV. Series.
BR141.S84   vol. 35
[BV176]
270 s–dc21
[264'.009]   99-36576

Details of previous volumes are available from Boydell & Brewer Ltd

Typeset by Joshua Associates Ltd, Oxford

This book is printed on acid-free paper

Printed in Great Britain by
St Edmundsbury Press Ltd, Bury St Edmunds, Suffolk

IN MEMORY OF

MICHAEL WILKS

CONTENTS

Preface   xi

List of Contributors   xiii

List of Abbreviations   xvii

Introduction   xxi

Continuity and Change in Early Eucharistic Practice: Shifting
Scholarly Perspectives   1
PAUL F. BRADSHAW

The Song of Songs and the Liturgy of the *velatio* in the Fourth
Century: from Literary Metaphor to Liturgical Reality   18
NATHALIE HENRY

The Carolingian Liturgical Experience   29
DONALD BULLOUGH

Change and Change Back: the Development of English Parish
Church Chancels   65
CAROL F. DAVIDSON

The 'Sample Week' in the Medieval Latin Divine Office   78
R. W. PFAFF

Message, Celebration, Offering: the Place of Twelfth- and
Early Thirteenth-Century Liturgical Drama as 'Missionary
Theatre'   89
BRENDA BOLTON

The Altars in York Minster in the Early Sixteenth Century   104
W. J. SHEILS

'One heart and one soul': The Changing Nature of Public
Worship in Augsburg, 1524–1548   116
PHILIP BROADHEAD

Transcendence and Community in Zwinglian Worship: the
Liturgy of 1525 in Zurich   128
BRUCE GORDON

Evaluating Liturgical Continuity and Change at the
Reformation: a Case Study of Thomas Muntzer, Martin
Luther, and Thomas Cranmer   151
BRYAN D. SPINKS

The *traditio instrumentorum* in the Reform of Ordination Rites
in the Sixteenth Century   172
KENNETH W. T. CARLETON

Expedient and Experiment: the Elizabethan Lay Reader   185
BRETT USHER

Giving Tridentine Worship back its History   199
SIMON DITCHFIELD

From David's Psalms to Watts's Hymns: the Development of
Hymnody among Dissenters following the Toleration Act   227
DAVID L. WYKES

Patristics and Reform: Thomas Rattray and *The Ancient
Liturgy of the Church of Jerusalem*   240
STUART G. HALL (*presidential address*)

The Mirage of Authenticity: Scottish Independents and the
Reconstruction of a New Testament Order of Worship,
1799–1808   261
DERYCK LOVEGROVE

'Shut in with thee': the Morning Meeting among Scottish
Open Brethren, 1840s-1960s   275
NEIL DICKSON

Goths and Romans: Daniel Rock, Augustus Welby Pugin, and
Nineteenth-Century English Worship   289
JUDITH F. CHAMP

'The Rector presents his compliments': Worship, Fabric, and
Furnishings of the Priory Church of St Bartholomew the
Great, Smithfield, 1828–1938   320
MARTIN DUDLEY

Prosper Guéranger O. S. B. (1805–1875) and the Struggle for
Liturgical Unity   333
PETER RAEDTS

A 'fluffy-minded Prayer Book fundamentalist'? F. D. Maurice
and the Anglican Liturgy 345
J. N. MORRIS

A New Broom in the Augean Stable: Robert Gregory and
Liturgical Changes at St Paul's Cathedral, London, 1868–1890 361
PENELOPE J. CADLE

A Broad Churchman and the Prayer Book: the Reverend
Charles Voysey 374
GARTH TURNER

'This Romish business' – Ritual Innovation and Parish Life in
Later Nineteenth-Century Lincolnshire 384
R. W. AMBLER

Continuity and Change in the Liturgical Revival in Scotland:
John Macleod and the Duns Case, 1875–6 396
DOUGLAS M. MURRAY

Anglican Worship in Late Nineteenth-Century Wales: a
Montgomeryshire Case Study 408
FRANCES KNIGHT

'Walking in the light': the Liturgy of Fellowship in the Early
Years of the East African Revival 419
EMMA L. WILD

'Austere Ritual': the Reformation of Worship in Inter-War
English Congregationalism 432
IAN M. RANDALL

Reservation under Pressure: Ritual in the Prayer Book Crisis,
1927–1928 447
IAN MACHIN

Reservation of the Sacrament at Winchester Cathedral,
1931–1935 464
T. E. DAYKIN

'The catechumenate for adults is to be restored': Patristic
Adaptation in the *Rite for the Christian Initiation of Adults* 478
EDWARD YARNOLD

Index 495

Professor Stuart Hall adopted the theme of 'Continuity and Change in Christian Worship' for the conferences held during his Presidency of the Ecclesiastical History Society in 1997–8. The contents of the present volume comprise the eight main papers delivered at the summer conference of 1997 and the January meeting in 1998, and a selection of the communications offered in the summer. The process of choosing the papers for inclusion here has necessitated hard and harsh decisions, to ensure a reasonable chronological balance and a volume which reflects the wide range of issues and approaches adopted in the many communications presented at St Andrews for the July meeting.

The Society wishes to thank the University of St Andrews, especially the staff of John Burnett Hall, for providing a memorable time. As an innovation, the winter meeting of 1998 was held at the Institute of Historical Research in London: the Society is grateful to the Institute and its staff for their assistance for the meeting.

* * *

The death of Professor Michael Wilks in May 1998 deprived the Society of one of its most loyal and dedicated members. He was President in 1986–7, and for many years held office as Treasurer, his reports on the finances being noted for their wit and humour. The dedication of this volume to his memory can be only an incomplete acknowledgement of the Society's debt to him.

Robert Swanson

CONTRIBUTORS

STUART G. HALL (President)
: Honorary Associate Research Professor, University of St Andrews

R. W. AMBLER
: Senior Lecturer in History, University of Hull

BRENDA BOLTON
: Senior Lecturer in History, Queen Mary and Westfield College, University of London

PAUL F. BRADSHAW
: Professor of Liturgy, University of Notre Dame

PHILIP BROADHEAD
: Lecturer in History, Goldsmiths' College, University of London

DONALD BULLOUGH
: Professor Emeritus of Mediaeval History, University of St Andrews

PENELOPE J. CADLE

KENNETH W. T. CARLETON

JUDITH F. CHAMP
: Lecturer in Church History, Oscott College

CAROL F. DAVIDSON
: Assistant Architectural Editor, *Victoria History of the Counties of England*

T. E. DAYKIN
: Vicar of Fordingbridge

NEIL DICKSON
: Research Student, University of Stirling

SIMON DITCHFIELD
: Lecturer in Early Modern European History, University of York

MARTIN DUDLEY
Rector of St Bartholomew the Great, Smithfield

BRUCE GORDON
Lecturer in Modern History, University of St Andrews

NATHALIE HENRY
Lecturer in Early Church History, University of Manchester

FRANCES KNIGHT
Lecturer, University of Wales, Lampeter

DERYCK LOVEGROVE
Lecturer in Ecclesiastical History, University of St Andrews

IAN MACHIN
Professor of British History, University of Dundee

J. N. MORRIS
Vice Principal, Westcott House, Cambridge

DOUGLAS M. MURRAY
Lecturer in Ecclesiastical History, University of Glasgow

R. W. PFAFF
Professor of History, University of North Carolina at Chapel Hill

PETER RAEDTS, SJ
Professor of Medieval History, University of Nijmegen

IAN M. RANDALL
Tutor in Church History and Spirituality, Spurgeon's College, London

W. J. SHEILS
Senior Lecturer in History, University of York

BRYAN D. SPINKS
Professor of Liturgical Studies, Yale University

GARTH TURNER
Rector of Tattenhall

BRETT USHER

EMMA L. WILD

DAVID L. WYKES
Director, Dr Williams's Library, London

EDWARD YARNOLD, SJ
University Research Lecturer, Campion Hall, Oxford

Abbreviated titles are adopted within each paper after the first full citation. In addition, the following abbreviations are used throughout the volume.

ActaSS   *Acta sanctorum*, ed. J. Bolland and G. Henschen (Antwerp, etc., 1643–)

AHR   *American Historical Review* (New York, 1895–)

Annales   *Annales: Economies, Sociétés, Civilisations* (Paris, 1946–)

BAV   Vatican City, Biblioteca Apostolica Vaticana

BL   London, British Library

BN   Paris, Bibliothéque national

CathHR   *Catholic Historical Review* (Washington, DC, 1915–)

CChr. CM   *Corpus Christianorum, continuatio medievalis* (Turnhout, 1966–)

CChr. SL   Corpus Christianorum, series Latina (Turnhout, 1953–)

ChH   *Church History* (New York/Chicago, 1932–)

CIC   *Corpus iuris canonici*, ed. E. Richter and E. Friedberg, 2 vols (Leipzig, 1879–81)

CSEL   *Corpus scriptorum ecclesiasticorum Latinorum* (Vienna, 1866–)

CUL   Cambridge, University Library

Davies,
  Worship, 1   Horton Davies, *Worship and Theology in England, from Cranmer to Hooker, 1534–1603* (Princeton, NJ, and London, 1960)

Davies,
  Worship, 2   Horton Davies, *Worship and Theology in England, from Andrewes to Baxter and Fox, 1603–1690* (Princeton, NJ, 1975)

Davies,
  Worship, 3   Horton Davies, *Worship and Theology in England, from Watts and Wesley to Maurice, 1690–1850* (Princeton, NJ, and London, 1961)

Davies,
  Worship, 4   Horton Davies, *Worship and Theology in England, from*

	Maurice to Martineau, 1850–1900 (Princeton, NJ, and London, 1962)
Davies,	
Worship, 5	Horton Davies, *Worship and Theology in England: the Ecumenical Century, 1900–1965* (Princeton, NJ, and London, 1965)
DNB	*Dictionary of National Biography* (London, 1885–)
EETS	Early English Text Society (London, 1864–)
EHR	*English Historical Review* (London, 1886–)
es	extra series
HBS	Henry Bradshaw Society (London/Canterbury, 1891–)
HistJ	*Historical Journal* (Cambridge, 1958–)
HThR	*Harvard Theological Review* (New York/Cambridge, MA, 1908–)
HWJ	*History Workshop Journal* (Oxford, 1976–)
JBAA	*Journal of the British Archaeological Association* (London, 1845–)
JBS	*Journal of British Studies* (Hartford, CT, 1961–)
JEH	*Journal of Ecclesiastical History* (Cambridge, 1950–)
JFHS	*Journal of the Friends' Historical Society* (London/Philadelphia, 1903–)
JMedH	*Journal of Medieval History* (Amsterdam, 1975–)
JThS	*Journal of Theological Studies* (London, 1899–)
JURCHS	*Journal of the United Reformed Church History Society* (London, 1970–)
LQF	Liturgiewissenchaftliche Quellen und Forschungen (Munster, 1957–)
MGH	*Monumenta Germaniae hictorica inde ab a. 500 usque ad a. 1500,* ed. G. H. Pertz *et al.* (Hanover, Berlin, etc., 1826–)
Cap.	*Leges 2, Leges in Quart 2: Capitularia regum Francorum*
Conc.	*Leges 2, Leges in Quart 3: Concilia*
SRM	*Scriptores rerum merovingicarum*
SRG	*Scriptores rerum germanicarum in usum scholarium*
SS	*Scriptores*
nd	no date
ODCC	*Oxford Dictionary of the Christian Church,* 2nd edn, ed. F. L. Cross with E. A. Livingstone (Oxford, 1974)
os	old series/original series
P&P	*Past and Present: A Journal of Scientific History* (London, 1952–)

PG   *Patrologia Graeca*, ed. J. P. Migne, 161 vols (Paris, 1857–66)

PL   *Patrologia Latina*, ed. J. P. Migne, 217 vols + 4 index vols (Paris, 1841–61)

PRO   London, Public Record Office

PS   Parker Society (Cambridge, 1841–55)

SC   Sources chrétiennes (Paris, 1942–)

SCH   *Studies in Church History* (London/Oxford/Woodbridge, 1964–)

SCH.S   *Studies in Church History: Subsidia* (Oxford, 1978–)

Speculum   *Speculum A Journal of Medieval Studies* (Cambridge, MA, 1925–)

SS   Surtees Society (Durham, 1835–)

ss   supplementary series

Traditio   *Traditio: Studies in Ancient and Medieval History, Thought, and Religion* (New York, etc., 1943–)

TRHS   *Transactions of the Royal Historical Society* (London, 1871–)

ZkT   *Zeitschrift für katholische Theologie* (Innsbruck, 1877–)

*   *   *

Canon law citations are laid out according ot the 'modern form' (see James A. Brundage, *Medieval Canon Law* [London and New York, 1995], app. 1), with quotations from *CIC*.

INTRODUCTION

Worship is the central activity of the Christian community. In its own terms, the Church exists to glorify God as made known in Jesus Christ. For that reason its worship is invariably historical. When Christians assemble, they read again from Scripture, from saints' lives or from homilies sanctified by time, the accounts of God's actions in the past and their duties in the present. They recollect and reiterate in psalms and hymns and prayers, and perhaps above all in sacramental acts, the central historical events they believe to have saving value. This has a double effect. One is radical, that what ought to be done is determined by past criteria: it might be the exact prescriptions or practices of Jesus himself or the New Testament Church, as for many Protestants; it might be the medieval Church as for some reformers in the nineteenth century; or the Church of the first five centuries as for Rattray and some contemporary Roman Catholic reformers. But alongside it goes another and largely inarticulate conservatism: practices are continued because they are what was always done, or because the reformer cannot see any way to do things except in the way he learned it himself.

When the Society adopted the theme of Continuity and Change in Christian Worship for its meetings in July 1997 and January 1998, it was acknowledged to be a vast topic. The gatherings at St Andrews and London produced a very wide range of contributions, high in scholarly competence and originality. The balance (or imbalance) of the present volume reflects not only the temporal spread of the main papers, but the interests of those who volunteered contributions. This has led to a predominance of modern and British material: while certainly broad and amazingly varied, the range of papers selected is by no means comprehensive. Byzantine, Orthodox, and Oriental church traditions are wholly absent, save for incidental references. Apart from one paper on the Rwanda Revival, Africa and South America, where contemporary Christianity flourishes as nowhere else, are absent too. One reason for this is that the study of worship is a practical as well as an historical science. People's interest is engaged, even when they are primarily working as historians, on topics which have a bearing on where worship is or should be today, and our contributors are mostly British. This is, furthermore, a volume of history and not of practical theology. The contemporary scene is consequently not directly in evidence. It is touched upon in the last paper, Edward Yarnold's study of the restored catechumenate in the Roman Catholic Church. We have not, however, considered the effects on worship of new technology in music, lighting, and visual display, or of the cascade of printed worship material from colourful publishers, or the widespread local production from clergy-run computers and copiers, all much in evidence in wealthier western Christianity. Some of what we have written may help believers to find a rational response to such things. But we have been writing history, and how the history is used is outside our brief.

You would expect Protestant leaders to evince the principle that Scripture only, or predominantly, should control the way worship is conducted. But we find Luther, Cranmer, and Muntzer, as Bryan Spinks describes them, continuing features of past practice in public worship. Indeed, Muntzer, socially and ecclesiastically the most revolutionary, turns out to be the most conservative liturgically. Zwingli and his Zurich associates, in Bruce Gordon's exposition, also begin with the framework of the existing mass as they frame their evangelical communion. Such continuity may be either conscious or unconscious. The English monarchs and bishops did not wish to make the break with the past too great when they reformed their ordination rites, as Kenneth Carleton shews: a form of *traditio instrumentorum* remained, even if it now centred upon the Bible. When we come to the Scottish Independents (Deryck Lovegrove) and Open Brethren (Neil Dickson) it is remarkable how the Presbyterian background intrudes and ritualization supervenes. Emma M. Wild describes the immediate and powerful revivalism which overtook the Christian communities of the Balakole, but finds there not only English evangelical features, but social bonding and forms of confession deriving partly from pre-Christian tribal and religious practice.

Some past writers certainly adopted norms for their liturgical reforms which do not stand examination, earnest and scholarly though they were. This is true of Thomas Rattray as I have expounded him: his conviction that an apostolic liturgy could be arrived at by purging the *Liturgy of St James* was rational, but in the last resort fanciful. So was the medieval Catholicism envisaged by the reformists Daniel Rock and Prosper Guéranger in the nineteenth century, as Judith Champ and Peter Raedts respectively shew. Views like theirs, however, and the vision of ancient Christianity recovered, caught the imagination of their century. The impact among Anglicans is illustrated by the contributions of R. W. Ambler and Frances Knight, among Scottish Presbyterians by Douglas M. Murray, and among English Congregationalists by Ian M. Randall. In all cases spiritual renewal goes hand in hand with liturgical reform. In some cases, as in the London churches of St Bartholomew (Martin Dudley) and St Paul's Cathedral (Penelope J. Cadle), reform of worship was part of a more general improvement, architectural, spiritual, moral, and musical. An important climax to such attempts to reform the Church of England's worship was the Prayer Book revision attempted in 1927-9, an episode of major importance now superseded by later more drastic changes. Ian Machin has given a clear, balanced summation, which will serve students well. Timothy Daykin's account of the ritualistic goings-on at Winchester Cathedral afterwards is a helpful accompaniment.

It would however be a mistake to try to force the papers here given into a unity. The reality with which we have to cope is many-sided. Most of the papers simply stand as sound, objective research in their own right. From chapters in this book we learn new facts about the initiation of nuns in the early Church (Nathalie Henry), the shape and structure of English church chancels (Carol F. Davidson), and the missionary use of liturgical drama as Innocent III envisaged it (Brenda Bolton). Both the latter correct current misconceptions about their subjects. Donald Bullough searches recalcitrant medieval texts for evidence of the lay people's part in Carolingian worship, and wrings serviceable water from the stones. New evidence on the making of the breviary is adduced by R. W. Pfaff, and important observations on the running of York Minster before and during the Reformation crisis are set out by W. J. Sheils. Philip Broadhead describes the vicissitudes of a ruling Council at Augsburg trying to unite a Protestant people in worship when the theologians were divided. Brett Usher's miniature on Elizabethan Lay Readers does honour to a class of church servants often wrongly disparaged, then as now. Simon Ditchfield has splendidly described the interweaving of Renaissance historiography with post-Tridentine liturgical reform, and has put history back where leading liturgiologists have denied there was any to be found. David L. Wykes shews that English Dissenting hymnody evolved more gradually, and earlier, than commonly believed. Two papers defy classification. That of Garth Turner on Charles Voysey shews how eliminating the historic element tips over the edge, since Voysey rejected biblical authority and the revelation in Jesus Christ, and is scarcely Christian at all (the Editor seriously doubted whether it could be included under this book's title). Voysey himself, however, could not escape the Anglican forms of worship. He denies the historical in principle, but affirms it in his habits of mind and liturgical writing. The other oddity is F. D. Maurice, whom J. N. Morris shews to have been not quite fluffy-minded, and not a 'Prayer Book fundamentalist'. Maurice's judgements on the Prayer Book, as on the Thirty-nine Articles, changed in response to developing criticism and pastoral considerations. Maurice remains an enigma. Dismissed for heresy by King's College London, he is now the theologian most honoured by that College; abused then and now for turgid obscurity, he commanded and commands admiration, respect, and discipleship because of his grasp of permanent principles in the face of rapid change and ecclesiastical dispute.

A final word goes to Paul F. Bradshaw's opening essay. It demonstrates the way in which the quest of scholars and liturgy-writers for an 'original' norm derived from the New Testament and the early Church has led to bad history-writing. Students of worship must be more open to the material before them and the facts we actually possess. This will mean that, among other things, multiplicity, variety, and debate are not aberrations from an original purity, but the continual accompaniments of serious engagement with the subject. If that is so, this multifarious volume stands in a good tradition. One of the main points of continuity in Christian worship turns out to be the very variety which church-people and scholars alike try to bring to a coherent unity. There is some sort of lesson in that.

Stuart G. Hall

CONTINUITY AND CHANGE IN EARLY EUCHARISTIC PRACTICE: SHIFTING SCHOLARLY PERSPECTIVES

by PAUL F. BRADSHAW

AS a result of the great advances that have been made in liturgical scholarship in the last few decades, we now know much less about early eucharistic worship than we once thought that we did. Indeed, it sometimes appears that if things keep on at their present rate, it is possible that we shall soon find that we know absolutely nothing at all; for a large part of what current research has achieved has been to demolish theories that had been built on unreliable foundations. As this paper will demonstrate, the older consensus that there had existed a large measure of continuity between the eucharistic practices of the various early Christian communities is slowly giving way to the acceptance that there are considerable gaps in our knowledge of the period, and that what evidence there is points more towards variety than towards uniformity of practice.

* * *

Scholars in the eighteenth, nineteenth, and even early twentieth centuries were generally quite confident that they had a clear picture of the pattern of eucharistic worship practised in the first few centuries of the Church's history. They began from the usually unspoken presupposition that in a matter as important as this, Jesus himself – or at the very least the apostles – would have left clear directives which all Christian communities would have followed. One had only to look, therefore, at the texts of eucharistic rites known to us from later centuries, determine what was common to them all, and those elements would be the very ones that had persisted through the earlier centuries for which evidence was so limited, and would ultimately go back to apostolic times. Inconvenient pieces of historical evidence, like that offered by chapters 9–10 of the *Didache*, which describe a ritual meal quite unlike that of all later known eucharistic texts, sometimes forced minor modifications of this theory of mono-linear development to be adopted. It was proposed, for example, that there had once been both a 'private' and a 'public' form of eucharistic celebration, or that two quite different kinds of eucharistic rite from very early times – Jewish-Christian and Pauline, according to Hans Lietzmann's hypothesis – had eventually coalesced. In addition there were always a few scholars who dissociated themselves completely from the whole idea; but the dominant view remained that eucharistic practice had evolved from uniformity to diversity, from a single archetype to the later varied rites of the regional patriarchates of East and West.[1]

As well as professing a strong belief in continuity in Christian worship traditions, such scholars were in effect employing philological rather than historical methods in their work, which is not surprising since most of them had been educated in classical literature rather than as professional historians. They were treating liturgical texts like other ancient manuscripts, comparing variant readings and trying to arrive at the original that lay beneath them all. A similar methodology was also employed by Jewish scholars in their search for the roots of their liturgy.[2] However, as F. L. Cross warned,

> Liturgical and literary texts, as they have come down to us, have a specious similarity. They are written in similar scripts and on similar writing materials. They are now shelved shoulder to shoulder in our libraries and classified within the same system of shelfmarking. . . . But these similarities mask a radical difference. In the first place, unlike literary manuscripts, liturgical manuscripts were not written to satisfy an historical interest. They were written to serve a severely practical end. Their primary purpose was the needs of the services of the Church. Like timetables and other books for use, liturgical texts were compiled with the immediate future in view. Their intent was not to make an accurate reproduction of an existing model.[3]

In other words, liturgical texts are much more prone to emendation than many other sorts of literature because they exist not to preserve antiquity for its own sake but to provide for the current needs of a living Christian community in a specific cultural setting. I would also

---

[1] See Paul F. Bradshaw, *The Search for the Origins of Christian Worship: Sources and Methods for the Study of Early Liturgy* (London and New York, 1992), pp. 131–6.

[2] See Richard S. Sarason, 'On the use of method in the modern study of Jewish liturgy', in W. S. Green, ed., *Approaches to Ancient Judaism: Theory and Practice*, Brown Judaic Studies 1 (Missoula, MO, 1978), pp. 97–172; reprinted in Jacob Neusner, ed., *The Study of Ancient Judaism*, 2 vols (New York, 1981), 1, pp. 107–79.

[3] F. L. Cross, 'Early western liturgical manuscripts', *JThS*, 16 (1965), pp. 63–4.

include within this category literary texts that deal with liturgical matters, for here too copyists or translators were inevitably tempted to bring what the text described into line with contemporary liturgical practice as known to them, since it would have been unthinkable for the customs of their own day not to have been observed in more ancient times.

Liturgical manuscripts are not unique in this respect. They belong to a genre which may be called 'living literature'. This is material which circulates within a community and forms a part of its heritage and tradition but which is constantly subject to revision and rewriting to reflect changing historical and cultural circumstances. It would include such diverse specimens as folk tales, the pseudo-apostolic church orders, and even some scriptural material, all characterized by the existence of multiple recensions, sometimes exhibiting quantitive differences (that is, longer and shorter versions) and sometimes qualitive differences (in other words, various ways of saying the same thing, often with no clear reflection of a single *Urtext*), and sometimes both.[4]

All of this is not to say that philological methods have no part at all to play in the study of early liturgical history, but only that their role is more limited than previous generations of scholars tended to assume. For we are not dealing here with the history of manuscripts in isolation but as tools employed within actual worshipping communities and so subject to all the forces operative in those particular historical contexts.

*   *   *

The attraction to philology as the key that would unlock the secrets of ancient liturgical practice has not been the only false trail that has led to erroneous conclusions being drawn, however. Early in the twentieth century there arose the notion that the development of liturgical rites was governed by certain scientific 'laws' intrinsic to their nature, and hence that through a knowledge of these laws one could determine how rites had arrived at their present state and what their previous forms must have been. This school of thought is most prominently associated with the name of Anton Baumstark and his book *Liturgie*

---

[4] See further Paul F. Bradshaw, 'Liturgy and "living literature"', in Paul F. Bradshaw and Bryan Spinks, eds, *Liturgy in Dialogue* (London, 1994), pp. 138–53.

comparée,[5] although he was not the first person to apply analogies from the world of science to liturgical study, nor the first to make use of the term 'comparative liturgiology'.[6] While it has commonly been assumed that Baumstark's work was inspired by the comparative study of language, Frederick West has shown that the ultimate source of all the comparative sciences was nineteenth-century German biological thought, the comparative anatomy of Georges Cuvier, and the evolutionary theory of Charles Darwin.[7] From here comparative linguists and the other practitioners of the comparative sciences of culture derived both a model and a method. The model was the living organism. The method was systematic comparison and consequent classification on the basis of a supposed line of descent from the origin of the species.

The basic flaw in this approach was a failure to recognize the essential difference between nature and culture: whereas nature is generated genetically, culture is transmitted socially. As the French anthropologist Claude Lévi-Strauss has observed, 'the historical validity of the naturalist's reconstruction is guaranteed, in the final analysis, by the biological link of reproduction. An axe, on the contrary, does not generate an axe.'[8] Since the cultural objects of study were not truly 'organic', they were not in reality subject to the same laws of development as other organisms, and hence the exact analysis and predictive power of the natural sciences was simply not possible in these cases.

Once again, all this is not to deny the value of the comparative approach advocated by Baumstark in helping to reconstruct liturgical history. Indeed, some form of comparison must necessarily be a part of any attempt to bridge the gaps in our knowledge; and a whole school of comparative liturgiologists has subsequently emerged. Their work, however, is much more cautious and sophisticated in its methodology. It proceeds from a close comparison of the similarities *and differences*

[5] Chevetogne, 1940; 3rd edn rev. Bernard Botte, Chevetogne, 1953; English translation: *Comparative Liturgy* (London, 1958).

[6] See Bradshaw, *Search for the Origins of Christian Worship*, p. 58; and also Martin D. Stringer, 'Style against structure: The legacy of John Mason Neale for liturgical scholarship', *Studia Liturgica*, 27 (1997), p. 235.

[7] Frederick Sommers West, 'Anton Baumstark's comparative liturgy in its intellectual context' (University of Notre Dame Ph. D. thesis, 1988); idem, *The Comparative Liturgy of Anton Baumstark*, Alcuin/GROW Joint Liturgical Study 31 (Nottingham, 1995).

[8] Claude Lévi-Strauss, *Structural Anthropology* (New York, 1963), p. 4.

between liturgical practices in different geographical regions, temporal periods, or ecclesiastical traditions to a hypothesis which attempts to account satisfactorily for the origin and development of those practices both in the light of the tendencies already observed in the evolution of other liturgical phenomena and within the context of their known historical circumstances.[9]

* * *

In his classic work, *The Shape of the Liturgy*, first published in 1945, Gregory Dix was one of the severest critics of the school of thought that had attempted to find a single original eucharistic text, and effectively brought about its demise. However, he did not really abandon the single-origin theory altogether, but merely revised it. In his view, the various forms of the Christian eucharist did have a common root, but this was to be sought in the overall structure or shape of the rite rather than in the particular wording of the prayers:

> the outline of the rite – the Shape of the Liturgy – is everywhere most remarkably the same, after 300 years of independent existence in the widely scattered churches. . . . The outline – the Shape – of the Liturgy is still everywhere the same in all our sources, right back into the earliest period of which we can as yet speak with certainty, the earlier half of the second century. There is even good reason to think that this outline – the Shape – of the Liturgy is of genuinely apostolic tradition.[10]

In the years since the publication of his book, Dix's influence has become all-pervasive and his methodology widely followed, even if some of the details of his conclusions would now be challenged. He has thus enabled the traditional theory of a single liturgical archetype to retain its position of pre-eminence in this modified form down to the present day.

Dix's principal concern was with the shape of the eucharistic rite as

---

[9] See especially Robert F. Taft's important studies, 'The structural analysis of liturgical units: an essay in methodology', *Worship*, 52 (1978), pp. 314–29; and 'How liturgies grow: the evolution of the Byzantine divine liturgy', *Orientalia Christiana Periodica*, 43 (1977), pp. 355–78. Both are reproduced in his collection of essays, *Beyond East and West* (Washington, DC, 1984), pp. 151–92.

[10] Gregory Dix, *The Shape of the Liturgy* (Westminster, 1945), p. 5.

a whole and he did not pursue connections between eucharistic prayers themselves beyond what he saw as their shared characteristic of thanksgiving, or more precisely a series of thanksgivings.[11] However, that has not stopped other scholars since then from going further and trying to find some common denominator to link together all later eucharistic prayers to their presumed apostolic and/or Jewish roots, no longer of course seeking verbal parallels but rather structural similarities. Thus a tripartite pattern – usually defined in terms of two thanksgivings and a petition, and alleged to mirror the profile of the Jewish grace after meals, the *Birkat ha-mazon* – has been a popular choice. The most recent exponent of this hypothesis is Enrico Mazza, although he has to exercise considerable ingenuity to make all extant forms fit within this framework.[12] Other scholars, recognizing the difficulties posed by such an approach, have preferred to look instead for an original bipartite structure, encouraged by Cesare Giraudo's contention that the Old Testament prayer form *todah* had such a pattern, composed of remembrance and supplication (anamnesis-epiclesis), into which an embolism explaining the grounds for the act might also be inserted.[13] Thomas Talley in particular, in attempting to do justice to the variety of extant anaphoral structures, has envisaged a quite complex process of development taking place, from an initial bipartite pattern, still visible in some ancient forms, to a later tripartite shape, normally resulting from the prefixing to the prayer of an act of praise for the Creator that culminated in the *Sanctus*.[14]

That scholars have had such difficulty in agreeing among themselves what constituted the original shape of the eucharistic prayer should of itself cause warning signals to sound as to whether what is being sought ever really existed. Why must we assume that eucharistic prayers all belong to the same family and have the same ancestor? Earlier generations were led in this direction because of their belief that Jesus had instituted the eucharist at the Last Supper, and that all

---

[11] Gregory Dix, *The Shape of the Liturgy*, pp. 216–37.

[12] Enrico Mazza, *The Origins of the Eucharistic Prayer* (Collegeville, MN, 1995).

[13] Cesare Giraudo, *La struttura letteraria della preghiera eucaristica* (Rome, 1981). For a critique of the whole idea, see Paul F. Bradshaw, 'Zebah todah and the origins of the eucharist', *Ecclesia Orans*, 8 (1991), pp. 245–60.

[14] See in particular his essays, 'The eucharistic prayer: tradition and development', in Kenneth Stevenson, ed., *Liturgy Reshaped* (London, 1982), pp. 48–64; and 'The literary structure of the eucharistic prayer', *Worship*, 58 (1984), pp. 404–19.

later eucharistic practice would have followed this original blueprint, including the pattern of its prayer. But many contemporary New Testament scholars would not now see the accounts of the Last Supper as historical records of the institution of the eucharist,[15] nor would they see New Testament Christianity itself as homogeneous in character. Diverse forms of primitive Christianity, therefore, are likely to have given rise to diverse forms of community meals, and of patterns of prayer used within them. Some prayers may certainly have exhibited a tripartite structure from early times, others may have been bipartite, while other ancient forms may even have been unitary in construction, consisting of the expression of praise alone,[16] as simple Jewish blessings over items of food appear to have been. And any of these, as Talley has suggested, may have mutated from one shape to another through the addition of a new element to the prayer.

Nor may we assume that Jewish table-prayers must have been the ultimate ancestor of all eucharistic prayers and so provide the common structural bond that binds them together. Not only does there appear to be more diversity in first-century Jewish prayer forms than earlier generations of scholars thought,[17] but we cannot presume that such Jewish patterns of praying would always have predominated at Gentile Christian eucharistic meals, or that meal-prayers would have been the only source on which later Christians would have drawn when seeking appropriate patterns of prayer for the larger and more formal worship assemblies of the fourth century. The Strasbourg Papyrus, for example, which appears to contain an early version of the Alexandrian Liturgy of St Mark, seems remarkably devoid of specific eucharistic reference for a prayer that has supposedly been used in a eucharistic context for several generations, and has much more the

---

[15] For recent contributions to this debate, see John Dominic Crossan, *The Historical Jesus: The Life of a Mediterranean Jewish Peasant* (San Francisco, CA, 1991), pp. 360–7; John Meier, 'The eucharist at the Last Supper; did it happen?', *Theology Digest*, 42 (1995), pp. 335–51.

[16] Geoffrey Cuming, developing a suggestion made by Louis Ligier, put forward this idea in his 'Four very early anaphoras', *Worship*, 58 (1984), pp. 168–72.

[17] See Stefan Reif, *Judaism and Hebrew Prayer: New Perspectives on Jewish Liturgical History* (Cambridge, 1993), pp. 22–87; Tzvee Zahavy, *Studies in Jewish Prayer* (Lanham, NY, 1990), pp. 14–16; Baruch M. Bokser, 'Ma'al and blessings over food: Rabbinic transformation of cultic terminology and alternative modes of piety', *Journal of Biblical Literature*, 100 (1981), pp. 557–74. For variants from what later became the standard Jewish grace, see also Jacob Neusner, *A History of the Jews in Babylonia*, 5 vols (Leiden, 1969, repr. Chico, CA, 1984), I, p. 161 n.3; Moshe Weifeld, 'Grace after meals in Qumran', *Journal of Biblical Literature*, 111 (1992), pp. 427–40.

appearance of a prayer of blessing for creation and general intercession that might originally have belonged to a non-eucharistic context, perhaps that of daily prayer, and was only much later adapted for eucharistic use.[18]

In addition to these doubts about the actual existence of a single archetypal structure from which all later forms of eucharistic prayer are ultimately descended, the nature of the quest itself also adds several significant methodological questions, to which we now turn.

* * *

First, there is the question as to what should be allowed to count, or not allowed to count, as a legitimate link in the chain of evidence for the structure and contents of these prayers. The texts in *Didache* 9–10 provide a very good illustration of this problem. Many scholars earlier this century – among them R. H. Connolly, Gregory Dix, and Joseph Jungmann – excluded these from consideration because they judged them not to be genuine eucharistic prayers but rather table prayers for some other sort of Christian community meal.[19] Even Louis Duchesne, who did regard *Didache* 9–10 as a eucharistic rite, still dismissed it from serious consideration because he thought it had 'altogether the aspect of an anomaly; it might furnish some of the features which we meet with in later compositions, but it is on the whole outside the general line of development both in respect of its ritual and style'.[20] More recently Willy Rordorf has maintained the older point of view, that this church order contains 'not a eucharistic liturgy in the strict sense, but prayers spoken at table before the eucharist proper'; and has claimed that this is 'the most common view today'.[21] The truth is, however, that the majority of scholars in the last thirty years have taken the opposite view, that it is a eucharist, and that therefore

---

[18] See further Paul F. Bradshaw, 'The evolution of early anaphoras', in Paul F. Bradshaw, ed., *Essays on Early Eastern Eucharistic Prayers* (Collegeville, MN, 1997), pp. 5–7. For an English translation of the Strasbourg Papyrus, see R. C. D. Jasper and G. J. Cuming, *Prayers of the Eucharist: Early and Reformed*, 3rd edn (New York, 1987), pp. 53–4.

[19] See for example R. H. Connolly, 'Agape and eucharist in the Didache', *Downside Review*, 55 (1937), pp. 477–89; Dix, *Shape of the Liturgy*, pp. 48 n.2, 90–3; Joseph Jungmann, *The Mass of the Roman Rite*, 2 vols (New York, 1951), 2, p. 12. For a summary of the various scholarly opinions on this question, see Kurt Niederwimmer, *Die Didache* (Göttingen, 1989), pp. 173–80.

[20] Louis Duchesne, *Christian Worship: its Origins and Evolution* (London, 1903), p. 54.

[21] Willy Rordorf, 'The *Didache*', in *The Eucharist of the Early Christians* (New York, 1978), p. 6.

theories about the evolution of eucharistic prayers must take this particular form into account in some way.[22]

Obviously, this major shift of opinion has had a profound effect on the way in which the history of eucharistic prayers is understood, and the same would be true if other pieces of evidence were either included or excluded from the picture. For instance, it has been customary only to give attention to prayers which conform, broadly speaking, to those that later became standard in the mainstream Christian tradition, and to ignore those that have a very different appearance (for example, lack an opening 'praise' section), especially if they are known to us solely from sources that appear to reflect less conventional forms of early Christianity, such as Syrian apocryphal texts.[23] But to pick from the debris of history only those pieces that fit the pre-conceived pattern and to ignore those that do not is to distort the picture. It may well be true that it is the pieces which most closely resemble the later forms that are best able to explain where those particular shapes came from, but they do not necessarily tell the whole story, nor do they accurately portray the situation in the earlier centuries. It would be rather like explaining later Rabbinic Judaism solely in terms of the Pharasaic traditions of the first century: while Pharasaism may have had the greatest influence in shaping what survived the destruction of the Temple, we do not understand Judaism properly or fully if we ignore the Sadducees, Essenes, and other groups within the earlier Jewish world.

Moreover, such an approach has another methodological weakness. It presumes that a sharp distinction can be drawn between 'orthodox' and 'heretical' groups in the Christianity of the second and third centuries, so that the eucharistic practices of the one were totally unlike those of the other. Yet this flies in the face of recent historical scholarship,[24] and indeed differs from the approach taken towards

---

[22] See for example Louis Bouyer, *Eucharist* (Notre Dame, IN, 1968), pp. 115–19; Louis Ligier, 'The origins of the eucharistic prayer: from the Last Supper to the eucharist', *Studia Liturgica*, 9 (1973), pp. 177–8; Mazza, *Origins of the Eucharistic Prayer*, pp. 12–97; Thomas J. Talley, 'The eucharistic prayer of the ancient Church according to recent research: results and reflections', *Studia Liturgica*, 11 (1976), pp. 146–50.

[23] See G. Rouwhorst, 'Bénédiction, action de grâces, supplication: les oraisons de la table dans le Judaïsme et les célébrations eucharistiques des chrétiens syriaques', *Questions liturgiques*, 61 (1980), pp. 211–40; Cyrille Vogel, 'Anaphores eucharistiques préconstantiniennes: formes non traditionelles', *Augustinianum*, 20 (1980), pp. 401–10.

[24] See for example the essays by Rowan Williams, 'Does it make sense to speak of pre-Nicene orthodoxy?', and by Richard Hanson, 'The achievement of orthodoxy in the fourth

early baptismal practice, where Syrian apocryphal texts constitute the principal source for the liturgical traditions of the region.[25] If we are to have a full and proper appreciation of the formation of the so-called 'classical' eucharistic prayers of the fourth century onwards, therefore, we need to cast the net much more widely and draw in all potential sources of evidence from the first three centuries.

* * *

A further methodological presupposition generally espoused by those engaged in the quest for the roots of eucharistic prayers is that what we are looking for is a unified composition. Many later eucharistic texts give the appearance of a seamless whole, flowing from initial dialogue to final doxology, and this is also true of the eucharistic prayer in the so-called *Apostolic Tradition* of Hippolytus. Since this latter text has customarily been dated to the early third century, the conclusion commonly drawn is that by that date, if not earlier still, all eucharistic prayers had a similar form. Many scholars would go further and presume that this had always been the case from earliest times, especially as written prayer-texts seem to have been virtually unknown before then and those responsible for leading public prayer were given liberty to improvise as they wished.

Yet, all these assumptions are highly questionable. Firstly, there are now serious doubts about whether the key piece of evidence in this hypothesis really should be identified as the *Apostolic Tradition* of Hippolytus or whether it does not belong, at least in its present form, to a somewhat later date.[26] Secondly, can we in any case really assume that eucharistic traditions everywhere were marching in step and exhibiting similar characteristics and changes at roughly the same time as each other? What we know of early Christianity in general suggests the opposite: that local churches tended to preserve quite different practices and theologies from one another until the fourth century, when the changed situation of Christianity caused them to begin to

---

century AD', in Rowan Williams, ed., *The Making of Orthodoxy* (Cambridge, 1989), pp. 1–23, 142–56.

[25] See for example Gabriele Winkler, 'The original meaning of the pre-baptismal anointing and its implications', *Worship*, 52 (1978), pp. 24–45; Baby Varghese, *Les onctions baptismales dans la tradition syrienne* (Louvain, 1989).

[26] See further Paul F. Bradshaw, 'Redating the Apostolic Tradition: some preliminary steps', in John Baldovin and Nathan Mitchell, eds, *Rule of Prayer, Rule of Faith: Essays in Honor of Aidan Kavanagh, O. S. B* (Collegeville, MN, 1996), pp. 3–17.

come more into line with one another.[27] Thirdly, improvization rather than the use of a written text does not necessarily mean that the speaker would always deliver a unified and coherent single prayer. After all, those who deliver speeches from notes or from a mental outline often produce a series of relatively unrelated points.

Finally, and most important of all, for those willing to take note of it there is quite a body of evidence to suggest that eucharistic prayers were from the first made up of a number of smaller discrete prayer units, and that only later were connecting phrases inserted to smooth out joints and give the impression of a single continuous whole. Jewish tradition, for instance, knew nothing of a composite blessing over bread and wine, but separate prayers were said over each item of food and drink. Jewish-Christians would surely have done likewise in their eucharistic practice, and even the Jewish grace after meals, the *Birkat ha-mazon*, often alleged to be the parent of Christian eucharistic prayers, is actually made up of three distinct units. So is the equivalent prayer in *Didache* 10 – thanksgiving for the holy name, praise for the gift of food and drink, and a petition for the gathering of the Church – and in each case these units have their own concluding doxological formula ('glory to you for evermore', or some variant of it). Furthermore, even in the account of the eucharist given by Justin Martyr in the middle of the second century, while it seems clear that the bread and cup were brought at the same time to the one presiding over the assembly, it does not follow that a single prayer was then recited over both together. Separate prayers could still have been used, and it may be significant that Justin says that the president 'sends up prayers and thanksgivings to the best of his ability'.[28] Even his next statement that 'the people assent, saying the Amen' could mean that this was done after each prayer-unit and not just once at the very end. The persistence of such separate prayers may also explain the otherwise enigmatic direction in the third-century Syrian *Didascalia Apostolorum* that if a visiting bishop does not wish to accept the invitation to preside over the whole eucharistic offering, he should at least 'say the words over the cup'.[29]

---

[27] See further Paul F. Bradshaw, 'The homogenization of Christian liturgy – ancient and modern', *Studia Liturgica*, 26 (1996), pp. 1–15.

[28] Justin Martyr, *First Apology*, 67.3.

[29] *Didascalia Apostolorum*, 2.58.3. See Michael Vasey and Sebastian Brock, *The Liturgical Portions of the Didascalia*, Grove Liturgical Study, 29 (Nottingham, 1982), p. 16.

Enrico Mazza has not only drawn attention to these two sources in this regard, but has also suggested that the unusual form of the narrative of institution in the later *Sacramentary of Sarapion* – where the account of the ritual of the bread is separated from that of the cup by the petition for the gathering of the Church drawn from *Didache* 9 – may be the remnant of an archaic structure of the eucharistic rite itself, in which a thanksgiving over the bread was followed by this short petitionary prayer and then by a thanksgiving over the cup.[30] In his recent detailed analysis of the *Sacramentary of Sarapion*, Maxwell Johnson has endorsed Mazza's theory.[31]

If this was indeed the pattern that early eucharistic praying once took, it means that the process of adding further components – such as the *Sanctus* and narrative of institution – that we encounter from the fourth century onwards does not represent an alien intrusion into what were formerly unified creations, but is simply continuing a tradition of combining smaller units together that was at the heart of the most ancient compositions. It also means that the connecting links that exist beween parts of these later prayers are unlikely to have belonged to their earliest stratum, but were more probably introduced at a later stage in order to smooth out the original roughness of the juxtaposition of discrete prayer units.[32]

* * *

Thus, if we are not able to say anything with certainty about a common pattern of eucharistic prayer shared by early Christians, is all that we are left with as universal the use of bread and wine within a common structure of a rite? Even this minimal claim will not stand up to close scrutiny. We have already alluded to the trend in modern New Testament scholarship to view primitive Christianity as essentially diverse in character, and to cast doubts on the accounts of the Last Supper as constituting reliable records of the actual institution of the Christian eucharistic meal. This robs of its sure historical foundation

---

[30] Mazza, *Origins of the Eucharistic Prayer*, pp. 59–60, 221–30.

[31] Maxwell Johnson, *The Prayers of Sarapion of Thmuis: A Literary, Liturgical, and Theological Analysis*, Orientalia Christiana Analecta, 249 (Rome, 1995), pp. 224–6.

[32] For example, the phrase in the Strasbourg Papyrus which links the petitionary material in the second half of the prayer to what precedes it, 'over this sacrifice and offering we pray and beseech you', is unlikely to be as old as what follows it, 'remember your holy and only catholic Church . . .', especially when we recall that the petitionary prayer in *Didache* 10 began simply: 'Remember, Lord, your Church . . .'.

Gregory Dix's hypothesis that the fourfold shape of later eucharistic rites – taking bread and wine, giving thanks over them, breaking the bread, and distributing them – evolved from the sevenfold pattern of the Last Supper. But in any case, his assertions that 'with absolute unanimity the liturgical tradition reproduces these seven actions as four', and 'in that form and in that order these four actions constituted the absolutely invariable nucleus of every eucharistic rite known to us throughout antiquity from the Euphrates to Gaul',[33] can only be sustained by very selective use of the evidence.[34]

First of all, there are sufficient signs of the existence in some early Christian communities of a different order altogether, in which cup preceded bread, to discourage us from concluding that bread first and then cup was necessarily always the 'normal' sequence. There is the 'shorter' text of the account of the Last Supper in Luke's gospel attested by a number of manuscripts, where the cup precedes the breaking of the bread and no second cup follows after supper (Luke 22.15–19). There is the passage in I Corinthians 10.16 where Paul mentions the 'cup of blessing' before 'the bread which we break': although some would see this as simply an inversion for rhetorical reasons, others believe that it reflects an actual ritual sequence known to Paul, very likely that of the Corinthian church which he is addressing.[35] And then there is once again the same pattern in *Didache* 9–10. In addition to these well-known texts, Andrew McGowan has recently drawn attention to another apparent instance of the same so-called 'inverted' sequence, in a fragment of Papias preserved in the writings of Irenaeus, and in a concluding footnote he observed that the same order appears to underlie the account of the community supper in the Ethiopic text of the *Apostolic Tradition* of Hippolytus.[36] All these can of course be dismissed – and indeed most of them have generally been dismissed – either as aberrations from so-called mainstream Christianity or as characteristic only of the *agape* and not of the eucharist itself in early Christianity. But the arguments used here are inherently circular: 'We know these can't have belonged to mainstream Christianity because

[33] Dix, *Shape of the Liturgy*, p. 48.

[34] See also the comments of Bryan D. Spinks, 'Mis-shapen: Gregory Dix and the four-action shape of the liturgy', *Lutheran Quarterly*, 4 (1990), pp. 161–77.

[35] For a recent analysis of the text from this latter point of view, see Mazza, *Origins of the Eucharistic Prayer*, pp. 66–97.

[36] Andrew McGowan, '"First regarding the cup . . .": Papias and the diversity of early eucharistic practice', *JThS*, 46 (1995), pp. 551–5.

they are unlike what we have decided mainstream Christianity to have been'; 'We know this can't have been a eucharist because we have decided that in a eucharist bread must always precede cup.'

A second objection to Dix's sweeping assertion is that we cannot assume that wine was used in all early Christian eucharists. Once again, there has been a tendency to relegate evidence for wine-less eucharists to the margins, to the categories of the abnormal and deviant, and so discount it from a consideration of the origins and early history of the 'true' eucharist. Yet, when divorced from *a priori* assumptions of what a proper Christian eucharist must have been like, the evidence is too plentiful to be ignored. In his recent doctoral dissertation, Andrew McGowan has subjected this material to careful analysis.[37] He has noted that not only are there sources in which it is clear that water rather than wine was used, and some where bread alone is mentioned, or bread with other foodstuffs, but in addition a number of early Christian writers – including the authors of some New Testament books – speak of the use of a cup without making reference to its content at all. There has been a natural tendency to interpret this silence in favour of the presence of wine, but this may not be true in every case, especially since there are numerous indications that the use of wine was controversial in early Christianity.

For example, Irenaeus, Clement, and other significant early witnesses to the use of wine all polemicize against the use of water in the cup, which would have been unnecessary were it merely the practice of a few deviant groups. Moreover, the importance attached by Cyprian to the mingling of both wine and water in the cup, while at the same time inveighing against the use of water alone, is suggestive of a deliberate compromise between variant practices rather than merely the continuation of a standard custom in the ancient world, which is the usual explanation advanced by scholars for the practice of the mixed chalice.[38] Indeed, long ago Adolf Harnack made the suggestion,

---

[37] Andrew McGowan, 'To gather the fragments: the social significance of food and drink in early Christian ritual meals' (University of Notre Dame Ph. D. thesis, 1966), forthcoming as *Ascetic Eucharists: Food and Drink in Early Christian Ritual Meals* (Oxford, 1999).

[38] The inclusion in the baptismal rites of some early Christian communities of a washing of the feet in addition to the immersion of the whole body in water appears to be another such liturgical compromise: see further Martin F. Connell, 'Nisi pedes, except for the feet: footwashing in the community of St John's Gospel', *Worship*, 70 (1996), pp. 20–30. The same may also be true of the combination of messianic anointing and water bath (in that order) in early Syrian baptismal practice, for which see the works cited in n.25 above.

which deserves more serious attention than it has ever received, that the references to wine had been interpolated into the accounts of the Christian eucharist in Justin Martyr's *First Apology*, and that the original text had referred to water alone.[39] It is certainly true that the phrase 'water and wine mixed with water' is an odd one for Justin to have used, and it would be truly ironic if the text constantly cited by scholars as the earliest description that we have of the 'conventional' Christian eucharist turns out to have originally been describing one with water alone instead of wine.

From his examination of the wide range of diverse evidence that exists, McGowan reaches the conclusion that quite a number of early Christian groups seem to have used water rather than wine not only for the cup of the eucharistic meal, but also for meals in general, and that this seems to be closely linked to another dietary restriction of a more general kind, the avoidance of meat. He suggests therefore that the rejection of both meat and wine by certain groups of Christians points to a form of asceticism which was based not so much on concern for the purity of the individual body as on marking out their particular group from others around them by the avoidance of all food and drink that was associated with pagan sacrifice.

* * *

The variations in ritual patterns among early Christians that we have traced, in the order and content of their eucharistic rites, are not merely differences in superficial details while the underlying meaning of what they were doing remained constant. Lietzmann and others after him may have tended to oversimplify in their assertions that there were just two types of eucharist in the primitive Church, but at least they rightly recognized that there was more than one.[40] Although

---

[39] Adolf von Harnack, 'Brod und Wasser: Die eucharistischen Elemente bei Justin', in *Über das gnostische buch Pistis-Sophia; Brod und Wasser: die eucharistischen Elemente bei Justin. Zwei Untersuchungen*, Texte und Untersuchungen, 7 (Leipzig, 1891), pp. 115–44.

[40] Hans Lietzmann, *Mass and Lord's Supper: A Study in the History of the Liturgy* (Leiden, 1979), pp. 193–208. Among variations of this duality hypothesis, see Oscar Cullmann, 'The meaning of the Lord's Supper in primitive Christianity', in O. Cullmann and J. Leenhardt, eds, *Essays on the Lord's Supper* (London, 1958), pp. 5–23; A. J. B. Higgins, *The Lord's Supper in the New Testament* (London, 1952), pp. 56–63; Eduard Schweizer, *The Lord's Supper According to the New Testament* (Philadelphia, PA, 1967), pp. 56–63; Xavier Léon-Dufour, *Sharing the Eucharistic Bread* (New York, 1987), pp. 90–101; Bernd Kollman, *Ursprung und Gestalten der frühchristlichen Mahlfeier* (Göttingen, 1990), pp. 142–52; and Gerard Rouwhorst, 'La Célébration de l'Eucharistie dans l'église primitive', *Questions liturgiques*, 74 (1993), pp. 89–112.

much further research is still required in this area, the evidence does not allow us to conclude that originally only a Jewish-Christian thanksgiving meal and a Gentile-Christian sacrificial memorial of the death of Christ existed, and that these two types of rite very quickly coalesced into a single composite form. On the contrary, significant variations in meaning as well as in structure seem to have persisted for some considerable time.

The sacrificial motif in particular is made up of a number of quite distinct strands that are gradually woven together in later sources but appear to have had an independent existence in earlier centuries. The idea that praise and thanksgiving constitute the Christian sacrifice in the eucharist, the notion that bread and wine are the gifts that are offered to God in the celebration, and the concept of the eucharistic rite as being a memorial of the sacrifice of Christ can all trace their origin to the first or second centuries; but they are at first quite separate concepts existing in parallel to one another that only from the third century onwards begin to be combined.[41]

Moreover, while it was frequently changes in the understanding of what the eucharist meant that brought about some modification in the structure of the rite or the wording of its prayers – on the principle of form following function – it also appears that sometimes the reverse may have been the case, that the form that the rite took altered the way that it was understood. In particular, this may be true of the emergence of the belief that the eucharist was a propitiatory sacrifice. Scholars have usually taken the statement in the *Mystagogical Catecheses* attributed to Cyril of Jerusalem in the fourth century, that 'we believe that [the souls of the departed] will obtain the greatest help if we make our prayers for them while the holy and most awesome sacrifice is being offered',[42] as the explanation for how eucharistic prayers came to include a wide range of objects of intercession, for the living as well as the departed, rather than just petition for the communicants, which is all that is found in some ancient texts. It was the idea of the eucharist as a sacrifice, it was thought, that led to the idea that it could be offered

---

[41] See further Robert J. Daley, *The Origins of the Christian Doctrine of Sacrifice* (Philadelphia, PA, 1978); R. P. C. Hanson, *Eucharistic Offering in the Early Church* (Nottingham, 1979); Kenneth W. Stevenson, *Eucharist and Offering* (New York, 1986); and Frances M. Young, *The Use of Sacrificial Ideas in Greek Christian Writers from the New Testament to John Chysostom* (Cambridge, MA, 1979).

[42] *Mystagogical Catechesis* 5.9. English translation from Edward Yarnold, *The Awe-Inspiring Rites of Initiation* (Slough, 1971), p. 92.

for others, which in turn led to the introduction of intercessions into the eucharistic prayer itself rather than at the earlier point in the rite after the ministry of the word that had been their original home. The Strasbourg Papyrus, however, suggests an alternative hypothesis. We have proposed earlier that the complete absence of any specific eucharistic reference in this prayer implies that it was originally used in a non-eucharistic context and only much later drafted into eucharistic usage. It may well be, therefore, that it was the adoption of prayers like this, already containing a substantial block of intercessory material, that helped to give rise to the idea of the eucharist as a propitiatory sacrifice, and not the other way around.

* * *

Thus what emerges from our survey of recent trends in the scholarship surrounding the origins and early history of the Christian eucharist is that the older vision of a broad continuity of thought and practice running from apostolic times through to the fourth century is slowly beginning to give way to a radically modifed perspective. This paradigm shift has come about to some extent as a consequence of the discovery of new data, but much more through the reinterpretation of existing evidence, and above all through the admission into the argument of testimony that at one time would have been dismissed or explained away. Once we cease to define what constitutes a legitimate eucharist solely by arbitrarily imposed criteria and are prepared to take into account all known examples of early Christian ritual meals, then a very different picture is revealed, one in which considerable diversity of practice and theology reigned. Only very gradually did a process of increasing standardization occur, sometimes by excluding from orthodox circles certain forms of celebration altogether; sometimes by tolerating them as features of the *agape* and other kinds of community meal but not as part of eucharistic practice as such; and sometimes by combining them with what was seen as the emerging mainstream pattern, as we have noted in the case of the mixed chalice. Thus, while the notion of continuity has tended to dominate the thinking of modern scholars, it was on the contrary change that marked the practice of the ancients.

University of Notre Dame,
Indiana, USA

THE SONG OF SONGS AND THE LITURGY OF THE *VELATIO* IN THE FOURTH CENTURY: FROM LITERARY METAPHOR TO LITURGICAL REALITY

by NATHALIE HENRY

JEROME and Ambrose often quote from the Song of Songs in their ascetic treatises. The writings of Ambrose on virginity contain no fewer than 130 quotations from or allusions to the poem.[1] Jerome's letter 22 to the young virgin Eustochium includes around thirty references to it.[2] It seems paradoxical for the Fathers to use the erotic images of the Song of Songs to encourage young women to keep their virginity.[3] How can we explain this phenomenon?

Were the Fathers simply seduced by the nuptial images of the poem? If so, Ambrose and Jerome were not the first. Before them Methodius of Olympus and Athanasius had already applied the Song of Songs to virginal life: Methodius in his *Symposium* and Athanasius in his letters to virgins.[4] Another possibility is that Ambrose and Jerome

---

[1] The writings of Ambrose on virginity include the following works: *De virginibus* (year 377), *De virginitate* (*c.*377/8), *De institutione virginis* (*c.*391/2), *Exhortatio virginitatis* (393). The Latin text of these works together with an Italian translation and abundant footnotes can be found in *Verginità e vedovanza*, ed. F. Gori, Biblioteca Ambrosiana, 14, 2 vols (Rome, 1989): 14/1 includes *De virginibus* and *De viduis*; 14/2 contains *De virginitate*, *De institutione virginis*, and *Exhortatio virginitatis*.

[2] Jerome, *Letter 22*, in *Sancti Eusebii Hieronymi Epistulae*, I. Hilberg, ed., 3 vols, CSEL, 54–6 (Vienna and Leipzig, 1910–18), I, pp. 143–211. English translation in F. A. Wright, *Select Letters of St. Jerome*, Loeb Classical Library (London, 1975), pp. 65–159.

[3] See J. Kelly, *Jerome* (London, 1974), p. 103: 'it is ironical to reflect that, in urging a young girl like Eustochium to crush the physical yearnings of her nature in the effort to surrender herself the more completely to Christ, he should feed her fantasy with such exciting images'.

[4] The Greek text of Methodius's *Symposium* is edited by H. Musurillo in SC, 95 (Paris, 1963). English translations of Athanasius' letters to virgins can be found in D. Brakke, *Athanasius and the Politics of Asceticism* (Oxford, 1995), pp. 274–302. These are translations of the Coptic and Syriac versions through which the letters are known to us. Athanasius quotes abundantly from the Song of Songs in his letters to virgins. It is possible that Ambrose did the same under his influence and that Jerome later imitated Ambrose in his application of the poem to Christian virgins. In letter 22 Jerome mentions Ambrose's treatise *De virginibus* (letter 22, 22). He had read the work and thought highly of it. On the similarities between Athanasius, Ambrose, and Jerome see Y.-M. Duval, 'L'originalité du *De virginibus* dans le mouvement ascétique occidental: Ambroise, Cyprien, Athanase', in Y.-M. Duval, ed., *Ambrose de Milan* (Paris, 1974), pp. 9–66.

quote from the Song of Songs because the poem was used in the consecration of virgins in their day. This is the question which is discussed below.[5]

Very little is known about the consecration of virgins before the fourth century. The oldest statement on the subject is found in the *Apostolic Tradition* of Hippolytus of Rome. Alluding to other consecrations which feature the laying-on of hands, he writes: 'Hands shall not be laid upon a virgin, for it is her personal choice alone that makes her a virgin.'[6] This shows that at the beginning of the third century the virginal vow was probably ratified by some kind of benediction or ceremony (public or private); but nothing allows us to come to any conclusion on the nature of the rite and its content.[7] In fact we have to wait until the end of the fourth century to find actual accounts of consecration ceremonies. They are to be found in the works of Jerome and Ambrose. In his letter 130 (dated 414) Jerome evokes the consecration of Demetrias, a Roman aristocratic lady.[8] In the *De virginibus* (written in 377) Ambrose describes Marcellina, his sister, receiving the veil from the hands of the pope in St Peter's church.[9] Furthermore, the *De institutione virginis* of Ambrose is a homily given in the year 391 or 392 for the consecration of the young Ambrosia, the grand-daughter of Eusebius (a friend or relative of Ambrose). The work ends with a beautiful prayer which constitutes an important document on the liturgy of the consecration of virgins at the end of the fourth century in Milan.

The patristic texts have been compared with the prayer for the consecration of virgins found in the Leonine Sacramentary, the earliest surviving book on Roman liturgy (see Table). The Leonine Sacramentary exists in a single manuscript preserved in the Chapter Library at Verona. The manuscript is dated to the early seventh century, but it probably contains compositions of Pope Leo I and other material of the fifth and sixth centuries. The prayer pronounced in the consecration of

---

[5] This question is briefly discussed in A.-M. Pelletier, *Lectures du Cantique des Cantiques* (Rome, 1989), pp. 164–7. She is extremely cautious, writing (p. 167): 'Les divers textes sur la virginité . . . interdisent de répondre de manière trop rapide et trop tranchée.'

[6] Personal translation from Hippolytus of Rome, *Apostolic Tradition*, 12: *Hippolyte de Rome, La tradition apostolique, d'après les anciennes versions*, ed. B. Botte, SC, 11bis, 2nd edn (Paris, 1984), p. 68.

[7] For a complete analysis of the passage see René Metz, *La Consécration des vierges dans l'Eglise romaine* (Paris, 1954), p. 77 n.1.

[8] Jerome, *Letter 130*, 2: Hilberg, *Sancti Hieronymi Epistulae*, 3, pp. 176–7.

[9] Ambrose, *De virginibus*, III, 1–14.

Comparative table: Leonine Sacramentary and patristic texts

1 7th-century manuscript/5-6th century material	2 Date: 391/392	3 Date: 414
Leonine Sacramentary, mense septembri, XXX: *Sacramentarium Leonianum*, ed. C. L. Feltoe (Cambridge, 1896), pp. 139–40. Respice Domine propitius super has **famulas tuas** ut virginitatis sanctae propositum quod te inspirante suscipiunt te gubernante custodiant per. Deus, castorum corporum benignus habitator, et incorruptatum Deus amator animarum [...] agnovit Auctorem suum beata virginitas et aemula integritatis angelicae Illius **thalamo** Illius **cubiculo** se devovit qui sic perpetuae virginitatis est sponsus quemadmodum perpetuae viriginitatis est Filius.	Ambrose, *De institutione virginis 107:* F. Gori, *Verginità e vedovanza*, 2, p. 186. Te quaeso ut tuearis hanc **famulam tuam,** quae tibi servire, tibi animam suam, tibi integritatis suae studium dicare praesumpsit. Quam sacerdotali munere offero, affectu patrio commendo, ut propitius et praesul conferas ei gratiam, quo **caelestium thalamorum** immorantem adytis sponsum excutiat, mereatur videre, introducatur in **cubiculum** [cf. S. of S. 1,4] dei sui regis, mereatur audire dicentem sibi: *Ades huc a Libano, sponsa, ades huc a Libano; transibis et pertransibis a principio fidei* [S. of S. 4,8]; ut transeat saeculum, ad illa aeterna pertranseat.	Jerome, *Epistula 130*, 2: Hilberg, *Sancti Hieronymi Epistulae*, 3; pp. 176–7 [to Demetrias, an aristocratic lady of Rome who has recently been consecrated]. Scio quod ad imprecationem pontificis, flammeum virginale sanctum operuerit caput; et illud apostolicae vocis insigne, celebratum sit: *Volo autem vos omnes virginem castam exhibere Christo* [II Cor. 11,2] [...] **Unde et ipsa sponsa laetatur ac dicit:** *Introduxit me rex in cubiculum suum* [S. of S. 1,4 Septuagint]. **Sodaliumque respondet chorus:** *Omnis gloria filiae regis intrinsecus* [Ps.44,14].

virgins is commonly known as the *Deus castorum corporum*. It is reused in later liturgical works such as the Gelasian Sacramentary, the *Missale Francorum*, the Romano-Germanic Pontifical, and the Roman Pontificals of the Middle Ages.[10]

In the three texts reproduced in the table, the taking of the veil is described as the entry into a wedding chamber.[11] The word 'cubiculum' is present in all three texts: in the prayer of Ambrose, in the prayer of the Leonine Sacramentary, and in Jerome's account of Demetrias's consecration. In Jerome's account the word apppears in a quotation from Song of Songs 1.4. The similarity between the patristic texts and the prayer of the Leonine Sacramentary is striking. It suggests that there must have existed already in the fourth century, at least in the Western Church, a set consecration prayer very close to the one in the Leonine Sacramentary. The existence of such a prayer is attested in a letter of Pope Siricius (384–99):

> If a virgin already consecrated to Christ, who has given a public testimony of her integrity, and who has received the veil from a priest who has pronounced upon her the benediction prayer; if such a virgin secretly defiles herself or, in order to conceal her crime, calls the adulterer her spouse, *taking the members of Christ and making them the members of a prostitute* (1 Cor. 6.15); and if in consequence of her actions she who was once the bride of Christ is now called the bride of a man; in the case of such a woman, there are as many causes [for dismissal] as offences. The intention to keep integrity has been changed; the veil is lost; the initial fidelity is corrupted and the woman is dismissed on grounds of invalidity.[12]

---

[10] H. A. Wilson, ed., *The Gelasian Sacramentary* (Oxford, 1894), c. CIII, p. 157; *Missale Francorum* in L. C. Mohlberg, ed., *Rerum ecclesiasticarum documenta*, Series Maior Fontes II (Rome, 1957), pp. 14–16; C. Vogel and E. Elze, *Le Pontifical romano-germanique du dixième siècle*, Studi e testi, 226 (Vatican City, 1963), p. 40; M. Andrieu, *Le Pontifical romain au moyen-âge*, 1, Studi e testi, 86 (Vatican City, 1938), pp. 157–8.

[11] See also Athanasius, *Second Letter to Virgins*, 31 in Brakke, *Athanasius and Asceticism*, p. 302: 'When you have found him, hold on to him, and do not leave him until he brings you into his bedroom. He is your bridegroom. He is the one who will crown you. It is he who is preparing the wedding garment for you.' The image of the wedding chamber is already used by Athanasius to describe the mystical union between Christ and the Christian virgin. The second letter to virgins does not contain any liturgical references. Images from the Song of Songs seem to be used as simple literary metaphors without liturgical resonance.

[12] S. Siricius papa, *Epistola X, seu canones synodi romanorum ad gallos episcopos*, PL 13, c. 1, col. 1182C: 'Si virgo velata jam Christo, quae integritatem publico testimonio professa, a

21

The existence of a set prayer inspired from the Song of Songs (in the style of that found in the Leonine Sacramentary) would explain why the Fathers so often quote from Solomon's poem in their writings on virginity: their works echo the prayer which was used in the consecration of virgins. It is possible that the person who composed the prayer (maybe Ambrose) took his inspiration from the biblical poem.

This would be one possible explanation for the quoting of the Song of Songs by the Fathers in their works on virgins. A second explanation could be that verses from the Song of Songs were sung by the virgin and her companions during the consecration ceremony. In letter 130 (see column 3 in the table above), Jerome describes the consecrated virgin singing Song of Songs 1.4. Her companions reply with Psalm 44, verse 14. Verses from the same biblical books are found in the antiphons of a liturgical work called the *Liber responsalis* attributed to Gregory the Great, which survives in a single extant manuscript at the Bibliothèque nationale in Paris.[13] The office for the vigil of a virgin saint (found under the title *In vigilia unius virginis, ad vesperas* in the *Liber responsalis*) includes the singing of three antiphons based upon the words of the Song of Songs:

> First nocturn: 'O quam pulchra est' (based on S. of S. 7.6)
> Third nocturn: 'Ista est speciosa' (based on S. of S. 1.5, Septuagint)
> 'Ista quae ascendit' (based on S. of S. 3.6)

It is worth mentioning that the text of the Song of Songs used for these antiphons does not seem to be that of the Vulgate but that of an old Latin version.[14] This is very important because it shows the antiquity of the antiphons of the *Liber responsalis*. The author of this work drew on old liturgical material which was in circulation before the time of Gregory the Great. Two of the antiphons found in the office of a virgin

sacerdote *prece* fusa *benedictionis* velamen accepit, sive incestum commiserit furtim, seu volens crimen protegere, adultero mariti nomen imposuit, tollens membra Christi, faciens membra meretricis [1 Cor. 6.15]; ut quae sponsa Christi fuerat, conjux hominis diceretur: in huiusmodi muliere quot sunt causae, tot reatus; integritatis propositum mutatum, velamen amissum, fides prima deprivata, atque in irritum devocata.'

13 MS Lat. 17436. Migne gives a basic edition of the text in *PL* 78, cols 828–9 (office of virgins).

14 See nn. 7, 33 of my critical edition of the *Liber responsalis* of Gregory the Great; below, pp. 24, 27.

saint of the *Liber responsalis* can also be found in the *Passio* of St Agnes, which is a fifth-century work falsely attributed to Ambrose.[15]

It can be suggested that the Song of Songs was sung during the consecration of virgins at the end of the fourth century in the Western Church. The virgin would have been surrounded by her companions and they would all have sung antiphons. Some of these antiphons would have been based on the words of the Song of Songs. The singing of antiphons for the consecration of virgins is attested in later liturgical documents: in the Romano-German pontifical and the Roman pontificals of the Middle Ages. The consecration ceremony in the pontifical of William Durandus (dated to the end of the thirteenth century) includes the singing of one antiphon based upon the words of the Song of Songs.[16]

In their ascetic treatises Methodius of Olympus and Athanasius used the Song of Songs as a literary metaphor to describe the life of Christian virgins. Perhaps at the end of the fourth century, what had been previously only a metaphor became a liturgical reality with the establishment of a ceremony inspired by the veiling of married women and accompanied by a prayer reminiscent of the Song of Songs, and by the singing of antiphons based on the text of the poem. During the ceremony the Christian virgin literally became the bride of the Song of Songs. The words of the bride became hers and she sang them with her companions.

It is in the light of this liturgy, imbued as it was with the verses of the Song of Songs, that the texts of Ambrose and Jerome must be read: the Fathers' application of the Song of Songs to virginal life reflects the fourth-century liturgy of the consecration of virgins in the Latin Church.

University of Manchester

---

[15] Below, pp. 25, 27, nn. 14, 23.
[16] Below, p. 25, n.12.

APPENDIX

Liber responsalis *of Gregory the Great: Office of virgins*
(BN, MS Lat. 17436, fols 94v–95r)

This is, to my knowledge, the first attempt to give a critical edition of the *Liber responsalis*. The aim of this edition is to underline the continuity in the use of the Song of Songs to describe virginal life. The footnotes provide references to the biblical verse upon which each antiphon is based as well as the location of parallel passages found in patristic texts or liturgical documents up to the thirteenth century.

IN VIGILIA UNIUS VIRGINIS

Ad vesperas

Vers. Specie tua.[1]
Ant. Simile est regnum coelorum homini negotiatori quaerenti bonas margaritas; inventa una pretiosa, dedit omnia sua, et comparavit eam.[2]

Ad invitatorium

Antiph. Regem virginum Dominum, venite, adoremus.

In primo nocturno

Ant. Ante thorum.[3]
Psal. Domine, Dominus noster.[4]
Ant. Haec est quae nescivit.[5]
Psal. Coeli enarrant.[6]
Ant. O quam pulchra est.[7]

---

[1] Ps 44.5. See *Responsoria de assumptione sanctae Mariae* in *Liber responsalis: PL* 78, col. 799A, In secundo nocturno: 'Specie tua et pulchritudine tua, intende, prospere, procede et regna.'

[2] Matt. 13.45.

[3] Cf. *Responsoria de assumptione sanctae Mariae, PL* 78, col. 799C, In Evangelio: 'Ante thorum hujus Virginis frequentate nobis dulcia capita dragmis.'

[4] Ps 8.2 (10) LXX.

[5] Cf. *Responsoria de assumptione sanctae Mariae, PL* 78, col. 799C, In Evangelio: 'Haec est quae nescivit thorum in delicto, habebit fructum in respectione animarum sanctarum.'

[6] Ps 18.2.

[7] Cf. S. of S. 7.6. Also found in the *Responsoria de assumptione sanctae Mariae, PL* 78, col. 798C: 'O quam pulchra et speciosa est Maria virgo Dei, quae de mundo migravit ad Christum.' The first part of the antiphon ('O quam pulchra et speciosa est') is based upon

Psal. Domini est terra.[8]
Vers. Specie tua.[9]

Responsoria unde supra

Resp. Diffusa est gratia.[10]
Vers. Myrrha et gutta.[11]
Resp. Veni, electa mea.[12]
Vers. Specie tua.[13]
Resp. Pulchra facie sed pulchrior.[14]
Vers. Specie tua et pulchritudine.[15]

S. of S. 7.6. It is interesting to note that it does not quite follow the Vulgate ('Quam pulchra est et quam decora'), reading 'speciosa' instead of 'decora'. The Vulgate was widely used at the time of Gregory the Great. The antiphon might be based on an old Latin version of the Song of Songs. If this is the case, this antiphon forms part of older liturgical material which was in circulation before the time of Gregory the Great and from which the author of the *Liber responsalis* took his inspiration.

[8] Ps 23.1.
[9] Ps 44.5.
[10] Ps 44.3.
[11] Ps 44.9.
[12] Reused by William Durandus in his pontifical. See M. Andrieu, *Le pontifical de Guillaume Durand* (Vatican City, 1940), p. 417 (33): 'Veni electa mea et ponam in te tronum meum. Quia concupivit rex speciem tuam.' The first part of this antiphon reminds us of S. of S. 2.10 ('Surge, veni, proxima mea, sponsa mea') or S. of S. 7.11 ('Veni, dilecte mi'). The second part of the antiphon comes from Ps 44.12. The Fathers frequently quote this verse when writing about consecration ceremonies or Christian virginity. See *De lapsu virginis consecratae*, V, 19, *PL* 16, col. 372A: 'Non es memorata qualis ad te die illo facta est allocutio: Aspice, filia, intuere, virgo, et *obliviscere populum tuum, et domum patris tui, et concupiscet Rex decorem tuum; quia ipse est Dominus tuus*' (Ps 44.11–12). See Jerome, *Letter 22*, 1, ed. Hilberg, p. 143: '*Audi, filia, et vide et inclina aurem tuam et obliviscere populum tuum et domum patris tui; et concupiscet rex decorem tuum* [Ps 44.11–12]. In quadragesimo quarto psalmo deus ad animam loquitur humanam [. . .]'. See Ambrose, *De virginibus*, I, 36 (in Gori, *Verginità e vedovanza*, 1, p. 136): 'Primum enim quod nupturae prae ceteris concupiscent, ut sponsi decore se iactent, eo necesse est impares sacris se fateantur esse virginibus, quibus solis contingit dicere: *Speciosus forma prae filiis hominum, diffusa est gratia in labiis tuis* [Ps 44.3]. Quis est iste sponsus? Non vilibus addictus obsequiis, non caducis superbus divitiis, sed cuius *sedes in saeculum saeculi. Filiae regum in honore* eius. *Astitit regina a dextris* eius *in vestitu deaurato varietate circumamicta* virtutum [Ps 44.10]. *Audi igitur, filia, et vide et inclina aurem tuam et obliviscere populum tuum et domum patris tui, quoniam concupivit rex speciem tuam, quia ipse est deus tuus* [Ps 44.11].'
[13] Ps 44.5.
[14] This antiphon is also found in the *Passio* of St. Agnes §1 (*PL* 17, col. 735B): 'Pulchra facie, sed pulchrior fide, et elegantior castitate.'
[15] Ps 44.5.

In secundo nocturno

Ant. Specie tua et pulchritudine.[16]
Psal. Eructavit.[17]
Ant. Adjuvabit eam.
Psal. Deus noster refugium.[18]
Ant. Dignare me laudare.
Psal. Fundamenta.[19]
Vers. Adjuvabit eam.

Responsaria unde supra

Resp. Virgo gloriosa semper.
Vers. Fiat, Domine, cor meum.[20]
Resp. Haec est virgo sapiens, quam Dominus vigilantem invenit, quae, acceptis lampadibus, sumpsit secum oleum, et veniente Domino introivit cum eo ad nuptias.[21]
Vers. Media autem nocte clamor factus: Ecce Sponsus venit, exite obviam ei. Et veniente.[22]

---

16 Ps 44.5.
17 Ps 44.2. Also found in the *Responsoria de assumptione sanctae Mariae* (PL 78, col. 799A), In secundo nocturno.
18 Ps 45.2 LXX.
19 Ps 86.1 LXX.
20 Ps 118.80(?).
21 Parable of the Ten Bridesmaids, Matt. 25.1–13. See Thecla's hymn in the *Symposium* of Methodius of Olympus (ed. Musurillo, pp. 310–21). The whole hymn is built around Matthew's parable. The chorus reads as follows: 'Chastely I live for you, and holding my lighted lamps, My spouse, I go forth to meet you' (trans. H. Musurillo, *St. Methodius, the Symposium* [London, 1958], Thecla's hymn at pp. 151–7). See Ambrose, *De institutione virginis*, 110 (ed. Gori, *Verginità e vedovanza*, 2, pp. 188–90): 'His igitur famulam tuam induc vestimentis, quae in omni tempore munda sint; mundum enim manet quidquid nulla interueniens culpa fuscaverit, ut ei iure dicatur: *Quoniam placuerunt deo facta tua* [Eccles. 9.7]. In omni tempore sint vestimenta sua candida, et oleum in capite non desit, quo faces suas mysticas possit accendere, ut cum venerit sponsus, inter illas sapientes virgines caelesti thalamo digna numeretur [cf. Matt. 25.10], quae devotionis ac fidei suae gravitatisque lumine munus sacrae professionis illuminet.' See also the end of the prayer *Deus castorum corporum* in *The Gelasian Sacramentary*, ed. Wilson, p. 157: 'Transeat in numerum sapientium puellarum, ut caelestem sponsum accensis lampadibus cum oleo praeparationis expectet; nec turbata improviso regis adventu, securata cum lumine ut praecedentium choro iungatur occurat, nec excludatur cum stultis. Regalem ianuam cum sapientibus virginibus licenter introeat, et in Agni tui perpetuo comitatu probabilis mansura castitate permaneat. Per Dominum.'
22 Cf. Matt 25.6.

Resp. Induit me Dominus cycladem in gyro textam, et immensis monilibus ornavit me. Et tamquam.[23]

In tertio nocturno

Ant. Revertere, revertere.
Psal. Cantate Domino.[24]
Ant. Haec est virgo sapiens.[25]
Psal. Dominus regnavit, exsultet.[26]
Ant. Tunc surrexerunt omnes.[27]
Psal. Dominus regnavit, irascantur.[28]
Vers. Elegit eam Dominus.

Responsoria unde supra

Resp. Veni, sponsa Christi, accipe coronam quam tibi Dominus praeparavit; pro cujus amore sanguinem tuum fudisti, et cum angelis in paradisum introibis.
Vers. Veni, electa mea, et ponam in te thronum meum, quia concupivit Rex speciem tuam. Et cum angelis.[29]
Vers. Propter veritatem, *ut supra.*[30]
Resp. Quinque prudentes virgines.[31]
Vers. Tunc surrexerunt.[32]
Resp. Ista est speciosa.[33]
Vers. Ista quae ascendit.[34]

---

[23] Cf. Isa. 61.10(?). The same antiphon is found in the *Passio* of St Agnes, §3 (*PL* 17, col. 736B).

[24] Ps 95.1; 97.1; 149.1.

[25] See n.12.

[26] Ps 96.1.

[27] Matt. 25.7.

[28] Ps 98.1.

[29] Ps 44.12. See n.12.

[30] Ps 44.5.

[31] Matt. 25.2.

[32] Matt. 25.7.

[33] Cf. S. of S. 1.5 (Vulgate 1.4). See *Responsoria de assumptione sanctae Mariae* (*PL* 78, col. 798B): 'Ista est speciosa inter filias Jerusalem'. I suggest that this antiphon is inspired by S. of S. 1.5 (Vulgate 1.4). The text of this verse in the Vulgate is the following: 'nigra sum sed formosa filiae Hierusalem'. In the antiphon the word 'speciosa' replaces 'formosa'. This could prove the antiquity of this antiphon as in the case of the antiphon based on S. of S. 7.6. See n.7 above.

[34] S. of S. 3.6. Cf. *Responsoria de assumptione sanctae Mariae* (*PL* 78, col. 798A): 'Quae est ista quae ascendit per desertum sicut virgula fumi, ex aromatibus myrrhae et thuris.' This antiphon is based word for word on the text of the Vulgate.

Resp. Haec est virgo sapiens et una.[35]
Vers. Media autem nocte.[36]
Resp. Specie tua et pulchritudine tua, intende, prospere procede, et regna. Dilexisti justitiam et odisti iniquitatem.[37]

In matutinis Laudibus

Ant. Haec est virgo sapiens, et una de numero prudentum.[38]
Ant. Haec est virgo sapiens, quam Dominus invenit vigilantem.[39]
Ant. Veni, sponsa Christi, accipe coronam quam tibi Dominus praeparavit in aeternum.
Ant. Media nocte clamor factus est: Ecce Sponsus venit, exite obviam ei.[40]
Ant. Benedico te, Pater, *ut supra.*
Ant. Inventa una pretiosa margarita, dedit omnia sua, et comparavit eam.[41]
Vers. Diffusa est.[42]

In Evangelio

Ant. Veniente Sponso, virgo prudens praeparata, introivit cum eo ad nuptias.[43]
Ant. Et quae paratae erant intraverunt cum eo ad nuptias.[44]
Ant. Et clausa est janua.[45]
Ant. Prudentes virgines, aptate vestras lampades, ecce Sponsus venit; exite obviam ei.[46]
Ant. Quinque prudentes.[47]

---

[35] Cf. Matt. 25.1–13.
[36] Matt. 25.6.
[37] Ps 44.5.
[38] Matt. 25.1–13.
[39] Ibid.
[40] Matt. 25.6.
[41] Matt. 13.45.
[42] Ps 44.3.
[43] Matt. 25.1–13.
[44] Matt. 25.10.
[45] Ibid.
[46] Matt. 25.6.
[47] Matt. 25.2

THE CAROLINGIAN LITURGICAL EXPERIENCE

by DONALD BULLOUGH

'THE Carolingian Liturgical Experience' may well seem, and indeed is, a recklessly broad topic for a single paper. 'Experience of the Liturgy in the Carolingian Period: some questions and not many answers' might be truer but not necessarily better. So I stay, uneasily, with my original title.

What that title does not portend is an interpretative essay comparable with (for example) Louis Marin's exploration of the eucharistic doctrines of Port-Royal, titled in its American-English version *Food for Thought*.[1] 'The discourse of assertion in the Catholic mass "This is my body"' followed by the prescriptive discourse 'Take, eat . . .' which 'institutes the space of the ecclesiastical community', we are told there, provide a theological model with 'far-reaching implications in the political sphere at a time when the French monarchy was headed straight toward absolutism'. And in case we have failed to grasp that model's even wider or profounder implications, an Introduction added to the American edition assures us that

> for the members of Port-Royal as well as for Saint Augustine, the communicational usage of signs and representations is nothing short of the manifestation of an irrepressible desire for the intense thrill to be derived from the Divine Body that is both replaced and realized by these very signs and representations. Once again it is apparent that the mystery of the Eucharist and the miracle of transubstantiation are the erotic core of Port-Royal semiotics. The displacements and transformations of the culinary sign in Perrault's *Tales* may be viewed as the figurative traces of this desire for the divine body.[2]

It may be that eighth-, ninth- and tenth-century understanding of and approaches to the eucharist and other sacramental actions can

---

[1] Baltimore, MD, and London, 1989; original French version, *La Parole mangée et autres essais théologico-politiques* (Paris, 1986). Neither version is in the University Library in St Andrews: but in the library of a Commonwealth university (Auckland, N. Z.) where I taught in 1996, the American edition was the most frequently borrowed work on the eucharist!

[2] Marin, *Food for Thought*, pp. 5 and xix.

fruitfully be examined in post-modernist terms or *à Barthes*. Indeed, something of the sort, specifically in relation to baptismal ceremonies, will be found in several chapters of Dr Peter Cramer's remarkable *Baptism and Change in the Early Middle Ages*, which a reviewer rightly praised for its 'judicious vocabulary and an appropriate sobriety of approach'![3] That is, however, certainly beyond my capacity and vocabulary. The approach here will be a more traditional and positivist one, with particular reference to the mass: this is the part of the liturgy where the essential forms remained much the same throughout these centuries, despite an accretion of new mass-sets, mass-prayers, and variable chants; and yet even the limited contemporary commentary literature shows how being in a particular place at a particular time or 'the refraction of different minds' (Cramer's words!) in different intellectual communities could effect changes of sense and under-standing.

The paper's theme is essentially the liturgical experience of the 'silent majority', the laity. It begins by defining the contexts, and more particularly the physical settings – in current jargon, the 'ecclesiastical space' – of Sunday or feast-day and of daily worship in the Carolingian centuries (defined as from *c.*750 to *c.*990); and goes on to consider the characterization of that worship in non-liturgical texts, and the evidence in those same texts for the regular and active participation of the lay faithful. It then considers what were the books that provided the textual basis of liturgical worship, by prescription and in practice: with a glance at the evidence for its musical settings (*cantilena* or *cantus* independent of the words these accompany). It looks, thirdly, at the rites of burial and baptism and their implications for a worshipping lay community. Finally, it turns to the evidence – if any – for attitudes to and experience of the central liturgical act, the mass, on the part of ordinary *fideles*.

* * *

First, then, the settings of the liturgy. It is now widely recognized that a distinction has to be made between 1) town cathedrals: in some places, other urban churches also; 2) churches associated with rural

---

[3] P. Cramer, *Baptism and Change in the Early Middle Ages, c.200–c.1150* [hereafter *Baptism and Change*], Cambridge Studies in Medieval Life and Thought, 4th ser., 20 (Cambridge, 1993): reviewed by Alexander Murray in *The Times Literary Supplement*, 25 March 1994, p. 3.

settlements, however defined but in general constituting quite small units of population; 3) the churches of religious communities, whether of monks or nuns *stricto sensu* or of canons and canonesses. But the implications of such distinctions for a correct understanding of the earliest extant liturgical books (which are, strictly, testimony only to the practice of the church for which they were written) are not always appreciated; and I shall necessarily concentrate on the first two groups.

* * *

We are bound to assume that the majority of western Europe's Christian laity would in this period normally have worshipped, if anywhere, in rural churches, whether these were located in a 'central place' and served probably by a small group of clergy who were also responsible for subordinate *oratoria* (*basilicae* etc.), or one of those oratories or chapels, typically on a private estate ('seignorial lands'), with a single priest who may only have been an occasional visitor. But estimating the number of these churches and oratories in the Carolingian centuries, and assessing how accessible they would have been to the inhabitants of scattered settlements, is only a little easier than trying to guess next week's winning lottery number.[4] We probably have a virtually complete record of the sixty-plus rural churches with 'parochial' rights in the ninth/tenth-century diocese of Lucca, together with a listing of the subordinate *oratoria* of some of them.[5] We can achieve a reasonable approximation of those in the diocese of Trier in the eighth and ninth centuries (fifty-plus?) and – on certain assumptions – even map the territorial parishes associated with them. In the Paris diocese, working backwards from its roughly 450 rural parishes on the eve of the Revolution, the evidence of medieval documentation, church dedications, and (sometimes) archaeology, has suggested a figure of *c.* 200 at the end of the tenth century, together with an unknown number of subordinate churches and chapels.[6] On

---

[4] For England, however, compare the more optimistic approach of R. Morris, *Churches in the Landscape* (London, 1989), ch. 4.

[5] L. Nanni, *La Parrochia studiata nei documenti lucchesi dei secoli VIII–XIII*, Analecta Gregoriana, 47 (Rome, 1948), pt 1, and esp. pp. 66–75: made possible by the remarkable collection of pre-1000 documents in the Archivio Arcivescovile, Lucca, and admirably edited already in the early nineteenth century.

[6] Trier: E. Ewig, *Trier im Merowingerreich: Civitas, Stadt, Bistum* (Trier, 1954), pp. 149–65, 182–282, with maps 3 and 4; and F. Pauly's several volumes with the common title *Siedlung*

one usage (or definition) of *parochia*, there is late but convincing evidence for ten, eleven, or twelve pre-Viking 'minster parishes', with up to twenty subordinate churches each, in the diocese of Canterbury.[7] Every regional specialist could doubtless extend this list without difficulty, although still leaving many blanks on the ecclesiastical map of Carolingian Europe.[8]

If, however, we ask what went on in those churches, for the greater part of this period we are faced with an almost total silence: a collection of contemporary texts descriptive of ordinary *fideles*, observant Christians joining in worship in their local church or oratory, would be at most a very slim volume, perhaps not even a short periodical article.[9] (Not that this has stopped scholars from making confident statements about, for example, the place of the homily or sermon in worship and evangelism in a nominally Christian countryside.) It is symptomatic that a substantial collective account of *Pastoral Care before the Parish* in the British Isles devotes only a few paragraphs to the Sunday or feast-day celebration of the eucharist,

---

und Pfarrorganisation im alten Erzbistum Trier in *Rheinisches Archiv* (Bonn) and *Veröffentlichungen des Bistumsarchiv Trier* (Trier) (1957–76); the final volume is *Zusammenfassung und Ergebnisse*. Paris: M. Roblin, *Le Terroir de Paris aux époques Gallo-Romaine et Franque*, 2nd edn (Paris, 1971), esp. pp. 151–4. Some aspects of Roblin's methodology have been seriously challenged; but he claimed no undue precision for this particular calculation.

[7] Namely, in the lists in the Canterbury 'Domesday Monachorum', in *The Domesday Monachorum of Christ Church, Canterbury*, ed. D. C. Douglas (London, 1944), pp. 77–9, cf. pp. 5–13: but for their interpretation, see further F. Barlow, *The English Church 1000–1066*, 2nd edn (London, 1979), pp. 180–2; T. Tatton-Brown, 'The churches of Canterbury diocese in the eleventh century', in J. Blair, ed., *Minsters and Parish Churches: the Local Church in Transition 950–1200*, Oxford University Committee for Archaeology Monograph, 17 (Oxford, 1988), pp. 105–18. According to Blair, 'Introduction: from minster to parish church', ibid., p. 1: 'For clarity, we have followed the artificial but now accepted usage of Latin *parochia* for minster parish, and English "parish" for the institution in its modern sense' since '*Parochia* originally meant a bishop's diocese [and] until the mid 12th century it was used more commonly in this sense' than for 'minster parish' or 'parish' as now understood. This is no doubt broadly correct: but it is worth noting that in one of very few relevant pre-ninth-century texts (other than Bede) Alcuin urges Archbishop Æthelhard of Canterbury to end his self-exile and return to ordain, preach, baptize, dispense alms, and care for the poor *per singulas aecclesias atque parochias* (*MGH. Epistolae* IV, ed. E. Dümmler (Berlin, 1897), no. 128 [p. 190] of 797).

[8] For eastern Brittany (dioc. Rennes) see below, pp. 60–1.

[9] Confirmed by A. Angenendt's 'Die Liturgie und die Organisation des kirchlichen Lebens auf dem Lande', in *Cristianizzazione ed Organizzazione Ecclesiastica delle Campagne nell'Alto Medioevo, i: espansione e resistenze*, 2 vols, Settimane di Studio del Centro Italiano di Studi sull'Alto Medioevo, 28 (Spoleto, 1982) [hereafter *Cristianizzazione ed Organizzazione Ecclesiastica*], i, pp. 169–226, which is almost entirely about 'ceremonies' and institutions or functions.

which is surely an integral part of that 'care'.[10] Alan Thacker's admirable contribution to that volume recognizes the problem; but he is forced back on Bede's prescriptions that layfolk should be receiving communion at least every Sunday and on major weekday feasts, and then goes on to show how the same writer's preconditions would make that virtually impossible.[11] A passage in Bede's *Comment-ary on Mark* which greatly appealed to Charles Plummer records that 'when we come to any estate-centre or [fortified?] settlement or any other place in which there is a prayer-house consecrated to God we enter it' and pray before getting on with our worldly business; and one of his references to lay communion occurs earlier in that commentary.[12] But he never, I think, describes an act of worship there. Similarly, the episodes relating to rural priests in the early-English *Vitae sanctorum* and in Bede's historical works never refer to the ordinary Sunday or weekday 'offices', although baptism and anointing of the sick figure there; and Alcuin, too, has nothing of substance on the subject – as I believe, because he simply wasn't interested in the Northumbrian *rustici*.

Texts like the decrees of the 747 Council of Clofesho and many of their Carolingian successors are authority-focused ('follow the Roman books'), and in that sense record aspiration, not reality.[13] A rare glimpse of the reality for some, as well as of the practice of worship, in a part of Europe that had been Christian for centuries is provided by one of the earliest documents relating to the protracted dispute between the dioceses of Arezzo and Siena, of the year 715. One of the witnesses recalls that an intruding bishop of Siena established a font in one community – S. Ansano in the Tuscan Val d'Arbia – and consecrated as priest a boy of no more than twelve 'qui nec vespero sapit nec

---

[10] J. Blair and R. Sharpe, eds, Studies in the Early History of Britain (Leicester, 1992) [hereafter *Pastoral Care*].

[11] 'Monks, preaching and pastoral care in early Anglo-Saxon England', *Pastoral Care*, pp. 137–70. The insistence on regular lay communion is in Bede's Letter to Egbert of York, c.15, in *Bedae Opera Historica*, ed. C. Plummer, 2 vols (Oxford, 1896), I, p. 419; for the preconditions see, e.g., his *In Marci evangelium expositio*, in *Bedae opera, Pars II, 3*, ed. D. Hurst, CChr. SL, 120 (Turnhout, 1960), p. 520, ll. 1217–27.

[12] Ibid., p. 575, ll. 1298–1303: 'cum forte villam aut oppidum aut alium quemlibet locum in quo sit domus orationis Deo consecrata intramus', etc. With *domus orationis* compare the 747 Council of *Clofesho*'s decree that priests should 'oratorii domum [the correct text-reading?] et cuncta ad cultum ipsius pertinentia sub sua cura conservare': A. W. Haddan and W. Stubbs, eds, *Councils and Ecclesiastical Documents Relating to Great Britain and Ireland* [hereafter H&S], 3 vols in 4 (Oxford, 1869–78), 3, p. 365.

[13] H&S, 3, pp. 367–8, cc.13, 15, 16, 18.

madodinos facere nec missa cantare'.[14] (If and when a priest of proper
age and capacity was installed in the church is not clearly documented.)
A rather different message is conveyed by a *cessio* of the bishop of Sens,
dated 808 and preserved among the *Formulae Senonenses*, which lays
down that the inhabitants of four named villages (*villae*) shall attend
mass, be baptized, hear preaching, and pay their tithes at a church
recently built and consecrated by him.[15] The response of the villagers
is unrecorded. The additional hurdles to be crossed in non-Romance
regions are reflected in the tenth of the Clofesho canons of 747. Not
only the congregations but also (it is implied) the priests themselves
may not really understand what they are saying 'in the celebration of
mass and the office of baptism': they should, accordingly, at least be
able to provide a vernacular version of the creed and the Lord's
Prayer.[16] Two and a half centuries later, admittedly after the
Scandinavian invasions of the North, a 'law' for priests in the York
diocese (Archbishop Wulfstan's?) includes among offences for which
compensation has to be paid: 'If a priest performs in a wrong order the
annual services of the church, by day or night'.[17]

As is well-known, the earliest *Continental* Germanic versions of both
creed and Lord's Prayer are in a manuscript of the late eighth century
that entered the library of St Gallen at an early date but probably did
not originate there; and other south-German examples are only a few
years younger.[18] Their relation to the liturgy is, however, not a
straightforward one. It must not be forgotten that at the time when

---

[14] *Codice diplomatico longobardo*, ed. L. Schiaparelli, 2 vols [hereafter *CDL*], Fonti per la
Storia d'Italia, 62–3 (Rome, 1929–33), 1, no. 19 (p. 74). Compare ibid., 2, no. 213 of 768, in
which a priest undertakes to reside in the 'private church' of S. Salvatore, 'casale Critianu',
Tuscania, 'et officio iuxta suo sapere in ipsa ecclesia singolis dies facere'. He also promises to
pay a penalty if, among other failings, 'non estudvero de lumen et incenso iuxta pecunia
ipsius ecclesiae aut aliquas exinde fraudavero'!

[15] *Formulae Merowingici et Karolini aevi*, ed. K. Zeumer, *MGH. Legum*, V (Hanover, 1886),
p. 217.

[16] H&S, 3, p. 366.

[17] D. Whitelock, M. Brett, and C. N. L. Brooke, eds, *Councils and Synods 1/i: A. D.871–
1066* (Oxford, 1981) [hereafter *Councils and Synods*], pp. 459–60.

[18] St Gallen, Stiftsbibliothek, cod. 911, pp. 320–2; complete facsimile (as *Das älteste
deutsche Buch. Die 'Abrogans' Handschrift*) with introd. by J. Duft and B. Bischoff and
transcription by S. Sonderegger (St Gallen, 1977); also B. Bischoff, 'Paläographische Fragen
deutscher Denkmäler der Karolingerzeit' [1971], in his *Mittelalterliche Studien* [hereafter
Bischoff, *MaSt*], 3 (Stuttgart, 1981), pp. 73–111, at p. 95. For the slightly later 'Freisinger
Paternoster' in Munich, Bayerische Staatsbibliothek, clm. 6330 (in fact from southern
Alamannia) and the 'Bavarian Paternoster' in clm. 14510 (this part written for a layman?), see
ibid. pp. 89–90, 99.

the first German-language versions were composed the creed had not yet established itself in the order of the mass; and in any case when it did, the version used was of course the one which we, like our medieval predecessors, call 'the Nicene creed', while the translations are of the 'Apostles creed' or perhaps the unrevised 'Old Roman' one! I return to this topic later.

A century of Carolingian legislation and the literally thousands of charters from the Empire and its successor kingdoms add detail to the fragmentary, and at times dispiriting, picture offered by those early texts, but little that is significantly new except in one area – the underpinning of books. The charters, of course, commonly include requests for masses for the souls of the donors and/or of deceased relatives; but even before the great age of Cluny and other reformed houses, they are overwhelmingly directed to monasteries and 'canonries'.[19] Prof. Jean Lemarignier calculated that surviving West Frankish royal diplomas from the death of Louis the Pious in 840 through to 987 record almost 400 'private churches' north of the Loire, three-quarters of them in the control of monasteries.[20] Their gifting, restoration, or confirmation, however, is almost never linked with an indication of what is involved in their exercise of a *cura animarum*, unless in the guaranteeing of their right to receive consecrated oil and chrism from the bishop without payment.[21] The more comprehensive provision in the private gifting of an existing church (*basilica*) at Cond, on the Moselle opposite Cochem, to the monastery of Stablo-Malmedy in 857, is very exceptional: the monastery was to ensure that 'sacerdos talis ad prefatam basilicam deputetur qui aptus sit officio sacerdotali fungi ubi eis conventicula prefate ville adunatur missam acceptura, sacrum baptismum precepturum [sic] et omnia spiritualia dogmata ab

---

[19] In 798, however, the Kentish minster (*familia*) of Lyminge, which had pastoral ('parish') responsibilities, was given land by ealdorman Oswulf in return for a precisely-specified annual commemoration (with feast!): P. H. Sawyer, *Anglo-Saxon Charters: an Annotated List and Bibliography* (London, 1968), no. 153.

[20] J. F. Lemarignier, 'Encadrement religieux des campagnes et conjuncture politique dans les régions du royaume de France situées au nord de la Loire de Charles le Chauve aux derniers Carolingiens (840–987)', *Cristianizzazione ed Organizzazione Ecclesiastica*, 2, pp. 765–800. For the way these figures were arrived at, compare the tables on pp. 770–5, compiled from his notes after his death.

[21] So, for example, in *Recueil des Actes de Charles II le Chauve*, ed. G. Tessier, 3 vols (Paris, 1943–55), 2, no. 349 (p. 279) – excluded geographically from Lemarignier's calculations – for the monastery of *Exalada* (subsequently St-Michel de Cuxa) and in later documents. The distribution of chrism implies that some or all of the dependent churches were ones with a baptismal font.

eodem sacerdote sine dilatione communicatura'.[22] Untypical in a different way is the grant to four Cluny monks in 983 by the bishop of Autun of the tithes of three churches where they are daily *in obedientia* and responsible for 'the cult of the holy religion'; which in the context is surely public worship.[23]

The overall picture from other regions and other royal writing-offices is similar, even if the language of the documents (their 'diplomatic') may be interestingly different. Italian church councils refer to the priest's reponsibility for *mysteria divina* or *mysterium divinum*, in the sense of 'eucharist', although I have not noticed either in charters. Indeed, following a centuries-old formulary, these seem much more concerned that priests should look after the lighting of their churches![24] A Bavarian document from the first year of Louis the Pious's reign records a transfer of property to the bishop of Regensburg by the executors of a deceased 'abbot', one of the conditions of which was that the bishop should 'una aecclesia fabricari' at Seissbach 'et ibidem posuisset aliquem sacerdotum [*sic in MS*] qui ibidem cantet'.[25]

[22] *Recueil des chartes de l'abbaye de Stavelot-Malmédy*, ed. J. Halkin and C.-G. Roland (Brussels, 1909), no. 32. The (later) dedication of the church, now de-consecrated and partly demolished, was to St Remaklus, the founder and patron of the abbey. Contrast with this the terms of the remarkable charter of 1092 (?unique before the twelfth century) in which the inhabitants of Saorge (France, dép. Alpes-Maritimes), who are individually named (including forty-seven wives), having assembled before their *capella ecclesia sanctae Mariae*, surrender it to the monks of Lérins on condition that they install 'monachi [vel?] presbiteri sub iussione eiusdem abas [*sic*] qui cotidie et vesperas sue matutinas in predicta capella canant': *Cartulaire de l'abbaye de Lérins*, ed. H. Moris and E. Blanc, 2 vols, Société des Lettres, Sciences et Arts des Alpes-Maritimes (Paris, 1883–1903), 1, no. 169 (pp. 164–9).

[23] *Receuil des chartes de l'abbaye de Cluny*, ed. A. Bernard and A. Bruel, 6 vols (Paris, 1876–1903), 2, no. 1628 (p. 665), quoted by G. Constable, 'Monasteries, rural churches and the *cura animarum* in the early Middle Ages', *Cristianizzazione ed Organizzazione Ecclesiastica*, 1, pp. 351–89, at p. 370.

[24] *Die Konzilien der Karolingischen Teilreiche, 843–859*, ed. W. Hartmann, *MGH. Conc.* III (Hanover, 1984), pp. 227 (c.14), 320 (c.4) etc. Compare, e.g., *CDL*, 2, no. 165 of 762 (Montalto near Lucca): 'omnem officium eclesiasticum et luminaria eidem eclesie faciat'; ibid., no. 213 (as n.14); *Le piu antiche carte dello Archivio Capitolare di Asti*, ed. F. Gabotto (Pinerolo, 1904), no. 23 of 892 (Mucegno, terr. Vercelli): 'missas canere et luminarias facere et officium seu sarcitectis [*sic*] eidem aeclesie sine ne[g]lectu . . . laborare et excollere'; *Codice Diplomatico Veronese*, ed. V. Fainelli, 2 vols (Venice, 1940–63), 2, no. 214 of 931 (an urban *oratorium* and *xenodochium*): 'solicitudinem habeant . . . ad concinnandas [*sic*, for *concinnandas*] lampades die noctuque in eadem eclesia et de ceteris ecclesiasticis officiis'.

[25] *Die Traditionen des Hochstifts Regensburg und des Klosters S. Emmeram*, ed. J. Widemann, Quellen und Erörterungen zur Bayerischen Geschichte, n. F. 8 (Munich, 1943) [hereafter *Regensburg*], no. 14 of Oct./Nov. 814. The bishop gave the church to *Ratolf monachus*, in spite of reiterated recent decrees (*Concilia aevi Karolini*, ed. A. Werminghoff, *MGH. Conc.* II/1 (Hanover and Leipzig, 1906), pp. 210, 215, etc.) that 'monachus nullo modo parrochiam regat'.

There seems to be nothing similar in the considerably more numerous Freising charters. These, on the other hand, are notable for their documentation of the founding of estate *oratoria* in the diocese, particular in the decades either side of 800, by both lay persons and clerics, with subsequent consecration by the bishop.[26] As private *oratoria* they would have had not a font or even a permanent resident priest, although the latter is something that bishops may have striven to achieve.

Among the admonitions in Charlemagne's comprehensive capitulary of March 789 is one requiring bishops to check that priests understand the mass-prayers; while the next one urges the laity to keep their minds on God when attending mass and not to leave before the final 'priestly blessing'.[27] Ninth-century *capitularia missorum* and episcopal statutes or *capitula* follow the royal lead and at times expand on it. The untypical first *capitula* of Bishop Ghaerbald of Liège (801/2) opens with a requirement that priests shall diligently maintain the structure of their church and care zealously for the relics with vigils and (daytime) offices, and follows this with the instruction to ring bells at the appropriate hours and teach the people how they should worship God at those hours.[28] Theodulf of Orleans's first *capitulare*, likewise of the opening years of the ninth century, seems to be the only one that assumes that morning and evening prayer will be said regularly in a rural church (*basilica*); he links it with a hope that those who cannot get to a church will offer up simple prayers on their own.[29] The same capitulary's next chapter (c.24) is one of the very few which, in the context of 'Sunday observance', speaks of the laity's

---

[26] *Die Traditionen des Hochstifts Freising*, ed. Th. Bitterauf, 2 vols, Quellen und Erörterungen zur Bayerischen und deutschen Geschichte, n. F. 4–5 (Munich, 1905–9) [hereafter *Freising*], 1, no. 391 of 818, is a typical record of the lay founding and episcopal consecration of an *oratorium*, while ibid., nos 394 of 818 and 421 of 819, are those of priest-founders: no. 421 records that the bishop, having consecrated church and altar and introduced relics, 'missarum solemnia statim ibidem celebravit'.

[27] *Capitularia regum Francorum*, ed. A. Boretius and V. Krause, 2 vols, *MGH. Cap.* II (Hanover, 1883–97), 1, no. 22, cc.71, 72.

[28] *MGH. Capitula Episcoporum*, 1 (Hanover, 1984), ed. P. Brommer [hereafter *MGH. Cap. Episc.*, 1], pp. 16–17. *Aedificare* in c.1 is clearly the counterpart of the Italian (and potentially unintelligible?) *sartatecta* etc.; drawing on the capitulary at the end of the tenth century for his 'Pastoral Letter for Wulfsige', Ælfric renders this passage as 'ðæt hi healdan heora cyrcan' (c.48: *Councils and Synods*, p. 206).

[29] So I interpret Theodulf cap. I c.23, *MGH. Cap. Episc.*, 1, p. 120. Since it is addressed to the laity and is concerned with *hora matutina vel vespertina* the editor's cross-reference (n.85) to *MGH. Cap.*, 2, no. 41 of 829 seems out of place.

presence with their offerings *ad missarum sollemnia*; although the importance of a *reponsio plebis* to the celebrant's salutation has previously been stressed in the last of three chapters concerned with the proper celebration of the mass by the priest (and other clergy, if any).[30] When the West Frankish bishops collectively take up the theme of 'Sunday observance' in 829, with direct reference to abstention from *ruralia opera*, the mass is not – in so many words – referred to: merely that the faithful shall join in singing and praise. What form this might take is, however, never made clear.[31] A few later Carolingian texts repeat or echo Theodulf. Only Bishop Rudolf of Bourges, who is particularly concerned to say what lay-people shall *not* do when mass is being celebrated, and the middle section of Archbishop Hincmar of Rheims's *Collectio de ecclesiis et capellis*, in the 860s or 870s, add anything of significance.[32] When, in the next century, an anonymous but presumably English 'author' put together the misleadingly-named *Excerptiones Egberti* from texts of different date and origin, and a succession of English bishops or episcopal amanuenses subsequently included parts of them in their pontificals, their instructions to priests, beginning 'Ut unusquisque sacerdos', were Ghaerbald of Liège's first capitulary *verbatim*![33]

The architectural setting of worship in rural communities – the liturgy's defining and confining 'space' – is properly the subject of a different paper, although on present evidence it would be quite a short one. There seems, however, to be a growing conviction among historians of buildings that the church of St John, Escomb, with its high, narrow nave and short square chancel, each with a north-side

---

[30] C.24, *MGH. Cap. Episc.*, 1, p. 121; cc.5–7, ibid., pp. 107–8. Compare Walahfrid Strabo's remarks in his *Libellus de exordiis et incrementis*, c.23 (*MGH. Cap.*, 2, p. 503) and the comment of Alice L. Harting-Correa in her *Translation and Liturgical Commentary* (Leiden, 1996), p. 281.

[31] *MGH. Conc.*, II/1, pp. 643–4 (c.50).

[32] *MGH. Cap. Episc.*, 1, pp. 233–68, esp. cc.5, 6, 10 and 28; Hincmar of Rheims, *Collectio de ecclesiis et capellis*, ed. M. Stratmann, *MGH. Fontes Iuris Germanici Antiqui*, 14 (Hanover, 1990) [hereafter Hincmar, *Collectio*], pp. 99–112. But see also Hincmar's first diocesan *capitula* (*presbyteris data*, an. 852), *PL* 125, cols 773–8.

[33] The most substantial item in 'the central witness', Oxford, Bodleian Library, MS Bodley 718 (so David Dumville, *Liturgy and the Ecclesiastical History of Late Anglo-Saxon England* [Woodbridge, 1992], p. 86 [85 n.111]) – probably a Christ Church, Canterbury book – is the Frankish penitential *Quadripartitus* (for which see esp. F. Kerff, *Der Quadripartitus: ein Handbuch der karolingischen Kirchenreform* [Sigmaringen, 1982]]), Bks II-IV: the Ghaerbald capitulary is at fols 3–5, the *Quadripartitus* at fols 22–178. A conveniently accessible text of the first section of the *Excerptiones* is *Anglo-Saxon Pontificals*, ed. H. M. J. Banting, *HBS*, 104 (London, 1989), pp. 5–8 (7–8).

doorway, is very far from being 'a typical early English village church': its substantial masonry construction suggests rather a monastic connection. Before the tenth/eleventh centuries, it is suggested, the majority of rural churches would have been of timber, with or without stone footings, commonly of a simple two-cell plan (often adopted also for the first masonry building on the site), with the main altar probably set forward in the chancel.[34] The situation in large areas of (lowland) Continental Europe may not have been significantly different, although excavators and others are still surprisingly reluctant to admit that the undiscovered 'first' church preceding the earliest approximately datable masonry *in situ* may well have been a wooden one.[35] Textual evidence, unsurprisingly, is uncommon but not entirely lacking – the *basilica lignea modica* at Michelstadt in the Odenwald included in Louis the Pious's gift to Einhard and his wife in 815; or the *ecclesia lignea* at nearby Schlossborn (in the Main-Taunus-Kreis), whose parish-bounds ('(de)terminatio cum universa decimatione') were established by Archbishop Willigis of Mainz *c.* 980 and which half a century later was 'in melius restaurata lapidea facta'.[36] North and central Italy may offer a partial exception; here too, however, many *plebes baptismales* of masonry construction once confidently attributed to the eighth or ninth century are now generally dated to the eleventh.[37]

[34] E. Cambridge, 'The early church in County Durham: a re-assessment', *JBAA*, 137 (1984), pp. 65–85; *Minsters and Parish Churches, passim*, but esp. the contributions of R. Gem (pp. 21–30) and R. K. Morris (pp. 191–9); Morris, *Churches in the Landscape*, pp. 120–1, 151–4, 165–7.

[35] Recent examples are C. Sapin, *La Bourgogne préromane* (Paris, 1986), pp. 123–40, 160–1, and M. Fixot and E. Zadora-Rio, *L'Église, le terroir*, Centre de Recherches Archéologiques, Monographie no. 1 (Paris, 1989), esp. pp. 51–69, 105–14. Compare, however, C. Ehrens, *Frühe Holzkirchen im nördlichen Europe* (Hamburg, 1981) (which I know only at second-hand), and H. Dannheimer, *Frühe Holzkirchen aus Bayern*, Kleine Ausstellungsführer der Prähistorischen Staatssammlung München, 3 (Munich, 1985).

[36] J. F. Böhmer and E. Mühlbacher, *Regesta Imperii, I: Die Regesten des Kaiserreichs unter den Karolingern, 751–918* (Innsbruck, 1908; repr. with additions, 1966), no. 569; *Mainzer Urkundenbuch*, ed. M. Stimming, 2 vols in 3 (Darmstadt, 1968–72), I, no. 284 of 1043. But when the later parish church of Dürrmenz (Germany, Enzkreis; south-east of Karlsruhe) was given to Lorsch in 835 it was already an *ecclesiam unam lapideam: Codex Laureshamensis*, ed. K. Glöckner, 3 vols (Darmstadt, 1929–36), no. 2337, which also records the giving with the church of two gilded reliquaries, a lectionary, a missal, priestly vestments, and two bells.

[37] Between 1951 and 1968 I visited more than 200 'rural' churches in Italy, Switzerland, Germany, southern France, and Dalmatian Yugoslavia which according to guide-books and older works of architectural history had structural features datable to the eighth, ninth, or tenth century. After the elimination of one-time abbeys, such as Ferrières and Münster in Graubünden, I concluded that no more than twenty, and probably less, might be so dated; and those included Einhard's Steinbach and the north-Italian (South Tyrolean) churches of

Simple (and wooden) construction was not incompatible with a degree of lavishness at and around the altar:[38] by the beginning of the tenth century, the more fortunate 'parish churches' could be surprisingly well-provided with liturgical vessels and ornaments in precious materials and with vestments, although it is hard to believe that (for example) the treasure of Eller on the Mosel – the centre of what German scholars call an *Urpfarrei*, and apparently still served by a clerical congregation in the tenth century – was typical even of churches in an economically-prosperous region which had escaped destructive violence.[39]

The Carolingian centuries witnessed a proliferation of belfries or bell-turrets, and eventually of bell-towers, in rural as well as urban churches throughout western Europe: bells to summon the faithful to prayer are already assumed to be normal by bishops on both sides of the Alps in the years either side of 800.[40] Evidence of popular or

S. Procolo, Naturno, and S. Benedetto, Malles Venosta, the remarkable frescoes and other decoration of which argue for major monastic and/or 'aristocratic' connections in the Carolingian period. (For the eleventh-century date of Agliate [Brianza, dioc. Milan], see E. Arslan, 'L'architettura romanica milanese', in [Fondazione Treccani degli Alfieri] *Storia di Milano*, 3 [n.p., 1954], p. 412.) My criteria and descriptions would hardly satisfy the present generation of architectural historians, but the conclusion seems sound enough. It has been strengthened subsequently by careful local studies, typified by I. Moretti and R. Stopani, *Chiese Romaniche in Val di Pesa e Val di Greve* (Florence, 1972), who found nothing pre-eleventh century even in the *pievi* (dioc. Florence) and oratories for which there is earlier documentary evidence.

[38] For *cancelli*, etc., dividing the *presbiterium* from the nave, see below, p. 53 and n.78.

[39] A list of Eller's altar-ornaments, liturgical objects, etc., and of its books was entered in the early tenth century in the Rheims-origin Gospel-book, London, BL, MS Harley 2826: ed. F. Pauly, 'Ein Dokument aus dem Britischen Museum zur Geschichte der Pfarrei Eller an der Mosel', *Archiv für Mittelrheinische Kirchengeschichte*, 8 (1956), pp. 348–50. The oldest item in the present-day treasury (but kept in the *Pfarrhaus*) is a late-Romanesque holy-water bucket. For other ninth- and tenth-century records of church 'treasures' (excluding books), see *Mittelalterliche Schatzverzeichnisse, I: von der Zeit Karls des Grossen bis zur Mitee des 13. Jahrhunderts*, ed. Zentralinstitut für Kunstgeschichte (Munich) and B. Bischoff, Veröffentlichungen des Zentralinstituts für Kunstgeschichte, 4 (Munich, 1967) [hereafter *Schatzverzeichnisse*].

[40] *MGH. Conc.*, II/1, p. 194 (Paulinus of Aquileia-Friuli), *MGH. Cap. Episc.*, 1, p. 17 (Ghaerbald of Liège); see also Walahfrid Strabo, *De exordiis*, c.5, with the commentary of A. Harting-Correa, *Translation and Liturgical Commentary*, pp. 214–16. The earliest *Ordo ad signum ecclesiae benedicendum* in the ceremony for the dedication of a church is in 'Frankish Gelasian' sacramentaries: e.g. the Sacramentary of Gellone, in *Liber sacramentorum Gellonensis: Textus*, ed. A. Dumas, CChr. SL, 159 (Turnhout, 1981), pp. 367–9 (nos 2440–6). The early evolution and chronology of bell-turrets and bell-towers have been much discussed, without conclusive results: a majority of architectural historians, however, denies that any tower is older than the tenth century, although turrets (even in some minor churches) may be earlier.

community participation in liturgical acts in cathedral towns, although often indirect, is considerably greater than for rural churches; but it, too, is very unevenly distributed in space and time. In the present century, and especially since the 1930s, archaeology has abundantly confirmed what texts had already hinted at – that before the great rebuildings of the twelfth and thirteenth centuries many episcopal churches were a complex of consecrated buildings rather than a single cathedral; or alternatively, as in several cities of north Italy including Pavia and Milan, were parallel structures (plus a free-standing baptistery) which, whatever their original functions, were commonly distinguished simply as *ecclesia maior* and *ecclesia minor.*[41] Such arrangements, together with other churches established within the walls of a city in the seventh and eighth centuries, made possible an *imitatio Romae*, where from an early date the pope had processed from the Lateran to a *titulus* or cemetery basilica – the *statio* – to celebrate a Sunday or festal mass. The earliest instance is, as is well known, at Metz under (Arch)bishop Chrodegang. A small number of other Frankish churches may have followed suit, although the (later) evidence from Rogation processions is of doubtful relevance. Any imitation was incomplete and imperfect: even at Metz it affected only a small part of the liturgical year – Lenten Sundays, Holy Week, and Easter Week and a few other feasts; and neither there nor elsewhere (in spite of some recent claims to the contrary) was there any attempt to match the dedications of the 'station churches' to those found in copies of the 'Gregorian' sacramentary and their associated lectionaries.[42] (In the

---

[41] For early medieval cathedrals as complexes of buildings, see especially J. Hubert, *L'Architecture religieuse du haut moyen âge en France* (Paris, 1952) (plans with minimal commentary) and E. Lehmann, 'Die frühchristlichen Kirchenfamilien der Bischofssitze im deutschen Raum und ihre Wandlungen während des Frühmittelalters' in H. Fillitz, ed., *Beiträge zur Kunstgeschichte und Archäologie des Frühmittelalters*, Akten zum VII. Internationalen Kongress für Frühmittelalterforschung (Graz, 1962), pp. 88–99. North-Italian 'double cathedrals' are discussed by J. Hubert, 'Les "cathédrales doubles" et l'histoire de la liturgie', *Atti del 1° Congresso di Studi Longobardi, 1951* (Spoleto, 1952), pp. 167–76, and by R. Krautheimer, 'The twin cathedral at Pavia', in his *Studies in Early Christian, Medieval and Renaissance Art* (London, 1971), pp. 161–80: pp. 176–80 are an important Postscript to the original 1936 article, responding particularly to criticisms of his use of evidence from Milan by A. De Capitani d'Arzago, *La "Chiesa Maggiore" di Milano: Santa Tecla* (Milan, 1952), pp. 45–76 and esp. pp. 45–56: the supposed 'first construction' in 836 is certainly a re-building *al.* re-dedication.

[42] The Metz list, on a two-leaf insertion in the (non-Metz) Gospel-book BN, MS. lat. 268, was edited by T. Klauser, 'Eine Stationsliste der Metzer Kirche aus dem 8. J.h., wahrscheinlich ein Werk Chrodegangs', *Ephemerides Liturgicae*, 44 (1930), pp. 162–93; also in T. Klauser, *Gesammelte Arbeiten zur Liturgiegeschichte, Kirchengeschichte u. Christlichen*

greater Carolingian monasteries, if we follow Dom Häussling, the *imitatio* took the form of a multiplication of altars within the conventual church and – sometimes – some subsidary ones.)[43] At Milan, although by the late ninth century (and probably much earlier) other churches in the city were linked liturgically with the cathedral on, for example, Palm Sunday and for the Ascension-tide litanies, the *ecclesiae minor* and *maior* had become respectively an *ecclesia hiemalis* and an *ecclesia aestivalis*; with the implication that all three Christmas masses would have been celebrated in the one 'winter cathedral' and not in three different basilicas as at Rome.[44]

These and a few other less well-documented instances of city-wide celebration of Sunday and feast-day masses may none the less always have been exceptional; and they cannot properly be used to throw light on the contemporary practice of (say) Lucca or Toulouse or York. There are, however, some very ambiguous indications that York was imitating Chrodegang's Metz in the late eighth century; and thanks to Alcuin, and in particular to the only partly-published *De laudibus Dei* compiled by him, it is possible to say rather more about the *content* of York's cathedral liturgy at that time than is generally

Archäologie, ed. E. Dassmann, Jahrbuch für Antike und Christentum, Erg.-Bd 5 (Münster, 1974), pp. 22–45. The very questionable attempts to interpret this text in the light of evidence from the monastery of St Riquier c. 800 are considered below. For the much later Cologne 'stational liturgy', see A. Wolff, 'Kirchenfamilie Köln. Von der Wahrung der geistlichen Einheit einer mittelalterlichen Bischofsstadt durch das Stationskirchenwesen', *Colonia Romanica*, I (1986), pp. 33–44; *Der älteste 'Liber Ordinarius' der Stiftskirche St. Aposteln in Köln*, ed. A. Odenthal, Studien zur Kölner Kirchengeschichte, 28 (Siegburg, 1994), pp. 51–91, with an instructive table at pp. 54–5.

[43] A. A. Häussling, *Mönchskonvent und Eucharistiefeier: Eine Studie über die Messe in der abendländischen Klosterliturgie des früheren Mittelalters und zur Geschichte der Messhäufigkeit*, Liturgiewissenschaftliche Quellen und Forschungen [hereafter LQF], 58 (Münster in Westfalen, 1973), esp. pp. 40–72, 298–347.

[44] A mass at S. Lorenzo before the Blessing of Palms and procession to the cathedral figures in the earliest Ambrosian sacramentaries as, e.g., the 'Sacramentary of Biasca', Milan, Biblioteca Ambrosiana, MS A 24 bis inf.: *Corpus Ambrosiano-Liturgicum ii: Das Ambrosianische Sakramentar von Biasca*, ed. O. Heiming, LQF, 51 (Münster, 1969), pp. 59–60 (no. lxv). The earliest evidence for the three days of litanies, halting at most of the churches in the city, and for the seasonal alternation of the cathedral *ecclesiae* is the Gospel-book and *capitulare evangeliorum*, Busto Arsizio, Biblioteca capitolare (S. Giovanni Battista) cod. M. I.14, of s.ix[2]. I have not seen this remarkable manuscript, and have been unable to consult any of the (partial) editions, for which see C. Vogel, *Medieval Liturgy: an Introduction to the Sources*, trans. and rev. W. Storey and N. Rasmussen (Washington, DC, 1986), pp. 331–2. But the single (unidentified) folio of the manuscript illustrated in E. Cattaneo, 'Storia e particolarità del Rito Ambrosiano', in [Fondazione Treccani degli Alfieri] *Storia di Milano*, 3, p. 793, shows the reading for the *dominica ante transmigratione[m] ecclesie* followed by the readings for the first day of the litanies, beginning *in sancto simpliciano*.

appreciated.[45] Yet I do not find in his letters a single reference to worshippers who are not themselves clerics; and if Alcuin's verse-compositions really do include a very early 'sequence' – *Summi regis archangele/ Michahel/* . . . , the chant-melody of which unexpectedly accompanies it in its unique eleventh-century manuscript testimony – it was evidently not for a lay congregation.[46]

* * *

In one of his letters to Archbishop Eanbald (II) of York, Alcuin, who was certainly a composer of mass-sets but not the compiler of the Supplement to the Gregorian Sacramentary which for at least a century was credited to him, rebuts his request for a new mass-book for the cathedral, and by extension perhaps for the diocese. His grounds for doing so are that the cathedral already has perfectly good Roman-type *libelli sacratorii* as well as enough of the larger missals of the older rite.[47] This somewhat surprising response is a convenient introduction to the well-worn topic of 'liturgical books' in Carolingian Europe, but hereafter particularly those used for celebration and worship in the innumerable rural (parochial) churches.

A 'pastoral instruction' which seems to be Arno of Salzburg's, at the very end of the eighth century, requires every parish priest to have a *sacramentorum* [sic] that his bishop has checked is of the proper form ('secundum ordinem'), but refers to no other books.[48] A widely-circulated capitulary of Bishop Haito of Basel, which is probably of before 813, declares on the other hand that no-one can properly call

---

[45] Details in D. A. Bullough, *Alcuin: Achievement and Reputation* (forthcoming, 2000), Pt II ch.1.

[46] Trier, Stadtbibliothek, MS 120/1170, fol. 'CLXXXIII^v'; *MGH. Poetae Latini aevi Carolini*, ed. E. Dümmler, 2 parts in 1 vol. (Berlin, 1880–1), pp. 348–9 (with a wrong manuscript number). The concluding (dedicatory) line as printed is no part of the poem in the manuscript and has no necessary bearing on its authorship: compare P. Dronke, 'The beginnings of the Sequence', *Beiträge zur Geschichte der Deutschen Sprache und Literatur*, 87 (1965), pp. 50–1. According to Edmund Bishop, *Liturgica Historica* (Oxford, 1918), p. 329: 'In a letter of Alcuin's we get a glimpse of the people joining in a litany of sorts; but in fact it all seems the noisy shout of a crowd just repeating the ejaculation of *Kyrie eleison*.' He gives no reference, and I do not know which letter he had in mind.

[47] Dümmler, *MGH. Epistolae*, IV, no. 226. The section of the letter of which this is the middle sentence presents considerable problems of translation and interpretation, which I have endeavoured to resolve elsewhere (as above, n.45).

[48] Ed. by R. Étaix, 'Un manuel de pastorale de l'époque carolingienne (Clm 27152)', *Revue Bénédictine*, 91 (1981), pp. 105–30, this passage at pp. 117–18, and previously from a single late manuscript in *MGH. Conc.*, II/1, pp. 198–201.

himself a priest unless he has a sacramentary, a lectionary, an antiphoner, a *baptisterium*, a computus, *kanon paenitentialis* (two books or one?), and a homiliary for the whole year for Sundays and feast-days. Similar lists in other capitularies, beginning with one of Bishop Ghaerbald of Lige, who died in 809 – still often improperly quoted as an Imperial capitulary of ?802 – tend to be less full, although commonly with the addition of a martyrology.[49] The occurrence of both martyrology and *baptisterium* among the 'prescribed texts' for priests in the Prologue of the Penitential of 'Egbert of York' (732–66)[50] is one of several reasons why almost all Continental scholars believe that it is a composition of the late eighth century (pseudo-Egbert, therefore), probably in some Continental centre, possibly the monastery of Lorsch. Since the oldest manuscript-text is apparently as early as any of the Frankish episcopal capitularies and has a heading that names Egbert – hardly, one would have thought, a familiar figure on the Continent *c.* 780–800 – and his see, I follow them only very reluctantly.[51]

That by mid-century prescription was partly matched by practice in widely scattered Frankish rural churches – ones that had evidently benefited from generous donors, lay and ecclesiastical, and presumably from actively interventionist bishops – is shown by lists of their possessions in charters and other texts. The polyptych of the estates of St Rémi, Rheims, in the early years of Archbishop Hincmar (845–82) records the treasures and books of churches on six of them. The books listed range in number from five to nine, always including at least one 'missal', the others being largely but not exclusively other liturgical texts: Aguilcourt (dp. Aisne) has both a 'missalis Gregorii cum evangeliis et lectionibus et breviarium antiphonarii' and 'alter missalis Gelasii'; another church has a 'missal' with the same additional matter and also an old (*vetustus*) Gelasian missal together with an old lectionary and an old antiphonary; a third church has a Gregorian

[49] *MGH. Cap. Episc.*, 1, p. 211 (c.6), pp. 39–40 (c.9).

[50] H&S, 3, pp. 416–30 (reprinting F. W. H. Wasserschleben's text of 1851 – in *Die Bussordnungen der abendländischen Kirche* – but giving variants from MS Bodley 718), at p. 417.

[51] I.e. BAV, MS Pal. Lat. 554, at fol. 5 (the text that follows omits cc. 14 and 15); for the manuscript, see B. Bischoff, *Die Abtei Lorsch im Spiegel ihrer Handschriften* (2nd edn, Lorsch, 1989), pp. 57–8, 124. My reservations have not been ended by R. Haggenmüller's intricate study of manuscript affiliations and textual development, *Die Überlieferung der Beda und Egbert zugeschriebenen Bussbücher*, Europäische Hochschulschriften, 461 (Frankfurt am Main, 1991), esp. pp. 148–95, 282, 295–8.

missal, together with 'alter manualis ex diversis causis', and separate lectionary, *collectaneus* and antiphonary; while a fourth has a Gelasian missal only 'with martyrology and penitential' in two volumes, as well as two lectionaries, a passional, a psalter, an antiphonary, and 'canons'.[52] The first of several lists of books given to or already in the possession of rural churches in the diocese of Freising (Bavaria) specifies the four *codices* bequeathed by a priest at Kollersdorf to the church at Attenkirchen in 830 as a missal, a *comes* (that is, a lectionary), an *officiale*, and an antiphonary. Twelve years later a priest at Puppling bequeathed his possessions to the cathedral, including *de ministerio ecclesiastico* two missals, a lectionary, a collectar, an *omeliarum dialogorum*, a *gradalem*, an antiphonary, and *canonem* and *penitentialem*. In contrast, when in 899 the church at Mauern was surrendered by its widow owner to the bishop of Freising to become a 'parish church' (which it still is) the books she conveyed with it were two missals, a lectionary, an antiphonary, a *gradalis*, and a homiliary; but it was unusually well provided with liturgical ornaments and vestments.[53] A fragmentary inventory of mid-tenth-century date from the diocese of Verona similarly records that the apparently recently-established 'plebs sancti Petri qui dicitur Tillida' (corresponding to the present-day San Pietro in Cantalovo, Bevilacqua), with two dependent churches, had one book combining a missal, a lectionary, and an antiphonary *de die*; a second in which a missal was combined with an antiphonary *de nocte*; a collectar that covered only Advent to St

---

[52] *Polyptyque de Saint-Rémi de Reims*, ed. B. Guérard (Paris, 1857), pp. 56, 78, 61–2, 38: for the type of book listed as *missalis gelasii* al. *gelasianus*, see below, n.58. Two churches have copies of Jerome on Matthew (*S. Hieronymi presbyteri opera, Paris I, 7*, ed. D. Hurst and M. Adriaen, CChr. SL, 77 [Turnhout, 1969]), two other churches have copies of Gregory the Great's *omilia XL*. The books of the Bavarian 'royal' monastery of Staffelsee *c.*810 (*Mittelalterliche Bibliothekskataloge Deutschlands und der Schweiz, III/1: Bistum Augsburg*, ed. P. Ruf [Munich, 1932], pp. 164–5) included Gregory's *Forty Homilies*, Jerome on Matthew and an anonymous *expositio Psalmorum* but no other patristic writings.

[53] *Freising*, nos. 597, 646, 1031. The Kollersdorf priest had previously bequeathed his books to the cathedral: ibid., no. 572, where the second book is indeed a *lectionarium*. These are among the eleven inventories in Freising, Regensburg, and Passau charters to 899 analysed by C. I. Hammer, 'Country churches, clerical inventories and the Carolingian Renaissance in Bavaria', ChH, 49 (1980), pp. 5–17. All these churches were in some sense 'proprietary' ones, as Hammer correctly remarks (pp. 12–13): but the possible differences between the books owned by established priests and those conveyed with a lay proprietary church are not explored; and note that the view attributed to me on p. 6 both misrepresents what I actually said (namely, that a general obligation to maintain and advance the Christian faith '*would be meaningless so long as* many of the clergy were' illiterate) and ignores the fact that I was referring to the situation *before* 'the Carolingian Renaissance'.

Stephen's Day(!); and unbound quires containing ten homilies of SS Augustine and Caesarius.[54]

These and similar lists elsewhere conceal as much as they reveal. Did the *lectionaria(-i)* include the occasional epistle/gospel-lectionary as well as the standard epistle-lectionary?[55] What was included in parish-church *antiphonaria* (unqualified, or *de die* and *de nocte* – which ought to be office-books)?[56] Does the presence of a collectar in only a minority of the lists indicate a significant difference of practice between those churches and others? Did the priests in the latter simply use the more limited range of *orationes ad matutinos* and *ad vesperos* included in their sacramentaries ('Gelasian' or 'Gregorian')?[57] Other than the several examples from the St Rémi 'proprietary churches', almost the only ninth-century book-list to categorize sacramentaries in the terms adopted by and sometimes misleadingly dominating twentieth-century liturgical scholarship is, of course, that from the abbey of St Riquier, compiled or copied in 831. Yet until recently there has been an almost

---

[54] *Inventari Altomedioevali di Terre, Coloni e Redditi* ed. A. Castagnoli *et al.*, Fonti per la Storia d'Italia, 104 (Rome, 1979), p. 109.

[55] The books prescribed by Haito of Basel and (?)Egbert of York and (above, p. 44 and nn.49, 50) include a *lectionarium* but no book of Gospel-readings; two centuries later Ælfric assumes in his first Latin letter to Archbishop Wulfstan (*Die Hirtenbriefe Ælfrics in altenglischen und lateinischer Fassung*, ed. B. Fehr, Bibliothek der angelsächsischen Prosa, 9 [Hamburg, 1914; repr. with supplement, Darmstadt, 1966], pp. 35–57, at p. 51) that the reference is to an epistle-lectionary – 'lectionarium quod quidam vocant epistolarium'.

[56] The mass-chants in Brussels, Bibliothèque royale, MS 10127–44 (below, pp. 48–9 and n.65) have the heading (fol. 90), 'In Dei nomen incipit antefonarius ordinatus a sancto Gregorio per circulum anni'.

[57] In the 'Old Gelasian' sacramentary, BAV, MS Vat. Reg. 316, III lxxxiv, lxxxv: *The Gelasian Sacramentary: Liber sacramentorum Romanae ecclesiae*, ed. H. A. Wilson (Oxford, 1894), pp. 291–2; *Liber sacramentorum Romanae æcclesiae ordinis anni circuli (Cod. Vat. Reg. Lat. 316/ Paris Bibl. nat. 7193, 41/56)*, ed. L. C. Mohlberg, L. Eizenhöfer, P. Siffrin, Rerum Ecclesiasticarum Documenta: series maior, fontes, 4 (Rome, 1960), nos 1576–94; a selection already in the 'Bobbio Missal' (from an Alpine-region or N. Italian village? *c.*700), *The Bobbio Missal: a Gallican Mass-Book (MS. Paris Lat. 13246)*, ed. E. A. Lowe *et al.*, 2 vols, HBS, 58, 61 (London, 1920–3; repr. as one vol., 61, 1991), I, pp. 171–2 (nos 563–73), and subsequently in 'Frankish Gelasian' and supplemented 'Gregorian' sacramentaries (*Le Sacramentaire Grégorien: ses principales formes d'après les plus anciens manuscrits*, ed. J. Deshusses, 3 vols, Spicilegium Friburgense, 16, 24, 28 [hereafter Deshusses, *Sacr. Grég.*] [Fribourg, 1971–82; 2nd edn of vol. 1 1979, preface only changed], I, nos. 1487–1509). For collectars and their contents, see especially Alicia Correa's introduction to her edition of *The Durham Collectar*, HBS, 107 (London, 1992), pp. 18–75. The earliest is St Gallen, Stiftsbibliothek, cod. 349, pp. 5–36 (= *Codices Latini Antiquiores*, ed. E. A. Lowe, 11 vols [Oxford, 1934–66], 7, no. 937), described by Correa, *Durham Collectar*, pp. 22–5; all extant Carolingian-period collectars are of monastic or cathedral-church origin (and use?). Episcopal statutes prescribing the saying of *horas canonicas tam nocturnas quam diurnas* are those of Haito of Basel and Radulf of Bourges (*MGH. Cap. Episc.*, 1, pp. 218 [c.2]), 239 [c.8]).

wilful refusal to take it at its face-value, because it records among the 'libri sacrarii qui ministerio altaris deserviunt' fourteen (or nineteen) Gelasian missals (the first certain occurrence of the term and referring, it is agreed, to our 'Eighth-century' or 'Frankish' Gelasian sacramentaries), but only three Gregorian ones, plus a *Missalis gregorianus et gelasianus modernis temporibus ab Albino ordinatus*.[58] If this was the situation in a monastery famous for its liturgical performance, what of the lesser churches with minimal resources, both before and after *c*.850? Did the 'missals of Gregory' in the St Rémi estate-churches' book-lists include the Aniane or some other supplement? When quite modest rural churches possessed two (unspecified) sacramentaries, were they of the same basic type, or of two different types? The answer to these and other similar questions is, surely, that we do not know. Neither the St Rémi listings nor the evidence of use of several of the surviving 'Frankish Gelasian' sacramentaries[59] encourages a supposition that they were commonly discarded within a year or two of their copying or acquisition. All extant ninth-century copies of the *Hadrianum* and of the Aniane Supplement were probably or certainly made in major monasteries or cathedral churches; although both are invariably one component of books that often are otherwise very varied in content; and it is not always certain where they were first used.[60] Only because of an excessive credence in the 'unifying' effect of early Carolingian liturgical reform or renewal has there been a widespread assumption that by the end of the century subordinate churches throughout Francia would normally have been celebrating the liturgy with some form of 'Gregorian' book.

At the level with which we are particularly concerned, that of the rural baptismal or other church (*oratorium*, etc.) served by a priest with the help of a boy and (at most) one or two other clerics, there is frustratingly little help to be found in extant manuscripts. Whole categories of book in the possession-lists have left no certain material

---

[58] Preserved only in Hariulf's early-twelfth-century *Chronicon Centulense*, ed. F. Lot, *Hariulf: Chronique de l'abbaye de St.-Riquier*, Collection de Textes pour servir à l'étude et à l'enseignement de l'histoire (Paris, 1894), p. 93; also in C. Vogel, 'La réforme liturgique sous Charlemagne', in *Karl der Grosse, Lebenswerk und Nachleben* [hereafter *Karlswerk*], 2: *Das Geistige Leben*, ed. B. Bischoff (Düsseldorf, 1965), p. 228. For *missalis gelasianus* etc., see Vogel, 'Réforme liturgique', p. 228 n.69 and B. Moreton, *The Eighth-Century Gelasian Sacramentary: a Study in Tradition* (Oxford, 1976), p. 170.

[59] Below, p. 49.

[60] Deshusses, *Sacr. Grég.*, 1, pp. 35–47; 3, pp. 19–59.

trace. It is possible that some of the ninth- and tenth-century sacramentary and lectionary fragments from southern Germany and north Italy are from books that once belonged to rural churches, even if written at their cathedral or in a neighbouring monastery; but it is not proved that they were, and they remain mute witnesses.[61] A Carolingian-period mass-book copied for and used in a rural *plebs baptismalis* is the Ambrosian sacramentary from Biasca (Switzerland, canton Ticino); but its church was, in the Carolingian and post-Carolingian centuries, a well-staffed collegiate one.[62] Going beyond the Carolingian period proper, there are a few late eleventh-century books from southern France that once belonged to country churches.[63] The one early-Carolingian 'liturgical' manuscript that was almost certainly produced for a country priest celebrating on his own, and is perhaps a lone survivor of a once-common type of book,[64] is the compendious but modest-sized Brussels, Bibliothèque royale, MS 10127–44, of *c*.800 or a little later. More than half of its 136 folios, mostly of poor-quality parchment, are a canon-law and penitential collection (the supplemented 'Vetus Gallica', magisterially expounded by Hubert Mordek), which is followed (to fol. 89ᵛ) by a collection of five *ordines* with two extraneous texts: neither section shows much

---

[61] B. Bischoff, *Die Südostdeutschen Schreibschulen und Bibliotheken in der Karolingerzeit* [hereafter Bischoff, *Schreibschulen*], 1, 2nd edn (Wiesbaden, 1960), 2 (Wiesbaden, 1980), *passim*.

[62] Edited by Heiming, *Das Ambrosianische Sakramentar von Biasca*. That it was intended from the start for a rural 'parish', even though it retained features proper to the cathedral town, is indicated by the language of the Lenten litanies, in which the *Pro civitate hac* of, e.g., the 'Sacramentary of Bergamo' (*Codex Sacramentorum Bergomensis*, ed. P. Cagin [Solesmes, 1900], pp. 37, 43; *Sacramentarium Bergomense*, ed. A. Paredi [Bergamo, 1962] [which was not available to me]), is replaced by *Pro plebe hac* (Heiming, *Das Ambrosianische Sakramentar von Biasca*, pp. 42, 47). An entry of *c*.840 (not '*c*.880') in the *Liber Viventium Fabariensis*, p. 42, under the heading *Hec sunt nomina presbitorum de Aviasca* (complete facsimile, Basel, 1973; *MGH. Libri Confraternitatum S. Galli, Augienses*, . . . , ed. P. Piper [Berlin, 1884]) lists an *archipresbiter* and seven *presbiteri*.

[63] A.-G. Martimort, 'Répertoires des livres liturgiques de Languedoc', *Cahiers de Fanjeaux*, 17 (1982), pp. 51–80; also idem, 'Sources, histoire et originalité de la liturgie Catalano-Languedocienne', ibid., pp. 27–9. For the Moussoulens sacramentary of *c*.1100, Carcassonne, Bibliothèque Séminaire, s.n., as a product of the monastery on which that village church was dependent, see A.-G. Martimort, 'Un sacramentaire de la région de Carcassonne des environs de l'année 1100', *Mélanges en l'honneur de Mgr Michel Andrieu* (Strasbourg, 1956), pp. 305–26.

[64] Compare the pre-Carolingian 'Bobbio Missal', which E. A. Lowe, *The Bobbio Missal*, 2, pp. 105–6, characterized as the work of 'an old cleric in an obscure village' who 'crowded into his Missal much more than properly belonged there' (e.g. *lectiones*), and the *missales cum evangeliis* etc. possessed later by St Rémi (Rheims)'s dependent churches.

evidence of use. The remaining forty-seven folios provide, successively, an early text of the 'Gregorian' mass-antiphonary, the leaves moderately worn; a baptismal *ordo* followed by a collection of blessings, both of which show considerable 'wear-and-tear'; and finally, under the rubric *Liber sacramentorum Excarsus* [sic], an evidently much-used assemblage of Gelasian-type masses, with lections in full, for eleven of the liturgical year's major feasts. These were ones, presumably, which a visiting priest was expected to celebrate for the local community in a seignorial or subordinate church. Whether or not the Brussels book once had a text of the canon and so on in a now lost quire, the assumption must certainly be that the putative early users will have had access to a complete mass-book at their principal church.[65] Likewise evidently written for secular, non-episcopal, use *c.*800, and showing extensive wear and damage (partly from the waters of a font?) before its acquisition by the monastery of Rheinau near Zurich, is another 'Frankish Gelasian' sacramentary, subsequently combined with mass-antiphonary and penitential.[66]

* * *

The picture of the first Carolingian century as one in which many more books, in a generally improved Latinity, were copied and

[65] J. Van den Gheyn, *Catalogue des Manuscrits de la Bibliothèque Royale de Belgique, 1: Écriture sainte et liturgie* (Brussels, 1901), no. 363 (10127-44) must be corrected and supplemented, for fols 1-79v, from H. Mordek, *Kirchenrecht und Reform im Frankenreich*, Beiträge zur Geschichte und Quellenkunde des Mittelalters, 1 (Berlin and New York, 1975), pp. 276-7, 219-21 and, for fols 79v-135v, from *Les 'Ordines Romani' du haut moyen âge*, ed. M. Andrieu, 5 vols, Spicilegium sacrum Lovanienses: études et documents, fasc. 11, 23-4, 28-9 (Louvain, 1931-61) [hereafter Andrieu, *Ordines*], 1, pp. 91-6. The mass-sets, baptismal *ordo*, and blessings are edited by C. Coebergh and P. de Puniet in *Testimonia Orationis Christianae Antiquioris*, CChr. CM, 77 (Turnhout, 1977), pp. 85-110. R. McKitterick, *The Frankish Church and the Carolingian Reforms, 789-895* (London, 1977), p. 127, cites this manifestly non-monastic book among her 'evidence' that 'the diffusion of the Gelasian type of sacramentary . . . was largely confined to the monasteries', in this instance St Peter's, Ghent. But it was almost certainly only after it had ceased to be used liturgically that it entered the monastic library (the *ex-libris* is of *c.*1200); and the added note on fol. 89v, 'De servitio domni episcopi et archidiaconi. De una matrice aecclesia mod. I de farrina *etc.* ad modum leodicensi' (Liège), shows that it was still a secular 'country church' book in s.ix/x.

[66] Zurich, Zentralbibliothek, cod. Rh.30: Moreton, *Eighth-Century Gelasian Sacramentary*, pp. 184-7; *Sacramentarium Rheinaugiense*, ed. A. Hänggi, Spicilegium Friburgense, 15 (Fribourg, 1970). It was written neither for Reichenau(!) nor Rheinau, as supposed by McKitterick, *Frankish Church*, p. 127: Rheinau's effective foundation was indeed a half-century later than the penning of the manuscript (on this see most recently H. Löwe, 'Findan von Rheinau. Eine irische peregrinatio im 9. Jahrhundert', *Studi Medievali*, ser. 3, 26 (1985), pp. 53-100, at pp. 63-75).

circulated, and even reached segments of society that had previously been book-less, is not to be questioned. But in trying to establish which of the familiar changes in liturgical forms and practice had become normative in rural (or indeed minor urban) churches, and when, neither surviving manuscripts nor the book-lists are of much help. We are in no position to say how many older books continued in use, with or without inserted leaves and added *libelli*, even after most cathedrals and monasteries had gone over to 'reformed' sacramentaries and their associated *ordines* – and were conceivably more intelligible to priests and congregations than the new ones.[67] The late Christopher Hohler, reviewing Gerald Ellard's *Master Alcuin, Liturgist*, forty years ago, already challenged the supposed rapid triumph of the 'Gregorian' sacramentary in its Hadrianic or any other form over the 'Gelasian'; although he characteristically linked this with a suggestion that many Frankish churches may have been abandoning their traditional Gallican rite even before the Carolingian 'reforms'.[68] Since then, of course, credit for the *Hucusque* supplement has been transferred from the Northumbrian Alcuin to the 'Goth' Benedict, which makes better sense of some of its non-Roman features.

Conversely, Hohler himself noted many more prayers of apparently Gallican origin in southern French mass-books, including the Moussoulens sacramentary, right down to the printing era; and others have reported even more striking survivals in that region in particular high-medieval festal observances, in the celebrant's *apologiae*, and in the occasional sacraments.[69] We should not ignore the possibility that the pre-Carolingian 'Bobbio Missal' (which cannot be shown to have been at Bobbio in any medieval century) has survived precisely because it continued to be used for centuries in some remote country church,

---

[67] John Harper's proposition that 'in most instances [parish churches] followed the Use of a larger church (often the local cathedral) rather than instigating their own customs' (*The Forms and Orders of Western Liturgy from the Tenth to the Eighteenth Century* [Oxford, 1991], p. 26) cannot be disproved; but it is quite unprovable for the earliest of the centuries with which he is declaredly concerned, and may indeed make the situation sound more regular and consistent than it then was.

[68] *JEH*, 8 (1957), pp. 222–6.

[69] For Benedict's 'authorship' of the Supplement and the earliest manuscript evidence for it see, most conveniently, Deshusses, *Sacr. Grég.*, 1, pp. 61–70, 3, pp. 66–75; also A. M. Mundo, 'Sur quelques manuscrits liturgiques languedociens de l'époque carolingienne', *Cahiers de Fanjeaux*, 17 (1982), pp. 81–95. For 'Visigothic' and 'Gallican' survivals, see Martimort, 'Sources, histoire et originalité', ibid., pp. 25–49, esp. pp. 31–41; A. Olivar, 'Survivances wisigothiques dans la liturgie Catalano-languedocienne', ibid, pp. 158–72.

whatever may have been the rite of its (unidentified) see-church. One way of giving, or potentially giving, continued currency to an old liturgical book was to hand it on to a new incumbent with other symbols of his office and specifying that it should be used. There is remarkable eleventh-century evidence for this from the chapter of the Seu d'Urgell in Catalonia; but if something similar is recorded elsewhere, and specifically at the level of the rural church, I have failed to notice it.[70]

The gulf between a monastic or a cathedral church and the rural churches that served most of the 'faithful' was at its widest, of course, in the even more elusive area of performance, the chant-settings of liturgical texts. Episcopal capitularies are as sparing as other sources on the actual – as distinct from the desirable – training of rural priests: and even assuming that some of them had spent time in adolescence in a cathedral or other *scola*, how much of what they had learnt and practised there was transferable to the churches of the villages in which they lived out their lives? The chant repertory that is still commonly referred to as 'Gregorian', although few musicologists today would regard it as more than incidentally pre-Carolingian,[71] and its alternatives in parts of Italy and in northern Spain, were phenomena of churches with specialist *cantores* to guide *pueri* and *clerici* in choir. Yet the Carolingian-period work with the best claim to be described as a musical 'teaching manual', Regino of Prüm's *De harmonica institutione*, does seem to have been written with a wider constituency in mind: Regino had, he told Archbishop Ratbod of Trier (d. 915), found the singing in churches under his authority marred by 'vocal confusion because of the discrepancy of the tone'.[72] The references in the book-lists to *antiphonarii* and *gradales* imply that at least a selection of the variable texts was widely available, although at that time without any form of musical markings (alphabetical or neumatic). Presumably most

---

[70] See J. Alturo, 'Les inventaires de livres en Catalogne du IXe au XIIe siècles', *Scriptorium*, 50 (1996), pp. 370–9, at p. 372 (on the basis of testaments in C. Baraut, *Els documents conservats a l'Arxiu Capitular de la Seu d'Urgell* [Urgel, 1979 et seq.], which I have not seen).

[71] For a good presentation of the arguments, see D. Hiley, *Western Plainchant: a Handbook* (Oxford, 1993), pp. 503–23, esp. 513–20.

[72] *PL* 132, cols 483–502 (without the accompanying tonary), at 483–4; a promised new edition by the musicologist Yves Chartier seems not to have appeared. The limited manuscript tradition offers both a shorter and a longer version: it is just possible that the former, which omits a long theoretical or philosophical section, was specifically directed at village priests.

priests continued to 'intone' them, more or less in line with local speech rhythms and occasionally even – on the evidence of conciliar prohibitions – with melodies that properly belonged to secular compositions.[73]

This, however, would always have been no more than than a marginal aspect of the laity's 'liturgical experience'. One of the paradoxes of 'Carolingian reform' is that the more successful it was in training the clergy in 'good Latin', with a traditional syntax and carefully articulated in ways that served clearly to distinguish it from the 'Romance' vernaculars in a direct line of descent from earlier spoken Latin – and thus far, although not much further, I follow Dr Roger Wright[74] – the less accessible the liturgy of mass and office became to the ordinary faithful in both Romance and Germanic regions. The independent developments that led to the praying of the canon in silence and subsequently to an equal 'secrecy' of the prayer *super oblata* – possibly in some areas already in pre-Carolingian times and apparently normal by the end of the ninth century – further weakened the prayerful bonds between celebrant and congregation.[75] The several hundred known extra-liturgical *preces privatae* must, even on a more optimistic or positive assessment of lay literacy than I am able to accept,[76] always have been the privilege of a very few.

It has been claimed that the bishops in their statutes were seeking to ensure that 'Their flocks were to feel the core of their religion in a great mystery, centred on the mass.'[77] But a widening of the gulf between the *ordines clericorum* and the ordinary faithful (tempered perhaps only by ignorance and the forms of misconduct which figure

[73] On which see especially *Clofesho* 747 c.12 (H&S, 3, 366): 'Ut presbyteri saecularium poetarum modo in ecclesia non garriant, ne tragico sono sacrorum verborum compositionem ac distinctionem corrumpant vel confundant, sed simplicem sanctamque melodiam secundum morem ecclesiae sectentur.'

[74] R. Wright, *Late Latin and Early Romance in Spain and Carolingian France* (Liverpool, 1982); R. Wright, ed., *Latin and the Romance Languages in the Early Middle Ages* (London, 1990), esp. Pt II.

[75] R. Cabié, *The Church at Prayer*, ed. A. G. Martimort, 2: *The Eucharist* (Collegeville, MN, and London, 1986), pp. 133–4; P.-M. Gy, 'La doctrine eucharistique dans la liturgie romaine du haut Moyen-age', *Settimane di Studio del Centro Italiano di Studi sull'Alto Medioevo, XXXIII: Segni e Riti nella Chiesa Altomedievale Occidentale* [hereafter *Segni e Riti*] (Spoleto, 1987), pp. 532–54, at pp. 537–9. But G. G. Willis, *Further Essays in Early Roman Liturgy* (London, 1968), pp. 123–9 ('The Secret'), argues for a very different chronology.

[76] As by R. McKitterick, *The Carolingians and the Written Word* (Cambridge, 1989) and elsewhere.

[77] J. M. Wallace-Hadrill, *The Frankish Church* (Oxford, 1983), p. 280. See also ibid., p. 283.

in almost all statutes) and an increasing emphasis on the exclusiveness of altar and 'choir' are not obviously helpful to that end. One of Bishop Haito of Basel's decrees already assumes (*ante* ?813) that this special 'sacred space' would have been marked off to the west by *cancelli*, that is, balustrades or low screens: altar linen that has to be washed can only be removed by clergy, who hand it over to women *ad cancellos* and subsequently receive it back there! Archaeological and art-historical evidence suggests, moreover, that these 'barriers' may have become more common in lesser churches during the ninth and tenth centuries; and curtains or veils, originally intended to shut out catechumens, may not have been peculiar to churches in Rome or to those of nuns and canonesses.[78] I have already suggested that even in Theodulf's capitularies – the first of which was exceptionally widely circulated through three centuries – there are really very few passages that deal with the mass, and even fewer that are concerned with layfolk's participation. The 'mystery of the mass' is a matter for clerics, and for not many of them, whether expounded by Amalarius of Metz – whose 'excessive' allegorizing provoked a successful accusation of heresy – or by his more traditionalist critic Florus of Lyons. The latter's *Expositio missae* was drawn on by both Hincmar of Rheims and the eleventh-century author of the *Confessio fidei* – John of Fécamp? – but a majority of the manuscripts are of the twelfth or thirteenth centuries. Amalarius's work survived its condemnation 'to inspire most liturgical writings down to the end of the Middle Ages'.[79] Paschasius Radbertus

---

[78] Haito: *MGH. Cap. Episc.*, 1, p. 215 (c.16). Architectural *cancelli* (cf. Walahfrid's *De exordiis*, *MGH. Cap.*, 2, p. 480 and Alice Harting-Correa's comments in her *Translation and Liturgical Commentary*, p. 222): the greatest body of evidence comes from south of the Alps, comprehensively published in the *Corpus della Scultura Altomedievale* of the *Centro Italiano di Studi sull'Alto Medioevo* (14 vols so far; Spoleto, 1959–); but the commentaries of the several editors show how very uncertain is their stylistic sequence and dating. Compare, for Carolingian Francia, the very selective account by E. Doberer, 'Die ornamentale Steinskulptur an der karolingischen Kirchenausstattung', in *Karlswerk*, 3: *Karolingische Kunst*, ed. W. Braunfels and H. Schnitzler (Düsseldorf, 1965), pp. 203–33, esp. pp. 205–17. *Vela, cortinae*: the many examples in secular churches recorded in *Schatzverzeichnisse* (see index s.vv.) obviously served more than one purpose; but Doberer, 'Ornamentale Steinskulptur', p. 212, assumes that the surviving (usually fragmentary) screen cross-beams will often have had curtains hanging from them. For the *velum* that conceals a female congregation see, e.g., *MGH. Conc.*, II/2, p. 455.

[79] A. Kolping, 'Amalar von Metz und Florus von Lyon, Zeugen eines Wandels im liturgischen Mysterienverständnis in der Karolingerzeit', *ZkT*, 73 (1951), pp. 424–64; P.-M. Gy, 'History of liturgy in the west to the Council of Trent', in A. G. Martimort, ed., *The Church at Prayer*, 1: *Principles of the Liturgy* (London, 1987), pp. 56–7. Florus's *Expositio* was ed. and commented on by P. Duc, *Étude sur l'Expositio Missae de Florus de Lyon* (Lyons, Thèse de Doctorat; Belley, 1937).

wrote *his* treatise on the eucharist for the monks of Corvey, although (he claimed) for ones at a fairly early stage of their education, 'those whom the tide of liberal education has not yet reached'.[80]

* * *

This, of course, is very far from being the whole story. In cathedral towns and in the vicinity of major monasteries (until reformers objected) these 'liturgies for an elite' were now commonly supplemented by processions of the kind implicit in the Metz stational-list, recorded in remarkable detail for St Riquier *c.* 800, and obviously to be inferred from the somewhat later texts from the churches of Milan and other cities.[81] Indeed, I do not doubt that the brief litany of the saints to be chanted as the bishop proceeded from the church to the free-standing baptistery which is a feature of the Gellone Sacramentary's *ordo baptisterii* for Holy Saturday really did involve active participation *ab omnibus* at Cambrai (or wherever was the book's original destination).[82] But here, as elsewhere later, its citizens can hardly have done more than chant a simple refrain with a 'popular' pronunciation; and by 807 the book, like its probable donor, had entered the southern French 'desert' monastery of Gellone where it quickly ceased to be used.[83]

---

[80] *De corpore et sanguine domini*, ed. B. Paul, *CChr. CM*, 16 (Turnhout, 1969), p. 5.

[81] The most recent edition of the only partly-preserved *Institutio Angilberti Centulensi*, from BAV, MS Reg. 235 and Hariulf's *Chronicon Centulense*, by K. Hallinger and M. Wegener (with limited liturgical notes by H. Frank) in *Corpus Consuetudinum Monasticarum*, 1: *Initia Consuetudinis Benedictinae*, ed. K. Hallinger (Siegburg, 1963), pp. 283–303, was unfortunately unknown to D. Parsons, 'The pre-Romanesque church of St-Riquier: the documentary evidence', *JBAA*, 129 (1976), pp. 21–51. Some of Parsons's textual points are of doubtful merit: but his criticisms of the claims of C. Heitz and others for precise parallels with Metz's more skeletally-documented liturgical practice earlier and with the ceremonies in *Westwerken* later (see esp. pp. 48–50), and his own alternative interpretations of Angilbert's account, are very much to the point. (For the St Riquier litanies, see now M. Lapidge's introduction to his *Anglo-Saxon Litanies of the Saints*, HBS, 106 [London, 1991] [hereafter Lapidge, *Litanies*], pp. 36–9.) The Metz list is apparently the earliest evidence in the West of a Palm Sunday procession, going from an extra-mural church to the intra-mural St Peter's. The 'Bobbio Missal', however, has a *Benedictio palme et olive* with the incipit *Ecce dies domine festa recolitur*: ed. Lowe, *The Bobbio Missal*, 1, p. 170 no. 558.

[82] Dumas, *Liber sacramentorum Gellonensis*, pp. 332–3 (no. 2313); Lapidge, *Litanies*, pp. 33–4.

[83] 'Tous ceux qui ont eu le privilège de feuilleter le célèbre sacramentaire de Gellone ont pu constater qu'il est pratiquement intact: preuve évidente qu'il n'a jamais été qu'un objet de musée pour ses possesseurs': so R. Amiet, 'Le plus ancien témoin du Supplement d'Alcuin', *Ephemerides Liturgicae*, 72 (1958), pp. 97–110, at p. 109; cf. McKitterick, *Frankish Church*, p. 127.

The sophisticated melodies to which the introductory *Kyrie eleisons* of litanies were later sung (so unlike Benjamin Britten's), as witnessed by – among others – a major chant-manuscript from St Vaast, Arras (now at Cambrai as Bibliothèque municipale, MS 61), surely excluded popular participation. It is indeed symptomatic that the early eighth-century *Ordo Romanus I* already credits the chanting of the *Kyrie* after the Introit to the *scola* alone and not (as formerly) to the whole congregation assembled at the 'station'.[84] *A fortiori*, the expansion of the repertoire of processional hymns in the ninth and tenth centuries could have done little or nothing for lay involvement. Just because some of us are accustomed to exuberant renderings of 'Hail thee, Festival Day' or 'All glory, laud and honour' (Theodulf of Orleans's *Gloria laus et honor tibi sit*), we should not be tempted into supposing that 1100 years ago our predecessors joined in the words and melody, or even in the alternate refrains, of Fortunatus's *Salve festa dies*.[85] English, and I am sure other, chant-manuscripts of the later Middle Ages give the singing of its main text to soloists, the choir providing the refrain. It needed Thomas Cranmer to produce a singable English-language version, and his comments are worth quoting:

> The Latin note as I think, is sober and distinct enough; wherefore I have travailed to make the verses in English, and have put the Latin note unto the same: nevertheless they that be cunning in singing can make a much more solemn note thereto – I made them only for a proof to see how English would do in song.[86]

* * *

Layfolk's limited access to the resources of the liturgy during the early medieval and Carolingian centuries seems to have made difficult even

[84] Andrieu, *Ordines*, 2, p. 84 (c.52), cf. *Ordo IV* (in Paris BN, MS lat. 974: Northern French but hardly St Amand) c.20: ibid., p. 159.

[85] With untranscribable neumatic musical setting, for the first time in the great St-Gallen book Stiftsbibliothek, MS 391, pp. 35–42; the melody in *Monumenta Monodica Medii Aevi* 1: *Hymnen*, ed. B. Stäblein (Kassel and Basel, 1956), p. 482 (no. 1008), cf. pp. 616–17, is from the fourteenth-century Kremsmünster, Stiftsbibliothek, MS 31. In the lost Sirmond manuscript of Theodulf's poetry the text of *Gloria laus et honor* etc. (*MGH. Poetae*, I, pp. 558–9) apparently had the rubric 'versus facti ut a pueris in die palmarum cantarentur'; the late-tenth-century *Regularis concordia*, c.36 (in *Regularis concordia*, ed. T. Symons *Nelson's Medieval Texts* [London and Edinburgh, 1953], p. 35), allocated the hymn to the monastic *pueri*, with the rest of the congregation singing the refrain; and similarly, with some variations, in later customaries etc.

[86] *Miscellaneous Writings and Letters*, ed. J. E. Cox, *PS* (Cambridge, 1846), p. 412: quoted by H. Gneuss, *Hymnar und Hymnen im Englischen Mittelalter* (Tübingen, 1968), p. 234.

a proper 'Christianizing' of burial. The testimony here is documentary and archaeological as well as liturgical: taken in conjunction, and with all its ambiguities, it leaves little doubt that the ceremonial, involving family and community, is only exceptionally in the church itself – unlike subsequent 'priestly' commemorative masses. The German (Lotharingian) diocese of Trier offers an unusually rich corpus of evidence for 'popular' funerary practice in the Carolingian period and again in the fifteenth and sixteenth centuries; but, for the earlier centuries, the more fragmentary documentation from other parts of Francia points in similar directions.[87] The liturgical vigil ('wake') by a corpse was for long peculiar to members of religious communities, occasionally extended to prominent lay people and especially founders of churches or their immediate descendants. Regino of Prüm's 'manual of canon law' represents the views of his archbishop at the end of the ninth century as trying to get laity to move their traditional wakes into the local church, and substitute *Kyries* and some Christianized 'song' (unspecified) for their secular *carmina diabolica*. Whether directly linked with Ratold's initiatives or not, the very recently published 'Echternach Sacramentary' of ?895/8 shows the process of Christianizing burial actually under way in the diocese in the rubrics of prayers for the dying and the dead, especially the one that begins 'In ecclesia autem requiescit corpus defuncti et ibidem psalmi sine intermissione cantantur', and in the specifying of three-fold *Kyries* after two of the *orationes* that follow.[88] The weight of the evidence is that these efforts

---

[87] The Trier evidence is spendidly exploited by N. Kyll, *Tod, Grab, Begräbnisplatz, Totenfeier*, Rheinisches Archiv, 81 (Bonn, 1972): for the Carolingian period, esp. pp. 30–41, 189–91. D. A. Bullough, 'Burial, community and belief in the early medieval West', in P. Wormald, D. Bullough, and R. Collins, eds, *Ideal and Reality in Frankish and Anglo-Saxon Society* (Oxford, 1983), pp. 177–201, uses selectively archaeological and textual evidence from other parts of Western Europe also; for this period see esp. pp. 198–201. P.-A. Février, 'La Mort chrétienne', *Segni e Riti*, pp. 881–942, ranges far more widely, chronologically and geographically. Almost no account is taken, however, of the extensive post-800 documentary evidence for 'rites'; and citing the evidence for commemorative masses, including one on the seventh day, in the eighth/ninth-century 'Autun sacramentary' (ibid., pp. 905–6; *Liber Sacramentorum Augustodunensis*, ed. O. Heiming, CChr. SL, 159B [Turnhout, 1984]). Février seems not to have appreciated that the mass-set rubric is one found already in the Vatican Gelasian (III, cv: Wilson, *The Gelasian Sacramentary*, p. 312; Mohlberg et al., *Liber sacramentorum Romanae æcclesiae*, before nos. 1690–5), while the other two quotations are from its final, penitential, section which is largely made up of extracts from one or other of the versions of Theodore's Penitential (Bk II in the *discipulus Umbrensium* version): *Die Canones Theodori Cantuariensis und ihre Überlieferungsformen*, ed. P. W. Finsterwalder (Weimar, 1929), pp. 318–19, 249, 265–6, 273.
[88] Regino, *Libri duo de synodalibus causis et disciplinis ecclesiasticis*, ed. F. W. H. Wasserschleben (Leipzig, 1840), pp. 24, 145, 243, and other passages quoted by Kyll, *Tod, Grab,*

were ultimately unsuccessful, although the 'devilish songs' reputedly died out. The circumstantial stories of miracles associated with the relics of St Matthias have been taken to mean that even in the twelfth century many lay people were still favouring *ludi* and popular songs over prayers for the recently deceased:[89] which, if typical also of other areas of western Europe, underlines the attraction in the intervening centuries of admission to a monastery *ad succurendum* with the right of burial and subsequent intercessory prayer.

In one sacramental rite, that of baptism, the involvement of the laity – as baptizee, as parents, and as godparents or sponsors – is inherent in the liturgical action or actions, with a corresponding personal and shared experience. The complex and often contradictory textual record of baptismal ceremonies between the early eighth and late tenth centuries is none the less testimony to significant and often enduring long-term changes in ritual and its language, simultaneously with the maintaining or even revival of more ancient practice. Frankish church councils and episcopal statutes reiterate the rule that baptisms should be restricted as far as possible to Easter Eve with the alternative of the eve of Pentecost: at many cathedrals in Italy, southern Gaul, and northern Spain, that may indeed have been the normal practice uninterruptedly since the age of the Fathers (at Florence, it apparently continued until at least the 1840s).[90] Professor Valerie Flint has graphically evoked the 'popular' atmosphere in church or baptistery at the time of these mass baptisms, and at the preliminary Lenten-season ceremonies ('scrutinies') which she supposes still preceded them in the mid-ninth century, attended by parents, relatives, sponsors, and of course *infantes*.[91] It is very doubtful, however, whether the sevenfold

pp. 30–1; *The Sacramentary of Echternach*, ed. Y. Hen, HBS, 110 (London, 1997), pp. 441–7 (nos 2290–2308). The rubric quoted (no. 2302) continues: 'missae celebrentur et offerantur ab omnibus. Post caelebrationem vero missae stat sacerdos iuxta feretrum et dixit oratio', which is the 'Mozarabic' prayer adopted as Aniane Supplement no. 1401 (Deshusses, *Sacr. Grég.*, 1, p. 458), *inc.* 'Non intres in iudicio cum servo tuo'; the *aliae orationes* have more than one source.

[89] *MGH. SS*, VIII (Hanover 1848/Leipzig 1925), pp. 231–2 (ed. G. Waitz); J. Hau, *Aus dem Altmattheiser Wunderbuch* (Trier, 1948), p. 63; Kyll, *Tod, Grab*, p. 39.

[90] *MGH. Conc.*, II/1, pp. 173, 261, etc.; *MGH. Cap. Episc.*, 1, pp. 19 (c.10), 211 (c.7), etc. The Easter baptisms at Florence were remarked on by several visitors from northern Europe in the seventeenth, eighteenth, and early nineteenth centuries.

[91] V. Flint, 'Susanna and the Lothar Crystal: a liturgical perspective', *Early Medieval Europe*, 4 (1995), pp. 61–86, at pp. 72–6. But Professor Flint's linking of the mass *Ad sanctam Susannam* on the third Saturday in Lent and its *lectiones* Dan. 13.1–62 and John 8.1–11 with one of the pre-baptismal scrutinies for parents, sponsors, and *infantes*, and the inferences she

scrutinies prescribed in the eighth-century Roman or Gallicanized Roman *Ordo XI* have any relevance to regular Carolingian Frankish baptismal practice, even in cathedral towns – the more if (as seems likely) the prohibition on parents receiving their own child from the font in one of the great reforming synods of 813 was one of wider application. It remains to be shown that their use for the reception of adult catechumens survived, or was revived in these same decades, in missionary regions.[92]

The commonsensical Hrabanus Maurus, as Archbishop of Mainz, was aware of the rule about 'the proper season' for baptisms, but regarded it as unwise and unnecessary, at least in rural areas. Half a century later Ratold of Trier recognized another reason for ignoring the rule, a fear of pagan attack.[93] The chronology of the introduction and dissemination of simplifed rituals particularly adapted to the now-

draws from that supposed link, depend entirely on an unfortunate confusion between the originally distinct 'Gregorian' (papal stational) and the 'Gelasian' (Roman presbyteral) liturgies. The *statio* (the only one at that church) and its mass-lections, including the story of Susanna, belong to the first-named. The scrutiny and its associated mass (originally on the Sunday but then moved back to Saturday) took place at the presbyteral and other churches with a font (which Sta Susanna did not have until the time of Leo III), the readings being – as *Ordo XI* makes clear – Ezek. 36.25–9 and Matt. 11.25–30, after which 'offeruntur oblationes a parentibus [infantium] vel ab his qui ipsos suscepturi sunt' (cf. Flint, 'Susanna', p. 74); 'finita missarum sollemnia communicent omnes praeter ipsos infantes': Andrieu, *Ordines*, 2, pp. 424–6 (cc.28–32, 36–8). Compare J. H. Lynch, *Godparents and Kinship in Early Medieval Europe* (Princeton, NJ, 1986), pp. 289–92, who observes that before the mass on the occasion of the fifth scrutiny the *infantes* are apparently handed over to a baby-sitter ('foris relinquunt ipsos infantes in custodia': Andrieu, *Ordines*, 2, p. 441 [c.73])!

[92] Early ninth-century commentaries on the baptismal liturgy, whether in answer to a questionnaire sent out in the Emperor's name or indirectly inspired by it, vary between those that include large parts of *Ordo XI*'s account of the sevenfold scrutinies (e.g. Theodulf of Orleans, *PL* 105, cols 223–40, or Jesse of Amiens, ibid., cols 781–91: a near-contemporary copy, although without the preface, in the St Amand-area manuscript St Gallen, Stiftsbibliothek, cod. 124, pp. 310–26) and those which, like Alcuin earlier, implicitly accept the notion of a single occasion. For the next century, see the *ordo scrutiniorum* in the *Sacramentarium Fuldense* (Göttingen, Universitätsbibliothek, cod. theol. 231), ed. G. Richter and A. Schönfelder (Fulda, 1912; repr. as HBS, 101 [Farnborough, 1977]), pp. 329–43 (nos 470–4), with the comments of Cramer, *Baptism and Change*, pp. 195–7. But Dr Cramer may not have recognized that the Sacramentary is here heavily dependent on, although not exactly identical with, *Ordo Romanus L* (ed. Andrieu, *Ordines*, 5) = *Le Pontifical Romano-Germanique du dixième siècle*, ed. C. Vogel and R. Elze, Studi e Testi, 226–7 (Vatican City, 1963) at pp. 226–7, which had itself drawn on the eighth-century *Ordo XI*; for some of the implications of this, compare Lynch, *Godparents and Kinship*, pp. 297–302. The prohibition is among the 'consanguinity' decrees of the 813 Council of Mainz, *MGH. Conc.*, II/1, p. 273.

[93] *Epistolae Karolini aevi, III*, ed. E. Dümmler et al., *MGH. Epistolarum*, V (Berlin, 1899), p. 522, from one of the letters known only from extracts in the Magdeburg Centuriators (who surely, rather than a medieval compiler – as supposed by Cramer, *Baptism and Change*, p. 140 – are responsible for the approving comment); *MGH. Cap. Episc.*, 1, p. 68 (c.21).

normal infant baptism remains, however, a matter of debate. Dr Cramer is among the scholars who, following Père Gy and others, favours a pre-800 date for the reduction of the scrutinies effectively to one and a change in the person (no longer the baptizee) to whom the credal interrogation was addressed.[94] This is indeed a particularly appropriate context for the innovatory vernacular creeds. Unsurprisingly, the wording of the bi-lingual *exhortatio ad plebem christianam*, the German version of which is for many decades the only extant Continental vernacular sermon, directly links it with a just-completed ceremony of baptism, and insists on the obligation of sponsors to know and teach the articles of faith.[95]

In his Supplement to the Gregorian *Hadrianum*, Benedict of Aniane 'canonized' the simplified and shorter rite (with 'ego te baptizo', etc., accompanying the three-fold immersion) as one part of an effort to separate adult and infant rites; and we are able to recognize, even if contemporaries did not, that this had major consequences for an understanding of the 'sign' in the baptismal ceremony.[96] It is surely unlikely that once the simpler forms were available, perhaps initially in an independent *libellus* rather than as a component part of another liturgical book (the mysterious *baptisterium* of the lists?), they were not the ones most commonly used by rural priests. Yet uncertainties and ambiguities persisted even in the minds of usually well-informed and clear-thinking diocesans. When Archbishop Hincmar of Rheims, addressing particularly the needs of rural parishes, writes that his priests should take care 'ut scrutinia per baptismales ecclesias fiant et baptizati mox post baptismum communicentur', he is hardly using *scrutinia* in its original or later extended 'institutional' sense; and he introduces a note of potential confusion when, in the next paragraph, his list of the rites that the same priests should memorize includes 'consignationem infantum tam masculorum quam et feminarum,

---

[94] P.-M. Gy, 'La formule "je te baptise" (et ego te baptizo)', in B. Bobrinsky, C. Bridel, *et al.*, eds, *Communio Sanctorum. Mélanges offerts à J. J. von Allmen* (Geneva, 1982), pp. 65–72; Cramer, *Baptism and Change*, pp. 139–41; above, n.92.

[95] Text: *Die kleineren althochdeutschen Sprachdenkmäler*, ed. E. von Steinmeyer (Berlin, 1916; repr. 1963), ix (p. 43). Manuscript: Kassel, Murhardsche Bibliothek und Landesbibliothek, MS 4° Theol. 24, 'nach Schrift und Inhalt bayerisch aus dem ersten Viertel des IX. Jhs' (Bischoff, *Schreibschulen*, 2, p. 185). It has only sixty leaves, the first part *canones*, the two leaves after the *Exhortatio* a Latin-German glossary; could it originally have been one of the books of a south-German country church? It was at Fulda only very much later.

[96] Cramer, *Baptism and Change*, pp. 141–51. For Mediterranean dioceses where the older rite was maintained, see ibid., p. 140 n.27.

unius vel plurium [sic!]', since *consignatio* is historically 'episcopal confirmation'.[97] At the same time Hincmar's words, together with a capitulary of Bishop Rudolf of Bourges – with a noteworthy reference to the responsibilities of godparents – and other texts, are testimony that giving the consecrated wafer (and wine) to a child re-born and freed from sin at baptism was, in line with the prescriptions of the *ordines romani* and less specifically of the Gregorian Supplement, acknowledged as the normal Frankish practice.[98]

The Easter and Pentecost baptisms in free-standing baptisteries at Florence, Pisa, Parma, and elsewhere may well have been – like city-walls – a major element (as has been claimed) in the creation of a sense of cohesiveness and identity.[99] Rural communities on both sides of the Alps seem more likely to have found a degree of cohesion in church-linked actions which commonly had no liturgical character. Professor Wendy Davies's fine study of the communities of eastern Brittany which reveal themselves in the pages of the Redon Cartulary shows some of the ways in which this might happen.[100] Although these seem in part to be a reflection of that region's distinctive social structures, other aspects have close parallels as far away as southern Bavaria. In both areas, for example, members of the community assemble in their

---

[97] Hincmar, *Collectio*, ed. Stratmann, pp. 101–2. (In his first diocesan *capitula* Hincmar, like earlier 'national' councils, had used the singular *scrutinium*: 'Ut scrutinium et omnem ordinem baptizandi nulli penitus liceat ignorare', *PL* 105, c.773.) The editor adds to the confusion with her cross-reference to *Sacramentum Gelasianum*, I, 75 (Wilson, *The Gelasian Sacramentary*, p. 117; Mohlberg et al., *Liber sacramentorum Romanae æcclesiae*, no. 615), which actually says – in the context of infirm catechumens – 'consignatur ab episcopo'. But *ordines* XI and XV and Benedict of Aniane in his Gregorian Supplement already use *confirmare* (Andrieu, *Ordines* 2, p. 446 [c.100], 3, p. 120 [c.119]; Deshusses, *Sacr. Grég.*, 1, no. 1088). Is Hincmar's *consignatio* the imposition of the cross by the priest at baptism?

[98] *MGH. Cap. Episc.*, 1, p. 249 (c.20): 'quamdiu in albis sunt, cotidie [sic!] a patrinis ad ecclesiam cum luminaribus deducantur, et corpus et sanguinem Christi usque in diem octavum aequali iure cuncti percipere studeant'; Andrieu, *Ordines*, 2, pp. 446–7 (cc.103–4), 3, p. 120 (cc.118, 120); Deshusses, *Sacr. Grég.* 1, nos. 1088, 1089. That it was normal practice also in pre-1066 England is indicated by the (eleventh-century) miraculous story of Rumwold, grandson of Penda of Mercia, who was baptized, communicated, and preached about the Christian faith before dying at three days old (quoted by S. Foote, '"By water in the spirit": the administration of baptism in early Anglo-Saxon England', *Pastoral Care*, pp. 171–2).

[99] Cramer, *Baptism and Change*, pp. 151–2, 267–70, 282–90. See also D. A. Bullough, 'Social and economic structure and topography in the early medieval city', *Settimane di Studio del Centro Italiano di Studi sull'Alto Medioevo, XXI. Topografia Urbana e Vita Cittadina nell'Alto Medioevo in Occidente* (Spoleto, 1974), pp. 351–99, esp. pp. 351–2, 360–2.

[100] W. Davies, *Small Worlds: The Village Community in Early Medieval Brittany* (Berkeley and Los Angeles, CA, 1988); *Cartulaire de l'Abbaye de Redon*, ed. Aurélien de Courson (Paris, 1863).

local church to witness the symbolic conveyance of land and the literal gifting of a book or books at the altar, or to hear a gift announced. In one Breton example the donor had apparently travelled to Redon for the reception of the body of St Marcellinus and stayed on *ad vesperum* to make his gift, although it was back in his community that his 'charitable gift' (*elemosina*) was witnessed by kindred and neighbours.[101]

There are other patterns of behaviour, with rather different implications. In 875–6/7 members of a well-documented Breton aristocratic family arranged for the future burial of its senior members with gifts to a local 'monastery' (Saint-Maixent). After the death of its head and his burial *in vestibulo* of the monastery 'secundum dignitatem', followed quickly by his widow's decease, their oldest son is reported twice to have paid Sunday visits (the first of them 'dominica prima') to their burial-places, and on each occasion 'after mass' made further gifts in the presence of other laymen. The document's wording makes it likely that the masses were the regular Sunday ones, not ones offered as commemorations of the deceased. But this was not the donors' 'parish' church; and it is not said, nor clearly implied, that the son and the other laymen actually attended the mass in the monastery church: like so many of their twentieth-century successors, they could have stood in the porch throughout![102]

With texts that so often fall silent at the very point at which the historian of worship hopes for at least whispers of past practice, the temptation to seek refuge in the concepts of anthropology or of 'the new criticism' is a strong one. It would indeed be unwise to 'pass by on the other side', if only to force us to look critically at our own understanding of and response to the liturgy. But we are equally being untrue to our craft if we do not turn back to the texts and see what they may, after all, record about lay experience of the eucharistic service, of 'the mystery of the mass'. Out of a very small number, all of considerable degrees of ambiguity, two will be reviewed here. Both, as

---

[101] Brittany: Courson, *Cartulaire de Redon*, nos. 190 (*ante* 863), 263 'in ecclesia Serent' (Sérent) on Sunday 20 July 878, cf. no. 115 of 848. Bavaria: *Freising* no. 480, of (Monday) 8 December 822: a gift of property to the church at Isen 'in ipsam altarem sancti Zenonis' etc., in the presence of eleven named witnesses; perhaps ibid., no. 646, of (Saturday) 1 July 842, of property and liturgical books at Puppling, before nineteen witnesses, possibly also ibid., no. 581a, of (Wed.) 17 March 829, before twenty-eight witnesses. I have not noticed any comparable instances in Italian Carolingian-period charters, although it is, of course, not uncommon for charters to be written *ante ecclesiam* of a rural community.

[102] Courson, *Cartulaire de Redon*, no. 236.

it happens, are from English sources and, strictly, are post-Carolingian, being of early eleventh-century origin; although they are referring back to the period of Carolingian-inspired 'reform' in the previous century.

The first is a text to which I have already drawn attention elsewhere, hoping – as it turned out in vain – that others would quickly resolve the ambiguities and uncertainties of Latinity and of content.[103] Byrhtferth, biographer of (Arch)bishop Oswald of York and Worcester tells a story of how, when he had celebrated mass in his northern cathedral, the adjacent *aula* was full of its citizens who, in accordance with 'an ancient English custom', wished to receive from the bishop an *offula* of bread previously blessed by him ('panis benedictus'). The bishop duly obliged and the bread was consumed by its recipients *gratanter*, although before he could get up and leave a wretched mouse nibbled a fragment of the bread and choked on it.[104] Was the *aula* the York cathedral nave (as Dorothy Whitelock supposed) or, as I now prefer, either the forecourt or some subsidiary building in the cathedral complex? If, as the recorded sequence of events and the avoidance of any mention of the *corpus domini* strongly suggest, the bread that was handed out had (probably) originally been brought as offerings by the *populus*, left unconsecrated and then blessed at the end of the mass (what Carolingian synodal *capitula* and other texts refer to as *eulogiae*),[105] we have a picture of layfolk presenting themselves for and obtaining a 'communion substitute' while being excluded from the eucharist proper.

The second passage, from Wulfstan of Winchester's *Life* of Æthelwold, must necessarily be quoted in the original Latin but is

[103] Donald Bullough, 'St Oswald: monk, bishop and archbishop', in N. Brooks and C. Cubitt, eds, *St Oswald of Worcester: Life and Influence*, Studies in the Early History of Britain the Makers of England, 2 (London and New York, 1996), pp. 17–18.

[104] Byrhtferth, *Vita sancti Oswaldi*, in *Historians of the Church of York and its Archbishops*, ed. J. Raine, 3 vols, *Rerum Brittanicarum medii aevi scriptores* (*Rolls Series*) (London, 1879–94), I, pp. 454–5.

[105] For *eulogiae* in this sense (for they can also be nominally freewill offerings by priests or ordinary faithful to their bishops and other senior ecclesiastics, as indeed in Hincmar's *Collectio*, ed. Stratmann, pp. 105, 108, etc.), see Hincmar's *capitula synodica* of 852, c.7 (*PL* 125, col. 774) and above all Hildegar of Meaux's ?unique decree of 868 (*MGH. Cap. Episc.*, 1, p. 199). This last gives the rationale for the laity's receiving the *eulogiae*, before repeating Hincmar's text of the blessing to be said by the priest before he breaks and distributes the bread. Is it merely coincidence that the only full text of this decree is a marginal addition (by John of Worcester himself, in the 1130s?) to the Worcester chronicle manuscript, Dublin, Trinity College, MS 503, fol. 59v?

happily quite short: 'Quadam namque die cum mater eius stipata civibus staret in ecclesia *sacrae missae celebrationi interesse desiderans* sensit animam pueri quem gerebat in utero venisse et in eum Dei nutu cuncta moderantis intrasse.'[106]

I hurriedly pass over the theological implications of the phrase translatable as 'when she felt that the soul of the child whom she was carrying in her womb had come to enter him at the will of Almighty God', merely recalling that the Congregation of the Doctrine of the Faith's 1974 Declaration on Procured Abortion specifically 'leaves aside the question of the moment when the spiritual soul is infused';[107] and concentrate on the seemingly simpler 'sacrae missae celebrationi interesse desiderans'. Does *interesse* here have the force of 'actively take part in'? or simply 'be present during the celebration'?[108] And does the association with a miraculous awareness imply that the mother's presence, or eagerness to take part, was something exceptional rather than normal? I do not know. Nor am I sure how we should interpret the subsequent story of the saint's nursemaid who, being determined 'quadam sollemni die' to go to her local church 'orationi incumbere' (words translatable in more than one way),[109] was prevented by heavy rain; but then after weeping bitter tears and praying, 'found herself with the baby sitting in the church she had planned to visit, where the priest was celebrating mass' and was frightened out of her wits 'at so inexplicable an event'.

Early medieval hagiographers occasionally describe the emotions of their heroes during a eucharistic celebration. Cuthbert, according to Bede (in a passage which he does not owe to the Lindisfarne biographer),

> was so full of penitence . . . that when celebrating Mass he could never finish the service without shedding tears. But it was indeed

[106] Wulfstan of Winchester, *Life of St Æthelwold*, ed. and transl. M. Lapidge and M. Winterbottom, *Oxford Medieval Texts* (Oxford, 1991), p. 6 (c.4).

[107] But by implication Wulfstan believes in the pre-existence of souls.

[108] 'Quando fideles missarum solemnibus interesse properant' and are 'not in a state of grace' to receive the Body and Blood is, according to Hildegar of Meaux, the reason why they should accept a *eulogia* of blessed bread: *MGH. Cap. Episc.*, 1, p. 199.

[109] The phraseology is that of the *Regula Benedicti*, c.4 ('the Instruments of Good Works'): 'orationi frequenter incumbere'. In the present context the words could equally well signify 'praying on her own' and 'following the Mass', with obviously quite different implications for our view of lay 'spirituality'. The entire chapter of the Rule, except its final sentence, had been taken over by Theodulf of Orleans verbatim in his first capitulary (c.21) and from him by Rudolf of Bourges (c.13): *MGH. Cap. Episc.*, 1, pp. 117–19, 242–3.

fitting that as he celebrated the mysteries of the Lord's Passion, he would himself imitate what he was performing, that is to say, he would sacrifice himself to God in contrition of heart. Moreover, he would urge the persons standing there to lift up their hearts and to give thanks to our Lord God, himself lifting up the heart rather than the voice, sighing rather than singing.[110]

Other writers of the ninth and tenth centuries provide exuberant and detailed accounts of the enthusiasm, joy, and even ecstasy displayed by layfolk in the presence of newly-arrived or long-familiar relics of saints and at the miracles associated with them. Perhaps among these folk there were a few who overcame the barriers between themselves and the celebrant at the altar, and experienced some of the emotions of living saints. But if they did, this remains for me as historian almost as much a mystery as 'the mysteries of the Passion' itself.

University of St Andrews

---

[110] Bede, *Vita Cuthberti* (prose), ed. B. Colgrave in *Two 'Lives' of St Cuthbert* (Cambridge, 1940), p. 213 (c.16).

CHANGE AND CHANGE BACK: THE DEVELOPMENT OF ENGLISH PARISH CHURCH CHANCELS

by CAROL F. DAVIDSON

THE eleventh-century core of the church at Wittering, North-amptonshire (Fig. 1a), is typical of the type of church which served local communities in the Anglo-Saxon period. It has a rectangular nave and a short, square chancel. Kilpeck, Herefordshire (Fig. 1b), is an equally typical example of a post-Conquest, twelfth-century local church.[1] It also has a rectangular nave, but it has a longer, apsidal chancel. Such early twentieth-century authors on the development of English parish churches as A. Hamilton Thompson and Alfred Clapham suggested that the use of apses for smaller, post-Conquest churches is an example of French/Norman influence over-riding the existing English/Anglo-Saxon forms.[2] They cite the wide-spread use of apses after the Conquest not only for smaller churches, but also for virtually every major church built in the wake of the Conquest, and the use of apses for churches of all sizes in France in the late eleventh and twelfth centuries. The use of square ends for later medieval parish church chancels such as those at Polebrook, North-amptonshire (Fig. 2a), or Linton, Herefordshire (Fig. 2b), Clapham suggested, marked a return to native English forms after the immediate impact of the Conquest had passed.[3] But is this actually the case? Or are the rectangular, square-ended chancels so typical of later medieval English parish churches a response to new demands being placed upon these buildings? This paper will explore this issue, and ask whether the use of square-ended chancels represents a continuity with, or a change from, older forms.

Recent archaeological excavations have brought to light much new evidence relating to the development of church plans which was

---

[1] The term *local* church is used here to encompass both parish churches and those churches which served local communities, but which had not yet attained parochial status.

[2] A. Hamilton Thompson, *The Ground Plan of the English Parish Church* (Cambridge, 1911), p. 53; F. H. Fairweather, *Aisleless Apsidal Churches of Great Britain* (Colchester, 1933), pp. 4–5; A. W. Clapham, *English Romanesque Architecture After the Conquest* (London, 1934), p. 101; G. H. Cook, *The English Medieval Parish Church* (London, 1955), p. 83.

[3] Clapham, *English Architecture*, p. 102; Gerald Randall, *The English Parish Church* (London, 1988), p. 27.

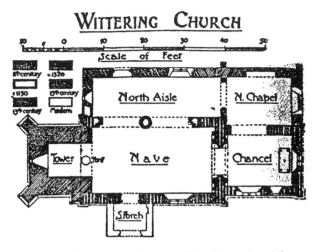

WITTERING CHURCH

Fig. 1a. Wittering, Northamptonshire. Reproduced from
R. M. Serjeantson and W. R. D. Adkins, eds, *History of Northamptonshire*, 2
(London, 1906), p. 540, by permission of the General Editor of the Victoria
History of the Counties of England.

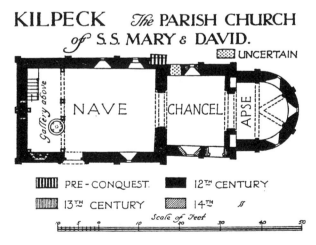

KILPECK *The* PARISH CHURCH *of* S.S. MARY & DAVID.

Fig. 1b. Kilpeck, Herefordshire, reproduced by permission of *RCHM(E)*;
Crown copyright.

unavailable to early twentieth-century authors such as Thompson and Clapham. With a few possible exceptions, the earliest standing local or parish churches, as opposed to minsters or other major churches, date only to the beginning of the eleventh century, and most seem to have been constructed between *c.*1050 and *c.*1125.[4] The archaeological excavations have shown, however, that on virtually every medieval parish church site investigated, a late ninth- or tenth-century wooden church, or churches, underlies the eleventh- or twelfth-century stone church.[5] While some of these early churches, such as that at Wharram Percy, East Yorkshire, were single-cell structures, most were of the rectangular nave and square chancel type found at St Michael Thetford, Norfolk, and Rivenhall, Essex (Fig. 3).[6] Whether single cell, or nave and chancel, all of these buildings had flat east ends. This means, therefore, that such a plan type was in use for several centuries before the Conquest.

Taylor attempted to date a few apsidal minor churches, including those at Dunham Magna (Norfolk), Pentlow (Essex), and Stanley St Leonard (Gloucestershire), to the years before the Conquest;[7] but his dating is tentative at best. It is now generally accepted that the earliest use of apses for local churches was *c.*1100, and that in most cases, churches like Kilpeck date to the second quarter of the twelfth century. This means that while these buildings do represent a change in the post-Conquest period from the designs used in the pre-Conquest period, this change came many decades after 1066. Therefore, it is unlikely that the use of apses was a direct result of Norman patrons and masons arriving in the wake of the Conquest.

Archaeological excavations have also revealed that apses were far more widely used for local churches in the twelfth century than might be guessed from the standing buildings. Previously unknown apses have been excavated at a diverse range of sites, including

---

[4] Richard Morris, *Churches in the Landscape* (London, 1989), pp. 165–7.

[5] See Richard Morris, ed., *The Church in British Archaeology*, Council for British Archaeology [hereafter CBA] Research Report, 47 (Oxford, 1983), fig. 24, and W. J. Rodwell, *Rivenhall: Investigation of a Villa, Church, and Village, 1950–1977*, CBA Research Report, 55 (Oxford, 1986), p. 89, fig. 62, for comparative tables of the plans of excavated churches.

[6] Maurice Beresford and J. Hunt, *Wharram Percy: Deserted Medieval Village* (London, 1990), pp. 60 1, figs 43–4; Rodwell, *Rivenhall*, p. 91.

[7] H. M. Taylor and J. Taylor, *Anglo-Saxon Architecture*, 3 vols (Cambridge, 1965–78), 3, p. 1028. The other churches on his list can all be identified as having been major monastic, or cathedral churches.

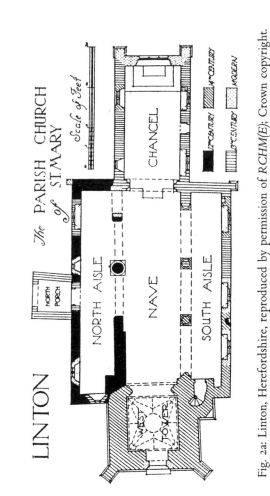

Fig. 2a: Linton, Herefordshire, reproduced by permission of *RCHM(E)*; Crown copyright.

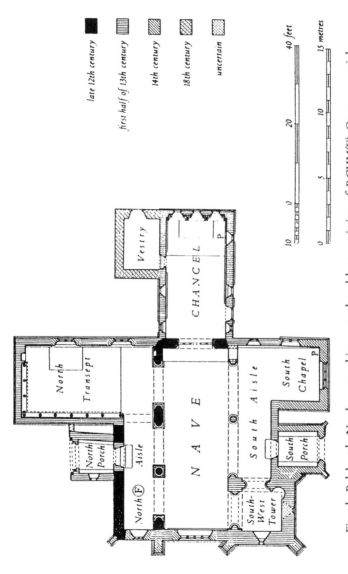

late 12th century

first half of 13th century

14th century

18th century

uncertain

North ⓕ Aisle

North Porch

North Transept

NAVE

South-West Tower

South Porch

South Aisle

South Chapel

CHANCEL

Vestry

P

P

Fig. 2b: Polebrook, Northamptonshire, reproduced by permission of *RCHM(E)*; Crown copyright.

10   0   5   10   20   40 *feet*

0   5   10   15 *metres*

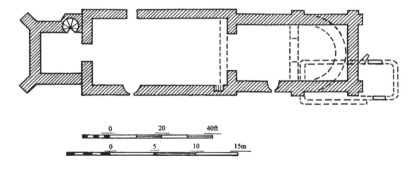

Fig. 3.   Rivenhall, Essex, after Rodwell.

Barton-on-Humber (Lincolnshire), Wharram Percy (East Yorkshire), Waterperry and Cumnor (Oxfordshire), St Bride's Fleet Street (London), Reedham (Norfolk), and Asheldam and Rivenhall (Essex) (Fig. 3).[8] A closer examination of some of the standing apsidal churches suggests that they, too, may have been built in this way.[9] For instance, at Pentlow, Essex, one of the churches which Taylor claimed had an Anglo-Saxon apse, the chancel plinth does not extend underneath the apse.[10] This suggests that the apse is a later addition to an Anglo-Saxon nave and square chancel. The same may be true at Kilpeck (Fig. 1b), where the presence of Anglo-Saxon quoining at the north-east nave angle suggests the ghost of an earlier, probably square-chancelled church.[11] Virtually every excavation of a later medieval rectangular parish church chancel has uncovered a late eleventh- or twelfth-century apse beneath it, and given the relatively few number of parish churches which have been excavated so far, this

[8]   W. J. Rodwell and K. A. Rodwell, 'St Peter's church, Barton-on-Humber: excavation and structural study, 1978–81', *Antiquaries Journal*, 62 (1982), fig. 3; Beresford and Hunt, *Wharram Percy*, pp. 60–1, figs 43–4; Taylor and Taylor, *Anglo-Saxon Architecture*, 2, p. 641; John Blair, Jane Croom, and Eddie Colman, 'The early church at Cumnor', *Oxoniensia*, 56 (1989), p. 41; W. F. Grimes, *The Excavation of Roman and Medieval London* (London, 1968), pp. 185–6, fig. 42; Edwin J. Rose, 'The church of Saint John the Baptist, Reedham, Norfolk: the reuse of Roman materials in a secondary context', *JBAA*, 147 (1994), p. 6; W. J. Rodwell and K. Rodwell, *Historic Churches: A Wasting Asset*, CBA Research Report, 19 (London, 1977), p. 58, fig. 25; Rodwell, *Rivenhall*, p. 93, fig. 65.

[9]   Ibid., p. 138.

[10]   Taylor and Taylor, *Anglo-Saxon Architecture*, 2, fig. 239.

[11]   Royal Commission on Historical Monuments (England), *An Inventory of the Historical Monuments in Herefordshire. Volume 1: South-West* (London, 1931), pp. 156–7.

indicates that apses were far more common in the twelfth century than might be guessed from the relatively few apsidal chancels still in existence today.

Churches with apsidal chancels make up a relatively small percentage of the total provision of the standing local churches in England.[12] In general, they are located in rural backwaters, and there are particular concentrations of apsidal churches in Herefordshire, Essex, and parts of Norfolk and Suffolk. As areas like Herefordshire had a high degree of Norman building activity in the early years of the twelfth century, these regional concentrations have been used to support the theory that the introduction of apses was primarily the work of the incoming Normans.[13] However, the archaeological evidence for the widespread use of apses suggests that these concentrations are not a reliable indicator of the situation in the twelfth century, and that surviving apsidal churches like Kilpeck were once part of a much larger group of similar churches in the twelfth century.

Most of the standing apsidal local churches have been virtually unrenovated since the twelfth century. Kilpeck, for instance, is a largely pristine example of *c.*1130 except for the insertion of a few new windows and a chancel door. The same is true of Steetley (Derbyshire), Manningford Bruce (Wiltshire), Flitton (Suffolk), and Hales (Norfolk), to name only a few. Both the additive renovation processes which produced composite churches like Linton and Polebrook (Fig. 2), and the late medieval building boom which created enormous single-build churches like Long Melford (Suffolk), Fairford (Gloucestershire), and Boston (Lincolnshire), passed them by. This means that the use of apses for Steetley, Kilpeck, Hales, and Flitton may be much less significant than it might seem. The archaeological evidence demonstrates that apses were widely used in the twelfth century, while the lack of subsequent work done on these churches suggests that no-one had the inclination or the resources to replace their apses at a later date. Therefore, these buildings are as much a product of later disinterest as they are of any particular interest in the first half-century after the Conquest.

Kilpeck, like Steetley in Derbyshire and a number of the other very finest local churches built in the middle of the twelfth century, has a

---

[12] See Fairweather, *Aisleless Apsidal Churches*, pp. 25–54, for a list of standing apsidal churches in Britain.

[13] Ibid., pp. 4–5.

two-celled chancel in which the western choir section of the chancel is separated from the eastern sanctuary section housing the altar by an additional arch. At Steetley and Kilpeck, and at most other churches with two-celled chancels built before c.1150, the eastern sanctuary compartment is apsidal. Those churches built with two-celled chancels built after c.1150, such as Stewkley (Buckinghamshire), Compton (Surrey), Coln St Denis and Elkstone (Gloucestershire), and Iffley (Oxfordshire), generally have a square eastern compartment, giving the church a flat east end. In general, however, two-celled chancels seem to have been limited to more elaborate buildings, perhaps because of the added expense of building a sanctuary and a chancel arch.

From the end of the twelfth century, long, rectangular, flat-ended chancels without any internal divisions like those found at Linton, Polebrook, and Rivenhall (final phase) were the favoured type for local churches, and were to remain so for the rest of the Middle Ages. Flat east ends also gained popularity for larger churches in the twelfth-century, being used, in various forms and usually as part of a rebuilding campaign, for churches such as Romsey, Kirkstall, Ely, Salisbury, Fountains, Lincoln, and Durham. Indeed, this becomes the typical English east-end type in the later Middle Ages.[14] For local churches, rectangular chancels were used in the late twelfth-century for newly-built churches such as Long Sutton (Lincolnshire), and West Walton (Norfolk). The chancels of older churches like Stoke d'Abernon and Brigstock were also renovated or rebuilt to bring them into line with this new type. Although churches like Linton and Polebrook have not been excavated, it seems reasonable to assume that they too had square chancels, and possibly apses, before their present long chancels were built at the beginning of the thirteenth century.

In general, this pattern of development still seems to agree well with the theory that the long-standing Anglo-Saxon form of flat-ended churches was replaced or altered by the Normans in the post-Conquest period, before being put back in a similar form in the later twelfth century after the immediate influence of the Conquest had passed. However, a number of things suggest that this may not be the case. First of all, although the use of apses for smaller churches in the

---

[14] M. F. Hearn, 'The rectangular ambulatory in English mediaeval architecture', *Journal of the Society of Architectural Historians*, 30 (1971), pp. 187–208.

post-Conquest period is a departure from pre-Conquest practices, apses had been widely used for larger buildings before the Conquest. The use of apses for major churches was particularly associated with those buildings using the basilican, Kentish-type plan, such as Canterbury Cathedral, Canterbury St Pancras, Brixworth, Deerhurst, Hexham, Lyminge, Reculver, Rochester, Sherborne, and Winchester Old Minster.[15] An Anglo-Saxon apse was recently discovered at Pershore,[16] and a similar arrangement has been suggested for Lady St Mary Wareham, Dorset.[17] Most of these churches were originally built in the seventh or eighth century; however, the Confessor's Westminster was an important, mid-eleventh-century apsidal building.[18] Although not every major pre-Conquest building was apsidal, these examples clearly indicate that the form was well-known in England before the Conquest, and therefore was not imported from the Continent by the Normans.

Secondly, when one takes a wider view of the development of parish church chancels in the twelfth century, it is clear that it is part of a larger pattern of experimentation with the form of the east ends of English churches of all sizes. To take only one, albeit rather dramatic, example: Canterbury Cathedral had four different eastern terminations between 1066 and 1186.[19] To be sure, two of these new east ends were the result of rebuilding after serious fires in 1067 and 1174; however, the marked differences in both size and arrangement between each new choir and its predecessor, especially between the first and second Romanesque choirs which were not separated by a fire, suggests that a considerable degree of rethinking of the liturgical and spatial arrangements was going on in this building in the twelfth century.

Similar patterns can be identified in parish churches. Especially in the period from *c*.1125–*c*.1175, there was a huge range of chancel types in use for local churches: single-, double-, and occasionally triple-celled, apsidal, and square-ended, in a wide range of combinations.[20]

[15] Taylor and Taylor, *Anglo-Saxon Architecture*, 3, p. 1028.

[16] Kevin Blockley, 'Pershore Abbey', *Current Archaeology*, 150 (1996), p. 218.

[17] Royal Commission on Historical Monuments (England), *An Inventory of Historical Monuments in Dorset. Volume 2, South East, pt. 2* (London, 1970), pp. 308–12.

[18] Geoffrey Webb, *Architecture in Britain in the Middle Ages* (Harmondsworth, 1956), p. 27.

[19] Francis Woodman, *The Architectural History of Canterbury Cathedral* (London, 1981), figs 11–13, 24, 28.

[20] Thompson, *Ground Plan*, pp. 44–52; Clapham, *Architecture After the Conquest*, pp. 101–5.

At many, perhaps even most, local churches, more than one of these chancel types existed during the course of the twelfth century. At Rivenhall, the late tenth- or early eleventh-century square chancel was made apsidal in the late eleventh or early twelfth century, before being made long and rectangular in the fourteenth. In other churches, however, these changes were much more rapid. Cumnor, for instance, had three different chancels between the end of the eleventh and the end of the twelfth century.[21] The wide variety of twelfth-century chancel forms, and the speed with which chancel types changed during this period, form a striking contrast to the homogeneity and stability of parish church chancel types in the earlier and later Middle Ages. This suggests that, having been stable for a long time, the demands placed on chancels changed quite rapidly in the twelfth century before settling down again towards the beginning of the thirteenth century. In view of the renovations being made at Canterbury and many other major English churches in the same period, it seems likely that these demands were functional rather than iconographic or nationalistic.

It is interesting to note that long, rectangular chancels were used not only for large, grand buildings like Bakewell, Derbyshire, but also for much smaller, less elaborate churches like Great Dunham, Norfolk. This suggests that such chancels fulfilled functions which were common to all sizes and types of parish churches after the end of the twelfth-century. One possible purpose of a flat eastern wall was the provision of space for splendid, large east windows of the type found at Barnack, Northamptonshire.[22] While the provision of additional light in the chancel was undoubtedly a concern in the late twelfth and especially in the thirteenth centuries, the use of large east windows in parish churches is probably as much a result of flat-ended chancels as it is a cause of them.[23] The type of lancet windows used in the thirteenth-century chancels at Bakewell and Polebrook (Fig. 2a), or those used for the small church of West Harnham, Wiltshire, could easily have been accommodated in an apse.

The main requirement for the east end of any church is the

---

[21] Blair, Croom, and Colman, 'Cumnor', p. 41.

[22] David Parsons, 'Sacrarium: ablution drains in early medieval churches', in L. A. S. Butler and R. K. Morris, eds, The Anglo-Saxon Church: Papers on History, Architecture, and Archaeology in Honour of H. M. Taylor, CBA Research Report, 60 (London, 1986), p. 107; Randall, English Parish Church, p. 28.

[23] C. F. Davidson, 'Written in stone: architecture, liturgy, and the laity in English parish churches c.1125–c.1250' (University of London Ph.D. thesis, 1998), p. 150.

provision of a suitable setting for the mass and the clergy. Medieval altars were one of the most serious casualties of the post-Reformation reordering of minor churches.[24] There is little doubt, however, that in English parish churches of the later Middle Ages the altar was positioned flush against the east wall, as the remains of image brackets, reredoses, and other liturgical fittings indicate. However, the altars in earlier Anglo-Saxon churches such as Reculver, Winchester Old Minster, and the first church at Raunds were apparently placed west of the chancel arch in the east end of the nave itself, while the small chancel served as a sanctuary space for the clergy.[25] This arrangement is similar to that of the early Christian basilicas, where the bishop and other clergy sat in the apse, while the celebrant said mass facing the congregation at an altar at the end of the nave.[26] By the eleventh century, however, the altar had been moved inside the chancel of English churches, although there still seems to have been a considerable amount of free space behind it to the east.[27] Archaeology on sites such as Raunds second church (*c.*1050), St Mark Lincoln (also eleventh-century), and Barton-on-Humber, has revealed features thought to have been altars in this position.[28]

The widespread use of apses in the late eleventh and twelfth centuries suggests that the altar was not yet at the far east end of the chancel in this period, as the curved wall of an apse would have made it difficult to place the altar flush against the east wall. Apses probably do indicate, however, that the altar was moving towards the east end of the chancel, as an apse highlighted the space around and directly behind the altar.[29] As in major buildings with apsidal eastern terminations, the altar was probably placed on the chord of the apse. At Rivenhall, for instance, Rodwell noted that the light from the windows in the *c.*1090 apse was directed to the centre of the chord of the apse, suggesting an altar in this position.[30] The movement of the altar into

---

[24] G. W. O. Addleshaw, *The Architectural Setting of Anglican Worship* (London, 1948), p. 26.

[25] H. M. Taylor, 'The position of the altar in early Anglo-Saxon churches', *Antiquaries Journal*, 53 (1973), pp. 53–4; Eric Fernie, *The Architecture of the Anglo-Saxons* (London, 1983), p. 41; Parsons, 'Sacrarium', pp. 101–5.

[26] Richard Krautheimer, *Early Christian and Byzantine Architecture* (Harmondsworth, 1965), p. 43.

[27] Taylor, 'The position of the altar', pp. 54–6.

[28] Parsons, 'Sacrarium', p. 106; Rodwell and Rodwell, 'Barton-on-Humber', fig. 6.

[29] Fairweather, *Aisleless Apsidal Churches*, pp. 25–6; Lawrence R. Hoey, 'Stone vaults in English parish churches in the early Gothic and decorated periods', *JBAA*, 147 (1994), p. 38.

[30] Rodwell, *Rivenhall*, fig. 97.

the chancel coincides with the beginning of a general increase in the secrecy surrounding the mass, including the silencing of the canon of the mass.

By the end of the tenth or the beginning of the eleventh century, the celebrant had ceased to celebrate facing the congregation, moving around the west side of the altar and turning his back on the congregation.[31] Changing the orientation of the celebrant would have required more space to the west of the altar where the priest now stood, and less space to the east of the altar. The resulting cramping of the space within the western end of the chancel may have helped to spur the movement towards longer chancels which provided extra space west of the altar while still permitting the altar to stand clear of the east wall. Initially, both apsidal and two-cell chancels may have provided satisfactory, if somewhat different, solutions to this problem.[32] They allowed the altar to be moved further east in the chancel, while also providing space for the clergy in front of it. They also highlighted the altar to a much greater extent than had previously been the case. The use of freestanding altars, however, meant that it was still possible to walk around the back of the altar. If the canon of the mass was meant to be entirely secret, this was undesirable. It was preferable, therefore, to push the altar back against the flat east wall of a rectangular chancel.

It is not altogether clear when the altar reached the east end of the chancel. Parsons notes that while St Martin, Thetford (Norfolk), seems to have had its altar against the east wall as early as c.1030, elsewhere the altar may have remained freestanding for much longer.[33] It would certainly have been possible to put the altar against the east wall of a square chancel, or even of an apsidal one, something which must have been done in some of the smaller apsidal churches which remained unrenovated throughout the Middle Ages. It seems likely, however, that the progressive extension of chancels in the twelfth century indicates a continuing movement of the altar towards the east, and that the use of long, flat-ended chancels from the third quarter of the century indicates that there was a desire to place the altar against the east wall by this time. This, more than the desire for larger windows, or

[31] Theodor Klauser (trans. J. Halliburton), *A Short History of the Western Liturgy* (2nd edn, Oxford, 1969), p. 101.

[32] Francis Bond, *Gothic Architecture in England* (London, 1905), p. 220.

[33] Parsons, '*Sacrarium*', p. 107.

an attempt to return to Anglo-Saxon plan types, was the reason for the use of square-ended chancels for parish churches from the late twelfth century onwards.

It is not possible, therefore, to agree with Clapham and Hamilton Thompson. Rectangular chancels do, in some ways, represent a formal continuity with the square chancels used in the pre-Conquest period. However, it is clear that they are part of a larger pattern of liturgical and architectural change in churches of all sizes in the twelfth century which is unrelated to nationalistic concerns.

Victoria History of the Counties of England,
University of London

THE 'SAMPLE WEEK' IN THE MEDIEVAL LATIN DIVINE OFFICE

by R. W. PFAFF

ONE of the apparent pillars of consistency in the medieval Latin liturgy is the divine, *alias* daily, office. Although scholars convincingly postulate forms of the office that both antedate the specific provisions for it which bulk large in the Rule of Benedict and reflect an urban secular (the so-called cathedral office) rather than a monastic context, in terms of actual books out of which the office was performed, not a great deal survives until roughly the eleventh century. By that time, if not before, thought is clearly being given as to how to present the contents of the office – given that much of it consists in the recitation of psalms – in a way that, while clear, minimizes repetition. This can most readily be done in the long stretch of the weeks after Pentecost and the shorter stretch (sometimes very short indeed, depending on when Easter falls) of the weeks between the octave of Epiphany and the beginning of Lent or pre-Lent (that is, from Septuagesima on). Although the structure of the office in this, to use the current phrase, 'ordinary time', remains the same as in the more exciting seasons of Advent, Christmastide, Lent, and Eastertide (plus, of course, the individual feasts of the Proper of Saints), the content of the various services is not driven by a particular time or saint, and so there is a somewhat abstract quality about it quite lacking from the great seasons and occasions of the liturgical year.

There are two problems to be addressed in the presentation of the ordinary-time office. The first is which forms to use, in the absence of seasonal or occasional considerations. Precisely how these choices were made, and beyond that who made them, belong to the misty *Ur*-history of the divine office that may never be completely uncovered. One useful organizational principle came to be the *Historiae*, the extensive sets of matins lessons drawn from the Old Testament during the post-Pentecost ordinary time. The commonest scheme for these seems to be Kings, Wisdom, Job, Tobit, Judith, Esther, Maccabees, Ezekiel.[1] Sets of

---

[1] Laid out succinctly in Andrew Hughes, *Medieval Manuscripts for Mass and Office: a Guide to their Organization and Terminology* (Toronto, 1982), no. 835.

responsories commonly accompany these lessons, and the Sundays during this time are sometimes referred to by the initial words of the responsories involved: for example, the words *Deus omnium* mean the first such summer Sunday, when they begin the responsory to the first lesson.

The second problem is how to lay out this office material for ordinary time, both the short post-Epiphany and the sometimes seemingly endless post-Pentecost seasons. This problem, involving for the long season a great deal of material, some of it very repetitious, was never quite satisfactorily worked out. (Indeed, the later medieval solution was in large measure responsible for Cranmer's complaint that it often took more time to find out what to read than to read it.) The problem is not so great when the office is performed in choir, with a mixture of books for individual parts – antiphoners, collectars, books of readings, pamphlets (*libelli*) – and reliance on memory. When, however, there becomes apparent a desire to have material for the complete office contained within a single volume, the problem of how to present the entire bulk of it for the long series of weeks in ordinary time became acute.

This paper is concerned with a rudimentary strategy, not I think hitherto noticed, for laying out the contents of the daily office during those times when there is no seasonal necessity. This strategy – what I am here calling a 'sample week' – is discernible in a tiny group of English witnesses to a formative stage in the construction of that complete medieval daily office which we find contained in the full English breviaries like those that have become familiar through accessible modern editions: Sarum, York, Hereford, and Hyde (English monastic).[2]

Any observation about the history of the liturgy in the Middle Ages must of course be qualified by caution as to how representative are whatever sources have survived towards solving a particular problem. It is nonetheless striking that the first two attempts I am aware of to develop this sample week idea are products of the same half- or even quarter-century, indeed possibly of the same decade; that one is monastic and one secular seems to make it all the likelier that what

---

[2] F. Procter and C. Wordsworth, eds, *Breviarium ad usum . . . Sarum*, 3 vols (Cambridge, 1879–86); S. W. Lawley, ed., *Breviarium ad usum. . . . Eboracensis*, 2 vols, SS, 71, 75 (1880–2); W. H. Frere and L. E. G. Brown, eds, *The Hereford Breviary*, 3 vols, HBS, 26, 40, 46 (1904–15); J. B. L. Tolhurst, ed., *The Monastic Breviary of Hyde Abbey, Winchester*, 6 vols, HBS, 69–71, 76, 78, 80 (1932–42).

is represented here is more than random survival. As it happens, each can be associated with some plausibility with a well-known English figure from the second half of the eleventh century: Wulstan, Bishop of Worcester (d. 1095), and Leofric, Bishop of Exeter (d. 1072). The books involved are generally known as the Wulstan Portiforium (Cambridge, Corpus Christi College MS 391)[3] and the Leofric Psalter (London, British Library MS Harl. 863).[4] Having examined these, we shall consider the additional light afforded by a curious manuscript of a hundred-plus years later and by a mid twelfth-century codex which presents so variant a phenomenon that it is best considered in an appendix.

* * *

The Leofric Psalter is in its main part datable to 1046–72.[5] For the first 116 folios the book contains what one would expect in a psalter of this period: the psalms in numerical order, canticles, litany, and miscellaneous prayers; and there was presumably a calendar, later replaced by one written some time in the generation after Becket's death in 1170. Thus the book provides much of the material for putting together the full divine office, but there would also be needed some sort of chant book, the texts of such hymns as were used, and, most important, the lessons to be read at nocturns (matins) with their responsories.

The aggregation of all this is of course what the breviary provides, in theory throughout the entire year: which in practice often means a division into two, or in modern usage four, seasonally-based volumes. What is supplied in the Leofric Psalter, in a section written by a new hand, is indeed all of that material – for one week. (This is the fair presumption; in fact, the leaves containing what must have been the services for Wednesday and, save for a few words, Thursday are missing.) Which week is not specified. The rubric which begins this section in mid-folio 117 reads merely 'Sabbato ad Vesperas'. But the hymn ('O lux beata Trinitas'), capitulum, and collect are those most commonly encountered on the Sunday after the Octave of Epiphany.

[3] Anselm Hughes, ed., *The Portiforium of Saint Wulstan*, 2 vols, HBS, 89–90 (1958–60).

[4] E. S. Dewick and W. H. Frere, eds, *The Leofric Collectar (Harl. MS 2961)*, 2 vols, HBS, 45, 56 (1914–21); vol. 1 carries the subtitle, *with an Appendix Containing a Litany and Prayers from Harl. MS 863*.

[5] Andrew G. Watson, *A Catalogue of Dated and Datable Manuscripts, c.700–1600, in the Department of Manuscripts, the British Library*, 2 vols (London, 1979), no. 638.

So it is clear that we are dealing not with the beginning of the liturgical year, whether Advent or Christmas, nor with its high point in the days surrounding Easter, but with a neutral time which is in fact no particular time at all: hence the term I have coined for this phenomenon, the sample week.

Again, the 'commenting' forms in the Leofric Psalter's sample week – antiphons and responsories, the textual purpose of which is to comment on or shape response to the psalms and canticles on one hand and to the lessons at matins (nocturns) on the other – are be found widely used in the weeks that begin the two ordinary seasons. But none of this is made specific in the pages of the book we are considering, and this non-specificity is greatly reinforced by the choice of lessons. All medieval office books that I know of draw the scriptural lessons for one of these 'dull seasons' from the epistle to the Romans. The Leofric book follows this arrangement for the Sunday (the first six lessons), Monday, Tuesday, and Thursday (all of Wednesday being missing), having got through most of chapters one to three by that time. The lessons in the third nocturn on Sunday are likewise unremarkable, being taken from a homily by Bede on the wedding at Cana – which is commonly an Epiphany-tide pericope.[6]

But on Friday and Saturday, when we would expect on each day three more lessons from Romans, exactly as on the earlier weekdays, there are instead short lessons from a patristic treatise on the incommutability of God: lessons basically from Gregory the Great, but in a form that corresponds almost exactly to the reworking by the seventh-century Spanish bishop, Taio of Saragossa, at the beginning of his *Liber sententiarum*.[7] The choice of this source is in itself inexplicable, but to our current purpose is the equally inexplicable fact that in no other comparable medieval office that I have encountered are lessons for an ordinary weekday patristic rather than scriptural. This seems to underline the nature of what the compiler of this section of the Leofric book (whether or not the compiler was also the scribe here) seems to have been trying to do: namely, to put together a template or, to use the phrase once more, a sample week. There is no particular week during which these forms could appropriately be used, but repetition of this format week after week, with other

---

[6] Bede, *Homiliae in Evangelia*, II.14, in *Bedae venerabilis Opera: Pars III, Opera homiletica; Pars IV, Opera rhythmica*, ed. D. Hurst, CChr. SL, 122 (Turnhout, 1955), pp. 95–6.

[7] *PL* 80, col. 731; based on Gregory, *Moralia in Iob* XII.33.

specifications as to where the variable forms go, would produce a breviary.

*   *   *

It is not that a breviary is self-evidently a desirable thing; but when we turn to the next book, the Wulstan Portiforium, we may be able to see something of the appeal of this more comprehensive format. Manuscript 391 of Corpus Christi College, Cambridge, is a fat book about nine inches high and six inches wide. The traditional nickname for it, *Portiforium Oswaldi*, which goes back at least as far as Nasmith's catalogue of 1777, is both correct and useful in its first part, which may well be rendered 'portable compendium'. (The 'Oswaldi' part, believed as long ago as the thirteenth century, is plainly wrong; the best dating range for it is 1064–9, early in the pontificate of Wulstan.)[8]

The variety of contents in this fascinating and as yet not satisfactorily explained book makes sense best on the supposition that Bishop Wulstan carried it around with him when he visited churches, and especially religious establishments, in his diocese. The clearest indication of this is the discrepancies between the calendar (which seems to be that of Worcester cathedral priory), which is integral to the book, and what seems to be its Sanctorale: the collection of just under two hundred saints' days (a few being vigils) for which, in all save twenty-one cases, only a collect is provided. This means that the possessor of the book could by reciting the appropriate collect preside at the divine office at a church which was celebrating a saint's day even if that saint were not in the book's calendar: say, Arnulf or Eadburga, both of whose days coincide with that of Kenelm on 17 July; only the latter appears in the calendar of the portiforium, but there are collects for all three.

It is important to establish the character of this book as an aid to what we might call peripatetic liturgical presidency, because it helps to explain what happens after the book seems to have ended. Like the Leofric book, this one contains the meat of a liturgical psalter: calendar, psalms, canticles, litany; it has also an extensive hymnal, and the monastic canticles needed for the Benedictine office. Then comes an extensive section of material which virtually constitutes what is called a collectar: the capitulum, response and versicle, antiphon to Gospel

---

[8] Pamela R. Robinson, *Catalogue of Dated and Datable Manuscripts, c.737–1600, in Cambridge Libraries*, 2 vols (Woodbridge, 1988), no. 157.

canticle (Magnificat at vespers, Benedictus at lauds), and collect, for each of the Sundays and major occasions – for example, Maundy Thursday – of the Temporale and for twenty-one of the greatest Sanctorale feasts. This is followed by the aforementioned supplement, of bare collects for the 181 saints' days which did not make it into the select Sanctorale just preceding. And finally, again in terms of what one would expect, come similar forms for the Common of Saints and for the dedication of a church, with a kind of appendix of private prayers, some of them in English. All of this take up some 320 folios, of which the final one (pp. 619–20 in the modern pagination) is blank, and concludes a quire.[9]

Now – at last – comes our point of interest. On a new gathering, after the book would seem to have been adequately complete, there are supplied full office forms, including the lessons at matins, for the Common of Saints, thus providing a second such Common, one which is much more complete than its predecessor in the collectar section. This pattern of full forms is then continued with first vespers and nocturns for Sundays in general (*Dominicis diebus*, p. 657), as though they were occasions as abstract as, say, a feast of one confessor in the Common of Saints until a particular confessor is named. The character of the lessons supplied for this abstract Sunday suggests that this office is deliberately offered as a model or template: each of the first eight is taken from a different New Testament epistle-passage. The final four lessons are drawn, as they would normally be, from a patristic homily on a Gospel-lesson: in this case from Bede on John 15.26, a passage widely-used on the Sunday after Ascension Day.[10]

Next come a few vespers forms for something labelled 'Dominica prima': presumably *prima* after Pentecost (octave), because this is followed by eight antiphons and one hymn ('Nocte surgentes', the most widely-used ordinary-time hymn for Monday matins), collectively labelled simply 'De istoria', as though they were a kind of introduction to the summer *Historiae* for Sunday matins that follow. There is again a kind of template quality to this section, which, though presumably meant to cover the entire season from post-Pentecost until just before Advent, consists mainly of eight extremely brief lessons (no more than three modern verses apiece, sometimes just one), with their

---

[9] One quire, almost certainly of eight leaves, is lost after p. 580, so the original book would have been even bulkier than it is now.

[10] Bede, *Homiliae in Evangelia*, II.16; Hurst, *Bedae Opera*, pp. 290–3.

responsories, from each of six *Historiae*, Kings, Proverbs (but headed 'De Iudit', Judith), Job, Tobit, Maccabees, and Ezekiel. (In later [Sarum] usage these would be lessons for the first, ninth, sixteenth, eighteenth, twentieth, and twenty-second Sundays after Trinity.) There are also four lessons drawn in the usual way from a patristic homily on the Gospel lesson for each of those Sundays.

This abstract 'Dominica prima', which in fact seems to comprise the entire summer, is followed by something quite concrete, the full forms for Trinity Sunday.[11] Here the first eight lessons are all taken from a treatise on the Trinity,[12] and the last four are from a homily on the beginning of John's Gospel.[13] This office seems to be quite usable, being even provided with a cross-reference (for the full Gospel reading after the *Te deum*, there is a rubric, 'require natale domini'). But after the Trinity Sunday office come the weekday forms that constitute the clearest sample week in this book. The days are headed simply 'Feria ii', 'Feria iii', and so on; each is provided with three hymns (incipits only), three capitula, and three collects (capitula and collects in full), incipits of antiphons, and so forth. And each has a single lesson at matins (this marks the season as summertime, when the Rule of Benedict prescribes just one lesson at weekday nocturns, the second nocturn being supplied with a capitulum instead). It is the lessons that most clearly mark the sample character of the week; each comes from a different biblical source, all save the first (from Lamentations) being from a sapiential book – quite the opposite of an underlying notion of *lectio continua*. Plainly thought has been taken towards supplying a complete format, but the thrust of the contents is strongly towards a sample rather than a usable segment of the whole.

* * *

[11] The modern editor, Anselm Hughes (*Portiforium*, 2, II.48), suggests that an inset page might be missing before this office begins; it would presumably have contained further antiphons and the monastic canticles for ordinary Sundays. If it was an inset page it would not figure in the collations of M. R. James (*A Descriptive Catalogue of the Manuscripts in the Library of Corpus Christi College, Cambridge*, 2 vols [Cambridge, 1909–12], 2, p. 242) or W. H. Frere (*The Leofric Collectar*, 2, p. xviii). The present argument is not materially affected either way.

[12] This seems to be a composite from Augustine, *De trinitate* IX.1 and *Sermo* 52: respectively, *Sancti Aureli Augustini, De trinitate, libri XV (libri I-XII)*, ed. W. J. Mountain, *CChr. SL*, 50 (Turnhout, 1968), and P. Verbraken, 'Le sermon LII de saint Augustin sur la Trinité et l'analogie des facultés de l'âme', *Revue Bénédictine*, 74 (1964), pp. 9–35 at 21.

[13] Bede, *Homiliae in Evangelia*, I.8; Hurst, *Bedae Opera*, pp. 52–9.

That these two eleventh-century books, one monastic and one secular, are not mere 'sports' is shown by the third witness to be considered, a book as little known as the Portiforium of Wulstan is well-known. This is MS 1 in the small collection at St Paul's Cathedral in London, a book summarily described as a psalter of about 1200.[14] A full discussion of this puzzling codex and what happened to it a century or so after it was written is given elsewhere; in brief, it came into the possession of Ralph Baldock, successively Dean and Bishop at St Paul's, who seems to have used it to interesting effect.[15] Here it is the original contents that are pertinent. Again we have a psalter of what might be called the old-fashioned type (that is, with the psalms in numerical order rather than divided according to their placement in the week's cursus, which is the essence of the so-called 'ferial psalter'): in this case, mainly calendar, psalms, canticles, and litany. The book has been handsomely produced, with (originally) ten gold and coloured major initials at the principal psalm divisions and ornamented initials to all the other psalms.

But this late twelfth-century book – the dating range seems to be 1173–1203 – has much more than the contents of the conventional psalter it at first glance appears to be.[16] It has been supplied with noted antiphons for the psalms as distributed in secular use throughout most of the hours; with hymns, capitula, Gospel-canticle antiphons, and collects for vespers and lauds; and with hymns, capitula, and hour-collects for prime, terce, sext, and none (compline is unaccountably ignored completely). And it has matins lessons (nine for Sunday, three for each of the six weekdays, with accompanying responsories) for a single week: once more, which week in the liturgical year is not stated.

How the Sunday lessons work is the most astonishing thing about this book. The weekday lessons are unremarkable Monday through Friday (they come from Romans), and only mildly remarkable on Saturday in being drawn from the Wisdom of Solomon and

---

[14] N. R. Ker, *Medieval Manuscripts in British Libraries, I: London* (Oxford, 1969), pp. 240–1.

[15] In my *Liturgical Calendars, Saints, and Services in Medieval England* (Aldershot, 1998).

[16] The strongest influence discernible on the calendar is that of Worcester, as seen especially in the two feasts for Oswald; there is also the joint translation feast of Nicholas and Andrew on 9 May, which seems, for reasons I do not understand, to be characteristic of the diocese of Worcester. That Wulstan, canonized in 1203, is absent from the calendar, seems to yield that year as *terminus ad quem*; but Becket, canonized 1173, is present, in the original hand.

Ecclesiasticus.[17] The Sunday lessons, however, are taken from no scriptural source at all, nor even from the Fathers, but rather are a jumble of nine sections drawn from what reads like a commentary on the psalms, probably originally in glossed form.[18] The responsories are those which in most other Uses and texts accompany the lessons from Romans which would generally be found for the first week after the octave of Epiphany. The resulting mixture is not remotely usable, of course, in practice; hence my conclusion that it must have been drawn up as a kind of template, although the handsomeness of presentation effectively disguises this practical uselessness. (Indeed, it is not clear that the scribe understood that he was writing liturgical nonsense; there are other signs that he was, although a splendid scribe, something of a dunderhead.)

It is the backward-looking nature of this book that hints at a logical connection with the eleventh-century instances already noticed. By the time the St Paul's book was written, *circa* 1200, the breviary was not unknown; but there may still have been a question as to how best to construct one. The way the 'sample weeks' have been stuck into the Leofric Psalter and the Wulstan Portiforium suggests that the problem of putting together a single volume out of which the divine office could be performed in its entirety was just beginning to be tackled in the second half of the eleventh century. Neither of their 'sample weeks' is truly usable: that in the Leofric Psalter seems to give up on lessons for the last two days of its week, supplying there the odd passage from Taio of Saragossa, while that in the Wulstan Portiforium cobbles together as the weekday lessons inconsecutive snippets, more like capitula in length, from five different books of the Bible. And a century or more later, the garbled week represented in the St Paul's book is all the more puzzling because it is in effect concealed – that is, signalled by nothing like a rubric – as though to entice the user into trying to recite the divine office from it, only to discover that the week's forms supplied do not constitute one week out of the many in ordinary time but rather a sample of how such a week might work.

---

[17] Wisd. 1.6–7, Ecclus. 5.1–2, and Ecclus. 7.31–3; the first is the same as the single lesson for Saturday in the Wulstan book.

[18] I have not been able to identify this commentary, either from the electronic resources of CETEDOC and the Patrologia Latina Database or from knowledgeable friends (the late Margaret Gibson, Philip Pulsiano, Joseph Wittig). I am especially grateful to Gill Cannell of the Parker Library, Corpus Christi College, and J. Joseph Wisdom of St Paul's Cathedral Library for repeated access to the MSS in their care.

The feature we have been tracing does not in itself affect the contents of any of the constituent parts of the divine office. In that sense, this step towards a new format represents only a change in arrangement of a service book, while continuity of substance is being preserved. Since how the breviary evolves structurally is a separable question from how its contents change (for example, in the number of saints whose offices supplant those of the Temporale), it may be useful to have laid out one point in the evolution of that intellectual, cultural, and spiritual monument, the fully developed divine office.

APPENDIX

The quasi-sample week in BL Royal 2 A.x.

MS Royal 2 A.x is generally described as a breviary, made at St Albans Abbey in the fifth decade of the twelfth century.[19] The characterization as a breviary is not quite exact, but the book certainly represents a stage in the making of the breviary beyond that of the Wulstan Portiforium. In addition to the contents of the expanded psalter as noticed earlier in the Leofric and Wulstan books – calendar, psalms, canticles, litany, hymns (these throughout the year, but only for major occasions, and with Temporale and Sanctorale intermingled), and monastic canticles – there is a set of items which collectively point towards but do not comprise a full breviary. Among these items are a section of collects for saints' feasts (fol. 83v) rather like that in the Wulstan book, followed by what the catalogue calls 'Services for the four Sundays after Epiphany, with the Feriae'.[20] This component begins with full forms for the First Sunday after Epiphany – first vespers, matins, lauds, second vespers. Then (fol. 93, without heading or specification) come full forms for Monday, including the little hours (prime, terce, sext, none); here the three lessons in nocturn I are taken from Romans 5, but this is preceded by a single lesson, so marked (Lc), from Lamentations 2.19. This means that the forms could be used for a

---

[19] R. M. Thomson, *Manuscripts from St Albans Abbey*, 2 vols (Woodbridge, 1982), no. 25 and *passim*.
[20] G. F. Warner and J. P. Gilson, *Calendar of Western Manuscripts in the Old Royal and King's Collections*, 4 vols (London, 1921), I, pp. 29–30.

Monday either in the post-Epiphany or in the post-Pentecost season, the later being the single-lesson period. This pattern continues for the remaining weekdays, the sets of three lessons being consistently from Romans; but forms for the little offices and vespers are repeated only after Tuesday, being presumably meant to apply to the other days as well. At the end of the Saturday forms come those for first vespers of Sunday, and the full forms (twelve lessons each) for the Second, Third, and Fourth Sundays after Epiphany.

What we have here is then a template or sample week set in the midst of the four Sundays that most clearly have that character, but with an alternative, and unexplained, single-lesson provision which gives a template aspect to these Sundays as well. All of this is followed by equally full services for the Purification, Assumption, Nativity of the Blessed Virgin Mary, and Annunciation (in that curious order), and by offices for the Trinity (presumably Trinity Sunday, but this is not stated), the two feasts of the Cross, commemoration of Mary, and Michaelmas (fols 126–45). The Common of Saints is quite full (fols 145–201), and it may well be that the book was to end there. But there are a further nineteen folios of, as it were, afterthoughts: twelve lessons for St Alban, collects for four April feasts omitted earlier, fuller forms for several late April-early May feasts and also 'De quolibet sancto a Pascha usque Oct. Pentecoste', as well as the services for no less an occasion than All Saints. Yet there is still no proper Temporale. It looks as though what began as a psalter-plus started to take on the character of a proto-breviary with the addition of the 'template' services noted above; the lengthy Common of Saints and provision in a separate section of collects for about seventy-five saints intensify this 'template' character. But, unlike the three MSS studied above, all the services in this book are thoroughly usable.

University of North Carolina,
Chapel Hill

MESSAGE, CELEBRATION, OFFERING: THE PLACE OF TWELFTH- AND EARLY THIRTEENTH-CENTURY LITURGICAL DRAMA AS 'MISSIONARY THEATRE'

by BRENDA BOLTON

THE Church of Christ, whether congregation, building, or organization, demands at all times continuity in the expression of its message to reinforce the faith of believers and in its purpose to spread the Word among non-believers. In the twelfth and early thirteenth centuries, the growth and development of liturgical drama assisted in the expression of a corporate faith, not only that of well-established communities of monks and cathedral clergy, but also that of the laity for whom dramatic presentations could provide the necessary stimuli to worship. On the frontiers of Christendom too, where missionary endeavour was crucial, the dramatization both of the liturgy and of biblical events helped to lay the foundations for a projected continuity of worship amongst neophytes and those whose faith was not yet secure. Problems inevitably arose as new situations provoked liturgical changes. It thus became essential to ensure that neither the central faith nor the purpose of worship were weakened, diminished, or lost in the face of such change.

Performing arts – music, dance, singing, and drama – all had a place in the religious life of the worshipping community at the turn of the twelfth century, and it was of importance to the ecclesiastical authorities that they were soundly based. Either separately or in combination, these performing arts served to make the liturgy more convincing and understandable.[1] Through them the Holy Spirit was able to work to enhance and spread the faith. Unfortunately, because of the contradictory motives of those dealing with these arts, many,

---

[1] Andrew Hughes, 'Liturgical drama: falling between the disciplines', in Ekhard Simon, ed., *The Theatre of Medieval Europe: New Research in Early Drama* (Cambridge, 1991), pp. 42–64; William Tydeman, *The Theatre in the Middle Ages: Western European Stage Conditions c.800–1576* (Cambridge, 1978), pp. 46–68; John Wesley Harris, *Medieval Theatre in Context* (London, 1992), pp. 23–46; Margot Fassler, 'Representations of time in *Ordo representacionis Ade*, in Daniel Poirion and Nancy Freeman Regalado, eds, *Contexts: Style and Values in Medieval Art and Literature*, *Yale French Studies* special issue (New Haven, CT, and London, 1991), pp. 97–113.

albeit clerics,[2] producers or performers, carried away by the moment, sometimes allowed themselves to stray into areas diverging from or even inimical to the faith.[3] Acceptable content from biblical sources was frequently supplemented by material from Apocryphal and non-biblical stories which was not so relevant.[4] By so doing, the clerical performers could be regarded, in the extreme, as engaging in 'the works of the Devil', and faced that whole list of disabilities in canon law which was usually reserved for actors.[5] Of course, there were, even in those days, large areas of drama and the other performing arts which, whilst not serving a religious purpose, did not stray too far towards the anti-religious or blasphemous. It is in this context that much criticism, analysis, and assessment has developed into a concern with the techniques, construction, and performance of these arts. So involved in this have been specialist historians that 'the play's the thing' has been their only concern.[6] How could any one of these arts, of itself, be moral or immoral? In putting forward this proposition, they have forgotten, ignored, or even denied that liturgical drama in any age, and particularly in the Middle Ages, should be presented as part of an act of worship. It was the message of faith combined with the celebration of the events and persons gone before (the ancient landmark of Proverbs 22.28) which were to be central to the performance. Any drama not so dealing with the liturgy could be opposed and rooted out by the Church. Such harsh treatment has been roundly condemned by drama historians as an unacceptable form of censorship of a particular performing art which, to them, was fulfilling its purpose merely by being presented. Nor would they have valued the performance of the actors as offerings of their talents to God in praise and thanks. It is important to realize this difference of approach when considering the place of liturgical drama in areas of on-going Christianization where it functioned as missionary theatre.[7]

[2] John W. Baldwin, 'The image of the jongleur in Northern France around 1200', *Speculum*, 72 (1997), p. 644.

[3] Idem, *Masters, Princes and Merchants: The Social Views of Peter the Chanter and his Circle*, 2 vols (Princeton, NJ, 1970), 1, pp. 198–204.

[4] Lynette R. Muir, *The Biblical Drama of Medieval Europe* (Cambridge, 1995), and the review by Alan K. Knight in *Speculum*, 72 (1997), pp. 865–7.

[5] 'Donare res suas istrionibus vitium est inmane, non virtus': D. 86 c.7: *CIC*, 1, col. 299; Baldwin, 'Image of the jongleur', p. 639.

[6] Hamlet, II, ii, [641]. For example, Stanley J. Kahrl, 'The staging of medieval English plays', in Simon, *Theatre of Medieval Europe*, pp. 130–48.

[7] For wide differences see E. K. Chambers, *The Medieval Stage*, 2 vols (Oxford, 1903), 2, p. 69; Karl Young, *The Drama of the Medieval Church*, 2 vols (Oxford, 1933), 1, pp. 80–5; O. B.

Whilst agreeing 'that the righteous should teach and advise one another, singing with grace in their hearts to the Lord',[8] St Paul had always been aware of the potential danger if all sought 'their own and not those things which are Jesus Christ's'.[9] He had warned that 'there should be neither filthiness, nor foolish thinking nor jesting, for these are not suitable'.[10] Ecclesiastical authorities could thus claim to have inherited apostolic authority to exert discipline by admitting to or excluding unsuitable actions from the liturgical life of the Church. For example, throughout the twelfth century, several French bishops had been concerned by the danger of activities surrounding the Feast of Fools. When clerics were seen to be behaving like actors – remembering their reputation – the purpose of Christ's Church was not being served. But these justifiable strictures, fully compatible with true Christian worship, have been used by some historians of medieval drama to condemn papal attitudes to this medium.[11] This view neglects some of the evidence. Whilst both continuity and change may occur in liturgical drama, the substance of the faith must remain. Innocent III (1198–1216) led this approach. Yet, in the best tradition of the melodrama, Innocent has been cast in the role of villain by historians of the Medieval Stage.[12] He has been labelled a kill-joy for acting like some grim, latter-day Censor, banning the performance of all those plays he decided to consider unacceptable.[13] In a letter which later became a decretal, Innocent had declared:

> From time to time, theatrical plays [*ludi theatricales*], are being produced in certain churches and not only are devilish masks being used in derisive parodies [*spectacula*], but also, during those

---

Hardison Jnr, *Christian Rite and Christian Ritual in the Middle Ages: Essays in the Origin and Early History of Modern Drama* (Baltimore, MD, 1965), and C. Clifford Flanagan, 'Medieval Latin music drama', in Simon, *Theatre of Medieval Europe*, pp. 21–41, for a discussion of recent historiography in this field.

[8] Col. 4.16.

[9] Phil. 2.21.

[10] Eph. 5.4.

[11] For a valuable synthesis see, Marianne G. Briscoe, 'Some clerical notions of dramatic decorum in late medieval England', in Clifford Davidson and John H. Stroupe, eds, *Drama in the Middle Ages: Comparative and Critical Essays*, second series (New York, 1991), pp. 210–22.

[12] Even the otherwise excellent Margot Fassler, 'The Feast of Fools and *Danielis Ludus*: popular tradition in a medieval cathedral play', in Thomas Forrest Kelly, ed., *Plainsong in the Age of Polyphony*, Cambridge Studies in Performance Practice, 2 (Cambridge, 1992), pp. 68–80, esp. p. 79.

[13] Chambers, *Medieval Stage*, I, p. 279; Briscoe, 'Clerical notions of dramatic decorum', pp. 218–19.

other festivals of the Church following immediately upon Christ's birth, deacons, priests and sub-deacons in turn presume to exercise their insane mockeries and by their obscene gesturing are demeaning their clerical office in the sight of the people.[14]

The basis of Innocent's belief was that the message of liturgical drama should be firmly founded on the tenets of the Gospel and the Bible generally; that feasts and holy days, particularly those commemorating the Life of Christ, ought to be occasions for celebration and that those who were performers should take seriously the offering of their talents to God. Since 'there are diversities of gifts but the same Spirit',[15] whilst 'some were apostles, some prophets, some evangelists, some pastors and some teachers',[16] these performers could sing, dance, create music, and act, all in the service of Christ the Saviour. If these conditions were fulfilled, an appropriate, balanced use of the arts for liturgical purposes would be achieved.

The liturgical calendar used then, as now, was based on the Life of Christ. It laid down the structure of the feasts of the whole Christian Church.[17] Beginning in Advent with the prophecies of Christ's coming, it proceeded from the Nativity to Easter and Pentecost. The Descent of the Holy Spirit led to the last part of the liturgical calendar with its celebration of the work and witness of the Church. Following the creed, the liturgy as a whole emphasised God as Creator, Redeemer, and Judge through the tradition of reading the Old Testament and relating it to the New. Readings from the prophets, especially Isaiah, formed part of the Lectionary during Advent whilst the Fall of Man was the subject of meditation from Septuagesima Sunday to the Saturday before Easter.

While Advent was marked by a period of severe, almost 'Lenten' penance, the week after Christmas was, in contrast, a time of exuberant expression, markedly different in character from the more reverential rejoicing which followed Easter. John de Beleth,

---

[14] *PL* 215, cols 1070–1.

[15] I Cor. 12.4.

[16] Eph. 4.11, and frequently cited by Innocent. Cf. *Die Register Innocenz' III, 2 Band, 2 Pontifikatsjahr: Texte*, ed. Othmar Hageneder, Werner Maleczek, and Alfred Strnad (Rome and Vienna, 1979), p. 273 (To all the faithful in the city and diocese of Metz, July 1199), ll. 14–15.

[17] Francis X. Weiser, *Handbook of Christian Feasts and Customs: The Year of the Lord in Liturgy and Folklore* (New York, 1958); Thomas Talley, *The Origins of the Liturgical Year* (New York, 1986).

writing in the mid-twelfth century, described the four *tripudia* or special offices and feast days assigned to the lower clergy following the Nativity.[18] On 26 December, the deacons celebrated the feast of St Stephen, the deacon; on the day after came the turn of the priests for their special feast of St John the Evangelist; *pueri* or choirboys enjoyed Holy Innocents' Day on 28 December; whilst the uncertain status of sub-deacons, which left them midway between the major and minor clergy, was reflected in the variable day of their celebration. Beleth stated that the so-called Feast of Fools, 'quod vocamus stultorum', was held by some at the Circumcision on 1 January but by others on Epiphany 'vel in octavis Epiphanie'.[19] Not only was the sub-deacons' feast confused as it possessed no special *ordo* of its own, but its coincidence with New Year celebrations became associated with particularly unsuitable improvizations and role reversals.[20]

Growing out of the celebrations of these liturgical seasons, 'drama' or 'church theatre' first began in a closed community of monks or cathedral clergy.[21] Monks or clerics as actors presented a scene to an audience and then the whole community was reunited in an act of worship. The distinction between performers and audience was a very fine one and remained so until lay congregations became involved. Whilst the Easter plays gave little or no cause for riotous frivolity, there were other instances of spectator participation which were more wild than worshipping. Yet, while the clergy accused its laity of pursuing non-essentials and demonstrating an inability to distinguish between sacred and profane activity, there were occasions when it was the actors themselves who were the ones to blame, and the pope fully shared this view. Particular events in Poland had given rise to his provocative letter of 1207, but other places were experiencing similar problems. In northern France they had existed for a very long time, and had aroused hostility from both theologians and clerics alike.[22] None of the *tripudia* was to escape stringent criticism from those in the circle of Peter the Chanter,[23] particularly Robert de Courçon and Thomas of

[18] John de Beleth, *Summa de Ecclesiasticis Officiis*, 2 vols, ed. Heribert Douteil, *CChr.CM*, 41A (Turnhout, 1976), cc. 70–2: 1, pp. 130–4.

[19] Ibid., c.72: 1, p. 133.

[20] Fassler, 'Feast of Fools', pp. 72–5.

[21] George Klawitter, 'Dramatic elements in early monastic induction ceremonies', in Davidson and Stroupe, *Drama in the Middle Ages*, pp. 43–60.

[22] Fassler, 'Feast of Fools', pp. 72–3.

[23] Peter the Chanter, *Verbum abbreviatum*, PL 205, col. 153; Baldwin, 'Image of the jongleur', p. 639 n.12.

Chobham.[24] In the Councils of Paris (1213) and Rouen (1214), Robert de Courçon attempted to dissuade the clergy from attending the *tripudia* celebrations altogether,[25] while Thomas of Chobham railed against the clerical parodies, obscene gestures, and masks.[26] The validity of the theologians' criticism is clear for even in the cathedral of Notre Dame, the priests presiding over the Office of St John the Evangelist were recorded as performing *negligenter et joculariter*, carelessly and like actors.[27]

In 1198 Peter of Capua, legate to France, wrote to Odo de Sully, Bishop of Paris, about the need for reform.[28] Odo responded by abolishing the customary processions to and from the church during which the clergy were prone to contort their bodies in 'histrionic gestures'.[29] Liturgical reforms were subsequently introduced at Beauvais[30] and at Sens, where Peter of Corbeil drew up a new office for the Feast of the Circumcision which was more worshipping than dramatic.[31] In the diocese of Auxerre, another reforming bishop, William de Seignelay,[32] believed in reforming abuses through 'well-ordered Christian substitutes that would succeed as replacements because they could offer some but not all of the most popular features of the abuse'.[33] Plays could thus be rewritten to bring them into line with the faith of the Church.

Innocent III was well aware that different strategies – didactic or

---

[24] Idem, *Masters, Princes and Merchants*, 2, p. 142 n.218; Thomas of Chobham, *Summa confessorum*, ed. Frank Broomfield, Analecta Mediaevalia Namurcensia, 25 (Louvain and Paris, 1968).

[25] *Sacrorum conciliorum nova et amplissima collectio*, ed. J. D. Mansi, 31 vols (Florence and Venice, 1759–93), 22, pp. 840–2, 919–20.

[26] Chobham, *Summa confessorum*, p. 291.

[27] Benjamin Guérard, *Cartulaire de l'église de Notre Dame de Paris*, 4 vols (Paris, 1850), 4, pp. 5–7, 121.

[28] Werner Maleczek, *Petrus Capuanus. Kardinal, Legat am Vierten Kreuzzug, Theologe (d.1214)* (Vienna, 1988), pp. 100–1. See also now the Italian translation of this work (by Fulvio Delle Donne), *Petro Capuano: Patrizion amalfitano, cardinale, legato alla Quarta Crociata, teologo (†1214)* (Amalfi, 1997).

[29] Constitutions of Odo of Sully, *PL* 212, cols 72 and 92; Henri Villetard, *Office de Pierre de Corbeil*, Bibliothèque musicologique, 4 (Paris, 1907), pp. 62–3.

[30] Wulf Arlt, *Ein Festoffizium des Mittelalters aus Beauvais in seiner liturgischen und musikalischen Bedeutung*, 2 vols (Cologne, 1970), pp. 42–51, 68–9.

[31] Villetard, *Office de Pierre de Corbeil*, p. 63.

[32] William de Seignelay, Bishop of Auxerre (1207–20), Bishop of Paris (1220–3); Constance Brittain Bouchard, *Spirituality and Administration: The Role of the Bishop in Twelfth-Century Auxerre*, Speculum Anniversary Monograph, 5 (Cambridge, MA, 1979), pp. 121–40.

[33] Fassler, 'Feast of Fools', p. 77.

dramatic – were used to promote and explain the liturgy, depending on the local circumstances. Those liturgical presentations, marking the great festivals of the Church's calendar, enriched and stimulated an existing stable faith. In other circumstances and in other areas, at the frontiers of Christendom for example, a different approach might be beneficial. Biblical history to which pagans could relate was often used for the purposes of their conversion. As with the wider variety of Innocent III's activities during his pontificate, little re-assessment has been undertaken. His attitude to liturgical drama is certainly an area where perhaps the views of many drama historians have held sway for too long and now need to be challenged.

In a reconsideration of Innocent's views and actions concerning ecclesiastical drama, certain important documents were included amongst Gregory IX's *Decretals* under the heading *De vita et honestate clericorum*.[34] These included Innocent's decretal *Cum decorem* of *c.*1210, which legislates on liturgical drama, and is essentially drawn from his letter of 1207 to the Polish bishops.

The letter *Cum decorem*, which came nineteenth in an unprecedented series of twenty-six letters which Innocent wrote to Poland over an eleven-day period between 2 and 13 January 1207, was mainly concerned with the actions of the Polish dukes in all aspects of their behaviour, and exhorted the clergy to set about implementing a thorough-going reform.[35] The particular situation which had provoked Innocent into such a spurt of letter-writing was the flight to Rome of his friend, Henry Kietlicz, Archbishop of Gniezno, who had arrived at the Curia just before Christmas 1206.[36] As always, Innocent was soft-hearted to those who made the long journey to see him! Kietlicz would most likely have told the Pope of the dire state of the Polish Church contrasted with that which he saw in Rome, particularly of the sequence of festivals following Christ's Nativity and the stational masses which he attended. These offices were numerous and deeply serious, commemorating the martyrdom of St Stephen on 26 December, the feast of John the Apostle and Evangelist on 27 December, the Slaughter of the Holy Innocents on 28 December, the martyrdom of Thomas Becket on 29 December, the feast of St Sylvester on

---

[34] X.3.12; *CIC*, 2, col. 452.

[35] *PL* 215, cols 1059–76; *Bullarium Poloniae I 1000–1342*, ed. Irena Sułkowska-Kuraś and Stanisław Kuraś (Rome, 1982), pp. 18–22.

[36] *PL* 215, col. 1061: 'venerabili fratre nostro, Gnesniensi archiepiscopo, ad sedem apostolicam accedente', 4 Jan. 1207.

31 December, the Circumcision on 1 January, and Epiphany or the Arrival of the Magi on 6 January.

What seems to have been happening in the Church in Poland was rather different, if we accept the version of Henry Kietlicz (as Innocent certainly did). Although the Pope was concerned about all aspects of the Polish Church, Kietlicz's description of the abuse of liturgical drama would certainly account for this letter and the consequent decretal. The letter does not concentrate entirely on plays in churches, but provides more evidence of the fragile state of the Polish priesthood. Innocent feared that the lamps of religion might be extinguished and the ministry of the Lord stained by so great a number of clerical irregularities as were taking place in Poland. Priests were 'married' or were openly consorting with women; the higher clergy were not ashamed to accept dignities and bribes, or to appoint their natural sons or close relations to high positions, whilst incontinent clerics fostered their own sons as priests. Spiritual feelings amongst the laity were beginning to dissipate as married priests and their illegitimate sons freely ministered at the altar (that is, at mass) where, as Innocent stressed, the only Son of the heavenly Father had suffered for the salvation of mankind. The honour of the Polish clergy was being tarnished at a time when it would have been more profitable to encourage the people by preaching the word of God.

Innocent's letter laid down strict provisions to ensure decent and honest behaviour by priests, ruling against their obscene theatricals. He was concerned by the corrupting custom of clerical mockery or parody (*ludibrorum*) which the bishops were to ensure was extirpated from their churches, 'lest both the sacred act of worship and the zealous practitioners of the sacred orders should be compromised'. He ends the letter on a dramatic note. 'The house of God mocks us and the reproaches seem to fall on us. Brothers, we command you to root out those customary parodies and commend the observance of divine and holy orders in your churches.'[37]

Innocent had hoped that Poland would be the springboard for the Christianization of nearby Pomerania, and so must have been disappointed by the calamitous state of the Church there. Perhaps he felt this all the more deeply for, at Regensburg and nearby areas in 1194,

---

[37] *PL* 215, col. 1071, 'praelibatam vero ludibriorum consuetudinem, vel potius corruptelam, curetis ab ecclesiis vestris taliter extirpare, quod vos divini cultus et sacri comprobetis ordinis zelatores'.

the custom had begun of performing exactly that kind of liturgical drama which was to prove so useful in the mission field, and which he must later have come to hope would be a feature of his pontificate.[38] At Regensburg a whole series of Old Testament plays were performed, including the *Ordo creationis angelorum*, the *Downfall of Lucifer*, *The Creation and Fall of Man*, and the *Ordo prophetarum* or prophet plays. Indeed, Chapter 31 of Innocent's own *De Miseria*, composed a year or two later while he was still Cardinal Deacon of SS Sergio e Bacco, was entitled *On the Pride and Fall of Lucifer*, and echoed the words used in the Battle between the Good and Bad Angels.[39] German crusaders, working closely with the Pope and engaged in the Christianization of Livonia and Estonia, seem to have used similar theatrical strategies. The *Gesta* of Albert of Buxhoven, bishop of Riga (1198–1229), chronicles the use of drastic but effective measures by these crusaders or *peregrini* to bring the faith to backsliding neophytes and pagans alike.[40]

> In that same winter (1204), a most well-organised *Play of the Prophets* was performed in the centre of Riga, so that the heathen might also learn the rudiments of the Christian faith through the evidence of their own eyes. The subject matter of this play or comedy was most carefully expounded by an expositor [*interpres*], not only to the neophytes but also to the pagans who were present. When Gideon's army was shown fighting with the Philistines, the pagans, frightened that they themselves were about to be slaughtered, began to run away.[41] They were brought back again and the performance continued, although they remained very wary. Within a short space of time the Church once more grew quiet.
>
> In spite of this, the play itself was a presentiment, a prelude and a forerunner of troubles yet to come. For in the play there were other battles, those of David, Gideon and Herod. The pagans were converted to the doctrines of the Old and New Testaments

---

[38] *Annales Ratisponenses*, ed. W. Wattenbach, *MGH.SS*, 17, ed. G. H. Pertz (Hanover, 1861), p. 590.

[39] Lotharii Cardinalis (Innocentii III), *De Miseria Humane Conditionis*, ed. Michele Maccarrone (Padua, 1955), 2, xxxi, *De superbia et casu Luciferi*, pp. 62–4; Muir, *Biblical Drama*, pp. 69–74.

[40] *Gesta Alberti Livonensis Episcopi* in J. D. Gruber, ed., *Origines Livoniae Sacrae et Civilis* (Leipzig, 1740), p. 34.

[41] They are actually Midianites in the Bible, but 'Philistines' was a more useful generic term in the dramatic licence of the time.

through these many battles and then were instructed how to come to a true peace and to everlasting life.

Innocent's concern for the successful Christianization of Livonia had led him in 1201 to intervene by urging the Germans to simplify their missionary strategy by uniting Cistercian white monks and black canons in one habit and regular way of life.[42] The purpose of the play mounted in Riga for the conversion of the populace no doubt was intended to help in this.

In order to get some feeling of the aims of missionary theatre, the work of Richard Trexler has provided invaluable insights in an essay on conversion in sixteenth-century Mexico.[43] Not only does Trexler make some interesting comments on the roles of mendicant preachers and soldiers involved in missionary theatre in a frontier situation, but his remarks on the Christianization of Mexico are highly instructive. To teach Christian behaviour there, historical events were theatrically re-enacted by the *conquistadores* so that the Indians would be shown the importance of both kneeling to God and the place of the altar in worship. Historical theatricalization using the verbal image of the Battle of the Good Angels with the Bad Angels announced the coming of evangelization (the Good Angels as agents of the Spanish Conquest and the Bad Angels, erstwhile leaders of the Indians).[44] These spectacles brought the Indians out into the public squares and open places, serving to increase their church attendance and, incidentally, ease the path of the conquerors. All this was truly reminiscent of the thirteenth-century missionary theatre on the frontiers of Poland and Livonia-Estonia.

Innocent III's letter of 1207, selected as being worthy of inclusion in the *Compilatio tertia* compiled by Petrus Beneventanus in *c.* 1210,[45] was followed by the decretal *Cum decorum* which sought to regularize the points of view Innocent had expressed. He hoped that if its provisions

---

[42] Michele Maccarrone, 'I papi e gli inizi della cristianizzazione della Livonia', *Gli inizi del cristianesimo in Livonia-Lettonia* (Vatican City, 1989), pp. 72–80; idem, *Studi su Innocenzo III*, Italia Sacra, 17 (Padua, 1972), pp. 262–3, 334–7.

[43] Richard C. Trexler, *Church and Community 1200–1600*, Storia e letteratura, 168 (Rome, 1987), pp. 575–613.

[44] Ibid., p. 580.

[45] Petrus Beneventanus in Emil Friedberg, ed., *Quinque compilationes antiquae* (Leipzig, 1882), cols 105–34; Kenneth Pennington, 'The making of a decretal collection: the genesis of *Compilatio tertia*', in his *Popes, Canonists and Texts 1150–1550*, Variorum Collected Studies Series, 412 (Aldershot, 1993), ch. VIII, pp. 67–92.

were followed, existing liturgical drama would be purified and regulated. Of course, many areas other than Poland – among them, as already mentioned, Riga and Regensburg – enjoyed liturgical drama acceptable to Innocent. Since the decretal was highly specific in that it related to the Polish situation, glosses to help other areas from being 'tarred with the same brush' appeared straight away.

The decretal *Cum decorem* clearly legislated a distinction between inappropriate and appropriate plays or dramatic representations. It was necessary for fear that any corrupt liturgical celebrations might lead to the derisive parodying of sacred matters instead of reinforcing the suitable commemoration of Christ's sacrifice upon the Cross – His offering of himself for Mankind. Reassurances, however, needed to be given to religious communities of monks or secular canons that the decretal did not really apply to their customary and decorous representations of certain suitable topics at high points of the liturgical year. These were not meant to be opposed by the papacy or hierarchy in their stringent dealings with corrupt practices. In 1208 Innocent visited Montecassino, spending several days there, and it may well have been there that the need for such early reassurances was brought home to him.[46]

Consequently, a canonistic gloss was rapidly produced:[47]

> It is not forbidden to perform *The Manger, Herod and the Magi,* and *How Rachel weeps for her Children,* and other plays which are relevant to that liturgical feast and which encourage men to worship rather than to wantonness and evil desires, just as at Easter *The Sepulchre* and *The Three Marys and the Gardener* are performed and other things which are staged to encourage devotion. And that these are to be performed is justified by [three citations:] *de con. di. I., Sel. christus,* and *d. iiii queris.* Rather it is permissible as this feast [Holy Innocents and St Stephen, in the margin] is a commemoration and sign of past times.

---

[46] *PL* 215, cols 1593–4; Brenda Bolton, '*Via ascetica*: a papal quandary', *SCH*, 22 (1985), pp. 161–91, esp. pp. 179–80.

[47] BAV, MS Vat. Lat. 1378, fols 57r–v: 'Et non prohibetur hic presentare presepe, herodem et magos et qualiter rachel plorat filios suos et alia que tangunt festa illa et alia pocius ad devotionem quam ad voluptatem et laquiam homines invitant sicut in pascha sepulcram tres marie ortholanus et alia que representantur ad devotionem exitandam et quod hec representari possunt est ar. infra de con. di. I. sel' christus et d.iiii queris. Immo quod licet festum est representatio et signum pretericarum rerum. lxxv.<di.> quod die.' Dr Peter Clarke kindly drew this gloss to my attention.

This was contemporary with Innocent III's handling of the issue of liturgical drama and is in the apparatus of glosses which Vincentius Hispanus wrote on *Compilatio tertia* around 1212.[48] As Vincentius was a well-known borrower, he probably took this from Laurentius Hispanus, his fellow Spaniard and glossator who was writing *c.*1210.[49]

Although we cannot know the precise texts which Innocent III and the glossator saw, it is possible to base some comments on the scattered plays of similar titles which have survived and which the gloss accepted as suitable to be performed. The eleventh-century Limoges play of the *Manger* resembles the Easter *Quem quaeritis* and may have been recited at the end of matins.[50] The *Officium Pastorum* play from Padua dates from the thirteenth century with clerics doubling as *pastores* and *obstetrices*.[51] The *Play of Herod* refers to the *Ordo ad representandum Herodem* which may have been performed on the Feast of the Innocents or for the *Festa Stultorum*.[52] The best version of this which had been composed in Freising *c.*1070 was widely diffused.[53] The *Magi* play clearly celebrated Epiphany whilst *Rachel weeping* was a re-enactment linking the massacre of the Holy Innocents with the prophecy of Jeremiah in Matthew's Gospel.[54]

The Sepulchre of the Lord or *Visitatio sepulchri*, the visit of the three Marys to the Tomb on Easter Day, is perhaps the oldest extant scene in biblical drama. The majority of plays also includes the meeting between Mary Magdalene and Jesus *in specie ortulani*, in the guise of a gardener.[55]

If these were the plays that the author of the gloss believed Innocent would permit, there is confirmation of an interesting distinction. Liturgical drama was licit when its purpose was to increase devotion and knowledge. It was not licit when it provided unthinking entertainment. Two citations from Gratian are given in the gloss:

---

[48] Vincentius Hispanus (fl. *c.*1210–*c.*1234); Kenneth Pennington, 'Innocent III and the divine authority of the pope', in his *Popes, Canonists and Texts*, ch. II, pp. 1–32, esp. pp. 12–15.

[49] Laurentius (fl. 1200–48); Brendan Mcmanus, 'An edition of Laurentius's *Apparatus glossarum in Compilationem tertiam*' (University of Syracuse, NY, Ph. D. thesis, 1991), pp. 450–1: 'Prohibitum est etiam causa ludibritii uti habitu monachali vel alio religioso. Et graviter punitur qui hoc fecit, in authen. de sanct. episc.'

[50] Young, *Drama of the Medieval Church*, 2, p. 9; Paul Evans, *The Early Trope Repertory of St Martial de Limoges* (Princeton, NJ, 1970).

[51] Young, *Drama of the Medieval Church*, 2, pp. 9–10.

[52] Ibid., pp. 102–24, 109.

[53] Peter Dronke, ed., *Nine Medieval Latin Plays* (Cambridge, 1994), pp. 24–51.

[54] Muir, *Biblical Drama*, pp. 104–10; Matt. 2.17–18.

[55] Muir, *Biblical Drama*, pp. 139–42; John 20.11–18.

Semel Christus mortuus est[56] and *Queris a me*,[57] both making the general point about the justness and importance of a proper remembrance of the past. Every time Easter is celebrated, the memory of the anniversary is made the more real by seeing an enactment of the Lord on the Cross. Hence, the deeply serious nature of this commemoration. The third citation, *Quod die*, seems to buttress Laurentius's statement that a celebration is a representation of past events, in this case the laying on of hands to bring down the Holy Spirit, as enacted by Paul and Barnabas.[58]

What, of course, is interesting is how well this gloss reflected Innocent's own views on liturgical drama. It is certainly possible to cite evidence of such plays being performed in his lifetime, and to stress the number of centres he had visited which produced them, such as Montecassino,[59] and St Martial, Limoges.[60] Any suggestions about Innocent's personal involvement with liturgical drama must remain somewhat tentative. That he was certainly well-acquainted with communal worship goes without saying. His early Benedictine education, his function as a cardinal-deacon concerned with papal ceremonial and liturgy, and the dramatic 'showman-like' skills which we know him to have possessed – all point in this direction.[61] Likewise, his role models – Gregory the Great,[62] Amalarius of Metz,[63] Notker the Stammerer of St Gall[64] – were those whose reputations had been built on the clearer transmission of the Christian message – didactically, dramatically, and musically – to believers and pagans alike.

Innocent's experience of liturgical drama started early. His first

[56] D.2 de cons. c.51: *CIC*, I, cols 1332–3.

[57] D.4 de cons. c.129: *CIC*, I, cols 1402–4.

[58] D. 75 c.5: *CIC*, I, cols 266–7. I am most grateful to Prof. Kenneth Pennington for an e-mail discussion on this matter.

[59] See n.50 above; Melody Sue Owens, 'The Montecassino Passion Play. Theatre in a Monastic Community' (University of California, Berkeley, Ph. D. thesis, 1987).

[60] *Chronicon B. Iterii Armarii monasterii S. Marcialis*, ed. H. Duplès-Agier, Société de l'histoire de France (Paris, 1874), p. 62.

[61] Brenda Bolton, 'A show with a meaning: Innocent III's approach to the Fourth Lateran Council, 1215', in Brenda Bolton, *Innocent III: Studies on Papal Authority and Pastoral Care*, Variorum Collected Studies Series, 490 (Aldershot, 1995), ch. XI, pp. 54–67.

[62] *PL* 217, Sermo XIII *de Sanctis. In festo d. Gregorii papae*, cols 513–22.

[63] Enrico Mazza, 'L'altare nell'alto medioevo: l'interpretazione di Amalario di Metz', *Arte Cristiana*, 80 (1992), pp. 403–10.

[64] Susan Rankin, 'The Song School of St Gall in the later ninth century', in James C. King, ed., *Sangallensia in Washington* (New York, 1993), pp. 173–97. For evidence of Innocent's interest in Notker, see *Vita B. Notkero Balbulo*, *ActaSS*, April I, 6 April, pp. 576–604, at p. 587.

recorded 'official' journey, undertaken to the Limousin in 1186 or 1187, was in the company of Hugh de Nonant, Bishop of Lichfield and Coventry, whose cathedral statutes (1188–98) record the earliest performance in England of liturgical plays at Christmas and Easter.[65] That great creative, artistic centre, the monastery of St Martial, Limoges, produced one of the earliest treatments of the *Ordo prophetarum* or *Procession of the Prophets*.[66] Based on the *Sermon against Jews, Pagans and Arians* attributed to St Augustine, the Limoges play calls forth thirteen prophets to bear witness to the Messiah.[67] The dramatic possibilities of this sermon are obvious. A presenter introduced each prophet, and his prophecy was delivered 'in character' by a deacon.[68]

An interesting possible side-effect of Innocent's knowledge of this play of the prophets is suggested by the so-called Lunette of Mentorella – the semi-circular decoration above the door which Innocent commissioned for the grill in front of the *Confessio* or tomb of St Peter.[69] On the front face, in the bottom row, are the prophets (or some of them) and others of the Old Testament – Amos, Hosea, Abdias (the servant of God), Daniel, Solomon, Habbakuk, Jonas, Joshua, Jeremiah, David, Moses, and Isaiah – each carrying phylacteries inscribed with well-known but incomplete phrases which announce the Coming of Christ.[70]

It is possible that Innocent had commissioned his own daily reminder of the *Ordo prophetarum* – this personal procession of prophets in Limoges metal work – from St Martial, the great monastery with the earliest text of a dramatic representation and collection of twelfth-century manuscript sources – which he knew well. Had Innocent III himself been compiling a list of plays that touched men's consciences and led them to worship and devotion,

---

[65] Young, *Drama of the Medieval Church*, 2, pp. 522–3; Lawrence M. Clopper, '*Miracula* and *The Tretise of Miraclis Pleyinge*', *Speculum*, 65 (1990), p. 904.

[66] M. F. Vaughan, 'The prophets of the Anglo-Norman Adam', *Traditio*, 39 (1983), pp. 81–114.

[67] Dorothy F. Glass, 'Pseudo-Augustine, prophets and pulpits in Campania', *Dumbarton Oaks Papers*, 41 (1987), pp. 215–26.

[68] Lynette R. Muir, 'Adam: a twelfth-century play translated from the Norman-French with an introduction and notes', *Proceedings of the Leeds Philosophical and Literary Society*, 13 (1970), pp. 155–201.

[69] Marie-Madeleine Gautier, 'L'art de l'émail champlevé en Italie à l'époque primitive du gothique', *Il Gotico a Pistoia nei suoi rapporti con l'arte gotica Italiana* (Pistoia, 1966), pp. 271–95.

[70] Ibid., p. 282.

rather than the canonists Laurentius or Vincentius Hispanus, he would most certainly have included the *Ordo prophetarum*. It is also possible to suggest that Innocent would have extended his list to include the field of missionary theatre – encouraging a far more flexible interpretation of suitable religious drama. The re-enactment of Old Testament battle scenes was part of his repertory. He knew what was going on in Livonia and Estonia and approved most of it, but his stress on the value of the plays of the prophets in Riga has not received the analysis he deserves.

This brief exploration, which began with liturgical drama in thirteenth-century Poland, has broadened to deal with similar abuses in other parts of Europe. Innocent III's response to the dangers of possible misuse of liturgical drama was a sharply-worded letter of instruction. His letter entered into *Compilatio tertia*, a decretal collection of 1210, and made him a target for vilification by some who have seen him as an implacably hostile opponent of all 'drama'. This view cannot be justified. Innocent was far too wise to disregard the inherent potential in dramatic representations as stimuli to worship and devotion. This attitude doubtless assisted the drawing up of the resultant contemporary gloss which clarified those commemorations approved by earlier authorities and allowed their continued use. The faithful were thus permitted decorously to observe their accustomed religious feasts, while recent converts on the frontiers were able to hold rather more rousing celebrations of their new faith via the medium of missionary theatre. Had drama historians been more appreciative of Innocent's approach, they would not have been quite so ready to condemn his significant place in the development of liturgical drama, particularly in the mission field.[71]

Queen Mary and Westfield College, University of London

---

[71] An important article by Susan Boynton, 'Performative exegesis in the Fleury Interfectio puerorum', *Viator*, 29 (1998), pp. 39–64, appeared after this volume went to press.

THE ALTARS IN YORK MINSTER IN THE EARLY
SIXTEENTH CENTURY

by W. J. SHEILS

'GOOD God! what a pomp of silk vestments was there, of golden candlesticks.'[1] The dismissive satire of Erasmus's pilgrim on looking down on Canterbury Cathedral not only brought traditional piety into disrepute among significant sectors of the educated, both clerical and lay, in early sixteenth-century England, but has also helped to colour the views of historians of the later medieval Church until recently. The work on parochial, diocesan, and cathedral archives since the 1960s, undertaken and inspired by the publication of A. G. Dickens' *The English Reformation*, has refined that view, which saw traditional piety as something of a clerical confidence trick designed to impoverish a credulous laity, and recovered the reputation of the early sixteenth-century Church.[2] The most recent, and most eloquent, account of the strength of traditional piety among the people is that by Eamon Duffy. His work has concentrated on the parochial context, where he has shown how intercessory prayer, through gilds, obits, and chantries, remained at the centre of a liturgical tradition which commanded great loyalty from the laity up to and, in some cases, beyond the dissolution of those institutional expressions of that devotion in 1547.[3] The place of such devotion within a cathedral context has largely been ignored, despite the recently published histories, and this paper sets out to fill that gap a little by looking at the minor altars of York Minster and the clergy which served them.[4]

Among some Henrician reformers the very purpose and existence of

---

[1] Quoted in P. Collinson, N. Ramsay, and M. Sparks, eds, *A History of Canterbury Cathedral* (Oxford, 1995), p. 154.

[2] See R. N. Swanson, *Church and Society in Late Medieval England* (Oxford, 1989), esp. pp. 275–99, for a recent overview.

[3] E. Duffy, *The Stripping of the Altars: Traditional Religion in England 1400–1580* (New Haven, CT, and London, 1992).

[4] S. E. Lehmberg, *The Reformation of Cathedrals: Cathedrals in English Society 1485–1603* (Princeton, NJ, 1988), pp. 13–25, discusses the minor canons. For a detailed study see N. Orme, 'The medieval clergy of Exeter cathedral, i. the vicars and annuellars', *Transactions of the Devonshire Association*, 113 (1981), pp. 79–102.

cathedrals as centres of cult was called into question, and the findings
of ecclesiastical visitation provided plenty of evidence of deficiency in
the performance of these functions.[5] This visitation material has been
interpreted by historians to suggest that much of cathedral worship in
the early sixteenth century represented the fitful observance, often by
poorly paid deputies, of an outmoded devotional pattern which
commanded little loyalty from either priests or people. Thus the
visitation of York in 1519 found that the hangings were covered with
dust, cobwebs, and wax, and 'dogges pysses of thame', whilst 'the
ragged and torn coverings of the little altars would have disgraced an
upland village, let alone a great cathedral.' Likewise, in 1544, the
visitors complained that the vicars choral did not take pains in doing
their duties, the chantry priests failed to observe the scheduled hours
allotted for their masses, and the copes and vestments were 'decayed'.
The picture conveyed by these sources was, in the words of the most
recent history of the Minster, one of 'tarnished splendour'.[6]

These findings of the visitors did not go unchallenged at the time; it
was noted that the furnishings and fittings of the chantry altars were
recorded and listed in a book kept by the chapter clerk, whilst the
timings of the masses at the altars had been adjusted so that 'than
might the pareshe messes be done afore our procession'; a necessary
arrangement as some of the chantry priests in the Minster assisted in
the poorly endowed parochial livings of the city, whilst others were
occupied at the high altar as vicars choral.[7] The question remains as to
how far the tarnished splendour was particular to the Minster at this
point in its history, and how far it can be explained by the nature of the
source. Deficiencies in the provision of things needful for the liturgy
were not confined to sixteenth-century visitations; in 1409 the
vestments, fittings, and plate of many of the Minster chantries were
found wanting, as were the furnishings of the annual, or obit, altar.[8]
Thus it would appear that, except perhaps in the wealth of detail
provided in their account, the overall impression to be gained from
visitation material between these dates is broadly similar. The context,
however, had changed significantly, for the fifteenth century had seen

[5] Lehmberg, *Reformation of Cathedrals*, pp. 69–76; D. Lepine, *A Brotherhood of Canons Serving God: English Secular Cathedrals in the Later Middle Ages* (Woodbridge, 1995), pp. 6–17.

[6] Claire Cross, 'From the Reformation to the Restoration', in G. E. Aylmer and R. Cant, eds, *A History of York Minster* (Oxford, 1978), p. 194.

[7] J. Raine, ed., *The Fabric Rolls of York Minster*, SS, 35 (1859), p. 269.

[8] Ibid., p. 245.

a great growth in chantry foundations in the Minster, culminating in the provision of a special college for the chantry priests in 1461.[9] That growth, however, had peaked by 1500, and here perhaps some signs of decay may be detected.

An early sixteenth-century listing records seventy chantries in the Minster at thirty altars and served by at least twenty-six priests. Of these chantries only one was a sixteenth-century foundation, that established at the Jesus and Mary altar in the Lady Chapel by Archdeacon Henry Carnebull for the soul of Archbishop Rotherham and, ultimately, for his own.[10] The terms of its foundation, however, indicated that the increasingly discriminatory and personal expressions of piety which characterized chantry ordinances of the later fifteenth century had carried on into the 1500s. It was to be served exclusively by a parson (that is to say, chantry priest) of the Minster who was required to carry out a quite elaborate range of masses as well as the Requiem, including the Jesus mass and the normal Sunday mass, to which was added the dirige, placebo, and commendation. Special prayers for Rotherham and for Carnebull were to be said after communion at each mass. Daily recital of the *Kyrie, Pater noster,* and *Requiem aeternam,* listing by name the souls for whom the chantry was founded, was required of the chantry priest who also, at the end of each daily mass, had to sing the *De profundis* at Rotherham's tomb, which was adjacent to the altar. The direct link between the masses and the soul of Rotherham was stressed further by a separate ordinance which provided for an additional daily ritual at the archbishop's tomb, to be performed by the vicars choral. They were required to sing the Antiphon and the *De profundis,* saying also the Lord's Prayer and the Hail Mary, on pain of a fine of 6s. 8d. to the Dean and Chapter.[11]

Although this is the only permanent foundation for which we have full documentation at this time, architectural evidence suggests that the tomb of Archbishop Savage was also designed to house a chantry, and in 1518 the precentor Thomas Perrott left an annual sum of eight marks for three years for a priest 'to syng for my saull in the chappell over the bodie of my lait lord, the bishop Savage, and for my said lodis saull, and all Christen saullis'.[12] The Jesus and Mary altar may have

[9] Lehmberg, *Reformation of Cathedrals,* p. 24.

[10] York Minster Library, Dean and Chapter Archives, M2(2)c, fos 19r–21r.

[11] Ibid., M2(4)b, fos 1r–4v.

[12] Raine, *Fabric Rolls,* p. 98; G. E. Aylmer, 'Funeral monuments and other post-medieval sculpture', in Aylmer and Cant, *History of York Minster,* p. 432.

been the only one to acquire a new tenant, as it were, at this time, but other Minster altars continued to attract new endowments by means of obits and, in the case of Savage's tomb, it would appear that there were plans to add to the number of altars available. Against these positive signs, however, we must place the findings of the visitors in 1519. If the altars were truly in the state suggested by the visitors then the foundations of Carnebull and Perrott can be seen as no more than isolated examples of a form of piety no longer central to the life of the cathedral.

The evidence of clerical numbers has been used to suggest that this may have been so. As at other cathedrals the provision of vicars choral had, by this date, fallen short of the official York figure of thirty-six, but this had been the case for some time and their numbers stabilized at around twenty for most of the early sixteenth century. Many of these not only served in the choir but also at the chantries, almost half of which were manned in this way.[13] The surviving wills of these men tell us little of their spiritual or social life, except that they retained a strong corporate sense of identity reflected in their bequests. A few, like William Burton, who died in 1520, made fairly specific arrangements for the masses they wished to have said at their burial day, and others, like John Usher, remembered particular altars and shrines in the Minster to which they had a special devotion; but this is all the specific detail we have.[14] Although almost all appear as loyal servants to each other and to the institution in which they made their livings, they were for the most part unexceptional men performing routine tasks, whose horizons rarely stretched beyond their families or their work place.

The remaining chantries were attended by the twenty or so cantarists living in St William's College. They too exhibited a strong collegial sense, almost all of them (like John Hixon, who served Rotherham's chantry from 1530 until his death in 1546) left money to the brethren of the college, making them the executors of their wills and bequeathing to individual cantarists the trappings of their calling – amices, tippets, and the like. In return for this they could expect a good turn-out at their burial and yearly obits from the college.[15] What

---

[13] Lehmberg, *Reformation of Cathedrals*, pp. 12, 23.

[14] C. Cross, ed., *York Clergy Wills 1520–1600: 1, Minster Clergy*, Borthwick Texts and Calendars: records of the northern province, 10 (York, 1984), esp. pp. 1, 6, 27–9, 46–7, 49–51, 81–4.

[15] Ibid., pp. 3, 27–9, 34–5, 47–9, 52–3, 77–80, 82–3.

distinguishes these chantry priests from the vicars choral, however, is the fact that more of them owned books, some of which suggested wider intellectual interests. John Nosterfield, who seems to have combined a succession of chantries with some parochial responsibilities but described himself as a Minster parson in his will, owned a copy of *Lyndwood* which he left to his more exalted colleague, Edward Kellett, doctor of laws and prebendary of Langtoft. John Fewlare, who served St Stephen's altar, listed nine books by name in his will of 1530, including among them Bede's *Life of St Cuthbert*, Balbus's *Catholicon*, and *The Golden Legend* of Voragine, sharing these among three of his fellow chantry priests. Among the possessions of John Hixon were listed the works of Hugh of St Victor and an English text glossing the Ten Commandments, as well as 'other olde written bookes'.[16]

Of course these books reveal minds of a conservative cast, but they were not empty ones; and the impression gained from the wills is that the founding of St William's College had achieved its purpose. Through it was provided a collegial sense of identity to a potentially atomized set of individual chantries; and within it the fruits of common experience, and even the minor accoutrements of clerical life, were passed on down the generations. The number of clergy may have been rather less than that formally established, but no altar was left unserved, those serving them seemed to believe in the efficacy of what they were doing, and some revealed an interest in wider spiritual concerns.[17] For some, at least, the communal life which they experienced at St William's College, based as it was on attendance at the Minster altars, may have recalled the pattern of their earlier careers in the religious orders. In the years following 1536 at least ten of the chaplains had been monks before the Dissolution, a fact which may also have contributed to the conservative tone noted in the probate evidence.[18] Despite the findings of the visitations, such disenchantment as there may have been could not be laid solely, or even primarily, at the door of the clergy whose task it was to officiate at these altars. But

---

[16] Cross, *Minster Clergy*, pp. 27–9, 77–80.

[17] Orme, 'Exeter clergy', pp. 96–7 reveals a similar pattern.

[18] C. Cross and N. Vickers, *Monks, Friars and Nuns in Sixteenth Century Yorkshire*, Yorkshire Archaeological Society Record Series, 150 (1995) pp. 66, 135, 151, 162, 181, 222, 276–7, 289, 320, 374, 401, 496, 498–9, 504, 515, includes some tentative identifications also. This was even stronger in former monastic cathedrals, I. Atherton, E. Fernie, C. Harper-Bill, and H. Smith, eds, *Norwich Cathedral: Church, City and Diocese 1096–1996* (London and Rio Grande, OH, 1996), pp. 518–19.

what were these altars like, for they too attracted the disapproval of the visitors?

In response to the diocesan visitors of 1519 it was pointed out that the Chapter clerk had the responsibility to maintain an inventory of those things belonging to the altars and such a list, compiled in 1483, existed. A new inventory, perhaps drawn up in response to the visitation, was made in 1521.[19] Its details repay consideration. The inventory covered twelve of the altars, most of which contained a rich variety of liturgical apparatus. The most richly endowed of these was the altar of St Christopher, which comprised a chantry for the souls of Richard II and his queen, Archbishop Arundel, and the earls of Northumberland and Westmorland. This altar was supported by the St Christopher gild in the city, whose members also benefited from the masses said there. Its copious array of vestments and altar cloths included all the liturgical colours, most of them richly adorned with embroidery, as was the black set with red birds and a green cross. Around the altar there were hangings depicting scenes from the life of the saint, images of Our Lady, St Christopher, and St John, and a little painted cloth of the Visitation. In addition there were other painted panels of a Rood, Our Lady, St Peter and St George, St Christopher, and St John, and the chapel had its own lectern and service books. Of course the support of the main civic gild made this an exceptional case but even the modest chantry at the altar of St John of Beverley which had been founded by Richard Taunton, an early fourteenth-century canon of the Minster, contained a good range of embroidered vestments, an altar frontal decorated with lions and other beasts, a missal, and a lectern. The ornaments at this chantry were significantly greater than those listed in the inventory of 1483 and suggest that, in the years around 1500, some of the minor altars were substantially re-equipped, often from gifts made by the chantry priests themselves and noted in the inventory. This continued into the 1540s when the modest altar of St James and St Katherine was provided with two service books, one of which was printed and thus relatively new, and a corporax which was the gift of a recently deceased chantry priest, Robert Johnson.[20] The inventories demonstrate that even if the prebendaries of the cathedral did not fulfil their statutory obligation

---

[19] Raine, *Fabric Rolls*, pp. 274–306, prints all the surviving inventories, arranged by chapel and chantry. There are some omissions in the published text. The original 1521 inventory is in York Minster Library, Dean and Chapter Archives, M2(4)a.

[20] Raine, *Fabric Rolls*, pp. 280–1, 287, 289; Cross, *Minster Clergy*, pp. 49–51.

to leave vestments to their church, the chantry priests and minor canons were, like Robert Johnson, more assiduous in this regard, providing vestments and altar fittings for the chapels they served. As was to be expected, these were usually modest gifts, like the towel given to the altar of St Blaise by John Nosterfield, whose will we have already noted. Small as they were, such gifts, usually made during the lifetime of the priest, testify to the close identification which these men had with their chapels. Of course, we cannot be sure of the condition of these ornaments, though the inventory does record broken clasps and occasionally describes an item as 'old', suggesting that some judgements were made by its compiler.[21] The impression left by the inventory is that things were not as bad as the visitation suggested and that, in so far as it was in their powers, the minor clergy of the Minster tried to maintain the altars which they served in decent order and that the picture of 'tarnished splendour' needs some modification. Just as at Exeter, the daily round of worship at the lesser altars of the Minster was neither neglected nor a mere formality in the years up to 1520, but expressed a conscientious continuity with patterns which had been established over the previous century and a half.[22]

By 1546, when the chantry commissioners surveyed the Minster, things appeared to have changed significantly. Of the chantries listed at the start of the century seventeen had disappeared and a further five had either been combined with another chantry or had suffered a reduction in provision.[23] Details of this process can only be uncovered in the case of one chantry, that of Thomas Haxey, which derived its income from an annual pension granted by the city and thus was dissolved alongside other civic chantries in 1536. In this case the economic problems of York were the key factor in the decision; but it would be wrong to see these financial problems as reflecting a disenchantment with the system. Even in the hard-pressed city the St Christopher and St George gild continued to support its prestigious patronal altar throughout these years.[24] A direct challenge to the endowments of a chantry was mounted in one other case, that founded

[21] Raine, *Fabric Rolls*, pp. 281–2, 299.

[22] P. Marshall, *The Catholic Priesthood and the English Reformation* (Oxford, 1994), pp. 50–9, discusses the greater demands of the laity on such priests at this date.

[23] W. E. Page, ed., *Yorkshire Chantry Certificates, ii, SS*, 92 (1895), pp. 429–50.

[24] A. G. Dickens, 'A municipal dissolution of chantries at York, 1536', *Yorkshire Archaeological Journal*, 36 (1944–7), pp. 164–73; E. White, *The St Christopher and St George Guild of York*, Borthwick Papers, 72 (York, 1987), pp. 7–9.

at the altar of St Stephen by Sir Thomas Scrope in 1449 for two chaplains. In 1546 ownership of the lands was claimed by the heirs of the Scropes, led by Sir Christopher Danby, who argued that the original foundation was for ninety-five years only. It is not surprising that in these circumstances the altar could only attract priests described as meanly learned.[25]

The decline in chantries led to a small diminution in the number of altars, but only three seem to have disappeared between 1509 and 1546, those dedicated to SS Jerome, Ninian, and Katherine. These seem to have been small altars with only one chantry attached and their removal did not result in the loss of the chantries, for in two cases the chantry had simply moved location. Ferriby's chantry transferred to the altar of the Holy Innocents where two other chantries were observed, and Felter's to that dedicated to the Holy Trinity and St Crux where Hammylton's chantry was also found; whilst St Katherine's altar seems to have been amalgamated with that dedicated to St James.[26] Clearly there was some rationalization taking place in these years but, in the absence of comparable records for an earlier period, whether such activity was peculiar to the sixteenth century or was a more common experience cannot be known. What is certain is that the chantries that had been lost were the less well endowed ones, and that the arrangements entered into at this time were designed to give each of the priests serving them a competent living. Nineteen of the chantries had an income of less than £4 a year, but these were almost exclusively reserved for vicars choral whose other duties would have brought their incomes close to £10 a year, and those who did not have this particular support usually held another post in the city or in the cathedral itself. The clear annual value of the remaining chantries was never less than £4 10s. and was usually considerably greater.[27] There was undoubtedly some stress in this situation and, not surprisingly, the terms of the original foundations (a number of which predated 1430) no longer produced the sort of income originally intended by the founder, especially where that income was drawn from urban properties whose value had

[25] Page, *Chantry Certificates ii*, pp. 440–1.

[26] Ibid., pp. 432–3, 438–9.

[27] Ibid. Details of the incomes are taken from this source *passim*, and vary somewhat from the view of A. Kreider, *English Chantries: the Road to Dissolution* (Cambridge, MA, 1979), pp. 19–25.

fallen significantly in the last half century.[28] These were the chantries that were lost, amalgamated, or reduced in status to obits. Despite these pressures, the chantries continued to represent collectively a substantial endowment, assessed at a clear annual value of £627 1s. 4d. by the commissioners of 1546, excluding the value of the goods and plate attached to the altars, and a further £54 11s. 10d. from obits.[29] Without making too much of the point, the reduction in numbers and the rearrangement of personnel can be seen in a positive light, not as decline *per se* but as a practical institutional response to external financial pressure. This leads us to consideration of those individuals whose incomes these measures were designed to protect.

Of the forty-six priests serving chantries in 1546, half were living in community in St William's College and most of the rest combined their chantry duties with those at the high altar as vicars choral. Two at least held livings in the city of York and probably resided in their parishes, and three others had unspecified posts elsewhere; whilst John Mell held a chantry in St Crux church and John Taylor one in Acomb as well as at the altar to St John the Evangelist. Over half of them were described as indifferently learned, including both the provost of St William's and the subchanter at the Bedern. Fifteen were found to be meanly learned, one of whom, Christopher Bentley, held two chantries and may also have been one of the principal songmen in the Minster, for the commissioners noted that he also sang the Lady Mass at the high altar. His skills may well have been liturgical rather than intellectual, and they were sufficiently highly regarded to bring him the substantial annual salary from his posts of £22 12s. 11d.[30] There were also seven chantry priests described as well learned, one of whom, William Robinson, was a graduate and said to be very well learned. Robinson was unusual in also holding a modest prebendal stall, that of Tockerington, and was, at least in age, the senior of the chantry priests at seventy, but not all of the well learned were in that age bracket.[31] Two of them, Thomas Webster and Thomas Wilson, were former monks in their thirties who combined their Minster chantries with other parochial responsibilities, but their abilities were probably combined with a traditional cast of mind, and neither of them

[28] D. M. Palliser, *Tudor York* (Oxford, 1979), pp. 205–6, 213–15.

[29] Page, *Chantry Certificates ii*, p. 450.

[30] Ibid., pp. 437, 441.

[31] Ibid., p. 434; J. Horn and D. M. Smith, eds, *John Le Neve, Fasti Ecclesiae Anglicanae, 1541–1857: iv, York* (London, 1975), p. 58.

prospered under the new religious regime.[32] Most typically the chantry priests, of whatever ability, were men who had probably achieved their career destinations, less than a quarter of them were under forty and half of them were over forty-five. The altars were being served by men who had already spent some years in the service of the Minster and who probably expected to remain in that service for the rest of their career. Unexceptional they may have been, but they were not devoid of some distinction, and the commissioners found them to be of uniformly honest conversation and life.[33]

These were not the men to stand up to a vigorous and determined policy of reform; but nor were they the ignorant and greedy figures of contemporary polemic; and the evidence of sources other than visitation suggest that right up to the eve of their dissolution the round of worship which had taken place for generations was being sustained at these altars. They continued to be well provided for in general, though the exception of that dedicated to All Saints, which seemed to specialize in 'old, ryven vestments', has coloured general views of the chantries at this date. Against that example can be set the altar of St Cuthbert, the furnishings and fittings of which remained stable at each inventory between 1483 and 1543, and others which had acquired printed service books in these years to add to their manuscript ones.[34] To the priests who served them these altars continued to sustain a spiritual purpose up to the very eve of their dissolution, and the corporate sense and mutual support which the college fostered was such that the commissioners recommended its retention, in a reformed mode, after 1546. The reprieve was shortlived and the assets of the college too tempting, so that it was dissolved in 1549, some of the profits being transferred to its sister institution, the college of vicars choral in the Bedern, which also handed over property to the Crown at this time.[35]

What then does this story reveal about continuity and change in Christian worship? Three issues arise: one of meaning, one of sources, and one institutional.

To begin with meaning. One of the main functions of a liturgy, that

---

[32] Cross and Vickers, *Monks, Friars and Nuns*, pp. 151, 401.

[33] Page, *Chantry Certificates ii*, pp. 430–48; Kreider, *English Chantries*, pp. 24–5.

[34] Raine, *Fabric Rolls*, pp. 274–5. All Saints is the first listed by Raine in his alphabetical arrangement, which might explain its influence on subsequent accounts.

[35] Lehmberg, *Reformation of Cathedrals*, p. 107; F. C. Harrison, *Life in a Medieval College* (London, 1952), pp. 194–202.

is the public worship of the church, is to provide a meaningful routine for the framework of praise and worship within the community. As the work of social anthropologists reminds us, such routine activity is often the least articulated, extremely difficult to interpret, and can thus remain elusive to the observer or dismissed as mere formalism.[36] In the absence of such articulation it is often the context and practice that provide the best evidence and, for the past, it is the silent witness of buildings, ornaments, and fittings which, as Professor Bullough has pointed out for the Carolingian Church, are our best guide.[37] This brings us to the sources.

Visitation returns and commissioners' reports were addressed to contemporary problems and spoke directly to them, and were thus invested with a powerful authority which has, until recently, given them a primacy in historiography also. The work of archaeologists, art historians, liturgists, and others has recently drawn attention to the visual and material aspects of worship at this time and, in the light of this, the inventories and listings that survive, supported by the documents produced by the clergy themselves, reveal a much stonger sense of continuity, albeit in stressful circumstances, than of decay brought on by neglect. At York there was neither 'pomp of silk vestments' nor 'tarnished splendour' but that dutiful endeavour reflected in the commissioners' judgement of the clergy as being of 'honest life and conversation'.

It has to be said, however, that such dutiful endeavour and continuity could not resist change when it came in 1547, and here we come to institutional issues. Faced with a variety of external pressures from the 1530s which are familiar to us – the intellectual challenge of an evangelical group of reformers to their intercessory role, the economic pressure from the declining value of the original endowments, and the threat of a predatory government – the chantries at York, as elsewhere, were quickly swept away. The losses, in terms of ornaments, have been described as staggering, and to the round of worship in the Minster they must have seemed just as great, removing a sizeable section of its personnel and of its

---

[36] I. M. Lewis, *Social Anthropology in Perspective*, 2nd edn (Cambridge, 1985), pp. 131–9, 144–8; J. Bossy, 'The mass as a social institution' *P&P*, 100 (Aug., 1983), pp. 29–61 esp. pp. 50–4.

[37] The British Archaeological Association has published volumes on the Medieval Art and Architecture of the following cathedrals: Wells, Gloucester, Lincoln, Ely, Worcester, Exeter, Salisbury, Hereford, Durham, and Winchester.

daily routine.[38] The speed of change owed more to external pressures than to internal problems, and these losses were not the inevitable consequences of neglect or complacency. During the first half of the sixteenth century the priests seemed to hold their altars and their calling in high regard, and the Dean and Chapter had endorsed some restructuring in order to retain the round of worship and protect the livelihoods of their inferior colleagues. Moreover, this was achieved at a time when the corporate energies of the canons were heavily committed elsewhere to the rebuilding of the fine parish church of St Michael le Belfrey, described as 'the swansong of English Gothic architecture'.[39] By 1550 the surviving altars in the Minster had gone,[40] but the speed of the change must not blind us to the earlier achievement. Change was largely imposed from outside, by the emergence of a new religious culture which rendered much of that worship redundant, and through the agency of a government which embraced that culture and also saw that there were distinct economic advantages to be gained. Visitation material, useful as it is, reflects those external pressures as much as the internal workings of the Minster, and to rely on it as a true record is to be misled.

University of York

---

[38] Kreider, *English Chantries*, for the general background; Lehmberg, *Reformation of Cathedrals*, pp. 118–19.

[39] Raine, *Fabric Rolls*, pp. 100–7; J. H. Harvey, 'Architectural history from 1291 to 1558', in Aylmer and Cant, *History of York Minster*, p. 188.

[40] Lehmberg, *Reformation of Cathedrals*, p. 116.

'ONE HEART AND ONE SOUL': THE CHANGING NATURE OF PUBLIC WORSHIP IN AUGSBURG, 1521–1548

by PHILIP BROADHEAD

EMANDS for the reform of public worship followed rapidly upon the outbreak of religious disputes in Germany in 1517. This was scarcely surprising, since some of the most important aspects of late medieval worship and devotion, including the mass, had become the focus of criticism. The reform of worship presented many difficulties to both spiritual leaders and secular authorities. In many cases they found it easier to identify the failings of Catholic worship than to devise new services which would be acceptable to all. It was also apparent that worship had not only to reflect the ideals and aspirations of the Church but also those of the wider community, and therefore worship impinged upon social and political life. This paper will look at how one community, the city of Augsburg, dealt with these issues. In particular it will consider the forces which shaped evangelical liturgy, and the reception given to the new forms of worship.[1]

Religious change proved contentious in Augsburg, and several phases of evangelical reform were experienced in the sixteenth century. The focus here is the crucial period between 1521 and 1548, for it was within these years, especially during the 1530s, that Augsburg gradually shaped its own evangelical Church and worship.[2] In the early years of the Reformation the ruling Council had refused to intervene directly, and although it had appointed its first evangelical preacher in 1524, it sanctioned no measures against the Catholic Church or clergy. By 1526 there were signs that religious reform had made progress, for there were married clergy in Augsburg, baptism was available without chrism, and communion was given in both kinds in some churches.[3] In most parishes change had been possible because of

---

[1] I wish to thank the British Academy for generously supporting this research, and the staff of the *Stadtarchiv* in Augsburg for their helpfulness.

[2] For a survey of this period see Friedrich Roth, *Augsburgs Reformationsgeschichte*, 4 vols (Munich, 1901–11).

[3] Clemens Sender, ed. F. Roth, 'Die Chronik von Clemens Sender von den ältesten Zeiten der Stadt bis zum Jahre 1536', in *Die Chroniken der deutschen Städte*, 36 vols (Leipzig, 1862–1931), 23, pp. 154, 174, 177.

the existence of preaching houses, which had been built in Augsburg from the middle of the fifteenth century.[4] They were funded by the parish and were under the control of elected parish guardians known as *Zechpfleger*. The freedom of the parish to control the preaching house allowed the parishioners to appoint evangelical preachers, and they were responsible for introducing changes to regular services. One of the consequences of this was that in most of the parishes there were evangelical services as well as Catholic services. These *ad hoc* changes at parish level meant that, even amongst the evangelicals, conflicting doctrines were taught and differing services were held. This was most evident in teaching on the sacraments, and a bitter dispute raged between supporters of Luther and Zwingli. The Council acted to end this in 1530 and imposed unified evangelical teaching on the sacraments. In 1534 it acted to forbid all Catholic preaching and restricted Catholic worship to a few churches in the city. Finally in 1537, following a decisive shift in favour of evangelical membership within the Council, all Catholic services were banned and uniform evangelical worship imposed.[5] The *Kirchenordnung* of 1537 was the culmination of a long process of reform, and it was also a turning point, for it gave the opportunity both to restore religious unity and to achieve changes in popular piety through preaching, worship, and discipline.

There is much evidence to show that the Council believed divisions in worship caused wider divisions in the community, and this argument was used by the government to justify the reforms of 1534 and 1537.[6] The restoration of religious unity nevertheless presented many difficulties and these could be solved only by a willingness to compromise or by the determination of the Council to impose solutions. Compromise between Catholics and evangelicals proved impossible; but it was also hard to gain agreement between evangelicals. Over the years both Lutherans and Zwinglians had established their own customs in worship based upon their differing teachings, and they were loath to make alterations. The preponderance

---

[4] Rolf Kießling, *Bürgerliche Gesellschaft und Kirche in Augsburg im Spätmittelalter* (Augsburg, 1971), p. 115.

[5] A detailed account of the course of the Reformation in Augsburg in the 1530s is given in Roth, *Reformationsgeschichte*, 2.

[6] Emil Sehling *et al.*, eds, *Die evangelischen Kirchenordnungen des XVI. Jahrhunderts* (Leipzig and Tübingen, 1902–, in progress), 12, pp. 44–5; Augsburg, Stadtarchiv [hereafter StadtAA], Evangelisches Wesenarchiv Akten, 492, pp. 37, 43.

of Zwinglians in the city, especially within the Council in the 1530s, meant that their views were likely to dominate. The attraction of Zwingli's teaching for the cities of southern Germany is well-established, and was based, at least in part, on the connection he made between the Church and the community, which he viewed as being co-terminous.[7] The need for secular authority to act in accordance with scriptural authority provided both the justification for ruling councils to introduce change, and also a means through which the gospel could be applied to the social and political life of the community.[8] Zwingli's ideas were also presented in a way which was comprehensible and attractive to those familiar with communalist institutions and ideas. His insistence on the need for the Christian to suppress self-love in the interest of brotherly love towards his neighbour coincided with traditional concepts of the need to subordinate self-interest to the common good of the community.[9]

Although Luther appears to have made less popular impact than Zwingli, by the mid-1530s, when measures were in hand to reform worship in the city, Lutheran views had to be treated as being significant. In 1536 Augsburg had agreed to the Wittenberg Concord, and with it accepted the terms of the Augsburg Confession. This agreement had only been gained through the mediation of Bucer and by the willingness of the Augsburg preachers, under pressure from the Council, to make concessions to Luther over their sacramental teaching. Many Lutherans remained suspicious of the sincerity of the changes, and it was to satisfy them that Johann Forster, a Lutheran, was invited to become a preacher in the city.[10]

The creation of new services began in May 1537. Bucer again was to play an important role and it was not until his arrival in the city that work began in earnest on the new liturgy. It is not known who devised the new forms of service. All the preachers were invited by Bucer to submit drafts, and four are known to have done so. A composite version was prepared by another of the preachers, but some felt that this little resembled the original drafts.[11] What was

---

[7] Bernd Moeller, *Imperial Cities and the Reformation* (Philadelphia, PA, 1972), pp. 85–7.

[8] Peter Blickle, *Communal Reformation. The Quest for Salvation in Sixteenth-Century Germany* (Atlantic Highlands, NJ, 1992), p. 137.

[9] Lee Palmer Wandel, 'Brothers and neighbours: the language of community in Zwingli's preaching', *Zwingliana*, 17 (1988), p. 367.

[10] Roth, *Reformationsgeschichte*, 2, p. 253.

[11] Wilhelm Germann, *D. Johann Forster der hennebergische Reformator, ein Mitarbeiter und Mitstreiter D. Martin Luthers* (Meiningen, 1894), p. 193.

clear was that the Council reserved the right to approve only those services which it considered to be the most appropriate, and that the role of the preachers in formulating them was no more than advisory.

Evangelical worship in Augsburg in the 1520s and 1530s had four distinct requirements: that Christian worship must serve to unite members of the community in common Christian endeavour; that worship should be centred on instruction; that worship should be participatory; and that the services must be clearly distinct from Catholic ceremonies. It is also necessary to remember that changes in worship were not in themselves considered sufficient to create a Christian Church. In addition Christian discipline was required, and this was supplied through the introduction of a separate Discipline Ordinance.[12]

Many aspects of Christian worship were intended to bring the Christian community together. Of great importance was the emphasis placed upon parish worship, especially on Sundays and major festivals. Before the Reformation people had identified with their parish, but could hear mass celebrated, attend sermons, or make their confessions in other churches. The closure of many Catholic churches in 1534 radically altered this situation, concentrating Catholic worship on the parish churches and evangelical worship on the preaching houses. At the same time, to ensure that the celebration of the mass was no longer considered to be the focus of parish worship, the Council ordered the removal of altars which had been used to celebrate morning mass from the naves of parish churches.[13] From 1537 all services were evangelical and held in the parish preaching houses, except in the case of St Moritz and the Cathedral, where services were transferred to the church. All people in the city were obliged to worship with their neighbours in the parish, and the importance of this was made explicit by a ruling of the Council of Thirteen in 1538.[14] The parish organization also had a system of discipline, and elders were appointed who had, amongst their responsibilities, the duty to see that parishioners were 'brought into true fellowship with Christ, through his Word, through the eucharist

---

[12] See Lyndal Roper, *The Holy Household. Women and Morals in Reformation Augsburg* (Oxford, 1989).

[13] Herbert Immenkötter, 'Die katholische Kirche in Augsburg in der ersten Hälfte des 16. Jahrhunderts', in R. Schwarz, ed., *Die Augsburger Kirchenordnung von 1537 und ihr Umfeld*, Schriften des Vereins für Reformationsgeschichte, 196 (Heidelberg, 1988), p. 23.

[14] StadtAA, Protokolle der Dreizehn, 1538, fol. 33.

and in their entire lives'.[15] The sense of belonging to the Christian community was therefore most clearly expressed through parish worship.

The most important part of worship was the celebration of the eucharist. In Augsburg, Zwinglian teaching on the eucharist had been dominant from the 1520s.[16] The Zwinglian understanding of the way in which Church and community were brought together in the eucharist appears to have had a strong appeal in Augsburg.[17] It was evident that there was a widespread rejection of any notion that Christ was physically present in the elements, in favour of Christ being represented by the faithful Christian community, which was considered to be the body of Christ now on earth. By 1535 the Augsburg preachers and Church had apparently joined Bucer in his gradual movement towards a more Lutheran understanding of the sacrament, but this was more of an illusion than reality, as Forster found to his cost. In 1535 he preached a sermon on the eucharist, which he said was in total accord with Luther's teachings. At the point when he said that the bread and wine in the eucharist contained the true body and blood of Christ, a wave of muttering began in the church and many people got up and left. Once outside he could hear them shouting that he was trying to force Christ back into the bread, to make the body of Christ out of bread, and to lead people back to popery.[18] The preacher Musculus appeared at Forster's house to complain about the sermon, and though Forster said he had spoken of Christ being 'mit oder unter brot und wein', in the way used in Wittenberg, Musculus insisted that the people in Augsburg did not wish to hear the sacrament described in that way.[19] There were further protests against Forster in the town and he was admonished by his fellow preachers for stirring up the people. Forster ruefully but accurately remarked that, in these matters, he had to let himself be judged by the people. He had other reasons to be concerned, reporting that he had heard one preacher describe the eucharist as a love feast, and that during communion a hymn was sung which was attributed to Müntzer and which had been used by Anabaptists.[20]

[15] Sehling, *Kirchenordnungen*, 12, p. 54.

[16] Sender, 'Chronik', pp. 178–9.

[17] W. Peter Stephens, *The Theology of Huldrych Zwingli* (Oxford, 1986), pp. 222–5.

[18] Germann, *D. Johann Forster*, p. 96.

[19] Ibid., p. 97.

[20] Ibid., p. 101; Peter Matheson, ed. and trans., *The Collected Works of Thomas Müntzer* (Edinburgh, 1988), pp. 399–400.

Forster was muzzled in his preaching on the eucharist and, when the service appeared in the *Kirchenordnung*, it emphasised that Christ gave his true body and blood in the eucharist, but was not mixed in any physical sense with the elements, having a spiritual presence only.[21] The variations in the way in which the service was conducted also made it clear that divisions continued, even though they were officially ignored. An account of the celebration of the eucharist from 1548 drew attention to the way that preachers with Zwinglian views raised the elements together at the consecration, but those who favoured Lutheranism elevated them separately.[22]

For the sacrament of baptism the *Kirchenordnung* stated that children should be baptized in public during a normal service.[23] The extent to which civic and spiritual values were intertwined was apparent in the explanation given for baptism's importance, for it was seen to confer 'himelischen burgerrechts'.[24] The relationship between the community and the individual also emerged in this sacrament, for as a result of the prayers of those in the congregation at the baptism, they were held to have become spiritual co-fathers (*mitväter*) and co-mothers (*mitmuoter*) of the child.[25]

The liturgy for baptism avoided doctrinal precision in order to remain all-inclusive to evangelical opinion. Two forms of the service were available. That for use in the Sunday service made no specific reference to the nature or role of the water, thus skirting round potential conflict with Zwinglians. It was said that one of the preachers, Keller, had previously performed baptism without water and, although the service now required that the head of the baby be wet three times, the purpose of this was not made explicit.[26] The service for use on weekdays emphasised that the water used was not 'base water as one has at home, but heavenly, blessed, holy and spiritual water', and was thus more acceptable to Lutherans.[27]

The most frequent services were those of daily prayers, and these were given great importance in the spiritual life of the community. By

---

[21] Sehling, *Kirchenordnungen*, 12, pp. 79–80.
[22] Ibid., pp. 93–4.
[23] Ibid., p. 63.
[24] Ibid.
[25] Ibid., p. 73.
[26] Gottfried Seebaß, 'Die Augsburger Kirchenordnung von 1537 in ihrem historischen und theologischen Zusammenhang', in Schwarz, *Die Augsburger Kirchenordnung*, pp. 54–6.
[27] Sehling, *Kirchenordnungen*, 12, p. 75.

1529 a service of morning prayer had been devised to replace the morning celebration of mass. The quotation from Acts of the Apostles which formed the introduction to the service gave an indication of the importance attached to religious unity as it stated that 'The multitude of them that believed were of one heart and one soul.'[28] Morning prayer was described as originating with the church of the Apostles, and its role was to draw people together through prayer, so that all would live together in brotherly love, in the unity of the Word, and in hope of eternal life. It was contrasted with the mass, which was said to divide the people by being in a foreign language and by offering, for payment of money, spiritual advantage to certain individuals.[29] In the service the congregation prayed for themselves, the Church, and the government. They also prayed for their neighbours, and that all should live in peace, unity, and brotherly love. The preacher also admonished all to give towards the support of the poor of the community.[30]

The second element of evangelical worship to consider is the instructional. The most important aspect of this was the sermon. The Council was unhappy about divisions in preaching and, prior to 1537, took measures to enforce unity. From 1535 preachers were required to agree to a contract which, amongst other things, placed controls on preaching.[31] They were to preach the gospel and to explain it using only scripture. Preachers were to speak out against sin, but not to identify individual sinners, and they were forbidden to preach or write on any point which was an innovation in doctrine without first having gained the consent of the Council and the agreement of the other preachers. If a preacher felt the government was acting contrary to God's teaching he was not to declare this from the pulpit, but must raise the problem privately with a mayor. At every opportunity he was to emphasise the duty of all subjects to obey the Council.

Detailed regulation was contained in the *Kirchenordnung* which stipulated the content and length of sermons. Although this gives little indication of what was actually said in the sermons, it indicates the main issues which were addressed. On Sundays there were two morning services. At the early service the preacher was to read from one of the four Gospels and to use his sermon to explain the text 'in the

---

[28] Acts 4.32.
[29] Sehling, *Kirchenordnungen*, 12, pp. 35–6.
[30] Ibid., p. 38.
[31] For Bonifacius Wolfart, Augsburg, Staats- und Stadtbibliothek, 2° Cod Aug, 345; for Johann Forster, Sehling, *Kirchenordnungen*, 12, pp. 46–8.

simplest way'.[32] Only preaching on the Gospels was permitted, and the preacher was to see that over the year the people gained a thorough knowledge of all the Gospels, by preaching from all of them and not concentrating on a small area.[33] In addition at the later service, which was attended by servants and the young, the preacher was to bring out the duty to love and obey parents and masters. He was to explain that God ordered all people to his will, making some to serve and others to rule, some rich and others poor.[34] Sermons were not to last longer than an hour, for the common people were not considered able to concentrate for longer.[35]

Sermons were given each morning, at six in the summer and seven in the winter, and were held on alternate days in the cathedral and St Moritz. These morning sermons were to be three-quarters of an hour long and were to draw upon all the books of the Bible.[36] Services and sermons also took place in the afternoons. There were twice-weekly afternoon sermons at St Moritz on the Acts of the Apostles, while in the Latin vespers, which were also held there, the sermons dealt with the Book of Joshua, the Psalms, the Gospels, Acts, and the Epistles of St Paul.[37] The parish elders were to oversee the work of the preachers, and were required four times each year to report on their performance.[38]

Sermons were used to influence civic affairs. In the weeks before the elections, almost certainly with the consent of the Council, the preachers instructed the guildsmen on how they should vote. In 1536 the preacher Musculus was reported as preaching that nobody should vote for a Catholic for guild office or a position in the Council. He defended this by claiming that it was necessary for the preachers to influence government for the good of the Gospel, for if the mayors and guildmasters were not evangelical the city would slip back into popery.[39]

One of the most contentious issues in the reform of religious practice proved to be deciding upon which form of confession was to

---

[32] Sehling, *Kirchenordnungen*, 12, p. 56.
[33] Ibid.
[34] Ibid., p. 62.
[35] Ibid., p. 58.
[36] Ibid., p. 59.
[37] Ibid.
[38] Ibid., p. 52.
[39] Germann, *D. Johann Forster*, p. 241.

be adopted. Forster was keen to restore private confession to Augsburg according to Lutheran practice elsewhere, for he saw it as the way of upholding religious orthodoxy.[40] According to him, where there was no auricular confession, as in Basle, Zurich, and Strasbourg, there one found sectarianism. When he announced in a sermon that he required people to attend confession before communion, there were complaints from both the laity and the other preachers.[41] Again the *Kirchenordnung* failed to grapple with this problem, stating that the laity, especially the young, should be instructed that if they needed guidance and comfort before communion they should talk to their preacher.[42] We have evidence from Ascham that by 1551, in the week preceding communion, the laity attended at church and were examined by the preacher; but this was done 'not secretly but by two or three at once'.[43]

The third issue involved in the reform of worship concerns the extent and the form of lay participation in the services. There were a number of ways in which this was evident. After 1537 the services, with one exception, were in German and involved prayers said jointly by preacher and congregation. An important feature of evangelical worship was the amount of singing in the services by the congregation. The singing of Psalms and the hymns of Luther and other writers was part of every service, and the first Augsburg hymn book was compiled in 1529.[44] Ascham noted in 1551 that all the congregation joined in the singing with great fervour, often without recourse to a book. The singing was led by a choir and was so hearty that Ascham could hear it from his lodgings.[45] The *Kirchenordnung* demanded that the singing be orderly, and to this end the children from the parish German schools were to learn the hymns and attend the parish church on Sunday to assist in the singing.[46] So that none should feel excluded from the services, the preachers were instructed that the sermons were not to be over the heads of ordinary people. It was also required that nobody should leave the service until it was over, for worship was considered

---

[40] See Martin Luther, *D. Martin Luthers Werke. Kritische Gesamtausgabe: Abteilung Werke*, 60 vols (Weimar, 1883–1909), 26 (ed. K. Drescher), p. 220; Ernst Bezzel, *Frei zum Eingeständnis. Geschichte und Praxis der evangelischen Einzelbeichte* (Stuttgart, 1982), p. 14.

[41] Germann, *D. Johann Forster*, p. 125.

[42] Sehling, *Kirchenordnungen*, 12, p. 63.

[43] Roger Ascham, *The Whole Works of Roger Ascham, Now First Collected and Revised, with a Life of the Author*, ed. J. A. Giles, 4 vols (London, 1864–5), 2, p. 269.

[44] Sehling, *Kirchenordnungen*, 12, pp. 26–7.

[45] Ascham, *Works*, 2, p. 270.

[46] Sehling, *Kirchenordnungen*, 12, p. 64.

to be a corporate matter, by the whole congregation and for the whole congregation.[47] Any who left early were summoned before the Discipline Lords to answer for their conduct.[48]

Participation in the service was influenced by the design of the churches. The preaching houses were simple buildings designed for hearing sermons rather than performing elaborate rituals. Ascham described a preaching house as being like a theatre, with each row of seats higher than that in front.[49] Around the walls were galleries, and the pulpit was placed in the centre. The altar was placed at one end of the building and around it were boards bearing scriptural quotations.[50] Where evangelical services were transferred into the parish church, as at St Moritz and the cathedral, the alterations made to the fabric of the building give some indication of the way the church was used. All altars and images were taken away. At St Moritz seating was installed and all the chapels were removed, as was the *Sakramenthaus* and the pulpit on the choir screen from which the Epistle and Gospel had formerly been read.[51] The main emphasis in the buildings was upon seeing and hearing, and anything which interfered with this was removed.

One of the main characteristics evident in these changes was the rejection of all that smacked of popery in worship. This had several aspects of which only a few can be examined here. In general there was a suspicion of ceremonies and all that went with them, and for this reason altars were replaced with wooden tables and no vestments were worn by the preachers.[52] The vessels used in the celebration of mass were disposed of. In the case of the Barfüßer (Franciscan) church, some were returned to the donors and their families, while others were sold by auction and the proceeds used for the poor.[53] Forster said that in Augsburg communion was distributed from tin beakers,[54] and in 1536, perhaps as a response to these criticisms, the Council provided silver

---

[47] Sehling, *Kirchenordnungen*, 12, p. 58.

[48] For example, StadtAA, Strafbuch der Zuchtherren, 1539, fol. 50a.

[49] Ascham, *Works*, 2, p. 269.

[50] Roth, *Reformationsgeschichte*, 3, p. 126.

[51] StadtAA, Katholisches Wesenarchiv, B7/8; Evangelisches Wesenarchiv, 658.

[52] Germann, *D. Johann Forster*, p. 54. In 1548 the Council had to provide the preachers with surplices in order to conform with the terms of the Interim, Paul Hektor Mair, 'Zwei Chroniken des Augsburger Ratdiener Paul Hektor Mair', in *Die Chroniken der deutschen Städte*, 32, pp. 37, 39.

[53] Sender, 'Chronik', p. 340.

[54] Germann, *D. Johann Forster*, p. 54.

gilt vessels for its churches, but to a design very different from those which had been used in the mass.[55]

Augsburg adopted the Zurich form of the Ten Commandments which emphasised opposition to images.[56] Pictures and statues were removed, but this was done in an orderly fashion by Council workmen, and iconoclasm was not tolerated. In 1529 Keller was one of a group of men who smashed a costly crucifix over the altar of the Barfüßer church. The ringleader, Sigmund Welser, was fined and imprisoned, but Keller was not punished.[57] A Mandate against iconoclasm was published immediately.[58] Whilst evangelicals used only the preaching houses the issue of images remained minor, but it flared up when worship was moved into some of the parish churches. It brought out the distinction between religious practice in Augsburg and the terms of the Augsburg Confession. Forster insisted that religious pictures and images were not harmful as long as they were not worshipped, and he insisted that, in common with the terms of the Augsburg Confession, they should be retained.[59] He turned to Bucer for support who, despite his personal misgivings on the subject, was obliged to concede Forster's point on the Augsburg Confession. From this time the preachers in Augsburg began a campaign against images and this found great support in the city, leading the Council to accept that images should be removed.[60] At any point when Forster or other Lutherans attempted to change liturgical practices and bring them closer to those in Wittenberg, and Nuremberg, they faced hostility from the laity and preachers based on a fear of a return to Rome. These problems arose with the measures over confession and images, and with the demand that a service of vespers in Latin be instituted. On the issue of vespers Forster was to have his way, but attendance was poor.

What conclusions can be drawn from this record of change? Firstly that changes in worship were used to make a statement concerning civic and corporate identity. Augsburg would not simply accept the model of Strasbourg, Wittenberg or anywhere else, but sought worship

[55] S. Sprusansky, *Freiheit und Ordnung. Reformation in Augsburg*, Ausstellungskataloge des Landeskirchlichen Archivs in Nürnberg, 13 (Nuremberg, 1987) pp. 54–6.

[56] Sehling, *Kirchenordnungen*, 12, pp. 67–8.

[57] Sender, 'Chronik', p. 214; G. Preu, 'Die Chronik des Malers Georg Preu des Älteren, 1512–37', in *Die Chroniken der deutschen Städte*, 29, pp. 43–4.

[58] StadtAA, Evangelisches Wesenarchiv Akten, 486.

[59] Germann, *D. Johann Forster*, p. 200.

[60] Roth, *Reformationsgeschichte*, 2, p. 329.

which corresponded to its own needs, problems, and character. The process was long and sometimes painful, but in the end the services commanded the support of the vast majority of people of all social groups in the city. Efforts by Charles V to reverse changes in 1548 proved difficult to enforce. Secondly, evangelical worship was, in general, very different from the Catholic worship which preceded it. There are obvious theological grounds for this, but one of the most striking consequences was the emphasis given to corporate worship and the role of worship in drawing together the community. Finally, within the process of change and the creation of new services and worship, we see that theological issues were not decisive. The Council remained the final arbiter on what was acceptable, and its views were shaped by political and practical judgements as much as by doctrinal considerations. In the end, a system of worship was created which was a doctrinal hybrid, but it was one around which most of the people, preachers, and rulers of the city could unite.

Goldsmiths' College, University of London

TRANSCENDENCE AND COMMUNITY IN ZWINGLIAN WORSHIP: THE LITURGY OF 1525 IN ZURICH

by BRUCE GORDON

ICONOCLASM, rather than liturgical formulation, usually springs to mind when one reflects upon the events in Zurich in the mid-1520s.[1] Indeed, historians of the Swiss Reformation have hardly interested themselves in liturgy, and one searches in vain the most recent and comprehensive treatment of Zwingli's theology for a discussion of the subject.[2] Ignored by both historians and theologians, the study of liturgy in the Swiss Reformation cuts the figure of the unknown guest at a party who everyone assumes is being entertained by someone else. The consequence has been that liturgy has not been allowed to inform our understanding of Swiss religious change; historians have preferred to leave it in the safe keeping of liturgists who, for the most part, have attended to the history of worship as a separate and distinct act of the community controlled by the clergy. This, surely, can only form part of the picture, for liturgy was perhaps the most inclusive act of the Church: worship was experienced by all levels of society, even if the people brought and took away a panoply of varied levels of comprehension and acceptance. As the central, public act of the Church, the early liturgies of the Reformation articulated the tangled web of convictions, needs, and requirements of communities in transition. Liturgies cannot be separated from either the beliefs which created them or the physical space in which they were performed. The ordered rhythm of words and actions in a particular locality was intended to engage the intellect and senses, drawing out responses at once emotional and cognitive. If we can glimpse something of the experience of worship, whether positive or negative, we shall have an insight into the mental world of the early Reformation.

The aims of this paper are twofold: first to look again at what Zwingli attempted in his liturgy formulations, and, secondly, to argue

---

[1] On iconoclasm, the most important work relating to the Swiss is Lee Palmer Wandel, *Voracious Idols and Violent Hands. Iconoclasm in Reformation Zurich, Strasbourg and Basel* (Cambridge, 1995).

[2] W. P. Stephens, *The Theology of Huldrych Zwingli* (Oxford, 1986) provides a detailed account of Zwingli's eucharistic thought, but has little to say on liturgy.

that whilst Zwingli's role in religious reform was crucial, it was not exclusive. His liturgical work was the trunk of a tree with many branches. At no point in the Church's history has liturgical change taken place in a vacuum, and in Zurich it formed one aspect of a larger undertaking which sought to interpret Scripture to a vernacular community. Hence it will be suggested that biblical translations, early works of devotional literature in Alemanic, and liturgy, must be uttered in the same breath. Posterity has given the name 'Zwinglianism' to that movement which arose out of the Swiss cities, and this has effectively camouflaged a whole circle of men whose particular talents are abundantly evident when one examines the range of material from the period. In addressing liturgy the figure of Leo Jud, Zwingli's friend and collaborator as well as one of the most distinguished translators of texts into the German language, must be discussed.

Huldrych Zwingli in Zurich and Johannes Oecolampadius in Basle provided the basis of Reformed worship by appropriating the medieval tradition, by working within that tradition with a set of assumptions about worship which demonstrated their belief in continuity.[3] They believed in continuity as an essential aspect of truth for the same reasons that every other Christian of the early sixteenth century was persuaded that the Church stood in lineal descent from its apostolic roots. Reform did not mean innovation, especially to Erasmian humanists like Zwingli and Oecolampadius, for whom Church history was far too sacred.[4] Nevertheless, the polemic of the age, their own interest in distancing their reforms from the abuses of the late medieval Church, and the confessional nature of subsequent historical scholarship, have served to mask the depth of Zwingli's intellectual, ecclesiastical, and emotional roots in the late medieval world. The careers of Zwingli and Oecolampadius as reformers, however, were brief, in both cases less than ten years.[5] Zwingli's 'heroic' death at Kappel in 1531, central to the iconography of nineteenth-century

---

[3] On the theme of continuity in Protestant thought, see Bruce Gordon, 'The changing face of Protestant history writing', in Bruce Gordon, ed., *Protestant History and Identity in Sixteenth-Century Europe*, 2 vols (Aldershot, 1996), 1, pp. 1–22.

[4] The literature on Erasmus and the Church is enormous. A helpful recent essay which explores this theme is Hilmar Pabel, 'The peaceful people of Christ: the irenic ecclesiology of Erasmus of Rotterdam', in Hilmar Pabel, ed., *Erasmus' Vision of the Church* (Kirksville, MS, 1995), pp. 57–93.

[5] The best biography of Zwingli remains G. R. Potter, *Zwingli* (Cambridge, 1976). On Oecolampadius, see Gordon Rupp, *Patterns of Reformation* (Chatham, 1969), pp. 3–46.

Swiss Protestant nationalism, has become ingrained in Swiss concepts of identity, and historians have demonstrated little inclination to look beyond Zwingli in considering the provenance of Swiss Reformed Protestantism.[6] The confessional, political, and cultural forces which have shaped Zwingli research over the past hundred years have delivered a figure at once heroic, isolated, and rather unhistorical. If one trawls through the pages of *Zwingliana*, the most prominent scholarly journal of Swiss Protestant church history, one finds intermittent attempts to identify the circle around the Zurich reformer, but these voices have not been brought into the mainstream literature. There can be no doubt that Zwingli was the central figure of the Zurich reformation of the 1520s; but the reformer understood something which historians have all too often failed to grasp, that in the hurly-burly of the 1520s Zwingli could only attend to a limited range of matters, primarily high politics and theological *apologiae*. In many other respects he was dependent upon the talents of the circle which gathered around him.

Liturgical reform in Zurich under Zwingli sheds light on the series of narratives which ran through worship, illuminating the degrees of conscious and unconscious crafting undertaken by the first-generation reformers. Liturgy for the Swiss reformers was not some mere external act of piety, but the temporal and spatial expression of the divine drama manifested in the local community.[7] This drama was re-enacted partly in ritual and in images, but primarily through language. Language, spoken in the reading of Scripture, the preaching of the word, in praying and singing (though the last not in Zurich), transformed the community.[8] Worship was not simply the casting back of the mind to some distant event; rather, for the Zwinglian reformers, it framed an encounter between God and humanity in dialogue. The Zwinglian liturgy was moulded as a narrative; it was the narrative of the Last Supper and the Passion of Christ, and those attending this service were not spectators, but disciples. This drama did

---

[6] On nineteenth-century Swiss religious monuments, see Karl Stockmeyer, *Bilder aus der schweizerischen Reformations-Geschichte zum 400–jährigen Reformations-Jubilaeum 1917* (Basle, 1916).

[7] The major works on Zwingli's liturgy are Fritz Schmidt-Clausing, *Zwingli als Liturgiker* (Göttingen, 1952); J. Schweizer, *Reformierte Abendmahlsgestaltung in der Schau Zwinglis* (Basle, 1954); and Markus Jenny, *Die Einheit des Abendmahlsgottesdienstes bei den elsaessischwen und schweizerischen Reformatoren* (Zurich, 1968).

[8] See Arnold Snyder, 'Word and power in Renaissance Zurich', *Archiv für Reformationsgeschichte*, 81 (1990), pp. 263–85.

not lack movement, for each of the images culled from Scripture was intended to serve the believer in the imitation of Christ. This was Zwingli's concept of recollection, for memory is movement, and through the liturgy the community comes to its defining memory, that Christ offered himself as the bread of life. Hence the centrality of John 6 to Zwinglian worship. Within this drama Zwingli employed a range of images and formulations which would have been familiar to the people; these images were not static, and in themselves had no purpose other than to serve as stimulants to individual and collective consciences in their journey of recollection.

The Swiss reformers understood very well the importance of language; they formulated a vocabulary of worship which moved in two different but compatible directions. The language of Scripture took people out of themselves; it made them more like Christ; it united them to Christ's invisible Church, which is beyond time and space. The language of worship, however, also clearly grounded the people in their local community; it was a statement of who they were and it made connections between Christian teaching and their immediate environs. No level of discourse among the Swiss which did not embrace communal identity (*Gemeinde*) could ever enjoy any currency. This localizing of faith is to be found in the Swiss formulations of the Zurich Bible, the liturgy, and vernacular religious texts.

The years 1523–5 were the most crucial for liturgical formulation.[9] Zwingli had resigned his position as *Leutpriester* at Zurich in November 1522 and the magistrates, following the example of other southern Imperial cities, created the office of a preachership for him.[10] The ruling council in Zurich was riven and beleaguered and was neither prepared nor inclined to accept radical religious change.[11] It was, however, clear to all that the old forms of religion were collapsing as many priests had given up celebrating the mass and few of the laity were communicating, even by medieval standards. Reform of worship,

---

[9] For a general outline of events, the most comprehensive work in English remains Potter, *Zwingli*. Palmer Wandel, *Voracious Idols*, pp. 53–101 is not a chronology but contains much useful information.

[10] On the late medieval preacherships, see Steven Ozment, *The Reformation in the Cities* (New Haven, CT, 1975), pp. 38–42.

[11] On the Zurich council see, Heiko A. Oberman, *The Reformation. Roots and Ramifications* (Edinburgh, 1994), ch. 6: 'Zwingli's Reformation between success and failure', pp. 183–200; W. Jacob, *Politische Führungsschicht und Reformation. Untersuchungen zur Reformation in Zürich* (Zurich, 1970); Hans Christoph Rublack, 'Zwingli und Zürich', *Zwingliana*, 16 (1985), pp. 395–426.

for Zwingli, was primarily directed at eradicating the 'false sacrifice' of the mass. Central to his polemic was his slogan that the repetition of Christ's once-offered sacrifice on the cross was blasphemy. His abhorrence of transubstantiation must not be confused with a desire to abandon the mass *per se*, for as we shall see, Zwingli tacitly accepted the intention behind the structure of the mass. In mapping Zwingli's intellectual and spiritual formation we are dealing with a man whose conception of God and creation were honed by late medieval scholasticism; a humanist in his approach to linguistic exegesis and church history; and a liturgist deeply sensitive to language and aesthetics and profoundly influenced by the mystical language of the Greek Fathers.[12]

To a certain extent the Zurich council had an ideal reformer in Huldrych Zwingli. From the summer of 1523 he was clear on the direction of liturgical reform, which he argued could only proceed at the behest of the ruling magistrates. This reform was envisaged as a gradual process by which the church would be weaned of error. Zwingli's first liturgical writing from the end of August 1523, following Leo Jud's liturgy for baptism composed earlier in the summer, provided a clear insight into Zwingli's cautious alterations. In the *De canone missae epichiresis* Zwingli simply excised the canon of the mass.[13] The dilemma, however, lay in how it was to be replaced. The growing number of radicals present in the city believed that this heart transplant operation on the mass should result in the replacement of the despised words which signified the change in substance of the bread and wine with a sermon.[14] The radicals further argued that the Lord's Prayer as taught by Christ was the only legitimate prayer

[12] Zwingli's intellectual background awaits thorough examination. See Gottfried Locher, 'Zwingli und Erasmus', *Zwingliana*, 13 (1969–73), pp. 37–61; Joachim Rogge, *Zwingli und Erasmus* (Stuttgart, 1962); J. F. Gerhard Goeters, 'Zwinglis Werdegang als Erasmianer', in *Reformation und Humanismus. Festschrift für Robert Stupperich* (Witten, 1969), pp. 255–71; and on Zwingli's university training, Ulrich Gabler, 'Huldrych Zwinglis "reformatorische Wende"', *Zeitschrift für Kirchengeschichte*, 89 (1978), pp. 120–35. Heiko Oberman has argued that Zwingli's proofs of God's existence place him in the tradition of the *via antiqua*: Oberman, *Reformation*, pp. 195–9.

[13] Huldrych Zwingli, *Huldreich Zwinglis Sämtliche Werke*, ed. Emil Egli et al., 14 vols (Berlin, Leipzig, and Zurich, 1905–89) [hereafter Z], 2, pp. 552–608. Zwingli wrote in reply to the arguments of the radicals, 'Ego a vobis discere cupio, ubi deus praeceperit preter orationem dominicam nihil orandem esse. Nonne Mosi, Isaiea, Masass, David aliisque prolixas orationes licuit effundere?' (Z, 2, p. 623, ll.4–7).

[14] On Zwingli's attitude towards the reformers on this point, see Snyder, 'Word and power', pp. 274–5.

and that the accretions of human-authored prayers were an abomination.[15] Zwingli explicitly rejected this position in his *An Apology for the Canon of the Mass* (1523).[16]

While Zwingli accepted the link between preaching and the eucharist, he was not prepared to take a sledgehammer to the older forms of worship. Further, his understanding of liturgy had little in common with the aspirations of the radicals, despite superficial similarities. Zwingli's position was intensely conservative, for he saw his position as a leader of the church to re-form that which was already in existence.[17] This concept of reform must be set in the context of worship in Zurich and the other Swiss cities on the eve of the Reformation. As in most of Europe, people confessed in Lent, often Holy Week, and communicated at Easter.[18] It is certain that at least until 1522 the connection between preaching and the mass remained intact in Zurich, for an important part of Zwingli's duties as *Leutpriester* was regular preaching from the pericope, which he famously abandoned to preach through the Gospel of Matthew (*lectio continua*).[19] Zurich, unlike Basle, did not have those established preacherships which were increasingly common in the southern cities of the Empire.[20] Swiss historians of liturgy have long established that there was a late medieval form of worship known as the *Pronaus* (taken from the medieval Latin *praeconium*) which took shape with the rise of preaching.[21] The liturgical form of the *Pronaus* is to be found in Johann Ulrich Surgant's *Manuale curatorum*, printed in Basle in 1503. The connection was not merely textual, as Surgant was teacher to both Zwingli and Leo Jud during their stays in Basle. Like Jud, Surgant was an Alsatian and he had become Professor of Theology in Basle shortly after 1479.[22] He was by all accounts a model priest and his lasting

[15] Jenny, *Einheit*, p. 34.

[16] *Z* 2, pp. 620–5.

[17] On Zwingli's view of reform, see Bruce Gordon, 'Die Entwicklung der Kirchenzucht in Zürich am Beginn der Reformation', in Heinz Schilling, ed., *Kirchenzucht und Sozialdisziplinierung in frühneuzeitlichen Europa* (Berlin, 1994), pp. 65–90.

[18] On confession, see W. David Myers, *'Poor, Sinning Folk': Confession and Conscience in Counter-Reformation Germany* (Ithaca, NY, and London, 1996). See also Karl Schlemmer, 'Gottesdienst und Frömmigkeit in Nürnberg vor der Reformation', *Zeitschrift für bayrische Kirchengeschichte*, 44 (1975), pp. 1–27.

[19] Potter, *Zwingli*, pp. 60–2.

[20] See Ozment, *Reformation in the Cities*.

[21] Jenny, *Einheit*, p. 35.

[22] *Historisch-Biographisches Lexicon der Schweiz*, 8 vols (Neuchatel, 1931), 6, p. 611. R. Wackernagel, *Geschichte der Stadt Basel*, 3 vols (Basle, 1907–24), 2, p. 857.

contribution was his efforts to reform the liturgy which bore fruit in the *Manuale* now held in the British Library.[23] The connection between the Zurich reformers and Johann Surgant is crucial to tracing the late medieval background to Reformed liturgical development.

The office of the *Pronaus* offered Zwingli a model of a preaching service well known to the laity. Indeed, it is likely to have been the most familiar form of worship in the cities of Basle, Zurich, and Berne. The significance of this office, however, extends beyond its familiarity, for it provided Zwingli with a crucial theological formulation for his liturgical reform. Although the *Pronaus* was essentially a preaching office which had grown apart from the mass, as was the tendency in the late medieval period, it retained its original orientation towards the blessed eucharist.[24]

The point of preaching was to prepare people to be shriven and then to communicate. The eucharistic focus of the *Pronaus* is evident from its structure, which concluded with a confession. This essential model of proclamation, confession, and communion is clearly to be seen in Zwingli's reforms. What Zwingli wanted to achieve was to unite again liturgically and spiritually the sermon and the eucharist. This was no new idea to the medieval Church.

To return to the narrative: Zwingli hoped that the Council might be persuaded to introduce his new liturgy in 1524, but the reticent magistrates, and his numerous opponents, were not to be moved.[25] The events in Zollikon in January 1525 served, however, to bring into sharp relief the unsatisfactory nature of a situation where the mass had virtually disappeared without being replaced.[26] In April 1525 a small majority of magistrates, in a poorly-attended session of the Council, voted for the abolition of the mass and the introduction of Zwingli's liturgy.[27]

[23] Johannes Ulricus Surgant, *Manuale curatorum predicandi prebens modum: tam latino que vulgari sermone practice illuminatum: cum certis alijs ad curam animarum pertinentibus: omnibus curatis tam conducibilis quo salubris* (Basle, 1503) (BL classmark 845.k.11; the BL also has a 1520 edition printed in Strasbourg, classmark 845.h.21).

[24] On late medieval preaching, see the excellent Larissa Taylor, *Soldiers of Christ. Preaching in Late Medieval and Reformation France* (New York, 1992).

[25] On opposition to Zwingli in Zurich, see Oskar Vasalla, *Reform und Reformation in der Schweiz. Zur Würdigung der Glaubenskrise* (Münster, 1958), pp. 49–71.

[26] Snyder, 'Word and power', pp. 278–9. See also Fritz Blanke, *Brothers in Christ. The History of the Oldest Anabaptist Congregation, Zollikon, near Zurich, Switzerland* (Scottdale, PA, 1961).

[27] Emil Egli, *Actensammlung zur Geschichte der Zürcher Reformation in den Jahren 1519–1533* (Zurich, 1879), no. 684. Zwingli's own description of events is found in *Z*, 4, pp. 476–82.

Zwingli took great care to give liturgical expression to his belief that worship involves a personal transformation in which no Christian can be passive. The *Ordo Romanus* provided him with the essential framework for this reform, though he intended the drama of the service to be played out quite differently. Zwingli attempted to resolve several issues which he believed had gone seriously wrong in the worship of the Church: he wanted to activate the laity, to free them from their subordinate role as observers to an essentially priestly event; he wanted to excise the false conflation of the spiritual and the material as he interpreted the teaching of transubstantiation; he wished to reunite Word and sacrament in worship. Far from turning his face against medieval liturgical forms, he employed them as his basic tools, knitting together elements which had become separated by embracing that which was faithful to Christ's message whilst abandoning error. The result, as it emerged in 1525, was a tripartite communion service in which each of the parts retained strong echoes of familiar late medieval services. The first part was drawn from the *Pronaus* of his teacher Surgant, the second served the purpose of the Catechumen Mass, and these two culminated in the *Eucharistia* of part three. This threefold division of worship contained various dynamics, the most evident of which was the ancient order of proclamation, response, and communion. Proclamation, response, and communion as the structure of Zwingli's liturgy mirrored the economy of salvation which he worked out in *De vera et falsa religione* of 1525, in which God's word is received by the individual as condemnation, followed by gratitude for the sacrifice of Christ. The third part of Zwingli's salvific formulation was the Christian life in the world in the imitation of Christ; hence the origins of Reformed theology's positive assessment of the Law as a moral guide. Zwingli's liturgy employs the name *Action*, catching the sense in which the union of Christ and believer finds expression in the active Christian life.

A second dynamic evident in this structure is the relationship of pedagogy and praise. Zwingli was interested in theology only insofar as it spoke to the Christian life. Liturgy, therefore, as an act of the community was to express the central belief of that community about God. In humanist thought act and teaching were intimately related, and Zwingli applied this principle to worship, demonstrating that the community in performing such worship is also instructed by its own actions. This is most clearly laid out in the first two parts of Zwingli's liturgy, taken from the *Pronaus* and the *missa catechumenorum*. Here

Zwingli balanced instruction and adoration. The sermon, as proclamation, leads to a general confession of sin and a collect which read as follows:

> Let us pray. Almighty, eternal God, whom all creatures rightly worship [*eerend*], adore and glorify as their Architect [*Werckmeister*], Creator, and Father, grant us that we poor sinners with true faith may render you the praise and thanksgiving which your only begotten Son, Our Lord Jesus Christ, has commanded us to undertake. Through our Lord Jesus Christ, your Son, who lives and reigns with you in the unity of the Holy Spirit, God in eternity. Amen.[28]

The collect is a petition that the people might perform what Christ has taught them, and his instruction was that they were first to praise God. The content of their actions was then outlined in the Epistle reading for the communion service, I Corinthians 11.20–9. These are Paul's strong words of admonition to the community at Corinth against faction and misuse of the Lord's Supper, warning that those who eat and drink unworthily will be answerable for the body and blood of the Lord. At the heart of Paul's text was the requirement that each person examine him or herself and then 'eat of the bread and drink of the cup' (v. 28). Zwingli's use of this text for the Epistle reading was to place the focus of the eucharistic act upon the response of the community as a whole and individually. The gift is given and its benefits are to be received, but only if the people are rightly disposed. Their liturgical response was then formulated first in the Gloria and then in the Creed. Zwingli followed the practice, found in the *Pronaus* and already implemented in Nuremberg and Strasbourg, of using the Apostles' rather than the Nicene Creed.[29]

This nuanced shift from instruction to adoration was given dramatic visual representation by the minister's change of location. Following the conclusion of the sermon, the minister would leave the pulpit and come down to a table placed among the people.[30] Here we find another dynamic at work which was profoundly Zwinglian in character. Raised above the people the minister delivered the sermon in his prophetic role as an 'outsider' bringing the Word of God to the

---

[28] Z, 4, pp. 17, 12–20.
[29] Ibid., p. 55.
[30] Ibid., p. 62.

people.[31] This spatial separation, although well known in medieval preaching, was another representation of Zwingli's concept of salvation. God's gracious Word is alien to the people; they have no access to it other than through his gift as revealed historically through the prophets.[32] This Word validates the community, providing its identity by making the people one with the Israelites; but it also reveals the unworthiness of the people to receive God's mercy.[33] While the eucharist is an act of the community, it is an act possible only when the community has been ignited by the Word from outside. The minister, as God's prophet, performs the very function which God gave to those men of the Old and New Testaments who were to proclaim His will that the people might respond. This accomplished, the minister, for the second part of the service, moved to the table where he assumed a different role in the unfolding drama. Now he was among the people, no longer the prophet, but the host at the table. The minister at the table would then read the appointed Epistle and Gospel lessons, I Corinthians 11 and John 6. Despite the changes in the order of service, Zwingli originally intended the Reformed minister to retain much which was familiar. The 1525 liturgy retained the kissing of the Gospel at the end of reading.[34] Indeed, it was not until the October disputation of 1523 that Zwingli decided against having ministers retain vestments.[35] The reading from the table was an important visual statement about the connection between the promises contained in Scripture and experienced in the Lord's Supper.

Zwingli's first liturgical performance on Maundy Thursday 1525 was carried out in the three main churches in Zurich, the Grossmünster, Fraumünster, and St Peter's, but it was Zwingli's own church, the Grossmünster, which he had in mind when defining liturgical space. Here the choir is separated from the main body of the church by

---

[31] Bruce Gordon, 'Preaching and the reform of the clergy in the Swiss Reformation', in Andrew Pettegree, ed., *The Reformation of the Parishes: The Ministry and Reformation in Town and Country* (Manchester, 1993), esp. pp. 63–8.

[32] Fritz Büsser, *Die Prophezei: Humanismus und Reformation in Zürich* (Berne, 1994), and Pamela Biel, *Doorkeepers at the House of Righteousness. Heinrich Bullinger and the Zurich Clergy 1535–1575* (Berne, 1991).

[33] On Zwingli's association of the people with the Israelites and the development of this idea, see Hans Ulrich Bächtold, 'History, ideology and propaganda in the Reformation: the early writing "Anklag und ernstliches ermanen Gottes" (1525) of Heinrich Bullinger', in Gordon, *Protestant History and Identity*, 1, pp. 49–59.

[34] Z, 4, pp. 20, 28. See also Jenny, *Einheit*, p. 36.

[35] Stephens, *Theology of Huldrych Zwingli*, p. 35 n.104.

a steep rise of steps. Hence the high altar was removed from the faithful by both distance and elevation. In Zurich, as in other parts of southern Germany, there developed in the late medieval period a *Volksliturgie* whereby the priest instead of using the pulpit would have stood on a preaching stool in the body of the church surrounded by the standing laity.[36] Outside the main urban churches, portable preaching stools were the norm for late medieval parish churches. When it came time for the eucharist, the people would move into the choir of the church, which in the case of the Grossmünster involved ascending the steps. Zwingli, undoubtedly familiar with this service, wanted to bring together Word and sacrament by removing the spatial displacement of preaching and eucharist.[37] Zwingli's primary break with the medieval Church lay not in the assertion of the unity of Word and sacrament theologically, but in taking the eucharist away from the altar and placing it among the people, in the same part of the church where the Word was proclaimed. Propinquity, for Zwingli, was an essential element of Christian worship, and although he developed his own dynamic of movement between pulpit and table, it had an immediacy which rejected physical and visual barriers.

The third part of the service began with an admonition from the minister with strong echoes of the text from I Corinthians:

> Now, beloved brethren, we wish to eat this bread and drink this drink according to the custom and intention of Our Lord. This ought, according to his teaching, to lead us to adoration, praise and thanksgiving that he suffered death for us and poured out his blood in order to cleanse us of our sins. Therefore, according to the words of Paul each must ask and examine himself what sort of trust and certainty he had in Our Lord Jesus Christ so that he does not believe himself to be a follower of Christ, even though he has no faith and is guilty of the death of Our Lord, and further, so that no one sins against the whole community of Christ, which is his body.[38]

Again the dialectal nature of the liturgy is evident. The experience of the individual in worship was to hear the external words spoken and to examine the internal working of these words on the self. At each

---

[36] Stephens, *Theology of Huldrych Zwingli*, p. 49.
[37] Ibid.
[38] Z, 4, pp. 21, 22–31.

moment the individual was to make decisions about his or her preparedness, to judge his or her response. The psychological nature of the liturgy is quite striking: it posed questions which the individual had to be able to answer, but it also provided that individual with appropriate responses. Here we must be sensitive to parallels with the catechetical literature which Leo Jud produced in 1525 in Zurich. Zwingli's liturgical formulation assumed the presence of faith in those attending, and it provided the form and setting for the working out of one's relationship to God whilst making clear that in itself, as an act, liturgy was of no value. The first two parts of the service were to prepare the people for the eucharist, but the people had to decide for themselves what they would make of Christ's gifts. If they were ready to receive, then the only appropriate response was the Lord's Prayer, which Zwingli retained in its traditional place in the *Ordo Missae* directly before communion. This is the one element of the mass he left untouched.[39] The dominical prayer was then followed by the communion prayer which is redolent of *Agnus Dei* and the prayer for peace (with kiss of peace) found in the *Ordo*:

> Lift up your hearts to God and say: Lord, Almighty God, you who has made us one body in the unity of faith through your Spirit, and commanded this body [*lyb*] to praise and thank you for the gift of mercy and favour which you have given in the death of your only Son, Our Lord Jesus Christ, for our sins: Grant, that we might in such devotion fulfil your commandment that we neither insult nor scorn with deceitful shame the pure truth. Grant also that we might be blameless in our lives as is appropriate to your body [*lychnam*], sons and family, that unbelievers learn to recognize your name and peace. Protect us, Lord, that your name and honour might not be slandered by the wrongness of our lives. Lord, ever increase in us the faith that is our undoubting trust in you that you, Lord, live and reign forever.[40]

Zwingli was unequivocal that the words of institution were not words of consecration. They did, however, form the heart of his eucharist experience, for recollection, or *anamnesis*, is the *Action* of the com-

---

[39] Jenny, *Einheit*, p. 59.
[40] Z, 4, pp. 22, 9–21.

munity. The minister remained key to this corporate act, as Zwingli had no intention of eliminating the priestly function of the minister in the Lord's Supper.[41] It was the minister's voice which was heard at the feast. This point of the residual power of the words of institution for Zwingli needs to be pursued. For whilst these words might have no effect upon the substantial nature of the bread and wine, they were the essential catalyst for the community's recollection of its true nature. The force of the words and their importance to the community was made clear by Zwingli's intention that they be read out by the minister not over the elements but while the people passed the bread and wine. This made the people the focus of the ritual and stressed the connection between Word and action in which the people gathered around the table were visually and spiritually connected to the Last Supper. Once the words of institution were pronounced the minister continued to read from John 13, the washing of the disciples' feet.[42] This connection between Christ as bread of life and as servant remained central to Zwinglian eucharistic thought.[43] The reading of the words of institution while the people communicated did not, however, last long, as Heinrich Bullinger sternly insisted that the words of institution were to be said over the bread and wine before they were distributed.[44] The reading of the Johannine text during the meal was central to Zwingli's understanding of what took place. Zwingli's intention of holding together confession and eucharist was in line with well established reform ideas of the late medieval Church.[45] Where Zwingli departs from other liturgical reformers was in the radical way in which he used Scripture to make God the central actor in the acts of forgiveness and thanksgiving. As only Christ's words can indicate God's mercy upon sinners, so too is the voice at the table that of Christ speaking to his disciples. Christ is the host and the people sitting in their seats around the table his true followers. This is found in the language of the prayers, where the faithful beseech God to make them faithful *Jünger*. The language of Zwingli's liturgy emphasises the place of the people as *Diener*, disciples. The physical position adopted by the people was also important. Benches were relatively new to the

---

[41] Gordon, 'Preaching and the reform of the clergy', p. 67. Also B. A. Gerrish, *Old Protestantism and the New* (Edinburgh, 1982), p. 129.

[42] On the debate in the literature on this point, see Jenny, *Einheit*, pp. 60–1.

[43] See discussion of Leo Jud below, pp. 145–51.

[44] Jenny, *Einheit*, p. 61.

[45] On the medieval background, see Myers, 'Poor, Sinning Folk', pp. 33–47.

principal churches of Zurich during Zwingli's time; in most rural churches the people would have stood. Nevertheless, where sitting was possible Zwingli stressed that this was the normal position for receiving the body of Christ, whilst kneeling was the position of prayer. The use of unleavened bread and the frequency with which Zwingli's beloved Gospel of John was quoted indicated that the event at the centre of this process of recollection was the Last Supper, and that the Christian community was being fed.

As to what actually happened at the communion there was an ambiguity which neither Zwingli nor his successors were able to resolve. Here it is evident that Zwingli's liturgical reforms did not form a seamless robe; medieval traditions and evangelical convictions were woven together in a manner suggestive of the panoplied character of influences, sometimes seemingly contradictory, present in reformers raised in the late medieval world. The attention paid to Zwingli as a humanist has distracted scholars from the traditional lines of ecclesiastical influence present in his thought. Lee Palmer Wandel has written a suggestive article about the woodcuts which accompanied the Froschauer edition of Zwingli's liturgy, and which helps to unravel Zwingli's more complex nature.[46] The figure of Christ was so represented in the woodcuts that the people would draw specific conclusions about its meaning, interpretations consistent with Zwingli's teaching. The Christ in these woodcuts is seated at an ordinary table surrounded by his Apostles. Palmer Wandel argued that Christ's representation marks a break with late medieval eucharistic imagery by denying any connection between Christ and the priest.[47] These images speak to Zwingli's teaching on the nature of Christ: on the one hand he is the historical person at the table with his followers, the man who would be crucified and resurrected and ascend to the side of the Father, where he is now. On the other hand, the image shows how Christ is present with the community by revealing that whenever his followers gather around the table he is among them, but in spirit, not corporally. Wandel's reading of these images is extremely helpful in opening the door to a more expansive treatment of the whole setting of Zwinglian worship. She has identified the dialogue which takes place between the images and those who had access to them as they

---

[46] Lee Palmer Wandel, 'Envisioning God: image and liturgy in Reformation Zurich', *Sixteenth Century Journal*, 24 (1993), p. 36.

[47] Ibid., p. 37.

were printed in pamphlet form.[48] This exchange, however, is not different from, but analogous to, what takes place in the liturgy. Zwingli set the community in dialogue with Christ through the use of ritual. Nothing in that ritual, above all else the bread and wine, was of especial importance, as nothing could contain or adequately represent God's actions. The use of ritual and biblical imagery was to offer the people the means to conceive of God, of understanding what God has accomplished in Christ.[49]

What emerges clearly from this liturgy is Zwingli's dependence upon older forms and rituals in making the Lord's Supper an act of thanksgiving, a profession of faith in which the community reveals itself to be the body of Christ. As a modification to Palmer Wandel's interpretation of the Froschauer woodcuts, Zwingli's association of Christ with the priesthood should not be dismissed too quickly. The figure of the priest looms large in Zwingli's liturgy. The minister leading the community in worship cannot be understood as anything other than a *figura Christi*. He alone can preach and, from the table, his was the voice of Christ in the words from John 6. He may not have consecrated, but in breaking the bread and passing the cup, as the Froschauer woodcuts for the 1525 edition of the liturgy suggest, what other image could have been intended than that of Christ feeding his disciples? It cannot be denied that Zwingli had a high view of the priestly office, and that the minister, the people, and the bread and wine embodied, in different ways, something which they were not *in essentia*.

If these different elements are drawn together they provide a sense of the layers of meaning with which Zwingli sought to convey Christ's presence in the liturgy of the Lord's Supper. In the overarching structure of the service, which drew upon the mass, the order of proclamation, confession, adoration, and communion played out liturgically God's reconciliation with the world in Christ. Within that structure the minister served as the voice of Christ summoning all to be disciples, to gather with Christ at the Last Supper. The minister had not his own voice, but spoke with Christ's words from Scripture. That Last Supper was ritually re-enacted around the table in the

---

[48] For an insightful treatment of pamphlet readership, see Miriam Usher Chrisman, *Conflicting Visions of Reform. German Lay Propaganda Pamphlets, 1519–1530* (Atlantic Highlands, NJ, 1996), esp. pp. 1–15.

[49] This is explored in Lee Palmer Wandel, *Always Among Us. Images of the Poor in Zwingli's Zurich* (Cambridge, 1990), pp. 59–76.

church, again with the minister physically placed as the host of the meal. Then the presence of Christ shifted crucially from the minister to the bread and wine, which were consumed as the people heard the words from John 6, in which Christ speaks of himself as the bread of life. Finally the movement was internalized with the eating of the bread which, as the whole liturgy had been structured to make clear, signified the believer's membership in the body of Christ. The believer takes nourishment from the bread, it is a meal, in which Christ offers himself to those who have faith. That moment of feeding takes the person out of the locality to become part of Christ's eternal body which is the Church. The imagery of the Zwinglian ritual was not static. The outward symbols shift in their significance in order to facilitate the inward journey of the believer. The culmination of this relation between word and action was the reading of John 13 during the sharing of the bread and wine. Christ's washing of his disciples' feet was for Zwingli the perfect act of selfless love. Those who have heard God's word and now feed in faith must respond in the imitation of Christ through the fulfilment of his command to love one's neighbour.

The Reformation mandate in Zurich decreed that the Lord's Supper was to be celebrated four times a year in the city: at Easter, Pentecost, All Saints, and Christmas. In this penumbral world of intention, there is no reason to believe that Zwingli did not support this arrangement. Yet how does this square with his desire to hold sermon and eucharist together liturgically? And how often did Zwingli think people should communicate? These question cannot be answered with certainty, and scholars such as Markus Jenny have argued that whilst Zwingli certainly accepted the principle of quarterly communion, this was a compromise with social and political realities with the consequence that preaching services became the regular fare of Sunday worship. Although in Basle weekly communion was preserved by ensuring that at least one of the civic churches celebrated the Lord's Supper each Sunday, the evidence for Zurich is less persuasive. Heinrich Bullinger, himself an accomplished liturgist deeply wedded to the spirit if not always the format of Zwingli's liturgy, has left no indication in his liturgical writings that preaching services represented any form of sacramental lassitude.[50]

---

[50] Markus Jenny, 'Bullinger als Liturg', in Ulrich Gäbler and Erland Herkenrath, eds, *Heinrich Bullinger 1504–1575. Gesammelte Aufsätze zum 400. Todestag* (Zurich, 1975), pp. 209–30.

Zwingli died violently in the night of 11 October 1531. The force of the reaction against his reforms, combined with the shock of disbelief which gripped his followers, almost managed to overturn the Reformation in Zurich. Zwingli's death left much unresolved, and many open wounds. There was no clear succession, and the torrid flow of events in the 1520s meant that the Reformed Church had not even begun to grapple with crucial questions surrounding the implementation of reforms. All eyes turned to Leo Jud. The preacher of the St Peter's church, however, was so traumatized that with tears of bitterness in his eyes he struck out at the Zurich council from the pulpit.[51] It had betrayed the great reformer, who was now dead. The magistrates never forgave Jud for his audacity, and ultimately Heinrich Bullinger was called to Zurich. Leo Jud, however, remained the most important reformer in Zurich until his death in 1542. He had been Zwingli's closest colleague, sharing the reformer's deepest theological convictions. Nevertheless, Jud was a different character. He had strong mystical inclinations and his gift was for works of translation and devotion, rather than theological tractates. Perhaps we find something in Jud's work of what Zwingli might have written had he lived; but what is certain is that Jud's writings must be brought into any discussion of the formation of Reformed worship and piety.

Zwingli was the leader of a circle of men with diverse talents, and his role within that cohort was as principal theologian, political leader, and polemicist. In conjuring the shade of Swiss Reformed spirituality the skeletal remains of Zwingli's liturgical formulations are of limited assistance. The experience of Zwingli's liturgy can only be reconstructed with the use of other, cognate sources. One of the richest seams to be mined is the corpus of writings left by Leo Jud, whose talents lay in making the faith accessible to the laity through preaching at St Peter's church, his work as a translator, and the writing of devotional literature. In the meetings of the *Prophezei*, after Zwingli and others had expounded the Greek, Hebrew, and Latin versions of Scripture, it fell to Jud to explain the fruits of this exegesis in dialect to the laity who gathered in the afternoon in the Grossmünster.[52] Jud was in many ways the public voice of the

---

[51] Biel, *Doorkeepers*, pp. 93–8. Also Wayne Baker, 'Church, state and dissent: the crisis of the Swiss Reformation, 1531–1536', *ChH*, 57 (1988), pp. 135–52.

[52] The fullest treatment of the *Prophezei* is found in Traudel Himmighöfer, *Die Züricher Bibel bis zum Tode Zwinglis (1531)* (Mainz, 1995).

Zurich reformers, responsible for transforming evangelical ideas into the language of the market place.

Leo Jud had, as Oscar Farner once rightly adjudged, a 'priestly heart'.[53] He could speak to the people as both a powerful preacher and a sensitive interpreter of sacred and devotional texts. Like numerous Swiss reformers he was not Swiss, but rather Alsatian, born in Schlettstadt.[54] He came to Basle to study medicine in 1499 and, like Zwingli, became a student of Thomas Wittenbach, who persuaded him to take up the study of Scripture. For those in Basle during these years Valla's *Annotationes* proved pivotal to the study of Scripture, and during his thirteen years in the city Jud fell under the influence of Erasmus.[55] When Zwingli was called to Zurich in 1519 he persuaded his abbot at the great Benedictine house at Einsiedeln to invite Leo Jud, who had returned to his native Alsace as a priest, to succeed him as preacher. Jud's Einsiedeln years mirrored Zwingli's to the extent that it was a time for reading the Fathers. We know that Jerome, Tertullian, Lactantius, Origen, and Cyril of Alexander formed much of his daily intellectual diet; but this was supplemented by the works of Erasmus and Luther which Jud devoured.[56] Crucially in these years, at least partially through the influence of Erasmus and Luther, Jud concentrated on the Pauline Epistles. This study had one purpose for Jud, the propagation of the evangelical message to the people, and this he did through preaching. Jud had various audiences: the brothers in the abbey, the local people in the villages around Einsiedeln, and, perhaps most influentially, the large number of pilgrims who made their way to Einsiedeln every year at Pentecost from Zurich.[57]

---

[53] Leo Jud, *Vom Leiden, Sterben und Auferstehen des Herrn*, ed. and trans. Oskar Farner (Zurich, 1955), p. 8.

[54] The literature on Jud is limited. The most recent monograph study is Karl-Heinz Wyss, *Leo Jud, Seine Entwicklung zum Reformator 1519–1523* (Berne, 1976). Gottfried W. Locher, *Die Zwinglische Reformation* (Göttingen, 1979), pp. 568–75, provides a useful overview of Jud's activities. See also Leo Weisz, *Leo Jud. Ulrich Zwingli's Kampfgenosse 1482–1542* (Zurich, 1942); idem, 'Leo Jud in Einsiedeln', *Zwingliana*, 7 (1942), pp. 409–31, 473–94. Charles Garside, *Zwingli and the Arts* (New Haven, CT, 1966), provides a good deal of information on Jud's role in the iconoclasm debates in Zurich. Jud's work with Zwingli is described in Potter, *Zwingli*, pp. 80, 83, 130–3.

[55] On the intellectual climate in Basle, see Edgar Bonjour, *Die Universität Basel von den Anfängen bis zur Gegenwart, 1460–1960* (Basle, 1971); H. R. Guggisberg, *Basel in the Sixteenth Century. Aspects of the City Republic before, during and after the Reformation* (St Louis, MO, 1982).

[56] Weisz, 'Jud in Einsiedeln', pp. 419–20.

[57] On pilgrimages from Zurich, see Magdalen Bless-Grabber, 'Veränderungen im

From 1521 Jud began his work as a translator by rendering Erasmus's paraphrases of the Pauline epistles into Swiss German. These translations appeared as pamphlets over the course of the summer of 1521. The appearance in Basle of Luther's 'September Bible' in 1522 spurred Jud onward in his endeavour.[58] The Saxon dialect of the Bible left many Swiss scratching their heads as to the meaning of the text. Jud believed that in order to make the gospel available to the people it would have to be translated into local dialect. In 1523 Jud had all of his translations of Erasmus's *Paraphrases* printed and bound with the Basle New Testament. In his dedicatory preface to the edition he outlined his approach to the task:

> With respect to my translations into German I am well aware that I have in many places not been able to follow the art and style of the Latin. Who could do that, especially for the adorned and florid Latin of the learned Erasmus? No one may judge what labour is required to render good German out of good Latin, or whether it has been well done, unless he has tried it. Therefore I have attempted to capture in my translation common, clear rather than high, courtly German, for this in my opinion is more useful for the common people, for whom my work is written. I seek to provide meaning with clarity and brevity rather than with flowery language which only serves to obscure the message.[59]

Jud continued to write that whilst texts by even learned and pious Christians, such as Erasmus, were not to be preferred to Scripture, most men 'are so weak and ignorant that they are not able to enjoy the solid food [*festen spyss*] [of the Gospel]'.[60] This text defined Jud's own understanding of his role in the development of worship and religious life in Zurich. 1523 saw the first liturgical reform in the city, Jud's baptismal order. Jud's emphasis on making literature comprehensible in regional dialects through philological precision above any aesthetic concerns was a hallmark of Bible activity in Zurich in the 1520s. The first Zurich Bible edition of 1524 was a translation of Luther's Wittenberg Bible into a written form of Swiss dialect, and the man

---

kirchlichen Bereich 1350–1520', in *Geschichte des Kantons Zürich*, 4 vols (Zurich, 1995), I, pp. 445–7.
    [58] Hans Rudolf Lavater, 'Die Zürcher Bibel von 1524 bis Heute', in *Die Bibel in der Schweiz* (Basle, 1997), pp. 200–2.
    [59] Quoted from Weisz, 'Jud in Einsiedeln', p. 482. Translation is my own.
    [60] Ibid., p. 482.

responsible for this was Leo Jud. Jud was at the forefront of an evangelical religious language, and this was furthered in 1525 with his 'Wall Catechism', a precursor to his large and small catechisms which would appear in 1534.[61] Thus, if Zwingli was the architect of liturgical reform, Jud provided the people with a vocabulary of worship.

The pedagogical function of Jud's devotional writings found expression in his *Larger Catechism* of 1534 in which, in contrast to other Protestant catechisms, the pupil put the questions and the teacher provided the explications.[62] In was in Jud's catechism that the Reformed enumeration of the Ten Commandments first appeared.[63] In answer to questions concerning the Lord's Supper, the teacher responded that Christ is indeed present, not in the act of eating, but in faith and comprehension.[64] Jud pressed this conception of Christ's presence:

> If, however, one says that the true body of Christ is really [*wahrhaftig*] in the Lord's Supper in terms of faith and contemplation of faith and that he is eaten and drunk by the faithful soul, this is true according to the faith and the whole of Scripture.[65]
>
> In fact when this happens Christ is more present than he was when he walked on the earth. Yes, faith makes us the body of Christ, his suffering on the cross and his pouring forth of blood on the cross much more present [*gegenwärtiger*] than when it was fleshly present. The spiritual presence of the body and blood of Christ, which is taken in through faith, is more precious and certain than the fleshly, as the spirit is more certain than flesh.[66]

Jud's writing on the sacrament of the Lord's Supper enables us to see more clearly how the liturgical work in Zurich was part of the transition from late medieval to early modern religious culture. His emphasis upon the Passion of Christ and his endeavour to employ the language of late medieval attachment to that Passion met with other detectable influences such as the imitation of Christ, which arrived in

---

[61] A modern German translation of the Larger Catechism, with Bullinger's preface, is to be found in Leo Jud, *Katechismen*, ed. and trans. Oskar Farner (Zurich, 1955), pp. 25–239. See also Farner's introduction to the text, p. 17.

[62] Locher, *Zwinglische Reformation*, p. 571.

[63] Ibid.

[64] Jud, *Katechismen*, p. 229.

[65] Ibid.

[66] Ibid., p. 230.

Swiss lands through both the *devotio moderna* and the mediation of Erasmus.[67]

This mixture of medieval and early modern forms finds expression in Jud's Passion book of 1534, entitled *The Suffering of Christ According to the Holy Evangelists*.[68] The work has few parallels in early Protestant writing, with the exception of Johannes Brenz's *Sermons of Johannes Brenz. The Good News from the Passion and Resurrection of Jesus Christ*, printed in Stuttgart at the same time.[69] While Brenz's work was clearly a collection of sermons preached in Schwäbish Hall and Stuttgart, Jud's 238-page book, of which only two copies have survived, was intended as both a lay guide for personal devotion and as a study aid for ministers preparing sermons. Jud attempted in this book a harmonization of the Gospels around various topoi pertaining to the suffering of Christ as the model for Christian spirituality. Jud's method, as he explains in the preface, was to weave together biblical texts with quotations from the Fathers. He anticipated criticism for his use of patristic sources, and his defence echoes the remarks he made to justify translations of Erasmus. The people need spiritual guidance in order to digest the Word of God; Jud claimed that he had taken from the Fathers that which was edifying and instructive whilst discarding that which was not in accord with Scripture. Again, we see here the Zwinglian emphasis on the authority of ministers to make decisions for the laity.

Significantly, Jud's treatment of the suffering of Christ begins with the topoi of the Lord's Supper. In two passages of instruction taken from the scriptural texts, Jud develops the themes of union with Christ and imitation of Christ. Jud's first meditation is upon Jesus as the Passover sacrifice, the lamb. He drew a parallel between the memory of the Jews of their liberation from Egypt and Christian remembrance of Christ as the suffering lamb of God.

> Because we have been washed, saved and purchased by so great a treasure, namely by the precious blood of Jesus Christ, the spotless lamb, we must never forget this good deed, but think on it at all

---

[67] On some connections between the *devotio moderna* and Zurich, see B. J. Spruyt, 'Wessel Gansfort and Cornelis Hoen's Epistola Christiana: "The ring as a pledge of my love"', in F. Akkerman, G. C. Huisman, and A. J. Vanderjagt, eds, *Wessel Gansfort (1419–1489) and Northern Humanism* (Leiden, 1993), pp. 122–41.

[68] A modern German edition of the text is found in Jud, *Vom Leiden*, pp. 33–284.

[69] Ibid., pp. 6–7.

times with gratitude: that Christ as our Easter lamb was slaughtered and put on the cross as a sacrifice, that we might live in purity, simplicity and innocence. And if we eat his body in the Lord's Supper [*Nachtmal*] with correct faith, and drink his blood that we are strengthened and fed to eternal life, so shall we dwell in him and in eternal life.[70]

The sensuousness of the imagery which Jud employed is arresting. Whilst adamantly denying a physical eating of the body of Christ, Jud asserted that the spiritual body is even more real than the physical. The work is suffused with images of touching and tasting, of personal closeness to Christ. The believer hungers for the body of Christ. There is even a physical response in the believer to receiving the body of Christ: the person who has been fed experiences joy, an excitement in being one with Christ. The immediate fruit of this feeding is love, and this is the subject of Jud's second meditation. The emotional fervour experienced by the believer is given outward expression in acts of love. Jud's account of the Passion and the believer's response is not simply resonant of Zwingli's liturgy, it is a meditative gloss. Jud gives voice to the struggle of the believer confronted by the unbearable reality of Christ's sacrifice: the confrontation and resolution played out in the liturgical drama. In Jud's text, as in Zwingli's liturgy, the central image is no longer the lamb, but the servant who washed the feet of his disciples. Jud argued that union with Christ is revealed in the imitation of Christ. It is not surprising, therefore, to note that during the 1520s Jud translated Thomas à Kempis's devotional text.[71] For Jud, what makes this imitation possible is the love which is engendered by the meal. 'We must learn to show how in our works of love towards our neighbours we are not ashamed to demonstrate the lengths to which we shall go in humility and readiness to serve our neighbour, even when he is a common, unimportant or rude man or when he has insulted or betrayed us.'[72]

Following Erasmus and Zwingli, Jud locates the imitation of Christ

---

[70] Jud, *Vom Leiden*, p. 37.
[71] *Nachvolgung christi vnnd verschmaehung aller ytelkeit dieser welt, soll von einem wolgelerten liebhabter Gottes vor vil jaren beschriben . . . widerum von nüwem uſzgangen* (Zurich, 1539) (the sole extant copy at Zurich, Zentralbibliothek, call no. Z Ax 5216). The nature of sixteenth-century translations of *The Imitation of Christ* is the subject of a St Andrews doctoral dissertation being written by Max von Habsburg.
[72] Jud, *Vom Leiden*, p. 39.

in the life of purity (*Reinheit*); all Christians must live free of sin, and this constitutes their daily sacrifice.[73] Christians must constantly reflect upon the suffering and death of Christ, for the reality of that event is the source of all Christian action.[74] Christ's sacrifice reveals God to be love, and Christ is present in the believer to the extent that he/she exercises love in the world. Jud treated the theme of Christian love (*Liebe*) as central to the feeding which takes place at the table. In *The Suffering of Christ* Jud provided a more profound treatment of Zwingli's view of love and faith in relating them to the sacrament, and he developed a sacramental piety with debts to Erasmian and other late medieval lines of devotion. With their meditations on preparation for the sacrament and prayer we find in Jud's writings the devotional depth which Zwingli's liturgical text suggests; just as the two men worked together, so also their writings formed a diptych. The bellicosity of Zwingli and the intense, if slightly morose, introspection of Jud belie a shared spirituality. Only one, however, lived to tell the tale.

Liturgical reform in Zurich was integral to the creation of a vernacular religious community. Liturgy gave shape to the ways in which people expressed their love of God and their gratitude for his mercy, but devotion requires form, order, and space and cannot, therefore, be seen as something separate from the locality in which it was performed. To understand what was undertaken between 1523 and 1525 in Zurich is to enter the tangled web of attitudes and convictions, sometimes contradictory, which linked late medieval and early modern cultures. Zwingli stood at the beginning of a long process of religious change, and that beginning point was shaped by the medieval inheritance which had produced him. He held assumptions which later Protestants would reject as unscriptural. Tracing the evolution of Reformed worship requires sensitivity to the stages of change and the intellectual, social, and cultural influences attendant at each point. To look at the printed version of Zwingli's 1525 liturgy tells the reader a great deal, but by no means everything. Only through an awareness of all aspects of the reforming endeavour can one sense how the Zurichers believed Christ to be present at the meal.

University of St Andrews

---

[73] Pabel, 'The peaceful people', p. 90.
[74] Jud, *Vom Leiden*, p. 57.

EVALUATING LITURGICAL CONTINUITY AND CHANGE AT THE REFORMATION: A CASE STUDY OF THOMAS MÜNTZER, MARTIN LUTHER, AND THOMAS CRANMER

by BRYAN D. SPINKS

I N his now classic work, *The Shape of the Liturgy*, first published in 1945, the Anglican Benedictine monk, Dom Gregory Dix, was concerned to demonstrate that in the origin and development of the eucharistic liturgy, and underneath the verbal differences, the cultural diversity, and the growth of the centuries, a particular unchanging core shape could be identified.[1] His study was primarily concerned with the eucharist from its institution in the New Testament to the sixth century, and it was not his intention in that work to survey in any depth the later medieval developments, East or West, or the Reformation. Nevertheless, as an Anglican in the Anglo-Catholic tradition Dix felt obliged to use his findings of the earlier period to embark upon a not too subtle criticism of the sixteenth-century Reformation liturgies, and particularly those revisions of his own denomination instigated and presided over by Thomas Cranmer. For Dix, the later medieval liturgical development saw a shift of emphasis to an unhealthy preoccupation with the Passion, and was brought to its logical unfortunate conclusion in the rites of the Reformation. With reference to Cranmer, Dix could thus write: 'With an inexcusable suddenness, between a Saturday night and a Monday morning at Pentecost 1549, the English liturgical tradition of nearly a thousand years was altogether overturned.'[2] We should note the phrase, 'inexcusable suddenness'. When combined with rhetoric such as 'a horrible story all round' and 'enforcement by penal statutes of a novel liturgy', it is clear that Dix was using a different set of criteria from earlier Anglican apologists. Compare Jeremy Taylor in 1658, who wrote: 'the Liturgy of the Church of England hath

---

[1] Gregory Dix, *The Shape of the Liturgy* (Westminster, 1945).
[2] Ibid., p. 686.

advantages so many and so considerable as not onely to raise it self above the devotions of other Churches, but to endear the affections of good people to be in love with liturgy in general.'[3]

A more recent example of disapproval of Cranmer's liturgical reforms are the views of Eamon Duffy in *The Stripping of the Altars*.[4] In this important study Duffy, a practising Roman Catholic and a revisionist Reformation historian, does not hide his lament at the dismantling and destruction of English medieval piety and spirituality. Cranmer's liturgical work is described as 'representing radical discontinuity' with the traditional liturgical tradition. He writes:

> Hindsight and the far more openly Protestant character of the second prayer-book of 1552 make it difficult for us now to capture any real sense of the radical discontinuity with traditional religion represented by the book of 1549. At an obvious level, of course, it preserved the basic pattern of parochial worship, matins, Mass, and evensong. But it set itself to transform lay experience of the Mass, and in the process eliminated almost everything that had till then been central to lay Eucharistic piety. The parish procession, the elevation at the sacring, the pax, the sharing of holy bread, were all swept away.[5]

Duffy describes how devotional practices which centred on the cult of the saints and the departed were swept away, together with eucharistic piety. He acknowledged that some parts of the new liturgy remained close to their medieval originals, citing the Office of the Visitation of the Sick, but suggests that the Tudor laity would have noticed the removal of the familiar symbolic gestures and ceremonial. What we have is a 'ritual impoverishment' which 'antagonized the laity'.[6]

These two less than enthusiastic evaluations of Cranmer's liturgical work raise important questions about historical and liturgical methodology. Both writers were aware of the standard source book for the making of the prayer book, F. E. Brightman's *The English Rite*.[7] Duffy had the added advantage of the important studies by Geoffrey

[3] Preface to *Forms of Prayer Publicke and Private together with the Psalter or Psalms of David after the Kings Translation* (London, 1658), sig. A6.

[4] Eamon Duffy, *The Stripping of the Altars* (New Haven, CT, and London, 1992).

[5] Ibid., p. 464.

[6] Ibid., pp. 466–7.

[7] F. E. Brightman, *The English Rite*, 2 vols (London, 1915).

Cuming.[8] These amply demonstrate that, at a textual level, Cranmer's work was not all novel, or discontinuous with the liturgical past. The Sarum rite, even if in translation, is a major source. It is true that Cranmer used Lutheran sources, but he also at one point drew upon Mozarabic or Visigothic material.[9] Dix approached these rites from the standpoint of a paradigm which he alleged could be found in the pre-sixth-century liturgical tradition. Duffy approaches the rites from a deep appreciation of, if not nostalgia for, English medieval piety; together with the conviction that everywhere the Reformation was imposed from above by a minority upon a reluctant but powerless general populace. Both Dix and Duffy, therefore, are able to highlight the change, and play down the continuity. Change there no doubt was, and much of it must have appeared drastic. Yet the Reformation rites were not intended to be *ex nihilo* creations, and it is also clear that they were not like Melchizedek, completely motherless and fatherless. The Reformers worked with the rites they inherited, and saw their task as purifying the tradition from later decomposition. Luther thus asserted:

> The service now in common use everywhere goes back to genuine Christian beginnings, as does the office of preaching. But as the latter has been perverted by the spiritual tyrants, so the former has been corrupted by the hypocrites. As we do not on that account abolish the office of preaching, but aim to restore it again to its right and proper place, so it is not our intention to do away with the service, but to restore it again to its rightful use.[10]

And he could assure Nicholas Hausmann: 'It is not now nor ever has been our intention to abolish the liturgical service of God completely, but rather to purify the one that is now in use from the wretched accretions which corrupt it and to point out an evangelical use.'[11] In the Preface to the 1549 Book of Common Prayer, Cranmer could claim: 'So yᵗ here you haue an ordre for praier (as touchyng the

---

[8] G. J. Cuming, *The Godly Order. Texts and Studies relating to the Book of Common Prayer*, Alcuin Club Collections, 65 (London, 1983).

[9] H. Boone Porter, 'Hispanic influences on worship in the English tongue', in J. Neil Alexander, ed., *Time and Community* (Washington, DC, 1990), pp. 171–84.

[10] *Concerning the Order of Public Worship, 1523*, in *Luther's Works* [hereafter *LW*], ed. J. Pelikan and H. T. Lehmann, 55 vols (Philadelphia, PA, 1958–86), 53, p. 11.

[11] *Formula missae et communionis pro Ecclesia Vuittembergensi, 1523: LW*, 53, p. 20.

readyng of holy scripture) muche agreable to the mynde and purpose of the olde fathers, and a greate deale more profitable and commodious, than that whiche of late was used.'

Given Luther's stated intentions and Cranmer's claim, is it legitimate to evaluate Reformation liturgies by alien criteria, such as some more ancient liturgical pattern, as in the case of Dix, or by the very practices which the Reformers openly admitted to wanting to suppress, as in the case of Duffy? A subjective element reflecting one's own liturgical preferences is perhaps inevitable. Yet it raises the question of what methodology or methodologies are legitimate in evaluating these rites, or indeed, any liturgical rite.

At present a number of methodologies can be found in liturgical studies, mostly modelled on methods in biblical criticism. There is the method of source criticism used in Brightman's *The English Rite* and in part, in Dix's study, where texts are set out in parallel to show common material. In the case of the early liturgy, it is normally to demonstrate literary dependence, in order to establish the earlier and 'more original' text. Often this method carries the *a priori* assumption that older means better. More recently there has been an extension of Dix's search for shapes and structures – rather like form criticism, but borrowing methodologies from anthropological studies. Associated with Juan Mateos and Robert Taft, this method concentrates on the deep structures of liturgical units, which then form the basis of judging change and development.[12] There is the approach more akin to redaction criticism, which seeks to evaluate how previous sources have been used, and therefore the theological interests of the compiler.[13] More recently still there has been a concern to utilize the linguistic methods associated with Ricoeur and Derrida, viewing the text as performance, and to evaluate the promised world that the worshippers are invited to appropriate as their own.[14] Generally, no

---

[12] See the many works on Eastern Orthodox rites by Juan Mateos, e.g. *La Célébration de la parole dans la liturgie byzantine. Étude historique*, Orientalia Christiana Analecta, 191 (Rome, 1971). For a summary, R. F. Taft, 'The structural analysis of liturgical units: an essay in methodology', in his *Beyond East and West: Problems of Liturgical Understanding* (Washington, DC, 1984), pp. 151–64.

[13] See for example my approach in 'The Anaphora of Nestorius: Antiochene Lex credendi through Constantinopolitan Lex orandi?', *Orientalia Christiana Periodica*, 62 (1996), pp. 273–94.

[14] For example, Joyce A. Zimmerman, *Liturgy as Language of Faith: A Liturgical Methodology in the Mode of Paul Ricoeur's Textual Hermeneutics* (Lanham, MD, and London, 1988); Bridget Nichols, *Liturgical Hermeneutics* (Frankfurt am Main, 1996).

one methodology is used to the exclusion of others, and perhaps more than one is necessary to achieve some balanced perspective.

This paper discusses continuity and change in certain liturgical rites compiled by three Reformers – Thomas Müntzer, Martin Luther, and Thomas Cranmer. The rites are the divine office, the mass, and baptism. It presents two evaluations. The first will be the traditional approach, concerned with the text and structure of the rites. The second will be concerned to place the compilations in the wider context of the possible intentions of the compilers.

*   *   *

Although Martin Luther had called for reform of the mass as early as 1519, and even gave strong hints as to how this was to be achieved, the Wittenberg Reformer seems to have felt that more time was needed before it could be given implementation. To his chagrin and extreme annoyance, it was Kaspar Kantz, Andreas Karlstadt, and Thomas Müntzer who took the initiative, and gave practical application to Luther's suggestions. Of these, Müntzer remains the most curious and imaginative.

Little is known of Müntzer's early life, and until recently interest in 'the Mystic with the hammer' was confined to Marxist studies. More recent treatment of Müntzer's works has discovered underneath the polemic an astute even if naive theologian.[15] Born in Stolberg probably *c.* 1488/9, he began studies in the arts faculty in Leipzig, but by 1512 was at the new university at Frankfurt an der Oder. He had been ordained priest by 1514, and already between 1516 and 1517 (when confessor to the nuns at the convent of Frohse) drafted an office for the patron saint, St Cyriacus. Of this liturgical compilation Gordon Rupp noted: 'Each consists of three Nocturns with Antiphons, Responsories and Versicles, and there is a much abbreviated Sequence. A similar text has been found in the Breviary of John of Hildersheim (1480) and the Book of Hours of Bishop John of Lubeck.'[16] What we have, therefore, is the compilation of a special Office, but structurally in agreement with the received tradition. It was an accomplished piece of traditional liturgy.

---

[15] Thomas Müntzer, *Schriften und Briefe*, ed. P. Kirn and G. Franz (Gutersloher, 1968).
[16] Gordon Rupp, *Patterns of Reformation* (London, 1968), p. 306.

From 1517/18 we know that Müntzer began an association with the Wittenbergers, and considered himself a disciple of Luther. Like Luther, he seems to have been deeply influenced by the sermons of Tauler. However, his own preaching developed a pronounced polemical style, which took the form of anti-clericalism. First at Jüterbog, then at Benditz and Zwickau, Müntzer managed to cause social unrest resulting in destruction of church property. Fleeing Zwickau, he emerged at Prague and arranged a form of disputation – using the theses which Philip Melanchthon had defended in 1519. According to Hans-Jürgen Goertz,

> Müntzer now developed fundamental principles which had already been hinted at in Brunswick, Juterbog and Zwickau: vehement anti-clericalism, traces of mystical piety centred on the spirit and on the Passion, and an apocalyptical understanding of history. Features which at first had stood independent of one another were now clearly connected in a properly articulated theological chain of thought.[17]

In March 1523 Müntzer arrived in Allstedt, where he became pastor in the main church of St John in the New Town. It was during his pastorate here that he compiled his Reformation liturgies in the German tongue. Müntzer wrote: 'This attribution to the Latin words of a power like the incantations of the magicians cannot be tolerated any longer, for the poor people leave the churches more ignorant than they entered them contrary to what God has declared in Isaiah 54, Jeremiah 31, and John 6, that all the elect should be instructed by God.'[18] There is here a concern for edification, and a certain egalitarianism.

In place of the Latin daily office, Müntzer provided a double service of matins and lauds, and a service of vespers, appropriate for five seasons of the calendar – Advent, Christmas, the Passion, Easter, and Pentecost. Though using German, he retained plainsong. The structure was little altered, and all the material has parallels in the Breviary of Halberstad, as listed in the Kirn and Franz edition of Müntzer's works. Thus matins for Advent begins with the traditional votum and versicles, though with some liberty in translation:

---

[17] Hans-Jürgen Goertz, *Thomas Müntzer. Apocalyptic Mystic and Revolutionary* (Edinburgh, 1993), p. 83.
[18] *The Collected Works of Thomas Müntzer* [hereafter *CTM*], trans. and ed. Peter Matheson (Edinburgh, 1988), p. 168.

V. Got sey unser hulff umb seynes namens willen.
R. der do geschaffen hat hymel und erden.
V. O Got, thu auff meyne lippen.
R. und lass meynen mundt deyn lob vorkundigen.
V. O Got, steh mir bey in meyner not.
R. Herr, kumm mir schwinde zu hulffe.[19]

Next comes an invitatory and antiphon from the first Sunday in Advent. The first Psalm is 25, followed by another Advent antiphon and then Psalm 80 which is taken from Feria V of matins. In other words, Müntzer follows a traditional structure for the service, and his material is all taken initially from the Breviary.

In his German Mass we again encounter a fairly traditional structure. The Introit is a whole psalm – Psalm 45 being provided, though he also provided Isaiah 45.8, *Rorate coeli*, and Psalm 19.2, *Coeli ennarrant*. Although the ninefold *Kyrie eleison* was reduced to a fourfold version, Müntzer defended this liturgical unit on the grounds that 'the friends of God, realising his eternal mercy, may praise and glorify his name'.[20] Likewise the *Gloria in excelsis* was retained, with the greeting 'Der Herr sey mit euch', the collect, epistle, alleluia, Gospel, and creed. An Offertorium was also provided, but gone are the prayers of the so-called 'Little Canon'. Yet Müntzer retained the *sursum corda*, with preface, proper preface, *sanctus*, and *benedictus*. Then come the words of institution, the Lord's Prayer, pax, *Agnus Dei*, collect and blessing. Following Luther's suggestions, Müntzer removed the *canon missae* because of its pronounced supplicatory and sacrificial terminology, and replaced it simply with the words of institution – though Aquinas and the canonists would have recognized this as a valid, if irregular, consecration![21] Since the canon was normally recited silently, the laity would have been none the wiser regarding its abolition. On the whole, the structure and most elements remained intact.

His baptismal rite too appears to have been a fairly tame revision. Though aligning himself with emerging anabaptist groups, and advocating believers' baptism, there is no evidence that Müntzer abandoned infant baptism. In his description of his rite Psalm 68 was read in German, then Matthew 3. Salt is still presented to the child,

---

[19] Müntzer, *Schriften*, p. 30.
[20] *CTM*, p. 170.
[21] Aquinas taught that the words of Christ must be recited for it to be valid; if the priest omitted (by accident) other parts of the canon, this would not invalidate the mass.

though its exorcistic role is spiritualized: 'N receive the salt of wisdom, so you may learn to distinguish good and evil in the spirit of wisdom, and never be trodden down by the devil.'

The creed was retained, with traditional renunciations and anointing. The post-baptismal anointing remained, though the formula also gives it a spiritual interpretation. A baptismal robe and candle were also retained. In terms of text and structure it is little wonder that Gordon Rupp could describe Müntzer's work as 'conservatively creative', but Cranmer's as the more radical abbreviation.[22]

It was the reforms made by Müntzer which spurred Luther into action. 1523 saw the appearance of his *Formula Missae* with advice about reforming the daily office, and also the publication of the first *Taufbüchlein*. 1526 saw the publication of his *Deutsche Messe*, further advice about the Daily Office, and the second *Taufbüchlein*.[23]

In revising the divine office Luther was as cautious as Müntzer and, apart from the Scripture readings, he retained Latin and followed the traditional structure and content – namely three psalms with one or two responsories at both matins and vespers, with lessons. Non-biblical canticles such as *Te Deum* were retained. The precise details though he left vague. In 1526 he advised as follows for Sundays:

> At five or six o'clock in the morning a few Psalms are chanted for Matins. A sermon follows on the Epistle of the day, chiefly for the sake of the servants so that they too may be cared for and hear God's word, since they cannot be present at other sermons. After this an antiphon and the *Te Deum* or the Benedictus, alternately, with an Our Father, collects, and *Bendicamus Domino*. . . . At Vespers in the afternoon the sermon before the Magnificat takes up the Old Testament chapter by chapter.[24]

For weekdays he suggested a few Psalms in Latin before the lesson, 'as has been customary at Matins hitherto'. Three chapters from the New Testament are read in Latin, followed by the same chapters in German. Then an antiphon, a German hymn, the Lord's Prayer, collect, and *Benedicamus Domino*, 'as usual'. For vespers he advised:

---

[22] Rupp, *Patterns of Reformation*, p. 323.
[23] Texts in *LW*, 53.
[24] Ibid., p. 68.

Likewise at Vespers they sing a few of the Vesper Psalms in Latin with an antiphon, as heretofore, followed by a hymn if one is available. Again two or three boys in turn then read a chapter from the Latin Old Testament or half of one, depending on length. Another boy reads the same chapter in German. The Magnificat follows in Latin with an antiphon or hymn, the Lord's Prayer said silently, and the collects with the Benedicamus.[25]

Note the words 'as usual', and 'as heretofore'. Apart from reducing the psalmody and introducing longer lections and German hymns, his intention was that matins and vespers remain virtually unchanged.

With the reform of the mass we again find simplification and omission rather than wholesale revision. The *Formula Missae*, still in Latin, has a whole psalm for the introit, together with Kyrie, *Gloria in excelsis*, collect, epistle, gradual with alleluia and Gospel. The only change was the suppression of the sequence or prose, 'unless the bishop wishes to use the short one for the Nativity of Christ, Grates nunc omnes'.[26] The creed is retained, but a sermon is mandatory. But as in Müntzer's rite, out go the prayers of the 'Little Canon' with their oblationary emphasis. The *sursum corda* and preface are retained, but then come the words of institution. Following Müntzer – who after all, was only following the suggestions which Luther had already made – the prayers of the canon were removed to be replaced only by the words of institution, ideally to be intoned to the same chant as the Lord's Prayer. Then came the *sanctus* and *benedictus* as a termination of the consecration, with the traditional ceremony of elevating the elements of bread and wine. The Lord's Prayer, *Agnus Dei*, and final collect with dismissal are retained, though the Aaronic blessing from Numbers 6.24–7 may be used. Although this was in Latin, and had no proper prefaces, and the position of the *sanctus* and *benedictus* had been changed, this was remarkably like the rite of Müntzer, and is still recognizably the mass.

Rather more changes were made in 1526. Now in the vernacular, a hymn may replace the psalm as introit. The Kyries are reduced to threefold. The collect, epistle, and Gospel are retained, though now the gradual is a German hymn. However, the traditional chants for epistle and Gospel are retained. A creed in German is used. Then comes the

---

[25] Ibid., p. 69.
[26] Ibid., p. 24.

sermon. The main innovation begins with a public paraphrase of the Lord's Prayer, and then the words of institution are chanted. The latter may be divided with the singing of a hymn between the words relating to the bread and those relating to the wine. Though in practice it was rarely carried out, the bread could be distributed before the words relating to the cup were recited. But the elevation was retained. In comparison with the 1523 rite, this German Mass could be interpreted as a more drastic departure from the traditional mass, though even if such an interpretation is correct, the derivation from the Western medieval mass is obvious.

Finally, baptism. In 1523 Luther put the service into German; but apart from the substitution of his famous 'Flood Prayer' for the blessing over the water, it retained much of the medieval rite. Simplification took place in 1526, with the abolition of salt, anointing, and the giving of a candle. But the textual material is nearly all taken from the Magdeburg Agenda, the medieval ritual of Luther's diocese.

Cranmer began his liturgical activity some twenty years after Luther and Müntzer, and had experienced at first hand some Lutheran forms of worship. Already in the 1530s he made private experiments with the reform of lauds and vespers, inspired in part by those reforms made by Cardinal Quiñones and Luther.[27] If this experiment was innovative, it was in the main inspired by the innovations of the Spanish Cardinal. Apart from the Litany of 1544, Cranmer seems to have made no further reforms of the liturgy. Reform of popular religion was another matter, and the whole apparatus of devotion to saints and to the Virgin and prayer for the dead was in the process of being dismantled. The 1548 Order of the Communion was an English communion devotion designed to be inserted into the Latin mass, and much of it was inspired by the order for Cologne prepared for Archbishop Hermann von Wied by Bucer and based on the Brandenburg–Nurnberg order. The Royal Proclamation which prefaced this 1548 devotion spoke of further 'godly orders', heralding that this was but the beginning of a programme of reform. An Act of Uniformity in 1549 put in place the first *Book of Common Prayer*, giving the entire liturgy in English. 1550

---

[27] See C. H. Smyth, *Cranmer and the Reformation under Edward VI* (Cambridge, 1926); D. Webb, 'Les Offices du matin et du soir dans l'Église Anglicane', in M. Cassien and B. Botte, eds, *La Priere des Heures*, Lex Orandi, 33 (Paris, 1962), pp. 317–31; Cuming, *The Godly Order*, pp. 1–23; Anthony Gelston, 'Cranmer and the daily services', in Margot Johnson, ed., *Thomas Cranmer* (Durham, 1990), pp. 51–81.

brought forth a new Ordinal based on that of Bucer, though adapted to maintain a three-fold ministry of bishop, priest, and deacon rather than Bucer's single order of ministry. Then in 1552 a second Prayer Book was enacted. There was a rumour amongst the Marian English exiles that Cranmer had prepared a further prayer book one hundred times better than the one in use (1552), but we have no evidence of the existence of a further liturgy.[28]

The daily offices of the 1549 Book show a development from Cranmer's earlier experiments. Two offices were given, matins and evensong. The former was constructed from material from the traditional matins and lauds. It began with the Lord's Prayer, and versicles and responses. The *Venite*, Psalm 95, was retained from the medieval services as an introduction to the psalmody for the day, but without an invitatory. Psalms followed, but now recited in course over a period of a month rather than over a week. Canticles after the first Scripture reading included the *Te Deum* and *Benedicite*; and after the second reading, the *Benedictus*. Then short suffrages and final collects completed the service. Evensong used material from vespers and compline, and followed a similar, though not identical, structure with *Magnificat* after the first lesson, and *Nunc dimittis* after the second lesson. The *Quicumque vult*, or so-called Athanasian Creed, was to be used after the *Benedictus* at matins on six festivals – here Cranmer quarrying a component of the Office of prime.

In 1552 Scripture sentences, an exhortation, a confession, and an absolution precede the Lord's Prayer, but on the whole the services remained substantially the same as in 1549. We may note that the material, apart from the additions at the beginning of the 1552 rites, is all culled from the traditional liturgical rites. The services were in English. Yet, as Geoffrey Cuming ably demonstrated, much of the phraseology was already found in popular vernacular primers such as Hilsey's, the King's and especially that of George Joye. In many places, as Cuming noted, 'the admiration usually lavished on Cranmer belongs to Joye: Cranmer's only contribution was to refrain from altering Joye's phrases.'[29] Of course, Joye's Primer was one which contained Protestant material. However, Cranmer's use of it should caution against the view that this liturgical material was novel and divorced from the

---

[28] *The Order of the Communion*, ed. H. B. Wilson, *HBS*, 34 (London, 1908); for general details see G. J. Cuming, *A History of Anglican Liturgy* (London, 1969).

[29] Cuming, *The Godly Order*, p. 28.

devotional life of ordinary people. The vernacular primers were very popular amongst the literate, both traditionalists and those of Protestant taste. But we should also not underestimate the novelty or creative ability of Cranmer here. The material was traditional, and some of the translations were contemporary popular devotional material. But out of this material Cranmer wove new services with their own particular logic. Anthony Gelston observes, for example: 'In Cranmer's services the psalms and the Old Testament lesson are linked to the New Testament lesson by a canticle, and the appropriateness of the *Magnificat* in this position at Evensong has always been recognised as one of Cranmer's master-strokes.'[30] More importantly, though, in comparison with the offices of Müntzer and Luther, those of Cranmer are structurally further from their medieval parental rites, and could be regarded as the most radical of the three.

A similar judgement could equally apply to Cranmer's reforms of the mass and the baptismal rite. In 1549 the mass was called that amongst other titles, and was celebrated in the traditional mass vestments. The altar was called the altar, and in most places that was still the traditional stone altar. The opening collect was all that was left of the English priest's pre-communion devotion. As with Müntzer and Luther, the Introit was a complete psalm. But the ninefold Kyrie, the *Gloria in excelsis*, collect, epistle, Gospel, and creed were retained. Innovations were the provision of a collect for the King, and the suppression of the gradual and alleluia. Exhortations followed, and sentences of Scripture concerned with the offering of alms replaced the prayers of the Little Canon. The traditional *sursum corda*, preface, proper preface, *sanctus*, and *benedictus* followed, but now the old *canon missae* was replaced by a complete new canon. Material from the 1549 communion devotion followed, and administration in two kinds. The *Agnus Dei* was retained, and the rite concluded with a post-communion prayer and a blessing. The shape was that of the traditional mass. The newly compiled canon and the exhortations arguably promoted a Protestant view of eucharistic sacrifice and presence. However, although Bishop Gardiner was able to pronounce the rite 'not distant from the Catholic faith', Cranmer's 1552 revision made any such judgement doctrinally and structurally untenable. Any hint of presence in association with the bread and wine was entirely rephrased to exclude such a suggestion. Although the basic structure of word and

---

[30] Gelston, 'Cranmer', p. 56.

sacrament remained, the Ten Commandments replaced the Kyries and
Gloria, the latter being removed to the end of the rite. The intercessory
part of the 1549 canon was now brought forward as a separate entity
after the offering of alms, but before any texts associated with the bread
and wine. The exhortations, confession, scriptural words of assurance
(that is, the Lutheran material) are moved forward. The *sursum corda*,
preface, and *sanctus* (but no *benedictus*) form a separate unit before the
prayer 'We do not presume'. A prayer containing the words of
institution was recited. Not until 1662 was it entitled the Prayer of
Consecration, and it is doubtful that Cranmer regarded it as con-
secratory in any traditional sense.[31] The administration of the bread and
wine followed immediately. The *Agnus Dei* disappeared. The post-
communion consisted of the Lord's Prayer, one of two prayers (one of
which was modified from the last part of the 1549 canon), the *Gloria in
excelsis*, and blessing. Once again we have a structure which is much
further from the parent rite than anything advocated by Müntzer or
Luther.

As for baptism, in 1549 Cranmer conserved the structure of the
Sarum rite, and preserved several of the traditional prayers, most of the
exorcism, and the presbyteral anointing. For the blessing of the font he
drew on a Gallican or Mozarabic source. It is uncertain where Cranmer
found this prayer, but this was an example of recovery of an older
Western usage.[32] He also incorporated Lutheran material, in particular
Luther's Flood Prayer. In 1552 the sign of the cross is moved to after
the baptism; according to Marion Hatchett this was applying the logic
of Thomas Aquinas's explanation of confirmation.[33] The exorcism was
omitted, together with the white garment and anointing. Here we have
something akin to Luther: first a conservative revision, followed by a
more radical revision. Of the three, however, Müntzer's rites remain
textually and structurally nearest the medieval paradigm.

* * *

If in using structure and text a case can be made to show that these
three Reformation liturgies were continuous with what went before,

---

[31] See Colin Buchanan, *What Did Cranmer Think he was Doing?* (Bramcote, 1982), for a
useful and judicious discussion.
[32] See Boone Porter, 'Hispanic influences'.
[33] Marion J. Hatchett, 'Prayer books', in S. Sykes and J. Booty, eds, *The Study of
Anglicanism* (London, 1988), p. 128.

other criteria yield a different picture. Duffy acknowledged, for example, that in the Office of the Visitation of the Sick Cranmer was close to the Latin text. Yet Duffy's criticisms[34] stem from the abolition of the supporting cult and devotional practices, as well as the change in decoration, ceremonial, and music. Here indeed change was most obvious. Müntzer had already attacked the traditional forms and ceremonies as early as 1520, and when at Allstedt had encouraged the destruction of the chapel at Mallerbach which housed the miraculous image of Mary.[35] The image together with all the furnishings were put to the torch. Müntzer celebrated mass on a wooden table without candles, and wearing a plain surplice. Yet although greatly concerned for the vernacular, he conserved plainsong. Luther was horrified at iconoclasm, believing that such things would disappear naturally in time. Luther therefore made considerable use of adiaphora, allowing vestments and ceremonies and even more popular devotions to remain until such time as there was agreement for their abolition. As Scribner notes, a number of Lutheran towns and cities retained 'Catholic' ritual and devotional customs well into the late sixteenth century.[36] In Sweden some of these were retained up to the beginnning of the eighteenth century.[37] Yet with Luther's introduction of the vernacular came a whole new musical tradition. Cranmer retained mass vestments and altar in 1549, but 1552 saw the use of surplice, tippet, and hood in parish churches, and the stone altar was replaced by wooden tables – though even in England practice was far from uniform. Music was not Cranmer's forte, and Diarmaid MacCulloch may well be correct in his estimation that most singing would have disappeared had Cranmer lived longer.[38] It cannot be denied, then, that from a visual and aural point of view, change abounded, and what is visual is often the most noticeable. Yet to criticize the Reformers for destroying popular piety because it was popular, as Duffy does, seems to miss the point. No doubt sacral prostitution was popular in ancient Israel, but popularity does not

[34] *Stripping of the Altars*, pp. 466–7.

[35] Goertz, *Thomas Müntzer*, pp. 114–15.

[36] R. W. Scribner, 'Ritual and popular religion in Catholic Germany at the time of the Reformation', *JEH*, 35 (1984), pp. 47–77.

[37] See E. E. Yelveton, *The Mass in Sweden*, HBS, 57 (London, 1920); Y. Brilioth, *Eucharistic Faith and Practice, Evangelical and Catholic* (London, 1930).

[38] Diarmaid MacCulloch, *Thomas Cranmer* (New Haven, CT, and London, 1996), pp. 621–32.

make a cultic act theologically appropriate. The Reformers believed those practices were inappropriate.

However, what of intention? One of Luther's criticisms of Müntzer's work was that the German translation was stilted, and that plainsong was not suited to the German language. Indeed, Luther's reforms seem to have been planned as specifically and intentionally as *German* reforms. A. G. Dickens has documented the growing concerns with German nationalism which formed the background to Luther's work. He noted that in the preface to the *Fragmenta* of Johann Pupper Luther discovers a tradition which had and still existed amongst the Germans. His *Germanica Theologica* was a retrieval of this specifically German tradition.[39] In 1520 Luther was to address the nobility of the German nation, and in that work there is constant reference to the German nation, the German people, German customs, German territory, and German land. 'We Germans', he wrote, 'are nothing but Germans, and will remain Germans.'[40] Commenting on Psalm 101.7 he could say: 'No virtue has been praised so highly in us Germans and, I believe, has elevated us to such a height and kept us there, as the fact that men have considered us to be faithful, truthful, and trustworthy people, who have let yes be yes and no be no, as many histories and books will testify.'[41]

Luther was of course concerned with the Kingdom of God, and the return to an evangelical Church. However, there is a sense in which Luther was not overly interested in what happened elsewhere, as long as Germany returned to the pure Gospel. His concern is given expression in his provision for a *Deutsche Messe* with German paraphrases and suitable music. He had written: 'I would gladly have a German mass today. I am also occupied with it. But I would very much like it to have a true German character.'[42] When Hans von Minkwitz sent him the rite which had been introduced in Sonnenwalde, he said in his reply: 'In time I hope to have a German mass in Wittenberg that has a genuine style.'[43] Of course, at one level Luther is concerned here with grammar, style, and syntax. He wanted a German liturgy according to German style, and not a wooden translation from Latin. And yet his concern for a German style is in harmony with his

---

[39] A. G. Dickens, *The German Nation and Martin Luther* (New York, 1974).
[40] *LW*, 45, p. 377.
[41] Ibid., 13, p. 218.
[42] Ibid., 40, p. 141.
[43] Ibid., 53, p. 54.

belief that there was a distinctive German approach to theology, and a distinct German character. Even his retention of Latin in the divine office and the existence of a *Formula Missae* alongside the *Deutsche Messe* he explained as a necessity for the education of German youth. It would be possible to exaggerate the point, but it was left to the 'third man' of the Wittenberg team, Bugenhagen, to undertake the mission work to Pomerania, Denmark, Iceland, and Norway, and to prepare liturgies for them – liturgies which are quite distinctive in being more traditional than Luther's rites.[44] Perhaps this too reflects Luther's lesser interest for things outside the Germany he knew. There is arguably a case for viewing Luther's liturgical work as the creation of a national liturgy, and therefore a break from what had become the common liturgy of Western christendom.

What of Cranmer? Surely the production of an English rite, buttressed with declarations of independency and prayers for the King and the High Court of Parliament was equally a national liturgy? That must be true. And yet can we detect in 1552 a wider concern? Diarmaid MacCulloch has brought to light Cranmer's early diplomatic career; and when he was Archbishop those skills and that experience were transposed to serve the Reformation cause. The Lutherans – perhaps rightly – did not trust the flirtations of Henry in the late 1530s. During the 1540s, when the political threat had lessened, Henry was able to dispense with Lutheran friendship. We know that Cranmer kept in contact with Archbishop Hermann von Wied of Cologne, perhaps seeing him as the only notable Reformation figure holding similar office and responsibility as himself. Cranmer was impressed with the attempted reforms for Cologne.[45] When that attempt came to grief, Cranmer seems to have regarded it as his duty to take an archiepiscopal lead. MacCulloch writes of Cranmer around the year 1549: 'A further and increasingly important dimension for Cranmer as he struggled to create acceptable formulae for the English Church, was his preoccupation with establishing English doctrine as a standard acceptable to the whole spectrum of evangelical truth on the continent, from the Lutheran to the Swiss.'[46]

MacCulloch's statement needs a little qualification, particularly as

---

[44] See the useful discussion in Dennis Marzolf, 'Johannes Bugenhagen and the Lutheran Mass', *Logia*, II:2 (1993), pp. 14–20.
[45] Cuming, *The Godly Order*, pp. 68–90.
[46] MacCulloch, *Thomas Cranmer*, pp. 392–3.

Cranmer seems to have abandoned the doctrine of eucharistic presence
that he once shared with Lutherans. However, he dispatched letters
inviting foreign divines to England, and he wrote to Bullinger, Calvin,
and Melanchthon in 1551 urging them to come to England to draw up
a united evangelical statement of faith to oppose the Council of Trent.
Amongst the foreign divines in England were John a Lasco, Martin
Bucer, Paul Fagius, Peter Martyr Vermigli, Valerand Poullain, Pierre
Alexander, and Marten Micron – all decidedly on the Reformed wing,
but by no means all of one school. As well as Melanchthon he invited
the Lutheran Osiander, though both declined. No Protestant ecumenical council materialized. But Cranmer's revision of the 1549 *Book of
Common Prayer* was undertaken within this context, when he still
hoped such a council might be convoked. In the revised communion
service Geoffrey Cuming observed three types of changes – in
structure, language, and ambience.[47]

At the beginning of the service the Ten Commandments are recited
– with the Reformed enumeration rather than the Lutheran. We find a
similar position in the rites of Bucer, Calvin, Poullain, and a Lasco.[48]
Echoing Bucer's Strasbourg rites, the intercessory part of the canon is
placed as a separate feature earlier in the rite. A new exhortation,
authored by Peter Martyr, was introduced. All the Lutheran penitential
material was retained. The *Gloria in excelsis* was retained, as in Lutheran
rites, but transposed to the post-communion to fit the Reformed
concern to emulate Christ and the disciples who had sung a hymn after
the supper. And what should we make of Cranmer's words of
administration in 1552? These are usually interpreted as reflecting
his complete departure from a doctrine of presence in association with
the elements. Indeed, similar words of administration are found in
John a Lasco's rite for the London Stranger Churches, and a Lasco was
close to Zwingli in his understanding of the eucharist.[49] But is
Cranmer's doctrine of the 'real absence' the only interpretation?
Cranmer knew that the understanding of the words 'This is my
body' had split the Reformation churches, first between Luther and
Zwingli, and then between French- and German-speaking Reformed.
All parties, however, were agreed that the object and goal of the rite

---

[47] Cuming, *History of Anglican Liturgy*, p. 105.

[48] See Bryan D. Spinks, *From the Lord and 'The Best Reformed Churches'. A Study of the
Eucharistic Liturgy in the English Puritan and Separatist Traditions, 1550–1633*, Bibliotheca
Ephemerides Liturgicae: subsidia, 33 (Rome, 1984).

[49] See ibid.; Dirk W. Rodgers, *John a Lasco in England* (New York, 1994).

was to take, eat. and drink this. Could it be that Cranmer's words of administration were the lowest common denominator, which he felt could not cause controversy?

And what of ambience? Here Cranmer takes a middle way between Lutheran adiaphora on vestments and ornaments, and the Reformed complete rejection of them. MacCulloch suggests that after the demise of Hermann von Wied Cranmer, as the only evangelical archbishop other than in Sweden, saw himself as in a position to bring together the Protestant factions in a united church.[50] The 1552 rite emerged during this time, and might, I suggest, be seen as blueprint for an international ecumenical Protestant liturgy.

But what of Müntzer? Müntzer too was concerned for a liturgy for German people, and we have noted already its conservatism in terms of structure and text. So why the harsh criticism from Luther? Was it merely that Luther objected to German sung to plainsong? According to Müntzer, the Wittenbergers had trapped the Spirit in the letter of Scripture. The Spirit spoke direct to the heart and soul, and was ushering in a new age. In his Sermon to the Princes in 1524, Müntzer expounded Daniel 2.[51] What Daniel had once seen in a prophetic vision was beginning to take place everywhere. The last Kingdom was falling into decay. In a letter to followers in Halle, on 19 March 1523, he could write: 'Let all the tares shoot up as much as they like: they will all have to come under the flail with the pure wheat; the living God is sharpening his sickle in me so that I will later be able to cut down the real poppies and the little blue flowers.'[52] The combination of mystical piety and suffering with the birth pangs of an apocalyptic upheaval led to his conviction that the princes to whom Luther could appeal had forfeited their role in the struggle for the Kingdom of God, and power was to be given to the people. The end result was to be the slaughter of the peasants at Frankenhausen, and Müntzer's execution at Muhl-hausen. It would of course be going too far to suggest that Müntzer's liturgies drove the worshippers to Frankenhausen; it was adopted at Erfurt without the same social unrest. But Müntzer himself was well aware of the nature and thrust of his liturgical reforms. Writing to Frederick the Wise in October 1523 he had said:

[50] MacCulloch, *Thomas Cranmer*, p. 393.
[51] See *CTM*, pp. 230–52.
[52] Ibid., p. 54.

And it has come to pass in me, that I have been eaten up by a burning zeal for the poor, wretched, pitiable Christian people, and that is why the godless have frequently loosed their insults upon me, Psalm 68, and have driven me without due course from one city to another Matthew 23 and have poured out the most hateful scorn when I defend myself. Jeremiah 20. All this has led me to cast back and forth in my mind Psalm 1 how could I throw myself forward as an iron wall to protect the needy Jeremiah 1, Ezekiel 13 and I have seen that the Christian people can only be saved from the mouth of the raging lion if one brings out the pure, refined word of God, removing the cover or lid which is concealing it. Matthew 5 and if one is quite frank about the truth of the Bible before the whole world Matthew 10, testifying to great and small Acts 26 presenting nothing but Christ, the crucified one, to the world 1 Corinthians 1, singing and preaching about him unambiguously and unwearingly, using a form of church service in which time is not wasted unprofitably, but which builds up the people with psalms and hymns of praise; the basic principles behind the services in German are set out quite clearly in Ephesians 5 and 1 Corinthians 14.[53]

In her thesis, Joyce Irwin observes that Müntzer's apparent traditionalism in liturgy was not based on any high ecclesiological sense, but rather on sound psychological understanding of the people for whom the liturgy was intended.[54] Because of the composition of his congregation – mainly cloth weavers and miners – his main goal was to make the Scriptures and liturgy available to the masses of the poor people in their own language. Müntzer was to write:

Hateful envy, however, has moved some learned men to take this exceeding ill of me. They have done their best to prevent them [his liturgies] being used, for they have come to the conclusion that I am trying in this way to bring back and justify the old papal ceremonies, masses, matins and vespers. Their accusation in fact runs clean contrary to my aim and intention, which is to rescue people's poor, pitiable, blind consciences by producing a shortened form of what the devious, false priests, monks and nuns had

---

[53] Ibid., pp. 68–9.
[54] Joyce Irwin, 'The theological and social dimensions of Thomas Müntzer's liturgical reform' (Yale University Ph. D. thesis, 1972), p. 8.

previosly chanted and read in the churches and monasteries in Latin, thus withholding it from the masses of the poor laity, to the destruction of the faith, the gospel, the word of God, and contrary to the clear, lucid teaching of the holy apostle Paul in I Cor.14.[55]

Irwin urges that the 'poor folk' were the inspiration not only for the fact but also the manner of Müntzer's translations.[56] He delighted in the use of colloquial and vivid expressions: the use of *geschuss* (cannon) rather than *bogan* (bow); singular becomes plural ('Lord, come quickly and help us'). He translates in order to remove distinction between clergy and laity, with the consequent placement of spiritual authority in the community of the elect. In his commentary on collects he wrote: 'Hence in the intercessory prayers which follow for the whole assembly of the great Christian church we raise up our prayers against the lamentable weaknesses which have penetrated it so deeply and which prevent the most glorious name of God from shining out before the entire world.'[57]

According to Franz, the reference to 'penetrated it so deeply' is a reference not to Ecclesiastics 34.18–26 as the original printed marginal notes suggest, but to Ezekiel 34, the woe to the Shepherds of Israel.[58] The terrible wrongs which have torn the Church and hindered the word of God are clearly the fault of the clergy; the laity are their innocent victims. Irwin notes that in the offices for Advent, it is the fear of God which is stressed, for the elect are known by their fear of God.[59] And the office for the Passion is no mere commemoration of the last days of Christ's life, but is an exhortation to imitate his suffering in the present. Wisdom 2 is chosen as a Lenten reading, which condemns worldly wealth. But Müntzer abandoned differences in his translation of enemy, sinner, and righteous; all are rendered either elect or godless. And in Psalm 48.14, God is now 'our Duke'. In his translation Müntzer provided worship for the poor, humble, and meek who are to expect exaltation, while the rich will be sent empty away. His liturgies carried a call to fear God, prepare for the suffering of the present age in transition, and the expectation of the ushering in of the final age.

[55] *CTM*, p. 180.
[56] Irwin, 'Theological and social dimensions', p. 22.
[57] *CTM*, p. 171.
[58] Irwin, 'Theological and social dimensions', p. 31.
[59] Ibid., pp. 86–97.

Underneath this conservative cloak was a sixteenth-century liberation theology. No wonder Luther feared these rites.

In conclusion, while the textual continuity must be acknowledged, in terms of theological intention there is reason for dissenting from Rupp's conservative estimate of Müntzer's theological work. Luther aimed at a liturgy for the German Nation, but with his doctrine of the two kingdoms, there was no place for civil unrest. Cranmer may have intended an international ecumenical Protestant liturgy, but all were to fear the magistrate, and should pray to be godly and quietly governed under lawful rulers. With Müntzer we have an eschatological liturgy which anticipated social change. And thus, in the guise of conservative-looking liturgies, we encounter the most radical departure from the traditional Western rites. Some, however, may see here also a continuity, or retrieval, of certain theological concerns as old as the New Testament itself.

Yale University

THE *TRADITIO INSTRUMENTORUM* IN THE REFORM OF ORDINATION RITES IN THE SIXTEENTH CENTURY

by KENNETH W. T. CARLETON

THE *traditio instrumentorum* is the ceremony in the rite of conferring holy orders in which an object or objects symbolizing the office to be conferred is handed to the candidate with an appropriate accompanying form of words. This ceremony grew in importance through the Middle Ages, to the extent that in Catholic theology it came to be seen as the essential act of ordination.[1] Eucharistic doctrine and the role of the Church in salvation were key areas of conflict in sixteenth-century Reform movements. The Church's ministry, therefore, being both intensely bound up with ecclesiastical structures and intimately concerned with the appropriate conduct of worship, was profoundly affected by these fundamental debates. A continuing need for some form of structured ministry was widely felt, though often understood as simply the appointment (for a time) of appropriate persons to the ministry of Word and Sacrament whose sacramental qualification for ministry was their own baptism, by which they entered into the priesthood of all believers, which was different from the unique high priesthood of Christ and completely replaced any sense of a sacrificing priesthood, which was tied up with the Old (and superseded) Testament. Looking to their Bibles for this, as for so much else in their ecclesiologies, the Reformers found only the apostolic laying on of hands with prayer in the conferring of ministry.

---

[1] Contemporary sacramental theology required two essential features for the valid administration of a sacrament: 'matter' (the medium used in the rite, such as water in baptism, or a specific action carried out by the minister) and 'form' (the words which accompanied the matter). Perhaps arising from a belief that all grades of order, minor and major, were sacramental, the confusion grew among late medieval scholastic theologians that the sole common action, the handing over of an appropriate instrument, itself constituted the matter (or essential rite) of the sacrament of order. Indeed, it was not until 1947 that Roman Catholic theology formally defined the first imposition of hands in silence as the matter of the sacrament of holy order, and then only with reference to ordinations after that date without prejudice to those carried out in the belief that the *traditio instrumentorum* was the essential rite. See L. Ott, *Fundamentals of Catholic Dogma* (Cork, [1952]), pp. 327–8, 454–5, and Pius XII, '*Sacramentum ordinis*', in H. Denzinger, *Enchiridion symbolorum definitionum et declarationum*, 33rd edn (Barcelona, 1965), 3857–61 (2301), pp. 765–6.

Sacrificing priests of the Romish sort, and the web of complex ceremonies by which they were ordained, disappeared from the ordination rites of the Reformers. It would indeed be surprising, in the light of their fundamentally different understanding of the ministerial function, were this not to be so. What is more surprising, however, and worthy of further consideration, is that the *traditio instrumentorum*, the medieval addition most closely associated with the Catholic understanding of priesthood and ministry, did not completely disappear, but in at least one Reformed ordination rite survived (in a much modified form) to the extent that it could even be taken to define the essence of ministry for that rite.

The late medieval rite of ordination in the western Church was the result of a process of growth and development, both in the understanding of the nature and function of holy orders and in the structure of the Church itself. The ceremony itself was adapted to the order being conferred, and by the end of the Middle Ages the seven sacramental grades of order (the minor orders of ostarius, lector, exorcist, and acolyte, and the major orders of subdeacon, deacon, and priest) had become a set of steps progressing to the highest of those grades. Between the major orders certain minimum periods of time, or *interstices*, were to be maintained, though these could often be reduced to as little as a day. The rite of entry to all the minor orders was essentially the same: the handing over of an object that represented the order being conferred, with an imperative formula. The first of the minor orders, that of ostarius or doorkeeper, was conferred by the handing over of the keys of the church. The lector received a copy of the book of readings, and the exorcist a copy of the book of exorcisms. An unlighted candle and an empty cruet were handed to the acolyte symbolizing his liturgical function at the altar. Minor orders had existed in the Church from early times, and the method of conferring them seems to have changed little between that time and the end of the Middle Ages. The *Apostolic Tradition*, a document dating from the early third century and usually attributed to Hippolytus of Rome, contains the earliest extant ordination rites.[2] Only one order, that of reader, was conferred by the handing over of an appropriate instrument (in this case, the book of readings). The same document gives orders for the conferring of the offices of bishop, presbyter, and

---

[2] English translation and introduction in G. Dix, *The Treatise on the Apostolic Tradition of St Hippolytus of Rome*, 2nd edn, rev. H. Chadwick (London, 1968).

deacon, all of whom were ordained by the laying on of hands and prayer. Several other offices (including that of subdeacon) are mentioned, though none received the laying on of hands of the bishop. The number and types of minor order varied in both East and West, and were not definitively settled by the time of the Reformation. Indeed, while the Council of Trent anathematized those who denied that by certain steps advance is made to the priesthood, nonetheless it did not specify which major and minor orders constituted those steps.[3]

Between Hippolytus in the third century and the end of the fifteenth century the rites for conferring major orders had gained a number of additional features and ceremonies. Ordination was ordinarily conducted during mass, and the various orders, minor and major, were conferred at appropriate points so that at least some of the newly-ordained could exercise their ministry for the first time in that mass. The subdeacon still received no laying on of hands, but was given an empty chalice and paten by the bishop, then cruets filled with water and wine, and a basin and towel from the hands of the archdeacon. After clothing in the tunicle he was handed the book of Epistles. In ordination to the diaconate the bishop laid hands on the candidate and handed him a book of the Gospels, with the imperative formula: 'In nomine sanctae Trinitatis, accipe potestatem legendi evangelium in ecclesia Dei, tam pro vivis quam pro defunctis, in nomine Domini. Amen.'[4]

Priestly ordination, by the later Middle Ages, had become a much more complex affair. The imposition of hands occurred twice in the rite, the first after the presentation of the candidates and a lengthy exhortation on the duties of the priestly office, when the bishop, followed by all the other priests present, laid hands on the candidate, in silence. This action was completed by an ordination prayer, read by the bishop, while he and the priests who had joined with him in the laying on of hands extended their hands over the candidate. The second imposition of hands took place at the end of the ordination mass when the bishop alone laid hands on the candidate with the imperative formula 'Accipe Spiritum Sanctum: quorum remiseritis peccata,

---

[3] *Decrees of the Ecumenical Councils*, ed. N. P. Tanner, 2 vols (London and Washington, DC, 1990), 2, p. 743.

[4] Minor variants in texts and rites exist throughout the late Middle Ages, though by the end of the fifteenth century they were generally standardized. Texts cited here are from extant English pontificals of the period, as edited and collated by W. Maskell, in *Monumenta Ritualia Ecclesiae Anglicanae*, 2 (Oxford, 1882) [hereafter: Maskell], p. 211.

remittuntur eis: et quorum retinueris, retenta erunt.' This action seems to have entered the western ordination rites at a relatively late date, perhaps as late as the twelfth century.[5] The ceremony of anointing the candidate's hands (which seems to have entered the Roman rite in the eleventh century from Gallican rites) followed,[6] after which came the central ceremony of the late medieval ordination rites, the handing over of a paten and chalice containing the bread and wine which were to be offered later in the ordination mass. This *traditio* entered western ordination rites around the tenth century, and like anointing could be justified by reference to Scripture.[7] The significance of the rite was expressed in the imperative formula which accompanied it, clearly defining the sacrificial nature of the priestly office: 'Accipe potestatem offerre sacrificium Deo, missamque celebrare tam pro vivis quam pro defunctis. In nomine Domini Jesu Christi.'[8]

Consecration to the office of bishop was more complex again. Two co-consecrating bishops placed and held an open book of the Gospels on the shoulders of the elect, saying nothing. One of the most ancient ceremonies in the episcopal ordination liturgy, this rite was already well established by the end of the fourth century when it appears in the *Apostolic Constitutions*, the Scriptures symbolizing the descent of the Spirit on the elect, though this was not a *traditio instrumentorum* in the strict sense of the term. The imposition of the Gospel-book was followed immediately by the laying on of hands by all the consecrating bishops, in some rites in silence, in others with the imperative formula, 'Accipe Spiritum Sanctum'. In all cases this was followed by a lengthy consecration prayer, in the form of a preface, by the principal

---

[5] Maskell, p. 231.

[6] Anointing at ordination probably originated in the Celtic Church, passing through Gallican rites into the Roman liturgy. The practice was derived from the Old Testament, e.g. Lev. 16.32, where the priestly succession is confirmed by anointing with oil; this passage was cited by Gildas (*Liber Querulus*, III, 21, *c*.545 AD), with reference to Celtic practice: G. Ellard, *Ordination Anointings in the Western Church before 1000AD* (Cambridge, MA, 1933), pp. 10–13.

[7] The connection is less obvious, but can be made. In the Old Testament the rite of conferring priesthood often includes an act of handing over the holy oblations, referred to as a 'filling of the hands [*mille' yadh*]', translated as *'pleroun tas cheiras'* in the Septuagint; see Lev. 7.29 and Exod. 32.29. In the New Testament there are possible allusions to this action, as in the high priestly prayer of John 17, or in Eph. 1.22–3, 3.19. John 3.35, 'The Father loves the Son, and has given all things into his hands', may also suggest the *pleroun tas cheiras* to a reader familiar with the Old Testament rite. T. F. Torrance, 'Consecration and ordination', *Scottish Journal of Theology*, 11 (1958), pp. 225–52.

[8] Maskell, p. 226.

consecrator alone. The elect was anointed twice, once on the head and a second time on the right thumb. The blessing and giving of other symbols of episcopal office followed, some of which are relatively early in origin. First the elect was given the pastoral staff, with the words 'Accipe baculum pastoralis officii: et sis in corrigendis vitiis pie saeviens, judicium sine ira tenens, in fovendis virtutibus auditorum animos demulcens, in tranquillitate severitatis censuram non deserens.'[9] The episcopal ring, which symbolized the marriage of the bishop to his particular Church, was placed on his finger and the mitre, sign of his authority and jurisdiction, placed on his head.[10] The giving of the ring and the staff was prescribed by the Council of Toledo in 633, the latter possibly being of Celtic origin.[11] Finally, the book of the Gospels was handed to the elect (a comparatively late addition), and the celebration of the consecration mass continued.

The addition of so many ceremonies reflected the growing import-ance of the eucharist in the life of the Church. Priestly ordination ensured and enabled the salvation of souls primarily through offering the sacrifice of the mass *tam pro vivis quam pro defunctis*, while episcopal consecration ensured the continuation of the sacerdotal office in the Church. It was essential, therefore, to ensure that the order was validly conferred. So many ceremonies had accrued, however, that late medieval theologians were divided about which of the various ceremonies in the ordination liturgy was the essential rite through which the candidate received all the sacramental power of the priesthood. Some theologians taught that the priesthood was conferred by two essential rites: the handing to the candidate the paten with bread, and the chalice with wine, with an imperative formula expressly conferring the power to offer sacrifice to God and to celebrate masses both for the living and for the dead, and the second imposition of hands with the formula, 'Accipe Spiritum Sanctum: quorum remiseritis peccata', and so on. This was first formulated around 1300 by Duns Scotus, and gained great currency after the Reformation, especially in

---

[9] Maskell, p. 289.

[10] The principal consecrator, placing the ring on the ring finger (*in digitum annularem*) of the elect's right hand, said: 'Accipe annulum fidei scilicet signaculum, quatenus Dei sponsam, sanctam Dei videlicet ecclesiam, intemerata fide ornatus, illibate custodias.' Maskell, pp. 289–90.

[11] Where given, the episcopal staff was sometimes called *cambuta*, a word of Celtic Latin origin; J. H. Crehan, 'Medieval ordinations', in C. Jones, G. Wainwright, and E. Yarnold, eds, *The Study of Liturgy* (London, 1978), pp. 324, 326.

Catholic circles in the seventeenth and eighteenth centuries, where it was sometimes extended to include also the first laying on of hands with prayer.[12] The majority view, and the one which prevailed at the end of the Middle Ages, was that the essential rite for conferring the priestly order was the *traditio instrumentorum* alone, the giving of the paten and chalice with bread and wine accompanied by the formula of sacrifice and offering. This opinion was first expressed in the thirteenth century, its exponents including St Albert the Great and his pupil St Thomas Aquinas, whose pre-eminent place in scholastic theology on the eve of the Reformation probably contributed much to the prevalence of this interpretation.[13] It was also the teaching of the *Decretum pro Armenis*, the instruction of Pope Eugenius IV to the Union Council of Florence in 1439.[14] In the sixteenth century, we find many exponents of Catholic Reform supporting this view against the greater simplicity of Protestant Reformed rites, which themselves expressed a fundamentally different conception of ministry in the Church.[15] As at the end of the fifteenth century, so in the sixteenth, the Catholic priesthood was understood primarily in terms of sacrifice. The priest was set apart for his office in a complex rite at the core of which (according to the majority of scholars) was a ceremony which conferred the office by a handing over of the instruments through and in which the miracle of transubstantiation took place and Christ's sacrifice was re-presented for the living and the dead. This edifice was rejected by the Reformers, who saw the notion of sacrifice as detracting from Christ's unique act on the cross. The primacy of the word of God in the life and doctrine of the Church quickly reshaped its liturgy, and through that transformed the office and role of the Christian minister. Some went further, to deny the need for a distinct ministry altogether, preferring to rely on the inspiration of the Spirit in the whole body of believers. Others, such as Luther, while not going this far, nonetheless

[12] First expressed in Scotus (on the fourth Sentence of Peter Lombard, *in 4. dist. 24. qu. unica, art. 3*), this definition is found in both later medieval texts and in Catholic theology at least as late as the nineteenth century. For a comprehensive list, see G. M. Van Rossum, *De essentia sacramenti ordinis* (Rome, nd), pp. 38–42.

[13] 'The conferring of a power is effected by giving to its subjects something which belongs to the proper exercise of that power': Aquinas, *Commentum in quatuor libros sententiarum*, XXIV, ii, 3, cited in Crehan, 'Medieval ordinations', p. 326.

[14] Denzinger, *Enchiridion*, 1326 (701), p. 336.

[15] For instance, in the writings of Cardinal Cajetan (Thomas de Vio) and Reginald Pole, amongst others. Details of sources for this view may be found in Van Rossum, *De essentia sacramenti ordinis*, pp. 13–14.

denied a permanent and irrevocable change undergone by the candidate in their setting aside for ministry, while retaining a distinct and separate body of ministers whose call was recognized and approved by the Church. Luther taught that baptism was the act by which an individual received the power to exercise ministry in the Church, and the rite of ordination authorized those called to ministry to exercise that power in the name of the Church. Indeed, it was some years before he compiled a formal order for conferring ministry in the Church, and his 1539 rite, The Ordination of Ministers of the Word, is simple and with few ceremonies. Primarily consisting of exhortation and reading of Scripture, the central act of ordination consists of the imposition of hands by the whole presbytery, while the principal minister (the ordinator, often Luther himself in the early days) recited the Lord's Prayer. All other ceremonies were wholly omitted.[16] Calvin was clear that the only ceremony required at ordination was the laying on of hands, and only then when it could be used without superstition.[17] In practice, however, the institution of ministers in Calvin's Geneva took place without the imposition of hands. The Ecclesiastical Ordinances of 1541 had prohibited this on account of the weakness of the times and the superstition which still attached to the act, substituting a declaration by one of the ministers denoting the office to which ordination was being made followed by prayer for grace for the new minister to discharge his office.[18]

The teaching of Martin Bucer on the appropriate ceremonies for ordination is summarized in a treatise, De ordinatione legitima, probably written some time in the two years preceding his death in 1551. His approach, at least at the end of his life, was perhaps more flexible than that of other Reformers, and the extent to which the English Ordinal of 1550 affected his thought is still a matter of debate. The central act of ordination should be the laying on of hands by the ordaining minister and the presbyters present after silent prayer for the candidates and a lengthy ordination prayer seeking the outpouring of the Holy Spirit. Although it contains set prayers and interrogatories, the treatise is not a complete order of service, and Bucer left open the

[16] Luther's Works, Vol. 53, Liturgy and Hymns, ed. U. S. Leopold (Philadelphia, PA, 1965), pp. 122–6.

[17] Institutes of the Christian Religion, ed. J. J. McNeill, Library of Christian Classics, 21 (Philadelphia, PA, 1960), IV, iii, 16; IV, iv, 15 (pp. 1066–8, 1083–4).

[18] Calvin: Theological Treatises, ed. J. K. S. Reid, Library of Christian Classics, 22 (Philadelphia, PA, 1954), pp. 59–60.

possibility of adding greater solemnity and length to the rite when a Superintendent or bishop was being ordained, though without specifying what this should or could involve.[19]

The election and admission of ministers in the Reformed Church of Scotland owed much to the teaching and practice of Calvin and his followers. The rite which found its way into the Book of Common Order was compiled by John Knox from a rite of John a Lasco, and first used in 1561.[20] The laying on of hands was omitted on account of superstition, following Genevan practice, a ceremony which was also rejected by the First Book of Discipline (1560). The act of taking the candidate by the hand to admit him to his charge seems to have been acceptable as a substitute. However, it seems that the imposition of hands on the head of candidates soon began to be reintroduced in Scotland. By 1578 the Second Book of Discipline included 'the impositioun of handis of the elderschippe' as one of the ceremonies of ordination, probably reflecting a widespread though by no means universal practice.[21] The 1597 synod of Fife declared that 'impositioun, or laying on of hands, is not essentiall and necessar, but ceremoniall and indifferent, in admission of a pastor'.[22] The 1620 Ordinal for the Church of Scotland, which was influenced in many respects by the English Ordinal, has prayer and the laying on of hands as the main ceremony for the ordination of ministers. It also includes the delivery of a Bible into the hands of the newly-ordained minister. In 1577 the (Catholic) Bishop of Aberdeen collated the (Protestant) Reader of the city to a vicarage by giving him a ring. Ten years later, a chaplain was inducted in St Giles, Edinburgh by delivery to him of 'ane Psalm Book [The Book of Common Order] as use is'. The 1620 Ordinal may have influenced the nature of the item delivered. In 1637, at Perth, a Reader was inducted by being placed at the lectern and being delivered of a Bible, and in 1640 the Presbytery of Strathbogie inducted a minister 'by delivering the Bible unto him as use is in such cases'. It seems that the ceremony of giving a Bible was still in use at Perth in 1700.[23] The

---

[19] E. C. Whitaker, *Martin Bucer and The Book of Common Prayer*, Alcuin Club Collections, 55 (Great Wakering, 1974), pp. 176–83.

[20] W. McMillan, *The Worship of the Scottish Reformed Church, 1550–1638* (London, 1931), p. 342.

[21] Ibid., pp. 343–4. 'How the personis that bear ecclesiasticall functionis are admittit to thair offices': *The Second Book of Discipline*, ed. J. Kirk (Edinburgh, 1980), p. 180.

[22] Ibid., p. 72.

[23] McMillan, *Worship*, pp. 351–2.

making of ministers in the Church of Scotland was intimately bound up with the giving of a specific pastoral charge. It seems very likely that the *traditio* of the Scottish rite was derived from the act of induction or institution rather than from the giving of any specific or independent power in the act of ordination. As such it is perhaps not a true *traditio*, in the sense that it does not confer an order or ministry within the Kirk as a whole, but is rather an action which relates to the commencement of a specific post in the particular congregation to which the minister is called.

The first English Ordinal appeared in 1550, and was annexed to the 1549 *Book of Common Prayer*, a revised version appeared with the second Prayer Book of 1552. The central ceremony in the ordination of deacons, priests, and bishops was the imposition of hands with an imperative formula. In both the 1550 and 1552 rites, the bishop laid his hands on the deacon with the words 'Take thou aucthoritie to execute the office of a Deacon in the Church of God committed unto thee: in the name of the father, the sonne, and the holy ghost. Amen.' Immediately after this he delivered a New Testament to him, saying 'Take thou aucthoritie to reade the Gospell in the Church of God, and to preache the same, yf thou bee thereunto ordinarely commaunded.'[24] In the 1550 rite for the ordering of priests, the rite of laying on of hands was a composite of the two impositions of the late medieval rite. The bishop and the priests present were to lay their hands 'severally' on the heads of the candidates, as in the first imposition, and with an imperative formula derived from the second imposition, but with an addition which clarified and defined the office being conferred according to the understanding of the priesthood in the English Church at the time:

> Receiue the holy goste, whose synnes thou dost forgeue, they are forgeuen: and whose sinnes thou doest retaine, thei are retained: and be thou a faithful dispenser of the word of god, and of his holy Sacramentes. In the name of the father, and of the sonne, and of the holy gost. Amen.[25]

This was followed immediately by the giving of a Bible to the candidate in one hand, and, significantly, of the chalice and bread

---

[24] *The First and Second Prayer-Books of King Edward the Sixth*, Everyman edn (London, 1910), pp. 301, 447.

[25] Ibid., p. 311.

into the other. However, the language of sacrifice which formerly accompanied this act was replaced by an imperative formula which expressed and reiterated the Reformed doctrine of the minister as dispenser of Word and Sacrament: 'Take thou aucthoritie to preache the word of god, and to minister the holy Sacramentes in thys congregacion, where thou shalt be so appointed.'[26] It was this *traditio*, perhaps, more than any other part of the Ordinal, which was the cause of dissent among those who believed that the Reformation in England and its liturgical expression had by no means gone far enough, and the 1552 Ordinal retained only the giving of the Bible. Arguing against the 1550 version, John Hooper (then Bishop of Gloucester) proposed that the font and water should be given as well as the bread, chalice, and book, 'for the one is a sacrament as well as the other'.[27] He saw the minister as an office-holder who was given authority to exercise the ministry only for as long as the office was held. There is an entry in the Gloucester diocesan records for December 1561 in which the curate of Stroud, Robert Byocke, was recorded as having been accused of unlicensed preaching. In his defence he claimed to have been 'made minister' by Hooper in a room of the episcopal palace, when the latter 'willed and charged him to go forward according to the words of the Bible, which he then did hold in his hand, and to preach the same and to minister the sacraments'.[28] It is interesting to note that the most radical of the bishops of the English Church seems to have used a form closely approximating to a *traditio* of the Bible to authorize an individual to minister.

The order of episcopal consecration in the 1550 Ordinal was more closely related to its medieval antecedents than perhaps any other Reformed ordination rite. The laying on of hands was performed, as before, by all consecrating bishops; but it was the principal consecrator, not the co-consecrators, who was to lay the Bible (not the open book of the Gospels) on the neck of the elect. The pastoral staff was given with words stressing the pastoral rather than the juridical nature of episcopal office:

> Be to the flocke of Christ a shepeheard, not a wolfe: feede them, deuoure them not; holde up the weake, heale the sicke, binde

---

[26] Ibid., p. 312.
[27] Third Sermon upon Jonas, 5 March 1550, *Early Writings of John Hooper, D. D.*, ed. S. Carr, *PS* (Cambridge, 1843), p. 479.
[28] Gloucester, Gloucester Diocesan Records, XVIII, fols 49–50.

together the broken, bryng againe the outcastes, seke the lost. Be so mercifull, that you be not to remisse, so minister discipline, that ye forgeat not mercy; that when the chief shepheard shal come, ye may receyue the immarcessible croune of glory, through Jesus Christ our lord. Amen.[29]

In the revision of 1552 the Bible was not laid on the neck of the elect but delivered to him instead of the pastoral staff, the two formulae accompanying those ceremonies being conflated into one single imperative. The omission of all other ceremonies is significant in considering how the office of bishop was understood in the English Church at the time. The loss of the pastoral staff in the revised rite, even though the pastoral language was retained, nonetheless removed a visible symbol of the image of the bishop as shepherd. It is interesting to note that the records of Matthew Parker's consecration as Archbishop of Canterbury in December 1559 are particularly emphatic in their assertion that the pastoral staff was not given to him after the *traditio* of the Bible (clearly conforming with the rite of 1552). The ring was a symbol of the marriage of the bishop to his church. This militated against the idea of the bishop, and indeed of any of the Church's ministers, as merely an officeholder whose tenure could end at any time, at which point their episcopacy would cease. There was at this time some uncertainty among the holders even of episcopal office as to whether they ceased being bishops if they were removed from their see, or if their ordination or consecration had effected some permanent change in them. Even more, there was a question of the appropriateness, even the propriety of the idea of wedding oneself to a particular church when one already had a wife and children.

At the Council of Trent Sacred Tradition was clearly defined as a source of revelation equal to that of Sacred Scripture.[30] Continuity in a context of steady growth since apostolic times (and a clear link with the apostles through an unbroken succession of validly ordained bishops) was one of the great strengths of the self-understanding of the Catholic Church as it passed from Catholic Reformation to Counter-Reformation. Consequently, the revision of ordination rites in the Catholic Church in the late sixteenth century left both doctrines and ceremonies fundamentally unchanged. The Pontifical of Clement VIII, published in 1595, contained essentially the same rites as the

---

[29] *Prayer-Books*, p. 317.
[30] Tanner, *Decrees*, 2, p. 663.

Roman Pontifical of 1485, with a few changes in the preface to the rites for conferring minor orders, citing decrees of the Council of Trent and making some small additions to the rubrics.[31] Catholic ordination rites conveyed in their words and ceremonies the clear understanding of the priest as one set apart to offer the sacrifice of the Mass for the living and the dead. In the consecration of a bishop, authority and jurisdiction were conferred in a pastoral context, with a growth in importance of the latter as the reforms of Trent sought to restore a balance in the office. The rites also conveyed a sense of continuity with apostolic times. Innovations and omissions in the rites of the Reformers invalidated their ministry, based as it was on faulty doctrine and a defective understanding of the Church and the eucharist. For their part, the Reformers sought to eliminate what they saw as medieval accretions, excising many or all of the ceremonies which in the Catholic rite conferred and guaranteed an authentic ministry.

The English Ordinal was unique among the orders for conferring ministry in the major Reformed churches in that it consistently included a *traditio instrumentorum*. It is worth noting that the iconography of the English Reformation had the image of the king handing the Bible to his bishops as a powerful metaphor of the royal source of all authority and power (perhaps even sacramental power) in the English Church. This image appears in a number of prominent places, including not only the well-known title page of the Great Bible, but also the frontispiece of Cranmer's Catechism of 1550, where it is Edward and not Henry who is seen handing the Bible to his bishops. The words which accompanied the handing over of the Bible in the ordination service conveyed the meaning and understanding of each distinct order in the English Church (the deacon to read the gospel and to preach; the priest to be a dispenser of Word and Sacrament; the bishop to be both pastor and judge). One of the principal arguments against the validity of Anglican orders in the nineteenth-century condemnation by Leo XIII was that they failed to distinguish between the grades of order in the words 'receive the Holy Ghost' at the laying on of hands. This defect was not repaired by the qualifying phrase 'for the office and work of a priest' (or deacon, or bishop) added in the liturgical reforms of 1662, as by that time a valid ministry had died out. Although this was by no means the sole consideration, nonetheless

---

[31] M. Dykmans, *Le Pontifical romain, révisé au XVe siècle* (Vatican City, 1985), pp. 156–7.

it might well be argued that the formula accompanying the *traditio* of the Bible was perhaps not fully taken into account at the time. In any ordination rite, what is omitted can at times say as much about the understanding of the Church's ministry as what is included. The imagery and symbolism of the *traditio instrumentorum* and their use or disuse convey a significant part of this picture.

EXPEDIENT AND EXPERIMENT: THE ELIZABETHAN LAY READER

by BRETT USHER

THE origins of the most senior office in the Church of England open to a layman, that of lay reader, are obscure. Sir Robert Phillimore confined himself to the observation that the office was 'one of the five inferior orders of the Roman church', adding only that

> in this kingdom, in churches or chapels where there is only a very small endowment, and no clergyman will take upon him the charge or cure thereof, it has been usual to admit readers, to the end that divine service in such places might not altogether be neglected.[1]

But when and how did it become 'usual'? There are no references to readers in Edward VI's Royal Injunctions of 1547,[2] presumably because those holding inferior Roman orders were still legally entitled to exercise their functions. Although the Protestant advances of the next six years removed all such from office there is no sign that the Edwardian regime made any attempt to appoint readers as an emergency or auxiliary measure. Probably there was no immediate need to do so: with the abolition of the chantries in 1549 most chantry priests went on to serve as 'stipendiaries', effectively slipping into the ranks of the unbeneficed as 'curates'. If anything there was a glut in the clerical market between 1549 and the restoration of Catholic orders in 1553.

The need for a lay-readership was nevertheless anticipated by advanced Protestants. During their brief imprisonment together in 1554/5, the proto-martyr John Rogers advised the printer John Day to recommend to the exiled leadership that when the gospel was again freely preached, a superintendent should be appointed for every ten churches, under whom there would be 'faithful readers,

---

[1] Sir Robert Phillimore, *The Ecclesiastical Law of the Church of England*, 2 vols, 2nd edn (London 1895), 1, p. 450.

[2] Edward Cardwell, *Documentary Annals of the Reformed Church of England*, 2 vols (Oxford, 1844), 1, pp. 4–31.

such as might be got; so that the popish priests should be clean put out'.[3]

Of course no such radical scheme was introduced in 1559, and the first priority of the new regime was to persuade incumbent clergy to subscribe the Oath of Supremacy. This strategy was to be carried through in the first place by means of a Royal Visitation, and deprivations were assumed to be inevitable.[4] The problem of manning the parishes was exacerbated by high mortality rates during the influenza epidemic of the late 1550s and the fact that, as in 1549, inferior Roman orders would no longer be valid.[5] In all these circumstances the need for lay help in running poorly-endowed parishes was at once perceived, and it is in the Injunctions issued by Elizabeth early in 1559 that the Protestant lay reader makes his first official appearance:

> That all ministers and readers of public prayers, chapters, and homilies shall be charged to read leisurely, plainly, and distinctly; and also such as are but mean readers shall peruse over before, once or twice, the chapters and homilies, to the intent they may read to the better understanding of the people, and the more encouragement to godliness.[6]

Whereas the Injunctions of 1547 were framed for the cosmetic reordering of the Henrician settlement, undisturbed by legislation until 1549, those of 1559 were looking forward to the situation which would pertain only weeks later. The new prayer book came into effect at midsummer and the Royal Visitation was planned for August. Although the Articles of Enquiry prepared for the visitors' use make no reference to readers,[7] they make none either to preaching licences, which the Injunctions specifically empowered such visitors to grant.[8] By analogy we may perhaps assume that readers were appointed during

---

[3] John Strype, *Annals of the Reformation*, 4 vols in 7 (Oxford, 1824), I/i, p. 267.

[4] The standard account of the process remains Henry Gee, *The Elizabethan Clergy and the Settlement of Religion 1558–1564* (Oxford, 1898).

[5] There is no evidence that any man below the rank of deacon was offered the Oath of Supremacy.

[6] Henry Gee and William John Hardy, *Documents Illustrative of English Church History* (London, 1896), p. 438; W. H. Frere and W. M. Kennedy, *Visitation Articles and Injunctions of the Period of the Reformation*, 3 vols, Alcuin Club Collections, 14–16 (London, 1910), 3, p. 25.

[7] Printed in Gee, *Elizabethan Clergy*, pp. 65–70, and in Frere and Kennedy, *Visitation Articles*, 3, pp. 1–7.

[8] Ibid., 3, p. 11.

the visitation as a holding operation until their position could be fully regularized by the new bench of bishops.

Following Parker's consecration in December 1559 they make a spectacular appearance in the record. On 8 January 1560 the Archbishop authorized Roland Meyrick, Bishop of Bangor, to carry out ordinations in his name in St Mary-le-Bow. Five men were ordained deacon and priest, and five *lector*.[9]

Although Strype speaks as if it were common practice at this time,[10] such 'ordination' is unique in the London and Canterbury records. Parker himself seems to have given serious thought to John Rogers's scheme for rural superintendency, evolving a system whereby pluralist clergy could supervise a circuit of parishes each staffed by a curate or reader. Thus the reader was to be *more* than an expedient, and his status was to be reflected by a form of ordination. Parker implemented such a system in Canterbury diocese, but abandoned it by the end of 1562. It foundered in part because lay patrons, jealous of their property rights, were unwilling to see the incomes from a group of parishes (the circuit) pooled and thereafter more equably distributed.[11]

But it may be hazarded that the Archbishop had made a serious tactical blunder in another sense. St Mary-le-Bow, mother church of Canterbury's peculiar jurisdiction in London, the Deanery of the Arches, was a highly public place. The Archbishop's courts met in its crypt, and it was moreover now in the possession of Robert Cole, one of the leaders of the secret Protestant congregation of the late reign. The 'ordination' of readers may have caused some offence to the godly, suggesting the recognition, however attenuated, of minor 'popish' orders.

Henceforth readers would only be *admitted*, by licence or 'toleration' of their Ordinary, on an *ad hoc* and unco-ordinated basis. The history of readers during the rest of the reign is fragmented and chequered, but its general outlines are clear: they were accepted as an expedient, probably in every diocese in England and Wales; were officially sanctioned at the Convocation of 1563; and survived the curious wording of the canons of 1571. During the 1580s, however, probably in

---

[9] W. H. Frere, ed., *Registrum Matthei Parker diocesis Cantuarensis, A. D. 1559–1575*, 3 vols, Canterbury and York Society, 35–6, 39 (London, 1928–33), 2, p. 339.

[10] Strype, *Annals*, 1/i, pp. 265, 267.

[11] Rosemary O'Day, *The English Clergy: the Emergence and Consolidation of a Profession, 1558–1642* (Leicester, 1979), pp. 130–1.

reaction to the strategy of non-conformist incumbents in hiring laymen to read services of which they did not approve in all points of liturgy – whilst they devoted themselves to the much more important business of preaching – the policy of appointing lay readers was rapidly abandoned.[12]

Parker had begun mapping out the duties and conditions of service which would be imposed on readers in his 'Order for serving of Cures now destitute'. Pluralist incumbents were to provide their parishes with a deacon, or else 'some sober honest and grave layman who as a lector or Reader shall give his attendance to read the order of service appointed'. He was not to 'intermeddle' with baptism, marriage, or holy communion, with preaching or with prophesying, but might also read the Litany and the prescribed homily in the absence of an ordained 'Pastor'. Readers were not to be appointed 'but with the oversight of the bishop or his chancellor, to have his convenient instruction and advertisement, with some letters testimonial of his admission, how to order themselves in the said charge'. They were removable 'upon certificate and proof of their disability and disorder'.[13]

Monitoring their activities certainly remained a cause for concern. Articles drawn up in 1560 for an abortive diocesan visitation assume their presence but enquired whether they were taking it upon themselves to baptize, marry, or celebrate communion, and whether non-resident incumbents were appointing them where they 'should find a minister'.[14] The following year Parkhurst incorporated these enquiries into his articles for Norwich.[15] Amongst the 'articles agreed upon at the Second Session in Lambeth' on 12 April 1561 by Parker and Young of York 'with the assent of their brethren the bishops', it was enjoined

---

[12] The evidence is most conveniently summarized in *Readers and Subdeacons. Report and Resolutions of the Joint Committee of the Convocation of Canterbury Appointed to Consider the Question of Restoring an Order of Readers or Sub-Deacons in the Church*, 'New Edition with Additions' (Westminster, 1938), pp. 30–9.

[13] Ibid., p. 32.

[14] Possibly Grindal's work, from the phraseology and the fact that when on 27 May 1560 Parker forbade his suffragan bishops to visit in their own names until he had conducted a metropolitical visitation, he emphasised that Grindal was not exempt from this ruling: John Bruce and Thomas T. Perowne, eds, *The Correspondence of Matthew Parker*, PS (Cambridge, 1853), pp. 115–17.

[15] Frere and Kennedy, *Visitation Articles*, 3, pp. 87–93 (at no. 25), 100–3. Oddly, Parker's Articles for his metropolitical visitation make no reference to readers: ibid., 3, pp. 81–4.

that readers be *once again* by every Ordinary reviewed and their ability and manners examined, and by discretion of the Ordinaries to remain in their office or to be removed, and their wages to be ordered. And the abstinence of mechanical sciences to be also enjoyned by the discretion of the said Ordinaries as well to ministers as to readers.[16]

The articles were signed by Parker, Grindal, and Cox of Ely, the three most active of the episcopal ecclesiastical commissioners. Since Grindal made his primary visitation of London diocese the following month he doubtless acted on the directives agreed at Lambeth.[17]

Strangely, no licences or tolerations to serve as reader are recorded at any point by Grindal's vicar-general. He had been appointing them nonetheless. In 1561 Grindal's visitors listed a total of fifty-two men who were now serving or had recently served as *lector*. In London, the only parish not exempt from him which supported one was St Mary Staining.[18] Three are found in Hertfordshire, four in Middlesex,[19] and the remainder in Essex – no fewer than five of them in beleaguered Colchester,[20] all of whose sixteen parishes were poorly endowed or else not endowed at all, several having been appropriate to the mitred abbey of St John's or to the priory of St Botolph.[21]

The effect of this visitation appears to have been marginal. Three months later, on 12 August 1561, Cecil was forced to inform Parker that the Queen, on progress in East Anglia, was furious with the clergy in general 'by reason of the undiscreet behaviour of the readers and ministers in . . . Suffolk and Essex. Surely here be many slender ministers.'[22]

Perhaps it was the Queen's personal intervention that decided Grindal on drastic action. On 24 March 1562 he evidently issued a mandate to his archdeacons to call before them all licensed readers and

---

[16] Ibid., 3, p. 95. My italics.

[17] No articles, injunctions, or act book of office survive.

[18] Call Book of Visitation: London, Guildhall Library [henceforth GL], MS 9537/2, fol. 29r.

[19] Ibid., fols 87v, 98r–100r. The return for the archdeaconry of St Albans is missing.

[20] For full details of the Colchester clergy in this period see Brett Usher, 'Colchester and Diocesan Administration 1539–1604', unpublished study undertaken on behalf of the Victoria County History, Essex (1993): copies at the Essex Record Office (Chelmsford and Colchester) under reference T/Z 440/1.

[21] GL, MS 9537/2, fols 39r–96v, *passim*.

[22] Bruce and Perowne, *Correspondence of Matthew Parker*, p. 148.

to inhibit them from celebrating divine office anywhere within the diocese after the feast of Pentecost next.

That, at least, is to extrapolate from the evidence found in one of the few contemporary surviving act books for the diocese, that of Archdeacon Mullins of London. The number of readers in the capital had risen to five and Mullins summoned them all on 2 May. Thomas Dawes of St George Botolph Lane (presumably the man of those names 'ordained' by Meyrick in 1560), John Joy of St Mary Staining, and William Wager of St James Garlickhithe all dutifully appeared on 2 May, as directed, and were suspended 'iuxta tenorem . . . mandati'.[23] Two men, '[ ] Trivergo' of St Olave Hart St, and John Pratt of St Margaret Lothbury, failed to put in an appearance. Trivergo does not reappear in the record and was presumably summarily suspended. Pratt turned up on 4 May and appears to have offered resistance since he exhibited Parker's licence allowing him to officiate. All to no avail: he was suspended according to the bishop's mandate.

If Grindal's action was part of a co-ordinated effort by the English bishops it suggests the possibility that no readers were officiating between Pentecost and the formal introduction of a new set of Readers' Injunctions during the Convocation of 1563.

Parker and the bishops, urgently needing to regularize life in the parishes, had began to 'interpret' the Royal Injunctions of 1559 almost immediately upon entering office. Various drafts exist amongst the Petyt and Parker Manuscripts,[24] and in one form or other – no finished, official version is known to have been printed at the time – these 'Resolutions' or 'Interpretations and Further Considerations' seem to have been adopted by the bishops, perhaps with the formal ratification of the 1563 Convocation and the verbal consent of the Queen, as a practical guide to the regulation of their dioceses.[25]

They have something to tell us about readers. To the forty-third injunction, concerning poorly qualified ministers, is tacked a final sentence, that readers 'neither serve in any great cure, nor where the

---

[23] Court Book of the Archdeaconry of London, 1562–3: GL, MS 9055, fol. 22r.

[24] London, Inner Temple Library, Petyt MS 538, 38 and 47; Cambridge, Corpus Christi College, MS 106, pp. 423–6.

[25] Printed in Strype, *Annals*, 1/i, pp. 318–24, 514–15. Fully edited, with an introduction, by W. M. Kennedy, *The 'Interpretations' of the Bishops & their Influence on Elizabethan Episcopal Policy*, Alcuin Club Tracts, 8 (London, 1908); reprinted in Frere and Kennedy, *Visitation Articles*, 3, pp. 59–73. Further discussed by V. J. K. Brook, *A Life of Archbishop Parker* (Oxford, 1962), pp. 101–8. Brook makes heavy weather of the simple fact that the bishops were thrashing around to find a *modus vivendi* with the 1559 Injunctions and eventually did so.

incumbents may be resident'. The second draft alters the final phrase to 'nor where is any incumbents', and the third alters it back to 'nor where any incumbent be resident'.[26]

Amongst the 'further considerations' is a reference to the contentious subject of private baptism *in extremis*. It is ordered to be 'ministered either by Curate, Deacon or Reader, or some other grave and sober man if time shall suffer'. This directive is, however, omitted from the third (Parker MS) draft.[27] Finally it is agreed 'that the ministers or readers out of service remove not from the diocese or cure, where they first began, and were admitted by the ordinary, except they bring letters testimonial of their removing, allowed by the ordinary'.[28]

One specific upshot of these episcopal deliberations was a set of twelve 'Iniunctions to be confessed and subscribed by them that shalbe admytted Readers'. What would seem to be a final version of these was transcribed both by Strype and by Cardwell, but ignored by Kennedy:[29] it was signed by the two archbishops and eight other members of the bench including Richard Cheyney of Gloucester, not consecrated until 19 April 1562. Thus it seems more likely than it did to Kennedy that these Injunctions were finalized for submission to Convocation in 1563, and ceremoniously signed by the bishops at that time.

The differences between the wording of this 'official' version and that of the Petyt MS draft are trifling and in no way alter the purport of the Injunctions overall. Readers were required to obey their Ordinaries under twelve heads:

1. Not to preach or interpret, but only to read what was appointed by public authority;
2. To read plainly, distinctly and audibly that all might hear and understand;

[26] Kennedy, *'Interpretations' of the Bishops*, pp. 31–2, 41.
[27] Ibid., pp. 32, 41.
[28] Ibid., p. 33.
[29] BL, MS Add. 19398, fols 59r–v, printed in Strype, *Annals*, 1/i, pp. 514–15; Cardwell, *Documentary Annals*, 1, pp. 302–4. Kennedy remained content with the draft/fair copy version in the Petyt MSS, though he must have recognized that Strype and Cardwell (who quotes no source) had transcribed an original document unknown to him: *'Interpretations' of the Bishops*, pp. 36–7. In reprinting the Injunctions two years later he merely noted that 'another copy' was to be found in Cardwell 'of later date' than 19 April 1562: Frere and Kennedy, *Visitation Articles*, 3, p. 67n.

3. Not to minister the sacraments or other rights, but only to bury the dead and purify women after childbirth;

4. To keep the registers;

5. To use sobriety in apparel, especially in church;

6. To 'moue men to quiet and concorde' and give no personal cause of offence;

7. To submit to the Ordinary testimony of good behaviour from 'the honest of the parishe . . . within one halfe yere next followinge' appointment;

8. To 'geue place upon convenient warning so thought by the Ordinarie' if a learned minister should be placed there at the suit of the patron of the living;

9. To claim 'no more of the fructs sequestered of suche cure where I shall serue: but as it shalbe thought mete to the wisdom of the Ordinarye';

10. Daily 'at the leaste' to read one chapter of the Old Testament and one of the New 'with good advisement to the increase of my knowledge';

11. [fol. 59v] Not to appoint a substitute by reason of absence or sickness, but to leave such appointment to the 'sute of the parishe' to the Ordinary;

12. To read only 'in porer parishes destitute of Incumbents' except in time of sickness 'or for other good considerations to be allowed by the ordenarie'.

A revised version of the Readers' Injunctions, incorporated into Parker's Advertisements in 1566,[30] partially explains why they rapidly became a thing of the past: none was to officiate without 'special licence of the bishop under his seal', and no allusion is made to burial of the dead and the churching of women. Some bishops evidently took this implied tightening of the existing rules as their cue to restrict readers' freedom of action: from 1568 William Alley of Exeter sometimes permitted them to bury the dead and church women and sometimes not. In the latter year Guest of Rochester ruled that none should be admitted to benefices worth more than £5 in the *Valor*.[31] In such circumstances their numbers were bound to dwindle.

The call books of the London visitations of 1565, 1568, and 1571 are

---

[30] Ibid., 3, pp. 179–80. They are now described as 'Protestations'.

[31] *Readers and Sub-deacons*, p. 33; Frere and Kennedy, *Visitation Articles*, 3, p. 335.

unfortunately missing; but in that for 1574, Edwin Sandys's second and last, the number of readers recorded had dropped dramatically to eleven, three of whom were serving in Colchester. At St Runwald, where there is no evidence that the cure had been in any way served since the beginning of the reign, Andrew Brownsmith survived in 1577 but was supplanted by a curate in February 1578.[32] At St Martin, likewise unserved for a generation, Richard Boniar reappeared as 'sequestrator' in 1577, but also gave way to a curate early the following year.[33] At outlying Berechurch John Watson remained until at least July 1580, but disappeared before the summer of 1583.[34]

Elsewhere in the diocese readers were few and far between by 1574 and under pressure to be gone. Outside Colchester only three are listed in Essex.[35] None is found in the City nor in Hertfordshire, and only four or five linger in Middlesex, all of them in a twilight world of abandoned perpetual curacies or chaplaincies.[36]

By 1577 the situation had not greatly changed, Colchester accounting for five of the thirteen men then in place.[37] Two others survived from 1574;[38] six more had perforce been appointed to impoverished parishes.[39]

But not for much longer. As the Colchester evidence shows, John Aylmer (consecrated to London in March 1577) made a determined bid to bring its derelict parishes under strict supervision, and generally set about erasing readers from the ecclesiastical landscape. Only in and

---

[32] GL, MSS 9537/3, fol. 84v, 9537/4, fol. 31r; London, Metropolitan Archives [henceforth LMA], DL/C/333, fol. 96v.

[33] GL, MSS 9537/3, fol. 84v, 9537/4, fol. 31r; LMA, DL/C/333, fol. 102v.

[34] GL, MSS 9537/3, fol. 85v; 9537/4, fols 32r, 93v; 9537/5, fol. 58r.

[35] Reginald Metcalf, Wix, ordered to cease officiating; farmer of benefice ordered to secure a perpetual curate for Aylmer's approval; Bartholomew Church, White Colne, ordered to account for his sequestration of the perpetual curacy; John Crane, Little Braxted (worth only £3 6s. 8d. in the *Valor*), inhibited: GL, MS 9537/3, fols 78v, 83r, 87r. Crane was in breach of the Injunctions since the benefice had since 1569 had a resident incumbent.

[36] William Anderson, Brentford; Richard Strange, Teddington; Richard Carpenter, Littleton (name struck through); John Carpenter, Houslow ('Carpenter' struck through and 'Corbett' substituted): GL, MS 9537/3, fols 32r, 32v, 33r, 35r.

[37] Brownsmith of St Runwald, Watson of Berechurch and Bongiar, now 'sequestrator' of St Martin, had been joined by one Bonde at Greenstead and John Middleton at St Mary Magdalen: GL, MS 9537/4, fols 31r, 32r.

[38] Strange at Teddington and Church at White Colne: GL, MS 9537/4, fols 9r, 34r.

[39] William Gyett, Brentford; John Pemberton, Belchamp Walter; Christopher Elkin (first appointed in 1561 but not found in 1574), Little Maplestead; Clement Lucocke, Little Holland; Thomas Freeman, Little Burstead; Thomas West, Doddinghurst: GL, MS 9537/4, fols 9v, 26v, 28r, 35v, 48v, 49r.

around Colchester do they survive by 1580;[40] and in 1583 the four men so designated – none of them in Colchester – were all absent from the visitation, almost certainly because they knew that they had become *personae non gratae*.[41]

* * *

What manner of man was the Elizabethan lay reader? He had been introduced in the first place as an expedient, 'to serve', as Strype later put it, 'for the present necessity: hoping in time that the universities might produce men of learning to occupy places in the church'.[42] Exactly so, and historians have always been quick to observe that Parker, Grindal, and their colleagues dispensed with his services at the earliest opportunity. They have been too quick, however, to make an elision with the underpaid and overworked curates whom non-resident incumbents were obliged by law to employ and with the humble 'artificers' hurried into the ministry in the early days of the new regime as an emergency measure.

There is a distinction to be drawn between the ordination of men whose credentials for the ministry were less than ideal, and the appointment of laymen to read service in the poorer parishes. Readers were not necessarily clerical poor relations. Jasper Baker of Bowers Gifford was a member of the parish's leading family, lords of the manor and patrons of the living:[43] in such a case it was obviously an advantage that church services should be in the hands of a man whom the village was expected in social terms to respect. John Barber of Netteswell was also probably a leading parishioner before he was appointed reader.[44] John Lufkyn of Salcott Wigborough and William

---

[40] Bongiar and Watson have been joined by Anthony Harrison at St Peter and 'Mr Middleton' at Little Horkesley: GL, MS 9537/4, fols 92v, 93r, 93v, 96r.

[41] Thomas True, reader and schoolmaster of Wimbish; John Pemberton (formerly of Belchamp Walter) of Finchingfield, inhibited from officiating; John Moore of Lammarsh; and John Lingwood of Inworth, also inhibited: GL, MS 9537/5, fols 49v, 52r, 54r, 64v. In every case the parish had an instituted rector or vicar. Pemberton had acquired a teaching licence in September 1577: LMA, DL/C/333, fol. 88r. Thus the office of reader, where it continued to exist, seems increasingly associated with the function of village schoolmaster: it was perhaps an elision designed to circumvent the provision that no reader should serve where the parish had a resident incumbent.

[42] Strype, *Annals*, 1/i, p. 267.

[43] Richard Newcourt, *Repertorium Ecclesiasticum Parochiale Londinense*, 2 vols (London, 1708–10), 2, pp. 100–2.

[44] See will of Elizabeth Wood: F. G. Emmison, ed., *Essex Wills (England) Vol. 1, 1558–1565* (Washington, DC, 1982), no. 885.

Lufkyn of Abberton were self-evidently members of the prominent and reasonably prosperous clan of Lufkyns scattered throughout the Stour valley. Bartholomew Church was granted the sequestration of White Colne in 1565, probably before he was appointed reader.[45] John Damsell of Greenstead-iuxta-Colchester had been before the Privy Council as early as 1546, along with one Robert Smythe and one William Harvey, for what were evidently Protestant activities. Since Smythe later emerges as a 'servant' of Sir Francis Jobson (kinsman of Northumberland, and Colchester's MP under Edward and Elizabeth), and William Harvey as curate of St Peter's in 1561, there are solid grounds for supposing that Damsell was part of a 'Jobson circle' which maintained a watching brief over Protestant affairs there after 1559.[46]

In other words, there is no reason to assume that men such as these were either poor or ignorant, let alone only formally committed to Protestant courses. It is more likely that they are representatives of a deliberate policy of appointing a species of ecclesiastical JP, drawn from the ranks of those whom the new regime had good reason to believe had been holding the fort for reformed churchmanship for years before the accession of Mary.

But the placing of lay readers also served as a quasi-liturgical *experiment*. Until a reformed university system could begin turning out an educated elite, able to satisfy the minimum demands of reformed churchmanship, what better way to train likely men than by means of practical experience in running a parish? Drawing on the diary of Thomas Earle, Strype noted that not a few of those who entered the church at the beginning of the reign had been 'designed for the universities, had not the discouragement of the times interposed'. Earle was forced into an apprenticeship which lasted throughout Mary's reign, to emerge briefly as a reader in London before ordination.[47] Others gained their training in the first place during the exile. Such a one was Peter Hawkes, found in Knox's Geneva congregation in 1557 as a cobbler: he returned to become a reader in Colchester by 1561 and was instituted to the nearby rectory of Layer Bretton in 1568.[48]

Indeed the majority of those we can identify in fact went on to take

---

[45] LMA, DL/C/332, fol. 122r.

[46] J. R. Dasent, ed., *Acts of the Privy Council of England*, 32 vols (London, 1890–1907), 1545–47, p. 485; 1552 54, p. 304; GL, MS 9537/2, fols 63v, 64v.

[47] Strype, *Annals*, 1/i, pp. 267–8.

[48] C. H. Garrett, *The Marian Exiles* (Cambridge, 1938), p. 181; GL, MSS 9537/2, fol. 65r, 9531/13, fol. 145v.

orders. At least ten of those in place in Essex in 1561 did so, including Hawkes. Five of these ten men were ordained by Grindal in the immediate aftermath of the visitation: John Goldring and John Walford as swiftly as 27 May, Philip Petty on 27 October, William Kended on 21 December, and Thomas Wade on 27 December.[49] This is surely further proof that a readership had been regarded as preparation for the ministry and that examination by Grindal's visitors was the final stage of their training – particularly in view of the Commissioners' order of April 1561, signed by Grindal himself, that readers should *once again* be examined and unsatisfactory ones summarily removed.

Certainly other bishops regarded the grooming of able readers as a useful additional tool in their battle for the parishes. On 16 November 1560 Thomas Bentham of Coventry and Lichfield wrote to thank Edwin Sandys of Worcester:

> for his paynes takying in my diocese as I am informed by one Cole, whome as he haithe licensed to read within his diocese, so I pray hym to helpe the said Cole in to the ministerye yf he geve orders before me and I shall acknoweledg yt a pleasure for I lack many good ministers.[50]

It is true that the hierarchy never publicly defended the office in terms either of its short- or long-term usefulness. It was an acute source of embarrassment that their Catholic opponents and continental friends could accuse them of ordaining unsuitable men, let alone of appointing readers, and on 15 August 1560 Parker had famously warned his bishops to be 'very circumspect' for the future: because of 'the great want of ministers' in 1559–60 they had all been guilty of ordaining

> sundry artificers and others, not traded and brought up in learning, and . . . some that were of base occupations: forasmuch now by experience it is seen that such manner of men . . . are very offensive unto the people . . . these shall be to desire and require you hereafter . . . only to allow such as, having good testimony of their honest conversation, have been traded and exercised in

---

[49] GL, MS 9531/1, fols 102v, 105r, 106r, 107r, 107v, 108v.

[50] Rosemary O'Day and Joel Berlatsky, eds, 'The Letter Book of Thomas Bentham, bishop of Coventry and Lichfield', in *Camden Miscellany, XXVII*, Camden Society Publications, 4th ser., 22 (London, 1979), p. 179.

learning, or at the least have spent their time with teaching of children, excluding all others . . . brought up and sustained . . . either by occupation or other kinds of life alienated from learning.[51]

Since as late as 1575 the author of *A Brief Discourse of the Troubles begun at Frankfort* could make the extravagantly pessimistic claim that 'in most places, the Ministry . . . consists of old Popish Priests, tolerated Readers, and many new-made ministers whose readings . . . are such that the people cannot be edified',[52] it was not likely that the hierarchy would rush to the hapless readers' defence. James Calfhill had done so only by contrasting 'the simple reader' with the corrupt 'Sir Johns' of the previous regime, 'in every respect worse'.[53] Grindal flatly told the Scottish regent that he should not follow the English church's example in putting up with 'readers instead of teachers'.[54]

But the decline of the lay readership in London diocese and Aylmer's attempts to kill it off in the early years of his episcopate were accompanied by an impressive rise during the 1570s in the number of graduate ordinands who were being instituted and collated to the parishes: that is to say, it was an experiment which had served its purpose.[55]

In sum, the Elizabethan lay readers have received less than their due. Some were responsible minor magistrates who took on a temporary brief pending the appointment of an ordained man. Some were

---

[51] Bruce and Perowne, *Correspondence of Matthew Parker*, pp. 120–1.

[52] Edward Arber, ed., *A Brief Discourse of the Troubles begun at Frankfort (1575)* (London, 1908), p. 230.

[53] James Calfhill, *An Answer to John Martial's Treatise of the Cross*, ed. Richard Gibbings, PS (Cambridge, 1846), p. 52.

[54] Patrick Collinson, *Archbishop Grindal 1519–1583* (London, 1979), p. 113.

[55] For the development of an educated Protestant ministry after 1558 see O'Day, *English Clergy*, pp. 126–43. In London diocese that development was more rapid than O'Day's account implies. Between January 1579 and December 1580 Aylmer instituted or collated to forty-eight vacant livings. Whilst twenty-three men were described only as *clericus*, seven were B. A. and sixteen M. A.; the latter were outranked by one bachelor and one doctor of civil law: GL, MS 9531/13, fols 195r–200r. Other factors, however, need to be weighed on both sides. Many ordinands by this time are described as presently or 'lately' (*nuper*) members of Oxbridge colleges: thus numerous clerics had some form of university training, even if they had not graduated; while others can be shown to have graduated later. On the other hand, many instituted men with higher degrees did not eschew (indeed, eagerly espoused) pluralism, and therefore left these 'new, improved' benefices in the hands of poor curates. That there was an inexorable – if, nationwide, only gradual – improvement in recruitment to the rural parishes is not to be denied. Its parameters, however, have been discussed in rather simplistic terms.

humble but nevertheless convinced Protestants who had received a form of clerical training by virtue of going into exile. Others like Thomas Earle had been deprived in the Marian years of the traditional route to the ministry, a university education.

So, perhaps, had William Wager. Born and bred in St James Garlickhithe, he stated that he was twenty-nine when ordained by Grindal on 24 August 1566:[56] he was probably just sixteen years old, therefore, at Mary's accession. By the end of the reign he was turning out pro-Protestant interludes which, like those of 'the learned clerk' Lewis Wager – ?his father – may well have played their part in the final demoralization of Mary's regime. Deprived of his readership by Archdeacon Mullins in 1562, he nevertheless went on to occupy two city parishes at the hands of the dean and chapter of St Paul's,[57] became an outspoken anti-papal London lecturer, and a friend of Thomas Wilcox.[58]

In other words, he was no mere 'tolerated' ignoramus; and a recruitment system which could prepare the likes of this fascinating man, or of Thomas Earle, for a fruitful career in the Elizabethan Church should not be accounted a complete failure.

---

[56] GL, MS 9535/1, fol. 126v.

[57] George Hennessy, *Novum Repertorium Ecclesiasticum Parochiale Londinense* (London, 1908), pp. 79, 249.

[58] *DNB*, s.v.; P. S. Seaver, *The Puritan Lectureships* (Stanford, CT, 1970), pp. 80, 162, 209–10; E. K. Chambers, *The Elizabethan Stage*, 4 vols (Oxford, 1923), 3, pp. 503–5.

GIVING TRIDENTINE WORSHIP BACK ITS HISTORY

by SIMON DITCHFIELD

Question: What is the difference between a liturgist and a
terrorist?
Answer: You can negotiate with a terrorist!

AS is well-known, humour – by juxtaposing like with unlike – can
make a serious point, concisely and memorably; and this quip,
too, has a serious import. To begin with, the source for this
joke was an Oratorian priest. As will become clear, this is of more than
passing significance – aside, that is, from the fact that their founder, St
Philip Neri was well-known for his use of humour to mortify the spirit
of his favourite disciples. For my principal concern in this paper is with
ecclesiastical erudition (something of an Oratorian speciality during
this period) and its relationship to the shape, content, and practice of
Christian worship.

One of the more unfortunate objects of St Philip's practical jokes
was Cesare Baronio, whom the saint considered as being of an
excessively serious disposition. Accordingly, the saint bullied Baronio
into getting up at the end of a wedding feast they both attended to
intone the *Miserere* before the startled guests.[1] Baronio is, of course,
rather better known for having written an account of the Church's first
twelve centuries, the *Annales ecclesiastici*, first published in Rome
between 1588 and 1607.[2] This project, crafted with painstaking
chronological thoroughness, sought to combat Protestant polemic by

---

[1] G. Calenzio, *La vita e gli scritti del Cardinale Cesare Baronio* (Rome, 1907), p. 29. Cf. L.
Ponnelle and L. Bordet, *Saint-Philippe Neri et la societé romaine de son temps (1515–1595)*, 2nd
edn (Paris, 1958), p. 166.

[2] The autograph manuscript may still be found in the Vatican library: BAV, MSS Vat. lat.
5684–95. Aside from Calenzio's exhaustive and anecdote-rich *vita*, which was the direct
product of the author's attempts to get its subject canonized, the most satisfactory
biographical treatment of Baronio remains H. Jedin, *Kardinal Caesar Baronius. Der Anfang
der katholischen Kirchengeschichtsschreibung im 16. Jahrhundert*, Katholisches Leben und
Kirchenreform im Zeitalter der Glaubensspaltung, 38 (Münster in Westfalen, 1978),
which is also available in an Italian translation, *Il cardinale Cesare Baronio: L'inizio della
storiografia ecclesiastica nel sedicesimo secolo* (Morcelliana, Brescia, 1982). See also now S. Zen,
Baronio storico: controriforma e crisi di metodo umanistico (Naples, 1994).

demonstrating the continuity which the Roman Church had always professed with its apostolic origins and earned him the sobriquet – bestowed by contemporaries as well as posterity – as father of church history.[3]

What is much less well-known, however, is the role played by Baronio's local counterparts in the recovery of the devotional history and traditions of dioceses the length and breadth of the Italian peninsula, using the full panoply of scholarly methods available to the world of late humanism. Amongst those who study the Italian Middle Ages, the achievement of Ferdinando Ughelli, as author of *Italia sacra*, might be occasionally acknowledged with a mixture of gratitude and scholarly condescension; but who has heard of Pietro Maria Campi, Lodovico Jacobilli, or the numerous other local Baronios active during the two centuries or so after closing of the Council of Trent in 1564? There can be no greater testimony to the scale and scope of their labours than the comment made by their master chronicler, the indefatigable Jesuit bibliographer Girolamo Tiraboschi (1731–94), that 'in no century and in no other country can [the writing of] history have been cultivated to such a degree as it was in seventeenth-century Italy.'[4]

Before proceeding any further with sixteenth- and seventeenth-century ecclesiastical scholarship, it is necessary to spend some time looking critically at its more recent counterpart, specifically that relating to the history of Roman Catholic liturgy. The task here, explicit in the title of this paper and only slightly less so in its opening quip, consists in tackling an enormously influential and prejudicial tradition of liturgical scholarship which has sought to remove liturgy as it has been practised in the Roman Catholic Church from the Council of Trent down to Vatican II from history altogether.

To begin with, standard accounts of the Reformation and Counter-Reformation (such as that provided, for example, in volume four of the authoritative *Handbuch der Kirchengeschichte*) which tend to view their subject matter in terms of development – whether it be of doctrinal

---

[3] The classic treatment of the role played by history writing in confessional polemic remains P. Polman, *L'Élément historique dans la controverse religieuse du XVIe siècle* (Gembloux, 1932). See also the useful account in E. Cochrane, *Historians and Historiography in the Italian Renaissance* (Chicago and London, 1981), pp. 445–78.

[4] 'in niun secolo e in niun paese direbbesi che fosse mai tanto coltivato la storia, quanto in Italia nel secolo XVII': G. Tiraboschi, *Storia della letteratura italiana*, 9 vols in 10 (Florence, 1812), 8/ii, p. 369.

difference or of the relations between church and state – have largely passed over liturgy, seeing it as apparently unchanging. In the index to the English edition of this volume, there are just three references to 'liturgy' in almost 800 pages. In every case it features as an example of Tridentine rigidity.[5]

Turning to scholars who work directly in the field, Theodor Klauser, in a study which for several decades has remained the standard introduction to the history of the Western liturgy, views his subject from 1568 – the year of the introduction of the revised Roman Breviary – to the opening of the Second Vatican Council in terms of rigid unification (*Einheitsliturgie*) and rubricism.[6] This last term, in particular, has become a value-laden symbol – perhaps only second to the Inquisition – of all that was reactionary and wrong with the Tridentine Church. J. A. Jungmann, another major scholar in the field, went further and adopted the word '*Geschichtlosigkeit*' (literally 'the state of the absence of history') to describe the Tridentine liturgy.[7] While for another mid-twentieth-century commentator, the Oratorian Father Bouyer, 'the false notion of the nature of liturgy [which he defines a few pages further on in terms of "a rigid and unintelligent traditionalism"] has been framed by the Baroque and Romantic mentality'.[8]

In place of such a static and fundamentally ahistorical picture, this paper seeks to construct one which does justice to the contention that these centuries witnessed a living liturgy – with universalizing and regularizing pretensions certainly, yet a liturgy which never ceased its dialogue with, or to take account of, the particular devotions practised in dioceses the length and breadth of the Catholic world. This is the first sense in which it aims to give Tridentine worship back its history.

---

[5] E. Iserloh, J. Glazik, and H. Jedin, *History of the Church vol. V – Reformation and Counter Reformation* (London, 1980), pp. 206, 510, and 644. Somewhat confusingly, this is a translation of volume *four* of the 2nd edn of the German original *Handbuch der Kirchengeschichte* (Freiburg im Breisgau, 1967).

[6] T. Klauser, *A Short History of the Western Liturgy: an Account and Some Reflections* (Oxford, 1968), pp. 117–52. This is a translation of the 5th edn of the author's *Klein abendländischen Liturgiegeschichte: Bericht und Besinnung* (Bonn, 1965).

[7] J. A. Jungmann, 'Liturgical life in the Baroque period', from his essay collection: *Pastoral Liturgy* (Tenbury Wells, 1962) pp. 80–9. This is a not entirely satisfactory translation of his *Liturgisches Erbe und Pastorale Gegenwart* (Innsbruck, 1960).

[8] L. Bouyer, *Life and Liturgy* (London, 1956), p. 5 (and for the parenthetical definition p. 8). Cf. Anton Mayer, 'Liturgie und Barock', *Jahrbuch für Liturgiewissenschaft*, 15 (1941), pp. 67–154, who concludes (p. 148): 'Der Barock als geistige Form eines Zeitalters ist und bleibt seinem Wesen nach unliturgisch.'

There is also a second sense, one which takes as its point of departure precisely that part of the breviary which, as we shall see shortly, occupied the attentions of liturgical reformers extensively during this period, the second nocturn matins readings from the lives of the saints. In their efforts to 'save the phenomena' of their local cults by demonstrating liturgical and, wherever possible, historical continuity between current practice and apostolic origins – for this age of confessional strife *the* litmus test of legitimacy and orthodoxy – the local Baronios were responsible for carrying out a quiet revolution in historical scholarship by enlisting non-literary sources in their task to an unprecedented degree, and by distinguishing primary from secondary sources. In the process, they constructed during the century after Trent a comprehensive census of the sacred.[9]

The paper therefore argues not only that Tridentine liturgy itself has a history consisting of negotiating the dialectical relationship between particular practice and universal precept, but also that the scholarly skills this process called upon and developed secure liturgy's status as a significant, unwritten chapter in the history of historical scholarship. So what follows may be seen not only to be giving Tridentine liturgy back its history but – by acknowledging the debt the latter owes to scholarship which was generated by liturgical concerns – to be giving history back its liturgy.

* * *

Before proceeding further, however, a couple of disclaimers are required. Firstly, the paper will not deal with the mass, but will instead focus on the breviary, or rather that part of the office book devoted to the Proper Offices of saints. This might seem perverse, but arguably the emphasis of scholars on the Tridentine Mass and its virtual exclusion of the participating laity has contributed in no small measure to the dominant historiographical problem this paper is addressing: the myth of *Geschichtlosigkeit*.

Secondly, in terms of geography, the following discussion is not based on Roman Catholic western Europe in general. Instead, it is

---

[9] See S. Ditchfield, *Liturgy, Sanctity and History in Tridentine Italy: Pietro Maria Campi and the Preservation of the Particular* (Cambridge, 1995), *passim*, esp. chs 10–12. For a survey of the wider context see now A. Grafton, *The Footnote: a Curious History* (London and Cambridge, MA, 1997), ch. 6, 'Back to the future 2: the antlike industry of ecclesiastical historians and antiquaries', pp. 148–89.

essentially restricted to the Italian peninsula. This is not just a pragmatic decision, but one founded on the reality that it was here that the attempts at liturgical regularization were most far-reaching, so that if the case can successfully be argued for devotional particularisms coexisting with Tridentine liturgical universalism for this part of Europe, the argument will be all the stronger. By contrast, in the French Church Gallicanism enjoyed vibrant liturgical expression as reflected, in particular, by the extremely limited adoption by French dioceses of the Roman Breviary until the campaign led by Prosper Guéranger at Solesmes to reclaim the Rite in the nineteenth century.[10] Not even Klauser or Jungmann, with their distaste for the stilted, showy rhetoric of baroque devotion, have tried to extend their freeze-frame view of Tridentine liturgy to France.

Chronologically, the scope is essentially restricted to the first hundred years after the closing of the Council of Trent in 1564. However, mindful of the polemical origins of the very label 'century' in the work of the confessional historian Flacius Illyricus and his colleagues (appropriately referred to as the Magdeburg Centuriators), the close of the paper will float the idea of a 'the long Tridentine century' to encompass the working out of the processes adumbrated at Trent by such figures as John Henry Newman as late as the nineteenth century.

A final disclaimer relates to the whole approach to liturgy and worship adopted here, which is self-consciously philological before it is social; textual rather than performative in focus. It is true that the history of liturgy as a scientific discipline was largely the creation of the period *c*.1550–1700: reform is often accompanied by and generates research, if only for the purposes of forging weapons of polemic.[11] The seventeenth century is therefore something of a golden age for liturgiologists with the publication of works by, among others, Mabillon, Martène, and Gavanti.[12] With notable exceptions (Mabillon

---

[10] The diocese of Orléans was the last to abandon its own breviary in 1875. For an illuminating discussion of Guéranger and his vision of liturgy as an 'imagined community' – visualizing the unity of the Church around the pope – in an age of unprecedented industrial change, see P. Raedts's paper elsewhere in this volume.

[11] Beginning with the studies of Greek and Latin liturgies of the early Church by Georg Cassander, *Liturgica de ritu et ordine dominicae coenae quam celebrationem Graeci liturgiam, Latini missam appellarunt* (Cologne, 1558), and James of Joigny (known as Pamelius), *Liturgica latinorum*, 2 vols (Cologne, 1571).

[12] B. Gavanti, *Thesaurus sacrorum rituum seu commentari in rubricas*, 1st edn (Milan, 1628); J. Mabillon, *De Liturgia Gallicorum* (Paris, 1685); E. Martène, *De antiquis Ecclesiae ritibus*, 3 vols (Rouen, 1700–2).

and Pamelius), the term 'liturgy' hardly occurs in works on the subject or in the official documents of the Church prior to the twentieth century. The preferred term, instead, is *de ritibus ecclesiae* or *de sacris ritibus*, reflecting the concern with understanding the individual elements of the liturgy via painstaking philological reconstruction of its textual tradition rather than its operation as a system of public worship.[13] This is the path that the present approach ultimately takes its inspiration from.

By contrast, for leading social historians of early modern religion such as John Bossy, Natalie Davis, Bob Scribner, or David Sabean, liturgy is considered above all as religion in action, and as having played a central role in the negotiation of conflict within local communities.[14] This is implicit in Scribner's use of the term 'economy of the sacred' to describe the part played by liturgy in helping to structure peoples' relations with the sacred and the natural world, thereby constructing a form of cosmic order.[15] Similarly, David Gentilcore, in his own study of religion and magic in the early modern Terra d'Otranto at the heel of Italy's deep south, prefers to view his subject as 'a system of the sacred' in order to do greater justice to the shared community of belief between so-called 'elite' and 'popular' cultures personified for him by the figures of bishop and witch.[16]

This focus on the functional role of liturgy and worship as a means of earthing and dissipating social tensions is also central to Henry Kamen's study of the Catholic Reformation in Catalonia – *The Phoenix*

---

[13] See, for example, A. G. Martimort, ed., *The Church at Prayer, vol. 1 – Principles of the Liturgy* (Collegeville, MN, and London, 1987), pp. 7–8. For Latin writers of the Middle Ages such as Isidore of Seville, John of Avranches, Pseudo-Alcuin, and Rupert of Deutz, the preferred title was *De ecclesiasticis officiis*.

[14] E.g. N. Z. Davis, 'From "Popular religion" to "Religious cultures"', in S. Ozment, ed., *Reformation Europe: a Guide to Research* (St Louis, MI, 1982), pp. 321–41; J. Bossy, 'The Mass as a social institution, 1200–1700', *P&P*, 100 (Aug. 1983), pp. 29–61; D. W. Sabean, 'Communion and Community: the refusal to attend the Lord's Supper in the sixteenth century', in his *Power in the Blood: Popular Culture and Village Discourse in Early Modern Germany* (Cambridge, 1984), pp. 37–60.

[15] R. W. Scribner, 'Cosmic order and daily life: sacred and secular in pre-industrial German society', in K. von Greyerz, ed., *Religion and Society in Early Modern Europe, 1500–1800* (London, 1984), pp. 17–33; idem, 'Ritual and popular religion in Catholic Germany at the time of the Reformation', *JEH*, 35 (1984), pp. 47–77. These are both reprinted in idem, *Popular Culture and Popular Movements in Reformation Germany* (London and Ronceverte, 1987), pp. 1–16, 17–47.

[16] D. Gentilcore, *From Bishop to Witch: the System of the Sacred in Early Modern Terra d'Otranto* (Manchester, 1992).

and the Flame (1993). Kamen in fact goes as far as to deny *tout court* the relevance of the concept of personal faith to most members of the communities he has studied. Instead, he asserts the complete coincidence of the practice of religion with the functioning of the community. In other words worship is 'more social than sacramental', and 'the rites on which Trent placed such emphasis played a subordinate role in the life of the community and the Church.'[17]

For Eamon Duffy, however, the popular rituals which Scribner, Gentilcore, and Kamen regard as having well-nigh swamped the sacramental significance of, say, the mass, provide proof of the extent of lay participation in the liturgy: 'It makes no sense to talk here about "an alienated liturgy of the altar" . . . lay people called the shots.'[18] For Duffy therefore, the learned language of the liturgy combined with the monopolistic role played by the clergy in its adminstration did not preclude lay involvement. On the contrary, socially holistic as the shared possession of the laity of all classes, liturgy is shown to have offered spectacle and instruction as well as having provided a communal context for affective piety. What Duffy proposes here therefore is a dynamic model: 'The liturgy was in flux, responsive to changes from below, a mirror of the devotional changes and even fashions of the age.'[19]

In contrast to all this, what follows might well appear somewhat old-fashioned; but no apologies are offered for this, as an attempt to retrieve for serious consideration by ecclesiastical historians the *spiritual* role of liturgy as the provider of a structure for prayer and meditation on the universal Church and its local manifestations as reflected, in particular, in the hagiographical readings as found in the breviary.

Ironically, in view of how liturgy has subsequently come to be regarded as the very symbol of the rigidity of Tridentine religion, the office books were among those matters left to papal discretion by the fathers of Trent as they hurried to wind up the Council's closing session in the harsh winter of 1563/4. The work of the commission subsequently charged by Pius IV with the reform of the Roman

[17] H. Kamen, *The Phoenix and the Flame: Catalonia and the Counter-Reformation* (New Haven, CT, and London, 1993), p. 29 (but see also pp. 99–103 and 117–32 for his emphasis on the community dimension to early modern Christianity).

[18] E. Duffy, *The Stripping of the Altars: Traditional Religion in England, 1400–1580* (New Haven, CT, and London, 1992), esp. part 1: 'The structures of traditional religion', pp. 11–376 (quotation at p. 114).

[19] Ibid., p. 45.

Breviary was, however, only the most recent of a succession of such bodies or individuals who during the sixteenth century had drawn up plans for its revision. Perhaps the most well-known and radical of these projects actually resulted in the publication of a text whose two editions – of 1535 and 1536 – went through over one hundred reprintings before the work was placed on the infamous Caraffa Index of Prohibited Books in 1557 and again in 1559.[20]

* * *

This work was the *Breviarium sanctae crucis*, so-called after its principal author, Cardinal Francisco de Quiñones, whose titular basilica was Santa Croce in Gerusalemme.[21] Quiñones' radical starting point was his decision to divorce the breviary from the its public context of recitation or singing in church choir, and to make it for private use only. This enabled him to simplify the daily offices in a dramatic fashion by abolishing almost entirely the differences of rank between the various feast days which previously had determined the number of lessons to be read. He thus made the offices of almost equal length and therefore less of a burden to recite. The second nocturn readings at matins were all restricted to three – one scriptural, one homiletic, and one hagiographic – with the same number of psalms to be read at every office; whereas before a so-called feast of double rank (duplex) had enjoyed up to three of each, and more in the case of a feast which enjoyed Octave status (that is, was commemorated over the course of an entire week). Quiñones also considerably (and during Lent totally) reduced the number of feast days he included so as to leave enough room for the recital of the ferial, that is to say ordinary, non-feast-day office.

[20] For a modern edition of both versions of this document – the only universal Roman Catholic index which was drawn up exclusively by the Holy Office – see J. M. De Buganda, ed., *Index des livres interdits, vol VIII – Index de Rome, 1557, 1559 et 1564* (Sherbrooke and Geneva, 1990), pp. 1–50.

[21] The two editions of Quiñones' breviary are most easily consulted in the critical editions by J. W. Legg, *Breviarium Romanum a Fr. Card. Quignonio editum et recognitum, juxta editionem Venetiis A. D. 1535 impressam* (Cambridge, 1888); idem, *The Second Recension of the Quignon Breviary. Following an Edition Printed at Antwerp in 1537*, 2 vols (the second containing a liturgical introduction, a life of Quiñones, appendices, notes, and indices), *HBS*, 35, 42 (London, 1908–12). For what follows see the standard accounts in S. Bäumer, *Geschichte des Breviers* (Freiburg im Breisgau, 1895), pp. 392–409, and E. Cattaneo, *Il culto cristiano in occidente: note storiche*, 2nd edn (Rome, 1992), pp. 301–3. Cf. J. A. Jungmann, 'Warum ist das Reformbrevier des Kardinals Quiñones gescheitert?', *ZKT*, 78 (1956), pp. 98–107.

In this way Quiñones was able to see to it that, if followed correctly, a user of his breviary would recite all 150 psalms every week and the whole of the Bible during the course of the year. In making these radical changes, the Cardinal believed he was simply taking the breviary back to the patristic age, whose worship had been built on a bedrock of Scripture supplemented by ecclesiastical history and the lives of holy men and women, many of whom had been accorded the palm of martyrdom. In the preface to the first edition of 1535, Quiñones had explicitly declared that it was only by a daily reading from Scripture, ecclesiastical history, and the lives of saints, that a priest could adequately carry out his roles as an example to his flock and their intermediary with God.[22]

To return to the revised Roman Breviary as actually published by order of Pius V in 1568, and known to posterity as the *Breviarium pianum* (but which henceforth, for simplicity's sake, will be referred to as the Tridentine Breviary) the reform centred on the calendar of saints which here was being offered for the first time as a standard for the whole Roman Catholic Church to follow. The reformers sought to strip this back to its original simplicity – in Pius V's words *pristina patrum norma*, 'the original standard of the fathers' – so as to permit (in common with Quiñones' reforms) the more frequent saying of the daily, ferial office centred on readings from the psalms and Scripture that was suppressed on feast days where much space was taken up by hagiographical readings. Over the centuries the ever-increasing number of accretions to the saints' calendar had resulted in the fact that by the early sixteenth century the daily office had become seriously distorted, and those who recited it became accordingly negligent of reading whole sections of the psalter and significant parts of the Bible in favour of hagiographical readings considered by many contemporaries to be of doubtful historical veracity.[23] It must

---

[22] 'Cogitanti mihi pater sanctissime, atque animo repetenti initia veteris instituti, quo sancitum est, ut clerici sacris initiati, vel sacerdotiis praesidentes singulis diebus perlegant horarias preces, quas canonicas etiam apellamus, tres omnino causae spectatae fuisse videri solent. . . . Tertia, ut religionis quoque futuri magistri quotidiana sacrae scripturae et ecclesiasticarum historiarum lectione erudiantur, complectanturque, ut Paulus ait, cum, qui secundum doctrinam est, fidelem sermonem et potentes sint exhortari in doctrina sana et eos, qui contra dicunt arguere': Legg, *Breviarium Romanum a Fr. Card. Quignonio editum*, pp. xix–xx. A little further on (p. xx) Quiñones laments the current state of affairs: 'Tum historiae sanctorum tam inculte, tam negligenti iudicio scriptae leguntur, ut nec auctoritatem habere videantur nec gravitatem.'

[23] Between 1100 and 1558 some 200 feasts were added to the calendar (Klauser, *Short*

also be said that the ferial office took longer to recite than that used on saints' days, which certainly goes no little way to account for the latter's popularity.

The *desiderata* for the second nocturn matins readings from the lives of saints determined by the reforming commission instituted by Pius IV included concision matched with clarity of exposition; closer attention to accurate chronology (particularly relating to the date and time of the saint's death); and as precise information as was possible of the current whereabouts of the saint's body or principal relics. As the secretary of the commission, the Dominican Leonardo Marini, put it in his report to Pius V:

> one reads many apocryphal things in the legends of the saints and in some of them one comes across little or nothing that pertains to the saint. Furthermore, this is often done in an unsuitable manner, using words that confuse simple minds, neither obeying decorum or Christian honesty. However, the members of the commission have discussed this at length and concluded that the best thing to do is to take from all the stories of saints the most reliable information and make a compilation for each saint in a concise and sober style suitable to the ecclesiastical content, mentioning only the most important things that might edify and satisfy those that read them.[24]

It must be emphasised, however, that this concern to prune back the calendar of saints was not new. It long predated Quiñones, coming

---

History, p. 125). Cf. F. Focke and H. Heinrichs, 'Das Kalendarium des Missale Pianum vom Jahre 1570 und seine Tendenzen', *Theologisches Quartalschrift* [hereafter *TQ*], 120 (1939), pp. 383–400 and 461–9.

[24] 'nelle leggende de S[an]ti si leggono molte cose apochriphe, et di alcune leggende si legge pochissimo e niente di quello appartiene alla vita del santo, et anco sconciamente e con parole che più tosto possono talvolta offendere le menti semplici non servando ne il decoro ne l'honestà Christiana, però sopra di ciò si è fatto più e più volte dalli sudetti Sig[no]ri Deputati [members of the commission] discussione e finalmente si è risoluto che miglior modo non si poteva tenere che cavando da tutte le historie de S[an]ti le cose più autentiche, si facci una compilatione e di ciascun santo in brevità et con un stile mediocre che habbia dell'ecclesiastico, toccar le cose più importanti che faccino ad edificatione et sodisfattione di quelli che le leggeranno': P. Battifol, *History of the Roman Breviary* (London, 1912), p. 228. The entire text of the report is transcribed by Battifol on pp. 223–9. The original may be found in the Archivio Segreto Vaticano [hereafter ASV], MS Concil. Trident 47, fols 312–18.

up for discussion, for example, during the Council of Constance (1414–18).[25]

However, a reading of the papal bull *Quod a nobis*, which prefaced the Tridentine Breviary, reveals at once a different order of ambition. For by explicitly forbidding the continued recitation of *all* existing local variants of the breviary which could not prove at least two centuries of unbroken use, it set out to provide a calendar of universal application.[26] Nevertheless, several breviaries specific to particular religious orders did satisfy the 200-year rule, and so continued to be legitimately used; as were certain liturgies of undisputed ancient tradition such as the Ambrosian rite of Milan and the Mozarabic rite of Toledo.[27] Moreover, significant allowance must also be made for the length of time it took local churches and their incumbents to purchase the new order books. Of these the Tridentine Breviary was but the first, to be followed by the revised Roman Missal of 1570, the so-called *Clementine Vulgate* of 1592, and by the issue of new editions of the *Pontifical* (giving those rites celebrated only by bishops) in 1596 and of the *Ritual* (giving the forms for the administration of various rites outside the mass such as baptism and marriage) in 1614. Henry Kamen, in his important recent study of the Catholic Reformation in Catalonia, makes much of these material obstacles to the reform of worship.[28]

Despite such caveats, the Tridentine Breviary nevertheless represented an unprecedented attempt to regularize saying of the daily office by priests, nuns, other religious, and pious lay people throughout the

[25] E. C. Rodgers, *Discussion of Holidays in the Later Middle Ages* (New York, 1940), pp. 107–9 (my thanks to Robert Swanson for alerting me to the existence of this useful study). Cf. H. von der Hardt, *Magnum oecumenicum Constantiense concilium*, 6 vols (Frankfurt and Leipzig, 1697–1700), 1, pp. 423 (for comments of Pierre d'Ailly), 733–4 (for criticisms by Jean Gerson).

[26] 'exceptis quae ab ipsa prima institutione a Sede Apostolica approbata vel consuetudine; quae vel ipsa institutio ducentos annos antecedat.' Cf. J. Schmid, 'Studien über die Reform des römischen Breviers und Messale unter Pius V', *TQ*, 66 (1884), pp. 621–64.

[27] The Benedictines, Dominicans, Carmelites, and Premonstratensians, for example, kept the use of their own breviaries. For a comprehensive list of editions of both breviaries specific to religious orders and those specific to certain dioceses see H. Bohatta, *Bibliographie der Breviere, 1501–1850* (Leipzig, 1937), and now R. Amiet, *Missels et breviaires imprimes (supplément aux catalogues de Weale et Bohatta): propres des saints (éditions princeps)* (Paris, 1990). The only diocesan breviaries printed in Italy 1568–1600 were for Milan (5 edns) and Como (3 edns).

[28] H. Kamen, *The Phoenix and the Flame*, pp. 93–96, 348. By contrast, the very brief account of the reception of the Tridentine Breviary given in Mario Righetti's *Manuale di storia liturgica*, 4 vols (3rd edn, Milan, 1959–69), 2, p. 673, is superficial and naively optimistic.

Roman Catholic world. Moreover, as Quiñones explicitly recognized, it contained in the psalter and its scriptural, homiletic, and the hagiographical readings, comprehensive instruction in Roman Catholic devotion and doctrine.

* * *

This awareness of the didactic role of reading as prayer was central to another sixteenth-century plan to reform the breviary which centred on the figure of Gian Pietro Caraffa (1474–1559), later Pope Paul IV, and founder with S. Gaetano da Thiene of the Theatine Order named after Caraffa's bishopric of Chieti (Latin *Theate*) in the Abruzzi. The chief object of this Order was to recall the clergy to an edifying life and, through them, the laity to the practice of virtue. The importance of liturgical reform to this project was reflected in the fact that the papal brief founding the Order – *Exponi nobis* of 24 June 1524 – specifically allowed the Theatines to develop and use their own breviary. Though this project did not come to fruition, its approach extensively influenced the work of the reforming commission instituted by Pius IV, whose membership overlapped with that of Paul IV's own advisory group on the matter. The reason for this degree of influence was that, in contrast to Quiñones, Caraffa and his associates had no wish to meddle with the basic structure of the breviary. They rather concerned themselves with bringing the texts of the component parts into line with what up-to-date scholarship suggested was proper to ancient usage, thereby in particular eliminating those passages from the hagiographical readings of doubtful historical accuracy and orthodoxy.[29] Historians who obsessively count the number of episcopal seminaries and their dates of foundation as a prime indicator for the diffusion of Tridentine reform therefore arguably miss the point by overlooking the quiet dissemination of that portable seminary – the revised Roman Breviary.

Before going any further, it might be helpful to outline briefly the genesis, structure, and *modus operandi* of the breviary. In essence, it contains the psalms, hymns, lessons, prayers, and responses to be

---

[29] 'ma qual stomacho deve poter più sopportar tante sciochezze et sogni di libri apocriffi con tante bosie et tanta indignità che se chi ne havesse cura mai lo potria tolerar': BAV, MS Barb. lat. 5697, fol. 37r, taken from a letter sent to G. M. Giberti dated 1 Jan. 1533. Cf. G. M. Monti, *Ricerche su Papa Paolo IV Caraffa* (Benevento, 1925), p. 152; G. B. Del Tufo, *Historia della religione de'padri chierici regolari*, 2 vols (Rome, 1609–16), I, pp. 8–16; G. Silos, *Historia clericorum regularium a congregatione condita*, 3 vols (Rome, 1650–6), I, pp. 95–8.

recited at the seven daily offices of matins, lauds, prime, terce, sext, none, vespers, and compline – the so-called canonical hours. Reflecting the Gospel injunction that the whole Christian life should be one of prayer, the offices came to be elaborated, particularly in the monastic context, where they were recited and sung in choir and required the assembly in one place of several service books: the antiphonal (containing the responses), the lectionary (scriptural homiletic and hagiographical readings), the hymnary, and the psalter. As its name suggests, the breviary constituted a slightly abbreviated fusion of these books into a single one in order to facilitate the requirement – initially of the papal chapel in the twelfth century – that religious be able to recite their offices on the move. This requirement was of particular relevance to the mendicant orders, epecially the Franciscans, who did much to diffuse its adoption throughout Christendom.[30]

From relatively early on, to enhance their portability, Tridentine breviaries were split into four smaller, self-contained parts – each of which covered a season of the year, beginning with the feast of St Andrew on 30 November. The first volume for the winter season was prefaced with the papal bull *Quod a nobis*, followed by a set of introductory general instructions of unprecedented thoroughness, known as the *Rubricae generales* (which is sometimes referred to in English as *The Pie* or parti-coloured, owing to the fact that this section of the breviary was usually printed in red and black). These instructions, whose purpose was to facilitate correct co ordination between the constituent parts of the breviary, had been anticipated by the Quiñones breviary, which also provided the basis for no fewer than eighty-seven of the hagiographical readings which were included in the 1568 Tridentine Breviary.[31] After these sections each volume followed the same structure, starting with a calendar of saints together with tables to calculate the dates of the moveable feasts such as Easter. Next there came the psalter or book of psalms together with hymns,

---

[30] E. Cattaneo, *Il Culto cristiano: note storiche*, 2nd edn (Rome, 1983), pp. 237–40; cf. S. I. P. van Dijk, *Sources of the Modern Roman Liturgy: the Ordinals by Haymo of Faversham and Related Documents (1243–1307)*, 2 vols (Leiden, 1963).

[31] According to Righetti (*Manuale di storia liturgica*, 2, p. 673), another source for the general rubric was the *Directorium divini officii* by Ciconiolano which had been approved by Paul III in 1540. For a list of the sources for the hagiographical readings included in the Tridentine Breviary see C. De Smedt, *Introductio generalis ad historiam ecclesiasticam* (Louvain and Paris, 1876), pp. 484–7 (reprinted in S. Bäumer, *Histoire du Bréviaire*, 2 vols (Paris, 1905), 2, pp. 178–80 n.2).

divided according to the days of the week and within each day by the office at which they were to be sung or recited. This was followed by the *Proprium de tempore* (Proper Office of the Season) which, beginning at the first Saturday of Advent, provided prayers, responses, lessons from Scripture, and homilies by the Church Fathers together with indications of the psalms and hymns to be sung for every day of the year – all of which made up the ferial office which was, however, suppressed on Sundays and feast days. After this were provided the generic offices for different categories of saints – for example for virgins, martyrs, or for confessors – who did not have their own dedicated office. Next came that section of the Tridentine Breviary which, as we shall see shortly, received the particular attentions of the reforming commission, the *Proprium sanctorum*, that is to say, the Special Offices of saints to be recited on their feast days in place of the offices given in the Proper Office of the Season. These were arranged consecutively, day by day, month by month. The main text of the breviary closed with an appendix of additional services such as those for the Blessed Virgin Mary and for the Dead.

However, the main point to emphasise here is the kinetic, interactive mode of breviary reading. What is striking is the degree to which the breviary user is frequently required to make connections between the constituent parts of the service book and explains why, by tradition, printed breviaries come to this day with a set of different coloured ribbons to facilitate the marking of several places in the text simultaneously.[32]

*   *   *

This kinetic and fundamentally interactive mode of reading was particularly suitable for accommodating that part of the breviary which has yet to be mentioned, and which is more often than not entirely neglected in accounts of the service book's structure and development. This is the Proper of local saints' offices containing the structure and texts of services for saints who enjoyed either special or exclusive devotion in a particular region or diocese. These Propers

---

[32] For an admirably clear explanation 'How to find the Office for the Day' see ch. 12 of 'The Pie' as given in the English literal translation of the Roman Breviary (incorporating also the changes made by Clement VIII, Urban VIII, and Leo XIII) by John Crichton-Stuart, Marquess of Bute, *The Roman Breviary*, 4 vols, rev. edn (Edinburgh and London, 1908), I, pp. xxxiii–iv.

were inserted at the end of the main breviary text, thereby making the Roman books truly proper in a given place. As the late Neils Rasmussen noted in what is, without doubt, the finest short introduction to the problems and possibilities of liturgical study for this period, these local propers, consisting usually of loose sheets bound at the end of existing breviaries, were rarely catalogued separately and so have remained largely invisible to the scrutiny of subsequent scholars.[33]

They are also extremely rare, as was discovered when trying to locate the complete text of the revised Proper for the church of the North Italian town of Piacenza near Milan, whose 1598 edition provoked an extended three-way correspondence between their author, Pietro Maria Campi (who was under the specific commission of his bishop); the bishop's senior theologian, Daniele Garatola; and members of the Sacred Congregation of Rites and Ceremonies in Rome (whose consultors included Cardinals Baronius and Bellarmine, both of whom were directly involved, at one time or another, in decisions relating to the Proper's revision).[34] This apparently unique survival of such comprehensive documentation enables us to study in some detail the processes whereby the Roman Catholic Church of this period sought to reconcile particular, local devotions with the universalizing and regularizing imperatives of Tridentine liturgy as reflected in its revised office books.

At the outset of the research, primed by the still dominant view of post-Tridentine Catholicism in terms of a centralizing papal monarchy which post-1600 did all it could to stifle the 'true spirit' of the Council – local, diocesan reform – I sought for corroborative evidence.[35] That

[33] N. Rasmussen, 'Liturgy and the liturgical arts', in J. O'Malley, ed., *Catholicism in Early Modern History: a Guide to Research*, Reformation Guides to Research, 2 (St Louis, MI, 1988), pp. 273–97.

[34] The only (incomplete) text of this edition which I have been able to find is in Rome, Biblioteca Vallicelliana, G. 104, fols 314r–46r. The titlepage, colophon, and six pages are missing. Other manuscript material relevant to the Piacentine Proper's revision at the Vallicelliana may be found in MSS H. 5, fols 143r–44r; H. 18, fols 031r–070v; G. 90, fols 264r–86r; G. 104, fols 314r–46r. See also Vatican City, Archivio della Congregazione per le Cause dei Santi (ex-Riti), Positiones decretorum et rescriptorum 1748. For a detailed account of the Piacentine Proper's revision 1598–1610 see Ditchfield, *Liturgy, Sanctity and History*, pp. 96–112.

[35] See, *inter alia*, G. Alberigo, 'The Council of Trent', in O'Malley, ed., *Catholicism in Early Modern History*, pp. 211–26; idem, 'Carlo Borromeo between two models of bishop', in J. M. Headley and J. B. Tomaro, eds, *San Carlo Borromeo: Catholic Reform and Ecclesiastical Politics in the Second Half of the Sixteenth Century* (Washington, DC, Toronto, and London, 1988), pp. 250–63; E. Cochrane (ed. J. Kirshner), *Italy 1530–1630* (London and New York, 1988), pp. 106–64. Although there are some signs of the weakening hold of this orthodoxy (e.g. D.

is to say, I expected to find the Piacentine church locked in an unequal struggle to justify its devotional diversity and local liturgical practices in the face of inflexible, standardizing Roman curial positivism. Instead, what I discovered was something significantly different: a three-way process rather than a two-way one, with the clash of argument not between the Sacred Congregation of Rites in Rome, on the one hand, and Pietro Maria Campi, canon of Piacenza cathedral and author of the revised local Proper on the other. Rather, disputes over the precise manner in which the local saints' offices were to be rewritten so as to bring them into line with Tridentine liturgical norms were between two canons of the cathedral – Campi and the bishop's chief theologian, Daniele Garatola, the latter responsible for ensuring that the Piacentine clergy were suitably equipped for preaching and theological instruction. In view of what has been said above about the didactic role of liturgy, Garatola's involvement is a significant one.

Within the Piacentine pantheon of saints, pride of place went to the fourth-century martyr and member of the Theban Legion, S. Antonino, principal patron of the city and of its first cathedral. His prominence can be seen if we consult the diocese's own breviary, which was traditionally ascribed to St Ambrose's contemporary and correspondent, S. Savino, second bishop of Piacenza, and testified to the city's special liturgical identity. This was reprinted twice during the sixteenth century, in 1503 and again in 1530. No fewer than forty-five lessons had been composed to be read out over the first five days of S. Antonino's octave, at the rate of nine per day. (It must be pointed out that the majority of these were very brief – often being only one or two lines long.)[36] However, in the Piacentine Proper as finally approved in 1610, there were only three, of which only the third dealt exclusively with the saint. What can be said about the criteria employed in this dramatic pollarding operation?

Sella, *Italy in the Seventeenth Century* [London and New York, 1997], esp. pp. 161–87), it has been given a new lease of life by Eamon Duffy in a work which is inevitably destined for the widest possible diffusion: *Saints and Sinners: a History of the Popes* (London and New Haven, CT, 1997), pp. 161–94. For a full consideration of recent and current trends in the historiography of Italian religious history of this period see S. Ditchfield, 'In search of local knowledge: rewriting early modern religious history', *Cristianesimo nella storia*, 18 (1998), pp. 255–96.

[36] *Breviarium divini officii secundum ritum et consuetudinem ecclesiae placentinae approbatum* (Venice, 1530), fols 294v–96v.

To start with, Garatola had considerable room for manoeuvre. The first nine lessons printed in the 1530 Piacentine breviary took the narrative only as far as the Theban Legion's refusal to make a pagan sacrifice. The nine to be read out on the second day were similarly short on specifics and long on hagiographical commonplaces, which here took the form of scarcely individualized miracles carried out by the saint. By contrast, in the three lessons included in the revised local Proper of 1610, the emphasis was on the Theban Legion, whose historical existence was already accepted. The saint's time in Piacenza, his conversion of several of the city's inhabitants, his martyrdom, and the subsequent discovery of his body by S. Savino (who had him translated with much pomp and ceremony to the recently built basilica of S. Vittore – subsequently rededicated to S. Antonino), were despatched in not many more than one hundred words.[37]

During the course of the revision of these lessons it was therefore readily acknowledged that very little was known about the saint, or indeed which saint of that name the frequently unreliable sources referred to. However, in the end, there was little doubt that S. Antonino had enjoyed an unbroken continuity of cult since time immemorial. As Cardinal Bellarmine argued in his report as a member of the commission entrusted with revising the Roman Breviary in 1592: if purely historical criteria were brought to bear the saints' calendar, which has so recently been re-presented with full scholarly apparatus at the command of Pope Gregory XIII as a new edition of the *Martyrologium romanum* in 1584, would almost be emptied at a stroke.[38] Instead, what he and others proposed was that only the most glaring and recent errors should be excised, and that the theological criterion of continuity of cult should be paramount.[39]

In the case of more recent members of Piacenza's pantheon of saints, Campi had more than just liturgical tradition to go on; and his archival detective work, frequently involving correspondence with scholars throughout the Italian peninsula and in visits to Rome, went beyond

---

[37] Vatican City, Archivio della Congregazione per le Cause dei Santi (ex-Riti), Positiones decretorum et rescriptorum 1748, fols 2r–3r, as given in two slightly differing versions approved on 19 April 1608.

[38] 'Quoniam Martyrologium iussu et approbatione Summi pontificis Gregorii XIII jam est editum, non poterunt fortasse sine magno scandalo tot sancti a Martyrologio dimoveri, quot ego dimovendos esse existimarem; id est enim totum fere Martyrologium abolere vel mutare': X.-M. Le Bachelet, *Auctarium Bellarminianum* (Paris, 1913), p. 461.

[39] See ibid., p. 459. Cf. E. A. Ryan, *The Historical Scholarship of Robert Bellarmine* (Louvain, 1936), p. 173.

revising the second nocturn lessons in the Proper to their comprehensive reminting and, on at least two occasions, to their composition from scratch. The most important of these last two concerned Campi's recovery for Piacenza in about 1600 of the cult of S. Corrado Confalonieri, a thirteenth-century hermit who had left Piacenza and gone to live just outside Noto in Sicily where he died and was venerated.[40] Campi was also entirely responsible for establishing that S. Folco Scotti, Bishop of Pavia, had in fact been born in Piacenza and, furthermore, occupied the post of bishop of his birthplace before he moved on to Pavia.[41] Finally, in the case of Bl. Gregory X, Campi went beyond his usual brief to save or relaunch local cults in an attempt to *create* a universal cult of Piacenza's only Pope by getting him canonized. Gregory's cause occupied him for over forty years and entailed five years' residence in Rome. Although unsuccessful during his own lifetime, he left the documentation and the strategy in place to ensure that at least Gregory's local cult would be confirmed by Rome, which it was in 1713.[42]

* * *

The role played by the Roman Congregation in the disputes over the revision of the Piacentine Proper was therefore essentially that of a referee rather than policeman. Certainly the ground rules were set by Rome, but the parties to the dispute willingly brought their case to the Congregation as they were aware that this was the only means permitted by *Quod a nobis* by which local variations to the Roman Breviary could be preserved officially as a particular counterpart to the

---

[40] P. M. Campi, *Vita di S. Corrado eremita* (Piacenza, 1614). For the fullest and most recent life of the saint and history of his cult see F. Balsamo, *S. Corrado di Noto: biografia critica e storia del culto* (Noto, 1991). Cf. F. Balsamo and V. La Rosa, eds, *Corrado Confalonieri: la figura storica, l'immagine e il culto, Atti delle giornate di studio nel VII centenario della nascita, Noto 24–25–26 maggio 1990* (Noto, 1992).

[41] This involved recourse to a full range of sources, from a manuscript copy of S. Folco's sermons held in the Dominican priory of S. Giovanni in Canale to notarial documents held in the archive of the Piacentine church of S. Eufemia where the saint had been provost. For Campi's account of S. Folco's episcopate see P. M. Campi, *Dell'historia ecclesiastica di Piacenza*, 3 vols (Piacenza, 1651–62), 2, pp. 100–15. See also relevant documents which Campi had copied in full from the cathedral archives and printed at the end of vol. 2 (nos. 58, 59, 62 and 64) on pp. 381–5.

[42] For a full account of Campi's campaign see S. Ditchfield, 'How not to be a counter-reformation saint: the attempted canonization of Gregory X, 1622–45', *Papers of the British School at Rome*, 60 (1992), pp. 379–422 (also in a revised and slightly expanded form as ch. 10 in idem, *Liturgy, Sanctity and History*, pp. 212–69).

forms of worship and prayer of universal validity provided by the latter office book.

Further evidence in support of this revisionist thesis may be adduced from the immediate prehistory to the foundation of the Congregation of Rites in 1588. Letters held in the Vatican Library reveal how as early as 1570 individual dioceses from Italy and elsewhere were seeking official Roman approval of their local liturgies.[43] A key figure here was Guglielmo Sirleto, from 1572 Cardinal-librarian. This is reflected in the number of requests which turn up in his *epistolario*.[44] Sirleto had been involved in considering liturgical reform during the pontificate of Paul IV Caraffa, as well as acting as a member of the commission responsible for revising the Roman Breviary under his two successors, Pius IV and Pius V.[45] Such experience made him well-qualified to deal with requests the tenor of which may be seen from the following, representative example. This is a letter addressed to Sirleto from the Cardinal-Bishop of Vercelli, Guido Ferrero, and dated 18 December 1570, scarcely two years after the publication of the Tridentine Breviary:

> From among all the other needs and requirements of my church, I would have favoured by Our Lord and by your authority . . . the reform of the Vercellese breviary which it behoves me to carry out. It comes to my notice that the new Roman one is better and that other prelates whose churches have their own customs have [reformed theirs]. However, I beg you, most illustrious sir, that you speak with His Holiness so that he might issue a brief or letter – whichever would be more expedient – requiring that my church follow the new breviary, adding only the feasts and octaves of my predecessors S. Eusebio . . . S. Emiliano, S. Honorato . . . and S. Pietro.[46]

---

[43] The nineteenth-century scholar J. Schmid listed some 22 Italian dioceses which during the 1570s and 1580s sought official Roman recognition of their cults: J. Schmid, 'Weitere Beiträge zur Geschichte des römischen Breviers und Missale', *TQ*, 67 (1885), pp. 468–87, 624–37. The checklist for Italian dioceses is on pp. 624–7.

[44] E.g. a single MS, BAV, Vat. lat. 6191 (parts I and II), contains letters relating to requests from the dioceses of Squillace, Naples, and Bologna.

[45] On Sirleto the best monograph is still G. Denzler, *Kardinal Guglielmo Sirleto (1514–1585): Leben und Werk; ein Beitrag zur Nachtridentinischen Reform* (Munich, 1964); but now see also P. E. Commodaro, 'Il cardinale Guglielmo Sirleto, 1514–1585', *La provincia di Catanzaro*, 3 (1985) with its useful appendix of documents.

[46] 'Vorria tra li altri occorrenzi et ordinationi della mia chiesa esser da N[ostri] S[ig]n[o]ri favorito et dal autorità di V[ostro] S[ignore] Ill[ustrissi]ma aiutato alla riforma che mi

The following spring the bishop sent Sirleto a copy of the revised office for S. Eusebio with a covering letter which expressed the sincere hope that, in the event that his cathedral chapter appealed to the pope against the bishop's action, His Holiness would support him, 'since with uninterrupted and toilsome residence I do everything for the greater glory of God and of his church as it is required'.[47]

Here we have a local bishop not only deferring to Rome but requesting the latter's help in the implementation of liturgical reform. This was particularly the case when the bishop had to deal with opposition from *within* his own diocese, when clerics bridled at such episcopal tinkering with long-established local tradition. Complete co-operation with Rome on matters liturgical – and the sensitivity of local clergy in such matters – was also the keynote to a letter written by Agostino Valier, Bishop of Verona and future biographer of S. Carlo Borromeo, on 17 November 1574. In it, the Bishop enclosed a report drawn up by some of his priests with regard to the lessons of local bishop-saints whose feasts had been celebrated for more than the 200-year minimum requirement set out by *Quod a nobis*. A certain Don Curzio – who on the evidence of Sirleto's *epistolario* appears to have been widely active as reviser of hagiographical lessons – had responded to this report by recommending that these particular lessons should be standardized ('fare simili') and printed separately from the Roman Breviary itself. Valier then wanted Sirleto's advice as to how he might make these recommendations more acceptable to his local priests whom he regarded with some indulgence 'since they are acting out of simple devotion'.[48]

convien far del Breviario Vercellese, acciò si venga al osservazioni de nuovo Romano come si vede esser meglio et lo fanno altri Prelati che hanno le chiese con loro solo costumi. Però supplico V[ostro] S[ignoria] Ill[ustrissi]ma che mi faccia parola con S[ua] S[anti]ta la qual si digni[sic] ordinarmi per una sua lettera o breve secondo sarà più espedienti che nella mia chiesa si osservi il detto nuovo breviario aggiungendoli solamente la festa et ottava di S[an]t[o] Eusebio . . . S. Emiliano, S. Honorato . . . e S. Pietro tutti miei precedessori': BAV, MS Vat. lat. 6181, fol. 271r. The letter is dated 18 Dec. 1570.

[47] 'poich' con la continua et laboriosa residenza tutto operò a maggior honor di Dio e . . . della chiesa come conviene': ibid., fol. 347r, dated 23 May 1571.

[48] 'Mando a V[ostro] S[ignoria] Ill[ustrissi]ma um memoriale datomi da alcuni buoni sacerdoti in proposito delle lettioni dell S[an]ti vescovi di questa città le feste de quali si celebrano già duecento anni o più. Essi dicono che M. Curtio deputato alla riforma del breviario ha loro risposto che si dovevano fare simili lettioni et farli stampare separate dal breviario perciò io presi la fatica. Ma in tutto mi rimetto alla volunta di V[ostro] S[ignoria] voglio ben pregar VS Illma a farmi scrivere risolutamente quanto ho a fare in questo negotio acciò ch'io posso in qualche modo dar satisfactione a quelli del clero in quanto si movino da pura divotione': BAV, MS Vat. lat. 6192, fol. 139r. There is also the well-known example of

Viewed from this perspective, the eventual formalizing of this process, with the foundation of the Sacred Congregation of Rites and Ceremonies in 1588, should be seen as the papal response to a frequently embattled episcopacy rather than as the setting up of an interfering watchdog intent on imposing a standardized policy which would not take local needs and priorities into account. Something of the perceived usefulness of the Congregation to contemporaries as they sought to square their local practices with the universalizing models offered by the revised Roman service books may be gauged from the fact that the standard (but by no means exhaustive) nineteenth-century printed collections of the Congregation's formal replies to queries concerning the full range of liturgical activity down to 1887 – not just relating to local propers – run to no fewer than 8,709.[49] So much for the claim that the Roman Catholic liturgical life of the post-Tridentine centuries was characterized by a one-way, top-down and, above all, static papal hegemony.

*   *   *

Let us now turn to consider more briefly the second sense in which Tridentine liturgy can be given back its history. This centres on the collective achievement of Italy's local Baronios in preserving the particularities of their churches' devotional practices in the face of the universalizing norms of Tridentine Breviary.

While in a liturgical context, in accordance with the decisions refereed by the Sacred Congregation of Rites, Pietro Maria Campi of Piacenza reined in his pious local patriotism, outside it his treatment of the life of his city's principal patron saint, S. Antonino, exercised no

---

the diocese of Bologna where the bishop, Gabriele Paleotti, had commissioned the leading late-humanist scholar Carlo Sigonio to revise the hagiographical lessons for the feast of the town's patron, S. Petronio. Here again, the watchword was collaboration rather than conflict and confrontation. See Ditchfield, *Liturgy, Sanctity and History*, pp. 63–6. Cf. P. Prodi, *Il Cardinale Gabriele Paleotti (1522–1597)*, 2 vols (Rome, 1959–67), 2, pp. 246–8.

[49] For the fullest edition see A. Gardellini, *Decreta authentica congregationis sacrorum rituum*, 3rd edn, 4 vols (Rome, 1856–8) plus 6 vols of *Supplementa*, ed. W. Mühlbauer (Munich, 1863–85). This contains 5,993 decrees but should be consulted together with the *Analecta iuris pontificii*, 7–8 (1864–6), fasc. 57–9, 66–8, which contain a further 2,716 issued between 1588 and 1700. The successive editions of *Decreta* were catalogued anonymously in 'De sacra rituum congregationis decretorum collectionibus', *Ephemerides liturgicae*, 44 (1930), pp. 433–48, and in 1954 by F. R. McManus, *The Congregation of Rites*, Catholic University of America Canon Law Studies, 352 (Washington, DC, 1954). There is also a useful (though inevitably incomplete) collection arranged by subject: P. Martinucci, *Manuale decretorum sacrae rituum congregationis* (Ratisbon, 1873).

such restraint.[50] Here the Holy Office enjoyed jurisdiction, yet so long as an author prefaced each volume with the disclaimer that the terms 'saint' and 'blessed' were not being used in the official, liturgical sense of the word, much greater latitude was permitted because privately, outside the context of public liturgy, one could venerate whomsoever one pleased. Hence, Campi drew fully on the traditional account of Antonino's life as preserved in the now censored Piacentine Breviary of 1530, and framed it in terms of the timeworn Ciceronian topos of history as *magistra vitae, lux veritatis* (*De Oratore*, II, ix, 36), before going on to take up the greater part of his text with the careful enumeration of relics, privileges, and indulgence enjoyed by the church where the saint's body lay.

This was the first of several separately published lives of local saints which Campi wrote.[51] Each of them betrayed its liturgical origins by including the text of its offices together with a comprehensive history of the cult and miracles. Collectively they consituted, to use a contemporary term, a local 'school of sanctity' (*scola di santità*) which set out a range of ideal types to inspire their audience: in S. Antonino, the early Christian martyr; in S. Corrado Confalonieri, the aristocratic hermit; in S. Franca Vitalta, the well-born nun; in S. Raimondo Palmerio, the lay helper of the urban poor; in Bl. Gregory X, the saintly pontiff; and in Margherita Antoniazzi, a visionary shepherdess. In this way, universal virtues were particularized in local saints with whom their compatriots could more easily identify. However, in his untiring efforts to match hagiographical content with local context and appropriate form, Campi was merely one example of a wider trend.

For the leading hagiographer of the Kingdom of Naples during the late sixteenth-century, Paolo Regio, 'these saints of ours intercede now more than ever in heaven before the Protector of the world on behalf of their fellow countrymen'.[52] Similarly, in the words of Campi's Umbrian

---

[50] P. M. Campi, *Vita di S. Antonino martire* (Piacenza, 1603). In the same year Campi also published a catalogue of the spiritual and material riches of the church where the saint's body lay, the misleadingly entitled *Insignium gestorum S. Antonini martyris Placentiae tutelaris*, out of whose 35 pages only 3 were devoted to an account of the saint's life.

[51] *Vita di S. Corrado eremita* (Piacenza, 1614); *Vita di S. Raimondo Palmerio* (Piacenza, 1618); *Vita di S. Franca Vitalta* (Piacenza, 1618); *Apologia dell'innocente e santa vita del glorioso pontefice Gregorio il decimo* (Piacenza, 1651; Latin edn, Rome, 1655); and *Vita di Margarita da Cantiga per cognome detta divota* (Piacenza, 1877).

[52] 'questi nostri santi intercedono ora più che mai in cielo presso il Protettore del mondo a nome del loro compatrioti': P. Regio, *Vite de'sette santi protettori di Napoli* (Naples,

counterpart, Lodovico Jacobilli, near the close of the latter's 1,800-page survey of his province's holy men and women published in 1661,

> In this school and mine of sanctity, each in his own vocation, has been able to gain from frequent reading of the histories of the lives of these Umbrian saints an abundance of most perfect actions to imitate and benefit from. So much more easily [can we do so] owing to the fact that the authors of these actions were made of the same stuff as us, were from the same region and province (or at least had died there), and flourished with sanctity at every age and in every century and that, furthermore, they unceasingly help us in Heaven with their prayers and intercession.[53]

This passage comes immediately after an eight-page section in which Jacobilli matched Umbrian saints to the full range of conditions of life, from servants to courtiers, criminals to popes. In common with countless other Italian hagiographers from this period, Jacobilli was also author of a history of his diocese of Nocera published in 1653.[54] Having surveyed the town's past, its buildings, and a selection of its famous citizens in Book One, Jacobilli devoted the entire contents of Book Two to an annotated episcopal catalogue beginning with S. Crespoldo da Gerusalemme, disciple of St Paul. It is therefore appropriate that his volume was prefaced by S. Carlo Borromeo's statement concerning the important normative role played by ecclesiastical history in the restoration of Catholic practice to the purity of the early apostolic Church, which had been included in the Constitutions of the widely-diffused and correspondingly influential Third Provincial Council of Milan of 1573:[55]

1579), preface. For a fuller appreciation of Regio's importance as the pre-eminent hagiographer of this period in the Kingdom of Naples – he wrote no fewer than 21 volumes which were published between 1573 and 1612 – see J.-M. Sallmann, *Naples et ses saints à l'âge baroque (1540–1750)* (Paris, 1994), index.

53 'In questa miniera e scòla [*sic*] di santità ciascuno adunque nella propria vocatione è stato procuri con la frequente lettione dell'Historia delle vite de'santi umbri di trovar abbondanza di attioni perfettissime da immitare e di approfitarsene; tanto maggiormente, che gli operatori di esse furono composti della medesima massa che siamo noi, e della medesima regione e provincia; ò vissuti, ò morti in essa e hanno fiorito in santità in ogni età e secolo, e questi del continuo ci aiutano in cielo con le loro orationi e intercessioni': L. Jacobilli, *Vite de'Santi e Beati dell'Umbria e di quelli corpi de'quali riposano in essa provincia*, 3 vols (Foligno, 1647–61), 3, p. 540.

54 *Nocera nell'Umbria e sua diocesi e cronologia de'vescovi di essa città* (Foligno, 1653).

55 E. Cattaneo, 'La singolare fortuna degli "Acta Ecclesiae Mediolanensis"', *La Scuola Cattolica*, 111 (1983), pp. 191–217.

The bishop, [as holder of] an office instituted at the very beginning of the history of the Church, should diligently collect together the names, character and pastoral actions of his predecessors, and he should make certain that all these things should be written down, arranged in order and put into a certain book so that the memory should be conserved of those things which have been done or instituted by those bishops so that they [the books] should be of perpetual use and assistance in the good governance of that church.[56]

This passage enjoyed the status of an *imprimatur* in the prefaces of countless volumes of ecclesiastical history published on into the eighteenth century from Palermo to Paris.[57]

Pietro Maria Campi's *Dell'historia ecclesiastica di Piacenza*, published posthumously in three volumes from 1651 to 1662, may thus be seen as the typical product of a Tridentine ecclesiastical scholar. It was also typical in its deployment of the full range of available historiographical genres to describe and justify its local devotional traditions. Even a cursory glance at its title page reveals Campi's deployment of at least five distinct genres, all founded on a solid Baronian annal structure divided into episcopates. They are: municipal chronicle, collective saints' lives, *viri illustri*/family history, the *registrum magnum* municipal collections of privileges, and the *descriptio urbis* catalogue of material and spiritual wealth.[58] When the preservation of the liturgical particular became a burning issue during the century or so after the

---

[56] 'Episcopus id quod ab initio nascentis ecclesiae institutum fuit, ut rerum episcopalium studio curaque gestarum monimenta existerent, conquiri diligentissime curet; tam singulorum episcoporum qui praecesserunt nomina, genus et pastorales eorumdem actiones. Quae omnia litteris consignari, ordineque conscripta in librum certum referri curet, ut eorum memoria conservetur, et quae ab eodem acta vel instituta sunt, ad aliquam ecclesiasticae disciplinae normam perpetuo usui esse possint atque adiumento in illa ecclesia bene gerenda': *Acta Ecclesiae Mediolanensis* (Milan, 1582), fol. 46v.

[57] See, e.g., the preface to R. Pirri, *Sicilia sacra*, 3 vols (Palermo, 1644–7), I, sig. 1r, and G. and S. Sainte-Marthe (rev. D. de Sainte-Marthe, completed by B. Hauréau), *Gallia cristiana*, 16 vols (Paris, 1715–1865), I, first page of the preface (note a).

[58] *Dell'historia ecclesiastica di Piacenza di Pietro Maria Campi Canonico piacentino; nella quale si spiegano le attioni de'Santi, de'Beati, e de'Vescovi della città di Piacenza, e l'antichissima immunità, e giurisditione di quella chiesa, con le fondationi di molti luoghi sacri, et insieme le varie donationi, e gratie riportate da'Sommi Pontefici, Imperadori, Re, e Principi; e si fa anche mentione di molte Famiglie, Huomini Illustri, e maggiori successi d'Italia; con l'origine de'nomi de'Villaggi, Terre, e Castelle del Piacentino. E nel fine l'Historia antichissima, ne mai più uscita in luce della fondatione della Città stessa di Tito Omusio Piacentino, con un Registro de'Privilegi, Bolle e altre Scritture latine citate in quest'Opera con più Tavole copiosissime.*

Council of Trent, local ecclesiastical *eruditi* like Campi had a long-established multi-genre tradition to draw on.[59]

Moreover, as should by now be clear, it was in the very nature of Tridentine ecclesiastical erudition – in its attempt to justify local traditions – to relate the particular to the universal and vice versa. Hence the need for Campi to frame the particular privileges and traditions of his *patria* in the context of a comprehensive narrative structure backed up by registers of documents and a range of supplementary treatises; the heterogeneous whole being bound together for the reader at the end of each volume by no fewer than five thematic indexes.[60]

*   *   *

This discussion of ecclesiastical erudition and its role in the preservation of the liturgically particular can end by briefly drawing attention to the collective achievement of the Italian peninsula's local Baronios. This may be carried out most easily by looking briefly at a work which, because it is most often consulted in its enlarged, second edition published at Venice in 1717–22, has perhaps not been viewed in its proper context. This is Abbot Ferdinando Ughelli's nine-volume *Italia sacra*, first published in 1644–62, which provided annotated episcopal catalogues for 320 of Italy's mainland dioceses.[61] As such it constituted the first comprehensive framework of ecclesiastical history truly Italian in geographical scope and complemented the similar survey for France, *Gallia cristiana*, whose first edition, in four volumes, was published in 1656.[62] What has also never been commented on until now is the fact

---

[59] For a fuller discussion of the Campi's sources for his *Dell'historia ecclesiastica di Piacenza*, see Ditchfield, *Liturgy, Sanctity and History*, pp. 298–301.

[60] 1. 'Delle chiese e monasteri dentro la città di Piacenza'; 2. 'Delle chiese e monasteri sú la diocesi'; 3. 'Delle famiglie di Piacenza nominate'; 4. 'Delle cose notabili'; 5. 'De'villaggi, castelle e terre del Piacentino'.

[61] *Italia sacra sive de episcopis italiae et insularum adiacentium, rebusque ab iis praeclare gestis deducta serie ad nostram usque aetatem opus singulare. In quo ecclesiarum origines, urbium conditiones, principum dontationes, recondita monumenta in lucem proferentur*. Vol. 1 came out in 1644; vols 2–3 in 1647; vol. 4 in 1652; vol. 5 in 1653; vols 6–7 in 1658, and vols 8–9 in 1662. All volumes were published in Rome: vols 1–3 'Apud B. Tanum' and the remainder by Vincenzo Mascardi.

[62] For a fuller account of what follows see Ditchfield, *Liturgy, Sanctity and History*, ch. 12, esp. pp. 331–51. Except for the pioneering work of Giorgio Morelli – in particular his 'L'abate Ferdinando Ughelli nel terzo centenario della morte (1670–1970)', *Strenna dei Romanisti*, 33 (1972), pp. 246–50, and the same author's more recent contribution cited in n.63 below – the only other recent scholarly discussion of Ughelli remains D. Hay, 'Scholars

that *Italia sacra* was not the work of a single scholar.[63] Rather, it was the result of extensive collaboration with correspondents the length and breadth of the peninsula, as can be seen from Ughelli's letter collection now to be consulted in the *fondo Barberiniano* at the Vatican Library.[64] The 1,533 letters from 438 correspondents were responses to what appears to have been a systematic campaign on Ughelli's part to solicit details about the history of individual dioceses. However, just as it is inaccurate to see Tridentine liturgical reform simply in terms of the imposition of universal norms on local churches by Rome, so the traffic of information was not just one way. There are just as many letters offering information about dioceses Ughelli had yet to write about, and corrections about those he had already written about, as letters from those seeking information or guidance from the scholar whose post as Abbot of the Cistercian abbey of Tre Fontane on the southern outskirts of Rome placed him close to the city's unrivalled library and archival riches.[65]

*   *   *

Some final thoughts can be devoted to dealing with what might be called the 'so what' factor. Even if we recognize that Tridentine worship had a history after all, and that attempts to preserve the particular devotions and integrate them into the universalizing norms represented by the reformed service books such as the Roman Breviary simultaneously enriched local devotions and historical scholarship in general, how does this help us to answer the $64,000 question that has exercised ecclesiastical historians of early modern Roman Catholicism

and ecclesiastical history in the early modern period: the influence of Ferdinando Ughelli', in P. Mack and M. C. Jacobs, eds, *Politics and Culture in Early Modern Europe: Essays in Honour of H. G. Koenigsberger* (Cambridge, 1987), pp. 215–27.

[63] Although the ever perceptive Tiraboschi had noted that the uneven quality of *Italia sacra* derived from Ughelli's need to rely on others. See Tiraboschi, *Storia della letteratura italiana*, 8/ii, p. 145.

[64] For an invaluable handlist of correspondents from this *epistolario* to which I am much indebted see G. Morelli, 'Monumenta Ferdinandi Ughelli, Barb. lat. 3204–3249', in *Miscellanea bibliothecae apostolicae vaticanae, IV*, Studi e Testi 338 (Vatican City, 1990), pp. 244–80.

[65] Something of the quantity of material which Ughelli was sent by local correspondents after the publication of his original accounts of dioceses may be seen by looking at the appendices to vols 2–9 of the 1st edn of *Italia sacra*. That to vol. 2, for example, ran to over 90 folio columns (993–1084). This material was subsequently integrated by the editor Coleti into the main body of Ughelli's text which he revised for the 2nd edn, published in 10 vols (Venice, 1717–22).

more or less constantly since the closure of the Second Vatican Council in 1965 clearly inaugurated a new era in the Church's history: how long was the Tridentine reformation?

The current orthodoxy here is still that sketched by John Bossy in his postscript to H. Outram Evennett's 1951 Birkbeck lectures, *The Spirit of the Counter-Reformation*. According to Bossy, the true spirit of the Catholic Reformation – centred on the pastoral office of the bishop as initiator of diocesan reform – was crushed by the papal monarchy in the early seventeenth century so that by the death of Urban VIII in 1644

> the moment would seem to have passed when Catholicism could have established itself at any depth in the heart of the rising civilization of Northern Europe. A hundred and fifty years of crippling immobility were to ensue, before, ironically, the progress of industrial change presented the papacy with a windfall which it had not entirely deserved and showed little imagination in exploiting.[66]

This Gibbonesque judgement has since been developed and amplified, particularly in Italy, where Giuseppe Alberigo has predated the death of the Tridentine Reformation by almost half a century to the pontificate of Paul V. Paolo Prodi has meanwhile painted an enormously influential portrait of the papal prince which bears more than a passing resemblance to Machiavelli's secular counterpart.[67] Even scholars less preoccupied with laying the ghosts of Italian church–state politics from Pius IX to John XXIII, such as Laurie Nussdorfer in her fine study of civic politics in the Rome of Urban VIII, leave readers with the impression that the institutional heart of the Roman Catholic Church was spiritually as well as financially bankrupt by the close of Urban's pontificate.[68]

However, perhaps we should spend less time writing 'decline and

[66] H. O. Evennett (ed. with a postscript by J. Bossy), *The Spirit of the Counter-Reformation* (Cambridge, 1968), p. 145.

[67] G. Alberigo, 'Carlo Borromeo come modello di vescovo nella chiesa post-tridentina', *Rivista storica italiana*, 79 (1967), pp. 1031–52; idem, 'Carlo Borromeo between two models of bishop', in Headley and Tomaro, *San Carlo Borromeo*, pp. 250–63; P. Prodi, *Il Sovrano pontefice. Un corpo e due anime: la monarchia papale nella prima età moderna* (Bologna, 1982). For a brilliant critique of this last work see the review by D. Fenlon, *The Scottish Journal of Theology*, 44 (1991), pp. 120–7.

[68] L. Nussdorfer, *Civic Politics in the Rome of Urban VIII* (Princeton, NJ, 1992).

fall' scenarios for the papacy and its bureaucracy in Rome (in which one historian has even come up with an unpleasant-sounding diagnosis which he calls 'the post-Tridentine syndrome'), and expend less energy measuring the slowness of the reception of Tridentine reforms as reflected, for example, in the infrequency of diocesan synods and in the fact that Trent's target of a seminary in every diocese was barely reached by the time Napoleon's armies cross the Alps.[69] If we did so and emptied our heads just for a moment of all the historiographical clutter that increases at an exponential rate, we might be able to hear the murmured invocations of the faithful kneeling before the shrine of their local patron saint, or the barely audible mumbling of a priest or devout lay person bent over their breviary, and so witness the prayer life of the Church sustained across the centuries by a liturgical continuum whose readings appealed to John Henry Newman precisely because they were 'very unexciting, grave and simple'.[70]

University of York

[69] H. Gross, *Rome in the Age of the Enlightenment: the Post-Tridentine Syndrome and the Ancien Regime* (Cambridge, 1990). The emphasis of much recent writing about the post-tridentine Roman Catholic Church has been on the slowness of reform and the necessity of adopting a long periodization (preferably at least down to the end of the eighteenth century): e.g. Gentilcore, *From Bishop to Witch*; Sallmann, *Naples et ses saints*; A. Borromeo, 'I vescovi italiani e l'applicazione del concilio di Trento', in C. Mozzarelli and D. Zardin, eds, *I Tempi del Concilio: religione, cultura e società nell'Europa tridentina* (Rome, 1997), pp. 27–105.

[70] *The Letters and Diaries of John Henry Newman*, ed. C. S. Dessain *et al.* (London and Oxford, 1961–, in progress), 6, p. 46: letter of 25 March 1837 to Henry Wilberforce. Cf. D. Withey, *John Henry Newman: the Liturgy and the Breviary – their Influence on his Life as an Anglican* (London, 1992), pp. 23–4.

FROM DAVID'S PSALMS TO WATTS'S HYMNS: THE DEVELOPMENT OF HYMNODY AMONG DISSENTERS FOLLOWING THE TOLERATION ACT

by DAVID L. WYKES

THE introduction of hymns and hymn-singing has been described as one of the greatest contributions made by dissent to English worship.[1] Yet, with the exception of specialist studies by hymnologists, church historians have largely ignored eighteenth-century hymns and hymn-singing, though it is clear they represented a powerful and popular source of contemporary religious expression. Hymns, that is compositions which depart too far from Scripture to be called paraphrases, have been one of the most effective mediums of religious thought and feeling, second only to the Bible in terms of their influence. The only recent academic studies have been in English Literature, where hymns have been examined as literary texts for their poetic value.[2] As a consequence neither the historical context of the development of the hymn in the decades following the 1689 Toleration Act, nor the liturgical significance of their introduction to public worship, has been addressed.

Although it is commonly held that 'the daring transition from psalm to paraphrase to hymn' was made by Isaac Watts with the publication of his book of hymns and psalms in 1707,[3] it is clear from the evidence for Leicester and elsewhere that the singing of non-scriptural texts in public by congregations was already gaining acceptance by the first decade of the eighteenth century. An account of the clerk of the joint Presbyterian and Independent Meeting in Leicester being tricked into 'lining out' a popular ballad instead of the intended hymn provides an early example of hymn-singing by a major provincial congregation before the publication of Watts's first collection. It was customary for the clerk of the Leicester Meeting to 'line out' the hymn, two lines at a

---

[1] M. Watts, *The Dissenters*, 2 vols (Oxford, 1978), 1, p. 308.

[2] M. F. Marshall and J. Todd, *English Congregational Hymns in the Eighteenth Century* (Lexington, KY, 1982); D. Davie, *The Eighteenth-Century Hymn in England* (Cambridge, 1993). J. R. Watson, *The English Hymn: a Critical and Historical Study* (Oxford, 1997), appeared after this paper had been completed.

[3] Davies, *Worship*, 3, p. 34.

time, from a manuscript text. The boys who were catechized by the minister on the Saturday morning,

> acquainted with the practice of laying the hymns on the clerk's desk that were to be sung the following day, contrived to put in their place the old song of Chevy Chase. After the Scriptures had been read, the clerk gave out, in a sonorous voice,
>
> God prosper long our noble king,
> Our lives and safetyes all;
>
> upon which the minister, leaning over the pulpit, cried 'John, John, you must be wrong'. 'No, master', replied the clerk, looking up, 'it is so', and stoutly began the tune, the congregation joining heartily. But upon coming to the third and fourth lines,
>
> A woefull hunting once there did,
> In Chevy Chase befall:
>
> The reverend pastor cried, 'Stop, stop, let me see it'. John having handed up the paper, the cheat was discovered.[4]

The account of this incident, which was published by William Gardiner in his discursive memoirs *Music and Friends* in the late 1830s, provides an early example of hymn-singing by a major provincial congregation before the practice became more widespread following the publication of Watts's collection of hymns. Gardiner's account of the clerk being tricked into 'lining out' a popular ballad instead of the intended hymn is independently corroborated by William Bickerstaffe, the Under-Usher at the Grammar School in Leicester. Bickerstaffe's account also discloses that the incident took place before the new meeting-house was built in Butt Close Lane in 1708.[5] This paper seeks to examine both the factors behind the introduction of hymn-singing and the history of its adoption by dissenting congregations.

* * *

---

[4] William Gardiner, *Music and Friends*, 2 vols (London, 1838), 1, pp. 1–3.

[5] Oxford, Bodleian Library, MS Eng. misc. e. 257, Antiquarian notes and drafts of letters of William Bickerstaffe (1728–89), fol. 154v: 'The Dissenting meeting house, was the Barn in Bonners or Mill Lane ye Horspool street, where the clarke began to sing chevy chase.' Bickerstaffe presumably had the account from his mother who was a member of the Great Meeting congregation during the ministry (c.1709–29) of Thomas Gee. See J. Nichols, *The History and Antiquities of the County of Leicester*, 4 vols in 8 pts (London, 1795–1811), 1 pt 2, p. 315 n.3.

Hymn-singing, as distinct from psalm-singing, was introduced by dissenters into their regular worship in the period after the 1689 Toleration Act, and was adopted rapidly from the beginning of the eighteenth century. It has been suggested that the practice of hymn-singing was a consequence of the new freedom enjoyed by dissenters no longer inhibited by the threat of persecution from advertising their presence.[6] Much more significantly, it was a major period of innovation and development in religious practice and congregational organization for dissenters. In 1689, with the advent of toleration, dissent was emerging from nearly three decades of persecution, which, if not continuous, had at times been extremely fierce, particularly during the early 1680s. This persecution had clearly hindered efforts by dissenters to maintain services and indeed to develop regular forms of worship. Many nonconformist groups had been scattered by the intense persecution which followed the Exclusion Crisis, re-establishing their meetings only after James II had issued his Declaration of Indulgence in April 1687. The twenty-five-year period following the 1689 Toleration Act, therefore, witnessed a remarkable period of transformation and saw the development of dissent from a series of harassed and often informal meetings into settled congregations. Dissent was no longer confined to an illegal, twilight existence, but had at last the opportunity to develop and grow. The permanent features of congregational organization associated with modern dissent, notably the establishment of regular services and a system of church government, the appointment of a minister, the acquisition of endowments and a building in which to worship, came only with the removal of the legal threat to nonconformists worshipping in public. As a result dissenters no longer had to rely upon a snatched sermon by a visiting preacher, but could maintain regular Sabbath services and week-day exercises.[7] It is clear, however, that there was very little uniform religious practice among dissenters, even if services usually had a common content of Scripture-readings, extempore prayers, and psalm-singing in addition to the sermon, which remained the principal element with discourses often lasting an hour.

In November 1689 Robert Kirk, a Scottish episcopalian minister on a visit to London, attended the services of a number of leading

---

[6] Watts, *Dissenters*, 1, p. 308; Davies, *Worship*, 2, p. 274.
[7] See D. L. Wykes, ' "The Settling of Meetings and the Preaching of the Gospel": the development of the dissenting interest after toleration', *JURCHS*, 5 (1993), pp. 127–45.

nonconformist ministers, including Richard Baxter, William Bates, and Daniel Burgess. It is clear there was little uniformity even amongst the Presbyterians in the pattern of services as Kirk himself noted: 'Not any two Presbyterian preachers do I find keep one way. Mr Baxter reads the scriptures and preaches. Dr Bates only has one sermon and two prayers. Mr Burgess lectures, preaches and sings [the] Doxology.'

Kirk only recorded attending one Congregational meeting in Aldersgate Street where George Cockayn was minister. Cockayn had 'no psalms before or after sermon'.[8] The New England Puritan Samuel Sewell was also in London in 1689. He attended Dr Annesley's meeting in Little St Helens, where he received the Lord's Supper. He later attended a Fast kept at Annesley's meeting: 'they began with singing and sang 4 or 5 times.' Services appear to have been little different in the major provincial meetings such as Coventry which Sewell visited.[9] Psalms and paraphrases appear to have been sung regularly by Presbyterians in public. There are no contemporary references to the singing of hymns, though the publication of printed collections as early as 1692 suggests they must already have been in use.

*   *   *

Before the introduction of hymn-singing only metrical versions and paraphrases of the psalms were used in public worship. The strength of psalmody in England was a result of the insistence by Protestant reformers that Scripture was the only language of praise allowed in divine worship, a view which was to dominate the employment of religious song until the early eighteenth century. To many the Bible was not only divinely inspired, but contained the songs of David himself. Furthermore, the language of the Old Testament, with its war-like imagery and relentless onslaught against God's foes, suited seventeenth-century Puritans admirably, particularly during the Civil War when Parliament's enemies were seen as God's as well.[10] The strength of metrical versions was a result of the popularity of the literal translations made by Thomas Sternhold and John Hopkins. The first

---

[8]   D. Maclean and N. G. Brett-James, 'London in 1689–90', *Transactions of the London and Middlesex Archaeological Society*, ns 7 (1934), pp. 143–5, 148–50.

[9]   *The Diary of Samuel Sewall 1674–1729*, ed. M. and H. Thomas, 2 vols (New York, 1973), I, pp. 208–9, 214, 218, 226.

[10]   E. Routley, *Hymns and Human Life* (London, 1952), pp. 52, 59; Davies, *Worship*, 2, pp. 269–70.

complete edition of their *Whole Book of Psalms*, published in 1562 and subsequently known as the 'Old Version', remained the authoritative text for more than a century. In addition to their fidelity to Scripture, the metrical psalms of Sternhold and Hopkins had the advantage of being written in easily memorized stanzas to simple ballad tunes in common metre that the whole congregation could sing.[11]

If the metrical psalms met the needs of the godly of the seventeenth century, the versions available were increasingly out of step with those of the eighteenth. Existing translations of the psalms upheld the principle of literal exactness to the original texts, but it often proved impossible to render Hebrew into English metres. The results were frequently unfortunate because of the forced rhymes, awkward inversions, and contorted phrases needed to make the translations fit the metre. The poor quality of the language of Sternhold and Hopkins's version was compounded by the limited variations in the tune and metre. Of the 150 psalms found in the 'Old Version', 134 were in common metre.[12] The uniformity of the English common metre had proved of great practical value in helping congregations to sing together without assistance, but inevitably the predictable stresses of the metre led to monotony. Increasingly, as Richard Baxter recognized, 'the ear desireth greater melody than . . . strict Versions will allow'.[13] The practice of the psalms being 'lined out' by the clerk added to the laboured, halting phraseology of the original. More serious than the dreariness of metrical psalmody was the inappropriate imagery and language of many of the psalms and the complete absence of references to the New Testament Christ. As Watts himself asked his reader, had there not been many occasions when

> your Spirits [have] taken Wing, and mounted up to God and Glory with the Song of David on your Tongue? But on a sudden the Clerk has proposed the next Line to your Lips . . . with Confessions of Sins which you never committed, . . . cursing such Enemies as you never had, giving Thanks for such Victories as you

---

[11] For an account of the history and complex relationship between the different editions, see R. Illing, 'The English metrical Psalter of the Reformation', *Musical Times*, 128 (1987), pp. 517–21; N. Temperley, *The Music of the English Parish Church*, 2 vols (Cambridge, 1979), I, p. 76.

[12] Routley, *Hymns*, p. 55; Davies, *Worship*, 2, pp. 278–9.

[13] *Mr Richard Baxter's Paraphrase on the Psalms of David in Metre, with other Hymns* (London, 1692), preface, sig. 5.

never obtained, or leading you to speak in your own Persons of Things, Places and Actions, that you never knew.[14]

The deficiencies of the 'Old Version' encouraged other editions, but none of them proved to have any lasting value, being too defective in metre and vulgar in style. Sternhold and Hopkins's monopoly in the Church of England was eventually challenged by Tate and Brady's *New Version of the Psalms of David*, published in 1696. The main competitors of the 'Old Version' amongst Puritans and dissenters, however, were the *Scottish Psalter* (1564) revised in English common metre in 1650, and William Barton's *Book of Psalms* (1644; fourth edition 1654) and his *Psalms and Hymns* (1651).[15] There is evidence that Barton's editions were fairly widely adopted by dissenters, certainly there are references to their use in Southampton and Cheshire during the late 1680s. There are also references to the use by English dissenters of New England editions of the psalms.[16]

Not all dissenters would sanction the singing of psalms in public. Most General Baptists were opposed to congregational singing because it promiscuously involved the unregenerate singing the praises of God. Others objected to metrical psalms because of the liberties taken with the biblical text in order to fit the metre. In London the Particular Baptists were also utterly divided on the question of congregational singing, though in their case the issue was as much about ministerial authority. According to Kirk in 1689, the minister of the Baptist meeting at Paul's Alley in the Barbican, 'for 4 days sung psalms, but many of his people forsaking him for it, because the scripture command it not, he desisted from it'. Watts found even as late as 1709 that some dissenters still believed 'All that arises a Degree above Mr Sternhold is too airy for Worship, and hardly escapes the Sentence of *unclean* and *abominable*.' On the other hand, Mary Price joined Matthew Mead's Independent Church at Stepney in December 1692

---

[14] I. Watts, *The Psalms of David Imitated in the Language of the New Testament* (London, 1719), p. xv; cf. idem, *Hymns and Spiritual Songs* (London, 1707), pp. iv–v.

[15] The *Scottish Psalter* was the Edinburgh edition of the English metrical psalter, which excluded the Canticles associated with the Common Book of Prayer and included the Form of Prayers and Catechism from Calvin's Order of Worship; see Illing, 'English metrical Psalter', pp. 517–19. For Barton, see E. Welch, 'William Barton, hymnwriter', *Guildhall Miscellany*, 3 (1971), pp. 235–41.

[16] London, Dr Williams's Library, MS 90.4.5, Sarah Savage to Matthew Henry, 12 Feb. 1686/7. Barton's Psalms were said to have been used at the Above Bar meeting in Southampton, when Isaac Watts was a boy: L. F. Benson, *The English Hymn* (New York, 1915), p. 113; Maclean and Brett-James, 'London in 1689–90', p. 145.

from a Baptist Church, she 'being dissatisfied with their way in not singing psalms, and bec[ause] of their unedifying ministry'.[17] Benjamin Keach began using hymns with his congregation at Horsleydown in the early 1670s, initially at the end of the Lord's Supper, but later on days of public thanksgiving, and finally in 1691 at the end of the Sunday service. Hostility to his attempts to introduce hymn-singing was so intense that a number seceded to found a new church. Keach published three hundred of his own hymns in 1691 and another hundred hymns and paraphrases in 1696. None of Keach's hymns were of much merit, but he has been seen as 'a pioneer who points the way to the future, from Old Testament paraphrase to Christian hymnody'.[18]

Some historians have argued that the Baptists had an important role in the development of hymn-singing by pioneering the transformation of Old Testament paraphrase into Christian hymnody, but have admitted that such efforts were of little direct relevance to the subsequent development of hymnology.[19] Caution on this point is necessary. The main source of evidence for the involvement of Baptists in early hymnody comes from the editions of hymns and spiritual songs they published after 1689, but the bitterness of the controversy amongst Baptists over the question of hymn-singing may explain the publication of so many of their works which otherwise would have remained in manuscript for use by individual churches. Hymns were in much wider use amongst dissenters generally than has perhaps been previously recognized. Matthew Sylvester, Baxter's literary executor, published *Mr Richard Baxter's Paraphrase on the Psalms of David in Metre, with other Hymns*, in 1692. According to Sylvester the manuscript had been 'left . . . compleated' by Baxter before his death in 1691. Baxter had himself written hymns and been in correspondence with William Barton and other hymn-writers. *A Collection of Divine Hymns* was

[17] R. Brown, *The English Baptists of the Eighteenth Century* (London, 1986), pp. 15, 38, 46–7, 58–9; Davies, *Worship*, 2, pp. 272–4; Maclean and Brett-James, 'London in 1689–90', p. 148; I. Watts, *Horae Lyricae*, 2nd edn (London, 1709), p. vi; London Borough of Tower Hamlets, TH/8337/1, Records of Stepney Meeting House, 1644–1974, fol. 9r. Quaker reactions to hymns and hymn-singing were discussed by Rosemary Moore in a paper given at the 1997 Summer Conference of the Ecclesiastical History Society, 'Quaker worship: a discontinuity?', which is to be published in the chapter on the development of Quaker worship in her forthcoming book.

[18] Benjamin Keach, *Spiritual Melody* (London, 1691); idem, *Spiritual Songs* (London, 1696; 2nd edn, 1700); Davies, *Worship*, 2, pp. 284, 509–10.

[19] Davies, *Worship*, 3, p. 135.

published in 1694 with contributions from six different authors, including Richard Baxter. Michael Harrison, the Presbyterian minister at Potterspury in Northamptonshire, published a scheme for a Gospel Church in 1700 and included twelve sacramental hymns, some of which were paraphrases of psalms written 'For the Lord's Day'. He had earlier printed four hymns with a sermon he published in 1691. Richard Davis, the Independent minister at Rothwell, Northamptonshire, more noted for his part in the break-up of the Happy Union, published the second edition of a volume of 168 hymns in 1694, which included hymns for funerals and days of thanksgiving. Samuel Bury, Presbyterian minister at Bury St Edmunds, after a careful study of the available hymns, issued a volume for use in families. A collection of *Psalms, Hymns and Spiritual Songs*, drawn up by the London minister Daniel Burgess 'through the Course of many Years', was published posthumously in 1714. Gardiner in his account of the substitution made by the schoolboys provides some additional details on the practice of hymn-singing by the Leicester congregation. According to Gardiner, before the publication of Watts's volume of hymns the text of the hymn 'was supplied in MSS by the more educated persons of the congregation'.[20]

The insistence upon a strict adherence to Scripture ruled out the use of almost all hymnody in public worship before the end of the seventeenth century. The important exception to this injunction was the Lord's Supper, where, because of the inadequacy of the psalms, the example of Christ and his disciples at the Last Supper was used to permit the singing of a hymn instead. Watts noted 'to what a hard Shift the Minister is put to find proper Hymns at the Celebration of the Lord's-Supper, where the People will sing nothing but out of David's Psalm-Book: How perpetually do they repeat some part of the XXXIIId or the CXVIIIth Psalm.'[21] As a consequence some of the earliest collections of hymns published by dissenters were written for use on such occasions. Joseph Boyse, one of the two Presbyterian

---

[20] *Calendar of the Correspondence of Richard Baxter*, ed. N. H. Keeble and G. F. Nuttall, 2 vols (Oxford, 1991), 1, p. 319; Michael Harrison, *A Gospel Church Describ'd* (London, 1700); idem, *The Best Match . . . Preached at Potters Pury in Northamptonshire, September the 29th, 1690* (London, 1691); Richard Davis, *Hymns Composed on Several Subjects*, 2nd edn (London, 1694), no copy of the first edition appears to survive; [Samuel Bury], *A Collection of Psalms, Hymns, and Spiritual Songs* (London, 1701); *Psalms, Hymns, and Spiritual Songs. By the late Reverend Mr Daniel Burgess* (London, 1714), p. iv; Gardiner, *Music and Friends*, p. 1.

[21] Watts, *Psalms of David*, p. viii.

ministers at Dublin, published a small volume of twenty-one hymns in 1693, all but two of which he had written, 'collected (chiefly) out of such passages of the New Testament as contain the most suitable matter of divine praises in the celebration of the Lords Supper'. The collection included a hymn relating to baptism and another to the ministry. Richard Davis, the Independent minister at Rothwell, included a number of hymns in his collection written by his predecessor, Thomas Browning (d. 1685), for use at the Lord's Supper.[22] The other exception to the use of hymns in public worship was on days of public thanksgiving.[23]

In addition, because of the limitations of metrical psalmody, the paraphrases of the original texts began gradually to be relaxed. Barton, whose hymns were widely used by dissenters before Watts, in his later works treated the biblical texts with increasing freedom, introducing different groupings of verses and even omitting some parts entirely. On the title-page of his first work, *The Book of Psalms in metre* (1644; second edition 1645), Barton testified that the edition was 'close and proper to the Hebrew'. Nevertheless in the preface, after quoting scriptural authority for the singing of psalms, he noted that 'the translation it self, since Hebrew must be made English, English must be made Verse, and Verse ryme, we must of necessity admit some alteration and amplification of words'.[24] The following year he published the *Choice and Flower of the old Psalms*, a selection of psalms, which also included eleven hymns at the end of the volume 'composed out of Scripture to celebrate some more speciall and publicke occasions'. The public occasions included Parliament's recent victory at Naseby as well as three hymns for the Lord's Supper. The practice of combining biblical texts, which characterized later paraphrases, was only a short step from transforming the scriptural paraphrase into the scriptural hymn.

If hymns continued to be largely proscribed in public worship, there was more freedom in family worship and private devotion. In 1701 Boyse published a further collection of *Family Hymns* in three parts

---

[22] J. Boyse, *Sacramental Hymns* (Dublin, reprinted London, 1693), see title and preface; Davis, *Hymns*, p. 146.

[23] For example, Davis, *Hymns*, p. 56; Charles Nicholetts, *The Devil's Champion foil'd* (London, 1707), p. 37, who published the hymn 'publickly sung at the close of the Sermon' delivered in December 1706 on the day of public thanksgiving to celebrate Marlborough's victories.

[24] W. Barton, *The Book of Psalms* (London, 1644).

with music, 'with some for the Lord's-Days; and others for several particular occasions'.[25] Matthew Henry, the celebrated biblical commentator, after failing to persuade his father, Philip Henry, to prepare a volume of psalms for family use, issued a volume of family hymns in 1695, where he provided an apology for placing different texts of Scripture together. He justified his action by citing the example of sermons which were often glosses on different texts. In public worship, however, he preferred scriptural psalms before 'those that are wholly of humane Composure', where 'the Fancy is too high, and the Matter too low', preventing their use in worship.[26]

The question of whether singing was permitted in public continued to concern dissenters. In 1699 John Clifford, in *Sound Words*, argued that the singing 'of Psalms and Hymns to the Praise of God' in public was a duty, and one that was 'both commended and commanded by the example and Exhortations of Christ and his Apostles': ''tis certainly a sinfull neglect in many that they sit silent in the publick Assembly, when others are singing'. He included in the volume 146 psalms and 50 hymns. The hymns were 'partly composed, but for the most part Collected with such Alterations, that the Metre might be Pleasant, and with such Choice that the Matter might be Practical'. They were taken from both the psalms and other parts of the Scriptures, and although the proofs were omitted to keep the volume in bounds, Clifford claimed that 'such as do know the Scriptures, will understand the Language of Canaan which is spoken by the Hymns as plain as Metre can speak it'. The psalms were chosen 'whose Principal Matter could be well comprized in Six Verses, which are commonly enough to be Sung at once with the Doxology'.[27] In 1702, Samuel Cradock added eight additional chapters to his well-known guide to salvation, *Knowledge and Practice*, in which he also commended the singing of psalms as a gospel-duty. He not only rejected the scruples of those unwilling to sing in 'mixt congregation, where wicked men join', because, as he argued, Moses and the children of Israel had sung psalms together, but

---

[25] J. Boyse, *Family Hymns for Morning and Evening Worship* (Dublin, 1701).

[26] Oxford, Bodleian Library, MS Eng. lett e.29, fol. 106r, Matthew Henry to Philip Henry, 3 Apr. 1693; M[atthew] H[enry], *Family-Hymns Gather'd (mostly) out of the best Translations of David's Psalms* (London, 1695), see 'Epistle to the reader'. New Testament hymns were not added until the 2nd and enlarged edn in 1702; W. Tong, *An account of . . . Matthew Henry* (London, 1716), p. 117.

[27] J. Clifford, *Sound Words: The Catechism of the Westminster Assembly* (London, 1699), pp. 7–8.

he commended singing as spiritually edifying in itself: 'Singing will affect, and raise, and quicken the heart to Praise God more than Reading'.[28] James Peirce in his *Vindiciæ* (1710), his celebrated defence of dissent written in reply to William Nicholls's *Defensio* (1707), argued not only that singing was commanded by Scripture, but that it could 'by its own virtue, excite devout and Spiritual affections in us', though he argued against the use of musical instruments in worship.[29]

Hymns were sung unaccompanied, though increasingly there were attempts to improve the quality of singing. In July 1699 the Independents at Rothwell agreed after a debate that 'any tune may be sung provided it be grave and is of divine institution'.[30] Congregations were much slower to accept the use of instrumental music. The clerk of the meeting was not only expected to give out the words of the psalm two lines at a time for the congregation to sing, but also in most cases to set the tune. It was not always easy to find someone sufficiently musical. At Portsmouth in 1710 the Presbyterian meeting agreed to allow Mr Knight £8 a year for his services as clerk, but 'upon proviso that he reads the Psalm and be content that another Tune it as soon as Mr Browne [the minister] thinks fit for the Introducing of regular Singing'.[31] According to William Gardiner, 'it was not uncommon for the clerk to give a flourish upon his voice before he commenced. The clerk in the Great Meeting, [Leicester,] however, was a person of more discreet manners, and by way of pitching the key, gently sounded the bottom of a brass candlestick, in the shape of a bell.' Nevertheless, 'as some of the most intelligent and wealthy families attended this place, and the taste for music improved, the direction of the psalmody was taken from the clerk, and given to a few qualified persons'. In about 1760 a choir was formed, of which Gardiner's father took the lead. 'At

[28] Samuel Cradock, *Knowledge and Practice* (first pub. London, 1659; 4th edn, 'corrected, and very much enlarg'd', 1702), pp. 226, 276–83, 146–7. He included 25 hymns, both personal and private, to be used in the family.

[29] J. Peirce, *Vindiciæ fratrum dissentientium in Anglia* (London, 1710). Although Peirce's *Vindiciæ* was extensively revised when the English translation was published in 1718, the third part, 'Concerning Discipline, and Modes of Worship', was little altered: *A Vindication of the Dissenters: in answer to Dr W. Nichols's Defence of the Doctrine and Discipline of the Church of England* (London, 1717), pp. 385–6.

[30] Rothwell, Northamptonshire: Rothwell United Reformed Church, First Church book of Rothwell Independent Church, 1655–1708, s.v. 3 Jul. 1699.

[31] Portsmouth Record Office, CHU 82/9/1, High Street Presbyterian Meeting, Portsmouth, Ledger of miscellaneous church receipts, 7 Nov. 1697–1 Aug. 1736, under 21 Feb. 1709/10.

this time he had just purchased Dr Croft's work, entitled *Musica Sacra*, a collection of anthems which could not be performed without an instrumental bass, and the society consented that a bass-viol should be procured of Baruch Norman for this purpose.'[32] By the late eighteenth century the congregation was described as 'genteel and numerous' with a noted choir. An organ was acquired in 1800, 'a valuable advantage to the choir, who form a musical society, cultivated with great care, and justly celebrated for its excellence'. Organs do not appear to have been common in dissenting places of worship until the last decades of the eighteenth century.[33] Gardiner himself was a provincial musician of some distinction, and indeed took part in the first performance of Beethoven's music in this country in 1794.[34]

*   *   *

Watts published his *Hymns and Spiritual Songs* in 1707, though his first efforts at hymn-writing apparently date from about 1695, as a result of a challenge from his father to improve upon the paraphrases then in use at the Independent meeting in Southampton. The collection consisted of 210 hymns, made up of 78 paraphrases, 22 communion hymns and 110 'free composures'. He deliberately only used 'three Sorts of Metre . . . fitted to the most common Tunes', and 'endeavour'd to make the sense plain and obvious'. The volume proved so successful that two years later he published an enlarged second edition with 345 hymns. This was clearly in response to the demand amongst dissenters for an improved collection. Watts himself had seen 'the dull Indifference, the negligent and the thoughtless Air that sits upon the Faces of a whole Assembly while the Psalm is on their Lips', and had been repeatedly importuned for his own collection. As a result, 'I have for some Years past devoted many Hours of leisure to this Service'.[35] His younger brother, Enoch, had attempted to persuade him to publish his collection of hymns as early as March 1700, urging him to 'consider how very mean the performers in this kind of poetry appear in the pieces already extant', and stressing the 'great need of a pen, vigorous and lively as yours, to quicken and revive the dying devotion of the

---

[32] William Croft, *Musica Sacra, or, Select Anthems in Score* (London, 1724). This edn is one of the first attempts in England to engrave music in score.

[33] Nichols, *History*, p. 547.

[34] B. Elliott and R. H. Evans, 'The French exiled clergy in Leicestershire from 1792', *Transactions of the Leicestershire Archaeological and Historical Society*, 64 (1990), p. 37.

[35] Watts, *Hymns*, pp. iii, vi, viii.

age'. 'Mason now reduces this kind of writing to a sort of yawning indifferency, and honest Barton chimes us asleep.'[36] It was not only the inadequacy of the paraphrases but the deadness of spirit with which they were sung.

Watts did not create the English hymn, for it is clear there were earlier authors who published their collections in the 1690s; nor was he responsible for the adoption of public hymn-singing by dissenters. The hymn evolved out of the increasing dissatisfaction with the metrical psalm as a vehicle for congregational praise. His achievement was his skill as a poet, together with his understanding as a minister, which resulted in the publication of a comprehensive collection of evangelical songs suitable for modern use by congregations. He succeeded overwhelmingly in what his predecessors had achieved only indifferently. His *Hymns and Spiritual Songs* were to prove so popular that they came to dominate the public worship of dissenters for more than a century, passing through over twenty English and American editions by his death, and an astonishing 111 English and 113 American editions by 1800.[37] It was the Wesleys who made the hymn the central feature of worship. Nevertheless, the development of hymn-singing amongst dissenters in the decades after toleration was to introduce a new and vital form of praise which was to transform the public worship of congregations.

Dr Williams's Library, London

---

[36] T. Gibbons, *Memoirs of the Rev. Isaac Watts* (London, 1780), p. 254; Enoch to Isaac Watts, March 1700, printed in T. Milner, *The Life, Times and Correspondence of the Rev. Isaac Watts* (London, 1834), p. 177.
[37] S. L. Bishop, *Hymns and Spiritual Songs* (London, 1962), p. ix.

PATRISTICS AND REFORM: THOMAS RATTRAY AND THE ANCIENT LITURGY OF THE CHURCH OF JERUSALEM

by STUART G. HALL

IN reforming Christian worship radical change often follows from the attempt to restore what was ancient. Nowhere is this more clear than among the liturgical scholars of the early seventeenth century, when advances in critical scholarship made it possible for some to believe they could restore the Church's worship to that of apostolic times. This is well illustrated in the work of Thomas Rattray (1684–1743),[1] a Scot of great learning, and among Scottish Episcopalians of lasting influence. Rattray was a Non-juror, one of those expelled or withdrawn from the churches of England and Scotland after 1689 for refusing obedience to the new regime. They pinned their hopes, and the survival of what they perceived as the true Catholic Faith, on the Roman Catholic House of Stuart in exile in France. Their hopes perished in blood on the field of Culloden in 1746. That was three years after Rattray's death. The Episcopalians hold Rattray's name in honour, both because of the part he played in fixing their Church's constitution, and because of one book of learning and ingenuity, called *The Ancient Liturgy of the Church of Jerusalem*.[2]

This work was published by subscription in London in 1744, the year after he died. Rattray's subscribing admirers numbered 324. Of these some ordered multiple copies: the Cotton family of Stretton in Bedfordshire apparently bought one each for John Cotton Esq., Mrs Cotton and two Misses Cotton. Of the subscribers about four-fifths are Scots. There were nests of Rattray admirers not only in Scotland (such

---

[1] See Alexander Gordon, 'Rattray, Thomas, D. D. (1684–1743)', *DNB*, 47, pp. 312–14; A. M. Allchin, 'Thomas Rattray: after 250 years', *Scottish Episcopal Church Review*, 4 (1995), pp. 50–63 (lecture given after a celebration of Rattray's liturgy in Edinburgh on 22 May 1994).

[2] *The Ancient Liturgy of the Church of Jerusalem, being the Liturgy of St. James, Freed from all latter Additions and Interpolations of whatever kind, and so restored to it's Original Purity: by comparing it with the Account given of that Liturgy by St. Cyril in his fifth Mystagogical Catechism, And with the Clementine Liturgy &c.* (London 1744) [hereafter *The Ancient Liturgy*]. See W. J. Grisbrooke, *Anglican Liturgies of the Seventeenth and Eighteenth Centuries*, Alcuin Club Collections, 11 (London 1958), pp. 317–32.

places as Aberdeen and Bamf [*sic*]), but in Huntingdonshire and Bedfordshire. The religious and social background of the subscribers would repay further investigation, as would their fate after the rebellion of 1745. But our concern is with the features that commended Rattray's work to these people, difficult and complicated as it was. Rattray was a creative liturgical reformer in a denomination deeply engaged with liturgical reform. Subsequent rewriters of the liturgy in Scotland have known and used his ideas, and these have in turn influenced Anglican churches overseas. The claim is even rashly made that the most recent compositions of the Scottish Episcopal Church bring to fulfilment what he intended.[3]

Rattray's book presents a synopsis, in Greek and in English, of the eucharistic prayer of the Liturgy of St James on one side, and the evidence of Cyril of Jerusalem and the Clementine Liturgy (that is, that in the *Apostolic Constitutions*) on the other. These are supplemented with a column of relevant material from the liturgies of St Mark, St Basil, St John Chrysostom, and the Maronites. Between these Rattray sets what purports to be the restored Ancient Liturgy of the Church of Jerusalem. Each opening of these five columns is followed by the same material in English. Footnotes are frequently present in some of the columns, and these are carried over into the pages of English synopsis. The whole is preceded by a learned Introduction, and followed by an English text of the restored Jerusalem Liturgy designed to be printed and published separately, with the rubrics and supplements necessary for liturgical use. The whole must have been quite a headache for the printer, even though it consists of only 122 pages of text and another twenty of introduction and subscribers' names.

Ever since the Reformation, textual and historical science had been deployed in the reform of worship. The Non-jurors had already embarked on significant patristic research. This was stimulated by one bitter issue. The English Non-jurors, though suffering deprivations of various kinds for their loyalty to the House of Stuart, were split over the Usages. These were eucharistic practices, observed to be present in the ancient and eastern Churches, but not in the English *Book of Common Prayer* of 1662. Some regarded them as essential, and craved their introduction without tarrying for any. While they argued their correctness on historical and scriptural grounds, no doubt the desire to

---

[3] Gianfranco Tellini, 'The Pittenweem manuscript Prayer Book of 1743', *The Royal Martyr Annual 1985* ([Edinburgh], 1985), p. 6.

do business with the Patriarch of Constantinople and other leading Orthodox figures affected their judgement. The leading Usager was Jeremy Collier (1650–1722),[4] who was ordained bishop in 1713. He was the most important English Non-juror after George Hickes died in 1715. Collier was called an 'Essentialist' because he held the Usages as essential to the conduct of the liturgy. The Usages were opposed by those who, while loyal to the Stuarts, were prepared to work with the Common Prayer Book of 1662 as sufficiently scriptural and Catholic, even if not ideal. They perceived political advantages in not disturbing the massive compromise between Zwinglian text and Anglo-Catholic rubrics which was the strength of the Holy Communion of 1662. Jeremy Collier is held responsible for the Liturgy of 1718, which included all the Usages, and he went as far as to forbid communion with those who held to the Common Prayer Book, thus generating open schism among the Non-jurors.

Rattray was in England while this quarrel was brewing, working for the Non-jurors. He and Nathaniel Spinckes translated into church Greek their overtures to the eastern patriarchs in 1716: co-operation was offered and recognition sought for their small but distinguished denomination. The Usages dispute called out an important publication, which Rattray refers to and which clearly influenced him. In his Introduction to *The Ancient Liturgy* he recommends 'Dr Brett's Collection of Lit.' as making Greek texts accessible to English readers.[5] This is Thomas Brett's *A Collection of the Principal Liturgies used by the Christian Church in the Celebration of the Holy Eucharist, particularly the ancient* (London, 1720). The title page specifies *the Clementine Liturgy as it stands in The Apostolical Constitutions, the Liturgies of S. James, S. Mark. S Chrysostom, S. Basil, &c.* Brett gives English versions of these texts 'by several hands' unnamed. It includes two forms of St Basil (the Constantinopolitan and Alexandrian), the Ethiopic, liturgies attributed to Nestorius and to Severus of Antioch, fragments of the Gothic or Gothico-Gallican, and of the Mozarabic, the Roman Missal, the Communion office of Cranmer's first Prayer Book of 1549 (which Non-jurors preferred to the later versions), and the Non-jurors' new communion office of 1718, 'A Communion Office, taken partly from Primitive Liturgies, and partly from the First English Reformed Common Prayer Book.' There follow patristic

---

[4] William Hunt, 'Collier, Jeremy (1650–1722)', *DNB*, 11, pp. 341–7.
[5] Note to p. vii.

descriptions of the eucharist from Justin Martyr (*I Apology* 85–7) and Cyril of Jerusalem (*Mystagogical Catechesis* V). The liturgical texts are followed by Brett's Dissertation, running to 437 closely printed pages, 'shewing', it is claimed on the title page, 'their Usefulness and Authority, and pointing out their several corruptions and Interpolations'.

The religious passion and scientific vision of the book are clear from Brett's last page:

> I most humbly and heartily beseech God, that as he has been graciously pleased to discover to this Generation a more general Knowledge of the Doctrines and Practices of the Primitive Church, than our Fore-Fathers for some Ages have had before us: (For though there were some as Learned Men in all Times since the *Reformation* as any now living, yet I am persuaded that as to the Knowledge of the Fathers, no Modern Age has had so many as the present) so he will be graciously pleased to infuse a Primitive Spirit into us, and make us not only *almost, but altogether such* as the Primitive Christians were, *except their Bonds.*

This hope was based on publications, many of which Rattray would use and cite. For the Alexandrian, Ethiopic, and oriental texts Brett used the massive study of Eusèbe Renaudot, whose *Liturgiarum orientalium collectio* had just come out.[6] Brett also used, as Rattray would, Jacques Goar for the liturgies of Basil and John Chrysostom,[7] and Jean Mabillon for the Gallican and Mozarabic.[8] For the Liturgy of St James he used the older *Bibliotheca patrum*.[9] Brett surely had also in mind such English authors as George Bull (1634–1710), whose masterwork demolished contemporary Arianism: *Judicium ecclesiae catholicae trium primorum saeculorum de necessitate credendi quod Dominus noster Jesus Christus sit verus Deus, assertum contra Simonem Episcopium aliosque* (Oxford 1694); and Joseph Bingham (1668–1723), whose *Origines Ecclesiasticae; or the Antiquities of the Christian Church* was appearing steadily in its ten great volumes from 1708 to 1722. Rattray in *The Ancient Liturgy* used the newer Johann Albert Fabricius for the

---

6 *Liturgiarum orientalium collectio*, 2 vols (Paris, 1716).
7 *Euchologium sive rituale graecorum* (Paris, 1647).
8 *De liturgia gallicana* (Paris, 1685) (= *PL* 72, cols 101–448).
9 *Bibliotheca patrum*, II (Paris, 1626).

Liturgy of St James,[10] and added the Maronite Liturgy from the same source and Renaudot, but is otherwise similar.[11]

Brett's collection had practical purposes. One was to justify and sustain from ancient sources and from the Common Prayer Book of 1549 the new liturgy used and commended among the Non-juring congregations, the Liturgy of 1718. If it demonstrated its dependence upon, and similarity to, the classic eastern liturgies, that could also help in promoting the negotiations with the eastern Churches. The second consequence was forcefully expressed in the Introduction, written by some other person than Brett, who is named and commended in the third person. It is the matter of the Usages, and their necessity. These are described in these terms:

> 1st That water is an Essential Part of the Eucharistick Cup. 2ndly That the Oblation of the Elements to God the Father; and 3dly, The Invocation of the Holy Spirit upon them are Essential Parts of the Consecration: And 4thly, That the Faithful departed ought to be recommended in the Eucharistick Commemoration.[12]

The matter is one to be resolved, this author says, by Scripture and Tradition, and Dr Brett has in this collection demonstrated the *universal* tradition, following the ancient texts. Brett's collection of eucharistic prayers, ancient and modern, is an Essentialist tract in the Non-jurors' debate over the Usages.

Back in Scotland the Non-juring bishops Alexander Ross (Rose) and John Falconer were called upon by both parties for support. They turned to Rattray to compose a reconciling paper. He did this, though it was a task he did not relish. He feared the spread of the schism to Scotland. On 11 March 1720 he wrote:

> as to the Success of any proposals can be made for healing these Breaches at present, . . . it was not my hope I had of that, which obliged me to write . . ., but purely in obedience to . . . Commands, and to take off that unjust aspersion with which I was loaded: Nay I humbly think it were most prudential not to Interpose betwixt them, but leave them Intirely to themselves till they have quite

---

[10] *Codex apocryphus novi testamenti*, 2 vols (Hamburg, 1703; rev. and enlarged, 3 vols, Hamburg, 1719).

[11] The publisher's note in *The Ancient Liturgy* quotes a letter from Rattray listing his textual sources on p. xvi.

[12] Brett, *Collection of the Principal Liturgies*, pp. iii–iv.

spent themselves, so as to give over writing on both sides, and then perhaps they may be more ready to harken to reasonable overtures for Peace.[13]

His own position is not neutral, however. He goes on to mark the differences between the English and Scottish situations: 'The only Shaddow of reason which I can see produced by those who are against the Alterations, viz. the former obligation they ly under, is what no way concerns us, who are intirely free from any former obligation.'[14] The English opponents of the Usages felt committed to the 1662 *Book of Common Prayer*, the Scots were not. Indeed, the Scots Non-jurors lived in a kind of liturgical vacuum, where the Lord's Prayer might be the only piece of liturgy widely used. Rattray could see the door wide open to restoring primitive liturgy.

At this point we might emphasise his commitment to the first of the Usages listed in the Preface to Brett's collection: that water is an essential part of the eucharistic cup. In *The Ancient Liturgy* he takes into his text at the point where the Last Supper is recounted the words of the Liturgy of St James: 'In like manner, after Supper, He took the Cup, and having mixed it of Wine and Water he gave Thanks . . .' In the synopsis he adds the footnote:

> So it is also in *Lit. Clem. Mar.* and *Basil*, not to mention many other latter Liturgies. And the Testimonies of the Mixture of Wine and Water in the Eucharistick Cup are so many and so early, that there can be no doubt of it's being an Apostolical Tradition, and consequently derived from the Practice of Christ himself.[15]

This revealing piece of reasoning is repeated in the last part of the book, which was intended for separate publication as a text for liturgical use. There, the patristic references for Justin, Irenaeus, Clement of Alexandria, Cyprian, and the Councils of Carthage and Orleans are added.[16]

Rattray does not in the published text replicate his enthusiastic discovery in 1719 that not only the mixed cup, but the symbolism of it, goes back to the Apostles:

---

[13] Aberdeen University Library, MS 2180/1, letter 11 March 1720, lines 19–26.
[14] Ibid., lines 27–9.
[15] *The Ancient Liturgy*, p. 30/32.
[16] Ibid., p. 117.

I sat down the other day to examine that difficult passage in Clemens Alexandrinus concerning the Mixture which I always thought Mr Johnson misunderstood; But Indeed I had a wrong notion of it my Self also, for I thought he had made the water to represent the Spirit, and the mixture of it with the wine the mixture of the Spirit with the Blood of Jesus, and with that view I began to translate and consider it, but I had not proceeded far when I discovered my mistake and to my no small satisfaction found that he made the water to represent mankind, or the people, exactly as St Cyprian doth.[17]

This agrees also, he claims, with Irenaeus, and he says that he is sending texts and translations, and asks his correspondent and friend to test his interpretation. If he is right, he says,

I think it will be as satisfactory as any thing I have yet mett with, in as much as it will shew that the Church in these Earlier Ages derived not only the Practise of the Mixture but also the Mystic interpretation of it from pristine tradition, for it is not to be thought that these three so very ancient Fathers could have agreed so Exactly in it if they had not received it from that Fountain.[18]

He would remain committed to this interpretation. In the Pittenweem Manuscript, which we shall mention later, one of the very few departures from the published text of The Ancient Liturgy is an addition after the final rubrics:

A Prayer used at the mixture in the Liturgy of the Latin Church Deus qui humanæ substantiæ dignitatem mirabiliter condidisti, mirabilius reformasti, da nobis per hujus vini et aquæ mysterium ejus divinitatis esse Consortes qui humanitatis nostræ fieri dignatus est particeps Jesus Christus.[19]

The Latin might be translated: 'God who wonderfully constituted the dignity of human nature, and more wonderfully restored it, grant us through the mystery of this wine and water to be partners of the

---

[17] Aberdeen University Library, MS 2180/1, letter 6 Oct. 1719 lines 8–16.
[18] Ibid., lines 25–31.
[19] St Andrews University Library, Deposited MS 84 [hereafter 'Pittenweem MS'] p. [192] (the pages are unnumbered).

divinity of him who deigned to become a partaker in our humanity, Jesus Christ.'

Rattray's reasoning is flawed. The Fathers are indeed unanimous about the mixed cup. But if we believe that Jesus mixed water with wine in the cup of his last supper, it will not be because of the patristic testimonies, but because it was general practice in the ancient world, including the Jewish. The Greek liturgies say that Jesus mixed wine and water in the cup, when it is not referred to in the New Testament accounts. This very fact should put us on our guard. The liturgical texts have been adjusted in the light of the practice of the Church, not in the light of critical historical analysis: the Church does it, so it must go back to Jesus. The same will apply even more to that interpretation found by Rattray to be 'pristine', that the water represents the people, and the wine the saving blood or deity of Christ. This is undoubtedly what Cyprian says.[20] But even if Cyprian, Clement, and Irenaeus were unanimous on this interpretation, that would not take us back to the practice of the apostles or of Christ. It is exactly that kind of ritual note which piety attaches to a liturgical practice, which may originally have had a merely practical purpose, or even a different symbolic one. The ritual generates the myth.

In fact Rattray's quest for patristic unanimity itself fails. Cyprian, opposing a tradition of offering a cup of water without wine at the eucharist, finds the symbolic meaning of the wine and water among his other arguments for the mixed cup. Clement, writing moral lectures on the disciplined use of alcohol, piles symbol upon symbol, in such a way that he includes the view that human nature and divine spirit as combined are signified by the mixed water and wine.[21] Clement is clear evidence for the Church's practice, but was quite fertile enough to create the interpretation for himself. Irenaeus uses the mixture to argue Christologically: the Ebionites reject the deity of Christ as they reject wine in the eucharist, and stick only with fallen Adam and water.[22] This also must be regarded as a secondary sophistry, rather than as a steady doctrinal tradition.

---

[20] Cyprian, *Ep.* 63: *S. Thasci Caecili Cypriani Opera omnia*, ed. W. Hartel, *CSEL*, 3, 2 vols (Vienna, 1868–71), 2, pp. 701–7, especially cc. 2, 13.

[21] Clement of Alexandria, *Paedagogus* II.ii.19–21: *Clemens Alexandrinus, erster Band: Protrepticus und Paedagogus*, ed. O. Stählin, Die griechischen christlichen Schriftsteller der ersten drei Jahrhunderte, 3rd edn (Berlin, 1972), pp. 167.15–168.30, especially 19.4–20.1 (p. 168.1–5).

[22] One reference in *The Ancient Liturgy*, p. 117, is to Irenaeus, *Adversus Haereses* V.2.3:

Between 1720 and 1743 Rattray rose in his corner of the Church to the highest eminence. The split over the Usages affected the Scottish Non-jurors, and partly coincided with their division between the College of Bishops sitting in Edinburgh, and the local churches and gentry who wanted bishops to have local sees. Rattray was at one with the gentry, and by diplomacy largely won his case in the 'articles of agreement' of 1731. The device of maintaining the Apostolic Succession by seating half a dozen bishops in Edinburgh, though convenient for King James's agent in Scotland, George Lockhart of Carnwarth, was theologically indefensible, and Rattray argued the necessity for lay election on patristric grounds. In the tangled course of events Rattray was himself ordained priest by 1724, and Bishop of Brechin in 1727. The Episcopalians constituted a 'privy kirk' as did the Scottish Protestants before 1560, and their strength lay in land-owning families, like Rattray's own. When the compromise was adopted, King James retained a veto over the appointment of the Bishop of Edinburgh and Primus, which is why Rattray was never installed in that top office after his election in 1739, though he was invited to assume the role *de facto* early in 1743, the year of his death.[23]

During this time Rattray worked on *The Ancient Liturgy*. He had in the first instance a scholarly or antiquarian object, and secondly a practical one. The Liturgy of St James, he says, is proven ancient by the references to the liturgical actions in Cyril of Jerusalem's fifth *Mystagogical Catechesis*. Only, it is demonstrably corrupted by added material.

> But then upon examining it more attentively, it appeared to me that all these Additions and Interpolations, of whatever kind, might easily be distinguished, and separated from it, and this excellent Liturgy of the Church of *Jerusalem* thereby restored to it's original Purity. And this induced me to bestow some Pains in attempting it; presuming that it would not be unacceptable to such as have a just Regard for Antiquity; and might prove useful.[24]

Irénée de Lyon, Contre les hérésies, livre V, ed. A. Rousseau, L. Doutreleau, and C. Mercier, SC, 153 (Paris, 1969), p. 34, ll. 37–42. Rattray also cites Irenaeus, *Adv. Haereses* IV.57, a reference I cannot find. Rattray presumably has in mind V.1.3 (Rousseau *et al.*, *Contre les hérésies*, pp. 24–7), where Ebionite rejection of mixing 'heavenly wine' with 'worldly water' is connected to their rejection of the union of deity with humanity in Christ.

[23] For this history see Gordon, 'Rattray, Thomas', pp. 312–14.
[24] *The Ancient Liturgy*, p. 1.

The antiquarian goal is achieved in the introduction, synopsis, and appendices.[25] The utilitarian goal is achieved in what is a separate or separable book, with its own title-page:[26] '*An Office for the Sacrifice of the Holy Eucharist, being the Ancient Liturgy of the Church of* Jerusalem, *to which Proper Rubrics are added for Direction, and some few notes at the Foot of the Page, &c.*' While clearly published together, since the pagination is continuous, there is no textual cross-reference between *The Ancient Liturgy* and the *Office*, and some repetition in the notes.

How shall we estimate Rattray's work? *The Ancient Liturgy* plainly has a narrow base. His key texts are of the Antiochene tradition: St James, Cyril of Jerusalem, and the Clementine Liturgy. St James is supposedly the original liturgy of Jerusalem, attested by Cyril. St James can be corrected from the Syriac version of it, which Renaudot had printed and Rattray diligently presents. It can also be corrected in the light of the Clementine Liturgy, which has not been used liturgically since it was incorporated in *The Apostolic Constitutions*, and therefore is without the later corruptions. Rattray allows its merits, but demurs at important points from the high praise others bestowed on it.[27] The supporting texts are of adjacent traditions: St Basil, St John Chrysostom, St Mark, and the Maronite. Brett had included Roman and oriental material in his collection. Rattray argues that the Roman mass is a mutilated rite, particularly in omitting the Invocation of the Holy Spirit upon the elements. He quotes John Johnson for the view that the loss occurred late in the sixth century.[28] The Gallican liturgies of Mabillon 'are but imperfect Fragments, and of no great Antiquity', though they still attest the oblation to the Father and the Invocation of the Spirit.[29] But they are useless for reconstructing the primitive Jerusalem Liturgy.

Rattray's method is circular. The texts tend to agree because they are all of one type, the Antiochene or West Syrian. St Mark is an exception, but is still near. One can seek a common root, and claim it as original. In some sense of course Christian worship, like Christian doctrine, goes back to Jesus and his immediate followers. The early Church believed

---

[25] *The Ancient Liturgy*, pp. 1–110.

[26] Ibid., pp. 111–22.

[27] Ibid., pp. v–x.

[28] Ibid., p. xii, citing [John] Johnson, *Unbl[oody] Sacr[ifice and Altar]* (London, 1714–18). There is an interesting discussion of Johnson's view in the light of Thomas Brett's opinion and other contemporaries in the publisher's note in *The Ancient Liturgy*, pp. xiv–xv.

[29] *The Ancient Liturgy*, pp. xii–xiii.

that the totality of doctrine and practice began with the apostles, and all changes were for the worse. But for practical purposes diversity precedes uniformity. The present is always being corrected by what is held to be the true original. But it always *needs* to be corrected. The diversity of the ancient liturgies offends the tidy minds of the faithful and of the scholar alike, but has to be accepted. West Syria, Alexandria, Rome, and the Gallican territories represent diverse families of eucharistic liturgies. Furthermore, in spite of all they have in common, the further back you go the more striking the diversities. Some examples will help.

Rattray argues that Cyril of Jerusalem comments upon the Jerusalem Liturgy of the fourth century, and tries to deal with the famous anomaly: Cyril goes straight from the *Sanctus* to the invocation of the Spirit upon the gifts, using his regular term, 'next' – 'Next, having consecrated ourselves with these spiritual hymns, we call upon the kindly God to send forth his Holy Spirit upon the offerings.'[30] Rattray, like many others, assumes that Cyril knew but passed over the account of the institution and the commemoration of Christ's work of salvation which come here in most liturgies. Recent editors of Cyril, Frank Leslie Cross in 1951 and Auguste Piédagnel in 1966, agree with Rattray, though all three use different arguments; and Gregory Dix had strongly criticized Frank Edward Brightman for defending the same position.[31] For seven openings of synopsis Rattray's 'Cyril' column is packed with densely-printed notes, arguing that we should not infer that the words of institution and the offering to the Father were lacking in Cyril's time, adducing patristic texts on the meaning of the liturgy in this passage.[32] It will be recalled that the offering to the Father is one of the four controversial Usages. Rattray cannot envisage early patristic texts without it. Dix is probably right, however, to conclude:

> On the whole it seems much more likely that Cyril means what he says, and that the invocation in the fourth century Jerusalem rite followed immediately upon the sanctus, however unexpected such

---

[30] Cyril of Jerusalem, *Mystagogical catechesis* V.7: *Cyrille de Jérusalem, Catachèses mystagogiques*, ed. A. Piédagnel and P. Paris, SC, 126 (Paris, 1966), p. 154 (my translation).

[31] Gregory Dix, *The Shape of the Liturgy* (Westminster, 1945), pp. 197–8, quoting F. E. Brightman, *Liturgies Eastern and Western* ([Oxford], 1896), p. 469.

[32] *The Ancient Liturgy*, pp. 15–27.

an arrangement may be to us, with our modern presuppositions as
to the 'proper' arrangement of a consecration prayer.[33]

Here a general point should be made about method. Liturgiologists
are prone to adapt the evidence to their theory of what is 'proper'. Dix
again rightly criticizes editors who would interpolate the narrative of
institution into the *Anaphora of Addai and Mari*.[34] E. C. Ratcliff, who
undoubtedly agreed with Dix about *Addai and Mari*, was himself guilty
of improving the anaphora of Hippolytus' *Apostolic Tradition* by adding
the Sanctus to it, albeit as a closing doxology.[35] The classic example is
the Didache or *The Teaching of the Twelve Apostles*, the most ancient
liturgical handbook surviving from ancient times. Here the recommendations for the Thanksgiving ($εὐχαριστία$) direct prayers over the
cup and over the broken bread, prayers which fail to refer either to the
Last Supper or to the death of Christ, and include neither Sanctus nor
invocation of the Spirit. Since these prayers fail to qualify as a mass for
Catholics, a Lord's Supper for Protestants, or a Liturgy for Orthodox,
scholars repeatedly try to prove it was a different rite, an *agapê*, or even
that it was a rite preliminary to the real thing, which was hidden under
the closing words, 'But allow the prophets to give thanks as much as
they like.'[36] Even Dix allowed himself to be taken in by the prevailing
school which found in it an *agapê*, and left it out of consideration as a
eucharistic liturgy.[37] It behoves us, however, to be more patient with
the ancient evidence, and let it speak for itself. In other fields, notably
doctrinal history and Gospel textual criticism, variety seems to precede
uniformity. Obvious though it may seem that there is a single original
and true text or doctrine, to which research should drive us back, in
practice one moves back through the firm uniformities of later texts to
looser and more varied manuscripts, the older they are, and through
the uniformity of orthodox creeds to the bewildering variety of early
Christian thought. In the same way we should expect the oldest

---

[33] Dix, *Shape of the Liturgy*, p. 198.

[34] Ibid., p. 179 n.1.

[35] E. C. Ratcliff, 'The Sanctus and the pattern of the early Anaphora', *JEH*, 1 (1950),
pp. 29–36, 125–34; cf. idem, 'The original form of the Anaphora of Addai and Mari: a
suggestion', *JThS*, 30 (1928), pp. 23–32; both reprinted in E. C. Ratcliff, *Liturgical Studies*, ed.
A. H. Couratin and D. H. Tripp (London, 1976), pp. 18–40, 80–90.

[36] *Didachê*, 9–10; the last view, with comprehensive documentation, is in *Die Didache.*
Erklärt von Kurt Niederwimmer, Kommentar zu den Apostolischen Vätern, 1 (Göttingen,
1989), pp. 173–9.

[37] Dix, *Shape of the Liturgy*, pp. 90–3.

liturgical texts to exhibit variety, which authority would later tame and reduce to uniform and orthodox standards.

It is time to return to Rattray. To him it is unthinkable that Cyril did not know a fuller text resembling the Liturgy of St James. There is consequently some circularity when he writes euphorically of the unanimity of all the most ancient liturgies, the ones he uses in his synopsis, in the main features of the eucharistic prayer. The same will be true of the congenial writers whose eucharistic theology he cites in support: Bingham, Johnson, and Hickes.[38] The contrary evidence of Cyril is set aside by assuming there are things Cyril leaves out, and that of the Roman canon is set aside because it fails to agree with the true, primitive consensus and must therefore have been changed.

Rattray's method leads however to important ideas. In considering what Cyril left out, he argues that there is a two-stage consecration, noticing that the patristic authorities like John Chrysostom are diverse: sometimes the conversion of the bread and wine into Christ's Body and Blood is associated with the words of institution, sometimes with the invocation.

> [T]he Christian sacrifice was not an Oblation only of the bare Primitiæ, to give Thanks to God as the Author of all the good things we now enjoy, and to acknowledge his Dominion over us; but that it was an Oblation of them as so far consecrated by the Words of Institution as to be made the Antitypes, or instituted Representatives of the Body and Blood of Christ.[39]

These Antitypes are then offered to the Father, and accepted through the descent of the Spirit: 'Which Oblation the Priest prays that God would accept of, not by sending down Fire from Heaven, as of old, to consume it, but his holy Spirit to transmute it ... and to make it truly, really, and effectually the spiritual and life-giving Body and Blood of Christ.'[40] Here is a splendid compromise between the Western view, that consecration is effected through Christ's words said by the priest in his name, and the Eastern view that the invocation of the Spirit is decisive. Had he known it, however, one of Rattray's key witnesses could be taken rather differently.

Letter 63 of Cyprian we have already noticed as a source of Rattray's

[38] *The Ancient Liturgy*, pp. xi–xii.
[39] Ibid., pp. 23, 25.
[40] Ibid., pp. 25, 27. The allusion to fire relates to such passages as Judges 13.15–20.

theory about the mixture of water with wine.[41] He relies heavily upon it for the offering to God of elements already consecrated as antitypes of the body and blood of Christ. He ignores the fact that Cyprian evinces but one side of the patristic miscellany, and that the typically western. By adding him to Irenaeus and eastern patristic evidence, one may conclude that both moments of consecration prevailed in the ancient Church. But this same letter of Cyprian has other uses. One could argue, with E. C. Ratcliff, that it demonstrates the origin of the crucial words of the Roman Canon in the Old Latin text of the Gospels. The notion that in the eucharist one repeats as closely as possible precisely what Jesus said and did at his Last Supper shaped the text and thought of the canon in perpetuity. If Ratcliff is right, that canon, and its concentration upon the words of Jesus, is the product of radical liturgy-writing in the third century, and evidence of one facet of the multitude of liturgical traditions in the early Church.[42]

Cyprian's letter, however, has other significance. It was written against those who used water only in the eucharistic cup, commonly supposed to be puritan or Ebionite heretics of one kind or another, and labelled 'Aquarii' or 'Hydroparastatae' by heresiologists. Cyprian's opening paragraph says that while most bishops throughout the world stick to Christ's command, some through ignorance or naiveté sanctify the cup and minister to the people otherwise than Jesus did and taught. This is plainly a custom observed in regular episcopal churches, not sects. He is writing so that 'if any are still held in that error, they may perceive the light of truth and return to the root and origin of the dominical tradition'.[43] Such churches may well have known no other custom, and the practice of using a cup of water, attributed to Ebionites, Encratites, Manichees, and others by the Church Fathers, and attested in New Testament Apocrypha,[44] may be part of the original variety. Certainly the Gospel traditions of the Last Supper reflect the Passover, and Jesus' references to 'the fruit of the vine' in that context make the use of wine apparent.[45] Paul

[41] See n.21 above.

[42] E. C. Ratcliff, 'The institution narrative of the Roman "canon missae": its beginning and early background', *JThS*, 30 (1957), pp. 64–82 (= Ratcliff, *Liturgical Studies*, pp. 49–65).

[43] Cyprian, *Ep.* 63,1: Hartel, *Cypriani Opera omnia*, 2, p. 701.

[44] Acts of Peter (Cod. Vercellensis 158) 2; Acts of Thomas 120, 152, 158; cf. F. Cocchini, 'Aquarii', *Encyclopedia of the Early Church*, ed. A. di Berardino, 2 vols (Cambridge, 1992), 1, p. 64.

[45] Matt. 26.29; Mark 14.25; Luke 22.18.

mentions only the cup, not its contents; yet even he knows of drunkards at what purports to be 'the Lord's Supper'.[46] Nevertheless to some extent the eucharist continues the feasts of Jesus in a variety of contexts, as represented by his notorious eating and drinking with sinners, and the miraculous feedings of multitudes in the wilderness. The essential point is not what is in the cup, but that it is shared. The Aquarian practice may go back to the very earliest congregations; the Ebionites, to whom it was attributed by Irenaeus, may well be vestigial remains of those Jerusalem churches which in earliest times broke bread from house to house.[47]

We have not gone through Rattray's synoptic reconstruction in detail. There is much more that could be said. But we have done enough to find his technique defective. He believed in an original apostolic liturgy, and sought it behind the evidence. What he was really handling was the evidence for liturgical reform in the fourth and fifth centuries. The reality was a colourful variety, which the emergence of the great Church through bishops like Irenaeus and Cyprian would progressively reduce to a very few models, each claiming venerable origin. The Liturgy of St James was not the ancient liturgy of the Church of Jerusalem. It was an earnest, practical compilation which reached Jerusalem after the time of Cyril's *Mystagogical Catecheses*. But in fairness it should be said that in terms of the times in which Rattray worked his error was understandable.

We now turn to the practical part of Rattray's book, the *Office for the Sacrifice of the Holy Eucharist*. He wanted to restore apostolic purity and sanctity to the Church of his day, to reform its worship on the best possible model. Having identified the perfect model to his own satisfaction, he wrote out that liturgy in English, with the necessary explanations and practical directions for performance. We cannot be sure that it was ever performed until 1994, celebrating the 250th anniversary of his death. How shall we rate it?

The first thing to say is that it represents only the *missa fidelium*. At the beginning, the priest washes his hands, the deacon dismisses 'those who ought not to join in this Service', the kiss of peace is shared, and the offertory made.[48] This uses words from various of the ancient liturgies, and offertory sentences from the Prayer Book.

---

[46] I Cor. 10.16, 11.25–9, with 11.21.
[47] Irenaeus, *Adversus haereses* v.1.3 (Rousseau *et al.*, *Contre les hérésies*, pp. 25–6); Acts 2.46.
[48] *The Ancient Liturgy*, pp. 113–15.

Thereafter the text follows the Jerusalem Liturgy as established in the synopsis, with occasional variations. It is not absolutely rigid: the opening greeting, 'The grace of our Lord Jesus Christ, etc.', follows Scripture and none of the variants of the ancient liturgies. There are minor rhetorical improvements: 'It is meet and right' becomes 'It is meet and right *so to do*'. The Intercessions follow the Liturgy of St James in a series of prayers over the consecrated gifts and an overlapping series led by the deacon. Rattray takes considerable liberties to improve these, changing the order and inserting petitions from liturgies other than James. He is perhaps aware that this is the most flexible and variable part of the ancient liturgies. Words of administering the communion are taken from Cyril. We are therefore offered a pedantic intention to restore the ancient text whole and perfect, which strays into creative liturgy-writing nevertheless. Rattray is certainly over-pedantic. At the commemoration of the passion of Christ one may compare the Communion Ofice of 1718, which uses the Liturgy of St James at this point. Collier, or whoever compiled the 1718 rite, wrote a commemoration which was not a translation, but a composition in English based on St James, which includes phrases reflecting the concerns of the Reformers and the authors of the Common Prayer Books: 'to satisfy thy Justice', 'to offer the Propitiatory Sacrifice of the Cross'.[49]

Of more importance is the use of the offertory sentences, said by the priest. These are based on those of the Scottish Prayer Book of 1637. They reflect the idea of God-ward offering which is typical of the Scottish liturgies. Of fourteen sentences, only eight are in the English books of 1549 and 1662. However, by staying with the principle introduced in 1549, Rattray shows his commitment to a fundamental point of Reformation eucharistic doctrine and liturgy: valid communion involves sharing of goods. In the eyes of Cranmer's critics the procession to the Poor Man's Box by the intending communicants turned the mass into a Yuletide game; it was the most conspicuous change the *Book of Common Prayer* made. One does not have to look far in the thinking of the Reformers, and especially of Martin Bucer, to find the justification for this approach. The eucharist originally involved the sharing of goods, and should even now represent it.

The reconstructed and adapted Jerusalem Liturgy was intended to

---

[49] Ibid., p. 117; Thomas Brett's edition of the 1718 Office in his *Collection of the Principal Liturgies*, pp. 144–5.

be performed. It could have been published separately as one of the 'wee bookies' circulating among Episcopalians for eucharistic worship this period.[50] The field was open. When episcopal synods had begun governing the Scottish churches in 1662, they did not attempt to impose the Prayer Book, least of all the provocative 1637 version. The English Prayer Book was used here and there, but all that was imposed was the use of the Lord's Prayer at every service, and the Doxology at the end of each portion of the metrical Psalms. The Westminster Directory was forbidden, but Knox's earlier liturgy was not, and was probably in use.[51] For Episcopalians a new rite compiled so learnedly by the elected Primus must have had practical potential and authority.

But how was one to start the service? Rattray acknowledges, 'We plainly find that the Service of the Church began with reading of the Scriptures, intermixed with Psalmody: After which followed the Sermon.'[52] When enthusiasts began in 1993 to prepare a realization of Rattray's liturgy to commemorate the 250th anniversary of its publication, they were at a loss as to how to start. One remarkable document saved them.

In the safe of St John's Church in Pittenweem I found in 1990 a neat leather-bound manuscript book. It is now Deposited MS 84 in the St Andrews University Library.[53] It had been known and studied by one earlier incumbent of St John's, Gianfranco Tellini, a considerable liturgical scholar. Tellini described it in 1984 in an address on the anniversary of the execution of King Charles I, 30 January. This was subsequently published in *The Royal Martyr Annual* of 1985, the official organ of the Royal Martyr Church Union.[54] That is an apt enough location in view of the Jacobite connections, but scarcely calculated to bring the Pittenweem Manuscript to a wide public. Tellini's presentation, though founded on accurate observation and sound scholarship, is not documented.

The little manuscript book is written in a beautiful steady longhand

---

[50] Since this lecture was given I have been informed by the Revd W. D. Kornahrens, Rector of Holy Cross Church, Edinburgh, that he has recently identified an early booklet printing of the text of the Pittenweem MS (see below, pp. 257–9) in the British Library, but no further details are available.

[51] See J. H. S. Burleigh, *A Church History of Scotland* (London, 1960), p. 243.

[52] *The Ancient Liturgy*, p. iii.

[53] It is 15.5 × 10 cm, with 214 written and 18 blank pages. How it got to Pittenweem is a matter of speculation.

[54] 'The Pittenweem manuscript Prayer Book', pp. 3–6.

of the eighteenth century. It is plainly intended as a manual of public worship. It contains

1. Lists of Psalms headed 'Introits for Sundays' and 'Introits for Holy-days';
2. A list of 'Lessons for Morning and Evening Prayer on Sundays and Holy Days', together with 'Proper Psalms on certain days' and 'Lessons for Ash Wednesday';
3. A table of 'Paschal Limits' (dates by which Easter is fixed);
4. A list of 'Proper Lessons for Morning Prayer' month by month throughout the year;
5. 'A Table of Moveable Feasts' calculated for 27 years (1744–70);
6. 'The order for Morning Prayer Dayly throughout the year';
7. 'The Litany';
8. A list of 'Proper Lessons at Evening Prayer' month by month throughout the year;
9. 'The order for Evening Prayer, Daily throughout the year';
10. 'An Order for the Sacrifice of the Holy Eucharist being the Ancient Liturgy of the Church of Jerusalem';
11. 'A Form of admitting a penitent to Pennance. To be used on Sunday morning immediately before the prayers for Penitents';
12. 'Form of absolving a Penitent. To be used on Sunday Morning'.

The book originally contained many blank pages. These were partly filled up in two later hands, with an exhortation to fortitude from 'Foster's Essays' and a Form of Confession and General Intercession to be used on Sundays. These earnest but disfiguring supplements indicate that the book was not being used for worship. The Table of Moveable Feasts was compiled in 1743, and that is probably the date of the Manuscript itself, or of its original as mechanically and anachronistically copied. The main part belongs to the year Rattray died, 1743.

Some of this material, such as the lectionaries and Litany, comes directly from the Scottish Prayer Book of 1637. A Prayer Book would still be needed to supply the Epistle and Gospel readings. The eucharistic rite is verbally identical with that of Rattray, published the next year in London. The manuscript should be taken as Rattray's own design for a manual of public worship, and was intended for publication and use.

Contents and annotations savour of Rattray. In Morning Prayer for various seasons the Apostles' Creed, the Nicene, and the Athanasian Creed are appointed. The Nicene Creed has the Holy Ghost, 'who proceedeth from the Father', and the footnote: 'The words And the Son do not belong to this Creed but are an after addition of the Latines, without the consent and ag^st the potestation [sic] of the Oriental Church: see Pearson on the Creed page 325 & 326 edit. 1692.'[55] The Athanasian Creed says unambiguously, 'The Holy Ghost is of the Father and of the Son: Neither made, nor created, nor begotten, but proceeding.' A footnote explains:

> He is the Spirit of the Father and the Son, and proceedeth from the Father and the Son, i.e. from the Father by the son. see Tert. adv. Prax cap. 4. The meaning of both expressions rightly understood is the same. For the Father as the fountain of the Deity hath the Spirit proceeding from him in & of himself; whereas the Son hath it in himself but of the Father, of whom he is begotten, and so receiveth all he is & hath as God. John XVI.15.[56]

The manner and concerns are Rattray's: ecumenical compromise between East and West over the controverted *Filioque*, based on patristic theology. Similarly, throughout this material typical patristic standards apply to the keeping of Eastertide and Sundays: there is to be no kneeling, and no Litany.

The forms of Morning and Evening Prayer and Litany have some variations from the Prayer Book, though basically like it. But the rubrics make Morning Prayer adaptable to begin the eucharistic Liturgy itself. Where an Epistle and Gospel are appointed, the Epistle replaces the second Lesson, and the Gospel follows Benedictus. The closing prayers of Morning Prayer are to be omitted, including the Lord's Prayer, and the service proceeds either to the Litany and eucharistic Liturgy, or straight to the Liturgy. When Rattray's Service of the Word was sought in order to celebrate his Liturgy on 22 May 1994, appropriate parts of the Pittenweem manuscript were transcribed.

It was a long performance in St Mary's Cathedral, Edinburgh, by the standards of the modern one-hour worship slot. In Rattray's day people expected to fill much of Sunday with church: in England, Mattins was followed by Litany and Ante-communion including sermon. Like that English practice, Rattray's service was repetitive: three sets of intercessions, for instance, one at Morning Prayer and two in the Liturgy.

---

[55] Pittenweem MS, p. [49].
[56] Ibid., p. [53].

This flowed partly from pedantic adherence to the model of St James. The most time-consuming part however was conveniently left out in 1994. For Rattray, the ancient disciplines must be re-established; 'None but the Faithful' are the opening words of his new Liturgy. Unbelievers, hearers, catechumens, penitents, heretics, and schismatics are explicitly excluded from the Liturgy and from the intercessions at Morning Prayer, where place for dismissal prayers is indicated.[57] The Sunday rites of penitence and absolution also belong here, and serious and time-consuming they would be.[58] In thus fencing the prayers and table, and requiring penance, Rattray was in step with contemporary Presbyterian practice: ever since the Confession of 1560 Scottish reformers had added 'Ecclesiastical discipline uprightlie ministred' as a third mark of the 'trew Kirk' to the two in which Calvin and the Thirty-nine Articles would agree.[59]

When we consider the claims of modern liturgists to be implementing Rattray's ideas, this is an aspect which should not be omitted. At Rattray's Liturgy in 1994, no one was required to leave, or to repent; spectators were welcome. Similarly the Kiss of Peace, which Rattray strongly encouraged, was performed without regard to his clear rubric: 'Note, This is not to be used but in such Churches or Chapels as are so ordered as that the Men and Women sit separate, as they ought to do. As to the Antiquity of it, there can be no question, since we find it so frequently mentioned in the Scriptures themselves.'[60] Rattray saw the Liturgy in the context of pre-Constantinian church discipline. Modern liturgically minded Christians do not.

But what of the content of the prayers? Undoubtedly the Scottish Prayer Book of 1929 implemented his programme with the Usages. Rattray argued for the double consecration, and marked it in his proposed Liturgy with the sign of the cross over the elements both at the words of institution and in the invocation of the Spirit; between the two came the commemoration of Christ's saving work and the offering of the gifts to the Father, and after it came intercession, including prayer for the dead. All of this the 1929 Prayer Book

---

[57] *The Ancient Liturgy*, p. 113; Pittenweem MS, p. [56].

[58] Ibid., pp. [199–205].

[59] *Scots Confession 1560 (Confessio Scoticana) and Negative Confession, 1581 (Confessio Negativa)*, ed. G. D. Henderson (Edinburgh, Glasgow, and Aberdeen, 1937), p. 75, Art. 18; *Calvin, Institutes of the Christian Religion*, ed. F. J. McNeill, 2 vols, Library of Christian Classics, 20–1 (London and Philadelphia, PA, 1960), 2, p. 1023; Thirty-Nine Articles, 19.

[60] *The Ancient Liturgy*, p. 113.

followed, and more. Rattray remains influential, and most Episcopalians still observe the double consecration by manual acts and devotional gestures, even when their modern texts do not require it. These modern texts, for which the claim is made that they implement Rattray more fully, fail to do so: the intercessions are moved out of the great prayer, and led, often by lay people, at the end of the service of the Word.

Rattray may have hoped, as many reformers do, that he was creating the definitive liturgy. At last, patristic research made it possible to restore the very words which Jesus' apostles had sung and said over bread and wine in upper rooms in Jerusalem. That was perfection, the goal of reform. It did not work, and it was not true. But the modern liturgy-writer, with far more books available, considering how believers should worship in a very different world, but no less fraught with perils, controversy, and mishap, may rightly recognize in Thomas Rattray a kindred soul, wedded alike to scholarly science and practical worship. We do well to honour him.[61]

University of St Andrews

---

[61] Rattray is commemorated in the present Calendar of the Scottish Episcopal Church on the anniversary of his death, 12 May.

THE MIRAGE OF AUTHENTICITY: SCOTTISH INDEPENDENTS AND THE RECONSTRUCTION OF A NEW TESTAMENT ORDER OF WORSHIP, 1799–1808

by DERYCK LOVEGROVE

The snuffy cobler now you mildly kiss,
And Cowgate damsels chuckle at the bliss.
By frequent salivations render'd fair,
They press your knees that envied bliss to share;
And, liquorish fish, wives piously begin
To think it sweeter than their morning gin.[1]

IN three satirical couplets the author of an anonymous pamphlet printed in 1812 suggests a possible reason for the popularity of the Haldane Tabernacle Connexion among the female population of Edinburgh at the turn of the nineteenth century.[2] In doing so he touches upon an important feature of the wave of evangelical Independency which swept across Scotland from the late 1790s: the appearance of new forms of worship that consciously sought to follow New Testament models. Reinforcing the verse this fiercely polemical work, which almost certainly comes from an establishment source,

---

[1] *Hypocrisy Detected in a Letter to the late Firm of Haldane, Ewing, and Co.* (Aberdeen, 1812), pp. 41–2.

[2] Robert Haldane (1764–1842) and his brother, James Alexander Haldane (1768–1851), who were members of a Perthshire landowning family, adopted evangelical views around 1795, and as a result applied their energies to the task of popular evangelism in Scotland. With their involvement in unconventional and suspect practices such as itinerant preaching, the establishment of Sunday schools, religious tract distribution, and the employment of laymen as catechists and travelling preachers, they quickly found themselves at odds with the Presbyterian religious establishment. A literal reading of the New Testament led to their preference for the congregational pattern of church government. However, the realities of mounting a national programme of evangelism led them to open large meeting places, known as tabernacles, in various centres across Scotland. The practical outcome was the emergence of the Tabernacle Connexion: a loose association of Independent churches bound together by a dependence for preachers and financial resources upon the generosity of Robert Haldane. While he remained a wealthy and influential layman, his younger brother was ordained in 1799 as pastor of the congregation that subsequently worshipped in the Edinburgh Tabernacle. In this satire the author refers to gin-sipping women who regarded the opportunity to exchange kisses with male members of the Tabernacle congregation as more exciting and daring than their customary glass of spirits.

takes the innovators to task for discarding reasoned biblical interpretation, flouting decency, and ignoring health dangers in their desire to resurrect long extinct practices from ancient Christianity.

Focusing upon the revival of the apostolic kiss of greeting, the critic suggests that 'it might be worth while to notice, how much oftener the young and sprightly women will be saluted than the old and ugly, and to keep an exact register.' Such intimacy will, the author believes, prove offensive and impractical.

> Suppose Mr. James Haldane's congregation to consist of five hundred persons, is the worthy pastor to slabber all those in turn, and they one another, several days would not suffice for the salutation; and then, what a conjunction of snuffy lips, snotty noses, foul breaths, ulcerous chops, &c. &c.: to confine the precept to kissing the next neighbour is ridiculous, it is general or nothing.[3]

In spite of such efforts to revive apostolic practice, the Haldane movement, at least in its early stages, was essentially pragmatic. In its resort to itinerancy, lay preaching, tract distribution, Sunday schools, seminaries, tabernacles, and especially in its undenominational aspirations, the dominant factor was the overwhelming conviction that the extension of the Christian message to the irreligious elements in society constituted the heart of the Church's task. For that purpose appropriate means had to be employed.[4] Yet, from the outset, pragmatism was modified by an equally strong biblical focus. In the end the preoccupation with scriptural correctness grew to such proportions that it did much to destroy what the former had achieved. At first the biblical emphasis merely provoked criticism of an underperforming and compromising Presbyterian establishment and led to separation from what was regarded as a vitiated church. Subsequently, it elevated the literal interpretation of the Scriptures to a position of absolute authority where it lacked the support of either confession of faith or existing church tradition. With virtually no indigenous experience of Independency to draw upon, the leaders of the new Scottish evangelical movement from 1799 onwards had little alternative but to construct a church order and the associated forms of

---

[3] *Hypocrisy Detected*, p. 43.

[4] Anon., *An Account of the Proceedings of the Society for Propagating the Gospel at Home, from their commencement, December 28. 1797, to May 16. 1799* (Edinburgh, 1799), pp. 7–12.

worship from scratch, using only their interpretation of New Testament practice. This was bound to involve a process of experimentation that would challenge existing conventions and in consequence provoke strong and hostile opinions.

At the heart of this process was the figure of James Haldane, who not only initiated the programme of evangelism in 1797, but also acted as principal architect and commentator on the forms of church order and worship that appeared in its wake. Throughout his long ministry he retained a fundamental concern for evangelism, but his acceptance of ordination in February 1799 as pastor of a group of converts arising out of the meetings held in the Edinburgh Circus signified an awareness of other responsibilities.[5] From that point onwards he demonstrated an equally strong interest in other aspects of New Testament practice.

In his writings Haldane devoted most of the next decade to exploring the scriptural evidence regarding church order and worship. His most comprehensive, if not final, statement on the subject appeared with the publication of *A View of the Social Worship and Ordinances observed by the first Christians* (Edinburgh, 1805).[6] In that book he argued that, while all churches were bound to display imperfections because of the fallibility of their human components, there was a perfect standard evident in the scriptural model of organization and worship to which all Christians were obliged to adhere. Wilful departure from that design led to disunity and schism, abuses, errors, weakness, and divine anger.[7]

Confining the role of miraculous features such as speaking in tongues to the exigencies of the New Testament period, he argued that the core of apostolic worship was essentially simple. It consisted in the regular observance of a cluster of ordinances every Lord's day: the apostles' doctrine, the fellowship, the breaking of bread, and prayers, together with singing the praises of God and, when appropriate, fasting and baptizing new members into the Christian community.

At the heart of the apostles' doctrine lay the unadorned proclamation of the gospel. That, together with the reading and teaching of the Scriptures, was the task of those appointed as elders in the church. However, in Haldane's understanding of passages such as Colossians

---

[5] A. Haldane, *The Lives of Robert Haldane of Airthrey, and of his brother, James Alexander Haldane*, 3rd edn (London, 1853), pp. 234–44.

[6] Hereafter referred to as *Social Worship*.

[7] Ibid., pp. 20–7, 441.

3.16, teaching and exhortation extended beyond the church's leadership to embrace all members who displayed appropriate gifts. Consequently, opportunity had to be given within the context of worship
for mutual exhortation. In 1805 he was prepared to confine this
exercise to the midweek meeting for church members.[8] Later his
opinion changed with damaging results.

Some aspects of apostolic worship presented relatively few problems.
Prayer raised minor questions concerning appropriate posture and the
extent of participation, while the subject of praise led the writer to
mount a brief polemic against those of conservative spirit who would
allow only psalm-singing or restricted hymnology to Old Testament
language.[9]

Far more conservative resistance might have been anticipated when
he came to review the Lord's supper and baptism. Already in 1802 he
had induced his own church to adopt a weekly observance of the
supper, in marked contrast to the infrequent celebrations which
characterized Scottish Presbyterianism. During the earliest period in
the life of his congregation he had observed the ordinance monthly in
order not to deter potential converts. But a careful study of the New
Testament had increasingly convinced him that it was not a matter for
private judgement; that the apostolic Church had commemorated the
death of Christ every Lord's day. In a tract published in 1802 he
rejected daily observance on the ground that the phrase 'breaking
bread from house to house' mentioned in Acts 2.46 may not have
referred to the Lord's supper. What was clear to him was that principal
congregations such as Corinth had exhibited a pattern of weekly
observance. To follow that example, he believed, would act as a
powerful attraction to outsiders.[10] Briefly he considered the objection
that frequent observance would necessarily lead to a loss of respect, but
he dismissed such fears on the ground that they betrayed the
continuance of the old superstitious veneration of the ordinance; the
elevation of communion above all other aspects of worship. In their
undue emphasis on preparation they also constituted a re-visitation of
the doctrine of good works.[11]

[8] *Social Worship*, p. 270.
[9] Ibid., pp. 285–6.
[10] J. A. Haldane, *The Obligation of Christian Churches to Observe the Lord's Supper Every Lord's Day, stated in a Letter to the Church of Christ assembling in the Tabernacle, Edinburgh* (Edinburgh, 1802), pp. 11–12, 15.
[11] Ibid., pp. 10–11.

With this tract on the Lord's supper Haldane seems to have succeeded in convincing any doubters within his congregation, for the 1802 change did not produce any noticeable division. Nor, it appears, did his 1805 pronouncements on the parameters of Christian baptism. In his book on apostolic worship and ordinances he argued on scriptural and theological grounds that baptism 'ought to be administered only to the children of believers, who are obeying, so far as they have opportunity, all Christ's commandments'.[12] Even within church walls the unbelieving hearer was still in a state of rebellion against God and, therefore, not a member of the covenant community. Hence baptism as the sign of that community was meaningless for the child of such an individual. Commenting on the tribal status of baptism in Scottish society at that time he observed, 'A person may, in this country, neglect the ordinance of the Lord's supper without being singular; but were he to allow his children to remain unbaptized, it would be thought very shocking and heathenish.'[13]

The radical implications of this volume for the worship of the new Independents lay in the rejection of traditional Presbyterian practices, and in the promotion of a pure church interpreting the Scriptures afresh in the formulation of its worship. Its radicalism did not primarily consist in the adoption of some of the stranger aspects of apostolic practice such as that seized upon by the anonymous critic of 1812. Indeed, features such as love feasts, the kiss of greeting, foot-washing and long hair for women were treated by James Haldane in 1805 either as insufficiently clear to be prescriptive, or as culturally related and therefore inappropriate for an authoritative model.[14]

Into this comparatively moderate situation two further elements obtruded. The practice of certain minority groups of eighteenth-century origin and the baneful influence of personality both introduced instability. By the turn of the century the Glasites and their slightly later antipaedobaptist counterparts, the Scotch Baptists, had existed for several decades, and had become locally influential. Both groups were devoted to a straightforward application of the words of Scripture, and since each was committed to a plurality of elders there were implications for the conduct of worship that in the case of the Scotch Baptists led to controversy and division. Some churches

---

[12] Haldane, *Social Worship*, p. 319.
[13] Ibid., p. 321.
[14] Ibid., pp. 85–9.

believed that the Lord's supper could be observed even if the elders were absent, while others disagreed with the concept of 'lay' administration. Through their writings both John Glas and Robert Sandeman for the Glasites, and Archibald McLean for the Scotch Baptists, exerted an unsettling influence upon the developing Tabernacle Connexion, especially in the case of its more literal-minded and incautious leaders.[15]

Contemporary commentators pointed the finger of blame at William Ballantine, a former Burgher Seceder. Ballantine, a product of the Burgher Divinity Hall at Selkirk and David Bogue's Gosport Academy, had assumed pastoral responsibility in September 1799 for a group of converts at Thurso created initially by the preaching of James Haldane in Caithness two years earlier. In March 1801 for health reasons he moved to Elgin, where he assumed the ministry of a 'Free Presbyterian Congregation'. With somewhat intemperate haste he set about forming a church out of the congregation, but as he began to develop his views on order and worship he found himself involved in an increasingly acrimonious dispute with the chapel managers.[16]

The Elgin congregation had occupied the position of an unrecognized chapel of ease, and as such evinced no desire to depart from Presbyterianism. In contrast Ballantine increasingly believed that he needed to review the hastily formed membership on an individual basis, and to exclude from the Lord's supper and the other privileges of membership those who were found to be unworthy and lacking evidence of true conversion. What was at stake was a conflict between two competing views of the church: the one a learning community of

---

[15] At least one commentator openly attributed the new ideas evident in the Tabernacle Connexion from around 1807 to Glas and Sandeman: G. Ewing, *Facts and Documents respecting the Connections which have subsisted between Robert Haldane, Esq. and Greville Ewing, laid before the Public, in consequence of Letters which the Former has addressed to the Latter, respecting the Tabernacle at Glasgow* (Glasgow, 1809), p. 95.

[16] Two leading Independents, John Aikman and Robert Kinniburgh, identified Ballantine as a prominent advocate of the new ideas. Aikman responded negatively to Ballantine in *Observations on Exhortation in the Churches of Christ* (Edinburgh, 1808), while Kinniburgh described his 1807 work on the elder's office as 'a withering blast . . . from the north, which was attended with direful consequences', Haldane, *Lives of Robert and James Alexander Haldane*, p. 357. Ballantine himself recorded the fact that he was accused by the chapel managers at Elgin of Glasitism, though he also denied the charge: W. Ballantine, *Observations on confessions of faith of human composition, the independency and discipline of Christian churches, weekly communion in the Lord's supper, church meetings &c. &c. in an address to the managers and others of the New Chapel at Elgin* (Edinburgh, 1804), pp. 55, 123–4.

saints and sinners; the other a group of individuals with personal experience of conversion.

In line with his more exacting view of the Church, Ballantine wanted to increase the frequency of the Lord's supper from the existing rate of twice yearly to a weekly observance of the ordinance. He advocated dispensing with the customary preparatory meetings on the grounds of a lack of scriptural warrant, and emphasised the desirability of the whole church membership sitting down together instead of the usual relays. His cavalier treatment of the Presbyterian sensibilities of his opponents culminated in an ultimatum from the chapel managers. The letter sent to Ballantine insisted that as their minister he 'must adhere to the doctrines of the Holy Scriptures, as explained in the Westminster Confession of Faith, the Larger and Shorter Catechisms ... not introducing unscriptural novelties, sneering at catechisms and confessions of faith, or at the pious and scriptural expressions of reputable divines.'[17] Public worship of God was to follow customary practice and the Westminster Directory without innovation. Any alteration in the psalmody was to be approved unanimously by the congregation.

Needless to say, Ballantine did not comply, and in March 1803 he left, becoming shortly afterwards the pastor of a small Independent church formed out of those who had been converted under his preaching. In this new situation, and apparently exercising some degree of influence over the thinking of Robert Haldane, the financial force behind the Haldane seminaries and tabernacle-building programme, he developed his ideas on apostolic worship. He argued in an 1807 pamphlet for Lord's day services in which all the ordinances were properly observed. Those ordinances would include mutual exhortation by private church members and, even more controversially, the exercise of discipline. His view was that concealment was wrong and that discipline was 'as much calculated to convert men as any other church ordinance'.[18]

Ballantine appears in the Tabernacle Connexion as a provocative figure; a restless man who never seems to have remained long in any position.[19] Influential over both James and Robert Haldane, he aroused

---

[17] Ibid. pp. 49–50.

[18] W. Ballantine, *A Treatise on the Elder's Office* (Edinburgh, 1807), p. 77.

[19] Strictly speaking, Ballantine's period as pastor of the Free Presbyterian Congregation at Elgin took him outside the Tabernacle Connexion. It was his attempt to steer that

the dislike of more stable Independents such as Greville Ewing of the Glasgow Tabernacle and John Aikman, pastor of North College Street Church in Edinburgh. Writing many years later, the widow of one of his successors at Elgin described him as 'a very overbearing person . . . rash and harsh . . . [who] went into things without proper consideration, when any fancy struck his mind'.[20]

In 1808 the crisis over apostolic organization and worship came to a head within the Tabernacle Connexion. Early that year John Aikman learned that James Haldane had introduced mutual exhortation into Sunday worship at the Edinburgh Tabernacle. Reacting against this innovation Aikman argued in a tract dated 4 February 1808 that while there was a clear duty to observe all of the Lord's ordinances, the new free-for-all in Sunday gatherings arose from a misunderstanding of the language of Scripture. It also owed much to a belief, which stemmed from Ballantine, that they could not be followers of the Lord or truly apostolic 'except an unlimited licence [were] constantly given, at the stated meetings of the churches on the first day of the week, to any brother who incline[d], or th[ought] himself fit for the service, to engage in it'.[21] Though he acknowledged (as had Ewing)[22] a place for mutual exhortation in the privacy of the church meeting, Aikman believed that the new exhortatory licence was completely at variance with the idea of an elected leadership.[23] Whereas the Scriptures divided the church into teachers and taught, mutual exhortation overturned that relationship. He believed it would destroy order and peace in the church, that it was calculated to offend uncommitted onlookers and work against the task of evangelism, and that it set aside the clear scriptural rules by which the Church should choose its public leaders. Aikman concluded by noting with alarm the even more damaging proposal to conduct discipline publicly on the Lord's day.[24]

In his response to this criticism Haldane's argument turned on the

congregation towards Haldane-style Independency that contributed to his dismissal, and led to his re-establishing open links with the Tabernacle Connexion as pastor of the newly formed Elgin Independent Church.

[20] Gleneagles, Perthshire: Haldane family papers: Catherine McNeil–Alexander Haldane, 27 May 1851.

[21] Aikman, *Observations*, p. 10.

[22] G. Ewing, *An Attempt towards a Statement of the Doctrine of Scripture on some Disputed Points respecting the Constitution, Government, Worship, and Discipline of the Church of Christ* (Glasgow, 1807), p. 169.

[23] Aikman, *Observations*, pp. 10–11.

[24] Ibid., p. 40.

nature of the local church. Noting that much of the New Testament was concerned with the nature and purpose of Christian assemblies and the manner of their organization, he refused to re-enter the debate as to whether unbelievers should be received into fellowship. Rather, he assumed that the church was in essence a pure body that existed to separate believers from the world and to strengthen their faith through observance of Christ's ordinances. He denied having suggested that mutual exhortation was the duty of all Christians, insisting that the possession of an appropriate gift was necessary. Nor did he believe that exhortation should in any way replace the teaching role of the elders. Indeed, he envisaged that the latter, in exercising their supervisory function, would be needed to encourage the diffident and to restrain the over-confident.[25]

Haldane admitted that, for those accustomed to a single individual leading worship who was trained in the art of public speaking, the involvement of untrained people might appear startling. Some ordinances were self-evidently justified; others appeared much less so despite their obviously scriptural basis. Pointing to the precedent offered by Jewish synagogues in the apostolic era, he denied that the exercise of mutual exhortation broke significant new ground.[26] Nor did it presuppose the continuance of the miraculous gifts recorded in the biblical narrative. As his argument developed he sought to resist two errors: the first, an undue focus upon the teaching office; the second, the belief that in the absence of miracles the Holy Spirit was no longer at work in the church.[27]

In his opinion the real value of exhortation had been diminished in the past by being confined to a weekday evening when no more than a third of the members were normally present. He argued that part of its worth derived from its role as the means by which members were able to choose wisely their future elders, although he insisted that it was never to be regarded as a trial of gifts.[28] Exhortation, he believed, should become an ordinance for the whole church. As an aside he suggested that the traditional fellowship meetings in the Highlands had failed to benefit the Established

---

[25] J. A. Haldane, *Observations on the association of believers; mutual exhortation; the apostolic mode of teaching; qualifications and support of elders; spiritual gifts, &c. in which Mr Aikman's Observations on Exhortation, &c. are considered* (Edinburgh, 1808), pp. 16–17.

[26] Ibid., pp. 29–31.

[27] Ibid., p. 40.

[28] Ibid., pp. 41–4.

Church as they might have done precisely because they had remained as quasi-autonomous gatherings.[29]

With this public disagreement over exhortation the Tabernacle Movement had become deeply divided, with figures such as Aikman and Ewing emerging as architects and leaders of a more formal and conservative group of Independent congregations.

The decisive blow to the unity of the evangelistically oriented connexion came in April 1808 over the ordinance of baptism. Up to that point, apart from one or two individuals who had left to become Baptists, all the members of the new Scottish Independent movement had maintained their belief in infant baptism even though it had come to be linked with the conversion and church membership of the parents. Now that consensus was to be blown apart.

James Haldane's views of the doctrine had been formed in the context of established Presbyterianism. An early reference to deviant practice as Anabaptism reveals the latent prejudice he had imbibed from his contemporaries.[30] Before he began his quest for apostolicity he had noted that ministers in the Established Church rarely made much of the scriptural basis of baptism. Even in his new phase as an evangelical his former distaste for antipaedobaptism was reinforced by the warnings of others that those who held such views were narrow and unevangelistic. As his views on the nature of the Church altered, so the combination of a literal reading of the New Testament and simple logic carried him inexorably away from the idea of baptism as a rite defining the boundaries of the wider Christian community, and towards the restriction of the ordinance to the children of believing parents. Ultimately, the same logic led him to reject infant baptism altogether.

At the Edinburgh Circus, and later at the Tabernacle, Haldane's twin concern was the task of reconciling his desire to form a pure fellowship of believers with the original purpose of allowing the building to function as a centre for preaching to the unchurched sector of the city's population. As he later explained to John Campbell of Kingsland Chapel near London, he had come to entertain doubts about the ordinance of baptism as early as 1804 and had resolved to make a full study of the subject.[31] The questioning had already commenced

---

[29] Haldane, *Observations*, pp. 44–5.
[30] J. A. Haldane, *Reasons of a Change of Sentiment & Practice on the Subject of Baptism* (Edinburgh, 1808), p. 2.
[31] Haldane, *Lives of Robert and James Alexander Haldane*, p. 359.

when *Social Worship* appeared the following year, with its resolute defence of the Independent paedobaptist position. Gradually Haldane's views changed until he reached the point in 1808 where he believed that infant baptism was inconsistent with the principles of a separated Church; that it belonged more naturally to the concept of religious establishment. Its deleterious effect was that it lulled people into a spiritual sleep, causing them to equate birth with entrance to the community of faith.[32]

Reviewing his own transition he noted that he had been struck by the confidence shown by the antipaedobaptists. They used the plainest New Testament passages dealing with baptism and made no attempt to shy away from the subject. Moreover, in spite of the allegations of their opponents, they displayed a strong propensity for making converts. None of their number ever moved in the opposite direction.[33]

By contrast he found paedobaptist arguments circuitous. Whereas apostolic practice in general was regarded as superseding Jewish religious customs, infant baptism was defended by its proponents on the basis of Old Testament parallels that he found obscure and unconvincing. Eventually, he concluded that the traditional covenant justification was invalid, and that the natural concomitant of a pure Church was the scriptural practice of baptising believers.[34]

Though Haldane hoped that this could be a matter for forbearance, both within his own congregation and the Tabernacle Connexion, the news of his change of view sundered the movement. Within a year nearly two hundred members of the Edinburgh Tabernacle, including his own brother, Robert, had embraced Baptist views. But many had left, some to return to the Established Church, others to join John Aikman's Independent congregation, while a third section formed their own assembly in hired rooms.[35] Across Scotland similar painful separations occurred within the Tabernacle congregations, some with the additional rancour caused by dispossession where Robert Haldane owned the title deeds.[36]

---

[32] Haldane, *Reasons*, p. 9.
[33] Ibid., pp. 4-5.
[34] Ibid., ch. 3.
[35] Haldane, *Lives of Robert and James Alexander Haldane*, pp. 359-61.
[36] At Elgin the small continuing Independent section of the congregation was made homeless and was forced to rent a former Episcopalian chapel. In the case of the Perth Tabernacle the Baptists as the minority group, having taken possession of Robert Haldane's building after the Independents had been evicted, were unable to collect a viable

The unhappy fate of the Tabernacle Connexion reveals how difficult it was in practice in the 1790s for even such a popular religious movement to disengage from the dominant ecclesiastical tradition. Though practical considerations had created the problem through the compulsion to evangelize the irreligious sections of society and to care for the resulting converts, a new basis of authority had to be found. The search had of necessity to be conducted outwith traditional Presbyterian structures and confessions of faith. The obvious alternative lay in the fundamental criterion of Reformed Christianity, the text of Scripture.

To many of the hearers the changes in worship that resulted reflected the egalitarianism they detected in the movement. Farm-workers, miners, fishermen, soldiers, women in humble circumstances, and members of the emerging urban proletariat listened to preachers and catechists from similar backgrounds to themselves, some speaking in the Gaelic tongue, and believed they represented a new and more relevant religion. Those drawn into the movement encountered a novel concept of the church in which members related to one another as those within a close family who shared an intrinsic equality and interdependence. Worship merely accentuated this ideal as the assembled brethren listened to their peers speaking publicly in prayer and spiritual reflection, shared in the practical exercise of Christian discipline, and sat down together around a common communion table.

To what extent was literalism to prevail in the quest for biblical authenticity? At times James Haldane's writings seem excessively concerned to follow the minutiae of early Christian practice, yet in other places he acknowledges that some of the most important teachings of Christ were figurative. Moreover, certain customs were dictated by cultural necessity. Even the central ordinances he seems to have prized as much for their didactic and evangelistic value as for their apostolic origin. To a greater extent than Ballantine, he resorted to reason rather than scriptural precedent to argue for the incorpora-tion or rejection of particular elements of worship, and exhibited a willingness to abandon what did not prove in practice to benefit the church. Writing much later to his son and biographer, Alexander

---

congregation. As a result of the division the premises were sold to the Methodists. H. Escott, *A History of Scottish Congregationalism* (Aberdeen, 1960), p. 262; R. Kinniburgh, *Fathers of Independency in Scotland* (Edinburgh, 1851), p. 127.

Haldane, the first historian of Scottish Congregationalism, Robert Kinniburgh, confirmed this characteristic:

> You are also right about the number of changes made by your late father. They were just four – Baptism he continued to hold to the last – I mean adult baptism by immersion – Exhortation he greatly modified – Public discipline and the salutation he abandoned. At all stages he was willing to forbear ... When he saw they did not tend to edification he either modified or abandoned them with the same singleness of heart that he adopted them.[37]

One essential ingredient of the process of disengagement from former ecclesiastical models was the new and disconcerting concept of built-in instability; of the Christian church as an experimental community, one that was continuously learning. Inevitably, among the critics of the Tabernacle Connexion this idea provided fertile ground for condemnation of what they regarded as restless innovation and a manifest tendency towards schism and disorder.

From the outset James Haldane recognized the force of this criticism. In 1802 he wrote:

> our practice [of following Scripture minutely] subjects us to what some will deem an inconvenience. It obliges us avowedly to follow the word of God, wherever it may lead us; and doubtless this may expose us to the charge of fickleness, inconsistency, and not knowing today what views we may adopt tomorrow. . . . What yesterday seemed to be duty, may not appear to be so today.[38]

As he continued he seemed to acknowledge the subjectivity of his position compared to that of the Presbyterian churches: 'as their standard remains the same, their character for steadiness does not suffer, so long as they nominally adhere to their subscription, . . . [whereas] the confession of our faith obliges us to act according to our present views of the word of God.'

In practice the evolution of worship brought mounting difficulties for the Tabernacle Connexion. By 1808, as changes in worship multiplied, local tensions of the type encountered at Elgin gave way to full-scale dislocation affecting every congregation. Though the

---

[37] Gleneagles, Perthshire: Haldane family papers: Robert Kinniburgh–Alexander Haldane, 11 March 1851.

[38] Haldane, *Lord's Supper*, p. [1].

changes initiated did not embrace the miraculous ingredient seen in the later charismatic developments under Edward Irving, they caused the new Scottish Independent movement to fracture, and as it fell apart the evangelical initiative passed back to mainstream Presbyterian bodies.[39] The divisions over worship were symptomatic of the loss of the original momentum that had been responsible for bringing the movement into existence a decade earlier.

The very occurrence of such divisions suggests that, although the original changes were prompted by organizational inertia, radical departure from accepted forms of worship, especially in the context of institutional flux, was never likely to find general acceptance. In the absence of any consensus as to what should succeed the traditional forms the impetus faltered, and the whole experiment became, at least to some degree, self-defeating. The instability of evangelical Independency during its experimental stage caused many would-be adherents to resort to more tried and tested expressions of corporate belief.

University of St Andrews

---

[39] James Haldane went out of his way to distinguish between miraculous gifts and the regular observance of the Christian ordinances: *Observations*, pp. 36–7. In a much later publication, in which he attacked Irvingism, he openly linked the supposed possession of miraculous gifts to doctrinal error: J. A. Haldane, *The Signs of the Times Considered* (Edinburgh, 1832), p. 31.

'SHUT IN WITH THEE': THE MORNING MEETING AMONG SCOTTISH OPEN BRETHREN, 1840s–1960s

by NEIL DICKSON

THE Brethren movement had its origins in the early nineteenth century in Ireland and the south of England, first appearing in Scotland in 1838.[1] The morning meeting gave quintessential expression to the piety of the members and was central to its practice. In the 1870s a former Presbyterian who was looking for the ideal pattern of the Church witnessed his first meeting in the village of K–.[2] Converted in the revivals of the 1860s, he was eventually to join the movement. A number of years later he described his initial impressions:

> The seats were plain, and all alike, and in the place where I would have naturally looked for the pulpit, there stood a small table, covered with a white cloth, and on it a loaf of bread unbroken, and a cup of wine beside it. . . .
>
> The worship of these simple, warm-hearted believers, was such as I had never seen or heard of before. There was no minister, no president; nearly all the brethren took part: some in giving out a hymn, some in prayer and thanksgiving, and several read short portions of the Word, making a few remarks. I particularly noticed that *all* directed our hearts to the Person and Work of Christ. There had been no pre-arrangement, yet everything done was in beautiful order and harmony. I had read of the guidance of the Holy Spirit in 1 Cor. xiv., but, like many others, I had thought it was something of the past: here I saw it before my eyes, and my heart was won by the simplicity and beauty of God's way. Then, after thanks being given, the loaf and the cup were passed round – not in that hasty manner I had been accustomed to, nor yet by officials set apart for the purpose, but from hand to hand among those there gathered; each slowly, reverently, partaking – in many

---

[1] Neil Dickson, 'Scottish Brethren: division and wholeness 1838–1916', *Christian Brethren Review Journal*, 41 (1990), pp. 5–41.

[2] During this period assemblies existed in Kirkfieldbank, Lanarkshire, and Kemnay, Aberdeenshire; the latter is the more likely identification in view of the origins of this anonymous individual's publisher, John Ritchie, in neighbouring Inverurie.

cases with tears – of the Divinely chosen emblems. Never before did Calvary seem so near and real.[3]

The account emphasises discontinuity with the spectator's previous mode of worship. It juxtaposes the ordinariness of the surroundings with the supernaturalism of the event. Its language and imagery, doubtless coloured by memory, stress simplicity, solemnity, and the lack of ritual; Christ as the focus of the gathering; the exclusion of human direction and an openness to the impulse of the Spirit. These were among the significant features of Brethren spirituality encompassed by the Sunday morning meeting or 'the breaking of bread'.[4] In 1848 the movement divided into 'Open' and 'Exclusive' factions,[5] a division which was antecedent to any significant Brethren growth in Scotland, where the Open party eventually became the majority. Although the discussion in this paper will primarily be concerned with the Open Brethren in Scotland from the 1840s to the 1960s, much of it will be applicable to the movement outside these imposed limits.

Scottish Brethren inherited the service having several strands of continuity with earlier Christian worship already woven into it. The breaking of bread held in Dublin in 1829, to which Brethren origins are traced, was held weekly, something which would be natural for most of the early leaders given their Anglican background. It had a set order of service, but gradually it allowed for spontaneous participation among its attenders.[6] Historians have speculated that a Scottish influence was at work in this transformation of worship.[7] The thinking of John Glas on mutual exhortation, it is surmised, could have reached the nascent movement through Thomas Kelly or John Walker who had founded congregations in Ireland in the early nineteenth century.[8]

---

[3] Anon., *How I was Led Outside the Camp* (Kilmarnock, nd), [pp. 5–7].

[4] For the latter term cf. Harold H. Rowdon, *The Origins of the Brethren: 1825–1850* (London, 1967), p. 299 n.190.

[5] For the various Brethren groupings see, F. Roy Coad, *A History of the Brethren Movement*, 2nd edn (Exeter, 1976).

[6] J. G. Bellet to James McAllister, [J. G. Bellet *et al.*], *Interesting Reminiscences of the Early History of 'Brethren' with Letter from J. G. Bellet* (London, nd), pp. 7–8.

[7] Derek B. Murray, 'The influence of John Glas', *Records of the Scottish Church History Society* [hereafter *RSCHS*], 22 (1984), pp. 45–56.

[8] Harold H. Rowdon, 'Secession from the Established Church in the early nineteenth century', *Vox Evangelica*, 3 (1964), pp. 76–88; idem, 'The problem of Brethren identity in historical perspective', *Biblioteca Storica Toscana*, 11 (1988), pp. 159–74; Grayson Carter, 'Evangelical seceders from the Church of England, c.1800–1850' (University of Oxford D. Phil. thesis, 1990), pp. 287–9.

Certainly the Brethren were aware of their teachings, but a direct influence has been impossible to prove.[9] When the Bristol pioneers Henry Craik and George Müller were moving their congregation away from clerical administration of the sacrament, they quoted James Haldane's phrase for participation, 'social worship', although this might reflect contemporary usage rather than familiarity with Haldane's thought, which itself was influenced by Glasite teaching.[10] The Brethren and Edward Irving had mutual interests for a period. Although spontaneous worship was accepted, they held back from Irving's pentecostalism,[11] leading Ian Rennie to describe their worship as a 'laundered charismaticism'.[12] Such worship was probably further developed by the accession of a number of prominent Quakers in the aftermath among them of the Beaconite controversy of 1835–6.[13] At least one Brethren Scot noted the similarity between the morning meeting and the Quaker use of silence.[14] However, it was the mode of worship described in I Corinthians to which appeal was exclusively made[15] – a decisive reason for not citing contemporary influences. The mixture of Glasite mutual edification and Quaker impulsive contribution was dictated by a desire for Christian primitivism which was, it has been recently maintained, the central concern in the formation of the movement.[16]

That the Brethren morning meeting showed continuity with the traditions of some Scottish dissenters would explain why it proved acceptable to some within Scotland.[17] John Bowes, a former Primitive

---

[9] Cf. W. B. Neatby, *A History of the Plymouth Brethren* (London, 1901), p. 28.

[10] [George Müller], *A Narrative of Some of the Lord's Dealings with George Müller, written by Himself*, 6 vols, 9th edn (London, 1895), 1, p. 281; cf. James Alexander Haldane, *A View of the Social Worship and Ordinances Observed by the First Christians* (Edinburgh, 1805).

[11] Timothy C. F. Stunt, 'Irvingite Pentecostalism and the early Brethren', *Christian Brethren Research Fellowship Journal*, 10 (1965), pp. 40–8.

[12] Ian S. Rennie, 'Aspects of Christian Brethren spirituality', in J. I. Packer and Loren Wilkinson, eds, *Alive to God: Studies in Spirituality* (Downers Grove, IL, 1992), p. 201.

[13] Timothy C. F. Stunt, *Early Brethren and the Society of Friends*, Christian Brethren Research Fellowship Occasional Paper, 3 (Pinner, 1970).

[14] A. Borland, 'The Lord's Supper', *The Believer's Magazine* [hereafter *BM*], 61 (1951), p. 122.

[15] Anon., 'Plain words about the morning meeting', *The Witness* [hereafter *W*], 57 (1927), p. 87; Robert Rendall to the editor, *W*, 75 (1945), p. 79.

[16] James Patrick Callahan, *Primitivist Piety: the Ecclesiology of the Early Plymouth Brethren* (Lanham, MD, 1996).

[17] The similarity of Glasite worship and that of the Brethren was shown by the reprinting among the latter of a correspondence initiated in New York (and printed there in 1820) among churches of a primitivist type as *Letters Concerning their Principles and Order from*

Methodist preacher who had adopted Glasite practices in his congregation in Dundee, made contact with the early Brethren movement in the south of England in 1839;[18] and for the following two decades he was the principal disseminator of Brethren ecclesiology within Scotland. During this period there were strong Glasite influences on Scottish Brethren worship. In 1847 the assembly at Newmains, Lanarkshire, which became one of the most influential in the county, evolved from an Evangelical Union congregation apparently independently of contact with Brethren elsewhere,[19] probably due to an infusion of Glasite ideas. The Glasite phrase, 'the church should edify itself', was used for ministry from among the members, and one of them presided at the first communion, a Scotch Baptist practice.[20] The pattern favoured by Bowes can be seen from the brief description he gave of the worship of the congregation he founded in Lochee, Angus: 'we meet to remember the Lord in the breaking of bread; three or four generally speak.'[21] Continuity with Scottish dissenting traditions gave an advantage, but discontinuity was sharp for those coming from the mainstream Presbyterian tradition. At Neilston, Renfrewshire, the difficulty in the 1850s was in getting the members to adopt unstructured, open participation and to cease relying on one person fulfilling a ministerial office.[22]

Mid-Victorian revivalism, itself shaped by Brethren influence,[23] became the dominant context out of which the Scottish movement emerged, and the practice of open worship continued to attract Scotch Baptists to the movement.[24] It is, perhaps, a shared background in

Assemblies of Believers in 1818–1820 (London, 1889). In this correspondence several Scotch Baptist churches in Scotland described their customs in terms sufficiently close to those of the Brethren to be mistaken later for an earlier form of the movement in the country by C. J. Pickering et al., 1865–1965: The Half-Yearly Meetings of Christians in Glasgow ([Glasgow, 1965]), p. 3.

[18] John Bowes, The Autobiography: or the History of the Life of John Bowes (Glasgow, 1872), pp. 221–32.

[19] David J. Beattie, Brethren: the Story of a Great Recovery (Kilmarnock [1939]), p. 202.

[20] John Smith–John Bowes, 12 Oct. 1848, quoted in Bowes, Autobiography, pp. 454–7.

[21] John Bowes, 'The work of God at Dundee and Lochee', The Truth Promoter [hereafter TP], 7 (1859–61), p. 11.

[22] 'Extracts from the journal of John Bowes', TP, 3 (1853–5), pp. 238–40; 6 (1858–9), pp. 127–8.

[23] John Kent, Holding the Fort: Studies in Victorian Revivalism (London, 1978), p. 116; D. W. Bebbington, Evangelicalism in Modern Britain: A History from the 1730s to the 1980s (London, 1989), p. 117.

[24] Neil Dickson, 'Brethren and Baptists in Scotland', The Baptist Quarterly, 33 (1990), pp. 372–87.

contemporary revivalism which, despite the discontinuities, gave the anonymous observer in K– the feeling that his searching was at an end when he witnessed his first morning meeting. A greater stress on extempore prayers and hymn-singing, more suited to impulsive views of the Spirit current in contemporary revivalism rather than the Glasite practice of exhortation, came to predominate at the morning meeting. This was not accomplished everywhere immediately. During the 1870s assemblies were formed in the north-east independently of Brethren elsewhere, and Scotch Baptist influences were initially present among them.[25] In 1873 the first breaking of bread at Insch, Aberdeenshire, was a series of Scripture readings, with a prayer of thanksgiving at the dispensing of each element, followed by a hymn and an exhortation.[26] But by the following year the service had been assimilated to the pattern of alternating prayers and hymns which John R. Caldwell, editor of the principal Brethren magazine, *The Witness*, stated was the normal pattern of a morning meeting.[27] His successor Henry Pickering described in 1934 what he termed 'the ordinary way', used in ninety per cent of some 10,000 assemblies worldwide, with 'each accredited brother being absolutely free to take part in hymn, prayer, reading, or ministry. The only arranged brother being one to give out names and notices.' But some assemblies in Glasgow had what Pickering called 'The Twofold Meeting', with the first hour following the 'ordinary' pattern and, after an interval, a further hour at which a pre-arranged preacher would speak.[28] The loose organizational structure of the Open Brethren movement meant that variations could be tolerated.

There were, however, a number of attempts to develop a firmer liturgy at the morning meeting which reflect the sociology of the movement. During the 1880s a group which had as its focus the magazine *Needed Truth* evolved, among other new thinking and practices, certain prescribed actions during the breaking of bread. F. A. Banks, the seminal teacher of the new ideas, maintained that the brother 'who says in the assembly, "Let *us* give thanks," ere he breaks the loaf *loses his individuality*, and is, for the time being, the mouthpiece of the church.' He should then publicly break the bread as a corporate

[25] Idem, 'Scottish Brethren', pp. 16–20.
[26] Insch, Fordyce Hall, Minute Book 1873–91, p. 1.
[27] J. R. Caldwell, 'Object of the Lord's Supper', *W*, 22 (1892), pp. 126–7.
[28] Hy P[ickering], 'The order of the morning meeting', *W*, 54 (1934), p. 85.

act.[29] Such prescriptions about the morning meeting led to controversy in many assemblies,[30] and eventually their advocates seceded in 1892–3 to form what became the Churches of God.[31] Other liturgical formats were developed, especially in the inter-war period of the twentieth century. The Brethren read the Old Testament typologically. Developing ideas contained in Exclusive Brethren writers,[32] some taught that during the morning meeting there should be a progression through the typological significances of the Levitical sacrifices: the sin, peace, meat, and burnt offerings; others favoured concentrating on either the meat offering (interpreted as a type of Christ's perfect humanity) or the burnt offering (thought to signify Christ's devotedness in death to God) only.[33] During this period the evangelist Isaac Ewan was the individual who developed the most exact liturgy of the occasion, based on the Old Testament sacrifices.[34] The worshippers were sympathetically retracing the life of Christ to the cross, and the morning meeting was to follow this progress.[35] The crucial moment of the service was when the brother who gave thanks for the emblems walked to the table on which they were placed and broke the bread and poured out the wine, thus 'shewing forth the Lord's death'.[36] The seeming oxymoron of a spontaneous liturgy in these uses of the Old Testament led to accusations of ritualism.[37] Those who promoted them were also wanting to intensify sectarianism. They combined with

[29] F. A. B[lanks], 'The feast of remembrance and testimony', *The Northern Witness* [hereafter *NW*], 16 (1886), pp. 74–5; cf. 'Question CCXXV', ibid., p. 80; 'Question CVI', *NW*, 12 (1882), p. 111; 'The believer's question box', *BM*, 37 (1927), p. 90.

[30] E.g., W. H. Clare, *Pioneer Preaching or Work Well Done* (London and Glasgow [1925]), p. 88.

[31] For a description of the breaking of bread in the Churches of God, see G. Willis and B. R. Wilson, 'The Churches of God: pattern and practice', in B. R. Wilson, ed., *Patterns of Sectarianism: Organisation and Ideology in Social and Religious Movements* (London, 1967), Appendix, pp. 285–6.

[32] J. N. D[arby], *Hints on the Tabernacle, the Sacrifices, the Day of Atonement, the Feasts, and the Coverings of the Holy Things* (London, nd), pp. 25–59; C. H. M[ackintosh], *Notes on Leviticus*, 2nd edn (London [1861]).

[33] A. Borland, 'The Lord's Supper', *BM*, 61 (1951), pp. 1–2.

[34] W. R. Lewis and E. W. Rodgers to the editor, *W*, 82 (1952), p. 120.

[35] I. Y. E[wan], 'When should the bread be broken?', *Present Testimony* [hereafter *PT*], 6 (1940–1), pp. 984–8.

[36] J. R[odgers], 'In the beginning', *PT*, 4 (nd), pp. 1110–12; Andrew Borland, 'The Lord's Supper', in J. B. Watson, ed., *The Church: a Symposium* (London, 1949), p. 78.

[37] A. Borland, 'The Lord's Supper', *BM*, 60 (1950), pp. 73–5; Lewis and Rodgers to the editor, *W*, 82 (1952), p. 120; G. C. D. Howley, 'The Church and its members', in *A New Testament Church in 1955* (Rushden [1956]), p. 21.

their teaching on the morning meeting a desire to exclude non-Brethren from participation in the Lord's Supper. The several liturgical formulae offered were part of attempts to evolve a sectarian distinctiveness, a recurring and significant phenomenon in Brethren history.

Mainstream opinion tended to be less doctrinaire and more pragmatic as, in Open Brethren fashion, some variety in belief was allowed (though within strict Fundamentalist limits). This can be seen in what was seemingly the principal liturgical issue to agitate the movement (if the number of occurrences in questions to *The Witness* is taken as an index): the permissibility of 'ministry' at the morning meeting. Worship was defined as being active,[38] whereas 'ministry' (or Bible teaching) was received passively. Applying this logic rigorously, the more sectarian individuals disapproved of devotional homilies or even Bible reading at the breaking of bread. However, the consistent advice from *The Witness* was that they should be permitted since precise rules could not be laid down.[39] Pragmatism too dictated whether one plate for the loaf and one cup only should be used. Some felt that the loaf should be passed round unbroken with each breaking bread individually, thus showing personal participation in Christ.[40] More than one cup was also resisted as it seemed to erode the symbolism of the participants' unity.[41] But, it was argued, larger assemblies needed to use two or more plates and cups to expedite the distribution of the emblems and, moreover, rules should not be established.[42] However, a line was drawn at using individual cups in case the 'Romish' practice of using wafers was also introduced.[43] The less sectarian wing of the movement also saw it as necessary to cultivate a proper understanding of the occasion.

The morning meeting was shaped by the central facets of Brethren practice and doctrine. By the inter-war period, certainly, the

---

[38] J. R. Caldwell, *Epitome of Christian Experience* (Glasgow [1917]), p. 111.

[39] See the correspondence in *NW*, 8 (1878), pp. 17–18; *W*, 29 (1899), pp. 82–4; *W*, 30 (1900), pp. 131–2; *W*, 33 (1903), pp. 34–6; *W*, 41 (1911), pp. 33–4; *W*, 44 (1914), p. 177; *W*, 45 (1915), pp. 176–7; *W*, 48 (1918), pp. 18–19, 26–8, 43–4, 60, 90–1; *W*, 55 (1925), pp. 112–13; *W*, 56 (1926), pp. 208–9, 384–5; *W*, 57 (1927), pp. 153, 159; *W*, 59 (1929), pp. 280–1; *W*, 60 (1930), p. 66; *W*, 74 (1944), pp. 95–6; *W*, 75 (1945), pp. 15–16, 21–2; *W*, 77 (1947), p. 141; cf. *BM*, 31 (1921), pp. 55–6.

[40] John Dickie to the editor, 4 July 1855, *TP*, 4 (1855–6), p. 95; 'The believer's question box', *BM*, 57 (1947), p. 317; Borland, 'The Lord's Supper', pp. 97–8.

[41] 'The believer's question box', *BM*, 45 (1935), pp. 22–3.

[42] See the correspondence in *NW*, 16 (1886), p. 80; *W*, 54 (1924), p. 422; *BM*, 45 (1935), pp. 22–3, 134, 190–1; John Ritchie, *BM*, 29 (1919), p. 71; *BM*, 43 (1933), p. 48.

[43] Hy P[ickering], 'Questions and answers', *W*, 49 (1919), p. 176.

preferred seating plan at the breaking of bread in many assemblies used the unfixed seats to form a square with the table carrying the elements in the middle.[44] It is a spatial arrangement that is not focused on one individual but which suggests the involvement and common status of the worshippers. In the Church all were clergy.[45] The use of the square pattern also suggested that the centre of the gathering was Christ. Much was made of Christ's promise to be 'in the midst' of those gathered in his name. 'It was decided', noted the minutes of one assembly when the square pattern was adopted in 1926, 'to alter some of the seats to permit of the table being placed in the "midst" on Lord's Day mornings'.[46] The service was also rooted in the doctrine of the movement. Brethren theology tended to concentrate on the redemptive significance of the second Person of the Trinity to the exclusion of the relationships of the other Persons to the world. The death of Christ had a central place. The cross was seen to be the foundation of the gospel just as salvation by blood was perceived as the principal theme of the Bible.[47] This primary focus in Brethren theology dictated the purpose of the morning meeting: the emphasis of the service fell on commemorating the person of Christ, especially his death.[48] Brethren belief in the believer's positional perfection in Christ,[49] and the freedom from introspection derived from their doctrine of assurance,[50] gave a confidence to their worship. But the focus on Christ's death meant that the tone of the morning meeting was sombre. Reference to the believer's subjective experience was excluded.[51] 'The special object for which the Lord assembles His people thus', wrote John Ritchie, the founding editor of *The Believer's Magazine*, 'is to "Remember Him"

[44] S. R. Hopkins, 'Questions and answers', *W*, 59 (1929), pp. 18–19.

[45] R. T. Hopkins, 'Friday's Conference', *Northern Evangelistic Intelligencer*, 2 (1872), p. 73; cf. [J. L. Harris], 'On Christian ministry', *The Christian Witness*, 1 (Jan. 1834), p. 9.

[46] Tillicoultry, Bankfoot Evangelical Church, 'Minute Record of the Assembly & Oversight Business Meeting. From 1st Jan. 1925 – Ann St. Gospel Hall, Tillicoultry', Half Yearly Business Meeting, 20 March 1926.

[47] J. R. Caldwell, *From the Cross to the Kingdom*, rpt (Glasgow, 1983), p. 188; Alexander Stewart, *Salvation Truths* (Kilmarnock, nd), p. 10; John Ritchie, *From Egypt to Canaan* (Kilmarnock, nd), pp. 21–3.

[48] J. R. Caldwell, 'The weekly gathering of saints', *W*, 38 (1908), pp. 173–5.

[49] Harold H. Rowdon, 'The Brethren concept of sainthood', *Vox Evangelica*, 20 (1990), pp. 91–102.

[50] Rennie, 'Brethren spirituality', p. 205.

[51] J. Murray, 'Cause and condition', *BM*, 57 (1947), pp. 178–9; cf. M[ackintosh], *Leviticus*, pp. 86–8.

in the breaking of bread.'[52] The morning meeting gave vital expression to both the Christocentrism of the movement and its liberty of ministry among male members.

Features of Brethren spirituality also controlled the occasion. Three of its defining ones will be isolated in the discussion which follows: supernaturalism, separatism, and cerebralism. The absence of a chairman or presiding minister at the morning meeting was stressed to emphasise that its centre was Christ. It was the supernaturalism implicit in this understanding of the service which had appealed to the anonymous observer at K–. Simplicity was perceived as an essential characteristic of the apostolic Church,[53] and the word was frequently used with reference to the breaking of bread. 'It is a simple ordinance,' Caldwell noted, 'observed in a simple manner, and by a simple people.'[54] The New Testament gave no liturgy; therefore, it was argued, one should not be developed.[55] The use of ecclesiastical art and architecture were strongly criticized,[56] a point underlined by the plainness of the surroundings in which the Brethren worshipped. Instrumental music at the morning meeting was also eschewed. The stress on simplicity helped to heighten the sense of the supernatural. The divine was not mediated through material objects and rituals, as in the Old Testament, but God worked directly on the human spirit. The dispensation of ritualism was past and Christians lived in the dispensation of the Spirit.[57] If the worship was directed, then it was the Holy Spirit 'as Guide and Sovereign Distributor of gifts' who was leading as he moved in the hearts of those present, using them as 'fit mouthpieces to express the assembly's worship'.[58] If there was a president, then it was the Lord himself who presided.[59] The direct faith that the Brethren had inherited from popular nineteenth-century Evangelicalism, with its strong sense of supernaturalism,[60] lent itself to this understanding of the morning meeting.

---

[52] John Ritchie, *Assembly Privileges and Responsibilities* (Kilmarnock, nd), p. 5.

[53] Callahan, *Primitivist Piety*, pp. 51–4.

[54] J. R. Caldwell, 'Christ the sin offering', *W*, 24 (1894), p. 56.

[55] Hy P[ickering], 'What is meant by the breaking of bread?', *W*, 56 (1926), pp. 283–4.

[56] J. R. C[aldwell], *W*, 24 (1894), p. 84; John Ritchie, 'The Church in its worship', *BM*, 28 (1918), p. 77; John Douglas, *Lessons from the Kings of Israel and Judah* (Ashgill, 1997), p. 14.

[57] G. A[dam] and J. R. C[aldwell], 'Questions and answers', *W*, 24 (1874), p. 84.

[58] Alexander Marshall, 'The Lord's two ordinances', *W*, 19 (1889), pp. 164–6.

[59] J. R. Caldwell, 'The breaking of bread: the meaning, mode, and practical observance. Notes on I Corinthians xi. 23–6', *W*, 39 (1909), p. 78.

[60] Bebbington, *Evangelicalism*, pp. 78–97.

Separatism and cerebralism also had a place in perceptions of the morning meeting. The world was excluded, and all were agreed that it was for believers only. Judas had left the Last Supper, J. R. Caldwell was at pains to establish, before Christ broke bread, for it was a feast for disciples only.[61] The division of the Sunday services into a morning meeting for Christians and an evening one for unbelievers emphasised the separation.[62] It was captured in a hymn by the Glasgow solicitor, Alexander Stewart:

> Shut in with Thee far, far, above
> The restless world that wars below,
> We seek to learn and prove Thy love,
> Thy wisdom and Thy grace to know.[63]

The verse also makes plain that central to the meeting was quietness so that there might be meditation on the love of Christ.[64] This requirement produced a leisurely service in which it was expected there would be silences.[65] Caldwell felt the ideal length of the morning meeting was two hours, with the participation in the Lord's Supper reasonably close to the start so that it 'might be lingered over in blessed meditation'.[66] Isaac Ewan wanted it nearer the end, moving towards it 'softly, reverently, meditatively'.[67] Caution was advised against too vocal a service, for silence involved all those present, including the women who were, apart from a period after 1863, excluded from audible participation in praying, announcing a hymn, or in ministry.[68] 'All should be exercised', counselled Ritchie, 'waiting upon God, meditating on Christ, during times of silence.'[69] The accounts which have survived of the earliest breaking of bread services bear testimony to the powerful awareness of the numinous that those present sensed. The observer at K– noted the participants' emotion; at Peterhead during the first morning meeting, it was remembered (perhaps with

---

[61] Caldwell, 'The breaking of bread', pp. 77–9.
[62] Caldwell, *Christian Experience*, pp. 102–3.
[63] *The Believers Hymn Book* (Glasgow [1885]), no. 129.
[64] J. R. Caldwell, 'The oneness of the Body', *W*, 38 (1908), p. 190.
[65] John Cowan, 'Self-control', *BM*, 60 (1950), pp. 255–6.
[66] J. R. Caldwell, 'Questions and answers', *W*, 22 (1892), p. 127.
[67] I. Y. E[wan], 'When should the bread be broken?', *PT*, 6 (1940–1), p. 987.
[68] Neil Dickson, 'Modern prophetesses: women preachers in the nineteenth-century Scottish Brethren', *RSCHS*, 25 (1993), pp. 89–117.
[69] Ritchie, *Assembly Privileges*, p. 4.

some exaggeration), the floor was wet with the tears of those present.[70] Although cerebralism was to become more dominant (as will be seen below), these gatherings when the movement was young could be emotional occasions.

Social and cultural influences were present in the spirituality which directed the morning meeting. The stress on simplicity and solemnity and the supernaturalism of the occasion arose out of the cultural context. They increased the state of awe favoured by nineteenth-century Romanticism.[71] Paradoxically, the desire for separation from 'the restless world' was formed in part by strong negative reactions to nineteenth-century society. The heavy reliance on meditation, like the adoption of an impulsive ministry, was possibly one of the Quaker influences on Brethren thinking.[72] But its use also pointed to the cerebralism of the movement. Rennie has noted that 'Brethren spirituality appears restricted, cerebral and serious.'[73] Among other things, this cerebralism was seen in the numerous conversational Bible readings held by Brethren, their love of the minutiae of the dispensational scheme of biblical interpretation, and the substantial publishing programme undertaken by the movement.[74] At the morning meeting it was evinced in the ability of the members to engage in silent meditation on doctrine and the text of Scripture and, during public participation, to cite effortlessly from memory biblical passages relevant to the theme of the prayers and hymns. These factors, combined with the prescription that the experiential should be excluded, ensured that the breaking of bread would become heavily weighted towards the use of the mind. Pentecostal churches, which appealed to similar social classes but were without the intellectualism of the Brethren, had to rely on a professional ministry;[75] but the Scottish Brethren movement was built on men such as Isaiah Stewart, a coal miner in Lanarkshire and

---

[70] [Alex Buchan], 'First Message in York Street Hall by Mr. Alex Buchan on 26th June, 1965' (cyclostyled sheet, nd: author's collection).

[71] Neil Summerton, 'The practice of worship', *Christian Brethren Review*, 39 (1988), p. 36.

[72] Stunt, *Brethren and the Society of Friends*, pp. 23–5.

[73] Rennie, 'Brethren spirituality', p. 195.

[74] Neatby, *Plymouth Brethren*, p. 278; G. M. Marsden, *Fundamentalism and American Culture: the Shaping of Twentieth-Century Evangelicalism: 1870–1925* (Oxford, 1980), pp. 48–62; J. A. H. Dempster, 'Aspects of Brethren publishing enterprise in late nineteenth century Scotland', *Publishing History*, 20 (1986), pp. 61–101.

[75] Bryan R. Wilson, *Sects and Society: a Sociological Study of Three Religious Groups in Britain* (London, 1961), pp. 63–75.

assembly member from 1882 until his death in 1934, who rose early to read the Bible before he started work at 5 a.m. and was prominent in his assembly for his participation at the breaking of bread.[76] The movement appealed to the more articulate members of the working classes and lower-middle class which had been produced by mass literacy. Alongside the emotional warmth infused by supernaturalism existed a colder cerebralism.

Not only did the principal features of Brethren spirituality shape the morning meeting, but the service was in turn expected to mould the lives of the members. The breaking of bread was the most significant moment of the week, 'the greatest privilege', Ritchie wrote, 'and the highest form of fellowship with God and His people, to which the believer is called upon earth'.[77] It was the service above all others at which attendance was obligatory.[78] The need for careful preparation of soul was stressed.[79] Because of the worshippers' dependence on the promptings of the Spirit, it was important that the individual's life was also kept open to his influence. 'If there is to be spirituality in worship on the first day of the week,' wrote Ritchie, 'there must be spirituality in life and godliness in walk, on the six days that precede it.'[80] The Brethren, as extreme anti-ritualists, held the commemorative, Zwinglian view of the Lord's Supper,[81] but individuals such as Caldwell and Andrew Borland, an editor of *The Believer's Magazine*, approached the Calvinist position, maintaining that the believer at the Lord's table fed by faith on Christ.[82] 'That will make better Christians of us,' wrote Caldwell, 'it will separate us from the world and its ways, bind us together in divine love and unity, and give us victory over sin and Satan.'[83] A link was made between the holiness of the occasion and

[76] Lesmahagow, Hope Hall, Roll Book 1876–1907, p. 67; 'Isaiah Stewart', *W*, 64 (1934), p. 167; J. McCallum, 'The Roll Call' (author's collection).

[77] J. Ritchie, 'The Lord's Supper', *BM*, 10 (1901), p. 140.

[78] Hy P[ickering], 'Witness Watchtower', *W*, 60 (1930), p. 114.

[79] J. A. Ireland, 'The breaking of bread', *W*, 78 (1948), pp. 43–4; R. Eadie, 'The Lord's Supper', *W*, 87 (1957), pp. 102–7; John Ritchie, 'Hints for behaviour in the assembly', *BM*, 16 (1906), p. 32; John Ritchie, 'The Church in its worship', *BM*, 28 (1918), p. 76; A. Borland, 'The Lord's Supper', *BM*, 61 (1951), pp. 1–2, 99, *BM*, 62 (1952), pp. 1–2, and *BM*, 63 (1953), pp. 17–19.

[80] Ritchie, 'The Church in its worship', p. 76.

[81] Peter Manson, 'A Sunday morning meditation', *W*, 78 (1948), pp. 17–18; Ireland, 'Breaking of bread', pp. 43–4.

[82] A. Borland, 'The Lord's Supper', *BM*, 60 (1950), pp. 97–8, 266; *BM*, 61 (1951), pp. 49–51; idem, 'The Lord's Supper', pp. 75–6.

[83] J. R. Caldwell, 'Christ the peace offering', *W*, 24 (1894), p. 137; cf. Ritchie, 'The Lord's Supper', p. 141.

the members' lives.[84] Although the debate over non-Brethren's participation in the Lord's Supper was never conclusively resolved, the majority view eventually was that they should be excluded.[85] Guarding the separateness of the morning meeting was the first line of defence in the battle to maintain the purity of the sect. Regarded as the crucial means by which spirituality was advanced, it became (to borrow a phrase from the Salvation Army) the holiness meeting of the movement, the core of the members' devotion.[86]

Cerebralism came to be dominant in the spirituality. The Brethren shared many of the concerns of the nineteenth-century holiness movement and they influenced Pearsall Smith.[87] In the north-east assemblies higher-life teaching was initially accepted.[88] The morning meeting suited this spirituality admirably, for both stressed surrender to the Spirit. A pseudonymous 'Crucified Man' criticized those who were too active during the service for 'Doing! Doing Doing!' Using an image favoured by Romantic poets and holiness teachers alike, he wrote that believers at the breaking of bread 'ought to be like the Aeolian harp, on which the winds of heaven play sweet music – the Holy Ghost playing sweet music on their soul to the glory of God, and His grace'.[89] Yet it was the intellectualism of the Brethren which eventually prescribed how the morning meeting should be conducted. The opening hymn set a theme for each meeting and participants were expected to follow it,[90] leading one individual to complain in 1964, with some rhetorical exaggeration, that the young 'find themselves concentrating on recognising the theme, seeking to link each hymn, prayer or meditation together, sometimes by a process of mental gymnastics little short of Olympic standard'.[91] It was presumed that the more intelligent contributions would show some familiarity with the typological significance of the Old Testament

---

[84] George Adam, 'The holiness of the Lord's Table', *W*, 30 (1900), p. 154.

[85] Dickson, 'Scottish Brethren', pp. 23–36.

[86] J. A. Ireland, 'Why I sit at the Lord's Table', *W*, 70 (1940), pp. 121–3; T. A. Kirkby, 'Why we prize the morning meeting', *W*, 71 (1941), pp. 203–4; Borland, 'The Lord's Supper', pp. 77–8.

[87] Bebbington, *Evangelicalism*, pp. 157–9; Roger N. Shuff, 'Open to closed: the growth of exclusivism among Brethren in Britain 1848–1953', *Brethren Archivists and Historians Network Review*, 1 (1997), p. 12.

[88] Dickson, 'Scottish Brethren', pp. 18, 38 n.62.

[89] A Crucified Man, 'Worship meetings', *The Northern Assemblies* (1872), pp. 5–6.

[90] J. R. Caldwell, 'Ministry at the Lord's Table', *W*, 41 (1911), pp. 33–4.

[91] W. E. Howie to the editor, *W*, 94 (1964), p. 230.

offerings.[92] The objective focus of the service required a capacity for abstract thought, and this need for intellectual understanding acted also as a brake on emotionalism.[93] Cerebralism produced a less spontaneous, more restrained service.

The Open Brethren in Scotland are an example of a sect which, unusually for Protestant Evangelicalism, gave a central place to a sacrament in the life of its members. Ironically, it gave them similarities with Catholic traditions.[94] The morning meeting was a perfect vehicle for Brethren theology, practice, and spirituality. However, spontaneity and change were suppressed over time, not just by those who attempted to enforce a stricter liturgy. The routinization of charismata also took place. By 1939 Henry Pickering was complaining of the monotony of the alternating hymns and prayers[95] and in 1945 one Glasgow lay preacher cited as proof of a spiritual deterioration the curtailment of the Spirit at the morning meeting.[96] The tension which existed in Brethren spirituality also restrained innovation.[97] A heightened supernaturalism produced an emotional sense of the occasion, but this coexisted with a drier cerebralism which eventually came to be dominant at the breaking of bread. The detailed understanding of the morning meeting which had been evolved constituted a powerful influence in repressing change to the received pattern of worship.

University of Stirling

---

[92] Ella [Jack] in *Central View* (the magazine of the Central Evangelical Church, Kilmarnock), 20 (March, 1994), pp. 10–11.

[93] Cf. Summerton, 'Practice of worship', p. 35.

[94] Ian M. Randall, 'Movements of evangelical spirituality in inter-war England' (University of Wales Ph. D. thesis, 1997), pp. 201–5, 218–20; Donald Bridge and David Phypers, *The Meal that Unites* (London, 1981), pp. 135–42, 175.

[95] Hy P[ickering], 'What place is given to scripture at the morning meeting?', *W*, 69 (1939), p. 109.

[96] W. A. Thomson, *W*, 75 (1945), pp. 15–16.

[97] Cf. Rennie, 'Brethren spirituality', p. 206.

GOTHS AND ROMANS: DANIEL ROCK, AUGUSTUS WELBY PUGIN, AND NINETEENTH-CENTURY ENGLISH WORSHIP

by JUDITH F. CHAMP

The Chant or music used by the Papal choir, and indeed in most Catholic cathedrals and abbey churches is, excepting in some instances, ancient. Gregory the Great collected it into a body and gave it the form in which it now appears, though not the author of it. The chant of the psalms is simple and affecting, composed of Lydian, Phrygian and other Greek and Roman tunes, without many notes, but with a sufficient inflection to render them soft and plaintive or bold and animating. . . . This ancient music which has long been known by the name of the Gregorian chant, so well adapted to the gravity of divine service, has been much disfigured in the process of time by the bad taste of the middle and the false refinements of the latter ages. The first encumbered it with an endless succession of dull unnecessary notes, dragging their slow length along, and burthening the ear with a dead weight of sound; the other infected it with the melting airs, the laboured execution, the effeminate graces of the orchestra, useless to say the least even in the theatre, but profane and almost sacrilegious in the church. Some care seems to have been taken to avoid these defects in the papal choir. The general style and spirit of the ancient and primitive music have been retained and some modern compositions of known and acknowledged merit, introduced on stated days and in certain circumstances. Of musical instruments, the organ only is additional in St Peters, or rather in the Papal chapel, and even then not always: voices only are employed in general, and as those voices are numerous, perfect in their kind, and in thorough unison with one another, and as the singers themselves are concealed from view, the effect is enchanting and brings to mind 'the celestial voices in full harmonic number joined' that sometimes reached the ears of our first parents in paradise, and 'lifted their thoughts to heaven'.[1]

---

[1] John Chetwode Eustace, *A Tour Through Italy*, 3 vols (London, 1813–19), 1, pp. 379–80. The several subsequent editions used the title *A Classical Tour through Italy*, which is therefore the title used in the main text.

THIS glowing commendation of plainchant and perhaps surprising assertion that it was one of the glories of papal Rome in the early years of the nineteenth century comes from an unexpected source. The author was John Chetwode Eustace, an English Catholic priest and in his time a famed travel writer, whose *Classical Tour Through Italy* became, in many editions, the *vade mecum* of English travellers to the south for two or three generations. Eustace was a controversial figure. He (and his employer Lord Petre, whose sons he accompanied on the Grand Tour) were part of the Cisalpine movement of the late eighteenth century which urged greater independence for English Catholics from papal control, in order to enhance their standing with their English contemporaries. His liberal Cisalpine views were expressed in his book and raised the fury of Bishop John Milner, the scourge of Cisalpines and Vicar Apostolic of the Midland District (to which Eustace was attached). Milner condemned the *Classical Tour* for containing 'insinuations of heresy, scandalous, schismatical, and the prevailing inducements to the indifferency and irreligion of the times'.[2] Eustace's expression of what were then regarded as liberal views, including recommending the use of the vernacular in liturgy and the reception of the cup at communion, won him sympathetic non-Catholic reviews which commended his lack of bigotry. In the Preface to the *Classical Tour*, while declaring vigorously his Catholicism, he makes a remarkable call for tolerance and understanding between Christians.

> Yet with this affectionate attachment to the ancient faith, he [the author] presumes not to arraign those who support other systems. Persuaded that their claims to mercy as well as his own, depend upon sincerity and charity, he leaves them and himself to the disposal of the Common Father of All, who we may humbly hope will treat our errors and our defects with more indulgence than mortals usually show to each other. In truth, reconciliation and union are the objects of his warmest wishes, of his most fervent prayers: they occupy his thoughts, they employ his pen; and if a stone should happen to mark the spot where his remains are to repose, that stone shall speak of peace and reconciliation.[3]

[2] F. C. Husenbeth, *Life and Times of John Milner* (London, 1862), p. 403.
[3] Eustace, *Tour through Italy*, Preface, p. XI.

Eustace's work is a clue to the possibility of looking afresh at the divisions within English Catholicism in the nineteenth century, which would eventually be passed on to the Church of England, between liturgical and religious revival in the mould of papal Rome or that of medieval England which diminished rather than advanced hopes of peace and reconciliation. He was a passionate and knowledgeable devotee of Rome, its classical history, the traditions of early Christianity there, and the Rome of the contemporary popes; yet Eustace is in no sense a prototype of the Romanizers of a later generation. If anyone fulfils that role it is his implacable episcopal enemy, Milner, whose first pastoral letter to his clergy celebrated the subordination of the 'whole vast body' of the Church to 'one Supreme Pastor, whose seat is the centre and rallying point of them all',[4] and who in 1814 introduced the popular Roman devotion of the Sacred Heart of Jesus into England. Yet even Milner himself stands as a warning against too easily categorizing the Gothics and the Romans. His ecclesiology was definitely that of a proto-Ultramontane, yet he was the author of a number of learned tracts on medieval church architecture and a history of medieval Winchester, and the builder of a neo-Gothic chapel for his mission there. What is important to Eustace and his fellow Cisalpine authors is the cultivation of a proper understanding of Christian history and appreciation of religious and liturgical practices, such as plainchant, which connect contemporary Catholics with the Church of their fathers throughout the centuries. It is the continuity of plainchant, despite its being 'much disfigured in the process of time' which is important. It is this, they believed, combined with generous tolerance, which would rebuild Catholicism in England.

Eustace was part of the tradition of English Cisalpinism or Gallicanism, which flourished in the late eighteenth and early nineteenth century, but which was gradually overwhelmed by the power of Roman Ultramontane ideology for which Milner stood. The Cisalpines advocated an approach which was designed to make Catholicism palatable to English tastes, by emphasising the loyalty of Catholics to the royal house of Hanover, their liberal religious opinions and Enlightenment spirit. The minimizing of direct papal interference in English Catholic life was a key tenet, hence the Cisalpine desire to re-establish bishops in ordinary and thereby emphasise the rights and obligations of local ecclesiastical authority, working in concert with

---

[4] John Milner, *Pastoral Letter to the Clergy of the Midland District* (London, 1803).

civil power. Ultramontanism, which emerged after the French Revolution, was the reverse of this, an ideology built upon an enhanced role for the person and office of the pope, rejecting all attempts by local churches to co-operate with civil government. These were the battle lines of nineteenth-century Catholicism, quickly adopted by the English. The leading exponent of English Cisalpinism, himself a gifted historian of Anglo-Saxon Christianity, was John Lingard. He lived till 1850, by which time Cisalpinism was dead and the term 'Gallican' had become a favourite term of abuse in ecclesiastical circles.

Lingard shared Eustace's desire to use history to bring about understanding and reconciliation. In 1806 he published his first historical work, *The Antiquities of the Anglo Saxon Church* (revised and enlarged in 1845).

> But even greater than his love of the subject which had so long occupied his thoughts and labours, than his desire to make that great period better known to his own people, was his longing to contribute somewhat towards lessening the antipathy and misconceptions of the great majority of his countrymen, with regard to a subject dearer to him than life itself. The great spring and motive of his writings, from the first to the last of his indefatigable labours, was to persuade his alien countrymen that they were mistaken in their estimate of his religion and its observers.[5]

Lingard was a reformer, who realized that liturgical and devotional life had to be renewed, in order to be intelligible to Catholics and non-Catholics alike.

> My notions are that the English Prayers should be such as would at least instruct and edify Protestants: that they should be read slowly, distinctly, devoutly, and that the sermon should be well composed and well delivered. For of the Mass, Protestants understand nothing, it is only by the prayers and sermons that you can induce them to repeat their visits and think of the doctrines of our religion.[6]

Lingard's understanding of liturgical reform was first demonstrated in his *Manual of Prayers for Sundays and Holydays*, published in 1833, in

---

[5] M. Haile and E. Bonney, *The Life and Letters of John Lingard* (London, 1910), p. 87.
[6] Quoted in J. P. Chinnici, *The English Catholic Enlightenment: John Lingard and the Cisalpine Movement 1780–1850* (London, 1980), p. 165.

which he tried to reconcile 'the taste of men of education' to 'our peculiar form of worship'. Lingard's *Manual*, intended for use before (or if necessary in place of) Sunday Mass, begins with the Sign of the Cross, dedication of the day, and the *Venite* psalm in translation, followed by various prayers about keeping the Sabbath and a dialogue Our Father. This is followed by a series of sequences, another psalm, a brief litany, and concluding prayer. The free translations of the psalms and the clear and simple structure are evidence that intelligibility was the paramount function. 'His intention was partly to produce a form of public prayer which would be attractive to potential Protestant converts; but he was also concerned, for its own sake, with the reform of Catholic worship and instruction, much of whose language he considered incomprehensible to ordinary people.'[7]

Daniel Rock stands in this tradition of historical scholarship with a polemical purpose, but rather that of nurturing possibilities of Christian understanding between Catholic and Protestant than bludgeoning non-Catholics into acceptance of the continuity in truth of Catholic practice. The historian of English Cisalpinism regards the date of publication of Lingard's *History of England* (1819) as the real end of Cisalpine influence.[8] Yet he names Rock among those who continued the literary tradition and indeed 'achieved definite literary ascendancy after 1825'.[9] The coherence of Cisalpinism (in so far as it had existed) had gone, but Rock was to take up the favourite Cisalpine issues of the restoration of the hierarchy and the rights of the clergy.

The interest in looking afresh at Rock, and the milieu within which he worked, comes from uncertainty about the fullness of our understanding of the Gothic-inspired battles in the nineteenth century. In this respect I am indebted to Mary Heimann for persuading many of us to revisit the Roman/Gothic skirmishes.

> Since the devotional change which English Catholicism underwent in the latter half of the nineteenth century has generally been held to have been that of a triumph of Ultramontanism over native or old-English traditions, whether imposed directly from Rome or via enthusiastic new converts on the one hand and the Irish immigrants on the other, the general perception seems to have been that, however interesting an examination of the

[7] John Bossy, *The English Catholic Community 1570–1850* (London, 1976), p. 374.
[8] Chinnici, *The English Catholic Enlightenment*, p. 135.
[9] Ibid.

minutiae of such a transfer of power might be, no new conclusions could be reached. Furthermore, the assumption that rigid distinctions existed between the supposed losers of this particular battle – the old or native or English or liberal Catholics – and the winners – the ultramontanes or Romans or converts or Irish or continentals – has meant that changes in devotional practice in the period have been interpreted only in this context.[10]

Eustace, Lingard, and Rock refuse to fit into that pattern of 'rigid distinctions' when applied, as they have readily been, to the nineteenth-century understanding of Christian history and liturgy. They are neither 'old-English' nor Roman, and yet share the passions of Pugin for the one and of Wiseman for the other. While sharing the determination of the Cisalpine party to see greater ecclesiastical democracy and to resist centralization in papal hands, they are insistent that the history of Christian liturgy and religious practice goes back in a direct line through the medieval and Anglo-Saxon Church, to the early Christian communities of Rome. Whereas Pugin and his fellow travellers stopped somewhere between the twelfth and fourteenth centuries for their ideal model church, Rock and Lingard were determined to take the story further back.

* * *

Rock's writings suggest the possibility of not having to be Roman and right or Gothic and wrong, of winning and losing, but of integrating a newly developed archaeological appreciation of early Christianity with the contemporary passion for all things medieval. His scholarship makes sense of the medieval by placing it in context, in a way in which Pugin never did. Rock was born in Liverpool in 1799 to a Catholic family and received a conventional Catholic education of its time for one destined for the priesthood. He was firstly educated by the Benedictine missioner at St Peter's chapel in Seel St and then at St Edmund's Old Hall Green, from the age of fourteen, where he was introduced to antiquarian studies. In 1818, he was one of the first group of half a dozen students, including Nicholas Wiseman, to colonize the newly restored English College in Rome after twenty years of Napoleonic occupation and disruption. Whether he was one of the few who could be provided with surviving remnants of the 'old

---

[10] Mary Heimann, *Catholic Devotion in Victorian England* (Oxford, 1995), pp. 4–5.

and hallowed costume of the English College' in order to meet the pope, is not recorded.[11] His seven years in Rome were to be vital in forming his scholarly interests and enthusiasms, as well as in shaping his future career. There he developed a passion for the history of the early Church and for collecting the evidence of its liturgical practice illustrated in the catacombs, which was to inform his later writings, and he also met while in Rome, John Talbot, later the sixteenth Earl of Shrewsbury.

Talbot's meeting with Rock took place towards the end of an eventful Grand Tour, during which he fled from the hideous sights of the Peninsular War and was captured by pirates. On his return to England and succession to his brother's title he invited Rock (now ordained and working at St Mary Moorfields in London) to be his chaplain at Alton Towers in Staffordshire. Shrewsbury's home was to be the centre of the Gothic-influenced Catholic Revival and itself was to be 'medievalized' in the 1830s by Pugin. It was here that Pugin and Rock met.

Daniel Rock has been described by the leading historian of English liturgy, James Crichton, as the most learned liturgiologist of his time, who almost certainly knew more detail of medieval rites than anyone – including Pugin.[12] Yet he is now largely unknown and overshadowed by the reputation of Pugin, whose work and knowledge owed much to Rock's influence. Pugin himself acknowledged this guidance, both in private correspondence,[13] and publicly in his *Principles of Christian Architecture*, in which, with typical dramatic flourish, he proclaims his dependence on Rock:

> I once stood on the very edge of a precipice in this respect from which I was rescued by the advice and arguments of my respected and revered friend Dr Rock, to whose learned researches and observations on Christian antiquity I am highly indebted and to whom I feel it a bounden duty to make this public acknowledgement of the great benefit I have derived from his advice.[14]

[11] Nicholas Wiseman, *Recollections of the Last Four Popes* (London, 1858), p. 11.

[12] James Crichton, *Lights in the Darkness: Forerunners of the Liturgical Movement* (Dublin, 1996), ch. 10: 'Daniel Rock', *passim*.

[13] Southwark Archdiocesan Archives [hereafter SAA], Rock Collection, Bundle 179, Lord Shrewsbury and Pugin to Rock.

[14] London, 1843, p. 67.

Rock and Lingard inherited an older Recusant antiquarian tradition and were taken up by the exponents of a newer 'Gothic mentality', and have thus been wrongly categorized. David Rogers argued as long ago as 1982, but in an article only recently posthumously published, that the English Recusants consciously clung to what they could of 'a past that was still their heritage'.[15] He suggested that among the great unwritten volumes of the early modern period would be an account of the preservation by Recusants of pre-Reformation sacred objects. However, as Rogers indicates, 'The interests of posterity as such were not, however, foremost in the minds of the Recusants as they guarded their treasures.' Lingard and Rock are the heirs of those who

> valued what they preserved – ancient service books, pictures, statues, vestments, stained glass, relics and plate, for example – not primarily as antiquarian rarities (which down the centuries they did in fact gradually become) but as sacred objects which, had the climate of religious opinion and the legislation in their homeland been less harshly hostile than it was, they would themselves have enjoyed using freely for their own spiritual life and for the service of their chapels and shrines.[16]

By the early nineteenth century that free enjoyment was becoming more possible and the purpose of the work of Daniel Rock, inspired by Lingard, was to reinsert English Catholicism back into the mainstream of English religious history, particularly in the development and continuity of its liturgical life. This meant not merely recovering one particular ancient pattern of liturgical practice and the fixtures and fittings which went with it, but demonstrating, by means of serious scholarship, the continuity of history from the earliest times to the present. This approach was not about reinstating a particular form of liturgy or architecture or vestments simply because that was the way in which Englishmen on the eve of the Reformation had done it, but about reclaiming the whole history of the pre-Reformation period for the Catholic Recusants and their heirs. Rock's view of the Reformation was of a violent dislocation of history which had thwarted natural development and the time had come to pick up the threads.

---

[15] David Rogers, 'The English Recusants; some medieval literary links', *Recusant History*, 23 (1997), pp. 483–507.
[16] Rogers, 'The English Recusants', p. 485.

But if those of our fellow countrymen who live separated from us in religious belief, manifest such a love for, and search out with so much ardour, those venerable monuments of Catholic antiquity, how much more ought we, who happily inherit the olden faith whole and unbroken, the olden liturgy, the olden practices, and exclusively retain the Apostolic succession of Catholic England, to show a deep, warm feeling for those glorious title-deeds and vouchers of the antiquity and unchangeableness of our heavenly faith.[17]

In this he differed from Pugin, whose view of the perfection of Christian life was much more static, having settled for that of the thirteenth and fourteenth centuries as the climax of development and the model to be imitated. This is a difference which has not been appreciated, and Pugin's has been the dominant perspective.

Lingard and Rock were on good personal and professional terms, although Lingard was the senior by nearly thirty years and a published author while Rock was still a student. Nevertheless when, in 1833, he received from the author a copy of Rock's *Hierurgia*, Lingard responded graciously, promising a copy of his own newly published *Manual*, 'but a mole hill for a mountain'. *Hierurgia*, he remarked, 'will do you great honour and at the same time promote that sacred cause in which we are all engaged'.[18] They corresponded frequently, discussing such matters as the validity of Anglican ordinations, which could not in Lingard's opinion 'be rejected as essentially deficient unless we also reject all the ordinations of all the Greek bishops down to the present day'.[19] Other subjects included Rock's campaign for a restored hierarchy, and insistence on full canonical rights for the clergy, including a voice in episcopal nominations.

* * *

A Catholic (Gothic-inspired) Romanticism took root in England in the 1830s, which appeared to find itself gradually drawn into conflict with the Roman or continental tastes increasingly in the ascendant, and as Heimann makes clear, that battle has been the context within which we have judged the Gothic revivalists. They were, in the language of *1066 And All That*, 'Romantic but wrong', while the nineteenth-

[17] Daniel Rock, *The Church of Our Fathers*, 3 vols (London, 1849–53), I, p. 342.
[18] SAA, Rock Collection, Bundle 172 Lingard–Rock (nd, 1833?).
[19] SAA, Rock Collection, Bundle 172 Lingard–Rock, nd.

century equivalent of the Roundheads were 'Roman but righteous'. Fuelling these judgements have been the condemnations heaped upon the old-English party because of their increasingly unfashionable liberal ecclesiastical views. To that extent at least, Rock and Lingard were tarred with the liberal brush and shared the condemnation.

In 1842 Rock addressed a circular letter to clergy advocating the restoration of episcopal hierarchy. Rock himself told of his increasing involvement in the hierarchy issue,

> Long had a yearning for such a measure [that is, a hierarchy] been growing in the minds of several among the secular clergy of this land; but for a combination of reasons none of them would venture on the first step in this direction. For myself it had been the darling of my younger days of missionary duty. . . . It was agreed then that I should at the next yearly meeting of the Midland clergy, begin to moot this point about the hierarchy. We met at Sedgley Park and at my suggestion a petition to His Holiness for the restoration of our long lost hierarchy was adopted and a committee of our elder clergy was chosen to draw it up and forward it to Rome.[20]

The Vicar Apostolic in the Midlands, Thomas Walsh, did not oppose the move by the clergy, but was not really in favour. Nicholas Wiseman, the leading champion of the 'Roman' school, who was to be the first Cardinal-Archbishop of Westminster in 1850, opposed any group which had its roots in clerical dissatisfaction, though he was certainly not antagonistic to the idea of a restored hierarchy.[21] As a result of Rock's campaign the Adelphi Club was formed to work to secure clerical rights, and clergy across the country were invited to join. In 1843 it began with twenty-six members attending monthly meetings, growing to 120. In 1847, when the hierarchy was pending, Rock was among twenty-two clergy who signed a petition to Rome asking that the clergy have a canonical voice in the appointment of their bishops and also seeking an alteration in the power of bishops to move clergy at will. The Earl of Shrewsbury (in other spheres an ally of Rock) reprimanded him and, while supporting the hierarchy and canonical status of clergy, he ridiculed the idea of their participation in

[20] K. O'Meara, *Thomas Grant* (London, 1874), pp. 66–7.
[21] R. J. Schiefen, *Nicholas Wiseman and the Transformation of English Catholicism* (Shepherdstown, 1984), p. 139.

nomination of bishops.[22] At a later stage the views of men like Rock were factors in Wiseman's opposition to the division of London into two dioceses, fearing difficulty in exercising control south of the river where could be found 'the worst anti-Roman clergy in England' – including Rock.[23] Thus Rock has been consigned to an ecclesiastical backwater, representative of outdated views of dubious orthodoxy, and been given scant regard by the mainstream historiography.

It has long been commonplace in nineteenth-century historiography to place Rock on the sidelines of the Gothic revivalists led by Augustus Welby Pugin, gathered around the Earl of Shrewsbury and including such characters as Ambrose Phillips de Lisle and George Ignatius Spencer. However, Rock stands in a different relationship to the medieval revivalists and represents a position which makes it more difficult to draw the rather crude battle lines between Romantics and Romanizers. If Pugin was the standard bearer for the Gothics, then Wiseman has been portrayed as the key opponent, standing trenchantly for all things Roman and deserting the Gothics over rood screens. Yet he and Rock were contemporaries as students in the English College in Rome and shared a passion for the archaeology of the Roman catacombs. Although Rock and Wiseman had disagreements at times, and later Wiseman believed Rock to belong to the 'cold antiquarian school, that never exhibits a spark of devotion, or tries to kindle one',[24] there was never on either side the fierce condemnation or sense of betrayal which Pugin felt towards Wiseman. After Wiseman's visit to England in 1839 he was reported by Shrewsbury to have disapproved of some of Rock's views. Rock presumed it was because he had criticized the architecture of St Peter's, Rome; but Wiseman dismissed this as a matter of taste, and pleaded for as much tolerance of others' opinions from the Gothic camp.[25] His real complaint was Rock's reference to the pope as 'patriarch of the West' and his argument for minimizing reference from the local church to Roman authority. In Wiseman's view this was the route to schism.[26]

It is widely believed that, given this difference of opinion over

---

[22] R. J. Schiefen, *Nicholas Wiseman and the Transformation of English Catholicism* (Shepherdstown, 1984), p. 157.

[23] Ibid., p. 193.

[24] Ibid., p. 217.

[25] SAA, Rock Collection, Wiseman–Rock (12 May 1840).

[26] Schiefen, *Nicholas Wiseman*, p. 134.

ecclesiastical politics, the heirs of Cisalpinism were hostile to the Romanizers and therefore natural allies of the Pugin camp. This was not necessarily the case. There was as much of a Roman tradition behind the work of Lingard and Rock, as a medieval English one, and therein lay the difference with Pugin and his insistence on the purity of Gothic. These Cisalpine historians, while influenced in ecclesiastical politics by a deep desire to minimize Roman influence in the contemporary Church and to restore the independence of local bishops and clergy in the face of a rising tide of Ultramontane centralization, were nevertheless at pains to emphasise the continuity from ancient Rome and the early Christians, through the medieval Church, across the Reformation gulf to their own day. They refused to fit the neat categories of Romanizers and Romantics, because they were scholarly historians and because the purpose of their work was to create understanding, not further division. They believed powerfully in the unifying power of continuity of worship, particularly in its effect on Protestants.

It is too simplistic to speak of Gothics and Romans in stark opposition to each other. The picture has been dominated excessively by Pugin's extreme views, and those around him were pushed into taking up positions. However, others in the circle of Catholic revivalists did not draw the same distinction, and shared as much of a passion for Rome as for Gothicism. Thus the divisions between 'old-English' and 'Roman' cannot be as sharply drawn as has been traditionally believed. The Roman roots of Anglo-Saxon and medieval practices were vital in asserting their validity. What Rock emphasised was that in the consistent English liturgical tradition, there was an authentic heritage to be restored and, therefore, there was no need for the importation of continental (Romanized) liturgical practices to restore English Catholic life. It was all there – Roman and English – in the ancient office books, missals, vestments, and artifacts. This accords with Rock and Lingard's ecclesial opinions about the restoration of the hierarchy and the canonical rights of clergy. It was a restoration of integrity to the English Church, not a Roman imposition. Rock referred to 'our long lost' hierarchy, and was disappointed in what emerged in 1850 with no mention of the rights of parishes or clergy.

* * *

The England to which Rock returned from Rome in 1825 was now obsessed with medievalism. In the Romanticism of the late eighteenth and early nineteenth centuries the ancient mysteries of medieval Christianity wielded a powerful influence. Castles and monasteries became a motto theme in its architecture and literature. Horace Walpole's *Castle of Otranto* (1763) was the first and most famous of a powerful literary genre of Gothic novels which forged the link between Romanticism and religion. Much of their mystery, romance, and terror stemmed from the fact that Gothic, in the shape of the medieval Church, was the culture of unreformed Catholicism. Fuelled by growing nationalism during and after the Napoleonic wars, Romanticism had one foot firmly in the English medieval past. This was encouraged visually by the survival of relics of medieval life all over England, including the magnificent cathedrals, which became the subject of vigorous, enthusiastic, but often damaging restoration. Monastic and secular ruins still littered the landscape picturesquely. Even the Classical influence of Inigo Jones had not quite destroyed English affection for native Gothic, and there were occasional, rarely successful, seventeenth- and eighteenth-century examples by Wren, Vanbrugh, and Hawksmoor.[27] These Gothic remnants were sufficient to convince the Romantic mind not only of the picturesque mystery of Gothic, but also of its inherent Englishness. It was part of the nation's heritage and must be restored and revived to counteract the foreign barbarities of classical and Baroque. This was a view shared, with a particular religious meaning and intention, by Lingard and Rock and by the Anglicans of the Camden Society.

Installed by the Earl of Shrewsbury as chaplain at Alton Towers, the epicentre of Catholic life, Rock was encouraged by his patron in his scholarly pursuits, and was subsidized by him for a further visit to Rome to study in the libraries and catacombs. Much of this work was to bear fruit in his first major publication, *Hierurgia; or the Holy Sacrifice of the Mass Expounded* (London, 1833). This work 'did much to educate Englishmen on the Mass and Roman liturgy'.[28] The second edition in 1851 was dedicated to the Earl of Shrewsbury as 'a monument of the grateful, and of the respectful but sincere attachment of the author'. The Shrewsbury family spent much of their time travelling abroad, so in 1840 Rock moved to be chaplain to Sir Robert Throckmorton at Buckland, in Berkshire, where he was known as an amiable man, little given to controversy and with no taste for public life, whose 'genial

---

[27] K. Clark, *The Gothic Revival* (London, 1950), ch. 1, *passim*.
[28] Schiefen, *Nicholas Wiseman*, p. 63.

disposition and solid piety won for him the love and respect of all who came into contact with him'.[29] After the Catholic hierarchy was restored in 1850, Rock was appointed a canon of Southwark diocese, but remained in residence at Buckland until 1854, by which time he had published his monumental work, *The Church of Our Fathers* (3 volumes, London, 1849–53), when he removed briefly to Sussex. The later part of his life was spent in London, living in his own house in Kensington, chosen for its proximity to the new South Kensington Museum. His last years were given to enthusiastic support of this new venture and he donated to its collection a portable altar and a copper gilt thurible which had belonged to Pope Boniface VIII. Rock was elected to the exhibition committee and his last published work before his death in 1871 was a highly regarded catalogue for the museum's exhibition of ecclesiastical textiles, *Textile Fabrics* (London, 1871). Daniel Rock died suddenly at his home in Kensington at the age of seventy-two.[30]

In *Hierurgia*, Rock 'sought to present doctrinal and historical support for the ceremonial and liturgical practices of contemporary Roman Catholicism'.[31] It was designed to demonstrate the continuity between the primitive Church and contemporary Roman Catholicism. In his later work, *The Church of Our Fathers*, he carefully and painstakingly sets out the continuity between the practice of the early Roman Christian Church, the Anglo-Saxon Church in England, and the practice of nineteenth-century Roman Catholicism. The point for Rock was not simply the restoration of pre-Reformation forms, but the assertion and historical proof of clear continuity from apostolic times to the present day.

Rock made a 'repeated inspection' of the catacombs while a student in Rome, which convinced him of their value and importance. His theological and historical opinions were strongly influenced by his encounter with these primitive cemeteries, and his *Hierurgia* was the first English work to make extensive use of the evidence they provided.[32] The rediscovery of the catacombs and the attention

---

[29] D. Rock, *The Church of Our Fathers*, 2nd edn, ed. G. W. Hart and W. H. Frere, 4 vols (London, 1905), 1, p. XXI: Memoir by Revd Bernard Kelly.

[30] J. Gillow, *A Literary and Biographical Dictionary of English Catholics*, 5 vols (London, 1885), 5, pp. 436–43.

[31] W. Meyer, 'The church of the catacombs: British responses to the evidence of the Roman catacombs, 1578–1900' (University of Cambridge, Ph.D. thesis, 1985), p. 144.

[32] Ibid., p. 144.

which this brought upon the history of early Christianity played an important propaganda role in English Christianity. The history of the early Christian community in Rome, the 'Church of the Catacombs' was increasingly explained in polemical terms, by Catholics asserting the historic continuity, and by Protestants arguing that theirs was the true heritage of the early Church. Wiseman was an important figure in this campaign to reclaim the catacombs, having shared Rock's fascination with them since his early years in Rome and used the evidence of them in his well-publicized lectures given in England in 1836. He was also close to the Tractarian-inspired Anglicans who sought their own history in the catacombs. The leading English catacomb archaeologist was James Spencer Northcote, a Tractarian convert and lifelong friend of Newman and Pusey.[33]

* * *

Some English Catholics found great reassurance in the fact that Gothic was English and Catholic. It embodied the verities of faith and encouraged them in the task of establishing corporate identity by forging continuity with the medieval past. Thus a specifically Catholic interpretation of the Romantic love of English medieval splendour and mystery came about. In practice it called for the revival of all possible outward forms of medieval religion. The restoration of medieval architecture, liturgy, music, and decoration would only be a reflection of the revived zeal and piety of the people. In turn, it would be a future inducement to piety.[34]

A group of Catholic Romantics took up the challenge which this offered, and the close personal friendships between Pugin, Ambrose Phillips de Lisle, George Ignatius Spencer, and John Talbot, sixteenth Earl of Shrewsbury, can give the impression of a radical movement which is perhaps exaggerated. The 'Good Earl', as he was to be nicknamed, was one of the most generous benefactors to the revived English Catholic communities in the 1830s and 1840s. His was the money which enabled Pugin to realize many of his dreams, supporting the building of cathedrals in Birmingham and Nottingham and churches all over the industrial Midlands, besides the convents and monasteries which enabled English Catholics to reclaim identity,

---

[33] Judith F. Champ, 'The rediscovery of the catacombs', *Catholic Archives*, no.17 (1997), pp. 12–13.

[34] E. S. Purcell, *Life and Letters of Ambrose Phillips de Lisle*, 2 vols (London, 1900), 2, pp. 49–51.

physical space, and liturgical practice. He was born in 1791, the second son of John Joseph Talbot, the brother of Charles, fifteenth Earl of Shrewsbury, and succeeded his brother to the title in 1827.[35] Despite his unstinting support of Pugin and devotion to medieval revivalism, Shrewsbury was also as much at home in Rome as in England. He spent long periods in residence there, married both his daughters to Roman princes (Borghese and Doria Pamphili) and finally ended his life in Naples in 1851. He therefore fails to fit the mould of an 'anti-Roman' Gothic devotee, and as has been suggested, was unimpressed by Rock's reluctance to embrace 'Roman' ecclesiology.

Another of those closely connected with Pugin, who sought and found reassurance and continuity in Rome (as well as plainchant) was Ambrose Phillips de Lisle, who wrote on hearing compline in the Roman basilica of Sta Sabina,

> I knelt down with a mixed feeling of heavenly awe and delight, and blessing God, that he had, of his infinite mercy, made me a member of his Holy Catholic Church, I thanked him that he had brought me to the threshold of the Apostles that 'New Canticle of the Lamb', the Divine chant of St. Gregory: I besought Him to confirm my faith, which I felt strengthened by this living image of the Church of the fourth century, the Church which is the same yesterday, today and forever.[36]

De Lisle was a remarkable convert, who made significant contributions to the shape of the English Catholic revival, including the erection of the first post-Reformation Cistercian Abbey at Mount St Bernard, Leicestershire. Although influenced by the movement to restore the medieval English grandeur of Catholicism, led by Pugin, he was also an ardent Romanophile. On his first visit in 1828 he wrote to a friend, 'I have been much delighted with my stay in Rome. How many profound and devout feelings are excited by a residence there . . . it is impossible for me to be in a more edifying place . . . the piety of the people is so great.' He found the popular religion warm, exuberant, and attractive – very different from what he had so far experienced in England.[37] His

---

[35] David Meara, *A. W. N. Pugin and the Revival of Memorial Brasses* (London, 1991), pp. 17–18.

[36] M. Pawley, *Faith and Family: the Life and Circle of Ambrose Phillips de Lisle* (Norwich, 1993), p. 42.

[37] Ibid., pp. 35–6.

life was greatly affected by the contacts he made in Rome in the small close-knit society of wealthy English Catholics. Among these were the Earl of Shrewsbury (with whom he was to collaborate on church-building projects in England), George Spencer, and Dominic Barberi. Thus even Pugin's immediate circle of patrons and supporters could not be said to share his exclusive and obsessive anti-Roman and pro-Gothic stance.

Pugin and those associated with him have come to dominate the accounts of liturgical and architectural revival in the nineteenth century. The volatile architect is seen as the leader of a campaign to eradicate three hundred years of history and to return English Catholics to the pattern of worship of the fourteenth century. He was not alone, sharing this passion with Anglicans who founded the Camden Society in the 1830s and published *The Ecclesiologist*, but his approach was single-minded and dogmatic. It is more than likely that the dominant figure of Pugin, in the context of the competitive view of nineteenth-century history noted by Heimann, has obscured a more subtle approach to liturgical history, which might have borne fruit in a different, less confrontational atmosphere – both for Catholics and Anglicans. There were those who, like Newman, had difficulties in appreciating Pugin's qualities wholeheartedly, and felt his single-mindedness to be misguided:

> Mr Pugin is a man of genius. I have the greatest admiration of his talents and willingly acknowledge that Catholics owe him a great debt for what he has done in the revival of Gothic architecture among us. His zeal, his innate diligence, his resources, his inventions, his imagination, his sagacity in research, are all of the highest order. . . . But he has the great fault of a man of genius, as well as the merit. He is intolerant, and if I might use a stronger word, a bigot. He sees nothing good in any school of Christian architecture except that of which he himself is so great an ornament. The canons of Gothic architecture are to him points of faith, and everyone is a heretic who would question them. . . . The See of St Peter . . . is pronounced by him to be pagan.[38]

Yet, under the direction of Pugin, attitudes hardened into an insistence that the future glory of English Catholicism rested in a

---

[38] Purcell, *Life and Letters*, 2, pp. 205–6.

complete reinstatement of ancient and traditional English religious practice. Italian-style devotions were the product of Renaissance and Reformation Europe, and in Pugin's view they were abhorrent, 'a perfect mockery of the real thing'.[39] Pugin always referred to Gothic architecture as 'Christian Architecture', which he believed to be not merely one possible style among many, and therefore a matter of taste, but a matter of principle. It was the only possible architectural setting for the revival of English Catholicism from what he regarded as its torpor.

> In the name of common sense, whilst we profess the name of Christians, whilst we glory in being Englishmen, let us have an architecture, the arrangement and details of which will alike remind us of our faith and our country – an architecture whose beauties we may claim as our own, whose symbols have originated in our religion and our customs.[40]

It was essentially Pugin's intolerance, possessiveness, and refusal to compromise which created the sense of isolation and hostility. Every opening of a Pugin church became a battle between Romantics and Romanizers. The publicity which surrounded them ensured a volley of fire from the increasingly vocal opposition. The intensity brought by Pugin to the cause was largely responsible for its success, but it also encouraged his opponents to take equally intransigent attitudes.

Conflicts between Romantics and Romanizers broke out wherever Pugin was involved, and although he was extreme in his views he clearly had some sympathetic support from others, including Rock. His letters to Rock are full of complaints about those who opposed him, including Wiseman, and about their failure to appreciate what he was attempting to achieve. In 1838 a ferocious argument broke out between Pugin and Wiseman over the desirability or otherwise of a rood screen at the newly built St Chad's Cathedral in Birmingham. Wiseman and the Romanizers abhorred rood screens as unnecessary and an example of medieval eccentricity. Pugin and his supporters, who saw Wiseman as a turncoat, believed the revival of screens to be essential. He wrote in despair to Phillips, 'An affair has happened at Birmingham which has gone through me like a stab. We have had a

---

[39] Purcell, *Life and Letters*, 2, p. 214.
[40] A. W. Pugin, *An Apology for the Revival of Christian Architecture in England* (London, 1843), p. 6.

tremendous blow aimed at us, and that from the centre of our camp. Dr Wiseman has at last shown his real sentiments by attempting to abolish the great rood screen.'[41]

Pugin's interest in his churches went far beyond their design and decoration. He was adamant that the proper services should be used. The traditional Catholic music, seventeenth- and eighteenth-century European in character, was abhorrent to him. Equally obnoxious was the European 'fiddle-back' style of vestments. In this, Rock and Pugin were of one mind. In *The Church of Our Fathers* an entire chapter is devoted to vestments, mostly to emphasising the continuity in the flowing shape of the chasuble, 'from the first preaching of the true belief amongst our forefathers, up to the change of the people's faith, brought about against the people's wishes, by the wickedness and wilfulness of our last Tudor rulers'.[42] Modern chasubles, according to Rock, were mostly continental imports and were the result of accident rather than design. 'The nibbling scissors cut away the old vestments every now and then; and when new ones were to be supplied, bad taste and parsimony whispered to each other, and made them small.'[43] Vestments were often specially designed by Pugin for his churches, in the medieval flowing style. On one occasion he refused to allow them to be used for the opening, and he and Lord Shrewsbury left the church in disgust at the female choir. A programme of operatic music had been arranged, in Pugin's view 'a perfectly disgusting display', and the local clergy refused to change it.[44] Consequently, Pugin attempted to take over the whole liturgy and reform it, to go with his churches. In May 1838 he had total control over the spectacular seven-hour ceremony for the opening of the new chapel at Oscott College, and

> It was here that the clergy wore for the first time the full Gothic vestments designed by Pugin in place of the 'Roman' or 'fiddle-back' chasuble. The acknowledgement of his liturgical authority was crucial for Pugin and it was at the seminaries that he hoped to begin the revolution in music, vestments and church fittings which for him was inseparable from the progress of the Gothic revival.[45]

[41] Purcell, *Life and Letters*, 2, pp. 213–14.
[42] Rock, *Church of Our Fathers*, 1, p. 315.
[43] Ibid., 1, p. 329.
[44] Purcell, *Life and Letters*, 2, p. 214.
[45] Roderick O'Donnell, 'Pugin at Oscott', in Judith F. Champ, ed., *Oscott College 1838–1988: a Volume of Commemorative Essays* ([Sutton Coldfield], 1988), p. 45.

Such freedom came rarely to Pugin, and in 1840 he wrote almost hysterically to Phillips, 'Every building I erect is profaned, and instead of assisting in conversions it only serves to disgust people. The church at Dudley is a compleat [sic] facsimile of the old English parish churches, and nobody seems to know how to use it. The present state of things is quite lamentable.'[46] To Rock, as perhaps the only priest he trusted to know what to do with his churches and fittings, he wrote, 'I am completely alone, and it is of little use building churches without men who will use them, and you, who would carry everything out, are set in a modern room. I live in hope that one of these days you will be rector of a real church.'[47]

Music was a frequent source of disagreement. The Gothic revivalists had only one type of church music – Gregorian plainchant, described by Eustace as 'simple and affecting', and by Lingard as the 'heavenly employment' of the Anglo-Saxon monks which 'assimilated them to the angels who are described in holy writ as constantly singing the praises of the Creator'.[48] Phillips, who had first encountered chant in Sta Sabina in Rome, wrote a treatise *On Church Musick* [sic] in 1847, parts of which read like a Gothic novel:

> Oh, my reader, if we could but transport ourselves but three centuries and could just pay a visit to some of our holy and venerable old churches, that are now perhaps but a confused mass of ruins and wherein nothing is now heard but the moaning of the wind through some broken casement, or the sad hooting of the bird at night![49]

In this treatise, Phillips describes plainchant as 'consecrated to the service of God', and he extolled the 'days of our faith and glory [when] it resounded beneath the vaulted roof of each parish church throughout our island'. Pugin fought endless battles to restore plainchant and eradicate European polyphony, but was forced to concede over the opening of St Chad's Cathedral in Birmingham. He had proposed plainchant for the opening and consecration on consecutive days. The showplace of English Catholicism, its first post-Reformation cathedral,

---

[46] Purcell, *Life and Letters*, 2, p. 214.
[47] SAA, Rock Collection, Bundle 179, Pugin-Rock (13 Dec. 1840).
[48] John Lingard, *The History and Antiquities of the Anglo-Saxon Church*, 2 vols (London, 1845), 2, p. 304.
[49] Purcell, *Life and Letters*, 2, pp. 189-90.

was entirely geared to converting those sceptical about the ideals of the Gothics. To Pugin's chagrin, a compromise was effected, after complaints to Rome, with plainchant for the consecration and a Haydn Mass for the opening.[50]

The passion for plainchant and the corresponding controversy were paralleled in the Church of England, where 'a largely antiquarian agenda motivated some of the leading figures in the choral revival.'[51] Those whom Bradley describes as 'musical purists' wanted to reinstate plainchant as an everyday part of Anglican worship and the publication of ancient texts was taking place from as early as the 1820s. This led to the institution of trained surpliced choirs in Anglican parish churches,[52] and the formation of the male cathedral choir at St Chad's Cathedral, Birmingham, by John Hardman, Pugin's glass and metal manufacturer. This accompanied the setting up of the Holy Guild of St Chad, into which the tradesmen of Birmingham entered with gusto, complete with black cloaks and collars and medieval-style white shields.[53] Although Rock described extensively the chanting of the Office of the Church in its familiar forms in *The Church of Our Fathers* he, perhaps surprisingly, makes no mention of the desirability or otherwise of its restoration in contemporary Catholic worship, but it may also be indicative of his interest primarily in content rather than form.

* * *

While Rock and Pugin did collaborate on certain projects, Rock was not an uncritical supporter. In 1844 he was reprimanded by Lord Shrewsbury (no longer his patron by then) for publicly criticizing Pugin's work: 'I am sure, Dr Rock, you will see, on reflection, that you are too hard upon him, and capable of doing Pugin much unintentional mischief by random criticism or by not understanding his meaning and object.'[54] Tellingly, Lingard warned Rock about the dangers of collaborating with Pugin, and the possibility that, if they collaborated, Rock would get nothing published. 'When Mr Pugin and you come to work together, many little differences of opinion will

---

[50] M. Trappes-Lomax, *Pugin: a Medieval Victorian* (London, 1932), p. 206.
[51] Ian Bradley, *Abide With Me: the World of Victorian Hymns* (London, 1997), p. 31.
[52] Ibid., p. 32.
[53] Birmingham Archdiocesan Archives, William Greaney MS, 'Notes on Catholic History'.
[54] SAA Rock Collection, Box J87, Shrewsbury–Rock (21 Dec. 1844).

arise, and perhaps lead to a dissolution of partnership. Look to this beforehand that you may not lose time and labour and expense.'[55] During his time as chaplain at Alton Towers (where he also received Pugin's wife into the Catholic Church), Rock naturally participated in the opening of Pugin/Shrewsbury churches,[56] and he provided designs for surplices illustrating an article of Pugin in 1840.[57] Towards the end of his life, Pugin provided drawings for *The Church of Our Fathers*, which for some unknown reason were never used.[58] Rock was not however, an advocate of rood screens, which to Pugin were *de rigueur*. He made no mention of rood screens in *Hierurgia*, though he wrote enthusiastically of the ancient practice of altar curtains and the Greek practice of the partition or screen between the sanctuary and people, 'which somewhat resembles the altar-screens and chancel-railings in our old English churches and venerable Catholic cathedrals'.[59] In his later work, he was clear that 'the revival of their use [that is, curtains], along with other memorials of the Church of our Fathers, cannot be too much applauded.'[60]

Rood screens came to denote to Pugin all that was proper about a Gothic church, and to his exasperated opponents all that was mere medieval frippery and nonsense. The arguments went on for years, culminating in a ferocious correspondence in *The Rambler* between July 1848 and January 1849, and in Pugin's *Treatise on Chancel Screens and Rood Lofts* (London, 1851). Lingard was also far from being an uncritical admirer of Pugin. Despite his passionate interest in the history and practice of the medieval Church, he is described as 'the consistent enemy of Gothic architecture'.[61] He vigorously opposed Gothic style for the new chapel planned at Ushaw College in 1840, preferring to extend the existing one and create something like a Roman basilica. He hated the rood screen put in place there. 'It is in my opinion, most frightful – and the four candles most ridiculous – and the rood and images above most unsightly. Do, I beg of you, sweep all away. Why must we put up roods, when for two hundred years they have been swept away in every country in Europe?'[62] Lingard, his

[55] SAA Rock Collection, Bundle 172, Lingard–Rock (nd).
[56] *Orthodox Journal*, 9, 14 Sept. 1839.
[57] Ibid., 10, 22 Feb. 1840, pp. 121–2.
[58] Margaret Belcher, *A. W. N. Pugin: An Annotated Bibliography* (London, 1987), p. 451.
[59] Rock, *Hierurgia*, p. 508.
[60] Rock, *Church of Our Fathers*, 1, p. 199.
[61] Haile and Bonney, *Life and Letters of John Lingard*, p. 144.
[62] Ibid., p. 310.

generation's leading historian of medieval religion, regarded rood screens as a monastic creation and responsible in part for the decay of religion. 'Do, I implore you, think well before you admit of such an incongruity. Let our churches be adapted to our wants, as those of ancient times were to the wants of those who built them. At all events have the church built so that all who attend may see the service.'[63] Thus Lingard and Rock demonstrate considerable historical understanding of liturgical development and symbolism, while Pugin was locked into a limited regard for historical or liturgical understanding.

The focus of both of Rock's works is the mass and its sacrificial nature and purpose. In both he is at pains to emphasise the continuity from the earliest times to the present day. In *Hierurgia* he makes extensive use of illustrations from early Christian sources, including the catacombs, and his frontispiece shows a chamber in the catacomb of S. Callisto. *The Church of Our Fathers* is built around a study of the Sarum Rite, a transcript of which became available to Rock through an acquaintance. He was also given a copy of an inventory of Salisbury Cathedral of 1222, which he published as an appendix. The text to which he had access dated from around the early thirteenth century and was almost complete, with the major exceptions of Good Friday and Holy Saturday. In many ways *The Church of Our Fathers* is a logical continuation of *Hierurgia*, since the first work dealt chiefly with the institution of the mass and its scriptural and patristic accounts. The work was published in three volumes over several years between 1849 and 1853, in the midst of which Rock republished *Hierurgia* in a new edition (1851). The later work has a strong theme of continuity and Rock sets out to prove that there is no break in the traditions of belief and practice between that brought from Rome by Augustine of Canterbury, the later Anglo-Saxons, the Normans, the medieval Church, and the surviving Roman Catholic Church in England.

> Both the Sacrifice and the sacraments were hallowed things, which the Normans looked upon with like deep reverence and holy feeling as the Anglo-Saxons; for each nation's belief upon these articles of Christian faith was identical, flowing as it did out of the self-same well-spring of truth – the Apostolic See, the chair of St Peter.[64]

---

[63] Ibid., p. 303.
[64] Rock, *Church of Our Fathers*, I, p. 11.

The point of his comparisons of Anglo-Saxon and Norman practice is to demonstrate 'how strikingly they agreed throughout with one another, and both of them with us Catholics of the nineteenth century, and in no point more so than the Holy Eucharist.'[65]

Volume one of *The Church of Our Fathers* is devoted to the mass and the architecture and vestments associated with it. Volume two continues the exposition of vestments and then contains a lengthy section on Purgatory. The third volume, which was published in two separate books, consists of further discussion of Purgatory, the invocation of saints, and the shrines and relics associated with them. The final part concludes with a survey of the canonical hours and the usage of the Sarum Rite, concluding with appendices containing St Osmund's *Treatise on the Divine Office*, extracts from the Ordinal of St Paul's, London, and a list of ornaments in Salisbury Cathedral *c.*1222. The most significant and inevitably controversial section is that on the mass, which bore fruit in the increasingly eucharistic emphasis of Catholic liturgy in nineteenth-century England in both the Roman Catholic and Anglo-Catholic traditions. In his initial discussion of the sacrificial nature of the mass and the belief in transubstantiation, Rock moves from the use of Scripture, universal early Christian authorities, and the contemporary practice of the Greek Church,[66] to the beliefs and practices of Anglo-Saxon England. Bede, Alcuin, and Aelfric are all brought to bear witness, and Protestant attempts to claim that Aelfric was speaking figuratively are briskly dismissed.[67] However, the key point (and hence surely the decision to republish *Hierurgia* simultaneously) is to demonstrate 'how thoroughly our Anglo-Saxon forefathers agreed with the rest of the Catholic Church in their times'.[68] To prove his point, Rock draws parallels with other western liturgies including the Ambrosian, but only in order to make clear 'how deeply rooted in the Anglo-Saxon mind was the belief in Transubstantiation'.[69] This point is repeated in a number of forms over several pages, but only in order to emphasise continuity. Lanfranc, Robert Pullen, Gilbert of Hoyland, and Stephen Langton are all claimed as authoritative proof of the long-lived belief in the doctrine.[70]

[65] Rock, *Church of Our Fathers*, p. 130.
[66] *Hierurgia*, pp. 124–82.
[67] Rock, *Church of Our Fathers*, I, pp. 24–5.
[68] Ibid., I, p. 28.
[69] Ibid., I, p. 37.
[70] Ibid., I, p. 63.

At various points during his discussion of the Anglo-Saxon form of the mass, Rock makes it clear that Anglo-Saxon practice in all its details was in line with that of the universal Church. This was true of employing the sign of the cross, 'a practice that had existed everywhere in the true Church from its beginning',[71] which lead him into a fifty-page digression taking issue with the Anglican scholar William Maskell over his accusation that multiple signs of the cross are 'intolerable' and 'of late introduction'.[72] The same is true of the mixing of water with wine in the chalice and reservation of the Blessed Sacrament (both among the 'six points' dear to the hearts of Anglican ritualists in the later nineteenth century which denoted 'proper' practice and created controversy). This was a ritual observance in which 'the Normans and Anglo-Saxons not only agreed with one another, but with all Catholic antiquity, which we reverently follow to the present day.'[73]

Having dealt in detail with the meaning and form of the Mass, Rock then discusses the architecture to which the liturgy has given rise. It is here that he is at his most historical and least in sympathy with the rigid Gothicism of Pugin, Phillips, and the rest, but at his most insistent that continuity is the key. He argues that Anglo-Saxon churches (though few fragments of evidence survive in England) would have been modelled on the early Christian basilicas of Rome, due to the influence of the likes of Benedict Biscop and Wilfrid of Hexham who returned from frequent Roman visits with artifacts, fitments, and designs. Rock suggests that S. Clemente in Rome was probably the model for the Anglo-Saxon minster, which in turn became the pattern for the Anglo-Norman cathedral; and that even after the pointed style of architecture took over, because of the unchanging liturgical requirements, English church architecture 'still shows itself to be the offspring of Rome, bearing about it, strongly marked too, the family likeness, as a true child of a Roman mother'. The differences, he claims, are 'more in appearance than reality'.[74] Such a view would scarcely have found credence with Pugin, for whom all things Roman were merely pagan, and who burst into tears on entering the basilica of St Peter in Rome.

*   *   *

---

[71] Ibid., I, p. 77.
[72] Ibid., I, p. 79.
[73] Ibid., I, pp. 159–60.
[74] Ibid., I, p. 192.

The Romantic cultural backdrop of the early part of the nineteenth century was as significant for the shift in taste among Anglicans as Catholics, and played a formative part in shaping the Oxford Movement. 'By the early nineteenth century romanticism and medievalism were dominating social attitudes as much as the escapism of Hollywood affected English-speaking society in the 1930s.'[75] Ecclesiastical factors were, however, significant. As Peter Nockles has made clear,

> The liturgical revival of the 1840s was not the product of Tractarianism alone. The roots of the revival can be dated back to at least as early as the first decades of the century. . . . The aim was to emphasise the 'catholic' and 'primitive' liturgical continuity of the Church of England. As early as 1797 in a sermon, revised and enlarged in 1817, Van Mildert had pointed out that the 'Ritual of the Romish Church, though composed in the Latin tongue and clogged with many superstitions and exceptionable forms, was yet in many parts of it truly Scriptural, and well calculated for the comfort and edification of pious worshippers'.[76]

In other words, the likes of Van Mildert were thinking along similar lines of reconciliation and understanding, and appreciation of the primitive roots of liturgical celebration, as their Catholic contemporaries, Lingard and Rock.

There were areas of convergent thinking for while, as Nockles puts it, 'Increasingly envious eyes were cast upon the Roman Breviary, described as "a treasure which was ours as much as" of Roman Catholics',[77] Rock was reported as telling his Tractarian friends that 'the Roman Catholics in England are about to adopt the Sarum Breviary'.[78] Rock certainly had Anglican contacts among the Oxford Movement, including Newman's curate Bloxam, to whom he gave an introduction to Mount St Bernards Abbey, Ambrose Phillips de Lisle's Cistercian foundation.[79] Bloxam visited Rock at Alton Towers and provoked a complaint to Bishop Bagot of Oxford for allegedly

---

[75] Nigel Yates, *Buildings, Faith and Worship: the Liturgical Arrangement of Anglican Churches 1600–1900* (Oxford, 1991), p. 129.

[76] Peter Nockles, *The Oxford Movement in Context* (Oxford, 1994), p. 219.

[77] Ibid., p. 221.

[78] J. H. Newman, *Letters and Diaries*, 21 vols (in progress) (London and Oxford, 1961–), 6, pp. 337–8: JHN–J. W. Bowden, 6 Nov. 1838.

[79] Pawley, *Faith and Family*, p. 115.

reverencing the consecrated host during Rock's celebration of a Roman Catholic mass in the chapel.[80] While not an intimate of Newman, Rock was certainly on corresponding and calling terms with him before 1845 as well as after. Indeed, he appears to have been one of Newman's first visitors at Littlemore, only three days after his confirmation in the Catholic Church.[81] Newman continued to regard Rock with respect, as one of 'our chief writers',[82] and for his avoidance of extreme opinions which made him (among others) more representative of English Catholic opinion than the exclusively Ultramontane Faber and Ward.[83] This is another hint perhaps that, had Catholics and Anglicans heeded the more 'representative' tones of Rock, the 'old-English' versus 'Roman' squabbles would have distracted them less from serious issues.

It may be said as much of Rock as Crichton said of Pugin, 'that the Anglicans inherited Pugin's legacy. It was they who in parish churches set up surpliced choirs, it was they who insisted on a devout liturgy and throughout the nineteenth century fostered good liturgical music.'[84] It was also the Anglicans who, in 1905, produced the only later edition of Rock's work, *The Church of Our Fathers*, despite the fact that much of its original purpose was polemic aimed at non-Catholics. The editors were well-known Anglican liturgical scholars, G. W. Hart and W. H. Frere, of the Community of the Resurrection, who acknowledged in the preface that, in its fifty years of existence, the effect of *The Church of Our Fathers* 'had been considerable, greater probably among those whom, as members of the English Church, Dr Rock continually attacked, than on his own co-religionists, to whom his appeals have been directed somewhat in vain'.[85] To Rock, in their view, was owed much of the liturgical development of the second half of the nineteenth century.

Nevertheless, Rock was not entirely in tune with Anglican liturgical writings. He took issue in *The Church of Our Fathers* with William Maskell, whose learned treatise, *The Ancient Liturgy of the Church of England*, was published shortly before his own work. Maskell 'did not himself support the Tractarian and Camdenite efforts at liturgical

---

[80] Newman, *Letters and Diaries*, 7, pp. 184–5: JHN–Bagot, 19 Nov. 1839.
[81] Ibid., 11, p. 24: Diary, 4 Nov. 1845.
[82] Ibid., 22, pp. 112–13: JHN–James Hope Scott, 26 Nov. 1865.
[83] Ibid., 22, pp. 203–4: JHN–Henry Wilberforce, 3 April 1866.
[84] Crichton, *Lights in the Darkness*, p. 79.
[85] Rock (ed. Hart and Frere), *Church of Our Fathers*, 1, p. XVII: Editors' Preface.

restoration',[86] but was clearly part of a growing band of liturgical archaeologists in the Church of England, who 'wedded themselves very firmly to the reintroduction of medieval ceremonial on the grounds that it represented the undisputed practice of the Church of England before the Reformation'.[87] In using the rites of Sarum, Bangor, York, and Hereford in his work, Maskell contrasted them unfavourably with present-day Roman Catholic liturgy. Rock, having devoted much of his first chapter (over sixty pages) to a trenchant defence of the antiquity of belief in transubstantiation, calling on sources from Theodore to the twelfth century to bear witness, triumphantly concluded, 'Thus do we behold the authoritative teaching, the writings, the ceremonial, the liturgical practices, the history, everything in fine belonging to the Anglo-Saxon Church, all unite in showing how thoroughly the people believed in the Catholic dogma of transubstantiation.'[88] He then takes issue directly with Maskell (in a passage tactfully removed in the only editorial amendment by Hart and Frere):

> We must in charity suppose that Mr Maskell was quite unaware of these and other ancient authorities upon this subject; for had he known them, notwithstanding those feelings of strong dislike towards many Catholic doctrines and practices, which he shows in so many places of his otherwise highly interesting works on our Old English liturgy, never would he have allowed himself to be betrayed into writing, that to hold that by the mere words of institution only, and by them alone, the Holy Eucharist is consecrated, is a 'novel figment'![89]

One of the key liturgical and theological shifts brought about by a combination of Tractarianism and the Ecclesiological movement within the Church of England was an increased emphasis on the eucharist which came to dominate its liturgical outlook. By the time of Hart and Frere's edition of *The Church of Our Fathers* it was becoming the predominant form of Anglican Sunday worship, so their interest in a work dominated by discussions of the history, liturgical forms, and physical setting of the eucharist is perhaps unsurprising. However, by

---

[86] Nockles, *Oxford Movement*, p. 222.
[87] Yates, *Buildings, Faith and Worship*, p. 144.
[88] Rock, *Church of Our Fathers*, 1, pp. 64–5.
[89] Ibid., 1, p. 65.

then the argument in the Church of England was not just over the acceptable extent of ritualism, but also over whether the Church of England should be trying to imitate contemporary Rome or recover medieval England.

> This question was of vital importance to the ritualist clergy and the more informed laity. It was debated endlessly within the ritualist societies established within the Church after 1850: the Society of the Holy Cross, the English Church Union, the Confraternity of the Blessed Sacrament and the Guild of All Souls. It became an absorbing interest among students at the Tractarian colleges, such as those at Chichester, Wells, Cuddesdon and Salisbury, institutions that were crucial instruments in the growth of ecclesiological principles among the clergy.[90]

The atmosphere was heightened by the Anglo-Roman exchanges over Anglican Orders in the 1890s, and by the no-Popery campaigns at the end of the century provoked in part by the publication of Walter Walsh's *Secret History of the Oxford Movement* (1897), which accused the ritualists of outright Romanizing.[91]

Crichton's assessment of Rock, from the perspective of a twentieth-century liturgical reformer, is dismissive: 'His pastoral interest was feeble and pastoral experience small. He was primarily a historian, collector and connoisseur, interested in objects for their own sake and as a manifestation of a past that he must have known could never return.'[92] In one sense that is true, as he did not share Pugin's determination to restore a vision of past glories and his archaeological and antiquarian work was taken up by others for polemical purposes. His purpose was to establish the continuity of liturgical practice from the earliest times to the present day and to argue for its unchange-ableness in fundamentals. If those fundamentals were preserved, then liturgy could be intelligible and powerfully symbolic again for a later generation. His work, like that of Lingard and Eustace, was a plea for understanding, and the misfortune of its adoption by the Church of England was that Anglicans also took up the polemical positions with which it had become unhelpfully associated. Perhaps there was more pastoral sense in Rock than Crichton is prepared to credit?

---

[90] Yates, *Buildings, Faith and Worship*, p. 144.
[91] O. Chadwick, *The Victorian Church*, 2 vols (London, 1970), 2, p. 355.
[92] Crichton, *Lights in the Darkness*, p. 84.

The value of looking afresh at Rock's work, and at his connections with Lingard, Pugin, Wiseman, and the Shrewsbury circle, is that it opens up a more nuanced understanding of the relationship between the old-English, liberal, Gothic-inspired school and the Roman Ultramontanism which dominated the later nineteenth century. In liturgical matters, as in the devotional world which Heimann explored to such effect, there is less conflict and less Roman imposition than at first appears. There is greater depth in nineteenth-century liturgical scholarship to be explored than the superficial disputes which caused such temper tantrums in Pugin. Arguably the differences between the Gothic and Roman schools were not fundamental. Rock wanted to reintegrate Catholic England into its liturgical past, which stretched as far back as the images of S. Clemente which Benedict Biscop, Wilfrid, and Theodore introduced from Rome to the Anglo-Saxons. He was scornful of Pugin's insistence on certain forms and of his archaisms of language and behaviour. Had Rock been an architect, or administrator of one of the new Catholic cathedrals, his influence in the nineteenth-century Catholic Church and Church of England might well have been greater than that of the noisier Pugin.

Before completing his first volume of *The Church of Our Fathers* with a detailed history of the form and usage of every possible item of liturgical vesture, almost incidentally Rock sets out, in a digression, his purpose in writing. It was a duty of Catholics, still more of clergy, to put to better account 'those many title deeds of faith bequeathed by the churchmen of Catholic England'. The purpose was catechetical, but not in the form of didactic insistence on one form alone to the exclusion of all others. Rock understood the use of imagination in religion and in drawing people to belief. To him, the strength of ancient Christian forms lay in their powerful and evocative symbolism, which were in danger of being rendered meaningless. Rock had clearly absorbed Lingard's lessons about attractiveness and comprehensibility:

> It seemed to me, that while we spoke to our countrymen through their ears, preaching the Catholic belief in English words; while we sought to instruct them, writing books in the English tongue – before we could do that work thoroughly well, we must try and talk to them through their eyes – by signs, as if they were deaf in a spiritual sense: by those symbols, in fact, which English architecture and her sister arts so readily furnish; – that we ought to make even the wayfarer, as he passed by a Catholic church, see, if he

would not step in and hear, Catholic belief; and have put before him, as he cast his eye upon the material building, some at least of the many English proofs which show the oldness of its growth in this land: to allow, in fine, everyone who went in, to behold by the distribution and adornments done after our old English manner, a kind of national catechism, which the poor as well as the rich, the bookless clown as well as the learned squire might be able to read and understand all alike – setting at one view, Catholic truths in native English characters before Protestant minds, and awakening Catholics themselves to the thought of living up to the ancient perfection of their venerable belief, besides remembering its ancient practices in this country.[93]

Oscott College

---

[93] Rock, *Church of Our Fathers*, 1, p. 345.

'THE RECTOR PRESENTS HIS COMPLIMENTS': WORSHIP, FABRIC, AND FURNISHINGS OF THE PRIORY CHURCH OF ST BARTHOLOMEW THE GREAT, SMITHFIELD, 1828–1938

by MARTIN DUDLEY

FOR nearly 900 years the Priory Church of St Bartholomew the Great has functioned as an expression of wider religious moods, movements, and aspirations. Founded in 1123 by Rahere, a courtier of Henry I, at a time when the Augustinian Canons gained a brief ascendancy over older forms of religious life, it represents the last flowering of English Romanesque architecture.[1] The Priory was dissolved by Henry VIII, became a house of Dominicans under Mary, and saw the flames that consumed the Smithfield martyrs. Since Elizabeth's reign it has been a parish church serving a small and poor but populous area within the City of London but outside the walls. Its history is fairly well documented.[2] Richard Rich lived in the former Lady Chapel. Walter Mildmay worshipped, and was buried, there. John Wesley preached there. Hogarth was baptized there. Parts of the church had been turned over to secular use. There was a blacksmith's forge in the north transept beyond the bricked-up arch of the crossing and the smoke from the forge often filled the building. A school occupied the north triforium gallery. The Lady Chapel was further divided, and early in the eighteenth century Samuel Palmer, a printer, had his letter foundry there. The young Benjamin Franklin worked there for a year in 1725 and recorded the experience in his autobiography. The church, surrounded by houses, taverns, schools, chapels, stables, and warehouses, was a shadow of its medieval glory; but between 1828 and 1897 it changed internally and externally almost beyond recognition. The process of change continued over the next forty years and indeed continues still. These changes in architecture and furnishings were closely linked to a changed attitude to medieval buildings, to issues of churchmanship, and to liturgical developments.

---

[1] A medieval account of the foundation is given in BL, MS Cotton Vespasian B. IX.

[2] The primary printed source is E. A. Webb, *The Records of St Bartholomew's Priory and of the Church and Parish of St Bartholomew the Great*, 2 vols (Oxford, 1921) [hereafter Webb].

The aspirations of individual rectors, especially of Panckridge and Savory, were expressed in a process of concrete change which nevertheless claimed continuity with Prior Rahere's original foundation.

On 8 February 1828, John Abbiss, Rector since 1819 and brother-in-law of the patron, William Phillips, wrote a letter to the Vestry. 'The rector presents his compliments to the vestry,' he began,

> having received a deputation . . . requesting his opinion as to the most proper site for the new pulpit and reading desk, which the vestry have obligingly agreed to erect at his recommendation, he begs to suggest that the best position in which they can be placed for the advantage of the congregation is in the two pews belonging to the rector situate one on each side of the aisle and opening into the church, and it is his wish, if agreeable to the vestry, that they should be placed there.[3]

The vestry agreed and on 15 February accepted a tender of £193 18s. for the new pulpit and desk and the altering of seats; £43 was expended 'in crimson silk and velvet hanging deep with fringe, the tops stuffed and covered with velvet' for the pulpit and desk; £7 12s. on a feather pillow and £21 10s. for 'two pairs of gothic bronzed branches for lamps for pulpit and reading desk'.[4] It is not entirely clear whether these pulpits[5] were intended to replace the original five-sided Gothic pulpit, but that was, apparently, destroyed in 1828 by the clumsiness of a workman attempting to remove it during repairs. Also in 1828 the extraordinary painted altar-piece which had filled the east end was removed and in due course replaced with an arcade of small arches in the Norman style with a plain wooden panelled screen behind the altar.[6]

A picture of the church drawn in 1838 shows therefore that it looked considerably different from the way it had in one drawn ten years earlier before the re-ordering was carried through. We may well describe it as a 'pre-Tractarian experiment' which, while not entirely successful, reasserted the orientation of the church and gave some

---

[3] Webb, 2, p. 376, quoting Vestry Minute Book 4, p. 625. He gives two dates for the letter – 8 and 18 February.

[4] Ibid., 2, p. 376.

[5] A similar pair survive in St George's, Portland (Dorset); photograph in Nigel Yates, *Buildings, Faith, and Worship: the Liturgical Arrangement of Anglican Churches 1600–1900* (Oxford, 1991), pl. 18.

[6] Webb, 2, p. 20.

priority to the altar, even if it was dwarfed by the pulpits. The emphasis on the east end continued in 1864 when there began what E. A. Webb, the church's historian, brother of Aston Webb, and sometime churchwarden, calls the 'first restoration'. The Church of England changed much in Abbiss's time, for he was Rector until 1883, but the most significant development as far as St Bartholomew's was concerned was the recovery of a sense of the importance of medieval buildings. The Cambridge Camden Society was formed in 1839 and *The Ecclesiologist* was published for the first time in 1841. As 'The Ecclesiological Society' from 1846, it promoted catholic churchmanship and the recovery of medieval ceremonial in Anglican worship. St Barnabas, Pimlico, and St George's in the East were some distance from Smithfield, but St Alban's, Holborn, and St Vedast, Foster Lane (whose Rector was imprisoned for ritual offences in 1880) were close at hand. Would St Bartholomew's, an ideal place for medieval ceremonial, follow the ritualist line? We do not know if and to what extent Abbiss was influenced by the Oxford Movement and all that followed from it, but, though seventy-four years old, he entered with enthusiasm on the restoration of the ancient proportions of the church and the reconstruction of the lost apsidal end. Sir Gilbert Scott, G. E. Street, Benjamin Ferrey, J. L. Pearson, and other eminent London architects acted as a consulting committee. Following their advice, the churchwardens applied for a faculty (in 1864) which included leave to replace the pews with chairs. The work was set in hand and the church closed for what eventually became four years. The apse was restored at ground level, but the fringe factory which now occupied the site of the Lady Chapel prevented a complete restoration. When the church reopened in 1868 the Bridge's organ of 1731 from the western gallery had been lost – it was inadvertently sold when the organ maker who stored it died – and Mr Abbiss purchased a small organ which was erected on the south side opposite Rahere's tomb. The sanctuary as it appeared before the second restoration shows only one feature that could be censured – a cross on the holy table.

In 1884, William Panckridge became Rector on the nomination of the patron, Frederick Parr Phillips, to whom he had been recommended by the then Bishop of Bedford, William Walsham Howe. Panckridge had previously been at St Matthew's, City Road, a living he had originally refused because of the Bishop's distasteful conditions with regard to ritual. Panckridge issued the first parish magazine for St Bartholomew's in April 1884 and announced the formation of a choir;

the choristers were admitted on Easter Eve. He told the congregation that 'the only addition at present to ordinary services of the Church will be a Celebration of Holy Communion on Sunday mornings at 8 o'clock.' He hoped to start Evensong at 5.00pm. During his first Holy Week he gave an address each evening on 'The Holy Communion; its Meaning, its Necessity, its Neglect, its Benefits'.[7]

The 'second restoration' began the following year, 1885, and its principles were set out in a report by the architect, Aston Webb, made to the Executive Committee. It included the completion of the eastern apse, begun in the previous restoration, at triforium and clerestory level; the re-roofing of the church; the removal of the boys' school from the north triforium; the removal of the blacksmith's forge and the rebuilding of the north and south transepts; the repair of the west end, the restoration of the Lady chapel; and the provision of 'Seating and necessary Furniture'.[8] The Executive Committee included three Fellows of the Society of Antiquaries and five members of Parliament; among the latter was J. A. Beresford Hope, son of the noted High Church parliamentarian J. A. B. Beresford Hope.

The temporary organ acquired in 1868, never adequate for its task, was replaced by one bought in 1886 from St Stephen's, Walbrook, which could only be placed in an organ loft at the west end. Rector Panckridge requested that the choir stalls, now occupied by a surpliced choir of men and boys, be moved to the west end and that the congregational seats should be arranged to face each other, as in the quire of a cathedral or college chapel. There was a flurry of enthusiasm and monies were offered for the loft, the stalls, and marble steps for the new high altar, and a brass lectern was also given.[9] A new altar was presented in 1886. It was raised on three steps and placed on the chord of the apse.[10]

Panckridge died in 1887 after only two and half years as rector. In June of that year there was a flurry of correspondence concerning ritualism. A letter, signed 'Long Lane' (which is one of the streets of the parish), pointed to 'clerical influence working at St Bartholomew's of a most disastrous character' and referred to a meeting there, for Evensong,

---

[7] The information here is drawn from a collection of leaflets and cuttings assembled by the churchwarden, E. A. Webb, now in London, Guildhall Library, MS 14,375/1.

[8] Aston Webb, *Report on the Proposed Restoration* (London, 1886), pp. 1–4.

[9] Webb, 2, p. 411.

[10] The original altar, possibly late sixteenth- or early seventeenth-century, is now in the north transept Chapel of Sacrifice. Ibid., 2, p. 52.

of the English Church Union. 'Old Bartholomewite' complained of the presence in the Priory Church of that noted ritualist Father Stanton of St Alban's, Holborn (who was deputizing during Panckridge's illness and in the interregnum) and spoke of 'extreme ritual' and 'Romanism in disguise'. A parishioner, Thomas Dixon, responded: 'I have attended the old church since 1853, and I have never seen the services conducted better, the congregation more satisfied, or a better attendance. And my advice is that those who do not approve of the ritual should go elsewhere.'[11]

Panckridge was succeeded by the Revd Sir Borradaile Savory, Bt, who continued his predecessor's work and style. In June 1888 we find him addressing an appeal letter to the members of the English Church Union. A choir screen was erected as a memorial to Panckridge and a subscription of £60 was diverted to it from the original purpose of providing a screen to the sanctuary. Canon Phillips, the patron, preached at its dedication on 8 June 1889. He praised Panckridge's 'conception of the office of an ideal priest',[12] and invoked the support of the parishioners:

> You who watched your late Rector's career, you know how he worked. You know his unwearied energy in urging on the restoration of our noble church. You know how much, through his exercise of patience and tact, much that disfigured and desecrated it, was swept away; – how much of its ancient beauty and proportions of its solemn features were opened to the eye. How by a higher tone of worship and deeper solemnity of ritual he sought to touch the hearts, to stir up the consciences, to reach down to the spiritual instincts, and to raise the souls of those 'over whom he had the rule' to the contemplation and hopes of better things above.[13]

Phillips's language about Panckridge, reminding the congregation that they would 'see him no more as once at the holy altar he consecrated the sacred elements of the body and blood of Christ, our great High Priest',[14] or recalling that at St Bartholomew's there 'never have the

[11] Cutting in Webb's scrapbook, London, Guildhall Library, MS 14,375/1.
[12] F. P. Phillips, *A Sermon preached in the Priory Church of S. Bartholomew Smithfield, on 8th June, 1889, the second Anniversary of the death of the late Rector, The Rev. W. Panckridge, M. A.* (Guildford, 1889), p. 8.
[13] Ibid., p. 9.
[14] Ibid., p. 14.

priests, the ministers, the stewards of [Christ's] word and sacraments, been wanting to celebrate the mysteries of the Holy Eucharist',[15] suggests that, at this point in the century, the Priory Church belonged at the catholic end of the Anglican spectrum.

Alas, there are no photographs and no descriptions to indicate just what that higher tone of worship under Panckridge might have been, or what the features were of the deeper solemnity of ritual; but a picture dated 1897, the tenth year of Sir Borradaile Savory's incumbency, shows six candles and a cross on the altar. This might be viewed as no more than artistic licence, but a further picture presented to Sir Aston Webb with an illuminated testimonial in 1898 also shows them, and so does a drawing dating from 1906. They do not appear in photographs dating from Rector Sandwith's incumbency (1907–29) which, as they show the brass eagle lectern, must date from before 1919 when it was replaced with one of oak.[16] It is not clear why or when they were removed. The inventory of 1906 is not very helpful for it lists three wooden altars in the church, three brass altar crosses, and seven brass altar candlesticks.[17]

Further additions were made in the later years of Savory's incumbency. Aston Webb erected a stone pulpit in 1893. It is described as being like an ancient ambo, having two flights of steps and had no canopy.[18] It was executed in Hopton stone at a cost of £117 and paid for out of a bequest from the late sextoness, Charlotte Hart.[19] In 1903 a new floor was provided for the sanctuary as a memorial to Canon Phillips.

The Ritual Question was again raised in the Church of England early in 1904 when a strong move was made for the appointment of a Select Committee of the House of Commons to inquire into ecclesiastical disorders. In March 1904 Archbishop Randall Davidson proposed that there should be a Royal Commission rather than a Select Committee. A. J. Balfour, the Prime Minister, agreed, and the Commission met for the first time in May. The inquiry lasted for two years and an immense amount of evidence was submitted.[20] It was

[15] Ibid., p. 15.
[16] Webb, 2, p. 49.
[17] Printed ibid., 2, pp. 505–6.
[18] Ibid., 2, pp. 22, 421, with reasons for omitting a canopy.
[19] Ibid., 2, p. 419.
[20] G. K. A. Bell, *Randall Davidson, Archbishop of Canterbury*, 2nd edn (London, 1938), ch. 25.

inevitable that St Bartholomew's, which was listed in the *Tourist's Church Guide* as one where vestments were worn, should receive some attention.[21] Evidence for submission to the Commission was gathered by a witness who attended Holy Communion at 8.00am on 8 September.[22] It was in the north transept chapel. There was a brass cross and two lighted candles. There were two persons in the congregation. Vestments were not worn; the priest wore surplice and stole. The Ten Commandments were omitted. There was a mixed chalice, the sign of the cross was made in the air at the absolution and the blessing, the manual acts were not visible, and both the paten and the chalice were elevated. Sir Borradaile replied to the Commissioners 'under advice': 'The clergyman who officiated is new to the parish, and he followed the use of the parish from which he came. Our use here is not even to omit the ten Commandments, and we do not use a mixed chalice, and it was done without my knowledge or consent.'[23] Savory seems too defensive, unwilling to enter a debate with the Commissioners, and possibly relieved that the witness had not been present on a Sunday when the six candles were lit. There is, however, no evidence for the use of eucharistic vestments. They are not recorded in the inventory of 1906. The sacristy is described as having '2 Cupboards for Robes for Clergy & Sacristans', but no further detail is provided.

*   *   *

The parish was poor and populous. Catholic ceremonial was believed to appeal to the working masses. How many of them came to church? The registers only tell us the number of communicants;[24] but in 1896 the congregation was counted on five occasions, resulting in the figures in Table I.[25] The congregation was also counted in 1897, giving the figures in Table II.[26]

---

[21] Abbreviated text in Webb, 2, pp. 505–7; full text in a bound volume in the church safe.

[22] *Minutes of the Evidence taken before the Royal Commission on Ecclesiastical Discipline*, in *Parliamentary Papers* (London, 1906), p. 33.

[23] Letter of 20 November 1904: ibid.

[24] The Service Registers replace Preachers' Books in 1884; that for 1887–92 is missing.

[25] Henry Clarke, *The City Churches* (London, 1898), p. 129.

[26] Ibid., p. 129.

Table I

Date	Morning	Evening
7 June	47	80
16 August	60	100
6 September	54	120
1 November	60	130
15 November	75	85

Table II

	25 April		16 May		13 June		18 July	
	M	E	M	E	M	E	M	E
Men	31	44	19	16	18	27	22	20
Women	43	153	47	90	50	88	40	91
Children	7	6	5	6	4	10	10	18
Choir	28	24	24	26	26	26	28	28
Clergy	2	2	3	2	2	3	2	2
Officials	2	2	2	2	2	2	2	2
TOTAL	113	231	100	142	102	156	104	161

Henry Clarke, who provides these figures, compares them with those at the 11am service on 1 May 1881, consisting of seven men, seven women, six officials with their families, and twenty-three school children, and admits that the contrast between 1881, under Rector Abbiss, and 1896–7 under Rector Savory is very remarkable. It is worth noting that the basic seating capacity of the church at 220 seats is not large, especially when compared to St Botolph, Aldersgate, and St Sepulchre without Newgate, with their galleries.

The Easter and Christmas communicant figures which are provided by the registers for the period 1892–1917 (Fig. 1) show a significant peak in the years following the completion of the restoration followed by a dip in the last years of Savory's incumbency. A proper interpretation of the figures would, however, require details about population and social trends which have not yet been obtained. It clearly was a parish populated by the poor and the sick, among whom the Mission Worker, Miss Towne, did good work. Replying to Bishop Mandell

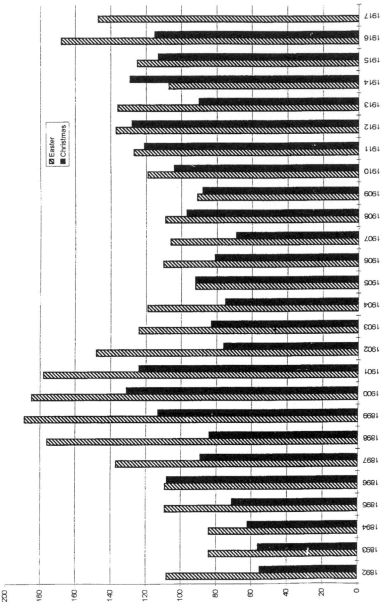

Fig. 1. Communicants at Easter and Christmas, 1892–1917

Creighton's letters of enquiry for his Primary (and only) Visitation in 1901, Savory said that there was a population of 1873, with an average Sunday congregation of 100 in the morning and 200 in the evening, but only twenty-five communicants at 8.00am, fourteen at 11.45am, and four on Thursday morning at 8 o'clock. Asked about the chief difficulties in the way of his ministry, Savory replied tersely: 'Apathy and Ignorance'. Asked what account he could give of the general moral condition of the parish, he replied: 'Drunkeness is our besetting sin.'[27]

We know almost nothing more about the worship than what we can gather from these snippets. No liturgical books other than the *Book of Common Prayer* appear in the Inventory compiled in 1906. The few extant parish magazines give us a programme of services and occasionally indicate hymn numbers. We know that the altars had frontals and super-frontals and that there were burses and veils, but nothing more. Savory died in 1906, probably worn out after twenty years of intensive ministry, and Captain Phillips nominated William Sandwith. On 25 January 1907, the *Church Times* reported his first meeting with parishioners and gives us the only indication of the type of liturgy he was inheriting:

> All would be pleased to hear that the rector's intention was to maintain the present character of the service, the dignified rendering of which, closely resembling (though with less ornate ceremonial) that in use at All Saints', Margaret-street, is loved by many and appeals to all. St Bartholomew-the-Great attracts many hundreds of people during the year from across the seas, and it would have been a matter of great regret, had the character of the services been altered. For the restoration of real church life and dignified worship at St Bartholomew's, one must go back to the days when that saintly servant of God, William Panckridge, was rector.

On 11 May 1908 the Bishop of Stepney, Cosmo Gordon Lang, soon to be Archbishop of York, preached at the dedication of Savory's three monuments in the church. That he should have had three – a personal memorial in the Lady Chapel, a large tablet in the west porch that records the process of restoration, and commemorative altar rails – is a tribute to his outstanding achievements as rector. Lang described Savory as having three great qualities – patience, thoroughness, and a sense of worship – and as fulfilling

---

[27] London, Lambeth Palace Library, Fulham Papers, Creighton 1/28.

the meaning of that old word – piety. A pious man was one who sought to preserve the heritage of his forefathers, of their devotion and faith, and if any man deserved the title of a man of piety, it was he who had spent his life in the restoration of that church. He was not a mere antiquary, but his efforts were made simply because he wished it be a House of God.[28]

Sandwith's registers of services give us occasional notes of the number attending church. On 25 April 1909, the Archdeacon of London, William Sinclair, was at St Bartholomew's; the Rector was away because of ill-health. Sinclair wrote in the register: 'I visited this glorious church for sermon and celebration. A thoroughly efficient choir, large and most devout and attentive congregation, a beautifully rendered service.' At Easter 1910 there were seventy-two present at 8.00am, with seventy communicants, 166 at 11.00am with forty-nine communicants, and 117 people at Evensong. At Christmas, falling on a Sunday, there were seventy-five at the early service with fifty-nine communicants, 128 at 11 o'clock with forty-five communicants; eighty-four people attended Evensong. On 31 December 1912 at 11.15pm the church was full.

Sandwith, however, was not able to maintain the number and style of services. In the absence of the register of services covering the period 1917–29 it is unclear how or why this happened. The last entry we have, 23 June 1917, the Third Sunday after Trinity, shows Holy Communion at 8.15am with eleven communicants, and at 11 o'clock with 160 people present but only thirteen communicants. There was catechism at 3.45pm and Evensong at 7.00pm when there were 129 people present. When the registers resume in 1929, the pattern of services had changed – there was Communion at 8.45am, with three or four communicants, Mattins at 11 o'clock and Evensong at 6.30pm, with a choral Eucharist on the third Sunday of the month – a familiar pattern of Anglican services but not one appropriate to a high-church parish. It seems unlikely that Canon Savage, Rector from May 1929, made these changes in his first week, and he must have inherited them from Sandwith.

* * *

28 Press cutting in E. A. Webb's scrapbook, London, Guildhall Library, MS 14,375/1.

The change in attitude to worship reflected in these changes to the pattern and style of services extended to the structure and furnishings of the church as conceived by Aston Webb with Panckridge and Savory. The process of change begun by Sandwith was continued under Savage. Webb's ambo was swept away and a new pulpit was erected. Panels of little artistic merit but illustrating the story of the founder were inserted into the choir screen. There was a new retable at the high altar and new altar silver. The set consisted of an altar cross, two altar candlesticks, four vases, and two large standard candlesticks designed by Omar Ramsden and made in 1934.[29] The stress in Savage's writings and appeals for money is on the historic importance and beauty of the building and on the quality of the music, but not on a higher tone of worship and a deeper solemnity of ritual.

There was one last anti-ritualist protest when the war shrine at the gate was dedicated by the Bishop of Willesden on 18 November 1917. The Bishop praised the inclusion of a crucifix in Sir Aston Webb's design and a protester asked him to read the second Commandment. The Bishop continued with the dedication both of this and of an image of St Bartholomew, a memorial to Sir Aston's son Philip. The protester, claiming this as an idolatrous desecration of the 'sacred soil of Smithfield', was the son of John Kensit, the notorious anti-ritualist campaigner who had caused Mandell Creighton endless difficulties.[30]

There is one part of the building that provides an indication of the liturgical spirit that animated the Victorian restorers of St Bartholmew's: the Lady Chapel. A great effort had been made in 1864 to purchase the fringe-maker's factory which occupied the site. It was unsuccessful, and the apse could only be restored at ground level with part of the factory extending into the church at triforium level. The factory was finally acquired in 1885, but there was really nothing left of the medieval fabric that could be restored.[31] In 1894 everything except the pre-suppression walls and the crypt beneath was demolished. The crypt was restored in 1895, and in the following two years Aston Webb created a remarkable chapel incorporating all the existing work but providing an entirely new east wall, without windows, so that direct light does not penetrate

---

[29] They were largely the work of the silversmith Samuel Coles: *Omar Ramsden 1873–1939, Catalogue of the Centenary Exhibition of Silver at the Birmingham City Museum and Art Gallery* (Birmingham, 1973).

[30] Report in *The Churchman*, published by the Protestant Truth Society, Dec. 1917.

[31] Webb, 2, pp. 82–3.

the quire or disturb the sombre effect of the ambulatory. There are, however, niches above the altar, with canopies and pedestals for figures. The chapel is separated from the ambulatory by a screen designed by Webb and erected in 1897, in time for the opening of the chapel, on 18 May in that year, by Bishop Mandell Creighton. Over the gates is a tall wrought-iron cross, supported by chains from the roof beam, with a figure of the Crucified in silver. It may not have been politic to place a crucifix on the high altar in 1897, but the priest standing at that altar, then as now, can look through the central arch of the apse to the crucifix above. The east end itself with curtains, hangings, gradine, cross, candlesticks and flower vases, sanctuary light, and altarpiece of the Madonna and Child with St Elizabeth (pronounced by the late Sir Alma Tadema to be a very fine copy of a painting by Murillo),[32] provides a marked contrast with the rest of the building. In its very limited changes through the early years of the century it remained a little catholic shrine, a church within a church, an indication of what Phillips, Panckridge, Savory, and the Webbs thought St Bartholomew the Great should be.

[32] Webb, 2, p. 85.

PROSPER GUÉRANGER O.S.B. (1805-1875) AND THE STRUGGLE FOR LITURGICAL UNITY

by PETER RAEDTS

ONE of the strongest weapons in the armoury of the Roman Catholic Church has always been its impressive sense of historical continuity. Apologists, such as Bishop Bossuet (1627-1704), liked to tease their Protestant adversaries with the question of where in the world their Church had been before Luther and Calvin.[1] The question shows how important the time between ancient Christianity and the Reformation had become in Catholic apologetics since the sixteenth century. Where the Protestants had to admit that a gap of more than a thousand years separated the early Christian communities from the churches of the Reformation, Catholics could proudly point to the fact that in their Church an unbroken line of succession linked the present hierarchy to Christ and the apostles. This continuity seemed the best proof that other churches were human constructs, whereas the Catholic Church continued the mission of Christ and his disciples. In this argument the Middle Ages were essential, but not a time to dwell upon. It was not until the nineteenth century that in the Catholic Church the Middle Ages began to mean far more than proof of the Church's unbroken continuity.

The sudden interest in the Middle Ages and in the medieval Church was certainly not an exclusively Catholic affair. On the contrary, it was outside the Catholic Church, in the circles of Romantic poets and of political enemies of the French Revolution, that the Middle Ages first appeared as an alternative to the cult of reason and the ideals of freedom and equality. For enthusiastic young Catholics, however, it was not so much the Revolution, as the way in which the ecclesiastical authorities handled the restoration of the Church after 1815, that made them think about a better future for their Church. To their deep disappointment the diplomats of the Roman Curia made no effort whatsoever to clean the slate but tried, where possible, to restore the situation as it had been before the Revolution: a close alliance between throne and altar and good relations with all the princes, not just the

[1] J. B. Russell, 'Interpretations of the origins of medieval heresy', *Mediaeval Studies*, 25 (1963), p. 28.

Catholic ones.[2] To maintain good relations the Roman authorities were prepared to make far-reaching concessions, as for example in the case of Poland. When in 1830 the Catholic Poles revolted against the Czar, their revolution was condemned twice by Pope Gregory XVI, for whom the principle of legitimacy was more important than the oppression of his Catholic children.[3] This condemnation caused a stir in all of Catholic Europe: the cowardice of Gregory XVI stood in sharp contrast to his heroic medieval predecessors, such as Gregory VII and Innocent III, both men who had not been afraid of anybody and of whom all princes of Europe had stood in awe. So it was the half-hearted policy of the Roman Curia that made young Catholics dream of an alternative: the restoration of the medieval Church, of the days when all the nations of Europe looked upon the pope as their leader, of the days when spiritual and political guidance was found *ultra montes*.

In no country was the unimaginative restoration policy of the Roman Curia more bitterly regretted than in France. The concordat of 1801 in fact restored the authority of the state over the Church. The government controlled the appointment of bishops, as it had done before 1789, and the education of the clergy in the seminaries was closely supervised by the *Ministère des cultes*. The French Church became once more, in the words of a prominent jurist, that branch of the civil service that saw to it that all Frenchmen received sufficient spiritual nourishment.[4] Probably the grip of the state over the Church was even more absolute than before 1789, because most of the ancient liberties and privileges that had once limited the power of the civil authorities remained abolished. Priests were treated like all other civil servants, which meant that they were completely subjected to the often arbitrary decisions of their civil and ecclesiastical superiors.[5] To gain some legal protection many younger priests began to look over the

---

[2] A. van de Sande, *La Curie romaine au début de la restauration; le problème de la continuité dans la politique de restauration du Saint-Siège en Italie, 1814–1817* (The Hague, 1979), p. 190: 'La Curie romaine suivait une ligne de conduite traditionnelle et ne se laissait pas impressionner par la tendance nouvelle de l'ultramontanisme, prônée surtout par des autres non-ecclésiastiques, issus des cercles contra-révolutionnaires. . . . On donnait la préférence à une voie diplomatique plus traditionnelle: le rétablissement de l'Alliance entre le Trône et l'Autel.'

[3] R. Gildea, *Barricades and Borders: Europe 1800–1914*, 2nd edn (Oxford, 1995), p. 118.

[4] J. Le Goff and R. Rémond, eds, *Histoire de la France religieuse. 3: Du roi très chrétien à la laïcité républicaine* (Paris, 1991), p. 117.

[5] N. Ravitch, *The Catholic Church and the French Nation 1589–1989* (London and New York, 1990), pp. 63–4; A. Gough, *Paris and Rome. The Gallican Church and the Ultramontane Campaign 1848–1853* (Oxford, 1986), pp. 12–13.

borders of their own diocese and of their country in the direction of Rome, in the hope that perhaps the pope might shield them from the worst vagaries and fancies of their immediate superiors and restore some liberty to the French Church.[6] The growing resistance of the younger clergy to the established Church was brilliantly articulated by the charismatic convert Hugues-Félicité de Lamennais (1782–1854), who in the years between 1820 and 1830 became one of the most influential thinkers in the Catholic Church, first in France, and later on also in the rest of Europe.

Lamennais' concern was not so much with the position of the Church as with the freedom of man. In the ever-growing power of the modern state he saw the main threat to that freedom. He was convinced that the only authority that could resist the modern state effectively was a free and independent Church powerful enough to see to it that all citizens could follow their own consciences. That is why he advocated a strong, unified Church under the direct leadership of the pope, as it had allegedly been in the Middle Ages, before the rise of the national states after 1300. The modern Church had to fight for the same *libertas* she had enjoyed in the glorious years between 1000 and 1300, when the popes had been the leaders in the fight against tyranny and state oppression.[7] Separation from the state was a necessary condition to re-establish that liberty. These ideas became very popular with the younger French clergy, so popular, in fact, that even the condemnation of Lamennais' ideas by Pope Gregory XVI in 1832 could not stop the rapid dissemination of the ideals of Ultramontanism all over Europe. Within a short span of thirty years Ultramontanism changed from a utopian dream of a few French hotheads into official Church policy. Few did more to spread the dream than Prosper Louis Guéranger.

*   *   *

Guéranger was born in 1805 in a small town to the west of Le Mans. In 1822 he went to the seminary of Le Mans, and was ordained a priest in 1827. During those years he became an ardent admirer of Lamennais' ideas about the renewal of the Church. Where Lamennais, however,

---

[6] R. Gibson, *A Social History of French Catholicism 1789–1914* (London and New York, 1989), pp. 60–1.

[7] H. J. Pottmeyer, *Unfehlbarkeit und Souveränität. Die päpstliche Unfehlbarkeit im System der ultramontanen Ekklesiologie des 19. Jahrhunderts* (Mainz, 1975), p. 29; Ravitch, *Catholic Church*, pp. 72–3.

saw a strong Church as a guarantee of civil liberty, Guéranger was fascinated by the idea of a centralized Church unified under a strong Roman authority as such: politically he always belonged to the extreme right. In that sense Guéranger was not unique. From the beginning Lamennais had not only inspired a Catholic liberalism but also an ideal of papal theocracy linked with all the right-wing political forces opposed to the French Revolution.[8] What Guéranger contributed to the development of Ultramontanism was not his passion for the pope, nor his reactionary political ideas, but his unique insight into the possibilities of the liturgy as a way of visualizing the unity of the Church and the authority of the pope everywhere in the Catholic world.

Liturgical unity was, in the nineteenth century, not a new idea in the Catholic Church. In 1570 Pope Pius V had prescribed the reformed Roman Missal for all Latin Christians. He had, however, exempted from that rule all dioceses and religious orders that had liturgies older than two hundred years. That exception meant, in fact, that most dioceses in France did not have to change to the Roman liturgy but were allowed to stick to their own traditions of which they were very proud, not in the least for political reasons. The existence of Gallican liturgies was, in their eyes, living proof that the French Church had always kept its distance from Rome, and was firmly resolved to keep it in the future as well. Therefore, in the seventeenth and eighteenth centuries most French dioceses had carefully reformed their liturgies and adapted them to the classical tastes of those days, which strengthened the conviction that the Gallican traditions were far superior to the Roman liturgy. The Revolution had brought no change in this respect; the French stuck to their own diverse rituals.

Guéranger was the first to complain about the liturgical diversity of the French Church. As early as 1830 he published four articles in the *Mémorial catholique*, an organ of Lamennais and his disciples, about the scandalous liturgical chaos in France.[9] Guéranger's firm conviction that liturgical unity was essential to the success of the Church's renewal was strengthened in the years after 1830, when he was able to realize his second dream, the restoration of monastic life in France. In 1833 he bought the abandoned priory of Solesmes and, with a few friends, he

---

[8] R. Gildea, *The Past in French History* (New Haven, CT, and London, 1994), pp. 234–8.
[9] A survey of these articles may be found in C. Johnson, *Prosper Guéranger (1805–1875): a Liturgical Theologian*, Studia Anselmiana, 89 (= Analecta liturgica, 9) (Rome, 1984), p. 31.

formed a monastic community there under the rule of St Benedict. In the new monastery the solemn celebration of the liturgy was to take precedence over everything else, just as, in Guéranger's imagination, it had been in the medieval monastery of Cluny.[10] It was in Solesmes that Guéranger wrote his most successful and influential work, the *Institutions liturgiques*, the first part of which was published in 1840.[11]

The *Institutions* are often described as a monument of that longing for the Middle Ages so characteristic of Guéranger's age.[12] That is not untrue, but the means and the end have to be distinguished very carefully. Guéranger wanted to be the champion of the Church of Rome and to restore all other churches to liturgical unity with the Roman See.[13] One of the means to reach that end was a review of the history of the liturgy, with an emphasis on the Middle Ages, when the unity that Guéranger so much wanted for his own time had existed for a short period. The thrust of the book is more political than historical; Guéranger did not so much want to describe the past as to change the present.

* * *

The main reason to introduce the Roman liturgy throughout the Church was, according to Guéranger, that it was the only tradition free from all stains of heresy.[14] Only in the Roman rite were all elements of the apostolic liturgy preserved; her *antiquité* stood in sharp contrast to the *nouveautés* introduced by heretics and schismatics in successive periods.[15] To prove his claim Guéranger sums up a number of very ancient rituals in the Roman liturgy, such as the breaking of the bread, the mixing of water and wine, and the kiss of peace.[16] He is absolutely certain that the Roman Canon is of apostolic origin. For, as he says, one cannot imagine that the apostles did not give exact rules for the celebration of the most fundamental of all Christian mysteries. As that is not imaginable, therefore it is impossible.[17] With this kind of

---

[10] Ibid., p. 129.
[11] Originally the *Institutions* appeared in 3 vols, published in 1840, 1841, and 1851. I use the 2nd unaltered edn, published in 4 vols (Paris, 1878–85).
[12] So for example Gough, *Paris and Rome*, p. 122.
[13] Guéranger, *Institutions*, I, pp. lxix–lxx, lxxv.
[14] Ibid., I, p. 200: 'La liturgie romaine seule est vierge de toute erreur, comme l'Église qui la promulgue.'
[15] Ibid., I, pp. 399–400.
[16] Ibid., I, pp. 30, 33, 36.
[17] Ibid., I, p. 34.

rhetorical trick several Roman traditions are traced back to apostolic times. Very cleverly he cites an ancient custom, preserved in the major basilicas in Rome, of the priest celebrating mass facing the congregation. That seemed to be much more like the habit of early Christians to gather around the altar than the later tradition of celebration where the priest had his back to the people, normal in all churches in Guéranger's own days. The conclusion must be that only Rome had preserved a link with the first, pure Christian community that had been lost in all other churches.

In this argument the medieval Church plays the same part as it did in the works of Bossuet and other Catholic apologists. The study of the liturgy of the Middle Ages is necessary to prove that there always has been a continuous development, that the Roman liturgy now is the logical conclusion to a long development reaching back to the first days of Christianity. This must be emphasised, because it qualifies the received wisdom that Guéranger belonged to a generation of romantics who wanted to restore the medieval Church. What Guéranger admired in the Roman liturgy was not its medieval but its apostolic character; it still breathed the spirit of the first Church gathered around St Peter in Rome. It had been the invaluable work of Pope Gregory the Great that the ancient Roman traditions, at the moment when they were threatened with extinction, had been collected and codified and been handed on to the barbarians who in the Middle Ages became the heirs to the Roman Church and Empire.[18]

The historic importance of the Middle Ages was that the whole of the Western Church between 500 and 1500 gradually introduced the apostolic Roman liturgy and thus began to form a visibly united society gathered around the Roman pontiff. At this point Guéranger is remarkably similar to other romantics: to him as to the others the Middle Ages were the time of order and unity, of a well-organized Christian society. He stressed two periods in particular, the Carolingian era and the age of Pope Gregory VII.

The first opportunity to unite all the western Church under Rome came with the alliance between the pope and the Franks in 751. After centuries of upheaval the Franks wanted to restore western Europe to political unity. For this they desperately needed the support of the papacy, because they themselves could not contribute much more than

---

[18] Guéranger, *Institutions*, 1, pp. 154–66.

military power to this project. Real cultural unity had to come from Rome. This step was taken when Pope Stephen II launched the proposal to make the Roman liturgy compulsory for all the Frankish king's subjects.[19] Guéranger emphasises that the initiative for this reform came from the pope, who now saw the opportunity to implement a policy designed by his predecessors, to elevate the papacy to the central position it ought to have had in western civilization a long time before. What was achieved was much more than liturgical unity. Because the liturgy is 'le plus grand mobile de la civilisation d'un peuple', unity on this essential point meant, in fact, the creation of a new Western-Christian culture.[20] The popes stood at the origin of that culture, and the Roman Church was its heart.[21]

This is a colourful but not very accurate description of what actually happened between the popes and the Frankish kings. It is true that the Frankish kings, Charlemagne in particular, wanted liturgical unity; but the initiative was theirs and not the pope's. It is also true that there was a cultural revival; but its centre was in Aachen and not in Rome. Guéranger must have been so obsessed by what he wanted for his own time that he perhaps could not see that the Frankish kings used the papacy to achieve a political and religious unity on their conditions and under their leadership. If the Franks had a model, it was the imperial government at Constantinople, not the Roman court. To Guéranger the eighth century was the time when the powerful Gallican Church gave up its independence and bowed its head before 'la Mère et Maîtresse des Églises . . . d'assurer à jamais dans son propre sein la perpétuité d'une inviolable orthodoxie'. It was a sad contrast with the French Church of later days, when the clergy became set upon destroying the unity with Rome and its apostolic liturgy.[22] Pope Gregory VII completed the work of his predecessors by adding the liberated areas of Spain to the Roman unity and forbidding the old Mozarabic liturgy. By 1100 the papal project was finished, all of western Europe was united in one Roman culture, the 'unité sociale catholique' was a fact.[23]

Alas, not for long. Despite the ceaseless efforts of the popes, quite

---

[19] Ibid., I, p. 235.
[20] Ibid., I, p. 243.
[21] Ibid., I, p. 237.
[22] Ibid., I, p. 233.
[23] Ibid., I, pp. 268–70, 278.

soon the Roman liturgy became overgrown again with the weeds of local traditions. The main reason was that the piety of medieval man was fervent, but 'peu éclairé', especially in the later Middle Ages. That is why Guéranger warns his readers not to be too uncritical in their praises of the Middle Ages. It is now the fashion, he says, to speak lovingly of those 'siècles catholiques', but one should not forget that in those days people were also ignorant and superstitious, and invented all sorts of strange rites that overran the purity of the ancient Roman liturgy.[24]

In the sixteenth century everyone agreed that a thorough reform of the liturgy was necessary. Many unfortunately turned their back on Rome and tried to reform the Church on their own. Guéranger's verdict on this reform is succinct: it resulted in nothing but an 'immense secte antiliturgique', and necessarily, therefore, heretical, because anyone who started opposing the liturgy ended by lapsing into heresy.[25] Fortunately, after the Council of Trent, the papacy took matters into its own hands and started the true reform: abolition of all medieval superstition, and restoration of the ancient Roman tradition. The result was the Roman Missal of 1570 which was to be the norm for all the Western Church. Unfortunately, what followed was a sad repetition of the later Middle Ages: local usage prevailed over the Roman liturgy once again, in France even more than in other countries. For his own time Guéranger saw it as his task to do what had been tried in the days of Charlemagne and of the Counter-Reformation; restoration of the Roman rite in all the Catholic Church.

Once again it must be noted that Guéranger's admiration for the Middle Ages was qualified. The liturgy that he so much admired originated not in the Middle Ages, but in apostolic times. Despite frantic efforts of the popes, medieval Christians were unable to understand the simplicity and purity of the Roman tradition. The only real merit of the medieval Church had been its quest for visible unity, and the subsequent efforts to spread the Roman liturgy all over the Church as a token of that unity. It had only been a very partial success, limited to the hundred years or so after the pontificate of Gregory VII, but that was the period and the unity to which Guéranger wanted the Catholic Church now to return.

*　*　*

[24] Guéranger, *Institutions*, I, pp. 320, 346–7.
[25] Ibid., I, pp. 391, 396.

The question that remains is why Guéranger considered unity in the celebration of the liturgy so important. The answer to that question is given in the first lines of the *Institutions*. The liturgy is far more than praying together instead of alone, it is 'la prière considérée à l'état social'.[26] Where the same words and the same rituals are used, Christians are welded together into one community of mind and heart. Guéranger saw very well that inward unity can hardly exist without outward conformity in word and gesture. His argument was that the Church is not a community of spirits but of people. And as in man the body is the expression of the soul, so in the Church the liturgy embodies the truth of the Catholic faith in signs and gestures. The Christian dogma penetrates deepest not when uttered in words, but where it is celebrated liturgically, when abstract truths through ceremonials and rites become concrete realities.[27] That is why heresies, such as Calvinism and Anglicanism, were so successful with the people. The first thing they did was put an end to the ancient liturgy and create new rituals and formulae. When that had been done, the preaching of the new faith started; the word of the preacher followed the change of ritual.[28]

The social character of the liturgy was not limited to its communal celebrations. Guéranger insisted that the private prayers of the clergy must follow the same rules as the Church's public prayers, because at every moment a priest should be aware that his prayers were not a private devotion but an 'acte de religion sociale'.[29] Guéranger rejected, therefore, the reform of the breviary, proposed by the sixteenth-century humanist Cardinal Quinoñez, because it made it too much a book for private meditation.[30] Such a distinction between private and public prayer was fundamentally wrong: even in their most personal prayers priests should be constantly soaking up the spirit and social unity of the Church.[31]

---

[26] Ibid., 1, pp. 1, 99.
[27] Ibid., 1, pp. 4–5: 'Et, comme l'Église est une société, non d'esprits, mais d'hommes, créatures composées d'âme et de corps, qui traduisent toute vérité sous des images et des signes, portant eux-mêmes dans leur corps une forme ineffable de leur âme; dans l'Église, disons-nous, ce céleste ensemble de *confession*, de *prière* et de *louange*, parlé dans un langage sacré, modulé sur un rhythme surnaturel, se produit aussi par les signes extérieurs, rites et cérémonies, qui sont le corps de la liturgie.'
[28] Ibid., 1, p. 397.
[29] Ibid., 1, p. 4.
[30] Ibid., 1, pp. 358–68.
[31] Ibid., 1, p. 379.

In the Middle Ages there had been a short period when all nations and races in Europe had been linked together in one common prayer and thus had been moulded into a 'nationalité unique en Occident',[32] a revealing expression because it betrays that Guéranger thought of the Church as a sort of superstate destined to embrace all nations in the one Catholic faith. That thought as such was not original. Many Ultramontane Catholics were convinced that the only true fatherland of the Christian should be the Church and not a secular state.[33] Guéranger's original contribution is that he emphasises that this ideal of an all-embracing Church state should be expressed in concrete ritual unity, so that to all it becomes visible that the Church does not recognize races and nations, but that to her all mankind is one united family, joined together in one common liturgy and one common language, both inherited from Rome.[34]

* * *

Guéranger's book was an immediate success. Although the first reactions were often very negative, with more than sixty bishops rejecting any proposal to introduce the Roman liturgy in their dioceses, the publication of the *Institutions* was a turning point in the relations of the French Church with Rome. In less than forty years the Roman liturgy was introduced in all French dioceses; the last diocese that gave up its own traditions was Orléans in 1875.[35] This is reason enough to ask why Guéranger's book was so immensely successful.

It cannot have been because of its scholarly qualities. Guéranger's quaint efforts to prove the apostolic origin of the Roman liturgy are uncritical to say the least. But perhaps that was an advantage, if social influence was what was really aimed at. In the *Institutions* Guéranger created a myth: the image that he gave of the Church's past was crystal clear, everyone could understand it, and, even more important, could use it as a weapon in the present. And the present was what Guéranger was really interested in. He was also very clever in attracting publicity for his ideas. He fully recognized the power of the modern media and used them to perfection. His great ally in the media circus was the notorious journalist Louis Veuillot, who in his weekly paper, *L'Univers*,

---

[32] Guéranger, *Institutions* 1, pp. 347–8.
[33] Gough, *Paris and Rome*, pp. 92–3.
[34] Guéranger, *Institutions*, 1, p. 278.
[35] Johnson, *Guéranger*, p. 204. The only diocese that kept some, but not much, of its own ritual was Lyons.

supported Guéranger's struggle with all available means, not always in the best of tastes.

To Guéranger's credit it must be said that he was original and far ahead of his time in one respect. He was the first to appreciate the crucial role of ritual in religious communities. Almost instinctively, and long before anthropologists said so, he saw that religion as a cultural system is not so much held together by words and by organizations, but by shared rituals that 'establish powerful, pervasive and long-lasting moods and motivations in men'.[36] Guéranger's curious diagnosis of the success of the Reformation, that the reformers had to change the ritual before their word could be heard, shows his conviction. Here it is stated explicitly, but it is implicit everywhere in the book, that the Christian faith has no firm roots and cannot stand united without a common liturgical tradition. What Guéranger does in the *Institutions* is to show a way to form a coherent religious community and to keep it alive and strong. And that might, in the last analysis, well be the real explanation for the phenomenal success of his work.

The date of publication, 1840, is crucial. It was in that year that France, and all of continental Europe, stood on the verge of revolutionary social and economic changes. The onset of industrialization and the development of modern transport were the end of face-to-face communities, the world of villages and small towns, that since the beginning of history had been the normal form of social life for the vast majority of people. Even if people in the days before industrialization belonged to a larger organization, that organization had an impact only through its local representative, in the case of the Church, the rector of the parish. The faithful were loyal to priest and parish, not to the universal Church. That is why liturgical unity, even if desired, was an impossibility before the second half of the nineteenth century.

All that changed after 1850. In the industrialized world loyalties could no longer be based on family ties and/or personal acquaintance. People started moving and travelling on a scale as never before and if they wanted to find roots, it had to be in much larger communities where loyalties were impersonal and abstract, because there were far too many people in them to know everyone personally. In a happy phrase the anthropologist Benedict Anderson invented the term

---

[36] 'Religion as a cultural system', in Clifford Geertz, *The Interpretation of Cultures* (New York, 1973), p. 90.

'imagined communities' to describe these new constructs. Very convincingly he shows that coherence and loyalty in these unnatural, constructed communities is only possible if their members, somehow, become aware that at the same moment they do the same things, which evoke the same feelings and the same thoughts. Such coherence must rest on a common language and a shared culture that usually forms its own organization in a unified and centralized political entity: the nation state.[37]

I have argued elsewhere that the Catholic Church in the second half of the nineteenth century underwent revolutionary changes similar to other European communities and cultures, and that in that period the Church responded in the same way to the challenges of industrial society by organizing itself in the form of a nation state, or as it was called in neo-scholastic jargon, a *societas perfecta*.[38] Guéranger was the man who showed the Catholics how to achieve it. He saw clearly that the days of many traditions and local diversities were over and that the Church, like secular society, had to be changed into a centralized organization with one language and one common culture. He shaped the dream that Catholics could form one community of mind and heart, because from Manilla to Alaska and from Oslo to Cape Town they prayed in the same language and used exactly the same gestures and rituals. Thus he showed Catholics how they could form an imagined community, of which no longer the parish, not even the diocese, but the universal Roman Church was the horizon. In his *Institutions liturgiques* he created the historical myths on which such a community could be founded. His plea for a return to the happy days of the Middle Ages when the popes in collaboration with Charlemagne had created a 'nationalité unique en Occident' showed the Church a way not just to survive the age of nationalism but through liturgical change to come to a new period of growth and prosperity.

University of Nijmegen

---

[37] Benedict Anderson, *Imagined Communities. Reflections on the Origin and Spread of Nationalism*, 2nd edn (London and New York, 1991), pp. 6, 76–7.
[38] P. Raedts, 'De christelijke Middeleeuwen als mythe', *Tijdschrift voor Theologie*, 30 (1990), pp. 146–58.

A 'FLUFFY-MINDED PRAYER BOOK FUNDAMENTALIST'? F. D. MAURICE AND THE ANGLICAN LITURGY

by J. N. MORRIS

The Liturgy has been to me a great theological teacher; a perpetual testimony that the Father, the Son, and the Spirit, the one God blessed for ever, is the author of all life, freedom, unity to men; that our prayers are nothing but responses to His voice speaking to us and in us. Why do I hear nothing of this from those who profess to reform it? Why do they appear only to treat it as an old praying machine, which in the course of centuries gets out of order like other machines, and which should be altered according to the improved mechanical notions of our time?[1]

* * *

NOTWITHSTANDING that fascinating quotation, F. D. Maurice might seem at first glance a figure marginal to the theme of continuity and change in Christian worship. One of the most creative and yet confusing Anglican theologians of the nineteenth century, he had little to say on the specific issue of the forms of Christian worship. He was not a liturgist by any stretch of the imagination, at least in the most common sense of the term. He was not interested in the study of liturgy as a technical subject. He was probably ignorant of almost all other liturgies except those of the Church of England and of the Unitarian churches in which he was brought up; at least his published work shows very little acquaintance with them. He showed little curiosity even in the remarkable upsurge of interest in the history and sources of the Anglican liturgy which took place during his lifetime, in the hands of · people such as William Palmer and John Mason Neale. He scarcely features in the relevant modern liturgical histories, such as G. J. Cuming's *History of Anglican Liturgy* (London, 1969), for example,

---

[1] F. D. Maurice, letter to the Revd Isaac Taylor, 10 April 1860, in F. Maurice, *The Life of Frederick Denison Maurice*, 2 vols (London, 1884), 2, p. 359.

or R. C. D. Jasper's more recent *Development of the Anglican Liturgy* (London, 1989).[2]

Yet the theological meaning and the continuing relevance of the Anglican liturgy were central preoccupations of Maurice. He returned to them time and again in sermons, in journal and newspaper articles, and indeed in the whole body of his published work.[3] Even if he was not in any sense a liturgist, clearly the liturgy carried a great deal of significance for him. Here, then, is the first of two apparent paradoxes: in an age of great revival in the study, development, and enrichment of the historic liturgical tradition of Anglicanism, Maurice managed at once to be entirely uninterested in the wealth of scholarship unfolding around him, and at the same time thoroughly committed to the defence and theological explication of the central texts on which that scholarship was based. The resolution of that paradox depends on an examination of the role the liturgy played in Maurice's understanding of the theology of the Church of England. In other words, the importance he attached to liturgy can only be understood in relation to his ecclesiology, and in that respect it is not going too far, perhaps, to assert that, whilst not a liturgist as such, he was nevertheless a liturgical theologian, perhaps the most substantial and influential defender of the *Book of Common Prayer* in the nineteenth century.

There is a second paradox, however, which emerges out of the first. The description of Maurice in the title of this essay as a 'fluffy-minded Prayer-Book fundamentalist' is a quotation from a recent essay by Sheridan Gilley.[4] It encapsulates a view of Maurice which is not wholly misleading, though it is, arguably, somewhat off-centre. For Maurice, despite his reputation as one of the founders of the Broad Church tradition of Anglicanism (a label which, incidentally, he always

---

[2] Cuming has just one reference in the main body of his text: p. 151.

[3] He first published a series of sermons specifically on the Prayer Book in 1849, under the title *The Prayer-Book Considered Especially in Reference to the Romish System*. The following year appeared a collection entitled *The Church a Family: Twelve Sermons on the Occasional Offices of the Prayer-Book*. John William Colenso extracted passages from these and other works of Maurice in a compilation entitled *The Communion Service from the Book of Common Prayer* (London, 1855). Further volumes of Maurice's sermons on public worship more generally followed: *The Worship of the Church. A Witness for the Redemption of the World* (London, 1857); *The Worship of God and Fellowship among Men: a Series of Sermons on Public Worship* (London, 1858); *The Faith of the Liturgy and the Doctrine of the Thirty-nine Articles* (London, 1860); *Dialogues between a Clergyman and a Layman on Family Worship* (London, 1862).

[4] S. W. Gilley, 'The ecclesiology of the Oxford Movement', in P. Vaiss, ed., *From Oxford to the People; Reconsidering Newman and the Oxford Movement* (Leominster, 1996), p. 69.

vehemently denied), usually took a firmly conservative line over the revision of the liturgy and of the historic formularies of the Church of England.[5] His own liturgical practice appears to have matched this: he was not an innovator in worship. He claimed throughout his life to adhere to the plain text of the Prayer Book, resisting absolutely the suggestion that the language of the sixteenth century should be jettisoned in the nineteenth: *'Reculer pour mieux sauter* is, I hold, the maxim of all true reformation. . . . Old charters have always been the barriers against prerogative, the grand helps to the assertion of eternal principles.'[6] And yet, once again, this is not actually the whole picture, because it is Maurice who has been taken by some liturgical scholars in this century as the fountainhead of the Anglican equivalent of the Liturgical Movement, the movement to instate the parish communion as the principal act of Christian worship, with all the implications that follow for church architecture, internal church organization, and the liturgical texts of modern Anglican worship.[7] In the hands of scholars such as Gabriel Hebert, Donald Gray, John Fenwick, and Bryan Spinks, this has become something of an orthodoxy.[8] Donald Gray, indeed, articulates my second paradox admirably: 'A fairly restrictive diet of Prayer Book worship with no frills or fancies easily satisfied all [Maurice's] needs in these matters', he says; even though the second and third generations of Christian Socialists, such as Stewart Headlam, Henry Scott Holland, Conrad Noel, Percy Widdrington and others, whose influence on the emergence of the parish communion was seminal, were all 'united in acknowledging that they in their turn looked back to F. D. Maurice for their fundamental theological inspiration'.[9]

A liturgical theologian, but not a liturgist; a liturgical conservative,

---

[5] On Maurice's resistance to his inclusion with the Broad Church party, see especially his letter to the editor of *The Spectator*, 2 April 1870, which appeared under the heading 'The Thirty-Nine Articles and the Broad Church', pp. 434–5.

[6] F. D. Maurice, 'Dr. Lushington, Mr. Heath, and the Thirty-Nine Articles', *Macmillan's Magazine*, 5 (1862), p. 156.

[7] The first exponent of this tradition of interpretation was Gabriel Hebert himself; as his biographer, Christopher Irvine, puts it, in *Worship, Church and Society* (Norwich, 1993), p. 60: 'he takes the thought of F. D. Maurice as the framework for his own arguments, and sets out to explain the view that the Church was both a human and a divine institution, given, as it were, to make tangible in the world, the catholicity of God's dealings with humanity.'

[8] G. Hebert, *Liturgy and Society* (London, 1936); D. Gray, *Earth and Altar. The Evolution of the Parish Communion in the Church of England to 1945* (Norwich, 1986); J. Fenwick and B. Spinks, *Worship in Transition. The Twentieth Century Liturgical Movement* (Edinburgh, 1995).

[9] Gray, *Earth and Altar*, p. 1.

whose work seems to have inspired a revolution in modern Anglican worship – these are striking paradoxes, and they suggest that the tension between continuity in Christian worship and the process of adaptation and change in the life of the Church is actually a central question for the interpretation of the work and influence of F. D. Maurice himself. This paper can only frame the most skeletal of attempts at understanding these related paradoxes, in three brief stages. First, it attempts to give greater substance to the brief description above of what Maurice actually said about the Anglican liturgy in his published work. Second, it turns to the related issues of Maurice's treatment of the Anglican formularies more generally, especially the Thirty-Nine Articles, the Act of Uniformity, and the location of the Athanasian Creed within the *Book of Common Prayer*. In this way, a slightly more nuanced view of Maurice than that of a 'Prayer-Book fundamentalist' will emerge. Finally, and briefly, it tries to place this description of Maurice's liturgical theology in the context of his wider ecclesiology, especially as it was developed in his most famous work, *The Kingdom of Christ* (1838). Drawing attention to his identification of fixed forms of prayer as one of the principal 'signs' of the Catholic Church, it demonstrates how his apparent inattention to the detail of liturgical scholarship was explicable in part in terms of his underlying conception of sacred history.

* * *

The natural starting-point for an exposition of Maurice's views on the Anglican liturgy is his first substantial collection of sermons on the subject, *The Prayer-Book Considered Especially in Reference to the Romish System* (1849). These were preached in Lincoln's Inn Chapel, of which Maurice had been Chaplain since 1846. They discuss the chief elements of the offices for Morning and Evening Prayer, treating both offices together, as the structural similarity of the offices permits, before turning to the Communion Service in the final chapters. Despite Maurice's asseveration that the communion service is the 'most sacred' part of the liturgy, it is actually the daily offices to which he devotes most attention.[10] The Preface to the second edition indicated the purpose of publication: 'I am sure the Liturgy will torment us so long as we continue selfish and divided, therefore I

---

[10] F. D. Maurice, *The Prayer-Book Considered Especially in Reference to the Romish System* (1849; 1880 edn, enclosing also *The Lord's Prayer*), p. 185.

would cling to it. I am sure it may be the instrument of raising us out of our selfishness and divisions.'[11] It is absolutely clear from repeated references in the text that the divisions Maurice has in mind are primarily ecclesiastical, and that this series of addresses goes right back, in its preoccupation with church unity, to one of the strongest and earliest themes in Maurice's published work, namely his resistance to the concept and reality of church party.[12] He attacks the idea which was common currency in the battles between Tractarians and Evangelicals that the Anglican formularies were a compromise, in which the Articles stood on the Evangelical side, and the Prayer Book on the Tractarian side; the Prayer Book itself is a witness against the sin of exclusiveness, he says.[13] Thus he stepped blithely over the considerable work devoted in various of the *Tracts for the Times* to demonstrating affinities between elements in the Prayer Book and earlier English and Latin liturgies. Maurice had been a student at Oxford from 1829 to 1832, not long after the death of Charles Lloyd, Regius Professor of Divinity, whose lectures on the history and structure of the Prayer Book attracted Newman, Pusey, Hurrell Froude, Robert and Isaac Wilberforce, and others. It is unlikely that he would not have been aware of these lectures (especially given his friendships with Samuel Wilberforce, Hugh Rose, and Charles Marriott); nor can he have been unaware of the liturgical work of other High-Church divines of the period. Again, however, they seem to have had no impact on his own understanding of the nature of the Prayer Book, though he shared with some of the High-Church leaders a horror at the idea of altering or revising its text.[14]

So Maurice's approach to the use of the Prayer Book resisted an archaeology of the text in which more Catholic elements, for example, might have been retrieved and re-emphasised by connection with the sources on which Cranmer drew. Maurice treated the book as a whole: it was, for him, the living voice of the Church. He even suggested that the Reformers deliberately eschewed liturgical artistry, in the interests

[11] Ibid., p. xvi.

[12] See, above all, F. D. Maurice, *Reasons for not joining a Party in the Church. A Letter to the Ven. Samuel Wilberforce* (London, 1841).

[13] Maurice, *Prayer-Book*, pp. xiii, 13.

[14] On the work of High-Church liturgical scholars, see P. B. Nockles, *The Oxford Movement in Context. Anglican High Churchmanship 1760–1857* (Oxford, 1994), pp. 217–23. Maurice even described Hugh Rose as 'afterwards a kind friend of mine', even though he seems, overall, to have regarded his time at Oxford as largely unprofitable: Maurice, *Life*, 1, pp. 179–80.

of constructing a liturgy which recognized that 'the spiritual is also the practical . . . that the whole realm of nature and art belongs to the redeemed spirit'.[15] This resistance to the burgeoning study of liturgical scholarship was probably deliberate; it had its starting-point in an ecclesiology which was at once Reformed, in its determination to exclude any kind of corporate, mediatorial role for the Church in the reception and transmission of revelation, and Catholic in its assumption that, nevertheless, God's providential ordering of history entailed that the visible Church, finally, was indefectible. There is not sufficient space here to trace in detail the lineaments of this ecclesiology, especially through all the twists and turns of the appeal to locality or nationality which it involved; but it should be evident that Maurice's treatment of the *Book of Common Prayer* was an expository, unified one, in which the primary purpose of the liturgy of the Church, to express the inclusivity of the economy of salvation, always determined the sense in which particular passages were read.

Two examples must suffice. In his sermon on the Absolution in the daily offices – the declaratory form 'Almighty God . . . pardoneth and absolveth all them that truly repent' – Maurice asserts that the function of the Absolution is to demonstrate to the penitent that there is an 'actual Deliverer', and to stand for the principle that 'God has redeemed men in His Son, and has claimed them for His own by His Spirit', against 'a multitude of notions coming forth from opposite quarters, Romanist and Protestant, foreign and English, orthodox and heretical which slander the character of God and war against the freedom of man'.[16] The same theme of inclusivity emerges in the sermon on the use of the Apostles' Creed in the daily offices. Maurice fastens on to the function of the creed as a baptismal formulary to assert that it demonstrates, once again, that the gospel 'is a continual protection against traditions, that when they try to force themselves upon us, we can always put this forward as a declaration . . . that it is the Eternal Name into which we are baptized, and in which the whole Church and each member of the Church stands'.[17] Precisely the same overall standpoint is adopted in the volume of sermons Maurice preached on the occasional offices of the Prayer Book later in 1849,

[15] Maurice, *Prayer-Book*, p. 12.
[16] Ibid., p. 43.
[17] Ibid., p. 147.

published as *The Church a Family* in 1850.[18] The service for infant baptism, for example, is claimed by Maurice to demonstrate that the proper principle of English society (since this is a national liturgy) is that all human society rests on its divine birth in redemption, and not on its natural birth. The service should liberate us from partisan struggles over baptismal regeneration: it is 'a witness that man is not his own saviour by his faith or by his works; it is for this that we plead for the old language, and ask for leave to construe it in a plain, homely, English manner'.[19]

This last comment gives the clue that Maurice's treatment of the *Book of Common Prayer* evidently depends on a connection between nationality and the doctrine of the Church, and the nature of that connection will become clearer in later discussion of his providential reading of history.[20] Maurice treats the liturgy as one for the whole nation: in his hands, it is read constantly as a symbol of the universal yet national character of the Church. With this principle in mind, his expository method is very simple: time and again, as we have seen, liturgical texts are placed within an overarching framework which draws explicitly on his primary theological assumptions. There is little actual textual exegesis and commentary, and there is little attention to structural considerations or analysis of influences on the composition of the liturgy. This eisegetical technique – reading *into* the text, practically, a prior theological framework – posed two particular and related problems for Maurice in the context of nineteenth-century controversies over the liturgy. The first is the fairly obvious point that his argument seemed to leave little scope for liturgical revision – hence the charge of liturgical fundamentalism. The second followed on from this: what if, notwithstanding Maurice's own stance, the liturgy was changed after all? Could his approach leave any scope for adaptation?

* * *

On both counts, Maurice's own published work suggests much more flexibility in his approach than his critics have tended to assume. This can be demonstrated by a brief examination of several specific issues which are related to his treatment of the Anglican formularies as a whole. First, two issues which had a direct bearing on the public

---

[18] F. D. Maurice, *The Church a Family: Twelve Services on the Occasional Services of the Prayer-Book* (London, 1850).
[19] Ibid., p. 32.
[20] Below, pp. 359–60.

liturgy of the Church of England in the mid-nineteenth century call
for attention. One is the question of the so-called 'State' services, the
seventeenth-century services to commemorate the death of Charles I,
the birth and restoration of Charles II, and the saving of Parliament
from the Gunpowder Plot, which had remained annexed to the Prayer
Book and renewed at the beginning of each monarch's reign.[21]
Surprisingly, perhaps – given his emphasis on the Prayer Book as a
national liturgy, and his general support for the principle of Establishment – Maurice did not support the continued inclusion and use of
these services. On perfectly consistent grounds, he condemned their
'long, vituperative addresses to God', and claimed that they had done
more harm than good, obscuring the fact that God was 'the real King
of the Nation'. Rather, they breathed 'the excitement and revenge of a
triumphant party'.[22] Consequently, we can infer that there was a
principle according to which Maurice thought revision possible – the
principle of inclusivity, or, as Maurice would surely have preferred to
put it, Catholicity. The second issue with a direct bearing on the public
liturgy of the Church of England was the Athanasian Creed, use of
which the rubric of the Prayer Book prescribed in place of the
Apostles' Creed at Morning Prayer on certain festivals. For most of
his life, Maurice was an ardent defender of that creed, and of its use.
Writing in 1864 to a clergyman who had supposed Maurice would
support its exclusion, on the grounds that its damnatory clauses would
be offensive to him, he asserted that it actually supported his
interpretation of the word 'eternal' (that is, as an ontological category
which, when used in relation to 'eternal life', described the present as
well as future state of the believer), and that 'I believe its very
vehemence has been a protection against the doctrine which it was
supposed [by his contemporary critics] to uphold.'[23] Here Maurice was
on the same side as his High Church detractors, Liddon and Pusey, for
example.[24] Objections to the Athanasian Creed fastened mainly on its
damnatory clauses, and were mounted by those such as Arthur Stanley,
Dean of St Paul's, who on many other issues were Maurice's allies.[25]
But when the issue was raised again by the Ritual Commission in 1870,

---

[21] Jasper, *Development of the Anglican Liturgy*, p. 48.
[22] Maurice, *Prayer-Book*, pp. 158–9.
[23] Maurice, *Life*, 2, p. 482.
[24] See J. O. Johnston, *Life and Letters of Henry Parry Liddon* (London, 1905), pp. 156–66.
[25] See R. E. Prothero, *Life and Letters of Dean Stanley* (London, 1893; 1909 edn),
pp. 385–90.

Maurice gave cautious approval to the idea that it should be banished from public services.[26] His change of mind was due simply to the recognition that his claim that the damnatory clauses expressed what *he* understood as 'eternal', and not what virtually everyone else understood, was simply no longer sustainable, in the face of the fierceness of controversy from both of the main parties in the dispute.[27] The only way, he concluded, to avoid the opposing parties' interpretations was to remove the creed from use. Once again, then, a proposal for change was adopted on the basis of the principle of inclusion, excluding what he took to be narrow and distorted interpretations.

Two further issues did not concern the liturgy as such, but have an important if indirect bearing on Maurice's approach to the Prayer Book. One of these was his well-known defence of subscription to the Thirty-Nine Articles at Oxford, advanced first of all in his pamphlet *Subscription no Bondage* (1835).[28] In this work, one of his earliest published forays into theology, Maurice advanced the remarkable argument that the Articles, far from being a form of confession of faith (after all, they were never imposed on the laity), were in fact educational principles or conditions, according to which all study at the historic universities ought to be undertaken. The argument laid him open to an obvious jibe by Thomas Carlyle, an acquaintance of his:

> Thirty-nine English Articles,
> Ye wondrous little particles,
> Did God shape his universe really by you?
> In that case I swear it,
> And solemnly declare it,
> This logic of Maurice's is true.[29]

Maurice's logic was, on the face of things, absurd. But was it absurd for one who took the national mission and identity of the Church of

[26] F. D. Maurice, 'A few more words on the Athanasian Creed', *Contemporary Review*, 15 (1870), pp. 479–94; see also Maurice, *Life*, 2, pp. 618–19.

[27] Maurice, 'A few more words'.

[28] F. D. Maurice, *Subscription no Bondage, or the Practical Advantages afforded by The Thirty-Nine Articles as Guides in all the Branches of Academical Education* (Oxford, 1835).

[29] J. A. Froude, *Life of Carlyle: A History of his Life in London, 1834–81*, 2 vols (2nd edn, London, 1897), 1, p. 41.

England so seriously? Maurice claimed that the catechism contained in the *Book of Common Prayer* taught that all people were called to be members of Christ, and that the Anglican formularies therefore 'expound to them what we believe to be that universal constitution. . . . We believe that we are admitted by baptism into this constitution, and laid under an obligation of making it known to other men as intended for them.'[30] So he linked explicitly the Articles as conditions of education with elements of the public liturgy of the Church for whose clergy the education at Oxford was intended. Maurice never abandoned this fundamental view of the central place of the Articles in training for, and the exercise of, ministry in the Church of England. But again the fact that scarcely anyone else took the same view gradually undermined his position. Ten years later, in 1845, against the background of the controversy over the proceedings against W. G. Ward, Maurice again advanced the view that the Articles and Prayer Book, and not any proceedings of the Convocation of Oxford, were the best defence against Romanism as well as against the more extreme views of some Reformers.[31] In 1870 he was still defending the view that the Articles were a means of preserving Protestantism and Catholicism without compromise, embodying 'the assumption that without individuality and nationality there can be no unity, no universality'.[32] And yet he appears to have begun to reconsider his stance on subscription itself at the universities as long ago as 1841, when Newman's *Tract XC* convinced him that not even those who were supposed to be teaching theology, let alone the students, took the Articles to be conditions of education; thereafter, he favoured abolition. And he even began, slowly, to change his mind on clerical subscription, eventually coming round to Stanley's view that enforcing subscription actually prevented the Articles from being taken as seriously as they should be.[33]

Perhaps the most striking instance of Maurice embracing the

---

[30] Maurice, *Subscription*, p. 45. This is one passage which strongly bears out Paul Avis's attempt to enlist Maurice in support of a baptismal ecclesiology for the Church of England: P. Avis, *Anglicanism and the Christian Church. Theological Resources in Historical Perspective* (Edinburgh, 1989), pp. 264–6.

[31] F. D. Maurice, *Thoughts on the Rule of Conscientious Subscription, on the Purpose of the Thirty-Nine Articles, and on Our Present Perils from the Romish System* (Oxford, 1845), pp. viii–ix.

[32] Maurice, 'The Thirty-Nine Articles and the Broad Church', p. 434.

[33] Both changes in Maurice's mind are described in a letter to Charles Kingsley dated 26 Oct. 1865, in Maurice, *Life*, 2, pp. 505–6.

possibility of change in the Anglican formularies comes towards the end of an article he submitted to *Macmillan's Magazine* in 1860 in response to a pamphlet by Isaac Taylor, which had supported Prayer-Book revision, and which had been published in the wake of controversy over the Evangelical peer Lord Ebury's proposals for revision. Maurice objected strongly to revision on two counts. First, if a change or clarification of doctrine was at issue, he believed that could only contract the inclusive character of the liturgy: 'even the younger Clergy who, of course, see much further than those of my age can, are yet not half as liberal and comprehensive as the Prayer-Book would make them if they allowed it to guide them.'[34] Second, if a mere modernizing of language or adaptation of services was at issue, Maurice would oppose it in the instance cited (note that he did not reject the idea of liturgical change *per se*), because the proposers of revision were those without what he called a 'healthy regard' for the rubrics.[35] Thus far, Maurice's argument was predictable: he was opposing liturgical revision in the interests of the inclusivity, and hence national character, of the national Church. But there was a twist in the argument. Revision would require an amendment to the Act of Uniformity, he suggested, whereas the Act should not be amended, but abolished. He acknowledged that his providential reading of the history of the Church could lead him to defend the Act, but suggested that 'Divine Wisdom' behind the passage of the Act in 1662 was not sufficient reason to keep it on the statute book in 1862. If Dissenters mounted a campaign for its repeal he would support it mainly because, he claimed, amendment would probably lead to more restrictive legislation, not less; but also because the Act gave the appearance of making the liturgy of the Church a mere appendix or schedule to an Act of Parliament.[36] Maurice scarcely began to work through what the implications of repeal would have been. This startling proposal to remove the sanction of law from the Church's use of the liturgy could surely have led to outright liturgical anarchy; it would at least, as Maurice recognized, have placed an even heavier burden of responsibility on the bishops than they already carried for ensuring that the worship of local churches was kept within the canonical limits of the Church.[37]

---

[34] F. D. Maurice, 'On the revision of the Prayer-Book and the Act of Uniformity', *Macmillan's Magazine*, 1 (1860), p. 425.

[35] Ibid., pp. 425–6.

[36] Ibid., pp. 427–8.

[37] Ibid., p. 428.

So, then, in a number of specific instances Maurice was prepared to countenance change in the liturgy of the Church – and in the overall pattern and use of the Anglican formularies which underpinned the liturgy – in a way which carried serious implications for worship. If he resisted the need for textual amendment as such, he was pushed, slowly but surely, towards supporting practical reforms which certainly, in the long run, were part of a process which saw increasing liturgical diversity in the Church of England. His underlying aims were invariably couched in terms of an appeal to inclusivity, depicting party strife in the Church as necessarily divisive, and carrying the hidden assumption that religious truth was a complex, multifaceted, but integrated whole, which could scarcely be captured by one group or party alone in the Church. But the very ubiquity of party division forced him back, step by step, it seemed. The great defender of the Prayer Book tradition in the nineteenth-century Church was always a reluctant reformer. Was this resistance to liturgical change little more than an innate conservatism, as some have suggested, or did it spring from deeper theological roots?[38] That it is the final issue to consider in this paper.

* * *

Attention has already been drawn to the way in which the principle of inclusivity is an abiding theme of Maurice's comments on the Anglican liturgy. In summary, he held the Church of England to be a national Church, carrying national responsibilities; therefore it ought in principle to be an inclusive Church. The claim that the Church of England is, or ought to be, 'comprehensive', is commonly taken to be Maurice's permanent legacy to Anglican ecclesiology.[39] Actually, Maurice rarely used the word 'comprehensive' itself in direct relation to the Church of England, perhaps because he would have been well aware that, if he did so, he could – quite mistakenly – be taken as favouring the schemes for inclusion of Dissenters into the Church proposed by Broad Church leaders such as Thomas Arnold in his *Principles of Church Reform* (London, 1833).[40] He faced a difficulty, however. The Church of England was comprehensive, he held: it

---

[38] On Maurice's alleged liturgical conservatism, see for example the judgement of Donald Gray, already mentioned above: *Earth and Altar*, p. 1.

[39] See in particular Stephen Sykes's critique of Maurice in S. W. Sykes, *The Integrity of Anglicanism* (Oxford, 1978), pp. 16–24.

[40] Maurice specifically criticized Arnold's scheme in *Subscription*, p. 117.

should include all the nation. Yet it was not a mere administrative arrangement, by which different worshipping communities with different theologies and different practices could be included under one overarching organization. It had a distinctive ecclesiology, one which seemingly was not recognized or accepted as such by a significant part of the nation. It was comprehensive in its aspirations, but far from comprehensive in its existence. How could its comprehensive mission and character best be supported?

Part of Maurice's answer to that question lay in the use and proper exposition of the liturgy itself, as we have seen. But that is not really explicable without the realization that his basic response involved a fundamental re-examination of the Anglican doctrine of the Church, in his treatise, *The Kingdom of Christ* (London, 1838).[41] Here, through a systematic examination of the major reformed church traditions in England, he sought to draw out those elements of their ecclesiologies which echoed the constitution of the Catholic Church in England, that is, the national Church. The central section of the work defines six 'signs' of the Catholic Church: baptism, eucharist, the Catholic creeds, the Scriptures, orders of ministry (the threefold order) and, surprisingly, fixed patterns of worship. If this last 'sign' is excluded, for the moment, it should be evident at once that Maurice's formula is significantly close to the fourfold formula of Scripture, ministry (episcopacy), creeds, and the two dominical sacraments later adopted by the Anglican Communion as a principle for Church unity and called the Chicago–Lambeth Quadrilateral.[42] The fact that fixed patterns of worship – liturgy – are included is startling, at first sight. It seems to give mere persistence over time a fundamental authority in helping to determine the Catholicity of the Church, and Maurice does not back away from that admission. But his view of the history of the liturgy is also affected by his assumption that 'all division comes through idolatry, that all union comes through the adoration of the one living and true God'.[43] Drawing on both Unitarian and English Platonic sources, Maurice's emphasis on unity

---

[41] F. D. Maurice, *The Kingdom of Christ, or Hints to a Quaker respecting the Principles, Constitution and Ordinances of the Catholic Church* (London, 1838; 2nd edn, rev., 1842; all page references are to the 4th edn, 1891).

[42] On the connection between Maurice and the Quadrilateral, see M. Woodhouse-Hawkins, 'Maurice, Huntington, and the Quadrilateral: an exploration in historical theology', in J. Robert Wright, ed., *Quadrilateral at One Hundred* (Oxford, 1988), pp. 61–78.

[43] Maurice, *Kingdom of Christ*, 2, pp. 28–9.

is expressed ecclesiologically in his constant reiteration that God is at one with his Church, and that all human beings through the Church are at one with each other; liturgy is the prayer of the whole body.[44] So the liturgy of the Church has a permanent, corporate character in principle, and the multiplication of different forms of liturgy is a sign of the perverse effects of human rebellion against God in division and disunity.[45]

Yet there is one exception to this account: there are *national* varieties of worship. David Young has characterized Maurice's theology as marked by a 'reverence for the earth': in his concern to stress God's unity with all his creation, Maurice implies that the Catholicity of the Church is fully compatible with – indeed necessitated by – local variation.[46] In Maurice's hands, the principle of locality – itself an important one in modern ecumenical dialogue – has a quite specific content, a thoroughly nineteenth-century concept of national identity, which Maurice goes so far as to describe as a Protestant principle.[47] Thus, for Maurice, the national Church is not defined as an amalgam of Catholic form and Protestant principle, balancing or qualifying each other; it is, rather, 'most Catholic when most Protestant'.[48] The six 'signs' of the Catholic Church are fully present within the national identity of the Church of England; therefore the liturgy of the Church of England has, for Maurice, a quite exceptional force, as both inheritor and guarantor of the Church's unique character as the Catholic and Apostolic Church in England.

Lurking behind all this, finally, was a view of history which refused to accept a distinction between sacred and secular. Maurice did not embrace the kind of narrow providentialism which claims to identify divine manipulation behind particular actions or people. He did, nevertheless, conceive God always to be at work in human history, such that the collectivities of family, Church, and nation were read as varying levels or types of divine influence. History was loaded with

---

[44] Maurice, *Kingdom of Christ*, 2, p. 37. The influence of English Platonic and Unitarian traditions of the thought on Maurice can be traced respectively in D. Newsome, *Two Classes of Men. Platonism and English Romantic Thought* (London, 1974), and D. Young, *F. D. Maurice and Unitarianism* (Oxford, 1992).

[45] Ibid., 2, p. 29.

[46] D. Young, 'A reverence for the earth: F. D. Maurice and his Unitarian roots', *Journal of the Association of Open University Graduates* (1990–1), pp. 15–17.

[47] F. D. Maurice, *Three Letters to the Rev. William Palmer* (2nd edn, London, 1842), p. 19.

[48] Ibid., p. 16.

theological meaning, and should be read as such: 'I do feel that we are in God's earth and that He is educating it, and that history is the record of His education.'[49] History, Maurice said, bears witness 'to that order which man has been continually violating', though this very violation prevented a simplistic reading into it of success or failure.[50] One of the 'signs' of the Catholicity of the Church, then, the liturgy of the Church of England, was not, for Maurice, 'an old praying machine' at all – that is, an instrument of merely human contrivance. It was a providential instrument, which enshrined within itself the other 'signs' of the Catholic Church, and which proved that 'I have a right to believe that the blessings of the day of Pentecost have been given once, and never withdrawn.'[51]

*   *   *

Some words are appropriate by way of conclusion. Even to many of his contemporaries, Maurice was an immensely frustrating writer, who dived headlong into controversy, often without sufficient theological and scholarly skills for the task in hand, yet whose contribution to Anglican theology in all sorts of ways was immensely creative.[52] His treatment of the Anglican liturgy was no exception. It was curiously detached from the main currents of liturgical controversy in his day. His seeming inability to address particular questions of detailed liturgical analysis and commentary does suggest – despite the laudable attempt to grasp the theology of the liturgy as a whole – that trying to make theological sense of liturgy is a dangerous exercise without adequate attention to liturgical scholarship. At least, it seems a fair complaint that his theological explication of the Prayer Book operates at such a general level that his defence could be mounted in favour of almost any specific liturgical text. It certainly prevented him from engaging in constructive, detailed controversy over proposals for revision of the Prayer Book.

Nevertheless, his concern to remind his contemporaries that the public worship of the Church in practice was a defence against the pressure of particular church parties represented a strong case. It did

---

[49] F. D. Maurice, 'Rough notes of some lectures on modern history', *Politics for the People*, 7 (1848), p. 113.

[50] F. D. Maurice, *Sermons on the Sabbath-Day* (London, 1853), p. 123.

[51] Maurice, *Kingdom of Christ*, 2, p. 29.

[52] The late Peter Hinchliff once replied to my complaint about Maurice's obscurity: 'Yes, but he was right on all the main issues.'

not prevent him from conceding the necessity of change in some instances. And it did suggest that, in the end, there was a theology of the Church of England which justified the continuing use of the *Book of Common Prayer*, and which marked a possible way forward through the maze of party controversy. What Maurice laid down as the principle of inclusivity, whatever its merits, has remained central to the principles by which liturgical revision proceeds in the Church of England. Ironically, then, he helped to fashion a method for change at the same time as setting his face against change. His theology of comprehension emerged as a defence against church pluralism; but it has become a central plank in the policy of containing and managing church pluralism.

Yet there may remain a sense of disquiet over the consistency and force of his case. Both of the paradoxes laid down at the beginning of this paper can be resolved by an attention to Maurice's ecclesiology and providentialism, but only at the cost of raising further and perhaps more fundamental difficulties, most obviously over the links between his view of God's involvement in history and his estimate of English national character and destiny. Henry Sidgwick is said to have commented:

> In Maurice's hands you feel like a horse being led up to a five-barred gate, which is your theological problem. How will you get over it? Maurice shows you the gate, dilates upon its bars, its height, its insuperability, strokes your nose a little more, and all of a sudden you find yourself looking at the gate from the other side. You know that you have not got over it legitimately, but how you find yourself on the other side you do not know.[53]

For Maurice, the defence of a historic liturgy in a time of increasing pressure for change may have seemed to be an almost insuperable problem. He managed to get over it. Whether or not he did so legitimately is perhaps a question for the systematic theologian, and not the historian.

Westcott House, Cambridge

---

[53] Quoted in H. G. Wood, *Frederick Denison Maurice* (Cambridge, 1950), p. 7.

A NEW BROOM IN THE AUGEAN STABLE: ROBERT GREGORY AND LITURGICAL CHANGES AT ST PAUL'S CATHEDRAL, LONDON, 1868–1890

by PENELOPE J. CADLE

THE fifth labour of Hercules required that he clean out, in one day, the thirty years of accumulated mess that the thousands of cattle owned by King Augeus had created.[1] The Augean Stable of St Paul's Cathedral had taken much longer to accumulate its liturgical mess, and would take much longer to clean out!

The difference between the theory and reality of cathedral life in the nineteenth century was stark. 'The principle feature of a Cathedral', according to Harvey Goodwin, then Dean of Ely, in 1858, 'is the maintenance of a daily service upon a grand scale.'[2] However, the reality behind this ideal left much to be desired. On Carlisle Cathedral, Mandell Creighton wrote in 1865 that

> the only daily service is at the Cathedral, and that is quite in the humdrum respectable line, so much a matter of course that they never take the brown holland off the altar for it – 'it is too much trouble, and gives the dust more time to settle,' was the reason the old verger gave me for not doing so, and he moreover added that he always used to take it off till forbidden by the Dean, I think it was, or else a canon, from motives of additional carefulness for the Church property! The small boy choristers amuse themselves all the time by squabbling and pinching each other in the middle of a chant, the men are perpetually turning over their music and restoring large folios to their place with a horrid bang in the middle of the lessons, while the precentor sits blinking above, looking down on all this irreverence, which he plainly sees, with an air of abject helplessness. I am sorry to say, since Christmas I have not gone nearly so often as I ought.[3]

---

[1] R. Graves, *Greek Myths*, 2 vols (London, 1990), 2, p. 116.
[2] P. Barrett, *Barchester: English Cathedral Life in the Nineteenth Century* (Chatham, 1993), p. 115.
[3] L. Creighton, *Life and Letters of Mandell Creighton*, 2 vols (London, 1904), 1, p. 25.

Retrospectively, Owen Chadwick has summarized the situation that cathedrals found themselves in in Victorian times:

> No one knew what cathedrals were for. By the beauty of their music and singing they set forth the glory of God; and yet it was confessed that if the choirs of Durham and Canterbury were models of decorum and of art, the choirs of some cathedrals, including St Paul's and Westminster Abbey, were renowned for slipshod irreverence.[4]

Problems at St Paul's in London went back to the eighteenth century. As early as 1703 a pamphlet referred to the cathedral as a place 'where men go out of curiosity and interest, and not for the sake of religion'.[5] Bishop Blomfield (Bishop of London 1828–56) declared in the House of Lords in 1840 that St Paul's was quite useless.[6] 'I wonder,' he said to Bishop Wilberforce of Oxford one day as they drove together up Ludgate Hill, 'I wonder what that great building has ever done for the cause of Jesus Christ.'[7] Edward White Benson, in his early days as Bishop of Truro and just after his chancellorship at Lincoln, wrote that a cathedral 'had distinct and progressive functions in relation to society and polity';[8] but went on to declare that many were 'enervated, paralysed, devitalised'[9] to such an extent that further damage was not possible. St Paul's in the mid-nineteenth century easily fell into this category, and had lost its way. No wonder that Londoners had little respect for it.[10]

Historically St Paul's had suffered badly from misuse, making it much more a centre of commerce than religion; that Shakespeare allowed Falstaff to buy a horse there in *Henry IV* was entirely realistic.[11] Aside from horse-trading in the north aisle, money lending in the south, bargains in a variety of other goods, fighting and meetings in-between,[12] it was also possible to find refreshment, seek shelter

---

[4] O. Chadwick, *The Victorian Church*, 2 vols (London, 1992), 1, p. 140.

[5] C. J. Abbey, *The English Church in the Eighteenth Century*, 2 vols (London, 1878), 2, p. 419.

[6] Chadwick, *Victorian Church*, 1, p. 524.

[7] J. O. Johnston, *Life of Henry Parry Liddon* (London, 1904), p. 135.

[8] E. W. Benson, *The Cathedral: Its Necessary Place in the Life and Work of the Church* (London, 1878), p. 1.

[9] Ibid., p. 3.

[10] Johnston, *Liddon*, p. 135.

[11] W. Shakespeare, *Henry IV*, part ii, act i, scene 2.

[12] Abbey, *English Church*, 2, p. 419.

from the weather,[13] and relieve yourself on the flagstone flooring. (It appears that this particular activity was so popular that the Latin inscription, *Hic locus sacer est, hic nulli mingere fas est* – 'This place is sacred. Nobody is allowed to urinate here', stood over each entrance warning visitors against taking such action.)[14] Or you could simply take a short cut, known as Paul's Walk, north to south across the transept, thus avoiding a somewhat longer walk around the outside.

Domestically, Canon William Hale's two-month closure of the building in 1842 for painting, dusting, and miscellaneous cleaning was a marvellous improvement.[15] Alas, he forgot that painting, dusting, and miscellaneous cleaning need to be done on a never-ending basis. Little wonder that a prospective visitor was warned in 1868 that he would find St Paul's 'horribly dirty'.[16]

The Augean Stables had taken thirty years to reach the state at which Hercules intervened. St Paul's had taken much longer to achieve the state whereby neglect affected every aspect of its life, reducing it to a haphazard and complacent manner of operation. It was against a backdrop of the most appalling lackadaisical attitude by the staff of St Paul's that Robert Gregory arrived from the parish of Lambeth in December 1868 as canon. Recognized as a man of opinions which he was not afraid to reveal, Gregory's appointment was not well received.[17] Almost from the start of his career, Gregory had never held back from doing what he felt was correct. As a curate at Panton, Lincolnshire, he did not shirk from confronting matters which he considered to be bad practice. On arrival he broke with the rector's practice of administering the sacraments to an entire rail of people with just one utterance of the appropriate words,[18] and in 1849 published a pamphlet, *A Plea in Behalf of Small Parishes, with Particular Reference to the County of Lincoln*, which dealt with various parochial matters, including the inadequate provision of Sunday services.[19] This outspoken work upbraided all levels of the clergy in one go: John Kaye, Bishop of Lincoln, accepted his own guilt and felt that much could be

---

[13] W. R. Matthews and W. M. Atkins, *A History of St Paul's Cathedral and the Men Associated with it* (Glasgow, 1957), p. 108.

[14] Ibid., p. 150.

[15] Ibid., p. 259.

[16] Ibid., p. 265.

[17] *Autobiography of Robert Gregory*, ed. W. H. Hutton (London, 1912), p. 157.

[18] Ibid., p. 41.

[19] Ibid., p. 43.

achieved through the publication, while Isaac Williams, curate of Bisley, commented that people had been sent to Botany Bay for less![20]

If Gregory had any doubts about the prevailing situation they were surely confirmed at his installation. He recalled in his autobiography:

> On a specially dark evening of the shortest day of the year, after the four o'clock service, every light in the Cathedral was turned out; some friends from Lambeth who had come to see me installed were compelled to leave the Cathedral before the service for my installation commenced, and the only persons allowed to remain were my wife and children. A procession was then formed; a virger walking first with a small taper in his hand provided the only light in the Cathedral, then myself and after me Archdeacon Hale; we walked to the high altar at the extreme east end of the Cathedral, and then the usual service was read by the Archdeacon, and I was placed in a chair instead of a stall, and we returned to the vestry. A more miserable and disgracefully slovenly service I never saw.[21]

This dreadful service of installation, though partly a fit of pique at the appointment of an 'undesirable' to the existing staff, also demonstrated that St Paul's suffered from liturgical complacency. This malaise did not affect St Paul's in isolation – it was endemic. Benson recognized, while he was still Master of Wellington College, that cathedrals generally were in a poor state. Later, in 1895, he wrote: 'From a boy I have prayed that God would revive the spirit which built Cathedrals – henceforth I pray that first we may know how to use those we have.'[22]

It was traditional at St Paul's that each of the newly-appointed canons set out to be the new broom that swept clean. Many had tried, made some progress, but ultimately failed. A review of the advice given to Gregory, shortly after his nomination, by a minor canon, the Revd J. H. Coward, reveals part of the reason why:

> The position you are about to fill is a very good one, and one that you may thoroughly enjoy; but do not imagine that you can make any changes or improvements. Every new Canon when he comes is full of plans for doing this, that and the other, by which he may

[20] Hutton, *Gregory*, p. 45.
[21] Ibid., p. 157.
[22] A. C. Benson, *Life of Edward White Benson, Archbishop of Canterbury*, 2 vols (London, 1900), 2, p. 655.

amend the existing state of things; but take my word for it, this is an Augean Stable that nobody on earth can sweep, therefore let things take their course, and do not trouble about them.[23]

He added: 'I know the Minor Canons do not fulfil their duties, but there is no fear of the Chapter finding fault with them, for none of them do the duties to which they are pledged.'[24]

Ultimately, Coward felt that the prevailing situation would continue until such time as a 'convulsion' occurred, and there was no way of knowing when that might be.[25] Little did he know, that 'convulsion' was sitting right in front of him. Although at the time this advice was given Gregory had yet to be installed, the challenge was already on the table. Gregory was one of those to whom Benson referred to when he wrote: 'The merits, the services, the earnestness of some who still worked and prayed in [cathedrals] kept up the belief that there was a vitality below worth preserving.'[26]

The opinions expressed by Bishop Blomfield and J. H. Coward make it clear that some people, at least, thought that change was necessary and inevitable. Coward also stressed that, although the appointment of each new canon brought with it the intention to bring about changes, these would not be welcome, nor would they succeed. The purpose of this paper is to comment upon some of the liturgical changes instigated by Gregory between 1869 and 1890, rather than to illuminate the responses they elicited from the existing cathedral staff. We must, however, also acknowledge that although Coward had effectively sought to warn off Gregory concerning his likely intention to improve St Paul's, there is always an underlying tendency for reformers to paint a darker picture of the institutions they mean to reform, a picture which ultimately adds some lustre to their own achievements.

It was Gregory's long-held opinion that on a parochial basis, the clergy generally saw no benefit in leading by example. They fulfilled their duties only in as much that they were in church when they were required to take a service, but preferred not to attend otherwise, considering this to be the complete fulfilment of their duty. Extra 'voluntary' attendance was usually only made in cases where an attendance fee was payable. Hearing Coward's words, Gregory would

[23] Hutton, *Gregory*, p. 158.
[24] Ibid.
[25] Ibid.
[26] Benson, *The Cathedral*, p. 3.

have been left knowing that this type of attitude was not limited to the parish clergy. It was common practice that the clerical staff on their preferment to a cathedral continued to hold on to their parishes in plurality; generally to the detriment of the cathedral, seldom to the detriment of the parish which continued to hold the greater part of the attention of its priest. (Gregory was encouraged to do likewise but declined.)[27] Even the Sunday morning services at St Paul's were held at such a time that Minor Canons with local benefices could leave the cathedral (albeit prior to the beginning of the sermon) in order that they arrive in time to take their own service.[28] Plurality was not limited to the minor canons; the deanery itself was similarly affected – between 1828 and 1849 Dean Copleston was also Bishop of Llandaff.[29]

If fulfilment of parochial duty was limited, fulfilment of cathedral duty was worse, as Gregory recalled:

> [T]he present Archbishop of Canterbury, Dr Temple, told me that when he was a young man he attended St Paul's one Sunday morning, intending to remain for Holy Communion. When the earlier part of the service was over, a virger came to him and said, 'I hope, sir, you are not intending to remain for the sacrament, as that will give the Minor Canon the trouble of celebrating, which otherwise he will not do.'[30]

Writing about the reality of the position of canon, Benson echoed Gregory's thoughts: 'although attendance at . . . worship was an essential part of their *life*, it was the *smallest* part of their *work*.'[31]

During his first months of duty at St Paul's, Gregory found that the cathedral was badly infected with indifference. His early observations revealed that the clergy did not appear to possess a single cassock between them, the choir was almost totally disorganized (and had been for several decades, despite Sydney Smith's attempts at improvement whilst he was a canon in 1831–45),[32] with attendance so haphazard that often the settings were changed at a moment's notice as the necessary voices had failed to arrive. Those who had turned up preferred to

---

[27] Hutton, *Gregory*, p. 166.
[28] Ibid., p. 165.
[29] *Concise Dictionary of National Biography*, 3 vols (Oxford, 1995), 1, p. 644.
[30] Hutton, *Gregory*, p. 160.
[31] Benson, *The Cathedral*, p. 22.
[32] Matthews and Atkins, *History of St Paul's*, p. 260.

spend their non-singing periods reading letters and chatting amongst themselves; and members who were less than punctual simply wandered in when, eventually, they did arrive. There was no organized procession at the beginning of services, straggles of choir and minor canons converging with the canon at the mouth of the choir for a silent entry. Throughout eucharistic services the bread and wine reposed upon the Holy Table, despite the Prayer Book rubric which requires that they arrive there immediately prior to the prayers for the Church. Attendance was poor, though a little less so on Sunday afternoons, and communicants minimal. Many of those who did attend were there not for their spiritual good, but to hear the anthem alone, after which they would promptly depart.[33] This brief survey of liturgical performance at St Paul's, as it greeted Robert Gregory, shows nothing of the coherent whole which worship in a cathedral should be, but a haphazard collection of half-hearted effort by a number of disinterested individuals whose interests lay elsewhere, and who sought only to fulfil their duties by the smallest possible exertion.

*   *   *

Space precludes a full discussion of the reform of St Paul's, an immense task which required many years, and whose full assessment would require many pages. Here only a few points on the way can be indicated, to demonstrate the scope and effect of change: the choir, the problems with ritual and the Purchas Judgement, and the controversy over the reredos.

Though not afraid to make his opinions known, it was not until 1869, almost a year after his appointment, that Gregory began his offensive in earnest – his first target being the choir. A practice room was provided and a joint procession into and out of services, against an organ voluntary, instituted. Those who arrived late or left early were marked as 'Absent' and not paid.[34] The choir was not a problem that would be easily put right. Henry Parry Liddon's comment that 'an elephant may be taught to dance, but the process is not a quick one',[35] could have been aimed specifically at St Paul's choir and its resistance to change. By 1873, four years after Gregory's initial offensive,

---

[33] Hutton, *Gregory*, p. 165.
[34] Matthews and Atkins, *History of St Paul's*, p. 267.
[35] Johnston, *Liddon*, p. 140.

problems had not been resolved nor, it seems, much been improved. Aspects of the choristers' behaviour raised between Liddon (a recent addition to the cathedral staff) and Gregory included their preference for standing about chatting, fully robed, before services; chatting whilst entering the Choir; sitting during prayers, with more chattering and the passing of notes (notes, Liddon added, that did not relate to the service); and irreverence immediately before and after receiving communion. Liddon was adamant that the cathedral needed religious men first, and musical ones if they could get them, second.[36]

Early attempts at cleaning out the Augean choir had clearly made little noticeable difference. B. J. Armstrong, in attending St Paul's twice, with an eighteen-year interval, noticed little change. In 1854 he was impressed by the size of the congregation but found the service 'noisy and undevotional'. In 1872 he commented, 'Service badly carried out, the music being of the lightest and most secular kind, and the whole thing misarranged.'[37] But change for the better (or otherwise) is never easy to achieve – resistance and controversy are easily provoked. Thus, in 1872, with the choir still wallowing in its disorganization, John Goss, the organist, was pressed into retirement and a new organist, Dr Stainer (who began his musical career as a chorister at St Paul's), was appointed. Where Gregory's earlier efforts had made little difference, Dr Stainer surged ahead. The choir size was increased from eighteen to forty, and cassocks and clean surplices supplied, but his 'excessive demands' – particularly that choir members attend rehearsals – caused grumbles from the vicars-choral and the resignation of the entire Sunday evening choir. But we are assured that Dr Stainer's tact and charm, along with an increase in salary and provision of a pension scheme, eventually won them over.[38] By 1877 the change in the musical quality of St Paul's, particularly of the Sunday evening voluntary choir, was communicated via *The Church Times*:

> I can remember the old Sunday Evening Choir; things are indeed changed. We were then located in a gallery over the south door: we had to buy our own music and surplices, and the admission for the public was by ticket. . . . But now how different. We are seated in the proper place in the choir, all music and surplices found, and

---

[36] Johnston, *Liddon*, p. 141.
[37] Barrett, *Barchester*, p. 126.
[38] Matthews and Atkins, *History of St Paul's*, p. 273.

everything done to make us comfortable; the whole of the Cathedral free to the public, and a thoroughly congregational service. . . . Dr Stainer and others have said we are not the same choir, musically speaking, we were a year ago; all thanks to Dr Stainer for that.[39]

The introduction of regular choral services was immensely popular and, as a long-term support, the choir school went through a period of re-constitution between 1873 and 1875. Nevertheless, the skills of Dr Stainer were not, and are not, remembered favourably by all. Dean Matthews (St Paul's, 1934–67) considered it quite lucky that much of his musical composition had been forgotten,[40] despite his many contributions to *Hymns Ancient and Modern*.

Meanwhile, problems with ritualism were sweeping the country, and as far as cathedral worship was concerned, Gregory and Liddon put St Paul's at the forefront of the controversy. Where St Paul's led, others soon followed. From his ordination in 1844, Robert Gregory had used the eastward position for celebrating the eucharist because, he said,

I carefully studied the rubrics in the Prayer Book, and desiring to obey its injunctions as closely as I could, I thought the proper place at which to celebrate Holy Communion was standing before the Table, at all events during the time of consecrating the elements. There was at the time no question about the positions, and I remember the first time I celebrated, Mr Thos. Keble, my vicar, acting as deacon, said, 'I think you are right in standing before the Table; I never do it.'[41]

Prior to the issue of the Purchas Judgement in 1871 Gregory, together with Liddon, introduced the eastward position at St Paul's, supported in their action by Dean Church. After the delivery of the judgement, which held the eastward position illegal,[42] they refused to adopt the more acceptable westward position, behind the altar. On the recommendations of Dean Church and Liddon, in 1876 Gregory published *The Position of the Priest Ordered by the Rubrics in the Communion Service interpreted by themselves*. Much correspondence passed between Gregory and Bishop Jackson, the current Bishop of London, the bottom line of

[39] *The Church Times*, 2 Feb. 1887.
[40] Matthews and Atkins, *History of St Paul's*, p. 273.
[41] Hutton, *Gregory*, pp. 107–8.
[42] *ODCC*, p. 1144.

which was that if Gregory was forced to comply with the Purchas Judgement on the eastward position he would be reduced to paying to Caesar what was due to Caesar, and little else.[43] It was suggested by Robert Cecil, Marquess of Salisbury, that Jackson should be provoked into bringing a prosecution against Gregory and Liddon for illegal use of the eastward position. Although he disapproved of such behaviour,[44] the Bishop refused.[45] The actions of Gregory and Liddon, which might seem reactive and deliberately provocative (and certainly invited much hostility from those around them),[46] were carried out on the basis that the Church itself had made no decision on the matter either way,[47] and the Prayer Book rubrics supported their stance: 'Then shall the Priest (or Bishop, being present,) stand up, and turning himself to the people, pronounce this Absolution.' If the priest had not been facing the altar, from where else could he logically be turning?

This was only a small victory, but it helped to make clear the sheer scale of the challenge posed by change at the cathedral. Whilst dealing with a recalcitrant choir and instituting aspects of ritualism, Gregory was also taking stock of the general state of decoration at St Paul's: 'I felt that the very little which had been accomplished only served to make more manifest the plainness and coldness of the blank, dirty walls of the Cathedral, which had been painted probably in the days of Sir Christopher Wren, and had been neither washed nor repainted since.'[48] Gregory resolved to continue the work begun by Henry Hart Milman in 1858, which introduced such comforts as fully glazed windows, draught exclusion, along with stained glass (though this was to be destroyed during World War II, and subsequently replaced with clear glass, as Wren had originally desired),[49] gilding in the choir, and mosaics in two spandrels of the dome.[50] At a public meeting at the Mansion House in 1872, at which the interior of St Paul's was discussed, Gladstone remarked on the 'cold, dark columns and its almost repulsive general condition'. The cathedral was, in his opinion, unfinished and unseemly.[51] The St Paul's of the late nineteenth

---

43 Johnston, *Liddon*, p. 149.
44 Barrett, *Barchester*, p. 140.
45 Hutton, *Gregory*, p. 115.
46 *ODCC*, p. 714.
47 Matthews and Atkins, *History of St Paul's*, p. 270.
48 Hutton, *Gregory*, p. 175.
49 Matthew and Atkins, *History of St Paul's*, p. 355.
50 Ibid., p. 264.
51 Matthews and Atkins, *History of St Paul's*, p. 270.

century was little more than an empty shell from the west end, through the nave and dome area, up to the choir. Though technically not entirely a liturgical matter, the decoration of St Paul's was an important issue, which formed part of Gregory's master plan that would 'make the Cathedral the centre of the religious life of the diocese'.[52]

As part of the plans for the decoration and embellishment of St Paul's, in 1883 the chapter invited G. F. Bodley, the renowned ecclesiastical architect, to submit a plan for a new reredos, the main focus of which was the scene at Calvary – a scene which appeared to be highly relevant to its position. With the chapter's approval, Bodley began the work in 1886, finishing two years later, when yet another controversial storm blew up. A petition signed by 9,000 London Churchmen demanded that Frederick Temple, Bishop of London since 1885, bring a case for the removal of the reredos under the terms of the Public Worship Act of 1874, using his authority as Visitor of the cathedral. It was not without logical thought that Temple refused to do so – he had dealt with a very similar case during his time at Exeter which had found the Exeter reredos to be legal. He said of his refusal to prosecute:

> I fail to understand how it can be considered compatible with the principles of the Reformation to draw nice distinctions between the figure of our Lord crucified and the figure of our Lord ascending [as featured in the Exeter reredos], and say that one tends to idolatry, and the other not. . . . It certainly would not tend to advance those principles, but rather to discredit them, if, in their name, the Dean and Chapter of St Paul's were required to remove the figure of our Lord upon the Cross, and were allowed to substitute the figure of our Lord in the act of the ascension. . . . there is not the slightest danger that any Christian in this country would be tempted to idolatry by any work of art, however lifelike or however beautiful.[53]

Temple was ultimately compelled to bring the case under a *mandamus* granted by the Court of Queen's Bench on the basis that his reasons for not bringing the case were 'insufficient and unreasonable'.[54] It was

---

[52] Hutton, *Gregory*, p. 167.

[53] E. G. Sandford, ed., *Frederick Temple, Archbishop of Canterbury*, 2 vols (London, 1906), 2, pp. 113–14.

[54] Ibid., 2, p. 112.

Temple's opinion that such a court case was a 'necessary evil' that would 'only be tolerable as a preventative of worse mischief that would otherwise follow'.[55] The initial judgement was that Temple's reasoning on the matter was 'so defective as to be irrelevant and nugatory'; the reredos was illegal and would have to be removed. An appeal by Bishop Temple with Dean Church and his chapter to the Court of Appeal was decided in their favour, as was a counter-appeal brought on behalf of the Church Association, which had originally demanded that the case be brought.[56] The figures in the reredos were judged to be historical in context rather than idolatrous.[57]

* * *

Though St Paul's was said to have been the only cathedral to reform itself voluntarily,[58] the success of Gregory – the new broom – was no accident. The cornerstone of the success at St Paul's lay in Gregory's appointment as Treasurer in 1869, which allowed him to fight for the funds that would be necessary to enable such a cathedral to fulfil its designated role within the community. It was Gregory's financial acumen that guaranteed success.[59] His plans were detailed in the extreme, business-like and realistic – he knew that if St Paul's was to fulfil its role with the appropriate degree of 'nobility and distinction' the budget allocated by the Ecclesiastical Commissioners would have to be generous. Though Gregory did not anticipate a bottomless pit of money, he did not intend that the implementation of change should be a shoe-string operation.[60]

The improvements brought about by the perseverance of Robert Gregory, aided by a team of like-minded colleagues – Henry Parry Liddon, Joseph Barber Lightfoot, and Richard Church – dragged St Paul's out of its earlier state of 'enervation and paralysis', revitalized it and made it a religious centre that the people of London could respect. It was no longer, in the words of Henry Scott Holland, 'cold, naked, and unoccupied', with its worship, such as it was, hidden in the choir.[61] Reforms that had seemed quite impossible at the time Robert Gregory

55 Sandford, *Temple*, 2, p. 115.
56 Ibid., 2, p. 117.
57 Ibid., 2, p. 116.
58 Hutton, *Gregory*, p. 239.
59 H. S. Holland, *A Bundle of Memories* (London, 1915), p. 85.
60 Hutton, *Gregory*, p. 178.
61 Holland, *Bundle of Memories*, p. 139.

dined with J. H. Coward had brought the cathedral back from the brink and returned it to the people of London as a focal centre for the worship and knowledge of God. When Mandell Creighton, that critic of Carlisle way back in 1865, attended St Paul's for his enthronement as Bishop of London in 1897 he found, according to his wife, that 'the reverences of its services and the beauty of its music completely satisfied his aesthetic sense. The ceremonial of his enthronement was ordered with all the simple dignity usual at St Paul's on great occasions.'[62] This simple dignity, which brought St Paul's back into the public's attention (and favour) began to develop in 1872, when the recovery of the Prince of Wales from typhoid was marked by a service of thanksgiving,[63] and continued throughout Gregory's time as canon and Dean, and beyond. Such was the scale of the change he and his circle achieved.

[62] Creighton, *Life of Creighton*, 2, p. 216.
[63] Hutton, *Gregory*, p. 183.

A BROAD CHURCHMAN AND THE PRAYER BOOK: THE REVEREND CHARLES VOYSEY

by GARTH TURNER

IF the heirs of the Tractarians were in Victorian Anglicanism most conspicuously dissatisfied with the Prayer Book, they were not alone: the Broad Church also had discontents, which focused largely upon the recitation of the Athanasian Creed:

> Whoever will be saved: before all things it is necessary that he hold the Catholick Faith.
> Which faith except everyone do keep whole and undefiled: without doubt he shall perish everlastingly.
> This is the Catholic Faith: which except a man believe faithfully, he cannot be saved.[1]

These damnatory verses repelled the moral sense of Broad Churchmen, and historical study persuaded them of the late, derivative character of the creed. Eminent among those voicing this distaste were A. C. Tait, A. P. Stanley, and Connop Thirlwall.[2]

But the Broad Church discontent was wider than this. Gladstone observed that

> the *bulk* of those who move against the Athanasian Creed are not firm in adhesion to dogmatic truth, desire and mean to go farther, demand this as an initial change only, and chiefly desire the excision of the Creed as a practical negation of the title or duty of the Church to proclaim the 'damnatory' message (for of necessity there is a damnatory message) of the Gospel.[3]

Gladstone's fears were personified in a foot-soldier of the Broad Church, Charles Voysey. Voysey was the son of an architect, and a

---

[1] 'At Morning Prayer': the first two and last verses of the Athanasian Creed, in the version in the *Book of Common Prayer*.

[2] Randall Thomas Davidson and William Benham, *Life of Archibald Campbell Tait*, 2 vols (London, 1891), 2, p. 128; Rowland E. Prothero, *The Life and Correspondence of Arthur Penryn Stanley, D. D.*, 2 vols (London, 1893), 2, pp. 224–5; *Remains Literary and Theological of Connop Thirlwall*, ed. J. J. Stewart Perowne, 2 vols (London, 1877), 2, pp. 321–9.

[3] D. C. Lathbury, *Correspondence on Church and Religion of William Ewart Gladstone*, 2 vols (London, 1910), 2, p. 409.

direct descendant of John Wesley's sister, Susanna Ellison.[4] He matriculated at Oxford in July 1847, aged nineteen, and graduated bachelor in 1851.[5] His society, St Edmund Hall, then had a strongly evangelical cast, the tone being set chiefly by the Vice-Principal, Thomas Hill. The testimony of contemporary Oxonians such as Gladstone and Thomas Mozley is that the evangelicalism of the Hall in Hill's years became extreme – a hot-house atmosphere, attractive only to men of narrow vision and self-satisfied, introspective spirituality, and repellent to the intellectually lively.[6]

Voysey must have fitted ill into this climate – 'I was a sceptic at Oxford', he told his atheist friend Thomas Allsop, years later.[7] But he was sustained as an undergraduate by a society 'for the support at the University of youths who felt a call to the ministry'. A termly report was required of his 'spiritual progress'. Voysey, mentally stimulated by the diversity of doctrines and interpretations of the Thirty-Nine Articles which he found in Oxford, bridled against those repeated interrogations, and 'this rebellion has ended in a liberty for which I have to thank that society and those sectaries'. Yet his rebellion cost him dear. The society withdrew its support, and only the munificence of the 'dear old saint', Thomas Hill, who despite his own distaste for Voysey's views respected his sincerity, enabled him to complete his degree.[8]

After ordination, Voysey continued to nurture doubts: 'I am thankful to say that I have been working at reform ever since I took orders.'[9] After a curacy of seven years in Yorkshire he went to Jamaica, where 'he had shown distinct signs of rebellion against orthodoxy, and had touched on dangerous controversial ground'.[10] Then, in the words of his own summary in *Who's Who*, he was 'Ejected from [the] curacy of St Mark's, Whitechapel, for preaching a sermon against endless punishment; began his career as a religious reformer by publication of a sermon entitled "Is Every Statement of the Bible About Our Heavenly Father Strictly True?"'[11]

---

[4] *DNB*: Voysey, Charles.

[5] Joseph Foster, *Alumni Oxonienses, 1715–1886*, 4 vols (Oxford, 1888–91), 4, p. 1476.

[6] J. N. D. Kelly, *St Edmund Hall: Almost Seven Hundred Years* (Oxford, 1989), pp. 74, 76.

[7] Oxford, Harris Manchester College [hereafter Man. Coll.], MS Misc. 6, Voysey–Allsop, 7 Jan. 1870.

[8] C. Maurice Davies, *Unorthodox London*, 3rd edn (London, 1875), pp. 43–4.

[9] Man. Coll., MS Misc 6, Voysey–Allsop, 7 Jan. 1870.

[10] Ethel Thomson, *The Life and Letters of William Thomson, Archbishop of York* (London, 1919), p. 212.

[11] *Who Was Who, 1897–1915* (London, 1929): Voysey, Rev. Charles.

In 1863 he became curate, and in 1864 vicar, of Healaugh, near Tadcaster in Yorkshire. The publication of the controversial sermon in 1865 first obliged Archbishop Thomson to remonstrate with him.[12] But it was only when pressed by 'the Ultra-Orthodox party in the Anglican church' (again to quote Voysey's entry in *Who's Who*) that Thomson felt obliged to initiate legal proceedings which, after an appeal to the Judicial Committee of the Privy Council, resulted in Voysey's deprivation from his living in February 1871.[13] It is reasonable to surmise that between his ordination as deacon in 1852 and his deprivation in 1871 – the years during which he held Anglican appointments – Voysey's rebellion within worship, his growing theological liberalism notwithstanding, was confined to the pulpit. There he resolved 'not to say one word . . . which he did not then and there believe to be true', though during his unbeneficed years he 'avoided openly attacking error'.[14] But there is no evidence that he treated the Prayer Book in a more cavalier way than other Broad Churchmen, and Broad Churchmen, generally speaking, were liturgically conservative, save that they wished to recite the creeds less frequently.[15]

Deprivation, however, delivered Voysey from the constraints of the establishment. 'I am not aware of any change in my convictions since my "condemnation"', he wrote to a friend; 'I have only been a little more emphatic than I was before.'[16] Thereafter he was free both to proclaim his beliefs and to clothe them in a suitable form of worship.

On the morning of Sunday, 1 October 1871, having in the morning preached at the Unitarian Church at Croydon,[17] Voysey delivered his *Inaugural Discourse*, in which he adumbrated the position that was to be his in the future. His task, he said, was 'to undermine, assail, and if possible, to destroy that part of the prevailing religious belief which we deem to be false'. Thus condemned were the doctrine of the Fall, the curse of God against our race, the need for atonement, the necessity for appeasing the imaginary wrath of God – every one of which 'involves a flaw in the moral perfection of God'. 'Only less noxious', he claimed,

---

[12] Thomson, *William Thomson*, pp. 213–23.

[13] For a modern account, see M. A. Crowther, *Church Embattled* (Newton Abbot, 1960), ch. 6. The 'Ultra Orthodox party' in fact comprised both high and low.

[14] Davies, *Unorthodox London*, pp. 45–6.

[15] Dennis G. Widmore-Beddoes, *Yesterday's Radicals* (Cambridge, 1971), pp. 79–80.

[16] Man. Coll., MS Misc. 6, Voysey–Allsop, 7 June 1871.

[17] Davies, *Unorthodox London*, p. 48.

were belief in the Devil, the doctrine of the Trinity, the Godhead, and even the superhuman divinity of Jesus Christ, the expectation of Christ's return as judge, the doctrine of the Church, of holy orders, the necessity of priestly interference, priestly intervention, at the burial of the dead. He would defend 'the right to use the Light of Nature within us', and repudiate 'revealed religion, contained in the Bible, or in the Church, or both'. 'The creed of Christendom', he told his hearers, 'is the cradle – nay, the mother of Atheism.'[18] Maurice Davies, in his account of the occasion, describes the address as concluding with Voysey's announcement that

> he hoped to establish a weekly service somewhere in London. . . . The devotional part of this he wished to make an expression of religious feeling without superstition or idolatry. He should call in the aid of music, and carefully avoid making his service too long or too 'rigid.' Any form that might be adopted would be subject to alteration to suit the tastes of the congregation.[19]

Founded upon such teachings, Voysey's Theistic Church took shape first in St George's Hall, Langham Place, then, after 1885, in premises of its own in Swallow Street, Piccadilly.[20] Davies, ever curious concerning the liturgical and doctrinal aberrations which he sought out, and possessed of an almost inexhaustible and indulgent good humour, confessed, on making a second visit in 1874, that he had been deterred from returning 'by a certain coldness pervading the ritual. . . . It seemed as though the body and bones of worship were there without the soul.' This time, however, he found the worship less cold, and enhanced by great improvements in 'the music and other aesthetic adjuncts'.[21]

After his deprivation, Voysey continued to describe himself as 'The Rev Charles Voysey, B.A. (Late Vicar of Healaugh, Yorkshire)'.[22] In his anniversary sermon in October 1874, he spoke of the objection of some of his followers to his wearing 'the raiment to which all his life he had been accustomed', and of 'some who prefer a methodistical to an ecclesiastical service'.[23] In another sermon he said, 'Though I have been

---

[18] Revd Charles Voysey, *Inaugural Discourse* (London, 1871), pp. 4–6, 11.
[19] Davies, *Unorthodox London*, p. 48.
[20] *DNB*: Voysey, Charles.
[21] C. Maurice Davies, *Heterodox London*, 2 vols (London, 1874), 1, pp. 274–5.
[22] See the title pages of his three service books (below, nn. 25, 32, 39).
[23] *Anniversary Sunday 1874. A sermon . . . preached by the Rev. Charles Voysey*, pp. 2, 3.

deprived of my benefice, I am as much a clergyman of the Church of England as ever, and I have my own good reasons for intending so to remain.'[24] Voysey was in truth ineradicably Anglican, and the worship of his Theistic Church was Anglican in style and, where his beliefs did not demand changes, in content. Maurice Davies's descriptions of his worship depict it as Anglican in ethos.

Voysey published three editions of what he called *The Revised Prayer Book*, the first in 1871, the preface being dated 1 October. It is recognizably based on *The Book of Common Prayer*.

The principal service is called 'The Order for Morning Prayer', as is the first service in the Prayer Book, and its pattern is that of the Prayer Book service. It begins with a selection of sentences from Holy Scripture with which the Prayer Book service starts, followed by the exhortation and the confession, shorn of the assertion that the purposes of worship include the hearing of God's most holy word, and of the profession by the worshippers that they have no health in them and are miserable sinners. The absolution is that from the Communion Service, though cast in the first person plural. The versicles and responses are as in the Prayer Book, though *Gloria patri* is amended to 'Glory be to God the Father Almighty, as it was in the beginning . . .'. The *Te Deum* is without the central, Christological, verses, from 'Thine honourable, true and only son' to 'whom thou hast redeemed with thy precious blood. Make them to be numbered with thy saints in glory everlasting.' There is no creed, and of the suffrages, that which refers to making thy chosen people joyful becomes 'And make all thy people joyful'. The Prayer Book sequence of weekly collects is abandoned, and the two fixed collects at Morning Prayer (and indeed all subsequent prayers throughout the book) are devoid of such concluding phrases as 'through Jesus Christ our Lord'. Of the two lessons, the first is to be 'taken from the Old Testament, or some other Ancient Writings, as selected by the Minister', and the second 'taken from the New Testament, or from some modern writings as selected by the Minister'.[25] When Davies attended the Theistic Church, he found Voysey to sit light to his own prescription of ancient and modern writings – on one occasion both lessons were from an article in the *Boston Index* on 'Worship in the Nineteenth Century'; on another the

[24] *God's Love versus Eternal Torment: A Sermon Preached* . . . [on] April 15 1877, p. 2.

[25] *The Revised Prayer Book for the Use of the Congregation Assembled at St George's Hall Langham Place, compiled by The Rev. Charles Voysey B.A. St Edmund Hall and late Vicar of Healaugh* (London, 1871), pp. 5–10.

first was from F. W. Newman's *Theism*, and the second from the *Heteropathy* of Miss Frances Power Cobbe. (In the second edition, the direction became simply that the lessons were to be 'as selected by the minister'.)[26] The psalms – in the second edition pointed for Anglican chanting – were chosen from a selection included within the book, 'after being relieved of those mournful complaints which had only or chiefly a temporary and local value'.[27]

In all of this, Voysey retained familiar Anglican forms, but adapted them consistently to the requirements of his principles: he removed from the service all phrases affirming belief in a fallen, erring, humanity; in Jesus as saviour; in a divine Trinity; in the uniqueness of Holy Scripture. The Prayer Book has been purged of 'what the Editor considered to be erroneous or superstitious', and 'stripped of all that has become obsolete and out of harmony with a pure Theism.'[28]

Voysey's Book is notable also for what is wholly omitted. In 1870, before his defeat in the courts, while still Vicar of Healaugh, he had written to his friend Allsop, 'I am myself quite averse to all religious rites as we have them. Baptism, ordination, Lord's Supper, Burial, and co. and co.'[29] In no edition of his Prayer Book did he provide a form of Holy Communion. Instead, from the first edition, for that and (he claims) for the Litany (of which in fact he retains an edited version) he substituted two new services: *A Service of Praise and Thanksgiving*, and *A Service Respecting our Duty*. The former, beginning with the Preface and Sanctus from the communion service, again embodies Voysey's belief in human perfectability and progress, without a saviour. 'For all that we have been, for all that we are, and for all that we shall become'; 'For every good work which we have ever been able to do, for every conquest of our self, and for every step onwards we have taken in the path of holiness and peace'; 'For the peace and security in which we dwell, for the civilization which is raising us step by step, and for all wise government and legislation', are among its clauses. It concludes with the singing of part of F. W. Newman's *Theism*.[30] *A Service Respecting our Duty* is built around the Summary of the Law, and is largely concerned with personal responsibility and civic duty:

---

[26] C. Maurice Davies, *Unorthodox London*, 2nd edn, series II (London, 1875), p. 105; idem, *Heterodox London*, I, pp. 277–80.

[27] *The Revised Prayer Book* (1871), Preface, p. 4.

[28] Ibid., pp. 3–4.

[29] Man. Coll., MS Misc. 6, Voysey–Allsop, 19 May 1870.

[30] *The Revised Prayer Book* (1871), pp. 20–2.

It is the Lord's will . . . that we should be diligent in our several callings . . . that we should endeavour to keep our bodies in health, and our appetites and passions under control . . . that we should live chiefly to make others happy and good, and not to seek only our own pleasure . . . that we should diminish the sufferings of mankind.[31]

Voysey published a second edition in 1875. According to the preface, the first edition was so successful that most of it must be retained. He treated most severely the penitential opening to *The Order for Public Worship*, as he now called the morning service, claiming that 'a large portion of conforming members of the Church of England also have completely outgrown the taste for the old "Dearly Beloved," "The General Confession," and "The Absolution." A clergyman who was and is perfectly orthodox, confessed to me that these were quite out of place in a mixed assembly.' He now hoped to set a tone of worship 'for well-conducted, happy people', and so the opening sentences 'are designed to set a more cheerful tone and to excite thoughts of God and His goodness, rather than reflections about ourselves and our sins'.[32]

By this stage Voysey evidently felt confident enough in his following to amend the Lord's Prayer in accordance with his own scruples: 'forgive us our trespasses, As we should forgive them that trespass against us. And leave us not in temptation' his congregation now prayed. He also began to retreat from his earlier distaste for all offices, adding to the book a number of new services – 'long in use among us' – chief of which are forms for the 'Dedication and Benediction of Children', 'for Matrimony', and for 'The Burial or Cremation of the Dead'.

The first of these differs markedly from the Anglican service of baptism, being devoid of any reference to regeneration, to sponsors and their renunciations and affirmations, to the use of water. The service is a form for the naming of the child, with thanksgiving to God for its birth and prayers for its future well-being and development, walking 'obediently in all the commandments of God, and [serving] mankind faithfully in brotherly love all the days of his life'.[33]

In 1871 *The Order of Service for Matrimony* had been the only

---

[31] *The Revised Prayer Book* (1871), pp. 18–20.
[32] *The Revised Prayer Book compiled by The Rev. Charles Voysey B.A. St Edmund Hall and late Vicar of Healaugh*, 2nd edn (London, 1875), Preface, pp. v, vi.
[33] Ibid., pp. 51–7.

exception to Voysey's dislike of occasional offices – 'I like a *marriage* ceremony to involve religion – but this is the exception', he had written to Allsop, adding, 'I do not defend the greater part of our marriage ceremony.'[34] Unsurprisingly, his form deviates widely from its Anglican counterpart. In the introduction, Voysey cannot refrain from a nagging didacticism: 'we must not regard [this service] as a charm, or a spell, or a sacrament, whereby the act of marriage can be rendered more sacred than it already is', the congregation is told; and the essence of the ceremony is the promise made by the bridegroom ('I call upon these persons present to witness that I A.B., to take thee, C.D., to be my lawful wedded wife') and reciprocated by the bride. A note states that 'these words foregoing constitute all that is sufficient for a legal marriage.' An exchange of rings – 'If it be agreeable to the Bridegroom and Bride' – may follow, the words for which 'are copied from a Jewish ritual'.[35]

The Office of the Burial or Cremation of the Dead also little resembles the corresponding office in the Prayer Book. If the emphasis in the Prayer Book is on the edification of the living, Voysey lays it on the comfort of those who mourn. To this end, not least in its assumption of the well-being of the departed, all its exhortations and prayers are directed: 'we commit . . . the body of our dear brother here departed . . . in sure and certain hope that his soul hath ascended into the rest of God, and is at peace in our Heavenly Father's home.'[36] Voysey, a founder of the Cremation Society for England,[37] envisaged the alternative of cremation, the minister then saying at the commital: 'we commit unto the flames the body of our dear brother here departed', the formula 'earth to earth, ashes to ashes, dust to dust' – one of the few echoes of the Prayer Book service in Voysey's – being reduced to 'dust to dust'.

This second edition ends with a selection of hymns. Many of them were familiar to Anglicans, yet adapted to Voysey's theology. The last line of the first verse of Reginald Heber's 'Holy, holy, holy' ('God in Three Persons, Blessed Trinity'), for instance, became 'Thou who are our Father, for all eternity'. Voysey's belief in human perfectability is evident in his amendment of the third verse:

---

[34] Man. Coll., MS Misc. 6, Voysey–Allsop, 19 May 1870.
[35] *The Revised Prayer Book* (1875), pp. 58–65.
[36] Ibid., pp. 66–72.
[37] *DNB*: Voysey, Charles.

though the darkness hide Thee,
Though the eye of sinful man Thy glory may not see

became

though we see but dimly,
As we make our progress onward daily nearer thee.[38]

In 1892 Voysey produced a further edition of his Prayer Book. There are changes of detail from the second edition, but most notable is the inclusion of new services, providing further non-sacramental alternatives to their counterparts in the *Book of Common Prayer*. A *Service of Self-Consecration to God*, held after 'a course of religious and moral education given by the minister', is for those 'on the threshold of manhood or womanhood [who] are impressed with the solemnity of the responsibilities of life, and desire henceforth to forsake evil ways, and to devote themselves heartily to the will of God. Such a service [is] commonly called Confirmation.' Voysey again nags a little: 'some Churches have erred in the mode of the ceremony ... and in importing into it a superstitious idea of Episcopal blessing.' His candidates 'are not to be distinguished by any special dress or badge'; there will be no laying-on of hands, 'partly to avoid the possibility of the entrance of superstitious ideas, and still more ... to impress on each candidate that the Consecration to God is his or her own act'.[39] Lastly – his final capitulation – Voysey added *The Service of Ordination to the Ministry*. An anti-sacerdotalist exhortation rails against the 'dire evils of superstition [which] have clustered around this natural and pious ceremony of ordination'; and while conceding 'that it is meet that some should be set apart for this office', he insists that 'every kind of lawful work to which we may be called, either as men or women, is equally sacred in the sight of God.'[40] Thereafter the service has two elements: an interrogation of the candidate, and a prayer. The emphasis of both is on the responsibility of the candidate to live a life, and to cultivate a personality, befitting a minister. Once more, the symbols of the

---

[38] *The Revised Prayer Book* (1875), p. 182.
[39] *The Revised Prayer Book for Use in the Theistic Church, by Rev Charles Voysey, B.A. (late Vicar of Healaugh, Yorkshire)* (London, 1892): quotations from 'Preface to the Service of Self Consecration to God', pp. 73–82.
[40] Ibid., pp. 101–11 (the 'Service of Ordination to the Ministry').

sacrament in the Prayer Book – the laying-on of hands, the presentation of the Bible – are removed.[41]

Maurice Davies suggested that Voysey's worship 'would indeed bespeak the Anglican Communion comprehensive could she be proved elastic enough to contain it. . . . He waits, in fact, until the Church of England is "broad" enough to welcome him back, like a theological Prodigal, to her maternal arms.'[42] She never did. Earlier in the nineteenth century than his, there were numerous revisions of the Prayer Book by Unitarians – less severe than Voysey's, but with which his deserves comparison.[43] Yet 'Unitarian' was an appellation he declined: 'I am no Unitarian.'[44] He remained, in his own eyes, a 'clergyman of the Church of England' – but one whose rejection of 'the creeds, biblical inspiration, the sacramental system, the divinity of Christ',[45] ensured that, to the end of his life, he remained outside that Church. Leslie Stephen, to whom Voysey once apologized for believing in God, though 'a very harmless one', thought his was the logical conclusion of the Broad Church position. He also thought the position untenable – 'I always feel as if I was the reality & they [Colenso and Voysey] the shams.'[46] Certainly, the changes which Voysey's beliefs led him to introduce into the forms he took from the Prayer Book could be held to place him, and his worship, beyond any perimeter of the Christian religion. His retention of the words, and frequently of the substance, of the services of the Prayer Book; his restoration in later revisions of his own book of rites which he had earlier omitted; his continued wearing of the robes of the Anglican clergy – these may appear inconsistencies in his ardent theism. Yet, exile though he was, sham though he may have appeared, his tenaciously Anglican manner and idiom form threads of continuity in all the vicissitudes of his life.

---

[41] Ibid.
[42] Davies, *Unorthodox London* (2nd edn), p. 101.
[43] Wigmore-Beddoes, *Yesterday's Radicals*, pp. 82–4.
[44] Man. Coll., MS Misc. 6, Voysey–Allsop, 10 March 1870.
[45] *DNB*: Voysey, Charles.
[46] *Selected Letters of Leslie Stephen*, ed. John W. Bicknell, 2 vols (London, 1996), i, pp. 143–5.

'THIS ROMISH BUSINESS' – RITUAL INNOVATION AND PARISH LIFE IN LATER NINETEENTH-CENTURY LINCOLNSHIRE

by R. W. AMBLER

I N February 1889 Edward King, Bishop of Lincoln, appeared before the court of the Archbishop of Canterbury charged with illegal practices in worship. The immediate occasion for these proceedings was the manner in which he celebrated Holy Communion at the Lincoln parish church of St Peter at Gowts on Sunday 4 December 1887. He was cited on six specific charges: the use of lighted candles on the altar; mixing water with the communion wine; adopting an eastward-facing position with his back to the congregation during the consecration; permitting the Agnus Dei to be sung after the consecration; making the sign of the cross at the absolution and benediction, and taking part in ablution by pouring water and wine into the chalice and paten after communion. Two Sundays later King had repeated some of these acts during a service at Lincoln Cathedral.[1] As well as its intrinsic importance in defining the legality of the acts with which he was charged, the Bishop's trial raised issues of considerable importance relating to the nature and exercise of authority within the Church of England and its relationship with the state.[2] The acts for which King was tried had a further significance since the ways in which these and other innovations in worship were perceived, as well as the spirit in which they were ventured, also reflected the fundamental shifts which were taking place in the role of the Church of England at parish level in the second half of the nineteenth century. Their study in a local context such as Lincolnshire, part of King's diocese, provides the opportunity to examine the relationship between changes in worship and developments in parish life in the period.

---

[1] In the Court of the Archbishop of Canterbury. Read and Others v. the Lord Bishop of Lincoln, Judgment, 21 Nov. 1890 (London, 1891), pp. 1–2; E. S. Roscoe, The Bishop of Lincoln's Case. A Report of the Proceedings in the Court of the Archbishop of Canterbury of the Case of Read and Others v. the Bishop of Lincoln (London, 1889), pp. 48–50.

[2] Geoffrey Rowell, The Vision Glorious: Themes and Personalities of the Catholic Revival in Anglicanism (Oxford, 1983), pp. 153–4.

The charges against King were specific, but the innovations in worship which aroused opposition and occasioned conflict at parish level embraced a wide spectrum of behaviour and had a variety of sources. Opposition to them had deep roots among a set of long-standing prejudices, attitudes, and assumptions of which one of the most enduring was anti-Catholicism. The nature of anti-Catholicism in Lincolnshire reflected in part the low profile of the county's Roman Catholic community which was moderate in its pretensions, so that when issues affecting Catholics did become prominent they arose largely in reaction to developments at national level rather than from within the county itself.[3] Yet while neither its more organized nor its more demotic forms were strongly represented in Lincolnshire, anti-Catholicism was a pervasive influence throughout the period when ritual innovation was an issue in church life.[4]

The stance of William Parker, a south Lincolnshire landowner, at his parish church of Morton illustrates the way in which anti-Catholic rhetoric was employed in disputes over innovations in worship. It also demonstrates the wide range of practice which excited opposition. In a letter to the local newspaper in 1868, headed 'Popery at Morton, near Bourne', Parker described how on Sunday 2 February, 'Father' Harris had appeared in the church during Holy Communion wearing three distinct kinds of vestments. Before the administration he had elevated the elements above his head with both hands. Although later correspondents pointed out that the vestments which his informants had described were in fact a cassock, surplice, and academic hood, Parker's concern to arrest the advance of 'Popery' had obliterated any understanding of the real substance of the practices.[5] At nearby Bourne, where the introduction of weekly offerings in aid of the restoration fund at the town's abbey church in 1871 had excited opposition, these parish disagreements found expression in dissension over the use of bags to make the disputed collections. They were perceived as 'ritualistic substitutes' for the pewter plates which had hitherto been

[3] J. Wolffe, *The Protestant Crusade in Great Britain 1829–1860* (Oxford, 1991), pp. 2, 9, 15, 21, 51, 145–6, 151, 153, 193–4, 318; Mrs Gutch and Mabel Peacock, *Examples of Printed Folk-Lore Concerning Lincolnshire*, County Folk-Lore, 5 (London 1908, repr. Lichtenstein, 1967), pp. 210–11; Mabel Peacock, 'Fifth of November Customs', *Folklore*, 14 (1903), p. 89.

[4] *Lincolnshire Returns of the Census of Religious Worship 1851*, ed. R. W. Ambler (Lincoln, 1979), pp. lxi–lxii; R. J. Olney, *Lincolnshire Politics, 1832–1885* (Oxford, 1973), pp. 61, 65, 131; Wolffe, *Protestant Crusade*, pp. 224, 293.

[5] *Lincoln, Rutland and Stamford Mercury* [hereafter *LRSM*], 21 and 28 Feb. 1868.

used. Although it was argued that they were simply more becoming replacements for the plates, it was said that 'the use of the bag and weekly offerings are practices originally introduced at Puseyite churches and copied from Roman Catholic custom.'[6]

These concerns were strengthened by the way in which latent anti-Catholicism had become subsumed in general charges of 'Puseyite' behaviour which was perceived as undermining the place of the Church of England in English life. When a Canwick correspondent to the same paper reported in 1870 that he had seen the papal crest – crossed keys – used on the pulpit of a Lincolnshire village church he noted that the Church of England would not assume its 'pristine vigour and excellence' until it rid itself of such practices.[7] Reports such as this were often the result of visits to other parishes in which innovations were seen out of context or even, like the reports from Morton, reported by hearsay. The way in which the innovations were described did not involve any reasoned appreciation of their precise origins and meaning. Just as the range of practices which excited condemnation extended far beyond what was to be more formally understood as Ritualistic, so the use of the term 'Puseyite' was not necessarily applied to behaviour which can be attributed to clergymen who had any particular association with the Oxford Movement.[8]

The sympathies of clergymen who were the agents of liturgical change can be adduced from their actions. They are confirmed by their affiliation to the various associations which united them to like-minded brethren, by their academic background, and by the patronage which they enjoyed. The Revd William Frederick Chambers who became Vicar of North Kelsey in 1854 was a clergyman whose position is clear in all these respects. In June 1867 the annual meeting of the north Lincolnshire district of the English Church Union – established in 1860 as a body for the general defence of the Church of England, but particularly concerned with Tractarians and Ritualists – was held in his parish. The choral celebration of Holy Communion which preceded it not only brought together a group of like-minded local

---

[6] Ibid., 6 Jan. 1871.

[7] Ibid., 8 July 1870.

[8] Wolffe, *Protestant Crusade*, p. 285; Rowell, *Vision Glorious*, pp. 71, 182; Frances Knight, 'The influence of the Oxford Movement in the parishes c.1833–1860: a reassessment', in Paul Vaiss, ed., *From Oxford to the People; Reconsidering Newman and the Oxford Movement* (Leominster, 1996), pp. 131–2.

clergymen but also demonstrated a clearly articulated set of liturgical practices which were common to them. Celebrant, deacon, and subdeacon were vested in alb and chasuble, a dalmatic, and a tunicle respectively. When the preacher for the occasion went into the pulpit he 'touched his breast in four places', spread out his hands and invoked the Trinity, while the celebrant was reported as making the sign of the cross on the forehead of each communicant when administering the bread. Candles were burning on the altar throughout the service.[9]

Chambers and his fellow clergymen at the Kelsey meeting were known to be Tractarians, and part of a group of some twenty-five clergymen identifiable as Tractarians who held livings in Lincolnshire at this time. For them Ritualism was an extension of their under-standing of the nature of the Church, but ritual innovation was by no means exclusively identified with them, and in fact only just under half – twelve – of these known Lincolnshire Tractarians can actually be identified as Ritualists.[10] The ministry of Canon Gordon Frederick Deedes exemplified the position of non-Ritualist Tractarians. When he died in his eighty-fourth year in 1898 he had been Vicar of Heydour, near Grantham, for forty-two years. This 'friend of Pusey and Keble' was an 'Old Tractarian', but he attracted attention only to praise his 'quiet but good work' set in a perfect pattern of family life.[11] Although 'A Village Incumbent' from Lincolnshire, writing in June 1867, said that 'the present pernicious ceremonial innovations' in the Church of England had sprung from 'the Tractarian school', Ritualist clergymen had moved into livings in the county who drew their inspiration from other sources.[12]

In the forty years before the trial of Bishop King there were forty-seven clergymen in Lincolnshire who were said to be Ritualists, but who lacked a direct connection with Tractarianism. They consisted of sixteen who can be identified from reports of their activities in the local press, and a further thirty-one whose churchmanship meant that they were included in a publication known as the *Tourist's Church*

---

[9] *LRSM*, 21 June 1867; G. I. T. Machin, *Politics and the Churches in Great Britain 1869 to 1921* (Oxford, 1987), pp. 4–5.

[10] C. P. S. Clarke, *The Oxford Movement and After* (London, 1932), p. 166; G. W. Herring, 'Tractarianism to Ritualism: a study of some aspects of Tractarianism outside Oxford from the time of Newman's conversion in 1845, until the First Ritual Commission in 1867', 2 vols (University of Oxford D. Phil. thesis, 1984), 2, *passim*.

[11] *LRSM*, 26 Sept. 1898.

[12] Ibid., 21 June 1867.

Guide. First published in 1874, and later edited by the Secretary of the English Church Union, it identified Ritualist churches by listing the hours of services in churches where Holy Communion was celebrated at least every Sunday and where eucharistic vestments and altar lights were used. Later editions noted whether the celebrant adopted the eastward-facing position during the service of Holy Communion. In doing this the *Guide* provides a more uniform body of evidence for the growth and extent of Ritualism than the more random, but informative, reports of the local press.[13] In 1874 services conducted in twenty-four Lincolnshire churches were included in the *Guide*. The growth in the number of incumbents whose practices can be clearly identified as Ritualistic meant that there were fifty-six by 1881.[14]

The backgrounds of these men are indicative of the complex influences which contributed to the development of Ritualism in Lincolnshire. One measure of this was the university at which these clergymen had been educated. Although there was not necessarily an association between an Oxford education and Tractarianism, the fact that only a minority, although a substantial one, of the Lincolnshire Ritualists were Oxford men is a further indication of how much wider the influences on the development of Ritualism were than any simple association with the Oxford Movement and the University of Oxford. While twenty-one Ritualists in Lincolnshire whose educational background can be identified were Oxford graduates, nineteen were from Cambridge and six from other institutions – including one from the new but important source of clergymen for the diocese of Lincoln, the Scholae Cancellarii, or theological college, at Lincoln.[15]

A further and potentially greater influence in the development of Ritualism can be located within the University of Cambridge, in the Cambridge Camden Society which had been formally established in 1839 for 'the study of Ecclesiastical Architecture and Antiquities'. Although its members were forbidden from entering into theological debate or religious controversy, membership led them towards the study of liturgy and an interest in ritual through a concern with the

---

[13] W. N. Yates, '"Bells and Smells": London, Brighton and South Coast religion reconsidered', *Southern History*, 5 (1983), p. 123.

[14] J. Carne Waram, ed., *Tourist's Church Guide 1874* (London [1874]), pp. 18–79; *Tourist's Church Guide 1881* (London [1881]), pp. 24–137.

[15] Herring, 'Tractarianism to Ritualism', 2, *passim*; James F. White, *The Cambridge Movement: the Ecclesiologists and the Gothic Revival* (Cambridge, 1962), pp. 26–7; *Crockford's Clerical Directory* (1875, 1881), *passim*.

'symbolical and material expression' of the Church's beliefs. Trinity College, the home of the Society, was a significant source of ritual innovators, and five of Lincolnshire's Ritualists were Trinity men. Yet while there were eleven Lincolnshire Camdenians in 1847, the Camden Society's influence was less marked at a local level. What became the Lincoln Diocesan Architectural Society had been founded in 1844, probably through the interests of a 'Louth Camdenian', as the Lincolnshire Society for the Encouragement of Ecclesiastical Antiquities. In its early days it cultivated an exclusively Anglican and largely clerical character; but only three of Lincolnshire's Camdenians were members of it by 1850. While Bishop Kaye felt able to give the Lincoln Society his cautious support as its President, he withdrew his patronage from the Camden Society because of what were seen as its Romanizing tendencies.[16]

The university and general intellectual background and associations of Lincolnshire's Ritualist clergymen can ultimately provide only an indication, and never a precise measure, of the wide range of influences which shaped their attitudes. Moreover, as the links between Camdenians and members of the local Architectural and Archaeological Society indicate, the ideas and attitudes of individuals were capable of change and development in the course of their ministries, so that the firmly-held convictions of newly ordained clergymen could be dissolved by the realities of a parish ministry. An increase in the number of Lincolnshire churches in the *Tourist's Church Guide* is evidence of the growth of ritual innovation in the county up to the time of the trial of Bishop King; but although a more rapid increase in the number of Ritualists nationally after 1880 was also felt in Lincolnshire, their numbers and influence have to be seen in the overall context of a total, by the beginning of the twentieth century, of 579 parishes in the county.[17]

While there is some evidence from south Lindsey that the party

[16] White, *Cambridge Movement*, pp. 19, 35, 37, 44, 67–8, 146, 225; James Bentley, *Ritualism and Politics in Victorian Britain: the Attempt to Legislate for Belief* (Oxford, 1978), p. 27; Terence R. Leach, 'Edward Trollope and the Lincoln Diocesan Architectural Society', in Christopher Sturman, ed., *Some Historians of Lincolnshire* (Lincoln, 1992), pp. 18–19; Sir Francis Hill, 'Early days of a society', *Lincolnshire History and Archaeology*, 1 (1966), pp. 58, 59, 62; 'The Thirty-Eighth Report of the Lincoln Diocesan Architectural Society', *Associated Architectural and Archaeological Societies Reports and Papers*, 16 (1881), pp. i–vi.

[17] *Tourist's Church Guide 1874*, pp. 18–79; *Tourist's Church Guide 1881*, pp. 24–137; Nigel Yates, *Buildings, Faith and Worship: the Liturgical Arrangement of Anglican Churches 1600–1900* (Oxford, 1991), pp. 143–4.

affiliations of clergymen in that part of Lincolnshire were becoming more pronounced by 1875, the attitude of the clergy as a whole appears to have been one of general tolerance towards their Ritualist colleagues. However, while their fellow clergymen might adopt a relatively neutral attitude towards this minority, opposition among the laity began to become more coherent.[18] Although anti-Catholicism was generally sustained by reaction to increased illiberalism in the Roman Catholic Church (with the Syllabus of Errors in 1864 and the promulgation of Papal Infallibility in July 1870) there is no evidence that these particular issues remained other than implicit in the continuing antagonism to ritual innovation in Lincolnshire.[19] However, at the time that lay concern for the nation's Protestant heritage became increasingly focused on it, the conduct of worship also became more significant as an expression of the authority of the clergy at a time when their general position in parish life was undergoing enforced change. The potential for friction in this situation was reflected in discussion of Viscount Sandon's parochial councils Bills of 1870 and 1871. Sandon, an Evangelical, sought to clarify the responsibilities of clergymen and their congregations in parish affairs. His measure, according to the writer of a letter to a Lincolnshire newspaper in 1870, gave parishioners, through their representatives, 'a check on the vagaries of the clergy'.[20]

The abolition of compulsory church rate in 1868, and the establishment in 1894 of elected councils for the secular administration of the parish, were stages in the separation of the sacred and secular which had considerable resonance in the lives of rural parishes. The changes which were taking place in the position and authority of incumbents were confirmed by the Burial Laws Amendment Act of 1880, by which clergymen lost formal control over churchyards, while the church building was becoming increasingly a place devoted solely to worship and the occasional offices. Moreover, the onset of agricultural depression in the 1870s meant reduced clerical incomes, especially in counties such as Lincolnshire where they were closely tied to agrarian prosperity. As their influence became confined to more exclusively ecclesiastical matters, Anglican clergymen were forced into a more

[18] James Obelkevich, *Religion and Rural Society: South Lindsey 1825–1875* (Oxford, 1976), pp. 122–3; John Henry Overton and Elizabeth Wordsworth, *Christopher Wordsworth. Bishop of Lincoln 1807–1885* (London, 1888), pp. 260–2.

[19] Machin, *Politics and the Churches*, pp. 6, 7, 21.

[20] *LRSM*, 8 July 1870; Machin, *Politics and the Churches*, p. 49.

specialized role as religious functionaries rather than as officers of the establishment. Ritualism, with its emphasis on the liturgical role of the priest, was a means of embracing and enhancing these new functions.[21] The actions of the parish churchwarden of Little Bytham, when in 1891 he led the opposition to liturgical innovation in the parish church, were seen in terms of a struggle for authority, with 'parishioners and churchpeople' pitted against an innovative clergyman caught up in 'this Romish business'.[22]

The growth and development of Ritualism can be understood in the context of these changes in parish life, but its geographical spread, particularly in rural counties such as Lincolnshire, was dependent on more contingent factors. The pastoral success of Ritualist priests in places as diverse as the East and West Ends of London, and along the south coast of England, has usually been explained in terms of the appropriateness of their ministrations for the congregations they served; but in Lincolnshire in the period up to the trial of Bishop King only the new and predominantly working-class parish of Holy Trinity Gainsborough was an exceptional Lincolnshire example of one of the types of parish which was a 'natural' home for Ritualism.[23] Moreover, like many of the other places in which Ritualism flourished in other parts of the country, the opportunity existed at Gainsborough for parishioners who were unsympathetic or opposed to it to go to another church in the town. This was an option which was not generally available in the villages, nor in most of the market towns of Lincolnshire, and so heightened the perception of Ritualism as an unwelcome innovation foisted on the people of a parish. The operation of the patronage system made its essentially intrusive nature even more marked. While lay patrons have been shown to have been significant in providing preferment for fifty-five per cent of the Tractarian clergymen in the whole diocese of Lincoln in the period 1833 to 1860, Ritualists tended to depend on other clergymen for their livings: a situation which not only confirmed the strong identification of

---

[21] Owen Chadwick, *The Victorian Church*, 2 vols (London, 1970), 2, pp. 193–9, 205–7, 322; Alan Haig, *The Victorian Clergy* (London, 1984), p. 15; R. C. K. Ensor, *England 1870–1914* (Oxford, 1960 edn), p. 141; Anthony Russell, *The Clerical Profession* (London, 1980), pp. 108–9; Frances Knight, *The Nineteenth-Century Church and English Society* (Cambridge, 1995), pp. 70–1.

[22] *LRSM*, 16 May, 12 Sept., 17 April, 24 April 1891.

[23] W. S. F. Pickering, *Anglo-Catholicism: a Study in Religious Ambiguity* (London, 1989), pp. 98–103; Ian Beckwith, 'Religion in a working men's parish 1843–1893', *Lincolnshire History and Archaeology*, 5 (1970), pp. 32–3.

Ritualism with clerical aspirations but distinguished it clearly from Tractarianism.[24]

While there had been a significant shift nationally which increased the amount of patronage that was in the hands of clergymen, and especially of bishops, the position of the Bishop of Lincoln was not as strong as that of many of his brethren. By the 1890s he only had the patronage of some six per cent of the livings in the county and even this was shared in some cases. The increase in the number of other clerical patrons in Lincolnshire was more marked: from 2.3 per cent to 12.2 per cent in south Lindsey, the type of predominantly rural area favoured by clergymen when they purchased advowsons. In addition there were livings in the gift of other church dignitaries such as the Dean and Chapter of Lincoln and other individual Cathedral officers, Oxford or Cambridge colleges, and those belonging to official patrons such as the Crown, Lord Chancellor, or Duchy of Lancaster. Nine of the sixteen Ritualists whose activities had attracted the attention of the local press between 1850 and 1889 had been presented to their livings by their fellow clergymen, and while the patron was a clergyman in twelve of the twenty-six Lincolnshire parishes in the *Tourist's Church Guide* for 1874, three were in the gift of Oxford and Cambridge colleges, and another three had official patrons. The living of Caistor, where there were recurring disputes over the conduct of church services, was in the gift of Walter Farquar Hook, Vicar of Leeds, by virtue of his office as Prebendary of Caistor in Lincoln Cathedral, until it passed into the hands of the bishop as a result of reforming legislation in 1840. The Revd W. F. Chambers had been presented to the living of North Kelsey by the Prebendary of North Kelsey, while the Revd W. J. Jenkins, a former Fellow, had Balliol College Oxford's country living of Fillingham.[25]

From 1865 the Church Association provided an institutional focus for the concerns of those who feared for the future development of the Church of England and in particular for its Protestant identity.[26] This change in emphasis can be seen first in Lincolnshire in the disputes which bedevilled parish life in the market town of Brigg in the 1860s

---

[24] Knight, 'Influence of the Oxford Movement', p. 138.

[25] *The Clergy List 1886*, p. 46; J. A. Venn, *Alumni Cantabrigienses, Part II: 1752–1900*, 6 vols (Cambridge, 1940–54), 4, p. 278; W. R. W. Stephens, *The Life and Letters of Walter Farquar Hook*, 6th edn (London, 1881), pp. 114, 193; *The Lincoln Diocesan Magazine*, 1, 6 (Oct. 1886), p. 77; *Crockford's Clerical Directory* (1878), pp. 173, 509; (1907), p. 1507.

[26] Wolffe, *Protestant Crusade*, pp. 21, 51, 151, 153, 318.

and 1870s. The town was in the parish of Wrawby until 1874, where the living was in the gift of Clare College Cambridge. It had been held by Canon John Rowland West since 1836. His Ritualism had led a local newspaper reporter to come away from Wrawby church in the 1870s wondering if he had 'not been in a Romish Mass House instead of a Protestant Reformed Church'. The 'ritualistic young men' who became his curates shared his attitudes to worship. They served with him the chapel of ease in the town of Brigg, a strongly nonconformist place where disputes over the burial of Dissenters and church rates had exacerbated divisions in the parish from the 1840s.[27] After a lull in the 1850s, dissension broke out between 'the priestly party' and members of the Brigg congregation and centred on the conduct of services. It was reported in 1870 that the 'Protestant laity' felt that their wishes and opinions were being treated too lightly and although they preferred peace, 'if the successive developments of Ritualism are not met with unmistakable marks of disapprobation, their very silence is taken to be consent, and is made the excuse for some further steps in the Ritualistic progress'.[28] Their response was to turn to the Church Association, whose first Lincolnshire branch was formed in the town in 1868.[29]

The Brigg Church Association did not survive the resolution of the disputes in the town, but it was significant for the way in which the basis on which disputes over ritual were conducted had been shifted. The case of the rector of Clee cum Cleethorpes was another stage in this process. Here the involvement of the Church Association brought a further level of significance to proceedings in the parish, for not only was Bishop King the patron of the living, but the dispute was also a step on the road to his prosecution. In 1886 complaints were made at the Clee Easter Vestry about the Ritualistic innovations of the parish's new rector. It was alleged that he had worn vestments and adopted the eastward-facing position at the celebration of the Holy Communion, used a mixed chalice (which he had rinsed afterwards), and made the sign of the cross when pronouncing the benediction.[30] Opposition was channelled into the formation of a branch of the

---

[27] Frank Henthorn, *A History of 19th Century Brigg* (Stamford, 1987), p. 40; *LRSM*, 11 Aug. 1876.

[28] *LRSM*, 24 Sept. 1870.

[29] *The Church Association Annual Report, 1868* (London [1868]), p. 14; *LRSM*, 10 and 21 Oct. 1867; Henthorn, *19th Century Brigg*, pp. 43–4.

[30] *Cleethorpes Gazette*, 5 May 1886.

Church Association in 1887. Its President was the elected churchwarden of Cleethorpes, Ernest de Lacy Read, and its Treasurer William Brown, a local solicitor. Both men were to be the main local agents in the prosecution of Bishop King in 1889, and it was King, as Bishop of Lincoln, who vetoed their attempts to prosecute the rector of Clee. The matter was taken to the Archbishop of Canterbury who refused to intervene.[31]

H. K. Hebb, another solicitor, had complained to the Archbishop of Canterbury in December 1886 that the Precentor had adopted an eastward-facing position during the celebration of Holy Communion at Lincoln Cathedral.[32] Hebb's involvement demonstrated the way in which solicitors were becoming active in the instigation of prosecutions for Ritualism in general, and in connection with the Church Association in particular. Like Brown, he was representative of the middle-class lay professionals with a largely urban perspective who sought to control clerical aspirations through the mechanisms they understood best: legal processes. In view of the importance of patronage in the diffusion of Ritualism, it is also significant that it was men of this type – the less deferential sections of the professional and commercial middle classes – who moved on to the offensive with regard to the reform of the patronage system in the second half of the nineteenth century. This was, however, a social group which in other situations might be active on behalf of different church interests. The involvement of these laymen in the politics of church life at a period when relationships between the clergy and leading laity were being redefined and redeveloped is as significant for its context as for their precise ecclesiastical affiliations.[33] For members of the Church Association their professional attitudes shaped their expectations of the role of a Protestant ministry. Many of these middle-class Protestant activists were men of substance, but without the traditional cultural and academic background of the clergymen whom they opposed. There was, according to Archbishop Benson, 'something in "Protestant truth" . . . very concordant with wealth' and its champions sought a degree of accountability on the part of clergymen which ran counter to the redefinition of their role implicit in Ritualism. In the county of Lincoln the paternalistic otherworldliness of its bishop, Edward King,

---

[31] *Cleethorpes Gazette*, 24 May 1887.

[32] *LRSM*, 31 Dec. 1886; Sir Francis Hill, *Victorian Lincoln* (Cambridge, 1974), p. 246.

[33] Jeremy Morris, 'The regional growth of Tractarianism: some reflections', in Vaiss, *From Oxford to the People*, pp. 150–1; Knight, *Nineteenth-Century Church*, pp. 198–200.

pointed up the distance which separated these sets of attitudes and assumptions.[34]

The charges brought against Bishop King belonged to the level of organized and systematic opposition to Ritualism. There is no evidence for any divisions over the conduct of worship in the parish of St Peter at Gowts before King's prosecution, and there were other churches nearby where Ritualistic practice was more developed. Although the two working men who provided the evidence for Kings prosecution were described as 'aggrieved parishioners' the case did not originate in the particular circumstances of parish conflict, although the ensuing 'trial' was a critical point in the definition of the framework of discipline which sustained the worshipping life of the whole Church of England. It was, however, representative of only one level of the process through which the basic relationship between the Church and the people to which it ministered was developed. Local opposition to ritual innovation, located among the transactions of parish life and contingent on their varied circumstances, was another part of the process through which that relationship between Church and people was beginning to be reshaped to meet new circumstances. Worship was at its centre.[35]

University of Hull

---

[34] M. J. D. Roberts, 'Private patronage and the Church of England 1800–1900', *JEH*, 32 (1981), p. 211; George W. E. Russell, *Edward King, Sixtieth Bishop of Lincoln, a Memoir*, 3rd edn (London, 1912), p. 146; Graham Neville, 'Right heart, wrong head', *The Modern Churchman*, 28 (1986), pp. 15–16, 19; I owe the point on the significance of solicitors to Dr D. M. Thompson.

[35] Hill, *Victorian Lincoln*, p. 245; B. W. Randolph and J. W. Townroe, *The Mind and Work of Bishop King* (London, 1981), p. 176; Russell, *Edward King*, p. 147; Roscoe, *The Bishop of Lincoln's Case*, p. 47; Mary Finch, *A Great Parish Priest: Andrew Chrysostom Ramsay, Vicar of St. Botolphs, Lincoln, 1876–91* (Lincoln, 1995), pp. 20–4.

CONTINUITY AND CHANGE IN THE LITURGICAL REVIVAL IN SCOTLAND: JOHN MACLEOD AND THE DUNS CASE, 1875-1876

by DOUGLAS M. MURRAY

URING the Liturgical Revival of the Victorian period, the worship of the Church of Scotland changed more radically than at any time since the seventeenth century. Those who favoured reform felt that the largely unstructured and didactic character of Presbyterian services no longer appealed to many sections of society. The upper classes, for example, were turning in increasing numbers to the worship of the Episcopal Church.[1] In addition some reformers wished the liturgy of the Kirk to reflect more clearly the doctrinal basis of the Reformed tradition. The innovations which were pioneered in this period included a change in the posture of the congregation for prayer and for singing, the introduction of prayers read by the minister instead of being delivered extempore; the use of set forms such as the Creed, the Lord's Prayer, and the Doxology; the singing of hymns as well as psalms; the use of organs to accompany praise; the observance of the main festivals of the Christian year; and the greater frequency of holy communion.

These changes were seen as being in continuity with the traditions of the Church and not as a radical departure from true Presbyterianism. The innovators would often justify them by an appeal to the past, that such practices were a return to the ways of worship of the Scottish reformers.[2] They would also seek to commend their innovations by explaining the theological rationale behind them, that they were liturgical expressions of the fundamental truths of the Christian faith. In addition, many of the leading liturgical reformers gave priority in their ministries to the traditional tasks of preaching and pastoral work. It was because these clergymen were perceived to be faithful preachers and pastors that their congregations came to accept liturgical change. These elements of change and continuity can be seen in the

---

[1] Douglas M. Murray, 'Disruption to Union', in Duncan B. Forrester and Douglas M. Murray, eds, *Studies in the History of Worship in Scotland*, 2nd edn (Edinburgh, 1996), pp. 88–9.

[2] Douglas M. Murray, 'The study of the Catholic tradition of the Kirk: Scoto-Catholics and the worship of the Reformers', *SCH*, 33 (1997), pp. 517–27.

ministry of the Revd Dr John Macleod (1840–98). When his innovations were challenged after he left Duns to become minister of Govan in 1875, his supporters appealed to the traditions of the Church. In both parishes the opposition was much less significant than it might have been because Macleod was held in high regard as a parish minister.

John Macleod was recognized as one of the most energetic and innovative ministers of his day. After a brief period at Newton-on-Ayr he became the minister of Duns in Berwickshire in 1862, and was then elected to Govan near Glasgow in 1874, the first minister to be so appointed to the parish following the abolition of patronage in the Kirk. In appearance Macleod was described as 'like a sea king, with the drooping moustaches of a Scandinavian chieftain'.[3] He had a forceful manner and tended to dominate his kirk sessions and congregations. He was used to getting his way and to overcoming opposition to his views. It is significant that the complaints about the worship at Duns only emerged early in 1875, after he had left the parish. His theological outlook was unusual if not unique at the time. He was a High Churchman, a leading member of the Scoto-Catholic group of ministers who formed the Scottish Church Society in 1892.[4] Yet he did not place so much emphasis on the continuity of the Church with the past as did other Scoto-Catholics. As his fellow High Churchman Henry J. Wotherspoon put it, his conception of the Church did not move 'longitudinally' with the stream of time in a doctrine of transmission of grace, but rather 'perpendicularly' between earth and heaven.[5] Macleod's emphasis upon the immediate relationship of the Church to Christ by the Holy Spirit was due largely to his connection with the Catholic Apostolic Church.[6] He came under the influence of members of this Church at the meetings of the Berwickshire Naturalist Club, which dealt with a wide range of subjects and brought together people of different ecclesiastical backgrounds from both sides of the border.[7] Macleod was concerned to recover what he considered to be

---

[3] Gavin White, 'John Macleod of Govan', in W. John Harvey, ed., *Govan Old Parish Church 1888–1988* (Glasgow, 1988), p. 12.

[4] Douglas M. Murray, 'The Scottish Church Society, 1892–1914: the high church movement in the Church of Scotland' (Cambridge University Ph. D. thesis, 1975), p. 64.

[5] H. J. Wotherspoon, 'John Macleod of Govan', *The Constructive Quarterly*, 8 (1920), p. 673.

[6] Douglas M. Murray, 'John Macleod of Govan: a distinctive high churchman', *Liturgical Review*, 8 (1978), pp. 29–30.

[7] James F. Leishman, *Linton Leaves* (Edinburgh, 1937), pp. 164–5.

'Catholic' elements in the worship of the Kirk, but they were most important in his view because they enabled the Church on earth to participate more fully in the continuing worship of heaven. It was this doctrinal point which he was most concerned to emphasise, and he gave priority to the task of teaching the central truths of the Christian faith. When his liturgical practices at Duns were challenged, however, those who defended them did so by appealing to the history of the Kirk. It was important that they were seen, not as mere innovations, but as a recovery of traditional elements which had been neglected or forgotten.

The changes which Macleod made in the worship at Duns were introduced gradually. An organ was installed in 1866, and two years later Macleod obtained the consent of the kirk session for the congregation to stand to sing and sit to pray.[8] Additional weekday services were later introduced; the main festivals of the Christian year were observed; and a monthly celebration of communion was started in 1871.[9] On leaving Duns in January 1875, Macleod recognized the support he had received from the kirk session, but he warned them that attempts might be made to change the pattern of worship which he had instituted.[10] In his farewell sermon to the congregation, he said that they should not take for their leaders 'those who would turn everything upside down, silence much of their praise, abridge and diminish the services, shut the church throughout the weeks on which the holy festivals recurred, and cut down their Communion seasons to four or two occasions in the year'.[11]

Not long after Macleod's departure a petition complaining of the forms of worship was presented to the Duns kirk session. The petition was signed by 116 out of the 580 members of the congregation. It complained of 'certain changes in the mode of conduct of public worship in the Parish Church, and in the seasons for the dispensation of the Lord's Supper, the observance of certain feasts of the English Church, and the introduction of Symbols foreign to a Presbyterian Church'.[12] Macleod was not on trial himself, nor was he able to appear

---

[8] Duns Parish Church, Duns, Berwickshire, Minutes of Duns Kirk Session [hereafter DKS], 10 March 1868.

[9] DKS, 3 Feb. 1871.

[10] DKS, 6 Jan. 1875.

[11] *Berwickshire News*, 12 Jan. 1875.

[12] DKS, 29 Jan. 1875.

in defence of his practices. The extent of his influence is shown, however, in that the kirk session, with only one exception, defended what he had introduced. The leading defender of Macleod's innovations was the session clerk, a local lawyer named Alexander Crawford.

The petitioners stated that they had not objected to these new practices before 'through respect to their late minister', thus indicating the influence of Macleod's personality. The case at first revolved round the question as to who should hear the petition, the kirk session or the presbytery of Duns. Since the kirk session was supportive of the innovations made by Macleod, the petitioners appealed to the presbytery to hear their complaints. This aspect of the case was taken on appeal to the General Assembly of 1875 which ruled that the presbytery should examine the contents of the petition.[13] In making this decision the Assembly was guided by an Act passed in 1865 concerning the worship of the Kirk. The Act had been proposed by Dr W. R. Pirie of Dyce, Aberdeenshire, a leading opponent of the liturgical changes which had been pioneered by Dr Robert Lee at Greyfriars Church in Edinburgh. The 'Pirie Act' was intended to stop innovations being made by a minister against the wishes of his congregation. It stated that arrangements with regard to worship were to be regulated by the presbytery and that 'even though no express law should exist with reference to such particulars, the decision of Presbyteries in each case shall be absolute and obligatory until they have been finally reversed by the competent court of review.'[14]

Intended as an absolute check to the progress of worship reform, the Act became in practice an 'awkwardly worded charter of liberty beyond which the Church did not find it necessary to advance'.[15] The Act depended on the vigilance of each presbytery, but not only were presbyteries reluctant to intervene in congregations unless invited to do so, when they did take action they would come to different conclusions as to what practices should be allowed. The members of the presbytery of Duns were on the whole opposed to innovations in worship, although a notable exception was the liturgical scholar Dr Thomas Leishman of Linton. At its meeting in July 1875, the presbytery upheld the complaints of the petitioners and ruled against

---

[13] *Acts of the General Assembly of the Church of Scotland 1875* (Edinburgh, 1875), p. 60.

[14] *Acts of the General Assembly of the Church of Scotland 1865* (Edinburgh, 1865), pp. 46, 48.

[15] J. R. Fleming, *A History of the Church in Scotland, 1843–1873* (Edinburgh, 1927), p. 204. Cf. Murray, 'Disruption to Union', p. 93.

the changes in worship at Duns. Thus in the Duns case the 'Pirie Act' was used for its original purpose, as a means of checking liturgical reform. Macleod's supporters appealed to the synod of Merse and Teviotdale in October 1875, and to the General Assembly in 1876, but the presbytery's judgement was upheld.

Five objections to the changes in worship at Duns can be identified. First, the petitioners complained about the 'symbol and letters' on the cloth covering the communion table, and the symbol on the cover of the baptismal font, which were thought to be unnecessary and needlessly offensive to Presbyterian feelings.[16] The cloth was embroidered with the letters 'I.H.S.', and there was a cross on the cover of the font. The presbytery ruled that these symbols should be removed.[17] The Revd J. H. Walker of Greenlaw, a prominent opponent of Macleod's practices, thought that the letters could mean either 'Jesus the Saviour of Men' (*Jesu Hominum Salvator*), or *in hac cruce salus*.[18] He thought that the doctrine of the real presence 'tended to materialise the whole views and hopes of the Redeemer, and to introduce what were the worst terrors of the Church of Rome'. Another opponent, the Revd David Swan of Smailhom, asked the synod: 'Whoever heard before of an altar cloth with the letters "I.H.S." in a Presbyterian Church?'[19] According to Dr John Macrae of Hawick, if an altar cloth was allowed, then all that followed was also permitted, 'candles, flowers, and the thousand inventions that were associated with the ritualistic party'.[20]

In defence of such symbols the session clerk of Duns, Alexander Crawford, said at the synod that he had never thought of the communion table as an altar and that the letters 'I.H.S.' meant 'Jesus the Saviour of Men'. The same letters were to be found in St Giles's Cathedral in Edinburgh where the General Assembly held its opening service.[21] A speaker at the Assembly in 1876 pointed out that these letters were to be found in other Presbyterian churches in Scotland.[22] The most telling point was made by Thomas Leishman when speaking at the synod. He said that the small representative communion tables

[16] DKS, 29 Jan. 1875.
[17] Edinburgh, Scottish Record Office [hereafter SRO], CH2/113/12, Minutes of the Presbytery of Duns [hereafter PD], 9 Feb. 1875.
[18] *The Scotsman*, 27 May 1875.
[19] Ibid., 13 Oct. 1875.
[20] Ibid.
[21] Ibid.
[22] Ibid., 24 May 1876.

now to be found in most churches in Scotland did not correspond with the real communion tables of old at which minister and people both sat to receive the sacrament. The battle of the altar, he said, should have been fought when the tables were thus reduced in size, not now on the point as to whether 'the table cloth should be more or less shabby'.[23] At the 1876 Assembly the maverick minister of Greyfriars in Edinburgh, Dr Robert Wallace, said amidst laughter that there was no law of the Church against table cloths. As for the letters 'I.H.S.', if there were periods between them, then they were the motto of the Jesuits, *Jesu Hominum Salvator*; but if there were no periods, they simply formed the first three letters of the name of Jesus in Greek. The proper procedure would be not to enjoin the removal of the letters, but to appoint a committee to go down to Duns to ensure that the periods were removed![24]

In ruling against these items the Assembly indicated the limit of what it considered to be permissible in the area of symbolism in church buildings. Yet, as had been pointed out during the debate, other church buildings contained these and other forms of symbolism. The decision only had reference to the church at Duns, and thus indicates the inconsistency of the operation of the 'Pirie Act'. At the root of the opposition was not so much the symbols themselves but the doctrine of the sacraments which they seemed to imply. Alexander Crawford said at the synod that there was no evidence that any member of the congregation held a Roman Catholic or High Anglican view of Christ's presence in the sacrament. The opponents of the symbols at Duns could have been reminded, too, that the *Westminster Confession*, the Kirk's subordinate standard in matters of the faith, states that Christ is 'really' and 'spiritually' present in the Lord's Supper.[25]

The second complaint in the Duns petition related to the observ-ance of the main festivals of the Christian year. In its ruling, the presbytery stated that while admitting the right and privilege of God's people to meet at any time for worship, 'they cannot approve of the commemorative observance of any of the Roman Catholic or Episcopal Feast or Festival days'.[26] At the synod Alexander Crawford stated that the congregation had held commemorative days as 'true Presbyterians,

---

[23] *The Scotsman*, 13 Oct. 1875.
[24] Ibid., 24 May 1876.
[25] *Westminster Confession of Faith* (Edinburgh, 1880), XXIX.7, pp. 94–5.
[26] SRO, PD, 20 July 1875.

and in no other way'.[27] At the Assembly Thomas Leishman pointed out that festivals such as Easter and Pentecost fell on Sundays, and that the courts of the Church could not forbid ministers from referring to certain doctrines on those occasions. And even with services held on weekdays, were they going to say that it was unlawful to meet for worship on certain days of the year? The point about such services, in his view, was to provide an opportunity of highlighting some of the great truths of the Christian faith. He pointed out, too, that such festivals were not particularly Episcopal or Roman Catholic, but were observed by 'every national Presbyterian Church in Europe except their own'.[28] Certainly the Scots Reformers had abolished the Christian year, but Leishman maintained that they had done so because of the superstitious observance of such days. Leishman would argue elsewhere that the evidence against these festivals in the years following the Reformation was not of a uniform character, and that the Kirk should now give liberty to congregations to observe them.[29] Although the observance of the festivals was forbidden at Duns, it was introduced in other places. Four congregations are recorded as having services on Christmas Day in 1873, and five years later James Cooper would be the first minister to hold Holy Week services, in his first charge at St Stephen's, Broughty Ferry.[30] John Macleod would proceed to observe the Christian year at Govan, and was not forbidden from doing so by the presbytery of Glasgow.[31] The verdict in the Duns Case thus represents a failure on the part of the opponents of liturgical change to halt a practice which was steadily increasing in the Kirk.

The petitioners at Duns complained in the third place about the monthly celebration of communion. They wished to return to a quarterly celebration with the traditional fencing of the tables, a warning against the dangers of partaking unworthily which was given immediately before the distribution of the elements.[32] They also wished the continuation of the twice-yearly fast days until such time that this practice was abandoned by the General Assembly. Fast

[27] *The Scotsman*, 13 Oct. 1875.
[28] Ibid., 24 May 1876.
[29] Thomas Leishman, *May the Kirk Keep Pasche and Yule?* (Edinburgh and London, 1875).
[30] Murray, 'Disruption to Union', p. 100.
[31] Glasgow, Libraries and Archives Department, City Archives [hereafter GCA], CH2/1277/7, Minutes of the Kirk Session of Govan Parish Church, 16 Jan. 1884, 28 March 1884.
[32] George B. Burnet, *The Holy Communion in the Reformed Church of Scotland, 1560–1960* (Edinburgh, 1960), pp. 39–41, 278. Cf. Murray, 'The Catholic tradition of the Kirk', pp. 524–5.

days were held on the Thursdays before the traditional celebrations of communion in the spring and the autumn; but by the middle of the nineteenth century they had become public holidays, with most of the population using them for leisure pursuits rather than for spiritual exercises.[33] The presbytery directed that communion should be held half-yearly or quarterly, and with the 'prayers and exhortations usual in Presbyterian Churches'.[34] The synod repeated this judgement, adding that the fast days should also be held.[35] According to Alexander Crawford, there had never been a celebration of communion at Duns without a preparatory service, and he had not thought that these services had to be held on fast days. In addition, communion had always been celebrated with the fencing of the tables.[36] Macleod had no doubt included an exhortation which had stressed the invitation to communicate rather than warning against unworthy participation. Thomas Leishman pointed out that there was no law of the Church about fast days. There was a treatise on fasting in Knox's *Book of Common Order*, but not in relation to the sacrament; and the *Westminster Directory* said that there should be a day of preparation before communion but did not specify a fast day.[37] Leishman did not point out, however, that some kirk sessions in the period following the Reformation did celebrate the sacrament in connection with a public fast.[38]

The General Assembly upheld the judgement of the presbytery and of the synod in relation to the celebration of communion at Duns. The observance of fast days, as the petitioners at Duns recognized, was on the way out in the Church of Scotland. John Macleod led the movement to abolish this custom in Glasgow in 1884, and the presbytery of Edinburgh would follow in 1887.[39] The traditional fencing of the tables also began to disappear, and the emphasis came

---

[33] Burnet, *The Holy Communion*, p. 289.

[34] SRO, PD, 20 July 1875.

[35] SRO, CH2/265/7, Minutes of the Synod of Merse and Teviotdale, 12 Oct. 1875.

[36] *The Scotsman*, 13 Oct. 1875.

[37] Ibid., 24 May 1876. Cf. George W. Sprott and Thomas Leishman, eds, *The Book of Common Order of the Church of Scotland, commonly known as John Knox's Liturgy, and The Directory for the Public Worship of God agreed upon by the Assembly of Divines at Westminster* (Edinburgh and London, 1868), pp. lii–liii, 150–91, 348–50.

[38] William McMillan, *The Worship of the Scottish Reformed Church, 1550–1638* (London, 1931), p. 333.

[39] Burnet, *Holy Communion*, p. 290; R. S. Kirkpatrick, *The Ministry of Dr. John Macleod in the Parish of Govan* (Edinburgh, 1915), p. 59.

to be placed more on an invitation to participate in the sacrament.[40] The more frequent celebration of communion was also a developing trend in the Kirk. Macleod introduced a monthly communion at Govan in 1884, and by the end of his ministry there were a total of eighteen celebrations during the year.[41] The judgement in the Duns case thus failed to slow down the pace of change in the Kirk regarding the celebration of the sacrament.

The fourth objection in the petition was to the posture of kneeling by the congregation at the benediction. The petitioners wished a return to the standing position as 'more consonant to Presbyterian belief that the blessing is pronounced by a Christian minister and not by a priest'.[42] The finding of the Church courts was that standing should be adopted since it was the 'immemorial usage' in the Church of Scotland.[43] Thomas Leishman thought that the congregation should be left free to decide which position to adopt. Standing for the benediction, he said, did not become the usual practice until the eighteenth century.[44] It was apparent in the debates on this issue that the reason for the opposition to kneeling was that it implied a 'sacerdotal power' in those who gave the benediction.[45]

The final objection to the forms of worship at Duns was not stated in the petition but lay behind the complaints. As could be seen in the opposition to the symbols on the cover of the communion table, and to the posture at the benediction, the underlying objection was that the innovations implied a different doctrinal standpoint from what was considered to be Presbyterian. J. H. Walker thought that the practices showed a tendency which was not in accordance with the Confession of Faith.[46] Alexander Crawford, however, said that nothing had been done from any idea of 'Ritualism' or from any 'superstitious idea'.[47] The real objection seemed to be to what the changes represented rather than the practices in themselves. Hence the forms of worship

---

[40] Burnet, *Holy Communion*, p. 278; G. W. Sprott, *The Worship and Offices of the Church of Scotland* (Edinburgh and London, 1882), p. 109.

[41] Douglas M. Murray, 'The worship of Govan Parish Church during the ministry of Dr. John Macleod', in Harvey, *Govan Old Parish Church*, p. 19.

[42] DKS, 29 Jan. 1875.

[43] SRO, CH2/265/7, Minutes of the Synod of Merse and Teviotdale, 12 Oct. 1875.

[44] *The Scotsman*, 24 May 1876. Cf. Thomas Leishman, 'The ritual of the Church', in R. H. Story, ed., *The Church of Scotland, Past and Present*, 5 vols (Edinburgh, 1890), 5, p. 401.

[45] *The Scotsman*, 13 Oct. 1875.

[46] Ibid., 14 April 1875.

[47] Ibid., 13 Oct. 1875.

were not so objectionable after the coming of the Revd Robert Stewart, Macleod's successor, later in 1875. Three of the leading petitioners wrote to the presbytery wishing to withdraw their complaints, since they could detect in Mr Stewart none of the 'ritualistic and sacerdotal element' which had given significance to Macleod's innovations.[48] The practices at Duns were seen by others, such as W. R. Pirie (the Pirie of the Act), as rather a continuation of the movement which had been begun by Robert Lee at Greyfriars, and which had inspired the founding of the Church Services Society in 1865.[49] Unless the Assembly took action in this case, he said, there was a danger that 'these extravagances would grow'.[50] The doctrinal basis of the changes at Duns was, however, very different from those at Greyfriars. Lee's theology was 'broad', while Macleod's was 'high'. One of Lee's main concerns in introducing liturgical change was to strengthen the position of the Established Church over against the Free Church and the Episcopal Church.[51] On the other hand, Macleod's practices were based on a desire to promote forms of worship which would promote the Catholic faith of the Church.[52] As would become apparent in his ministry at Govan, it was the doctrinal basis of worship which was of primary importance. The underlying basis of liturgical reform was therefore crucial, but it was rather different from that envisaged by the opponents of change.

Following the Assembly of 1876 the forms of worship at Duns were brought into line with the decision of the Church courts. Robert Stewart, the new minister, reported to the presbytery that 'In the forms and time of worship, there is nothing that is not thoroughly Presbyterian, and the Duns Church is now as destitute of adornment as any other ecclesiastical structure in Scotland.'[53] Stewart concluded by saying that the congregation was 'thoroughly evangelical in its doctrine, thoroughly impatient of sacerdotalism, and thoroughly free from symbol worship'.

At Govan Macleod proceeded to introduce many of the practices which he had observed at Duns, such as the use of an organ, changing

---

[48] Ibid., 8 Dec. 1875.
[49] Murray, 'Disruption to Union', pp. 91–7.
[50] *The Scotsman*, 24 May 1876.
[51] Murray, 'Disruption to Union', p. 91; Fleming, *The Church in Scotland*, p. 119.
[52] Edinburgh, New College Library, Church Service Society Papers, Letter No. 46, J. Macleod–G. W. Sprott, undated.
[53] SRO, PD, 13 July 1876.

the posture of the congregation at prayer and for singing, the observance of the Christian year and the greater frequency of communion. In addition, a new church building was opened for worship in 1888 and contained a great deal of symbolic decoration. It was designed by the architect R. Rowand Anderson and consisted of a nave, chancel, and baptistery, with stained glass windows executed by Charles E. Kempe portraying various aspects of the gospel in pictures.[54] Above all, at Govan as at Duns, Macleod sought to explain the doctrinal basis of worship to the congregation in a series of sermons and addresses.[55] Changes in worship, said Macleod, would give him little satisfaction 'apart from the conviction that the grounds on which they rest are intelligently received'.[56] According to his fellow High Churchman, James Cooper, Macleod never undervalued preaching and never disparaged doctrine. He was totally removed from the position of the mere aesthete: 'If he sought beauty, it was never for its own sake – but only and always as a means to set more fully the truth which God had revealed.'[57] Macleod was a faithful preacher and pastor and his liturgical changes were received by the congregation because he did not neglect these traditional roles of the parish minister.

When opposition to his ministry at Govan surfaced, it was from a very small number of parishioners, twenty-six out of a total membership of 1,724.[58] Complaint was made to the presbytery of Glasgow in 1884 about the 'irregular dispensation' of communion and the holding of special services during the week. Macleod, however, could point to the unity of the congregation and the support of the kirk session for the changes which had been made. He had, he said, 'devoted himself in the main, not to changes in external form', but to 'the higher and more spiritual departments of pastoral work'.[59] The presbytery dismissed the petition.[60] The only other complaint to be made to the presbytery was in the following year, concerning Macleod's doctrinal views of Purgatory and prayers for the dead, and alluded to his membership

---

[54] Anthony Wolffe, 'Govan Old Parish Church (1888–1988)', in Harvey, *Govan Old Parish Church*, pp. 23–30.

[55] Murray, 'The worship of Govan Parish Church', pp. 15–18.

[56] Kirkpatrick, *Ministry of Dr. John Macleod*, p. 30.

[57] James Cooper, *The Christian's Love for the House of God* (Edinburgh, 1904), p. 33.

[58] *The Glasgow Herald*, 8 May 1884; GCA, Minutes of the Kirk Session of Govan Parish Church, 25 March 1884.

[59] *The Glasgow Herald*, 12 June 1884.

[60] GCA, CH2/171/11, Minutes of the Presbytery of Glasgow, 11 June 1884.

of the Catholic Apostolic Church.[61] This petition was not received by the presbytery on procedural grounds and the petitioners appealed unsuccessfully against this decision to the synod of Glasgow and Ayr and the General Assembly in 1885.[62] Macleod answered the accusations against him in a letter which was published in *The Glasgow Herald*.[63] He denied teaching either a belief in a purgatorial state after death, or that the prayers of the living influenced the state of the dead. He did not deny or confirm that he was a member of the Catholic Apostolic Church, but he denied that he had ever followed courses which could be proved to be divisive or at variance with his position as a loyal minister of the Church of Scotland.

As at Duns, the underlying reason for the objections to Macleod's ministry at Govan was because his views were thought to be 'inconsistent with the Protestant Faith'.[64] Yet his doctrinal position was not condemned by the courts of the Church. Furthermore, the practices which had been prohibited at Duns were not condemned at Govan, and came to be widely practised in the Kirk. During the course of the Duns case, however, Macleod watched the events anxiously from a distance, and was in regular contact with his friend George Sprott.[65] According to James Cooper the case clouded his soul for some time; and although the verdict was thought at the time to be a calamity, it would later be seen 'as a mere absurdity'.[66] The case failed to stop the progress of change in the worship of the Kirk. The supporters of liturgical reform had been able to show that many of the practices were in continuity with the Reformed tradition of the Kirk, and that in addition Macleod had given priority to the traditional tasks of the parish ministry.

The University of Glasgow

---

[61] Ibid., 25 March 1885.

[62] *Acts of the General Assembly of the Church of Scotland 1885* (Edinburgh, 1885), p. 56.

[63] *The Glasgow Herald*, 25 May 1885.

[64] SRO, CH1/2/305(i), General Assembly Papers, Church Cases, 1885, p. 29.

[65] G. W. Sprott, *The Doctrine of Schism in the Church of Scotland* (Edinburgh, 1902), p. 63; New College Library, Church Service Society Papers, Letters 33, 42, J. Macleod–G. W. Sprott, and fragments, 1875–6.

[66] Cooper, *Christian's Love for the House of God*, p. 35.

ANGLICAN WORSHIP IN LATE NINETEENTH-CENTURY WALES: A MONTGOMERYSHIRE CASE STUDY

by FRANCES KNIGHT

I N 1910, the *Royal Commission on the Church of England and the Other Religious Bodies in Wales and Monmouth* revealed that the Church of England was the largest religious body in Wales, and attracted over a quarter of all worshippers.[1] This indicated a significant improvement in the Church's fortunes in the previous half century, and a different picture from that which had emerged from the 1851 Census of Religious Worship, which had suggested that the established Church had the support of only twenty per cent of Welsh worshippers.[2] The purpose of this paper is to shed some light upon the Church's improving fortunes between 1851 and 1910 by exploring the liturgical patterns which were evolving in a particular Welsh county, Montgomeryshire, in the late nineteenth century. Montgomeryshire is part of the large rural heart of mid-Wales, bordered by Radnor to the south, Cardigan and Merioneth to the west, Denbigh to the north, and Shropshire to the east. The paper considers the annual, monthly, and weekly liturgical cycles which were developing in the county, and how the co-existence of the Welsh and English languages was expressed in different styles of church music and worship.

At three o'clock on Easter Sunday 1895, the Revd William Gwynne Vaughan read himself in as vicar of Bettws Cedewain, a rural parish near Newtown in Montgomeryshire. Like many clergy in the county, he was young, and a graduate of St David's College, Lampeter. Vaughan's first year in the parish was to be characterized by liturgical innovation. On his first Sunday he introduced coloured stoles, and in

---

[1] *Royal Commission on the Church of England and the Other Religious Bodies in Wales and Monmouthshire*, 8 vols in 9, *Parliamentary Papers*, 14 (London, 1910–11), 1, p. 20.

[2] P. M. H. Bell, *Disestablishment in Ireland and Wales* (London, 1969), p. 236; E. T. Davies, *A New History of Wales: Religion and Society in the Nineteenth Century* (Llandybie, 1981), pp. 27–34; D. T. W. Price, *A History of the Church in Wales in the Twentieth Century* (Penarth, 1990), p. 2; Matthew Cragoe, *An Anglican Aristocracy: The Moral Economy of the Landed Estate in Carmarthenshire 1832–1895* (Oxford, 1996), p. 191; idem, 'A question of culture: the Welsh Church and the bishopric of St Asaph, 1870', *The Welsh History Review*, 18 (1996), p. 228.

the months which followed he promoted a high level of liturgical activity. The Sunday pattern was fortnightly holy communion, either at 8.30am or at 11.00am after mattins. If there was no communion, Mattins would be followed by the litany. Sunday school was at 2.30pm, evensong at 6.00pm, and choir practice at 8.00pm. Once a month, there was a special children's service at 3.00pm. The biggest congregation was at Evensong, when there would be over one hundred present (the population of the parish was five hundred). The smallest was at holy communion, where there were usually fewer than ten communicants. Like many other Anglican clergy at this period, Vaughan regarded increasing the number of communicants as a top priority. On Easter Day 1896, after a year in the parish, a note in the service register expressed pleasure at having increased the number of communicants by fourteen to forty-eight.[3] 150 worshippers attended the biggest service of the day, the 'fully choral' Easter Evensong.

Under Vaughan's direction the parish had prepared for Easter 1896 with considerable seriousness. Two Ash Wednesday services were held, and during Lent the meetings of the Guild of St Bueno, a Wednesday evening group which Vaughan had formed 'for prayers, Bible reading, church history and amusements', were suspended in order to make way for an evening service. Holy Week was observed with daily Mattins and ante-communion, and additional choir practices. On Good Friday, a three-hours service was held, with a 'very satisfactory' attendance of fifty-four. It was the first time that such a service had taken place at Bettws Cedewain. In the evening, the choir gave a performance of *The Story of the Cross*, a Good Friday choral work which they were to repeat each Easter in subsequent years.

Elsewhere in Montgomeryshire, Easter in the 1890s was marked in a similar fashion. It was not, however, to be the Easter services which attracted the biggest congregations. The largest crowds were reserved for harvest festivals, which in the late nineteenth century were sometimes large communal celebrations which lasted for several days.[4] In November 1880, the Berriew parish magazine reported that the church had been 'tastefully decorated' with evergreens, corn,

[3] Aberystwyth, National Library of Wales [hereafter NLW], St Asaph Parochial Records [hereafter St APR]: Bettws Cedewain 93, Service Register 1895–1901 (no foliation). All the material relating to Bettws Cedewain has come from this service register.

[4] R. W. Ambler, 'The transformation of harvest celebrations in nineteenth-century Lincolnshire', *Midland History*, 3 (1975–6), pp. 298–306.

fruit, vegetables, flowers, and bread and butter.[5] Everywhere, worshippers thronged the churches.[6] At Llanllwchaiarn, the attendance at the 1885 harvest festival was described as the 'largest congregation ever seen in this church within the memory of man', and in 1894 it was described as 'overflowing'.[7] At Bettws Cedewain there were usually about three hundred at the principal service on Friday evening; in the late 1890s there was never any standing room, and crowds gathered in the churchyard. 1896 was a typical year, in which the church's celebrations began on Friday 18 September, with two communion services, one at 8.30am and one at 11.00am, producing between them 102 communicants. There was luncheon in the schoolroom, and then an intoned litany at 3.00pm, followed by an organ recital with sacred solos and quartets. Tea followed, and then at 6.30pm Evensong – a service with no standing room. On Saturday, there was a mission service with magic lantern at the schoolroom, which raised money for the Church Army. On Sunday the harvest festival services of the previous Friday were repeated, with another large crowd attending in the evening. This was followed by a final mission meeting, organized by the Church Army.

William Gwynne Vaughan's approach to his parishioners' enthusiasm for harvest celebrations was supportive, but he also tried to steer it in an ecclesiastical direction. Thus harvest became an occasion for the best-attended communion services of the year, and also to raise awareness of missionary work. Many of the Welsh clergy were the sons of farmers and most had been brought up in rural Wales, and they were therefore naturally in sympathy with the harvest-time mood of their parishioners.[8] They would not be likely to ridicule it as 'the Feast of St Pumpkin' or to have wondered, with Henry Scott Holland, why 'we only have to wave a potato round our head and the church is

---

[5] NLW St APR: Berriew 119, *Berriew Parish Magazine*, Nov. 1880.

[6] The desire to celebrate the harvest was not restricted to the countryside. Jeffrey Cox has shown that harvest festival was also the most popular service in inner Lambeth at this period. See Jeffrey Cox, *The English Churches in a Secular Society: Lambeth 1870–1930* (Oxford, 1982), pp. 103–4.

[7] NLW St APR: Llanllwchaiarn 12, Service Register 1884–1901 (no foliation).

[8] Throughout the period from 1827 to 1897 more of the students admitted at St David's College Lampeter were the sons of farmers than any other occupational category. See D. T. W. Price, *A History of St David's University College Volume I: to 1898* (Cardiff, 1977), pp. 207–10. See also D. Parry-Jones, *Welsh Country Upbringing* (London, 1948), pp. 77–8 for an account of Anglican harvest celebrations in Carmarthenshire in the 1890s.

packed from end to end'.[9] The Anglican liturgical cycle in Montgomeryshire at this period was therefore marked by major celebrations at harvest and, to a lesser extent, at Easter. Advent and Christmas were less keenly observed, varying from parish to parish. Richard Gibbings at Llanmerewig introduced week-night services in Advent from 1896, but this seems to have been unusual.[10] There were no special services in the days immediately before Christmas, and the number of Christmas Day communicants was often quite small. At Bettws Cedewain on Christmas Day 1895, there were thirty-five communicants out of the fifty-three who came to church. Much more important in Welsh society was '*Dydd Calan*' – New Year's Day – and '*Calan Hen*' – old New Year's day, on 12 January.[11] Bettws Cedewain was probably not the only church which held social events and bell ringing to see in the new year, and in many places carols were sung at Epiphany.

During the 1890s and 1900s, it became increasingly common throughout Montgomeryshire to hold services on Ash Wednesday and Ascension Day, and to mark major saints' days with an early communion service. For the rest of the year the Sunday pattern was morning prayer at about 11am, evening prayer at about 6pm, a monthly service for children, and a monthly communion service. The most obvious trend at this time was the gradual introduction of weekly or fortnightly communion. As in England, the enthusiasm of the clergy for more communion services was rarely shared by the laity.[12] There were usually twice as many people at the service as there were communicants. At Llanwddyn, 1900 was the year when weekly communion was introduced, and the communicants' register reveals that of the approximately sixty-five communicants in the parish, only four began to receive three or four times a month. They were the vicar, a female member of his family, the parish clerk, and another female worshipper.[13] In Montgomeryshire, the service of

[9] Henry Scott Holland, *A Bundle of Memories* (n.p., 1915), p. 250. Cited by Cox, *English Churches in a Secular Society*, p. 103. Cox makes the point that Scott Holland was gently ridiculing the clergy who took this position, not expressing the view as his own.

[10] NLW St APR: Llanmerewig 7, Service Register 1890–1905 (no foliation).

[11] Trefor M. Owen, *Welsh Folk Customs* (Cardiff, 1959), pp. 41–7; Parry-Jones, *Welsh Country Upbringing*, pp. 75–6, 78–9.

[12] See Frances Knight, *The Nineteenth-Century Church and English Society* (Cambridge, 1995), pp. 35–6, 81, 203, for a discussion of this phenomenon.

[13] NLW St APR: Llanwddyn 5, Service Register 1899–1907 (no foliation). Many of the service registers contain communicants' registers at the back, and they were often diligently completed by the clergy.

choice of the majority of Church worshippers was undoubtedly choral Evensong.

This was a reflection of the great interest in singing which is evident among many of the Anglican worshippers of late Victorian Montgomeryshire. It may have been the result of an attempt to prevent all the musical life of the community being focused upon the chapel. In practice, the shared interest in music probably resulted in an improvement in relations between the church and chapel, as Matthew Cragoe has suggested in the context of Carmarthenshire.[14] Every church had its choir, and a great deal of the congregation's resources, both in time and money, were devoted to maintaining and improving the standard of the music.[15] At Llanwddyn, in addition to the established Victorian composers such as Stainer and Crotch, the choir performed chant by the early eighteenth-century composer Luke Flintoft, so-called 'Spanish chant', settings by Tallis, and music by Spohr and Gounod. All this was in addition to the performance of material in Welsh. Choirs made their distinct contribution to Sunday worship, and often prepared ambitious programmes for Easter, harvest, and Christmas. It was clearly understood that choral services attracted large congregations, and so they were crucial to the church's mission. Choirs developed their own momentum; at Llanwddyn they had a separate weekly Bible class, in addition to their schedule of rehearsals.[16] They also had their social side, with choristers entertained by the clergy at new year choir suppers, and children treated to outings to Aberystwyth. Concerts were important for fund-raising. Every New Year's Eve the singers at Bettws Cedewain gave a concert in aid of the new National school.[17] At Newtown, the parish council used a financial surplus accrued from the choral festival to pay off a debt on the new vestry and to buy stained glass for the east window.[18]

Church choirs played a wider role in local society by representing

[14] Cragoe, *Anglican Aristocracy*, p. 244. See also Owen, *Welsh Folk Customs*, p. 33, where it is noted that in Caernarfonshire, Merionethshire, and Montgomeryshire the parish church *plygain* attracted both church and chapel people, this being one of the few days when religious differences were laid aside.

[15] NLW St APR: Llanwddyn 4, Service Register 1891–9. Accounts at the back of the register reveal how much was spent on the choir.

[16] NLW St APR: Llanwddyn 48, Church Choir Book 1893–6 (no foliation).

[17] NLW St APR: Bettws Cedewain 93, Service Register 1895–1901 (no foliation).

[18] NLW St APR: Newtown 8, Parish Council Minute Book 1878–85, entry for 25 Aug. 1884.

their church at choral festivals, which were major events in the local calendar. There were separate English and Welsh events, usually a few weeks apart, reflecting the co-existence of two completely different musical traditions. The *plygain* (a service of Christmas music, traditionally sung in the early morning), the *cymanfa ganu* (hymn-singing festival), and the *eisteddfod* (a competitive arts festival) provided important occasions for Welsh religious singing.[19] In the deanery of Cedewain, the parishes in the eastern portion held an English choral festival and the parishes in the western portion one in Welsh.[20] A similar arrangement took place in the deanery of Llanfyllin, with the bilingual choir of Llanwddyn taking part in both.[21] The Newtown choral festival, which began in the late 1870s, aimed to promote the English cathedral sound in this anglicized Welsh town.[22] No expense was spared to further this objective; the parish church appointed a new organist to train their boys' choir, and other local choirs, in order to get them to an appropriate standard for the festival. They paid him £50 a year plus a complimentary offertory, and he also took pupils. When he left they advertised the post nationally in *The Musical Times*.[23] In 1881, in preparation for the festival, they spent £46 having the Willis organ cleaned and repaired, £45 adding a new bourdon stop to the instrument, and £20 hiring 'Special Cathedral Singers'. The money came from private subscription.[24] In 1883, the church council invited Sir Frederick Ouseley, one of the most celebrated church musicians in Victorian Britain, to give an address at the festival.[25]

The co-existence of parallel traditions of English and Welsh musicmaking in Montgomeryshire raises questions about language in worship among the Anglicans in the county. It is evident that the provision of separate, and virtually equally balanced, English- and Welsh-medium

---

[19] See Owen, *Welsh Folk Customs*, pp. 28–35 for the *plygain*. Traditionally associated with Christmas morning, in late Victorian Montgomeryshire it more usually took place in early January.

[20] NLW St APR: Manafon 6, Ready Reference Register 1905–14 (no foliation).

[21] NLW St APR: Llanwddyn 48, Church Choir Book 1893–6 (no foliation).

[22] Peter Crossley-Holland, 'Wales', in Stanley Sadie, ed., *The New Grove Dictionary of Music and Musicians* (London, 1980), 20, pp. 159–71, states that the Newtown Festival began in 1920. Presumably the choral festival of the 1870s was a precursor of the later festival, helping to lay the foundations for the town's musical tradition.

[23] NLW St APR: Newtown 8, Parish Council Minute Book 1878–85. Entries for 6 June 1878, 14 Aug. 1879.

[24] Ibid., entries for 7 April, 23 June, 8 Aug. 1881.

[25] Ibid., entry for 20 Aug. 1883.

worship had existed in the county for some decades. Forty-eight Anglican places of worship in Montgomeryshire may be identified from the census returns of 1851.[26] Seventeen of these only held services in English, nineteen only used Welsh, and twelve used both English and Welsh, although the two languages were not mixed (officially at least) at the same service. A clear picture of liturgical language use at mid-century emerges. Welsh only was used in the parishes around Llanidloes in the south-west, and Pennant Melangell in the north west. The parishes in the Newtown area, and eastwards into Shropshire, used English exclusively. Parishes on the border, such as Llandyssil, Berriew, and Welshpool, also used English. The parishes in Llanfyllin registration district, in the north east and central regions of the county, were most likely to provide services in both languages. Here the most common pattern was to offer services alternately in English and Welsh. Meifod, in the north of the county, was typical of a parish making this form of provision. The vicar, Richard Richards, reported on his Census form that 'The morning congregation, whether Welsh or English, is always largest.'[27]

This pattern of more or less equal provision of services in Welsh and English was sustained for the next thirty years, until 1880, when there began to be a dramatic increase in the amount of English used. Statistics derived from the diocese of St Asaph, of which most of Montgomeryshire was a part, reveal the extent of this development. In 1880, 274 English Sunday services were recorded as having taken place in the diocese, and 259 in Welsh – a mere fifteen more. By 1890, 394 English Sunday services were recorded, a sharp contrast with the 264 Welsh ones – 130 more.[28] Another ten years would see an even greater acceleration in English-medium worship, with an accompanying drop in provision for Welsh speakers. In the 1910 Report on the Welsh Church the number of English services in the diocese was recorded as

[26] Data derived from Ieuan Gwynedd Jones, ed., *The Religious Census of 1851: A Calendar of the Returns Relating to Wales, Vol. II North Wales* (Cardiff, 1981). The 1851 Census did not ask a question about the language in which services were conducted, but this deficiency has been overcome in Jones' edition of the Census by means of the incorporation of data taken from a government report of 1849, entitled *Number of Services performed in each Church and Chapel [in Wales]*. See Ieuan Gwynedd Jones, ed., *The Religious Census of 1851: A Calendar of the Returns Relating to Wales, Vol. I South Wales* (Cardiff, 1976), p. xxxii.

[27] Ibid., p. 83. It is also worth noting that 85% of the parishes in Montgomeryshire are recorded as holding two or more Sunday services in 1851.

[28] NLW St APR: Berriew 101.

443, and the number of Welsh as 236 – 207 more.[29] Unsurprisingly, the increase in the amount of English used at worship in the more anglicized Montgomeryshire was even greater than in the rest of St Asaph, which encompassed the more solidly Welsh-speaking county of Denbigh, as well as parts of Merioneth and Caernarfon.

Paradoxically, this acceleration in the amount of English-medium worship happened just at the moment when, it has been argued, the cultural transformation of the Church from being upper-class and English to being middle-class and Welsh was reaching completion.[30] This was particularly symbolized in 1870 when, after a protracted selection process, Gladstone appointed Joshua Hughes to St Asaph: he was the first Welsh-speaking Welshman to preside over a Welsh diocese since the time of Queen Anne. No longer was it sufficient for an English bishop in Wales to learn Welsh like Connop Thirlwall, or to brush up his previous knowledge, like Alfred Ollivant. By 1870, the majority view was that he should be of the same blood as the people of Wales.[31] Hughes was selected as Bishop of St Asaph because he was believed to be a good Welsh preacher, just at the moment when it appeared that his diocese would have a greater demand for good English preachers.[32]

The suddenly increased emphasis on English-medium worship in St Asaph sits uneasily with the strongly-held belief that Welsh was the language of religion. In the nineteenth century, the spectacular success of Nonconformity in Wales, and particularly Calvinistic Methodism, was attributed to their use of Welsh. Welsh was the language which God had providentially appointed in order to speak to the people of Wales. It followed that the use of English resulted in a dilution of God's revelation, and the exposure of the faith to all manner of hostile alien influences. Furthermore, Welsh was regarded as a Protestant language. It had been the language of the Reformation, and it could be traced back to the Celtic Church, which was also idealized as untainted

---

[29] *Royal Commission on the Church of England and Other Religious Bodies in Wales and Monmouthshire*, 1, p. 20.

[30] Cragoe, 'Question of culture', p. 231.

[31] Ibid., pp. 230–2. See pp. 231–44 for a discussion of the way in which the relationship between Welsh identity and the Church changed in the period from the 1840s to the 1870s.

[32] Commenting on Hughes's appointment, the *Globe* remarked that it was not by 'pandering to the Dissenters' love of extempore preaching' that people would be bought back to the Church, but by 'gratifying the national taste for music and singing'. Both Churchmen and Dissenters would be attracted to 'a hearty choral Church Service'. Quoted in *The Times*, 18 March 1870, and cited by Cragoe, 'Question of culture', p. 252.

by Rome.[33] Observers regarded it as a matter of no surprise that the Welsh Church should have been overtaken by Nonconformity after 1715, when non-Welsh-speaking Englishmen began to be appointed as bishops. The extent to which these views had been accepted by Anglicans in the second half of the nineteenth century is, of course, reflected in the campaign for a Welshman for the sees of St Asaph in 1870 and Llandaff in 1883, and in the continued importance which was given to the training and promotion of Welsh-speaking clergy.

By the 1890s, however, the picture had become more complicated. An influx of monoglot English speakers contributed to a fall in the percentage of Welsh speakers in Wales, who were estimated at 54 per cent of the population in 1891, 50 per cent in 1901 and 44 per cent in 1911.[34] It was becoming clear that English influences could not be contained at Offa's Dyke. Indeed, by the end of the century English was once more being seen in some quarters as the language of social prestige, and Anglicans were particularly susceptible to this type of cultural shift. But they were not alone. Ieuan Gwynedd Jones has noted that by the 1890s even some Nonconformist ministers were making strenuous efforts to perfect their command of English, and were using it on every possible occasion.[35]

In Montgomeryshire, where 52 per cent of the population were monoglot English speakers in 1901, the clergy had already responded with an increase in the provision of English-medium worship. As has already been shown, many of the parishes in the east of the county and around Newtown had used no Welsh at mid-century, and they did not attempt to introduce Welsh-medium worship in the second half of the century.[36] Bettws Cedewain, where two services in Welsh had been held at mid-century, had entirely switched to using English by 1871; and by the time Vaughan arrived in 1895 it was very firmly part of the English language belt.[37] Llanwddyn had also only used Welsh at mid-

---

[33] Ieuan Gwynedd Jones, 'Language and community in nineteenth-century Wales', in Ieuan Gwynedd Jones, ed., *Mid-Victorian Wales: The Observers and the Observed* (Cardiff, 1992), pp. 59–63.

[34] Ibid., p. 56. Jones makes the point that due to overall population growth, there were still more people who could speak Welsh in 1901 than there had been in 1801.

[35] Ibid., p. 67.

[36] This is apparent from NLW St APR: Berriew 101.

[37] Jones, *Religious Census of 1851, Vol. II*, p. 38 and NLW St APR: Berriew 101. The switch of language may have occurred in 1854 when Henry James Marshall of Corpus Christi Oxford became vicar. See D. R. Thomas, *A History of the Diocese of St Asaph* (London, 1874), p. 319.

century, but had introduced an English service in addition to the Welsh at some point between 1877 and 1880.[38] They experimented with bilingual worship; by 1891 Sunday services were being held at 10am, 11.30am and 6pm, with six different liturgical combinations used in rotation. They were: Welsh Mattins and sermon; English holy communion with litany and sermon; English Evensong and Welsh sermon; Welsh litany, ante-communion and sermon; English Mattins and sermon and Welsh Evensong and English sermon.[39] Change did not always come this early, however. Llangadfan, a parish with a population of 354 in the west of the county, may have been among the last Anglican churches in Montgomeryshire to abandon a Welsh-only policy. English services were introduced for the first time in 1913.[40]

One reason for increasing the amount of English-medium provision may sometimes have been financial. This was an unwelcome recognition of the voluntary nature of Welsh religion. The vicar of Llanwddyn kept a separate note of the amounts raised from collections at English and Welsh services. About the same number of collections were held each year; but in 1891–2 the English collection produced £27 2s. 4d. whereas the Welsh merely yielded £4 4s. 9d. In the financial year 1898–9, when the parish accounts had been in deficit for the previous two years, it was decided to step up the number of English collections. The result was a considerable increase in the overall amount of giving from £27 1s. 7d. in 1897–8 to £45 6s. 3d. in the next financial year. This was achieved from forty-two English collections which had yielded £36 0s. 11d. and twenty-eight Welsh ones which had produced £8 15s. 4d.[41] The overdraft was cleared. It was probably also the case that those English-medium worshippers who had paid the piper were also calling the tune. In November 1902, the first of what was to become a regular feature in the service register was recorded, a 'special service for English people', presumably one in which no Welsh at all was used. In the previous year, the vicar had also established separate English and Welsh children's services, thus encouraging from an early age the division of his congregation along linguistic and ethnic lines.

The experimental reintroduction of Welsh to English-speaking parishes, which was likely to be attempted by enthusiastic Lampeter

---

[38] NLW St APR: Berriew 101.
[39] NLW St APR: Llanwddyn 4, Service Register 1891–9 (no foliation).
[40] NLW St APR: Llangadfan 6, Service Register 1910–31 (no foliation).
[41] Ibid.

graduates, also appears to have been short-lived. Welsh services at Manafon, for example, had ceased at some point between 1877 and 1880. William Morgan tried to reintroduce a Welsh Sunday evening service when he arrived in the parish in 1905, but attendances dwindled, and he gave up the experiment in 1907. He began to put his energies into the Mothers' Union, the Church Defence League, and English church music.[42]

It is evident that Anglican worship in late nineteenth-century Montgomeryshire was undergoing a period of rapid transition. For many worshippers the high points in the calendar remained the traditional festivals of harvest and new year, although the numerous liturgical innovations which now clustered around Lent and Easter would certainly have made their mark on regular churchgoers. The Welsh clergy were usually sympathetic to existing popular custom, and welcomed the large crowds who turned up at harvest. Nevertheless, it was unsurprising that by the end of the century clergy should have been giving new emphasis to the other seasons in the Church's year. They experimented with additional services and more frequent communions, which resulted in a new prominence for Ash Wednesday, Holy Week, Easter, and Ascension, and in some cases also for saints' days. The energy of this largely young or middle-aged body of clergymen is reflected in the support which they gave to an ambitious variety of liturgical, musical, and social activities; and they drew quite naturally on both the Welsh and the English traditions. It was the particular task of the Welsh Church to minister to people from a number of distinctly different backgrounds, who used, with varying degrees of proficiency, two very different languages. In a border county such as Montgomeryshire, the issues which arose from this would be resolved differently in different parishes, but it was clear that despite the attempts to make the Welsh Church more Welsh, it was still very ready to assimilate the influences of its English neighbour.

University of Wales, Lampeter

---

[42] NLW St APR: Manafon 6, Ready Reference Register 1905–14 (no foliation).

'WALKING IN THE LIGHT': THE LITURGY OF FELLOWSHIP IN THE EARLY YEARS OF THE EAST AFRICAN REVIVAL

by EMMA L. WILD

URING a Christmas convention at Gahini mission station in Rwanda in 1933, a large number of people publicly confessed their sins, resolved to turn from their present beliefs and embraced the Christian Faith. From then on, missionaries of the Ruanda Mission wrote enthusiastically to their supporters in Britain of people flocking into churches in South-West Uganda and Rwanda, of 'changed lives', of emotional confessions followed by 'tremendous joy', and of the spontaneous forming of fellowship groups and mission teams.[1] Ugandans working at Gahini saw an opportunity for 'waking' the sleeping Anglican Church in Buganda and elsewhere which had, they believed, lost its fervour. Following in the tradition of the evangelists of the 1880s and 1890s they travelled vast distances to share their message of repentance and forgiveness with others. This was the beginning of the East African Revival, long prayed for by Ruanda missionaries and the Ugandans who worked alongside them. Max Warren, General Secretary of the Church Missionary Society, writing in 1954 when the Revival was still pulsating through East Africa, perceived the revival phenomenon as 'a reaffirmation of theology, a resuscitation of worship and a reviving of conscience . . . for the church'.[2] All three were in evidence from the early years of the East African Revival, but perhaps the most dramatic change was the form taken by the 'resuscitation of worship'.

Studies of the Revival have emphasised the similarity of its worship with the evangelical Anglican tradition brought to and spread from Buganda since 1877. Zeb Kabaza, an influential elder in the revival movement, was a teenager in the 1930s. He believes that 'the worship in the church didn't change' as a result of revival, it continued its

---

[1] The Ruanda Mission (CMS) worked in Rwanda and in South-West Uganda. It used the colonial spelling for Ruanda which has been retained when referring to it and its missionaries. For the country and its people the present spelling has been used.

[2] M. Warren, *What is Revival? An Enquiry* (London, 1954), p. 20.

familiar pattern of solemn Prayer Book worship.[3] The influence of the
Keswick spirituality of the Ruanda missionaries on the revivalists has
been stressed. Keswick was known for its testimonies, temperance, and
fellowship and all these are present in the East African Revival. Such
teaching may have acted as a catalyst for the spontaneous and popular
acceptance of Christianity but it does not sufficently explain the
Revival phenomonen. An assessment of elements of traditional African
worship and belief present in the Revival is fundamental to such an
understanding but it has often been neglected, not least because the
revivalists themselves declared a complete break from their 'evil',
'pagan' past. Despite this they naturally and unconsciously permeated
Revival Christianity with patterns of worship learned from their own
tradition, and which were remodelled on their contact with British
revivalism. Traditional worship fused with Keswick holiness as interpreted by East African Christians brought about an innovative style of
revival worship which developed outside the Prayer Book Sunday
worship. Kabaza says, 'the difference I've seen is the Fellowship
Meeting'. The revivalists, known as 'Balokole' , or 'saved ones',[4]
developed a ritual of regular fellowship which arose from the
spontaneity of the initial conversions and became the hallmark of
the revival in East Africa. By the late 1940s the Fellowship Meeting had
spread from Uganda and Rwanda into Burundi, Tanzania, and Kenya,
following in the wake of the revival. 'A sort of liturgy seems to have
developed', explained one observer, 'in that all meetings, in different
centres follow the same pattern.'[5]

Fellowship Meetings took place two or three times a week. Leaders
were usually lay Christians chosen for their charisma and their good
conduct. Leadership was fluid and a high level of participation was
expected of all members. Whilst people gathered hymns were sung,
starting with what became the theme tune of the revival, 'Tukutendereza Yesu' (We praise you, Jesus). This was followed by a time of
mutual sharing and confession, known as 'walking in the light', which
ended with prayers of thanksgiving for forgiveness. The second part of
the meeting was a Bible Study, preceded by extempore prayer and a
hymn. The meeting ended with the exchange of news, usually

[3] Interview, Kampala, 12 May 1997.
[4] 'Balokole' is the Luganda word most commonly used but each language group has its
own term. 'Balokole' is the plural form, 'mulokole' being the singular.
[5] Warren, *What is Revival?*, p. 118.

including reports on the latest mission and plans for the next one, and the saying of the Grace. Through this 'liturgy of fellowship' the formality of the Prayer Book was complemented by a more relaxed, intimate style of worship, which nevertheless retained a clear order. It has been said of the Revival Fellowship, 'all of its activities were informal yet on the whole uniform.'[6] The following study of two aspects of the Fellowship Meeting, the confession of sins and the hymns, and their effects on worship outside the intimate Fellowship groups, will demonstrate that unity among the Balokole and the ritual of the meeting by which that unity was sustained was the dynamic on which the early Revival was based.

'Walking in the light', the time of sharing experiences and, more particularly, confessing sin, is a unique aspect of Balokole worship. Although similar in many ways to the close fellowship of early Methodists it does not have any direct historical links with this strand of revivalism but rather takes its worship pattern from Traditional Religion. For the Balokole, to confess sins once, at the moment of conversion, was not sufficient. Admitting and repenting of sins committed since the last meeting was part of the ritual. Nothing was to be left hidden, rather Balokole were to 'walk in the light', as instructed in I John 1.7, so that they could 'have fellowship with one another and the blood of Jesus . . . [which] cleanseth from all sin'. To walk in light meant to have communion and transparency between Balokole. The cleansing process demanded ritual confession of sin, starting with the words 'I repent of . . .'. Although it was not part of the official teaching some of the Balokole felt that God's forgiveness was aided by public admission of sin.[7] Salvation, they had been taught by the missionaries, was an individual decision. Their experience, however, taught them that it could not be sustained alone. Unity and frankness with others was part of the salvific process. Confession in Fellowship Meetings was followed by advice or correction from the group, 'putting someone in the light'. The recipient of the correction was expected to receive the criticisms of others in an attitude of 'brokenness'. They were humbly to accept the advice following the example of Jesus. He had been broken for their sin on the cross, likewise they should be broken over their sin.

[6] A. Kagume, 'Church and society in Ankole, Uganda: an analysis of the impact of evangelical Anglican Christianity on ethnic and gender relations in Ankole 1901–1961' (University of Bristol Ph. D. thesis, 1993), p. 155.

[7] H. H. Osborn, *Revival – A Precious Heritage* (Winchester, 1995), p. 84.

Missionaries were not exempt from being 'put in the light' by the Balokole. Dr A. Stanley Smith, a founding member of the Ruanda Mission, was accused by Balokole leaders of being hypocritical and cowardly because he 'gave soft soap to people instead of reproving them of sin'.[8] He 'showed brokenness', but others found it harder to accept correction, especially when challenged about the reality of their own conversion or their arrogance towards Africans. The latter criticism was evidence of a wider trend: the breaking down of racial barriers within the Fellowship groups. The intimacy and trust which was displayed in the frankness of the Fellowship served to reinforce the sense of equality among the members regardless of tribe or race. Cattle keepers and agricultural tribespeople who had been living inter-dependently for centuries in a relationship of mutual usefulness and mistrust were able to break the cycle of suspicion and share meals and property together, much to the chagrin of those outside the Fellowship who saw in this a corruption of traditional values. The tight-knit tribal and clan groupings which gave people their traditional identity were replaced for the Balokole by equally tight-knit egalitarian Fellowship groups. The same religious experience and a commitment to right living in accordance with clear pragmatic rules bound the Balokole together and allowed all members a place of equal importance. Egalitarianism among the Balokole came, at least in part, from the fact that anyone could confess their sins. Since 1877 membership of the Church had been through baptism, which for the first converts involved proof of intellectual aptitude by learning first to read and understand the catechism. 'Kusoma', the verb 'to read', had come to mean 'to worship'. Before the Revival worshippers were those who, having learnt to read, now read from a book in church. The Balokole changed this conception. Women, for example, who had not learnt to read could confess their sins and become members in the Revival movement. They were encouraged to memorize biblical passages and to preach. Moreover, reading the Confession from the Prayer Book was not considered true confession. One could read the words without being sincerely penitent.

During confession sins were often recounted in graphic detail. Stealing, dishonesty, and tribal hatred were frequent themes, but drunkenness and sexual misdemeanours were also common. Mission-aries and non-saved alike were horrified by the vivid descriptions some

[8] Ibid., p. 100.

Balokole gave when recounting their sins. Joe Church, the missionary most closely associated with the Revival, accepts these zealous confessions as a sign of true repentance, believing that conviction of sin 'makes people do what no self-respecting African does: confess sins no-one knew about!'[9] In this, however, Church exhibits his lack of knowledge of African Traditional Religion. To him it was all evil paganism. In fact one aspect of African Traditional Religion which had been growing in importance during the previous century hinged upon a radical acceptance of wrong before one was worthy of worship. By the twentieth century there was a powerful cult worship which spread from south-west Tanzania, through Rwanda, Kigezi, Ankole, and into parts of Buganda; exactly the areas in which the Revival was strongest. The spirits worshipped were the Emandwa of the ancient royal Cwezi dynasty. Through them the creator God was made immanent to worshippers, and each family had at least one initiate to intercede on their behalf. The initiation ceremony lasted several days and was surrounded by much feasting, singing, and dancing. At the central point of the ceremony the initiates were expected to confess the shameful things that they had done, from theft to inappropriate sexual intercourse. Confession was often graphic, and accompanied by play-acting the shameful deeds.[10] These revelations were seen as a means of purification in which the former life was set aside and the initiates entered a world 'totally independent from the norms of secular society'[11] to become part of the family of initiates. Many of the Balokole had been Emandwa cult initiates,[12] and despite their rejection of all things 'pagan' they had necessarily brought to their new faith some elements of the old. The beer drinking and tobacco smoking which was part of the original ceremony was condemned; but the rite of entry into an elite cult by the open confession of shameful sins remained intact and became the hallmark of the early revivalists. Initiation into the Christian religion, like initiation into Emandwa cult, was seen as new birth, a break with old customs, a cathartic act on the

---

[9] J. E. Church, *Quest for the Highest: A Diary of the East African Revival* (Exeter, 1981), p. 136.

[10] D. J. Stenning, 'Salvation in Ankole', in M. Fortes and G. Dieterlen, eds, *African Systems of Thought* (Oxford, 1965), pp. 263–4.

[11] B. Turyahikayo-Kigyewa, *Philosophy and Traditional Religion of the Bakiga* (Nairobi, 1983), p. 40.

[12] Y. K. Bamunoba and F. B. Welbourn, 'Emandwa initiation in Ankole', *Uganda Journal*, 29 (1965), p. 13.

threshold of a new life, and an entry into intimate fellowship with other members.

The Balokole initiation differed in that its cult unity cut across tribal divides and that confessions were no longer 'once and for all' but an integral part of the bi-weekly fellowship liturgy. Confession to the wider public was also expected. Mission teams prefaced their evangelistic addresses with an explanation of sins committed. This angered traditional leaders and horrified people from areas outside the influence of the Emandwa cults. The Iteso refused to accept revival preaching in the late 1940s because it was accompanied by lurid details of sexual sin.[13] Confessions were expected in sermons as part of the testimony of the preacher. No Mulokole began a sermon without first giving a personal introduction on how he or she was saved, and from what particular sins. This frequently included stories of dreams, visions, or voices which had convicted the recipient of sin, and led to emotional repentance and dramatic action to right the wrong. Through these sermons the worship of the Fellowship Meetings began to have some influence on Sunday worship.

The need to confess sins to another human being has generally been rejected by Protestants. Certainly the evangelical Anglican missionaries working in East Africa saw little value in it. As a result of the influence of Emandwa initiation practices, however, confession had gained a position of importance analogous to its place in the Roman Catholic church; a vital rite for the spiritual well-being of the Christian. The difference between the two lay in the egalitarian, community nature of confession in the Balokole tradition, as opposed to the hierarchical and private penance of the confessional box. The Balokole took it in turns to be both confessor and confessant, admitting their faults and pronouncing the appropriate restitution for the faults committed by others.

The theology of 'walking in the light' features in the Balokole hymns sung during the Fellowship Meeting. They emphasise liberation from sin and membership of a community of elect through a radical change from the old life by a confidence in the purifying blood of Christ and confession of sin. A few songs which were composed by Balokole themselves survive from the early days of the Revival, handed down orally or occasionally finding their way into an early hymn book.

---

[13] O. Obote, 'Why the Revival Movement has failed in Teso' (Makerere University, Diploma in Theology dissertation, 1978), p. 5.

Certain themes recur in these compositions. Often songs list the sins from which they have been saved: 'He healed me from my prostitution, . . . my drunkenness'. There are hymns for the instruction of new converts, and challenges to outsiders. Traditional African beliefs were also condemned in song, as this millennial hymn makes clear:

> The world is going to burst
> With its over-turned Nyabingi.[14]

Nyabingi was a royal ancestral spirit around whom an important cult was centred, which the missionaries and later the Balokole deemed to be satanic. Veneration of ancestors was also attacked by the Balokole as they warned people of worldly pleasures:

> You who trust in the things of the world,
> Why are you never satisfied with them?
> For even your ancestors
> Were not satisfied with them.[15]

Not only was African Traditional Religion being attacked by the Balokole, theirs was a radical life-style which demanded as much change from Christians as non-Christians. Several hymns emphasise the distinction between the saved and the unsaved, asking

> You who have good manners . . .
> You who are a church teacher,
> Teaching many people,
> But without taking them to the cross,
> Why do you labour in vain?[16]

Church members cannot put their faith in their job, their compliance with customary etiquette, nor in the traditional respect for authority; only repentance in the light of Christ's brokenness on the cross can save them.

---

[14] Unpublished hymn in C. E. Robins, 'Tukutendereza: a study of social change and sectarian withdrawal in the Balokole Revival of Uganda' (Columbia University Ph. D. thesis, 1975), p. 259.
[15] *Ebyeshongoro Eby'okujunwa* [*Hymns for Salvation*] (London, 1951), no. 27: this is the Kigezi Hymn Book.
[16] Ibid., no. 50.

Most of the songs and hymns used during the Fellowship Meetings were translations of English hymns. The theme which appealed to Balokole and Ruanda missionaries alike was that of the efficacy of Christ's atoning blood. 'What can wash away my sin?' and 'My hope is built on nothing less than Jesus' blood and righteousness', were among the popular hymns. The constant refrain of 'Tukutendereza' emphasised the importance of this particular understanding of salvation. This most popular hymn punctuated Balokole meetings, it was sung as an appreciation of a testimony shared or a word preached, and its first line was used as a greeting. The words,

> We praise You, Jesus,
> Jesus, Lamb of God,
> Your Blood cleanses me.
> I praise You, Saviour

are an adaptation of the hymn, 'Precious Saviour, Thou has saved me', which like many other revival hymns is found in the Keswick hymn book, *Hymns of Consecration and Faith*. Such a comprehension of redemption was easily accepted in a culture which demanded sacrifices at points of crisis in order to deal with wrong-doing. In African Traditional Religion sacrifices were made to restore broken relations between two parties and to appease and show respect for the ancestors. When members of the Ruanda Mission introduced hymns which emphasised Christ's sacrifice they found a ready audience. Perhaps this is one reason why it was Ruanda missionaries and not those from the parent organization, CMS, who were the catalysts for the Revival. The Christian faith of the Ruanda missionaries was largely formed by Keswick holiness. They brought with them not simply a search for a 'new blessing' and a desire for committed Christians who sought holiness in their lives, but also the hymns which expressed that theology. Hymn-singing was an integral part of the Keswick Conventions the missionaries had attended, and they carried this tradition with them to East Africa, translating the songs which meant most to them into the local vernaculars.

The emotion and piety in these songs appealed to the Balokole, and they made them their own, contextualizing even the manner in which they were sung. In the early days of the Revival hymn-singing continued through the night, at times accompanied by drumming and (modest) dancing. Some missionaries looked on aghast, fearful that the sober transformation of lives was being hijacked by unnecessary enthusiasm. The Balokole, however, were expressing themselves through the African tradition of vigorous celebrations after dark. East African traditional songs are often repetitive, the rhythm and the tune are just as important as the words, and worship involves the whole person.[17] Singing is usually a community activity.[18] The missionaries' hymns were altered to reflect this. The hymns gained a syncopated rhythm which better fitted not only with the vernacular but also with the clapping and swaying which accompanied the singing. Often they would be sung antiphonally, and frequently a chorus or a single verse was repeated several times. Nasanairi Mukasa,[19] a Balokole student at Bishop Tucker Theological College in 1941, recalls that the group arose at 4am for corporate prayer and praise, choosing hymns which were felt to have a special message for the day or which touched a member of the group. Any 'revelations' which came from this time were then preached from the top of the college water tank at 6am, along with an explanation of the 'system of salvation'.[20] Many of the songs sung at the Fellowship Meeting were introduced into the Sunday service, and so Anglican worship in large parts of East Africa came to be invested with a similar message.

It was not only hymns which were imbued with the characteristics of fellowship and 'walking in the light'; they affected all aspects of Balokole life. For example conventions, which gathered together large numbers of Balokole for further teaching and mutual encouragement, and missions which evangelized the unsaved, displayed these central Balokole concerns. Conventions and missions had been the places of the first signs of revival. From 1931 Joe Church, the Baganda brothers Simeon Nsibambi and Blasio Kigozi, Lawrence Barham, and Yosiya Kinuka, organized teaching teams for large meetings in Rwanda and West and Central Uganda.[21] At the Gahini Convention of Christmas

[17] J. H. Kwabena Nketia, *The Music of Africa* (London, 1975), p. 244.

[18] Ibid., p. 30.

[19] Interview, Kampala, 26 April 1996.

[20] The Balokole group of students eventually left the college because their early morning worship, missionary zeal, and literal understanding of the Bible came into conflict with the obedience demanded by the staff, particularly the CMS warden, John Jones.

[21] For many years Nsibambi was the most important Balokole leader. His close relationship with Church, whom he met in 1929, was influential in the Revival. Kigozi was in charge of the Gahini Evangelists' training and the primary schools before his untimely death in 1936. Barham was a clergyman from the Ruanda Mission who worked in

1933 the themes chosen were Sin, the Holiness of God, the Second Birth, Repentance, Faith, Prayer, the Holy Spirit, Sanctification, and the Christian Walk. Similar themes were used in the following years as the Revival snowballed. By 1940 a change in theme is evident as the organizers believed that they were preaching to the truly converted. The Victorious Life (a popular Keswick theme) was the subject chosen for the first Balokole Convention held at Namirembe, Kampala, in August 1940, in order to teach how to continue to follow 'the victorious Christ' in all aspects of life. This convention was called, by some, 'Namirembe Keswick'. Similar appellations were given to other conventions. The Keswick Conventions in the United Kingdom had had a profound impact on British evangelicalism. Many of the Ruanda missionaries looked back fondly to the Conventions they had attended as moments of great significance in their own lives. They enjoyed the warmth generated by meeting those of like minds, and hoped to duplicate the intense spirituality of Convention week in their work in Africa. The results were beyond their expectations. Balokole learnt together, worshipped together, and 'walked in the light' together; this, they thought, was the only way to renew the Church. Whilst sound teaching was considered a vital component of a convention, the bringing together of scattered Balokole for fellowship was seen as being equally important; the convention was the Fellowship Meeting writ large. Organized whenever it was felt necessary, conventions were the high days of the Balokole calendar. The priority of fellowship amongst the Balokole ensured that they would sacrifice much to attend conventions held in different parts of the country. Missions also displayed the importance of fellowship, and many Balokole would volunteer for missions beyond their locality. Teams were composed of those accustomed to 'walk in light' and pray together, those who together would seek the prompting of the Holy Spirit for the mission programme. As the Balokole saw it, the climax of corporate worship was going out to preach the word of God to others; but equally they believed that evangelism was not considered effective if it had not been preceded by frequent meetings for prayer and fellowship. Fellowship was never a question of choice for Balokole; they believed it was the orbit in which their Christian life was to be lived.

Kigezi. Kinuka, a Muhima from Ankole, was on the hospital staff at Gahini when the Revival began.

The perceived needs of the Fellowship groups rather than the seasons of the ecclesiastical year drove the calendar of the Balokole. Its informal dynamic outlived the first years of spontaneous and enthusiastic conversions. The twice- or thrice-weekly Fellowship Meetings were the base of the calendar. Regional or national conventions were not to be missed. Weekly team missions were also staple fare for Balokole. All these events were considered a vital part of Christian living and as such had a greater prominence in the minds of the Balokole than the traditional Christian festivals which had been introduced in Uganda with Anglicanism.

Easter and Christmas were seen as occasions for holding conventions or missions. The traditional Anglican practice of celebrating Holy Communion on these feast days was discouraged by Barham and Church, and brought them into conflict with Bishop C. E. Stuart. They felt that too many people participated in communion without having changed their lives in accordance with biblical teaching. This was one of the points which Blasio Kigozi prepared to bring before the Synod in 1936 before he died. Why, he asked, was the Lord's Table 'being abused by those who are known to be living in sin being allowed to attend and partake?'[22] For him it was more important that people learnt of salvation than to celebrate a sacrament which, it was felt, was misunderstood. A similar attitude towards infant baptism was held amongst the missionaries, who disagreed with the theology of baptismal regeneration and tried to avoid the baptising of some children, including their own. On this issue the Balokole differed from the missionaries. 'It was their problem', said Zeb Kabaza. 'We saw these were kinds of legalisms . . . changing things for its own sake wouldn't do anything . . . the Lord wanted us to be humble and belong to our church.'[23] Belonging to the Church meant accepting the theology and practice of the sacraments which were already in place in the local churches, along with the *Book of Common Prayer* which gave them liturgical form. During 1941 and 1942 Church and others thought that the divisions between revivalists and non-revivalists over issues such as sacraments would split the Church. In reality the Balokole had little desire to leave the Anglican Church and they accepted the structure it imposed. In Kigezi District, for instance, the number of baptisms quadrupled in the years between 1935 (*c.*380

---

[22] J. E. Church, *Awake! An African Calling* (London, 1937), p. 44.
[23] Interview, Kampala, 12 May 1997.

baptisms) and 1940 (over 1200),[24] and this in the area which was most affected by the Revival and which came to be led entirely by Balokole. The Balokole emphasised word rather than sacrament, experience rather than structure; but they were content to channel their separatist tendencies, their spontaneous worship, and their insistence on high moral conduct, into the exclusive fellowship groups.

The Fellowship Meetings were considered a vital supplement to Sunday worship where 'saved' mingled with 'unsaved' but baptized Christians, and where worship had less warmth and intimacy. The meetings allowed Balokole to continue to accept the Anglican pattern of inclusiveness of worship based on parish structures whilst emphasising membership of elite groups by dramatic confession of sins. Such a tension has frequently led to secession, not least in Africa, where charismatic, decentralized movements challenge the order and clericalism of the missionary-established churches. In East Africa, with rare exceptions, the Balokole remained within the Anglican Church and respected its framework, whilst adapting its worship to suit their own spiritual needs. The worship within the Balokole movement, centred as it was around 'walking in the light' at Fellowship Meetings, has no parallels in the Anglican Church. Whilst comparisons can be made with the intimate communion of believers born out of the American and British Revivals of the eighteenth century, the order of worship of the Balokole was largely indigenous and was informed by their particular cultural background. Ironically, the Balokole were uncompromising in their rejection of those aspects of their culture which did not fit with their understanding of Christianity. Those aspects of African culture which they, often unconsciously, found appropriate were adapted. They recognized the importance of 'whole' worship which involved body as well as mind, and which had radical consequences for daily behaviour. The startlingly frank confessions of personal sin, and the intimate corporate relationships with other Balokole, were more intense than anything the Keswick-influenced missionaries had ever experienced. Their Keswick teaching had fused with a vigorous Traditional cult ritual to form a lively expression of African Christian worship. The honesty and unity of close, corporate worship and of 'walking in light' with the brethren was the fulcrum on which all other aspects of faith balanced. The liturgy of fellowship which developed in the early days of the Revival contained the

[24] Robins, 'Tukutendereza', p. 269.

explosive spirituality of the Balokole, and played a significant role in preventing secession. It significantly altered the worship of Anglicans in East Africa, and still has repercussions, for better and for worse, on the Church today.

Institut Supérieur Théologique Anglican,
Bunia, Congo

'AUSTERE RITUAL': THE REFORMATION OF WORSHIP IN INTER-WAR ENGLISH CONGREGATIONALISM

by IAN M. RANDALL

WRITING in 1965, Horton Davies, in his magisterial examination of worship and theology in England, gave a glowing account of advances made in Free Churches over previous decades towards 'a worship that is deeply reverent, sacramentally rich, ecumenically comprehensive, and theologically faithful'.[1] This study examines the pressure for reformation in worship which emerged, particularly in the 1930s, within English Congregationalism. Pressure came from an exploration of the Reformed and Puritan roots of the denomination and from the influence of wider forms of corporate devotion. By 1943, Nathaniel Micklem (1888–1976), Principal from 1932 of Mansfield College, Oxford, and the most formative theologian espousing new versions of Reformed thought, could write *Congregationalism and the Church Catholic*, affirming that 'by the faithful preaching of the Word, the believing celebration of the sacraments and the exercise of Gospel discipline, the Church is kept in the doctrine and fellowship of the apostles and stands in true succession'.[2] The inter-war years, a period of marked Anglo-Catholic dominance, saw Anglican and Free Church leaders who had been shaped by evangelical theology re-examining their practices in the light of higher forms of worship.[3] In Congregationalism, which with almost 300,000 members in England was the largest of the older Dissenting denominations, this process had distinctive features deriving from its own history.

Much Free Church theology and worship in the 1920s had been characterized, as J. W. Grant puts it in *Free Churchmanship in England*, by a belief in 'the supremacy of spirit over form and of spontaneity over tradition'.[4] Calvinism was widely repudiated. W. B. Selbie (1862–1944) advocated in 1928, when Mansfield College Principal, a Free Church-

---

[1] Davies, *Worship*, 5, p. 397.

[2] N. Micklem, *Congregationalism and the Church Catholic* (London, 1943), p. 54.

[3] For Anglicanism see I. M. Randall, 'The truth shall make you free: the growth of the Anglican Evangelical Group Movement', *Anglican and Episcopal History*, 65 (1996), pp. 314–56.

[4] J. W. Grant, *Free Churchmanship in England, 1870–1940* (London, 1955), p. 272.

manship which abjured 'obscurantist evangelicalism' and embraced instead the freedom of the Holy Spirit.[5] Famously, Albert Peel (1887–1949), editor of the scholarly *Congregational Quarterly*, was to define divine guidance as following 'the gleam'.[6] The most extreme expression of an anti-doctrinal tendency was seen in a group which gathered at Blackheath Congregational Church, London, for a conference during the 1932 Congregational Union meetings. Frank Lenwood, a respected Congregationalist who had moved away from orthodox Christology and who found communion services 'perplexing', and Thomas Wigley, the Blackheath minister, had prepared the ground.[7] Invitations to Union delegates attracted about seventy-five people and further discussions followed. A provocative 'Re-statement of Christian thought' appeared in *The Christian World* of 9 February 1933.[8] Micklem, quick to enter the fray, asserted that the Blackheath Group's statement bore no clear relationship to the Christian faith.[9] Public controversy was soon raging. By May 1933 Micklem, who would gain a reputation – which he gladly exploited – as an 'arch-anti-liberal', was contending that the 'historic gospel', and thus the authenticity of the Church itself, was at stake.[10]

Four years later, Albert Peel dismissed Blackheath, writing rather bitterly: 'So far as I see them, most Congregationalists are not disposed to wander with the wizards on the Blackheath, nor do they propose to fall down and worship the dogmatic image which Nathaniel the Principal set up.'[11] Micklem was nearer the truth in regarding his contretemps with the 'Blackheathens', as he termed them, as a defining moment – the bursting of a boil.[12] Powerful new emphases on the historic gospel were beginning to set the agenda in Congregationalism. Grant uses the term 'Genevans' to describe those Free Church leaders

---

[5] W. B. Selbie, 'The rebirth of Protestantism', *The Congregational Quarterly* [hereafter *CQ*], 6 (1928), p. 286.

[6] A. Peel, *Inevitable Congregationalism* (London, 1937), p. 114; A. Argent, 'Albert Peel: the restless labourer', *JURCHS*, 4 (1989), pp. 319–36.

[7] T. Wigley, *Christian Modernism – Impact and Challenge* (London, 1958), p. 16; F. Lenwood, *Jesus – Lord or Leader?* (London, 1930), pp. 4, 302; idem, *A Re-Statement of Christian Thought* (London, 1934), p. 7. For Lenwood see B. Stanley, 'Manliness and mission: Frank Lenwood and the London Missionary Society', *JURCHS*, 5 (1996), pp. 458–77.

[8] *The Christian World* [hereafter *CW*], 9 Feb. 1933, p. 7.

[9] *CW*, 16 Feb. 1933, p. 9.

[10] *CW*, 4 May 1933, p. 5; N. Micklem, *The Religion of a Sceptic* (London, 1975), p. 53.

[11] Peel, *Inevitable Congregationalism*, p. 113.

[12] J. Huxtable, *As It Seemed to Me* (London, 1990), p. 14; N. Micklem, *The Box and the Puppets* (London, 1957), p. 82.

in the inter-war years and subsequently who drew inspiration from Calvin's theology and practice in Geneva. The Genevans, against the background of the prevailing liberal theological climate within Congregationalism in particular, called for the espousal of a refashioned, broad Calvinism.[13] Genevans were not, however, engaged simply in theological protest: they were also deeply concerned for the reformation of Congregational worship. Thus Bernard Manning (1892–1941), Bursar and later Senior Tutor of Jesus College, Cambridge, a Congregational layman and a brilliant medieval historian, urged in 1923 the recovery of Dissent's 'stately and austere ritual', and his defence of plain Calvinistic worship was being quoted in Mansfield College in the 1930s.[14] A sense of history was growing stronger. Another Congregationalist who was fired by this Genevan vision, John S. Whale (1896–1997), President from 1933 of Cheshunt College, Cambridge, lucidly explained John Calvin's thinking about preaching and eucharistic services.[15] Attempts to foster the renewal of Congregational worship drew from earlier tradition while calling for changes to existing Congregational practice.

* * *

A manifesto which was drafted in 1939 by Micklem, Manning, and Whale, and was circulated to Congregational ministers, strikingly summed up the Genevan vision. It called for an increase in the number of Congregationalists who 'devoutly and conscientiously use the means of grace: Bible, Sacrament, Public Worship, Church Meeting'.[16] Biblical preaching was, in line with Reformed priorities, a pivotal issue. Campbell Morgan, minister at Westminster Chapel, London, embodied the grand style of expository preaching, but his conservative biblical stance attracted limited support within Congregationalism.[17] The broader evangelicalism of the Genevans emphasised preaching which, rather than according uniform authority to all parts of Scripture, had a Christological focus. Speaking at the International Congregational Council in 1930, Manning argued that

---

[13] Grant, *Free Churchmanship*, p. 325.

[14] B. L. Manning, 'Nonconformity at the Universities', *CQ*, 1 (1923), p. 187; *Mansfield College Magazine*, June 1932, p. 128.

[15] J. S. Whale, 'Calvin', in N. Micklem, ed., *Christian Worship* (Oxford, 1936), pp. 168–71; R. T. Jones, *Congregationalism in England, 1662–1962* (London, 1962), p. 451.

[16] E. Routley, *The Story of Congregationalism* (London, 1961), p. 166.

[17] *CQ*, 8 (1930), p. 408.

through 'the Word and the Sacraments and the fellowship' the Church brought people to 'the Word that was once incarnate'.[18] In similar vein Micklem, adducing and reshaping John Owen's view that Christian proclamation rested on the Bible and the experience of those who believed it, maintained in 1934 that the Church's foundation was 'Christ as revealed in Holy Scripture and in the worship of the Church Catholic'.[19] The contention was that preaching which declared the acts of God in Christ had been central to Reformed worship and was in urgent need of recovery.

The phrase 'the worship of the Church Catholic' was also intended to stress wider Christian tradition. Reformed formulations were subject to the gravitational pull of ideas of catholicity. Indeed Congregational preaching was on occasions compared unfavourably with Catholic worship. In 1927 Micklem contrasted the power of an Easter mass which he had attended in Budapest, in which there was a triumphant proclamation that 'the Lord is risen', with a Congregational Easter sermon he had heard a year later which began: '*Prima facie* the Resurrection presents us with a problem.'[20] In 1932 W. E. Orchard, minister of the Congregational King's Weigh House Church, Mayfair, and an ardent sacramentalist, embraced Roman Catholicism.[21] On the other hand Peel, in 1938, was finding the calming atmosphere of worship among the Society of Friends congenial.[22] A few months later, addressing the Congregational Union assembly, Manning could not have put the Reformed alternative more forcibly. All those who neglected 'Word and sacraments', he stated, even if they had liturgies and crosses, had forfeited 'the soul of our worship'. He saw it as profoundly damaging that the Reformation inheritance was being lost, with pulpits being shrunk to reading desks or flattened to platforms, and preaching degenerating into 'flabby platitudes'.[23] Preaching was portrayed as the vehicle for conveying historic truths.

But it was not simply that the content and place of preaching required attention; so too did the preachers. In a pungent weekly column in *The British Weekly* – which like *The Christian World* was

---

[18] B. L. Manning, *Essays in Orthodox Dissent* (London, 1939), p. 109.
[19] N. Micklem, 'The Holy Spirit and a new Creed', *CQ*, 12 (1934), pp. 547–8, 551.
[20] N. Micklem, 'Radicalism and Fundamentalism', *CQ*, 5 (1927), p. 334.
[21] E. Kaye and R. Mackenzie, *W. E. Orchard: A Study in Christian Exploration* (Oxford, 1990), ch. 7.
[22] *CW*, 10 Feb. 1938, p. 5.
[23] *CW*, 20 Oct. 1938, p. 6.

widely read among Congregationalists – Micklem devoted considerable attention to this theme. He commended, in January 1933,
preaching which was 'real' and sprang from 'experience', but he
cautioned against the purveying of 'private visions' rather than 'the
one, holy, universal, apostolic faith'.[24] A few months later, against the
background of the Blackheath controversy, Micklem was more
specific, insisting that ministers must be called, broken, and re-made
by God's word, and be able to affirm with evangelical conviction:
'Nothing in my hand I bring; simply to Thy Cross I cling.'[25] Yet clearly
there were tensions for Micklem. He wished to avoid the narrow
biblicism of Fundamentalism and, on the other hand, the subjectivism
of nondescript spirituality. The solution, as he expressed it in 1934, was
that ministers should cease to say, 'One feels, does one not . . .?', and
should restate the 'ever-living message' of the Reformation with the
words: 'Thus saith the Lord'.[26]

The commitment of Genevans to the recovery of authoritative
preaching is somewhat overshadowed in J. W. Grant's analysis by the
stress on Genevan high churchmanship.[27] Alan Sell is also restrictive
in interpreting the process by which the Genevans 'shunned the
individualistic nineteenth century, and exalted Owen and others' in
ecclesiological terms.[28] A higher view of Church and sacraments was
undoubtedly being promulgated by the Genevans, but in the mid-
1930s Micklem and Whale were using every opportunity to raise the
profile of preaching. Delivering a sermon to the London Missionary
Society in May 1935 Whale, then in his thirties, gave an impassioned
call for crucicentric preaching. His concept of the 'word of the cross'
was drawn from the outstanding Congregational theologian P. T.
Forsyth, whose influence on Genevans was considerable. Whale
himself spoke of the 'evangel of the Atonement'.[29] It is clear that
other Congregational ministers could not avoid these new voices. A
commentator in The Christian World noted, after Whale's address,
that theological modernists in Congregationalism were becoming
accustomed to pulpit rebukes from eminent preachers.[30] At the

---

[24] The British Weekly [hereafter BW], 26 Jan. 1933, p. 334.
[25] BW, 23 Nov. 1933, p. 163.
[26] BW, 26 April 1934, p. 71.
[27] Grant, Free Churchmanship, chs 6–7.
[28] A. P. F. Sell, Saints: Visible, Orderly and Catholic (Geneva, 1986), p. 97.
[29] CW, 23 May 1935, p. 11.
[30] CW, 30 May 1935, p. 9.

Congregational Union assembly a few months later Micklem was unrelenting. During what *The Christian World* said would have been described in a previous era of Congregationalism as 'a truly evangelical discourse', Micklem argued that if preaching which was faithful to the Bible 'as the revelation of the Word of God' was neglected 'it is a sure sign that we have fallen away from our most holy faith'.[31] Such austere ritual, it was being argued, preserved Reformed tradition.

* * *

Fresh approaches to the sacraments, also drawing from older tradition, characterized the new Calvinistic thrust in inter-war Congregationalism. In the 1920s a symbolic understanding of the sacraments was, as Grant shows, widely accepted.[32] Forsyth had argued in 1917 in *The Church and the Sacraments* that the 'idolatry of the popular preacher needs to be balanced by more stress on the Sacraments'.[33] But an article in *The Congregational Quarterly* in 1924 gave an (intentionally exaggerated) insight into popular perceptions of infant baptism. 'Our minister is perfectly sweet at christenings', said one Church member, 'he never lets the water touch the little dears.'[34] Manning was predictably outraged. Baptism, he expostulated in 1927, mattered. He deplored the fact that Congregationalists and Baptists were giving the impression that their differences over baptism were insignificant, although Baptist idiosyncrasies did not surprise Manning since among them were ('by nature and sometimes by grace') to be found 'cranks and fads'.[35] Yet there were signs that the sacramental scene was changing. E. J. Price, who as Principal of the Congregational Yorkshire United College identified with Reformed thought, said in 1927 that churches must recover the eucharist as 'a real communion with Christ'.[36] In 1929 Manning observed that all orthodox Dissenters, even Baptists, stood for 'a regular use of the sacraments with what they believe to be apostolic austerity'.[37]

Higher views gained much more credence in the 1930s. Again the

---

[31] *CW*, 17 Oct. 1935, p. 7.

[32] Grant, *Free Churchmanship*, pp. 274–7, 291–2.

[33] P. T. Forsyth, *The Church and the Sacraments* (London, 1917; 2nd edn, 1947), pp. 229–32.

[34] J. A. Quail, 'A Congregational doctrine of baptism', *CQ*, 2 (1924), pp. 81–2.

[35] B. L. Manning, 'Some characteristics of the older Dissent', *CQ*, 5 (1927), p. 296.

[36] E. J. Price, 'The eucharist in history and experience', *CQ*, 5 (1927), p. 147.

[37] B. L. Manning, *The Making of Modern English Religion* (London, 1929), p. 108.

past provided stimulus. Writing in the *Congregational Church Monthly* in 1932, Whale outlined how the Church could learn from the seventeenth-century Puritans about the sacraments as channels for the Spirit.[38] By 1935 Micklem was happy to commend the Calvinistic position on the Lord's Supper (as distinct from the Zwinglian one) taken by the 1658 Congregational Savoy Declaration.[39] A year later Micklem argued in *The British Weekly* that movements such as the Methodist Sacramental Fellowship, which were making communion central, were true to Protestant tradition.[40] John Calvin and John Wesley were, he commented, united over the ideal of weekly communion.[41] At the same time Whale and Manning were pressing for the view that the sacraments constituted God's action.[42] Thinking had moved so far by 1937 that in a piece entitled 'The views of the Congregational Church' Whale could refer to Calvin's high concept of the Lord's Supper as basic, and speak of the sacraments as offering 'spiritual reality'.[43]

Although such thinking was rooted in early Congregationalism, it was unfamiliar to an ecclesiastical culture which had increasingly emphasised individual preference.[44] In 1933 Manning had felt the weight of current Congregational opinion against him when he expressed deep unhappiness about church members for whom baptism and communion were matters of indifference.[45] Albert Peel exemplified the strand of inter-war Congregationalism which regarded benefits gained from sacraments as dependent on temperament.[46] A 1936 Congregational *Manual for Ministers*, embodying liberal and memorialist approaches to the sacraments, enjoyed some popularity, but two other books in that year were to prove much more significant: Micklem's robust *What is the Faith?*, and the composite *Christian*

[38] J. S. Whale, 'Things most surely believed', *Congregational Church Monthly* (May, 1932), p. 132.

[39] *BW*, 4 July 1935, p. 207.

[40] *BW*, 22 Oct. 1936, p. 63. For Methodist developments see I. M. Randall, *Quest, Crusade and Fellowship* (Horsham, 1995).

[41] *BW*, 3 Dec. 1936, p. 235.

[42] *BW*, 2 April 1936, p. 8; *CW*, 9 April 1936, p. 7.

[43] J. S. Whale, 'The views of the Congregational Church', in R. Dunkerley and A. C. Headlam, eds, *The Ministry and the Sacraments* (London, 1937), pp. 214–18.

[44] Grant, *Free Churchmanship*, p. 298.

[45] B. L. Manning, 'The gospel and the Church', *CQ*, 11 (1933), p. 163; idem, *Church Union: The Next Step for Congregationalists* (London, 1933), p. 15.

[46] *BT*, 26 May 1938, p. 409; A. Peel, *Christian Freedom* (London, 1938), p. 80; cf. *Congregational Year Book* (London, 1936), pp. 108, 116.

Worship, in which Whale set out Calvin's liturgical views and Micklem wrote on the sacraments.[47] A *Congregational Quarterly* editorial in 1938 reflected Peel's perspective. Recalling Selbie's prophetic sermons at Mansfield ('as the very voice of God'), Peel could not envisage a greater realization of God than through such preaching. For Peel these experiences refuted Whale's case for the centrality of the Lord's Supper.[48] But communion as a 'second service' following the end of a preaching service, or as a brief prelude to worship,[49] was gradually to give way within Congregationalism to an integrated liturgy of word and sacrament.

A new appreciation of the Lord's Supper was evident in an ecumenical submission by the Free Churches in 1941 which stated that most Free Church ministers now believed that the grace of Christ 'is conveyed and sealed to faith as well as expressed: there is the Real Presence, and the real Communion with Him'.[50] This statement partly resulted from the ubiquitous influence of higher Anglican practice. In 1936 Micklem was prepared to consider the merits of an 8.00am Anglican-style communion.[51] Free Church leaders were not, however, simply assimilating hitherto alien patterns. Adrian Hastings wonders why Micklem, whom he sees as intellectually (and socially) an Anglican, remained in 'increasingly irrelevant' traditional Congregationalism.[52] Certainly Micklem, a cultured Oxonian from a privileged background, and Manning, who spoke quite unselfconsciously of the liturgical tastes of the 'well-bred Dissenter',[53] fitted Anglican society. What Hastings does not appreciate is the power of Dissenting consciousness. In a pugnacious address to the Congregational Union in 1938, Manning described a parish eucharist he had recently attended: 'A few sentences of the Word were read. An apology for preaching it was made for five minutes. . . . Bread and wine were consecrated. . . . But these things, the essentials, were smothered by

[47] B. D. Spinks, *Freedom or Order?: The Eucharistic Liturgy in English Congregationalism* (Allison Park, PA, 1984), pp. 146–51 and ch. 10; N. Micklem, *What is the Faith?* (London, 1936); J. S. Whale, 'Calvin', in N. Micklem, ed., *Christian Worship* (Oxford, 1936), pp. 154–71; N. Micklem, 'The sacraments', ibid., pp. 243–56.

[48] *CQ*, 16 (1938), pp. 259–61.

[49] *CW*, 20 Oct. 1938, p. 7.

[50] G. K. A. Bell, ed., *Documents on Christian Unity*, 3rd ser. (London, 1948), p. 116.

[51] *BW*, 14 May 1936, p. 123.

[52] A. Hastings, *A History of English Christianity, 1920–1990* (London, 1991), p. 271.

[53] Manning, 'Nonconformity at the Universities', p. 187.

other things.'[54] It was a distinctively Reformed sacramentalism which Manning advocated.

* * *

Debates and disagreements over 'Word and sacraments' were related to differences between Congregationalists who cherished spontaneity and those favourably disposed towards set liturgy. Although the picture was not straightforward, the more theologically progressive were sometimes those least attracted by ritual. Thus Selbie believed it would be disastrous if spontaneous prayer was abandoned, and his own prayers were memorable.[55] It was those pressing for a return to Reformed values who were prominent in advocating liturgical services. A primary reason was that set forms gave worship theological substance. Manning argued in 1927 that scriptural content had been lost through 'freedom of thought' – for him 'a euphemism for lack of thought'.[56] By 1935, after the experience of Blackheath, Micklem confessed that he had changed his mind over the use of creeds, and he defined public worship as a confession of faith, the recital of a creed.[57] Much depression in modern spiritual Christian experience would, he argued, be countered if the dogmas of sin and evangelical grace were affirmed.[58]

The actual experience of worship was, therefore, a second factor stimulating calls for change. Micklem described attending churches only to 'come away feeling suicidal'. Nothing was worse than hearing prayers which did not meet with any audible 'Amen' or congregations droning 'Hail, Thou once despised Jesus' in an atmosphere appropriate to an atheist's funeral. Worship conducted with cold formality was anathema to Micklem. Indeed he preferred 'happy fellowship' in a small hall.[59] But structured prayers and praise had merit, especially when compared to artificial enthusiasm. Manning's view was that although extempore prayers could be memorable – he instanced those of Hubert Simpson at Westminster Chapel – in practice they were often tedious.[60] In a penetrating essay in 1935 on extempore praying,

---

[54] Idem, *Essays*, p. 53.
[55] *CW*, 10 Sept. 1931, p. 4; G. F. Nuttall, *The Puritan Spirit* (London, 1967), p. 327.
[56] Manning, 'Older Dissent', p. 296.
[57] *BW*, 1 Aug. 1935, p. 347.
[58] *BW*, 21 Nov. 1935, p. 151.
[59] *BW*, 10 Dec. 1931, p. 203; 4 April 1935, p. 7; 16 May 1935, p. 127.
[60] B. L. Manning, 'Common Prayer', *CQ*, 28 (1950), p. 117.

Micklem affirmed the tradition deriving from John Bunyan, Owen, and Isaac Watts, of a 'charismatic ministry of prayer', but argued that free prayer could not compel the Spirit's presence and that supposed freedom could become mere form. On the other hand forms, rightly employed, could mean that congregations drew on the worship of the universal Church. Ultimately, Micklem saw debates about liturgy as secondary to the deeper need for 'a revival of the evangelical faith'.[61]

Although Congregational fathers such as Owen had rejected liturgical prayer, there were Congregational theologians who had embraced the use of set responses. P. T. Forsyth's perspective, that opposition to liturgy had more to do with antipathy to the Church of England than sympathy with the Holy Spirit, was being quoted in the 1920s in the context of calls for a 'deepened spirituality' and 'the return of awe'.[62] Under H. C. Carter's ministry, Emmanuel Church, Cambridge, where Forsyth had been minister, became a fruitful inter-war setting for Manning and Whale. Emmanuel's worship was liturgically austere and its music powerful.[63] H. F. Lovell Cocks, who became Principal of Western College, Bristol, and was indebted to Forsyth, called for profounder prayer 'under the shadow of Golgotha'.[64] In the 1940s these trends within Congregationalism produced a Church Order Group and a journal, *The Presbyter*, which Daniel Jenkins, the editor (a student of Micklem's in the 1930s), saw as committed to renewing the Calvinist tradition.[65] Micklem, in 1941, published set prayers for each day in *Prayers and Praises*. Introducing these prayers, he opposed notions that written formularies were crutches for those lacking evangelical experience. After drawing attention to Puritan concepts of kindling the spiritual fire by Scripture and hymn-singing, Micklem argued that liturgy could ensure that praise did not depend on subjective moods.[66] Creative changes did not imply discontinuity with Congregational tradition.

Change was also due, however, to liturgical influences from outside Congregationalism. There was predictable concern for, as Micklem put it, Nonconformity to be 'more catholic in the forms of its

---

[61] N. Micklem, 'Extempore prayer in the Congregational Church', *CQ*, 13 (1935), pp. 328–34.

[62] G. H. Russell, 'Public worship', *CQ*, 3 (1925), pp. 460–1.

[63] Clyde Binfield to the author, 18 April 1997.

[64] H. F. Lovell Cocks, 'The meaning and value of prayer', *CQ*, 3 (1925), p. 305.

[65] Editorial, *The Presbyter*, 3/iii (1945), p. 2.

[66] N. Micklem, *Prayers and Praises* (London, 1941), pp. 7–10.

devotion'.[67] Micklem became committed to exploring wider spirituality, furnishing an ante-chapel at Mansfield for daily prayer. His brother Romilly, Mansfield's chaplain, supplied a small chamber organ.[68] Horton Davies suggests that Micklem's use of liturgy, such as that found in the 1930 *Rodborough Bede Book* (from Rodborough Tabernacle, Gloucestershire), meant that Mansfield provided 'a standard of worship that led all the English Free Churches from 1933 onwards';[69] although it is equally significant that despite studied opposition Micklem introduced into college worship traditional evangelical hymns celebrating Christ's atonement.[70] In a series of articles in 1935 Micklem highlighted weaknesses in Free Church devotion, by contrast with Catholic approaches to prayer, and one Baptist minister, F. C. Spurr, responded that many were leaving Free Churches to seek the 'numinous' in worship. Micklem's own reading at this stage included Ignatius Loyola and John of the Cross, and he was keen to recommend spiritual direction and the use of silence.[71] Two years later Micklem reiterated that people in Free Churches were turning to Catholic spirituality, yet his conviction was that those entering into the experience of Bunyan could not be content with Thomas à Kempis.[72] Peel found Micklem's statements about the attraction of Catholic devotion wild,[73] but it was Genevan thinking, rather than that represented by Peel, which was in touch with a growing desire within Nonconformity for the exploration of richer forms of devotion and corporate worship.

* * *

The re-assessment of preaching which was undertaken within Congregationalism highlighted the calling of ministers as heralds of the gospel. In a brilliant paper in 1936 on the Genevan inheritance of Dissent, Micklem explored the role of 'ministers of the Gospel' as ministers of word and sacrament. 'The minister in our Churches', he wrote, 'is *verbi divini minister*. From the Word he derives his authority,

[67] *BW*, 30 Jan. 1936, p. 367.
[68] E. Kaye, 'Mansfield spirituality', *Reformed Quarterly*, 1 (1993), pp. 5–8. I am grateful to Elaine Kaye for her help.
[69] Davies, *Worship*, 5, p. 373.
[70] Micklem, *Box and Puppets*, p. 76.
[71] *BW*, 17 Jan. 1935, p. 319; 23 May 1935, p. 147; 25 July 1935, p. 327; 30 Jan. 1936, p. 367.
[72] *BW*, 1 April 1937, p. 3.
[73] *BW*, 22 April 1937, p. 66.

his message and his power. Between Romanists and Rationalists we stand as ministers of the Word and the Word alone.'[74] It was this sense of prophetic proclamation which led to the historic manifesto sent to all Congregational ministers in 1939. Drafted by Manning, Whale, and Micklem, it was signed by other well-known figures: Sydney Cave, Principal of New College, London; J. D. Jones, the outstanding minister of Richmond Hill Congregational Church, Bournemouth; H. F. Lovell Cocks; E. J. Price; and John Short, who followed Jones at Richmond Hill.[75] Observers saw the 1939 message as embodying 'ultra-High Churchmanship' in worship.[76] In 1940, as the effects of the manifesto were being felt, Peel was finding older Congregational ministers more progressive while (to his chagrin) their younger contemporaries 'lean towards conservatism'.[77] While Genevans were broad rather than conservative in their evangelicalism, they undoubtedly exuded fresh confidence in the proclamation of the gospel.

Genevans were also in tune with wider European developments. Micklem had taken a keen interest in Karl Barth since 1927 and he closely followed European politics. On 4 March 1938 Mansfield staged a reception for Barth on the occasion of his receiving an Oxford honorary degree.[78] Micklem's subsequent comment was that in Germany 'Pauline' Christians (the Confessing Church) were likely to find themselves in concentration camps. With heavy irony, in the light of his own battles, he added 'where doubtless they belong'.[79] Nonconformist defiance was being stirred. A few weeks after Barth's visit to Oxford Micklem, accompanied by Alec Whitehouse (a Mansfield student who would become a leading Barthian scholar), visited Germany and met Confessing Church representatives.[80] Barth's view of the Church, as well as the thinking of Lovell Cocks and Micklem, provided inspiration for Daniel Jenkins. In 1942, in *The Nature of Catholicity*, Jenkins argued that 'the supreme mark of the

[74] N. Micklem, 'The Genevan inheritance of Protestant dissent', *The Hibbert Journal*, 25 (1937), p. 201.

[75] A copy of the manuscript is in the Lovell Cocks papers in Dr Williams's Library, London. It is reproduced in Routley, *Congregationalism*, pp. 164–71.

[76] *CW*, 30 March 1939, p. 8.

[77] Editorial, *CQ*, 18 (1940), pp. 244–5.

[78] E. Kaye, *Mansfield College, Oxford: Its Origin, History and Significance* (Oxford, 1996), p. 208.

[79] *CW*, 24 March 1938, p. 9.

[80] W. A. Whitehouse, *The Authority of Grace* (Edinburgh, 1981), p. vii.

Church's catholicity is its acceptance of and continuity with the testimony of the Apostles'.[81] In the same year a number of Congregational ministers associated with the Church Order Group met for a conference in Oxford on themes connected with the 'historic gospel' and ecclesiology. Those of liberal views, such as C. J. Cadoux, Mansfield's Church History Professor, lamented the signs of 'theological cleavage'.[82] Like their contemporaries in European neoorthodoxy, however, the Congregational Church Order ministers were convinced that the traditional means of grace – Scripture, prayer, preaching, the sacraments – constituted the path to renewed ecclesiastical vitality.[83]

The impact of demands for change was felt with increasing force within Congregational worship from the later 1930s. Micklem called for shorter agendas at Congregational gatherings and for more *Te Deums*.[84] In *Prayers and Praises*, in 1941, Micklem warned that corporate Congregational devotional life was 'at a dangerously low ebb',[85] and in the late 1940s it was noted that theological changes in Congregationalism and Presbyterianism – which produced a joint commitment to 'the traditions of Reformed Churchmanship' – had 'yet to permeate the spiritual atmosphere of our Churches'.[86] Nonetheless, by the early 1950s the emphasis on continuity with the past was enriching Congregational worship. *A Book of Public Worship* was compiled in 1948 by four members of the Church Order Group – John Huxtable and John Marsh, who had been students under Micklem, James Todd, who had been trained by Whale, and Romilly Micklem – and was of enormous liturgical significance. Todd produced a companion volume in 1951 for Christian festivals.[87] Erik Routley, a gifted musician, joined the Mansfield staff in 1948 and helped to produce the fine 1951 denominational hymnbook, *Congregational Praise*.

The way in which the Genevans implemented their ideas in local churches may be illustrated from Emmanuel Church, West Wickham,

---

[81] D. T. Jenkins, *The Nature of Catholicity* (London, 1942), p. 21.

[82] C. J. Cadoux, 'The present theological cleavage in Congregationalism', *CQ*, 20 (1942), pp. 230–9.

[83] J. Marsh, ed., *Congregationalism Today* (London, 1942), p. 28.

[84] *BW*, 15 June 1939, p. 179.

[85] Micklem, *Prayers and Praises*, p. 13.

[86] *The Presbyter*, 6/ii (1948), p. 10; *Congregational Year Book* (London, 1950), p. 96.

[87] Davies, *Worship*, 5, pp. 372–7; J. Huxtable, J. Marsh, R. Micklem and J. Todd, eds, *A Book of Public Worship* (London, 1948); J. M. Todd, *Prayers and Services for Christian Festivals* (London, 1951).

Kent. James Todd, who was to become known as Congregationalism's leading liturgiologist, was inducted to Emmanuel in May 1952, having been recommended by John Huxtable. Emmanuel's ministerial committee was informed that Todd had done 'all the donkey work connected with the Book of Congregational Worship'.[88] Three months after his arrival, Todd announced the integration of communion, which had been a separate event, into the preaching services. 'The point of the new procedure', said Todd in the church's *Bulletin*, 'is to emphasise the unity of the Service of Word and Sacrament.'[89] Within a year Todd had preached a series at Emmanuel on the Apostles' Creed and was hosting a conference on the subject of 'Ministry', at which, he announced, his friend Daniel Jenkins, minister of the Church of the Peace of God, Oxted (a strongly liturgical Congregational church), was speaking.[90] Todd was associate editor of *The Presbyter* and visiting pastor at Mansfield College under John Marsh's principalship, with his local ministry contributing to his wider reputation. By the end of the 1950s Emmanuel, which could attract over five hundred worshippers to its liturgical services, was a noted London Congregational church.[91] The vision for reformation of worship which had taken shape in the 1930s was steadily affecting the grass-roots of Congregational life.

*   *   *

Changes in Congregational worship which sprang from the 1930s were rooted in continuity with the past. 'If we offer to our people any substitute for this holy and historic Sacrament', said Manning in 1933 of baptism, 'we shall move into a false position, false alike to Holy Scripture, to the Reformation, to our own traditions, and to the spiritual experience of many of us.'[92] The past was used as a critique of the present. Instead of the traditional solemnity of 'Scripture read and prayer offered', many sermons, hymns, and prayers were, according to Manning and Micklem, about mountain scenery, emotional states, and psychological maladjustments. Sermons gave the impression of 'a bird

---

[88] A. Green to R. E. Palmer, 19 Dec. 1951. Letters and notes regarding Todd's settlement are in the Emmanuel Church Ministerial Committee archives, held in Emmanuel Church, The Grove, West Wickham, Kent. See *The United Reformed Church Year Book* (London, 1978), p. 270.

[89] *The Bulletin*, Aug. 1952.

[90] Ibid., Oct. 1952; March 1953.

[91] Ibid., June 1955; March 1957; Sept. 1959.

[92] *CW*, 25 May 1933, p. 13.

that flits and hovers over the waters but never dives to catch a fish'.[93] Peel, who had little sympathy with calls for reformation of preaching and sacramental practice, vividly summed up the differing approaches when he spoke of the beating of the Barthian drum, the jazz music of Fundamentalists, and the ballet of modernists.[94] From the standpoint of Reformed renewal, however, there was increasing convergence, not divergence. The coming together of Congregationalists and Presbyterians on the basis of their Reformed heritage led to the establishment in 1972 of the United Reformed Church – which has been called 'Micklem's Church' – with John Huxtable as its General Secretary.[95] There were also broader convergences. The hymns of the evangelical revival, Manning argued, mirrored the emphasis on the cross of Christ found in ancient liturgies such as 'O Lamb of God that takest away the sins of the world, Have mercy upon us.'[96] In all its austerity, Congregational worship was seen as the conveyer of the diverse riches to be found in Catholic, Reformed, and evangelical worship.

Spurgeon's College, London

---

[93] Manning, 'Older Dissent', p. 296; *BW*, 23 July 1936, p. 327; *CW*, 20 Oct. 1938, p. 6.

[94] *CW*, 17 Nov. 1938, p. 5.

[95] D. W. Norwood, 'The case for democracy in Church government: a study in the reformed tradition with special reference to the Congregationalism of Robert William Dale, Peter Taylor Forsyth, Albert Peel and Nathaniel Micklem' (University of London Ph.D. thesis, 1983), p. 150.

[96] Manning, *Essays*, p. 19.

RESERVATION UNDER PRESSURE: RITUAL IN THE PRAYER BOOK CRISIS, 1927–1928

by IAN MACHIN

THE Prayer Book controversy of 1927–8 was not merely 'the echo of dead themes', as was alleged by A. J. P. Taylor.[1] Disputes between Evangelicals and Anglo-Catholics, which lay at the root of the crisis, were still at a height in the 1920s and 1930s. Anglo-Catholic confidence was shown in their vast Congresses, commencing in 1920 (and lasting until the 1960s), and in the celebrations and publications which marked the centenary of the Oxford Movement in 1933.[2] Such confidence naturally caused Evangelicals and Broad Churchmen to look to their defences. Moreover, while in England anti-Romanism was less marked than before 1914, in Scotland it reached a high (if belated) peak in the 1920s in reaction to Irish Catholic immigration.

Over the question of growing Ritualism in the Church of England there had been a long dispute since about 1860, which reached its final peak in the Prayer Book crisis of the 1920s.[3] Ritualism was feared as importing 'idolatry' into the Church of England against the more pronounced doctrinal ideas of the Reformation, a process which might result in leading England back to Rome. The general concept of Ritualism embraced not merely vestments, ornaments, and ceremonial, but doctrinal concepts of which the vestments and ornaments were symbols.

Belief in the Real Presence in the consecrated elements in holy communion (whether the presence was believed to be spiritual alone, or corporeal as well) was the clearest doctrinal tendency of Ritualism. Reservation of the sacrament, and the possibility of worship before the reserved sacrament, were among the leading matters of ecclesiastical dispute in the early twentieth century. Perpetual reservation (as

---

[1] A. J. P. Taylor, *English History, 1914–45* (Oxford, 1965), p. 259.
[2] W. S. F. Pickering, *Anglo-Catholicism: A Study in Religious Ambiguity* (London, 1989), pp. 48–63.
[3] G. I. T. Machin, *Politics and the Churches in Great Britain, 1869 to 1921* (Oxford, 1987), pp. 70–86, 234–55; O. Chadwick, *The Victorian Church*, 2 vols (London, 1966–70), 2, pp. 311–12, 319, 324; A. Wilkinson, *The Community of the Resurrection: a Centenary History* (London, 1992), pp. 104–17.

opposed to temporary reservation for the purpose of communicating the sick) was first adopted in an Anglican church (All Saints', Plymouth) in 1882. The report of the Royal Commission into Ecclesiastical Discipline in 1906, however, stated that only thirty out of a total of 559 ritualist churches in England and Wales practised perpetual reservation, though this was probably an under-estimate.[4] Archbishop Frederick Temple discouraged reservation in a declaration of May 1900, and a letter of the archbishops and bishops to their clergy in January 1901 called for compliance with this pronouncement. In spite of the episcopal appeal, reservation spread widely in the succeeding twenty-five years. This is indicated by an estimate of 1929 that about seven hundred Anglican parish churches in England, and eighty Anglican chapels not linked to parishes, practised perpetual reservation.[5] Reservation had come to be a major defining mark of pronounced Anglo-Catholicism, and the matter generated much heat. Although more relaxed views on the subject may eventually have come to prevail, the early decades of the twentieth century were not a time when compromise on reservation was likely to be reached – perhaps on the basis that there might be a Real Presence in the sacrament, not necessarily through transubstantiation but through some other operation of the powers of an Almighty God. Instead there was only likely, for the most part, to be the repetition of entrenched opinions on both sides of a strong traditional division.

Yet a compromise on the subject was what the Revised (or Alternative, or Deposited) Prayer Books of 1927 and 1928 attempted to achieve. A Royal Commission was appointed in 1904 to try to end the 'crisis in the Church' by proposing methods for establishing 'greater elasticity' and better liturgical discipline.[6] The Commission's report in 1906 put forward ten unanimous proposals. These would permit the use of confession, prayers for the dead, and (in practical terms) incense, but recommended the prohibition of practices which were declared to be 'clearly inconsistent with and subversive of the teaching of the Church of England'. These included reservation of the sacrament under

---

[4] I owe this information to Dr Nigel Yates, who is preparing a full-scale study of Ritualism.

[5] Pickering, *Anglo-Catholicism*, pp. 61–2; note by Archbishop Davidson, Feb. 1926 (London, Lambeth Palace Library, Davidson Papers [hereafter DP], 455, fols 162–3).

[6] G. K. A. Bell, *Randall Davidson, Archbishop of Canterbury*, 2 vols (Oxford, 1935), I, pp. 454–61; W. Joynson-Hicks, *The Prayer Book Crisis* (London, 1928), pp. 89–90.

conditions which might lead to its adoration, processions with the sacrament, and benediction with the sacrament.

The Commission recommended that Royal Letters of Business be issued to the Convocations of Canterbury and York to propose liturgical changes. The Revised Prayer Book of 1927 was the eventual outcome of the Convocations' deliberations. These discussions were protracted by the gravity and controversy of the subject; interruptions caused by the First World War; and the need to have the Convocations' proposals examined at length by a new governing body in the Church, the National Church Assembly. This body was established by the Church and recognized by the State in the National Assembly of the Church of England (Powers) Bill (or 'Enabling Bill') – passed by Parliament at the instance of the Church in 1919.[7] This measure was intended to devolve upon the Church a more efficient means than direct parliamentary legislation for introducing changes to its government. But it was still left to Parliament, through the intermediacy of an Ecclesiastical Committee, to decide in cases where it was sought to make such a change the law of the land and not simply a resolution of the Church.

The commission given to the Convocations in 1906 stated that they should prepare revisions to be placed before Parliament. From 1919 it was intended that, after the National Church Assembly had approved the revisions, it should seek the backing of legal enactment in Parliament for them. This solicitation of parliamentary approval occurred unsuccessfully in 1927 and again in 1928.

That the revisions, in the form of an alternative Prayer Book, failed to gain the approval of the House of Commons (though they were easily carried in the House of Lords) was not the result of a desire by the Commons to vindicate its remaining powers over the Church. The rejection reflected the differences among members of the Church, including those in the House of Commons, over doctrine and liturgy and especially reservation. It also reflected the fact that Parliament contained not only Anglicans, but men and women of different denominations and religions, and of no religion. The non-Anglican vote on the Revised Prayer Book was divided. The Roman Catholic M.P.s abstained from the debates and divisions, and by no means all non-Anglican Protestant M.P.s opposed the measure.

---

[7] Machin, *Politics and the Churches*, pp. 317–20.

But enough non-Anglican M.P.s voted against it to sway the divisions and cause the Book's defeat.

* * *

During the early and mid-1920s, the matter proceeded to its climax, or rather anti-climax. The Convocations drew up a reply to the Letters of Business issued in 1906. This was considered by a committee of the National Church Assembly, and resulted in the presentation of a Revised Prayer Book Measure to the Assembly in 1923, together with a Schedule prepared virtually by the Convocations. The Measure and Schedule received general approval and were then considered in detail by each of the three Houses (of Bishops, Clergy, and Laity) in the Assembly.[8] The Archbishop of Canterbury, Randall Davidson, submitted a final draft of the House of Bishops' proposals to a joint session of the two Convocations on 7 February 1927.[9] Davidson was allegedly not deeply concerned about the changes he was advocating, but he was anxious for more peace and discipline in his Church.[10] He informed the Convocations that the Revised Prayer Book was intended as an alternative to the existing *Book of Common Prayer* of 1662, not a replacement of it. No clergyman need abandon any use of the 1662 Book, which would be included (with only some small changes regarding the minor Offices) in the new composite volume. The revised parts of the latter represented an attempt to bring peace to the Church by enlarging the comprehensiveness of the Book.[11]

Among the matters of detail treated by Davidson in his speech were the controversial matter of an Alternative Order for holy communion, and what he described as 'the anxious question of the Reservation of the Consecrated elements for the Communion of the Sick . . . and for no other purpose'. In resemblance to a traditional practice of the Scottish Episcopal Church, the Revised Book would permit continuous reservation for the purpose of communicating the sick and dying, but it would not allow any services of worship before the reserved sacrament.[12] These limits, it would soon be seen, were too generous

[8] Bell, *Davidson*, 2, pp. 1327–35.

[9] *Chronicle of the Convocation of Canterbury*, 7/vi, pp. 3–31 (7 Feb. 1927). Cf. draft of Davidson's speech, dated 28 Jan. 1927: DP, 450, fols 48–80.

[10] Bell, *Davidson*, 2, pp. 1331–3; H. Hensley Henson, *Retrospect of an Unimportant Life*, 2 vols in 1 (London, 1943), 2, p. 162.

[11] *Chronicle of the Convocation of Canterbury*, 7/vi, p. 13 (7 Feb. 1927).

[12] Ibid., pp. 16–17; A. Hastings, *A History of English Christianity, 1920–85* (London, 1986), pp. 203–5.

for some and not capacious enough for others. In his concluding remarks, Davidson stressed his belief that 'nothing that we have suggested makes any change in the doctrinal position of the Church of England'.[13] Archbishop Lang of York, who spoke after Davidson, emphasised that the discretion of a clergyman to use the revised sections of the composite Book would be dependent on the agreement of his Parochial Church Council; and that he could also consult his parishioners generally about the changes he proposed to make. The provisions in the composite Book could also be supplemented by special forms of worship issued by a bishop for use in his diocese.[14]

The debates and voting in Convocation following the formal presentation of the Prayer Book Measure on 29 and 30 March revealed that some Evangelicals were in favour of the measure and some Anglo-Catholics were against it, as well as *vice versa*. The Upper (episcopal) House of York Convocation voted unanimously in favour of the measure. But in the Upper House of Canterbury Convocation twenty-one bishops voted in favour and four against – the latter being Lord William Cecil of Exeter, Ernest Pearce of Worcester, Bertram Pollock of Norwich, and Ernest Barnes of Birmingham (who, as a scientific modernist, gave the opinion that reservation encouraged fetish worship).[15] The Lower House of York Convocation voted 68–10 in favour of the measure, the well-known Anglo-Catholic G. C. Ommanney of Sheffield opposing; and the Lower House of Canterbury voted 168–22 in favour, the prominent Anglo-Catholic canons Sparrow Simpson and Darwell Stone (Principal of Pusey House) expressing opposition.[16]

The measure was then submitted to the Church Assembly, and debated and voted on there on 5 and 6 July 1927, in a final official airing before it was presented to the Ecclesiastical Committee of Parliament. In the Church Assembly debate Darwell Stone again voiced Anglo-Catholic doubts about the measure, and the Home

---

[13] *Chronicle of the Convocation of Canterbury*, 7/vi, pp. 17–18 (7 Feb. 1927).

[14] Ibid., pp. 23–4, 27.

[15] For Barnes's view on this subject, see F. A. Iremonger, *William Temple, Archbishop of Canterbury, his Life and Letters* (London, 1948), p. 348.

[16] *Chronicle of the Convocation of Canterbury*, 7/vi, pp. 73–162 (division lists, pp. 158–61) (29–30 March 1927); Bell, *Davidson*, 2, pp. 1335–6. For some of Sparrow Simpson's views on reservation, see his speech in Convocation, 28 April 1920 (*Chronicle of the Convocation of Canterbury*, 3/v, pp. 336–42). See also Darwell Stone, ed., *The Deposited Prayer Book, by a Group of Priests* (London, 1927); F. L. Cross, *Darwell Stone, Churchman and Counsellor* (London, 1943), p. 176.

Secretary (Sir William Joynson-Hicks, known as 'Jix') and the Solicitor-General (Sir Thomas Inskip) expressed Evangelical opposition.[17] Joynson-Hicks had long been known as a prominent opponent of Ritualism, and in 1925 had given an address (later printed) to a meeting of the World's Evangelical Alliance, entitled *The Reformation: a Clarion Call to Britain*. He had already failed, in correspondence with Davidson, to obtain the absolute assurance he wanted, in relation to the provisions of the Revised Book, that any clergyman who wished to use the reserved sacrament for purposes of adoration could have 'no part or lot in the future of the Church of England'.[18] Majorities in favour of the Book, however, were very clear in all three Houses of the Assembly: in the House of Bishops, 34–4 (the four bishops already mentioned providing the minority); in the House of Clergy, 253–37; and in the House of Laity, 230–92.[19]

Well before this, the issue had extended far beyond official Church bodies to become a matter of widespread controversy. 'The interest in the country', wrote Bishop Bell in his substantial account,

> was extraordinary. All through the year the papers were full of news, speeches, and letters: and an immense flood of pamphlets was produced. . . . There were objections to the Book from very different camps – that it was too modernist, too old-fashioned, too rigid, too loose, that there were too many prayers for the dead, and too few prayers for the King.[20]

The question, in the revised sections, of reduced prayers for the sovereign – what Lang called 'the absurd agitation about the alleged treatment of prayers for the King' – was of considerable importance in the disputes.[21] It might actually have had some weight, said Bishop E. S. Talbot in a letter in *The Times*, if the episcopate was notorious for its republican opinions.[22] As for prayers for the dead, they were

---

[17] Bell, *Davidson*, 2, p. 1340; A. Fox, *Dean Inge* (London, 1960), p. 215.

[18] Bell, *Davidson*, 2, pp. 1336–9; memo. of Davidson, 7 March 1927 (DP, 451, fol. 76); Joynson-Hicks–Davidson, 18 March 1927 (ibid., fols 144–5); Davidson–Joynson-Hicks, 21 March 1927 (ibid., fols 156–8).

[19] Bell, *Davidson*, 2, p. 1340; Fox, *Inge*, p. 215.

[20] Bell, *Davidson*, 2, p. 1339.

[21] J. G. Lockhart, *Cosmo Gordon Lang* (London, 1949), p. 303; Waldron Smithers, MP–Lang, 12 July 1927 (DP, 452, fols 191–2); Lang–Smithers, 15 July 1927 (ibid., fols 193–4). See also Lang Papers (London, Lambeth Palace Library), 57, fols 274–90.

[22] *The Times*, 10 Dec. 1927, p. 13. Cf. ibid., 9 Dec. 1927, p. 10 (letter from Lord Daryngton).

condemned by a meeting of Liverpool laity said to have been attended by 3,000.[23] But neither of these matters rivalled reservation as the chief point at issue. The main controversy, as Archbishop Garbett of York noted when later reviewing the crisis,

> raged ... round the proposal to allow the consecrated elements to be reserved for the communion of the sick, and the new Order of the Holy Communion. Both were fiercely attacked; the Evangelicals feared that Reservation would lead to superstition, and to services of adoration usual in the Roman Catholic Church; the extreme Anglo-Catholics were afraid that they would be hindered in the devotional use they desired to make of the reserved sacrament.[24]

* * *

Archbishop Davidson's correspondence amply reveals the different opinions on the issue, and the foremost position of reservation in the case. Opposition to the proposed changes came strongly from 'the extreme Evangelicals and the advanced Anglo-Catholics',[25] while acquiescence in them came – not without a good deal of heart-searching in some cases – from more moderate members of both these groups. The League of Loyal Churchmen and Protestant Alliance sent an appeal to the archbishops and bishops saying that, judged by the Bible as the Standard of Truth, 'the Reservation of the Sacrament for any purpose whatever is condemned'.[26] John Alfred Kensit expressed his fear that, while the proposals 'might only go halfway in the Anglo-Catholic direction', 'the other half' might not be 'definitely disallowed and suppressed'.[27] The United Council of the Principal London and Provincial Protestant Societies resolved to call on all Protestants to try and 'ensure the defeat of this ignoble attempt to secure a legalised footing for Romish and Rationalistic teaching and practice within the National Church'.[28] The Revd H. W. Hinde, Vicar of Islington, told

[23] Davidson–Ronald McNeill, 10 March 1927 (copy); DP, 451, fol. 93.

[24] C. Garbett, *Church and State in England* (London, 1950), pp. 212–13.

[25] From leaflet issued by the League of Loyalty and Order in support of the Prayer Book Measure: DP, 452, fol. 22.

[26] 'A further appeal to the Bishops with reference to the Revision of the Prayer Book', enclosed in Revd E. G. Bowring and H. Fowler (Secretaries to the League of Loyal Churchmen) to Davidson, 10 Jan. 1927: ibid., 450, fols 11–12.

[27] Kensit–Davidson, 13 Jan. 1927: ibid., 450, fol. 15. Cf. Kensit–Davidson, 21 Feb. 1927 (ibid., fols 217–18); Joynson-Hicks–Davidson, 24 Feb. 1927 (ibid., fols 249–53).

[28] 11 Feb. 1927; DP, 451, fols 103–5.

Davidson that 1,500 clergy had signed a memorandum against reservation for any purpose whatsoever.[29]

Nearly a hundred Anglican incumbents who formed the Protestant Parsons' Pilgrimage in Defence of the Reformation (which was linked to the Fellowship of Evangelical Churchmen) argued that the Revised Book went a long way towards re-introducing the Roman mass, and should be abandoned.[30] A small deputation to Davidson from this group said that they could remain in the Church of England if they were fully assured that they could use the existing (1662) Prayer Book exactly as it was; and, moreover, if they were given, under the licence of the Archbishop of Canterbury, 'a special set of Bishops with a roving commission to enter any diocese and conduct services strictly and exclusively along the lines of the present Prayer Book.'[31] Davidson replied that he could not sanction such a surprising scheme, as it would clearly divide the Church of England.[32] Bishop Barnes feared that acceptance of the Revised Book would make it impossible to restore discipline in the Church.[33]

Nonconformists reacted in different ways to the Revised Book even when they belonged to the same denomination. Among those who were very suspicious of the revisions was Dr W. B. Selbie, Principal of the Congregationalist Mansfield College, Oxford. He informed the Protestant Dissenting Deputies that 'if the Established Church of the land ceased in any way to be a Protestant Church', the question of disestablishment in England would have to be revived.[34] Similarly, the Baptist annual assembly in April 1927 resolved that the Church of England should seek the liberty to adopt whatever changes it wished by means of disestablishment alone.[35] The Liberation Society, on the other hand, said that it was 'completely neutral' towards the Revised Book, but it wanted Parliament to reject it, because this action might promote a desire for disestablishment within the Church of England.[36]

---

[29] Hinde–Davidson, 2 March 1927 (ibid., fol. 31); 14 Oct. 1927 (ibid., 453, fol. 200).

[30] Revd G. Denyer–Davidson, 14 Mar. 1927; ibid., 451, fols 124–9.

[31] Memo. of 11 July 1927; DP, 452, fol. 173. Cf. Revd G. Denyer–Davidson, 14 July 1927 (ibid., fols 189–90), giving more details about this scheme.

[32] Memo. of 11 July 1927; ibid., 452, fol. 173.

[33] *The Times*, 13 Dec. 1927, p. 9.

[34] *British Weekly*, 8 Dec. 1927, p. 278.

[35] *Baptist Handbook*, 1928, p. 191. Cf. Revd M. E. Aubrey (General Secretary of the Baptist Union of Great Britain and Ireland) to the Secretary of the Ecclesiastical Committee of Parliament, 15 Sept. 1927; DP, 453, fols 58–62.

[36] Letter from Viscount Wolmer in *The Times*, 9 Dec. 1927, p. 10.

On a very different plain from the Evangelical hostility to the proposals was the opposition of the more extreme Anglo-Catholics, who objected to the restrictions on reservation in the Revised Book. Illustrating such opinions was a memorandum of the Central Council of Catholic (that is, Anglo-Catholic) Societies, representing the views of the English Church Union, the Federation of Catholic Priests, and the Confraternity of the Blessed Sacrament. This document called for the revision to be postponed for further discussion, and stated that 'a large body of Anglo-Catholic opinion' could not accept rubrics which prohibited 'all corporate worship of our Lord in the Holy Sacrament when Reserved'.[37] Davidson issued a circular letter to his bishops in July 1927, warning them to resist some Anglo-Catholic efforts in regard to the Revised Book.[38]

The emphatic opposition of extreme Anglo-Catholics continued to develop. In November 1927 the General Secretary of the Federation of Catholic Priests (Revd Dudley Dixon) informed Davidson that the Federation had resolved, regardless of the restrictions in the Revised Book, to teach the people 'to offer the same worship to our Lord in the sacrament when reserved as within the action of the Liturgy'; and, moreover, 'to support those of its members who, convinced of the need, reserve the Blessed Sacrament in their Parish Church when the Diocesan prohibits the practice'.[39]

There was clearly much dislike of the Revised Book from opposite sides. But there was also enthusiastic clerical and lay support for accepting the proposed changes, shown in letters and at meetings.[40] At the diocesan conferences which voted on the new Book, the total vote in favour was 8,415, and the total against was 1,969.[41] Many Anglo-Catholic clergy seemed ready to accept the proposals, finding in them at least some satisfaction for their sacramental views and other liturgical wishes.[42] Some leading Nonconformists also showed their

[37] The memorandum was sent to Davidson by Revd Arnold Pinchard, Secretary of the English Church Union, 1 March 1927; DP, 451, fols 22–4. Cf. Revd L. A. Matthew–Davidson, 9 Sept. 1927 (ibid., 453, fols 48–50).

[38] Circular letter from Davidson, 22 July 1927 (ibid., 452, fols 207, 253, 260–2); Bishop of Bath and Wells (St John Wilson)–Davidson, 24 July 1927 (ibid., fol. 253).

[39] Dixon–Davidson, 7 Nov. 1927; ibid., 454, fol. 47.

[40] E.g. Revd E. Swords–Davidson, 11 Feb. 1927 (ibid., 450, fols 153–4); Revd H. W. Blackmore–Davidson, 11 and 17 Feb. 1927 (ibid., fols 146, 173).

[41] Iremonger, *Temple*, p. 351.

[42] Revd C. Harris–Davidson, 24 March 1927 (ibid., 451, fols 238–9); Revd F. Underhill–Davidson, 25 March 1927 (ibid., fol. 245), 19 Aug. 1927 (ibid., 453, fols 33–5), 27 Sept. 1927 (fols 100–2).

readiness to accept the reform, notably the Wesleyan Scott Lidgett, the Congregationalist A. E. Garvie, and the Presbyterian Carnegie Simpson.[43] Garvie said in a letter to *The Times* that 'it is not the duty of Free Churchmen to advise any hostile action in Parliament.'[44] Simpson stated that, in the new Book, there was not 'such a specific denial of reformed doctrine and evangelical religion as would demand uncompromising opposition'.[45] But he wanted assurance that discipline would be firmly applied in support of the new options if they were carried, so that variations would not occur between dioceses in accordance with the liturgical inclinations of the individual bishops.[46] In similar vein, the chairman of the Anglican Evangelical Group Movement, Revd H. Montagu Dale, informed Davidson that his organization acquiesced in the new Book on the understanding that it would restore discipline in the Church.[47]

* * *

After the Revised Book had passed the Church Assembly in July, the next procedure was to deposit the Book (hence one of its names, 'Deposited Prayer Book') for consideration by the Ecclesiastical Committee of Parliament. The Ecclesiastical Committee appointed a sub-committee which considered objections to the Book from a variety of quarters in the late summer and autumn of 1927. The sub-committee's report was thought sufficient for the Ecclesiastical Committee to declare, on 24 November, that 'no change of constitutional importance is involved' in the proposals, and, in particular, nothing to infringe the Coronation Oath 'to maintain the Protestant Reformed Religion established by law'.[48] The Prayer Book Measure was then submitted to Parliament and was debated first in the Lords and then in the Commons in mid-December.

The general opinions already noted appeared again in the parliamentary debates, together with others. Davidson opened the debate in the Lords on 12 December by moving that the measure be approved

---

[43] Lidgett–Davidson, 11 July 1927 (ibid., 452, fol. 271).

[44] 12 Dec. 1927, p. 15.

[45] Simpson's address as Moderator to the Free Church Federal Council, on 'The Free Churches and the New Prayer Book', 19 Sept. 1927; DP, 453, fol. 86.

[46] Ibid., fol. 89, also fol. 92; and note of discussion between Simpson and Davidson at Lambeth Palace, 6 Oct. 1927 (ibid., fols 191–3).

[47] Dale–Davidson, 31 Oct. 1927; ibid., 454, fol. 314.

[48] Bell, *Davidson*, 2, p. 1342.

and presented to the king for the royal assent.[49] The impressive three-day debate concluded late on 14 December with a division of 241 to 88 in favour of the measure, the House having waxed theological to a considerable degree.[50] There were some notable speeches of an evangelical cast against the Book because of its reservation provisions.[51] Opposing from an Anglo-Catholic viewpoint was Viscount Halifax, former and future President of the English Church Union. He said he would abstain from voting, but seemed to be trying to deepen Evangelical fears of the Book by denying that it could establish discipline over reservation: 'How . . . will they deal with the view of the clergy who deny the right of any Bishop to forbid the reservation of the Blessed Sacrament?'[52] The divisions in the Church of England, he suggested, might be reduced through conciliatory discussions between the differing groups, but certainly not by an Act of Parliament.[53]

After passing the Lords the measure immediately went to the Commons. Here, it had been suggested, the passage would be easier; but in fact the Commons rejected the Book after seven hours' debate on 15 December. Although shorter than the debate in the Lords, the exchanges in the Lower House were more intense and impassioned, perhaps as befitted the commonalty. The dominant strand in the opposition to the measure in the Commons was strongly Protestant, displaying zealous defence of the Reformation against what was seen as the Book's threat to it. The Evangelical opponents of the measure among the M.P.s had been organizing their forces well before the debate. A preparatory inter-party meeting of about a hundred M.P.s, at which Joynson-Hicks presided, was held on 30 November. Four Whips were appointed to marshal opposition, and an executive committee of six was elected, including Joynson-Hicks, the Labour M.P. Rosslyn Mitchell, and Sir Thomas Inskip (Solicitor-General) – all of whom were prominent in denouncing the measure in the Commons' debate.[54]

On 15 December William Bridgeman, First Lord of the Admiralty,

[49] *Parliamentary Debates (Official Report)*, 5th ser. [hereafter *Hansard*]: House of Lords, 69 (8 Nov.–22 Dec. 1927), cols 771–93.

[50] Hastings, *English Christianity*, pp. 205–6.

[51] *Hansard* (Lords), 69, cols 793–807, 815–17, 852–9, 866–79, 895–903,937–51, 957–68.

[52] Ibid., col. 844.

[53] Ibid., cols 844–5.

[54] *The Times*, 1 Dec. 1927, p. 16.

moved adoption of the measure in a cautious and diffident speech which won him no thanks.[55] The next speaker, Joynson-Hicks, launched into a much more powerful oration which, according to the contemporary accounts, did much to sway the House. He held that the alternative communion service in the Book would bring the Church 'nearer to the mediaeval ideas which were abolished by us at the time of the Reformation'; and that, despite the restrictions in the Book, the sacrament could not be reserved without encouraging general worship: 'Although it is only reserved for the purposes of the sick, it is placed in a specific spot in the church itself . . . and men and women do, and probably must, from their own religious point of view, use it in an act of worship.'[56] He gave examples of adoration of the Blessed Sacrament which were currently taking place in Anglican churches, and urged that Reservation should not be legalized or sanctioned.[57] In addition, he deplored that the measure permitted archbishops and bishops – men who had failed to impose discipline on the Church – to adopt additional regulations without the authority of Parliament.[58]

Joynson-Hicks was supported later in the debate by the equally powerful speech of Rosslyn Mitchell, a lawyer who represented Paisley in the Labour interest and was a member of the United Free Church of Scotland. Mitchell 'fulminated like an old Covenanter', according to Dean Inge.[59] He used illustrations from English Reformation history (rather than Scottish) in appealing to the House against the measure. Archbishop Davidson, who heard the debate from the gallery, deplored the speech as being probably more effective than any other in winning votes.[60] Mitchell claimed that the Revised Book encouraged belief in transubstantiation. He alleged that, by adopting the Book, 'in one generation . . . you can swing over all the children of England from the Protestant Reformed Faith to the Roman Catholic Faith.'[61] After Mitchell came several other strong speeches against the measure –

[55] *Hansard: House of Commons*, 211 (28 Nov.–16 Dec. 1927), cols 2531–40; P. Williamson, ed., *The Modernisation of Conservative Politics: the Diaries and Letters of William Bridgeman, 1904–35* (London, 1988), pp. 211–14. For the debate see Bell, *Davidson*, 2, pp. 1345–6; Lockhart, *Lang*, pp. 304–6.

[56] *Hansard: House of Commons*, 211, cols 2543–4.

[57] Ibid.

[58] Ibid., col. 2549; H. A. Taylor, *Jix, Viscount Brentford* (London, 1933), pp. 253–60.

[59] Fox, *Inge*, p. 216.

[60] Bell, *Davidson*, 2, p. 1346.

[61] *Hansard: House of Commons*, 211, cols 2560–7.

including those of Sir John Simon, Stephen Walsh, Sir Douglas Hogg, and Sir Thomas Inskip.[62]

Among speeches by supporters of the Book were those of Sir Henry Slesser, an Anglo-Catholic, who emphasised that sacramentalism was not necessarily Romish; and Stanley Baldwin, the Prime Minister, who argued that the Book reflected the traditional dual nature of the Church of England in regard to the eucharist.[63] But these could not match the eloquent force of the Book's opponents. The defenders of the measure were 'strangely ineffective', commented Bishop Garbett; 'they seemed to be surprised and taken aback at the strength of the opposition'.[64] The defenders included C. G. Ammon, a Wesleyan, who held that 'the Deposited book in no way contravened the Protestant religion'.[65] Lord Hugh Cecil, who it was hoped would be the main oratorical champion of the measure, disappointed expectations. He defended the Protestant credentials of the Book but failed to reassure enough of his audience on this score.[66] Bishop William Temple, who strongly favoured the Revised Book, said that 'the one effective speaker on our side [in the Commons] was a Baptist minister!'[67] This was Revd Herbert Dunnico, Labour M.P. for Consett, County Durham, who said: 'there is nothing in the Reservation of the Sacrament under the rules laid down in the Revised Prayer Book that I could not conscientiously and honestly accept and vote for.... If you reject this Measure, will you stop the Romeward tendency? You will aggravate it.'[68] A final one-sentence contribution to the debate came from another Labour M.P., and perhaps reminded the House that the General Strike had occurred only eighteen months before: 'I want to say this, on behalf of the great mass of the workers of this country, that they are more interested in the rent book than they are in the Prayer Book.'[69]

In the division the opposition triumphed, the measure being lost by 238 to 205. The 'no' votes given by some of the non-Anglicans carried

[62] *Hansard: House of Commons*, cols 2571–8, 2603–7, 2620–5, 2637–48.

[63] Ibid., cols 2615–20, 2648–52, 2597–603, 2632–7.

[64] Garbett, *Church and State in England*, p. 213.

[65] *Hansard: House of Commons*, 211, col. 2559.

[66] Ibid., cols 2578–92.

[67] Iremonger, *Temple*, p. 352; *Church Times*, 23 Dec. 1927, p. 743.

[68] *Hansard: House of Commons*, 211, cols 2627–9.

[69] Ibid., col. 2652. See also S. Ball, ed., *Parliament and Politics in the Age of Baldwin and MacDonald: the Headlam Diaries, 1923–35* (London, 1992), pp. 135–7 (also pp. 143, 148–9).

the day, against the majority of Anglican M.P.s and the majority of M.P.s for English constituencies.[70] For example, the Baptist Lloyd George joined the Scottish United Free Churchmen Rosslyn Mitchell, Thomas Johnston, and the Revd James Barr, the Congregationalist Sir John Simon, and a Communist Parsee, Sapurji Saklatvala, in the 'no' lobby. The M.P.s for Scottish constituencies voted 33–6 against the Book, and the M.P.s for Welsh constituencies 18–2 against, though there were many abstentions in both cases.

* * *

The question whether the Church Assembly, having had its measure rejected by Parliament, should seek disestablishment in order to pursue its aims in freedom, was considered by some. The bishops, however, were intent on trying to persuade the Commons to accept a modified (or re-revised) Book. The two archbishops issued a statement on 23 December 1927, on behalf of the House of Bishops in the Church Assembly, that it had been decided to submit a revised measure.[71] The ensuing alterations, however, caused fresh dispute. Certain Anglo-Catholics – such as Bishop Frere and Canon B. J. Kidd, Warden of Keble College – had found the first measure the very most they could accept, and could not acquiesce in the proposed new version. The restoration of prayers for the monarch at morning and evening services was a non-controversial alteration, and the addition of the 'Black Rubric' against transubstantiation to the Alternative Order for Holy Communion apparently aroused little Anglo-Catholic perturbation. But there was alarm among some Anglo-Catholics over the more closely defined restrictions on continuous reservation for communicating the sick.[72] Darwell Stone, who had not accepted the first Revised Book, wrote in a new pamphlet that, while the 'Black Rubric' was 'not incompatible with the doctrine that the consecrated Sacrament is the body and blood of Christ, and that Christ is therein to be adored', the conditions on which reservation was to be allowed made

---

[70] *The Times*, 20 Dec. 1927, p. 16.

[71] Davidson–Lang, 29 Dec. 1927 (DP, 454, fols 270–3); Marquess of Salisbury–Davidson, 30 Dec. 1927, and enclosures (ibid., fols 286–301); also correspondence in DP 455, fols 18–66, and London, Lambeth Palace Library, Minutes of the Council of the English Church Union, 18 April 1928.

[72] Copy of letter, 'Anglo-Catholics and the Prayer Book', 31 Jan. 1928 (DP, 454, fol. 117); *Chronicle of Convocation of Canterbury*, 7/vii, pp. 1–5, 31–8 (speeches of Frere and Kidd), 94–5 (speech of Sparrow Simpson) (28 March 1928).

no concessions at all to the many Anglo-Catholics who desired more open practice.[73]

On the other hand, the alterations did not achieve their aim of obtaining more Evangelical support for the Book.[74] The Commons' rejection had perhaps encouraged more Evangelicals to oppose the Book, or at least to withhold support. In the Convocations and the Church Assembly the majorities for the re-revised Book, although still large, were smaller than for the first one. In April 1928 the majority in the Church Assembly as a whole was 396–153, compared with 517–133 for the first Book – a drop of 141.[75]

The 'Amended Deposited' Book therefore entered the House of Commons in a weakened rather than a strengthened state. After a debate on 13–14 June the Book was defeated by a rather larger majority than in December (266–220).[76] The same views came largely from the same speakers as before, and again reservation was the core of their comments. 'The question of Reservation is the crux of the whole matter', said Joynson-Hicks; 'It was the crux in December, and it is the crux today.'[77] The Church's lengthy efforts to obtain an agreed or at least a tolerated legal settlement were again overturned by the Commons.[78]

Nevertheless, the prospect of a disestablishment campaign was not markedly enhanced. From its main base among some Nonconformists the demand had ebbed since the First World War, and indeed before it, and there was little sign that the claim was now being clearly transferred to sections of the Church of England. The Commons' rejection in December 1927 did give the claim one episcopal supporter – the disputatious Bishop of Durham, Hensley Henson, who had strongly supported the Revised Book and described the opposition to it as 'an army of illiterates led by octogenarians'.[79] Although a previous champion of the Church's Established status, Henson now declared

---

[73] D. Stone, *The Prayer Book Measure and the Deposited Book*, 2nd edn (London, 1928), pp. 10–11.

[74] Declaration by the League of Loyal Churchmen and Protestant Alliance, 25 Jan. 1928: DP, 455, fol. 118.

[75] Joynson-Hicks, *The Prayer Book Crisis*, pp. 140–56.

[76] *Hansard: House of Commons*, 218 (5–22 June 1928), cols 1003–1139, 1197–1324.

[77] Ibid., cols 1121–39, 1197–1211, 1230–41; Taylor, *Jix, Viscount Brentford*, pp. 261–6.

[78] Bell, *Davidson*, 2, pp. 1347–51; Lockhart, *Lang*, pp. 307–8; Garbett, *Church and State*, pp. 214–15; explanatory memo. on 'Prayer Book Measure, 1928', March 1928 (DP, 455, fols 194–5).

[79] Quoted in Hastings, *English Christianity*, p. 206.

that only disestablishment could give the Church full spiritual authority and independence.[80] But his addresses and publications in favour of his new cause fell generally on stony ground. His campaign was virtually a one-man effort and did not last. In 1935 the report of a Commission on the relations of Church and State rejected disestablishment as a solution.[81] Disestablishment might have attracted more support if the conflict over the Revised Book had been more clearly one of Church against State. It was partly such a conflict, but was also one between opposing groups in the Church as well as the State.

The Church had to decide how it would cope with the liturgical diversity which had caused the divisions shown in 1927 and 1928. Parliament had refused to make the book of 1928 the law of the land, but it could still be made a rule of the Church – although it might be disregarded as not being part of the civil law. 'The Bishops must ... do the best they can without law by their own authority', wrote Lord Hugh Cecil to Davidson immediately after the defeat in December.[82]

Perhaps encouraged by these sentiments, and by a letter from Lord Birkenhead in *The Times* suggesting this course of action, the meeting of bishops on 23 December (already referred to) declared unanimously that the Church should maintain its 'inalienable right' to formulate its faith and liturgy.[83] A similar resolution followed the second rejection in June 1928. Accordingly, the 1928 Book was published at the end of the year. In 1929 Lang, the new Archbishop of Canterbury, declared that 'during the present emergency and until further order be taken' the bishops would permit the use of any liturgical additions or deviations (to the *Book of Common Prayer*) within the limits of the rejected Book.[84]

'The present emergency' still continues. Despite sporadic calls for action, there was no effective move to end it. The Church of England adopted (officially illegally) diverse liturgical forms, without incurring any action by the civil law or by Parliament. This remained the case in

[80] O. Chadwick, *Hensley Henson* (Oxford, 1983), pp. 203–8; E. Norman, *Church and Society in England, 1770–1970* (Oxford, 1976), pp. 342–5; H. Henson, *Disestablishment: the Charge Delivered at the Second Quadrennial Visitation of his Diocese* (London, 1929).

[81] Norman, *Church and Society*, p. 342.

[82] Cecil–Davidson, 18 Dec. 1927, enclosing memo. of that date: DP, 454, fol. 211.

[83] Hastings, *English Christianity*, p. 207; Birkenhead's letter reprinted in full in *Church Times*, 23 Dec. 1927, pp. 749–50.

[84] Lockhart, *Lang*, pp. 309, 338–40; Garbett, *Church and State*, pp. 218–26; Bell, *Davidson*, 2, pp. 1358–9; R. C. D. Jasper, *George Bell, Bishop of Chichester* (London, 1967), pp. 165–200; Pickering, *Anglo-Catholicism*, pp. 62–3.

spite of the fact that episcopal dispensations were exceptionally given to allow devotional services before the reserved sacrament. Nor has there been any strong demand that a Church acting in this independent way should be disestablished. On the one hand, Parliament would not grant the Church Assembly what it wanted in 1927–8; on the other, it would not prevent the desired course being pursued without the support of civil law. Liturgical liberty has spread in the succeeding years – and particularly in the last three decades as the 'alternative services' of the present time testify. Amidst this licensed diversity, different conceptions of reservation and its meaning have continued to flourish.

University of Dundee

RESERVATION OF THE SACRAMENT AT WINCHESTER CATHEDRAL, 1931–1935

by T. E. DAYKIN

THE Revised Prayer Book, though twice rejected by Parliament, was published in 1928 with the notice: 'The publication of this Book does not directly or indirectly imply that it can be regarded as authorized for use in the churches.'[1] The bishops set out in July 1929 three principles by which they would guide parishes wishing to use the 1928 Book:

1. They would not regard as inconsistent with loyalty to the Church of England the use of the additions to or deviations from the 1662 Book contained in the 1928 Book. They would regard 'any other deviations as inconsistent with Church Order'.

2. They would 'endeavour to secure that the practices which are consistent neither with the Book of 1662 nor with the Book of 1928 shall cease'.

3. They would only permit 1928 usage if agreed to by the Parochial Church Councils and by the parties concerned at occasional offices.[2]

Amongst the bishops there were those like Frere of Truro who strongly promoted the Revised Book's use.[3] Barnes of Birmingham, who regarded the bishops' line as flouting parliamentary authority, urged the Archbishop to get Parliament to adopt the non-controversial parts of the Book.[4] Headlam of Gloucester and Garbett, then at Southwark, followed the general line.[5] The policy met with considerable opposition from Anglo-Catholic clergy and laity. In the diocese of London the Bishop's Regulations met with both resistance and

[1] *The Book of Common Prayer with The Additions and Deviations Proposed in 1928* (Oxford, 1928), p. v.

[2] G. K. A. Bell, *Randall Davidson, Archbishop of Canterbury*, 2 vols (London, 1935), 2, pp. 1358–9.

[3] C. S. Phillips, *Walter Howard Frere* (London, 1947), p. 140.

[4] John Barnes, *Ahead of His Age: Bishop Barnes of Birmingham* (London, 1979), pp. 220–1.

[5] Ronald Jasper, *Arthur Cayley Headlam* (London, 1960), p. 191; Charles Smyth, *Cyril Forster Garbett* (London, 1959), p. 406.

antagonism.[6] The situation remained little changed until 1947 when steps were taken to allow the Church of England greater freedom over its liturgy.

This paper describes the introduction of reservation of the sacrament, permitted by the 1928 Prayer Book, into the Cathedral at Winchester by the Dean, Edward Gordon Selwyn. Drawing mainly on correspondence generated in response to the change, it shows how one man's desire to take advantage of the Book's provisions to introduce one particular change in practice could flare up into a much broader conflict.

Selwyn was born in Liverpool in 1885 (where his father was Headmaster of Liverpool College), and moved to Uppingham as a young child. Educated at Eton and King's, Cambridge, he became a Fellow at Corpus Christi College with the influential Anglo-Catholic layman Will Spens. At twenty-eight Selwyn became Headmaster of Radley College, a post from which he was removed in 1918 after an incident involving the corporal punishment of a boy. He then settled into a country parish near Portsmouth where he launched *Theology*, being the first editor, and edited *Essays Catholic and Critical*. He served on the Church Assembly, was a member of the Doctrinal Commission, and preached and lectured in this country and overseas.

When the Deanery of Winchester fell vacant in 1930 it was first offered to F. A. Iremonger, who declined and was later appointed Director of Religion at the BBC.[7] Selwyn was installed as Dean of Winchester in January 1931 at the age of forty-five and remained there until retirement in 1958. Edward Carpenter describes him as 'ultra-orthodox, theologically-minded but awkward'.[8] When Mervyn Haigh was translated to Winchester in 1942 his biographer comments that he would come into contact with a Dean whose 'expectations of bishops were perhaps never likely to be exaggerated'.[9]

Before Selwyn came to Winchester the sacrament had been reserved informally on a number of occasions at the Cathedral for the communion of the sick. He was quick to raise the matter and wrote to the Bishop of Winchester, Theodore Woods, on 5 October 1931 that it was the 'general wish that the Blessed Sacrament should be

---

[6] F. L. Cross, *Darwell Stone: Churchman and Counsellor* (London, 1943), p. 206.

[7] Kenneth M. Wolfe, *The Churches and the British Broadcasting Corporation 1922–1956* (London, 1984), p. 58.

[8] Edward Carpenter, *Archbishop Fisher: His Life and Times* (Norwich, 1991), p. 303.

[9] F. R. Barry, *Mervyn Haigh* (London, 1964), p. 171.

continuously reserved in the cathedral'.[10] The sole purpose was for the communion of the sick, a purpose he defended throughout the controversy that followed, and more especially for 'a number of old or infirm people' who regarded the Cathedral as their parish church. Selwyn admitted there was a difference of opinion in the Chapter about the details of the conditions under which the sacrament was to be reserved; 'but all are', he thought, quite prepared to feel that this was 'a matter which rests primarily with the Dean and to accept his discretion.'

In giving consent for reservation at the Cathedral, Woods was careful to point out that in the case of the Cathedral, the Dean and not the Bishop was the Ordinary and hence it was not a matter over which he strictly had jurisdiction. Selwyn was concerned to abide by the general regulations issued by the Bishop for reservation of the sacrament in the diocese, and suggested that there should be an experimental period of six months. Woods subsequently became ill and died in February 1932. He was succeeded in June by Cyril Garbett. Selwyn raised the matter with the new Bishop who was prepared to continue the permission granted by Woods on the assurance that the initial request had been 'unanimously endorsed by the Chapter', and that it proved of 'real use in communicating the sick'.[11]

In September Garbett received a letter from a lay-reader, William Cobb of Baughurst in the Basingstoke Deanery, informing him that he had been asked to sign a Memorial 'against the practice of Reservation lately introduced in our Cathedral'. Cobb wrote again to the Bishop on 5 November, and enclosed a copy of the Memorial. The Memorial itself, with over four hundred signatures, was presented to the Bishop in April 1933. At this stage Cobb admitted to the Bishop's Secretary that it has been drawn up by the Church Association, and that the Church League approved of it. The Church Association was formed in 1865 to maintain the Protestant ideals of faith and worship in the Church of England, and actively engaged in anti-ritual litigation. In 1950 it became the Church Society, which continues to exercise considerable patronage in the appointment of Church of England clergy.

[10] Winchester, Cathedral Archives, Selwyn Papers, Letter to Frank Theodore Woods [hereafter FTW] from Edward Gordon Selwyn [hereafter EGS], 5 Oct. 1931. All further unreferenced citations of original letters are from documents in the Selwyn Papers.
[11] Letter to EGS from Cyril Foster Garbett [hereafter CFG], 7 July 1932.

Cobb wrote to Garbett on 15 September 1932, enquiring 'whether necessary steps have been or are being taken to stop this grave irregularity'.[12] Garbett replied on 26 September:

> The Consecrated Elements have been reserved in the Cathedral for nearly a year. The Dean and Chapter were unanimously in favour of doing this, and my predecessor, Dr Woods, gave his consent. As you are no doubt aware, the Dean is Ordinary of the Cathedral, and I have no intention of attempting to over-rule, even if I have the power, the decision which was made by him and the Chapter and consented to by my predecessor.[13]

Should Garbett have been in any doubt about the churchmanship of Cobb, a letter from Mrs Edith Cobb expelled it. On 1 October 1932 she assured the Bishop she 'would pray God might open your eyes' that he might ' "SEE" ', and that he should 'repent in dust and ashes', as she herself had done before her vision of a personal Saviour. 'God', she continued 'is not asking for forms and ceremonies.'[14]

The Parochial Church Council at Baughurst on 13 October 1932 passed a resolution 'that this Council views with dismay the introduction of permanent Reservation in our Cathedral, and the Quota is being put on one side and withheld until the practice stops'.[15] Garbett sensed that reservation at the Cathedral had the potential to become a major controversy, something he was anxious to avoid within four months of his enthronement. He contemplated writing to the Rural Dean to ask him to speak against the Baughurst Resolution at the Ruri-Decanal Conference and wrote on 17 October to the editor of the *Diocesan Chronicle* to prevent publication of the Resolution.[16]

Cobb had impressed upon the Bishop that the action had been taken in 'our Cathedral'. He later pointed out that the Dean had only consulted the four Residentiary Canons and not the full Chapter and hinted that the church courts would be able to settle the precise nature of the Bishop's jurisdiction in the Cathedral, especially in the case of an illegal practice.[17]

During the debate at the Ruri-Decanal Conference on 4 November

12 W. H. Cobb–CFG, 15 Sept. 1932.
13 CFG–W. H. Cobb, 26 Sept. 1932.
14 Edith Cobb–CFG, 1 Oct. 1932.
15 W. S. Stegall–CFG, 15 Oct. 1932.
16 CFG–Dr Smith, 17 Oct. 1932.
17 W. H. Cobb–CFG, 5 Nov. 1932.

a letter from Selwyn was quoted giving an assurance that the sacrament 'was reserved for the sick only and was often used by the Bishop himself in his illness when he was unable to have a celebration in his room'.[18] Selwyn was referring to the late Bishop Woods. A procedural motion ensured that the Baughurst resolution did not come to a vote. The Baughurst Council paid their quota of £12 together with an additional contribution from Cobb of £3.

When Garbett first had sight of Cobb's Memorial in November 1932, he immediately (on 9 November) sent a copy to Selwyn explaining that he intended merely to acknowledge it and then provide a full reply or refer the matter to the Dean and Chapter suggesting that: 'So far the agitation seems to have been engineered by the Cobbs and some Society which is behind them.'[19] Replying, Selwyn considered it to be a '"got-up" business', as he had received no complaint 'either from regular worshippers or from visitors – so the vergers tell me'.[20] As already noted, Cobb was in fact advised and supported by the evangelical Church Association, no stranger to litigation or controversy, especially over ritualistic practices.

Garbett doubted his right to interfere in such a matter as reservation at the Cathedral and on 9 November raised the matter with the Chancellor, Guy H. Guillum Scott.

> For your private information I might add that personally I am sorry that there is Reservation in the Cathedral. I never allowed it at Southwark, where the need was greater, as I felt that the custom might prevent Evangelicals feeling the Cathedral was their Mother Church. On the other hand I should feel it quite impossible to raise difficulties about a practice which was approved so recently by my predecessor, and which has been found of real use in communicating the sick. Moreover the conditions of reservation are almost ideal: for though there is a lamp, the Aumbry in which the Consecrated Elements are kept is within a locked Chapel.[21]

Meanwhile the Archdeacon of Winchester, Alfred E. Daldy, pursued his own enquiries and on 10 December raised the matter with Lord

---

[18] *Hants and Berks Gazette*, 11 Nov. 1932.
[19] CFG–EGS, 9 Nov. 1932.
[20] EGS–CFG, dated 8 Nov. 1932, probably incorrectly.
[21] CFG–Guy H. Guillum Scott, 9 Nov. 1932.

Selborne, Chairman of the House of Laity of the Diocesan Conference.[22] Discovering this, Garbett wrote to Selborne on the 18th, urging that Selwyn 'should know what some of the leading laity think', and that there was no-one who would influence Selwyn more than he would. Garbett reveals his own dislike of reservation, commenting that the Archdeacon, in favour of reservation at the Cathedral, does not seem to realize 'what a serious controversy may arise'.[23]

The relationship of Cathedral and diocese was also of concern to Garbett, and on the same day he wrote to Selwyn to stress that as the Mother Church of the diocese 'reasonable members of all parties should feel at home'. He further questioned the assertion that perpetual reservation for the communion of the sick was necessary; and that such need as there was would be known to the Dean and Chapter and could be met by occasional reservation. He warned Selwyn: 'Unless there is an unanswerable case for perpetual reservation, you and the Chapter may find yourselves against all your wishes in the midst of a controversy which might sharply divide the Diocese and gravely injure the Cathedral.'[24] Responding to the Bishop on 19 December, Selwyn wrote:

> I can't help asking myself how many Church-people would be disturbed at what we do, if they knew it. If I had strong Protestant leanings (and I have a good many) I should welcome the fact that the Cathedral set an example of Reservation under conditions which appeared to offer permanent safeguards against the ostentation, *cultus* etc:, which are so undeniable elsewhere.[25]

Selwyn also wrote to Selborne to justify introduction of reservation at the Cathedral and recognized the inherent danger of misunderstanding:

> It has been associated with so much teaching and practice that are inconsistent with the traditions and standards of the Church of England that it is supposed (erroneously, but no less sincerely) to carry with it the whole Roman doctrine and *cultus* of the Sacrament. On the other hand, it is a very old principle that the abuse of a thing does not detract from its legitimate use, and I think one may fairly

[22] A. E. Daldy–CFG, 10 Dec. 1932.
[23] CFG–Lord Selborne, 18 Dec. 1932.
[24] CFG–EGS, 18 Dec. 1932.
[25] EGS–CFG, 19 Dec. 1932.

claim that the central Churchmen should not condemn, or fear, any practice which is unquestionably Catholic, merely because it is also found in the Church of Rome. Otherwise, indeed, very little of the Prayer Book would be left to us.[26]

Selborne was assured by Selwyn that the experimental period of six months had demonstrated that the utility of continuous reservation had been proved by experience, and that the communion of the sick had been adhered to. Nor did he know of any sign that the chapel in which the sacrament was kept was 'becoming in any special way a focus for devotion'. He claimed that the Cathedral was 'the most desirable' place in which the sacrament should be reserved. The letter to Selborne was published in the *Hampshire Chronicle* on 31 December 1932.

Garbett was unimpressed with Selwyn's argument:

> to be quite frank, it does not convince me, nor do I think it will convince most of the parochial clergy or laity, that continuous Reservation is necessary at the Cathedral. The arguments you advance for it would be equally applicable to the smallest country parish in which there are aged persons. The 1928 Book clearly did not intend Reservation on such an extended scale.[27]

Writing to the Archdeacon, Garbett commented:

> The Ordinary parish priest or layman will find it impossible to understand why the Cathedral with its Canons and Minor Canons is unable with occasional Reservation and private celebrations to meet the needs of the small group of elderly and infirm people who regard the Cathedral as their parish Church.[28]

The first signed copy of the Memorial was received by Garbett in January 1933. It contained twenty-three signatories. Writing on 10 January, Cobb took the opportunity to raise again the matter of the Bishop's jurisdiction claiming that 'according to the Prayer Book of 1928, under which alone Reservation is admissible at all, the Bishop is the sole authority who can permit Reservation'. Moreover, the Bishop may grant a licence for Reservation which unlike a Faculty was not

---

[26] EGS–Lord Selborne, nd.
[27] CFG–EGS, 21 Dec. 1932.
[28] CFG–A. E. Daldy, 31 Dec. 1932.

'once for all' but 'a permit for a practice always requiring justification for its continuance'.[29] He also noted that there were eleven clergy at the Cathedral and a resident population in the Close of fifty-five.

The Bishop's position was strengthened when he received a statement from A. T. P. Williams (Headmaster of Winchester College and later successively Bishop of Durham and Winchester), and a minor canon, A. W. Goodman, claiming that the means by which reservation at the Cathedral had been established was unconstitutional. No resolution had been passed by the Dean and Chapter and recorded in the Minute Book, and the Register of Services revealed that during the past five weeks the reserved sacrament's only use has been for an elderly canon, himself opposed to perpetual reservation, on Christmas Day and on the subsequent Sunday mornings immediately after the 8am celebration in the Cathedral.[30] An inspection of the Cathedral service registers confirmed this was the general pattern since the introduction of reservation.

Garbett now had reason to intervene. Before doing so, on 1 February he consulted the suffragan Bishop of Southampton, also a Residentiary Canon, C. H. Boutflower, to confirm that he had no 'recollection whatsoever of giving a formal vote in favour of perpetual Reservation'.[31] This he did the next day, although with the admission that whilst it was not put down as a formal item it may have come up under '"Dean's correspondence"'. Boutflower was in favour of occasional reservation for the sick and hence had approved of the purchase of an aumbry. However, 'on hearing arrangements for the purchase of a Sanctuary lamp (not I think brought up in Chapter) I wrote my own objection privately to the Dean, because this to my view exactly crossed the line between reservation for use pure and simple, and reservation for devotional interest also.'[32]

Armed with the information from Williams and Goodman, on 2 Februry 1933 Garbett wrote to Selwyn stating that the procedure for establishing reservation was unconstitutional on the grounds that no record of the resolution passed by the Chapter existed. Garbett clearly believed himself to have been misled by Selwyn's assurance that the desire for reservation was the 'deliberate and unanimous wish of the

[29] W. H. Cobb–CFG, 10 Jan. 1933.
[30] A. C. Goodman and A. T. P. Williams–CFG, 31 Jan. 1933.
[31] CFG–C. H. Boutflower, 1 Feb. 1933.
[32] C. H. Boutflower–CFG, 2 Feb. 1933.

Chapter'. He concluded by telling Selwyn that he may have 'in-advertently' gone beyond the wishes of the Chapter and that he proposed to go into the matter when he made a formal visitation of the Cathedral.[33] That evening Garbett and Selwyn met, following which the Bishop made a formal written request that the matter be placed before the Chapter and told Selwyn that he had had 'more anxiety over reservation at the Cathedral than over any other problem, since coming into the Diocese', and again emphasised his own misgivings about the need for reservation at all. He continued:

> I find it most difficult to continue my permission for perpetual reservation. But before I come to a final decision I should be grateful if you will obtain from the Chapter its deliberate opinion as to whether it regards continuous reservation as necessary at the Cathedral. . . . Unless the Chapter is of one mind on the principle of its desirability I do not see how the Bishop can give his approval.[34]

Selwyn replied that same day, to say that the Chapter would consider 'on its merits and without prejudice, the desirability of continuing the present arrangements in the Cathedral with regard to Reservation'. He further disputed the Bishop's claim to have been misled:

> Further from time to time when the Blessed Sacrament was reserved each week, no member of the Chapter has ever raised any question about it at Chapter meetings, whether formal or informal. This would be incredible if any member had supposed that the procedure had been irregular or (to quote Canon Goodman's phrase) unconstitutional. 'Passive acquiescence' would fairly describe the light, but not in regard to continuous reservation itself.[35]

This letter marks a more conciliatory tone in Selwyn's approach. Further discussion about the use of the term 'unanimous' to describe the view of the Chapter and Selwyn's failure throughout to contradict it led Selwyn to write on 6 February: 'If I had [contradicted its use], you would have asked which members of the Chapter objected – and, so

---

[33] CFG–EGS, 2 Feb. 1933.
[34] CFG–EGS, 3 Feb. 1933.
[35] EGS–CFG, 3 Feb. 1933.

far as I know, there were none.' Selwyn clearly felt let down by the Chapter who had allowed him to publish the letter to Selborne without any criticism 'on this score of corporate responsibility'.[36]

The Bishop's letter was considered at the Chapter meeting on 28 February 1933. Only the Dean and Canon Leonard Hodgson, the Anglo-Catholic theologian new to the Chapter, were present. The Minute Book simply recorded the exchange of letters between the Dean and Bishops Wood and Garbett since 1931, and left the matter in abeyance in the absence of the other members of the Chapter.[37] Due to illness and absence the Chapter failed to consider the matter; while on 28 February Selwyn assured Garbett that the sacrament was required each week and that the practice at Winchester did not go beyond that at York Minster, where it was reserved in similar manner when there was sickness.[38] The failure of the Chapter to consider his letter displeased Garbett, who told Selwyn that if he had to speak publicly about the matter he would state that it 'was now solely the responsibility of the Chapter'; and went further in saying that it would now be impossible for him to attempt to conceal from individuals that he was not convinced of the necessity of reservation at the Cathedral.[39]

For over a year the matter remained unresolved and the practice of perpetual reservation continued. In November 1934 it was raised again when Selwyn informed the Bishop that it was to be discussed by the Chapter and he wished to place before them the Bishop's view.[40] Responding on 8 November, Garbett asked the Chapter to pass a resolution to the effect that it regarded perpetual reservation at the Cathedral as necessary for the sick and dying and requesting that permission be granted upon such grounds, as they were the only grounds upon which permission can be granted if he was to remain loyal to the 1928 Book.[41] On 12 November Garbett wrote to the Bishop of Southampton, A. B. L. Karney, a member of the Chapter, to say: 'Personally I am in favour of Reservation at a Cathedral provided it does not upset people of the diocese.' At the same time he was determined to ensure adequate safeguards to prevent the doors being

---

[36] EGS–CFG, 6 Feb. 1933.
[37] Winchester, Cathedral Archives, Dean and Chapter Minute Book 1933.
[38] EGS–CFG, 28 Feb. 1933.
[39] CFG, 'Reservation at the Cathedral', a dictated note made after a conversation between CFG and EGS, 9 May 1933.
[40] Note signed F. W. S.
[41] CFG–EGS, 8 Nov. 1934.

opened 'very wide to customs and practices of which we should all disapprove'.[42] This represents a softening of the Bishop's position. Preparing Karney for the Chapter debate Garbett wrote on 29 November:

> If the Dean is really difficult, I think it would be best if the Chapter decided 'that as continuous Reservation is now unnecessary the practice be discontinued.' This would avoid a diocesan controversy between Bishop and Dean, and would save a doctrinal controversy: the strongest Anglo-Catholic cannot press for perpetual Reservation if those responsible state 'it is now unnecessary.' This is only a suggestion.[43]

Garbett had written the previous day to a former member of the Chapter, Robinson, to say that he had suggested that Karney might consult him, as reservation had come up again. Garbett was planning a trip overseas. He confided to Robinson:

> The whole thing could be settled so simply if the Dean would agree to reserve only when the sacrament was required for the sick and dying. But I am afraid he is going to be very awkward and difficult, and possibly plunge the Diocese in controversy.[44]

On 11 December Karney reported to Garbett the outcome of an interview with Selwyn and the Chapter meeting at which the Bishop's letter was discussed:

> I had a long interview with the Dean and found him very sticky, continually coming back to the point that he resented your harping on the string that he had not consulted the Chapter – a guilty conscience, I fear! We talked quite amicably, and I asked him what his reaction would be if I moved a resolution (which I knew both Lang and Moor would vote for, though I did not tell the Dean this) in the following terms 'That in the opinion of this Chapter perpetual Reservation is not at present necessary in the Cathedral at Winchester, and that the practice should be discontinued.' The Dean said at once 'I should exercise my veto.' As you can imagine, this cost me some hours' sleep. I communicated with Goodman, having told the Dean I should do so; and

[42] CFG–A. B. L. Karney, 12 Nov. 1934.
[43] CFG–A. B. L. Karney, 29 Nov. 1934.
[44] CFG–A. G. Robinson, 28 Nov. 1934.

Goodman, though personally upset, said that the Dean had the right to do so. I went to see Robinson after my Confirmation at Horle School, and he agreed that the Dean had the right to do so. I also got a long statement out of Robinson which I wrote down and he signed, and which I read to the Chapter. The Chapter threatened to be very difficult. The Dean began by reading a long Minute which he proposes to enter in the Minute Book at the formal Chapter meeting at the end of this month. I proposed to add a statement that the Bishop of Southampton wished it minuted 'that in the above statement the Dean is expressing his own views and not speaking for the Chapter.' I believe I have a perfect right to do this. So far so bad. Then gradually the spirit changed, and the Dean agreed that he would write to you a letter, which was first of all to have the approval of the formal Chapter at the end of the month.[45]

Selwyn wrote formally to the Bishop on 30 January 1935:

I am afraid there is no possibility of an agreed answer in regard to the 'necessity' of continuous Reservation. On the other hand we agreed that in a matter of this kind it is most undesirable that there should be a difference of policy between the Bishop and the Cathedral, and we shall therefore feel it to be our duty (without prejudice to our statutory rights and privileges) to defer in the matter to your wishes as Bishop of the Diocese, and to revert, if necessary, to our former custom of Reservation for particular sick persons. We gather that you are of the opinion as Bishop, that the present arrangement is, or may easily become, prejudicial to the welfare of the Diocese; and on receiving from you a definite expression of your wish that it should be modified, steps would be taken to give it effect.[46]

In an accompanying personal letter (dated 1 February) Selwyn revealed his true feelings about reservation:

In the Cathedral here the Reserved sacrament is hardly needed at all 'for help of devotion', in the sense that people say their prayers there. But there is a large number of Church-people, including some of the most devoted, to whom the Reserved Sacrament is the

[45] A. B. L. Karney–CFG, 11 Dec. 1934.
[46] EGS–CFG, 30 Jan. 1935.

plainest and most impressive of all symbols of the Love of God; and to that extent it has naturally proved to be a very great aid to the witness and ministry of the Cathedral.[47]

To the Dean's formal letter the Bishop replied on 14 February, that as there was no 'practical unanimity of the Chapter' over the desirability of perpetual reservation at the Cathedral, it was impossible for him to continue permission for the practice. For the sake of 'unity and peace in the Diocese', it was his hope that the Dean and Chapter would revert to 'their former custom of Reservation for particular persons'.[48] Before Selwyn reported the Bishop's decision to the Chapter he wrote again, on 8 March, to say of the division amongst the Chapter: 'I feel bound to point out that, as far as I know, there would have been no such division, if your Lordship's action had not created it.'[49] This was refuted by Garbett who wrote to Selwyn to say that in fact he had been misled about the mind of the Chapter. Sending a copy of this letter to Robinson for his 'candid opinion' Garbett remarked on 14 March, 'I have been very patient with him [Selwyn] for two and half years, but I feel the time has come when I must write to him very frankly and plainly.'[50]

At their meeting on 15 March 1935 the Dean and Chapter decided to discontinue the practice of perpetual reservation. The Dean had intended to circulate his final letter to the Bishop, and in response the Bishop proposed to circulate his 'plain' reply. Selwyn suggested that the Chapter should not see either. Garbett readily agreed and wrote to Selwyn, on 16 March:

> I should be more sorry than I can say if difference of opinion over Reservation at the Cathedral led to any breach in personal friendship: and I agree that further correspondence might not make matters any easier for either of us. We both have had a very difficult problem.[51]

In a letter to Karney of the same date, Garbett confessed that whilst he was glad Selwyn was not going to encourage propaganda, it 'was a little strange' that he should have received two letters from members

[47] EGS–CFG, 1 Feb. 1935.
[48] CFG–EGS, 14 Feb. 1935.
[49] EGS–CFG, 8 March 1935.
[50] CFG–A. G. Robinson, 14 March 1935.
[51] CFG–EGS, 16 March 1935.

of the English Church Union before receiving the Dean's formal reply as to the decision of the Chapter.[52] The English Church Union had played an active part in promoting Prayer Book revision in order to provide opportunities for reservation.

The provisions of the 1928 Book rapidly became the controlling authority for the bishops, despite being twice rejected by Parliament. This paper has illustrated a particular instance in which a bishop sought to hold the 1928 line in the face of a clear desire to go further and to establish, in this case, at the very least the opportunity for private devotional practices associated with reservation. Those who sought to embrace the provision of reservation still had to confront other equally principled and determined churchpeople who had opposed Prayer Book revision, and saw Parliamentary defeat of the Book as affirming their view of the proper practice of the Church of England. The various parties in the Church of England had yet to learn how to co-exist within the comprehensiveness which is perhaps its most enduring characteristic.

Selwyn would be delighted to know that the sacrament is today reserved in Winchester Cathedral.

---

[52] CFG–A. B. L. Karney, 16 March 1935.

'THE CATECHUMENATE FOR ADULTS IS TO BE RESTORED': PATRISTIC ADAPTATION IN THE *RITE FOR THE CHRISTIAN INITIATION OF ADULTS*

by EDWARD YARNOLD

AT the end of the third session of the Second Vatican Council in 1963, the bishops were able to make a beginning to their legislative work by promulgating two documents which they fondly hoped would be uncontroversial: the unremarkable *Decree on Mass Media*, and the much more consequential *Constitution on the Liturgy*. Among the principles for the revision of the Roman Catholic Church's sacraments contained in the second of these documents, instructions are given for the revision of the rites of initiation, including the following:

> The catechumenate for adults is to be restored [*instauretur*] and broken up into several steps [*gradibus*], and put into practice at the discretion of the local ordinary. In this way the time of the catechumenate, which is intended for appropriate formation, can be sanctified through liturgical rites to be celebrated successively at different times. In mission territories, in addition to what is available in the Christian tradition, it should also be permitted to incorporate ceremonies [*elementa*] of initiation which are found to be customary in each society, provided they can be adapted to the Christian rite.[1]

In another document the Council gave more detailed indications of the form it wished the adult catechumenate to take. The fact that these indications are contained in the *Decree on Missionary Activity* shows again that the desire for a restored catechumenate sprang from pastoral concerns and not from an antiquarian fascination with the remote past. The decree speaks of the 'spiritual journey' (*spirituale iter*) which leads the potential Christian under the influence of grace from 'initial . . . conversion' (*conversio . . . initialis*) to the reception of the sacraments of

---

[1] *Sacrosanctum Concilium*, 64, 65. The translation here and in other quotations from the Vatican II documents is my own; the Latin text can be consulted in *Decrees of the Ecumenical Councils*, ed. N. P. Tanner, 2 vols (London and Washington, DC, 1990).

initiation. Progress along the journey is to be marked by liturgical rites. The catechumenate itself is not

> a mere exposition of dogmas and precepts, but a training in the Christian life as a whole and a probation [*tirocinium*], to be prolonged as need be, by means of which disciples become united with Christ, their Master. Catechumens, therefore, should be initiated in a suitable way into the mystery of salvation and the practice of the moral teaching of the gospels, and introduced into the life of faith, liturgy and charity of the people of God through sacred rites to be celebrated successively at different times.[2]

The Council thus provides us with a case study to illustrate the topics of continuity and change, while adding a third factor, namely restoration. This paper examines the influence these factors exerted in the drafting of the new rites of initiation; it then considers a number of questions which are raised by the restoration of an ancient liturgy.

The rites of initiation which were duly composed according to the Council's specifications were not the Church's first attempt at restoring an adult catechumenate: in 1962, the very year the Council opened, the Sacred Congregation of Rites had published an *Ordo baptismi adultorum per gradus catechumenatus dispositi*.[3] An Introduction explained that it had been devised in response to a request from the missions for a process of initiation which would comprise a number of steps (*gradus*). The rite duly consisted of seven steps to be spaced out throughout the process of catechesis. At the first step the candidates formally handed in their names; after receiving fundamental catechesis, they ritually renounced their former errors and sought salvation with Jesus Christ; they were exorcized, and signed with the sign of the cross.[4] At the second step the candidate was given blessed salt. The third, fourth, and fifth steps took the form of solemn exorcisms, which were intended to arouse in the candidates a progressively deeper experience of conversion. The sixth step involved the immediate preparations for baptism: the teaching of the creed and the Lord's Prayer, a last exorcism, the *Apertio* or Opening of the candidates' lips

---

[2] *Ad gentes*, 13, 14.

[3] Published in *Acta Apostolicae Sedis*, 54 (1962), pp. 310–38.

[4] There are signs that St Augustine's *De catechizandis rudibus* was one of the sources of these celebrations.

and nostrils, recalling Christ's restoration of speech and hearing to the deaf mute,[5] a renunciation of the devil, and an anointing with oil as a sign of strength for the coming struggles. Finally at the seventh step the candidates professed their faith, were baptized and signed with chrism – a rite not to be confused with confirmation, which is not included in these rites. In fact the 1962 *Ordo* was less original than it appears, and has been criticized for doing little more than divide the already existing rite into seven stages.[6]

* * *

The *Rite of Christian Initiation of Adults* (RCIA) which was eventually promulgated in 1972, though superficially similar to the rite of 1962, differed from it radically in two respects.[7] First, whereas the earlier rite was a series of liturgical ceremonies, the later version places the rites in the context of the catechumens' 'spiritual journey' of growing faith, deepening conversion, and progressive assimilation into the life of the local Christian community. Secondly, whereas the earlier rite ends with the reception of baptism, the new rite includes the two further sacraments of confirmation and first communion, which are linked together to form the 'sacraments of initiation'.

The new rite is divided into four 'periods [*tempora*] for making inquiry and for maturing', linked by three 'steps' (*gradus*), which are 'the major, more intense moments of initiation and are marked by three liturgical rites'.[8]

The first period is that of *Evangelization and Precatechumenate*. It is a time 'for inquiry and introduction to gospel values, an opportunity for the beginnings of faith'.[9] This first period reaches its end when the

---

[5] Mark 7.32–6.

[6] See A. Bugnini, *The Reform of the Liturgy 1948–1975* (Collegeville, MN, 1990), p. 585.

[7] The normative Latin text was entitled *Ordo initiationis christianae adultorum* (Vatican City, 1972). The official English translation, made by the International Committee on English in the Liturgy, Inc. (ICEL), has appeared in several editions and recensions according to the pastoral needs of each English-speaking region throughout the world. One edition of the version authorized for use in Britain is entitled *The Rite of Christian Initiation of Adults: a Study Book* (London, 1988) [hereafter *RCIA*]. Because of these regional adaptations, no standard system of paragraph numbers has been devised, though many editions give marginal references to the original Latin; moreover the ICEL version sometimes conflates two distinct paragraphs of the Latin text. In this paper I give two numbers for each reference: the first refers to the British edition, the second, in square brackets, refers to the Latin.

[8] *RCIA*, 6 [6].

[9] *RCIA*, Table appended at 36 [not in Latin].

candidates arrive at 'the point of initial conversion and wishing to become Christians' after 'the beginnings of the spiritual life and the fundamentals of Christian teaching have taken root'.[10] In the first step of *Acceptance into the Order of Catechumens* the candidates express their desire to 'respond to God's call to follow the way of Christ'.[11] In response the Church, as represented by the local community, accepts them as catechumens, and assigns them to sponsors who will help them to 'find and follow Christ'.[12] This acceptance will not take place unless the candidates show that they are ready to take this step; there must be evidence of 'first faith', and an 'initial conversion'. 'Consequently, there must also be evidence of the first stirrings of repentance, a start to the practice of calling upon God in prayer, a sense of the Church, and some experience of the company and spirit of Christians through contact with a priest or with members of the community.'[13]

The parish should not decide to accept a candidate without careful consideration. 'With the help of the sponsors . . ., catechists, and deacons, parish priests . . . have the responsibility for judging the outward indications' of the candidate's dispositions.[14] This is especially necessary as catechumens are admitted to a formal relationship with the Church: 'From this time on the Church embraces the catechumens as its own with a mother's love and concern. Joined to the Church, the catechumens are now part of the household of Christ, since the Church nourishes them with the word of God and sustains them by means of liturgical celebrations.'[15] A catechumen is treated as a Christian in marriage and burial.

The second period is that of *Catechumenate.* It is described as the time 'for the nurturing and growth of the catechumens' faith and conversion to God'.[16] The Rite recognizes that no length of time can be fixed for the process, as much will depend on the grace of God and on various circumstances, but states that it may take several years.[17] The bishop or bishops' conference may lay down guidelines. The catechumenate should be 'long enough . . . for the conversion and faith

---

[10] *RCIA,* 6 [6], 42 [15].
[11] *RCIA,* 36, Table.
[12] *RCIA,* 53 [81].
[13] *RCIA,* 42 [15].
[14] *RCIA,* 43 [16].
[15] *RCIA,* 47 [18].
[16] *RCIA,* 36, Table.
[17] *RCIA,* 7 [7].

of the catechumens to become strong. . . . By their formation in the entire Christian life and a sufficiently prolonged probation the candidates are properly initiated into the mysteries of salvation and the practice of an evangelical way of life.'[18] However, the catechumenate is not just a course of what used to be called 'convert classes'. The instruction given 'should be of a kind that while presenting Catholic teaching in its entirety also enlightens faith, directs the heart towards God, fosters participation in the liturgy, inspires apostolic activity, and nurtures a life completely in accord with the spirit of Christ'.[19] Various rites, such as exorcisms and blessings, are celebrated to mark and encourage progress in the catechumenate. Local hierarchies are given authority to make minor adjustments.

When the candidates are ready to receive the sacraments of initiation, the second step of *Election* or *Enrolment* takes place, when the Church as represented by the local community recognizes their suitability (makes its 'election'), while the candidates express their decision to seek entry into the Church. Their names are inscribed in a special book after the godparents they have chosen publicly vouch for their worthiness. When baptism is celebrated at the Easter Vigil, this rite normally takes place on the first Sunday of Lent. A joint ceremony for the whole diocese may be conducted under the presidency of the bishop.

The third period, which lasts throughout Lent, is that of *Purification and Enlightenment*. 'This is a period of more intense spiritual preparation, consisting more in interior reflection than in catechetical instruction, and is intended to purify the minds and hearts of the elect as they search their own consciences and do penance.'[20] The three *scrutinies* play a vital part in this process. Originally an opportunity for the bishop to judge from the candidates' reaction to exorcism whether they had the right dispositions for baptism, they have now become 'rites for self-searching and repentance', intended to 'complete the conversion of the elect and deepen their resolve to hold fast to Christ'.[21] After listening to a specially chosen Gospel,[22] while the

[18] *RCIA*, 76 [98].
[19] *RCIA*, 78 [99].
[20] *RCIA*, 126 [cf. 22, 153].
[21] *RCIA*, 128 [25, 154].
[22] The Gospels for the three scrutinies are all taken from John, and each highlights a different symbol of Christ's saving work; they are respectively the stories of the Samaritan woman ('living water': 4.5–16, 19–26, 39–42), the cure of the man born blind ('the light of the world': 9.1, 6–9, 13–17, 34–8) and the raising of Lazarus ('the resurrection and the life': 11.3–7, 17, 20–7, 33b-45).

congregation supports them with silent prayer, the candidates also in silence examine their own hearts. (The requirement of silence is mentioned three times in one paragraph;[23] I know of no other place in the whole of the Church's liturgy where silence plays such an integral part in the ritual.) They then undergo solemn exorcisms. Later in this period the formal *'presentation'* is made of the Creed and the Lord's Prayer. In the early Church the presentations were a practical necessity, because the texts of these two formulas were considered so sacred that they were kept secret from the unbaptized; in modern conditions the purpose is rather spiritual: to 'enlighten the elect', 'suffuse(s) the vision of the elect with the sure light of faith' and 'fill(s) them with a deeper realization of the new spirit of adoption by which they will call God their Father'.[24] Finally on Holy Saturday the candidates take part in the *Preparation Rites*, which in England include the Opening, the formal Recitation of the Creed by the candidates, and the anointing with oil, symbolizing 'strength to accept the challenges of Christian life'.[25]

The third and all-important step consists of the three *sacraments of initiation*, namely baptism, confirmation, and first communion. If possible they are celebrated at the Easter Vigil, in order to show that the candidates, in dying to their old way of life and rising to a new, are brought into union with the death and resurrection of Jesus Christ.

> Through this final step the elect, receiving pardon for their sins, are admitted into the people of God. They are graced with adoption as children of God and are led by the Holy Spirit into the promised fullness of time begun in Christ and, as they share in the eucharistic sacrifice and meal, even to a foretaste of the kingdom of God.[26]

Before the baptism the celebrant performs the *Blessing of the Water*, in which he recalls with thanksgiving the various ways in which God has associated water with the process of salvation: the waters of creation, the flood from which Noah and his family were saved in the ark, the Red Sea through which Moses and his people escaped to safety, the Jordan in which Jesus was 'baptized by John and anointed

---

[23] *RCIA*, 139 [162].
[24] *RCIA*, 134 [25].
[25] *RCIA*, 193 [207].
[26] *RCIA*, 198 [27].

with the Spirit', and the water which flowed from his side on the cross. The celebrant's action of lowering the Easter candle into the water and lifting it out again has more than one meaning: it recalls not only Christ's rising after his three days in the tomb, but also the link between Jesus' baptism and that of the Christian. Thus one version of the blessing includes the prayer:

> Praise to you, God the Holy Spirit, for you anointed Christ at his baptism in the waters of the Jordan, that we might all be baptized in you.[27]

Between the blessing of the water and the baptism, other rites are celebrated which express the removal of obstacles to rebirth in Christ. First comes the Renunciation, by which the candidate either explicitly rejects 'Satan, and all his works, and all his empty promises', or less personally renounces sin and the 'glamour of evil'.[28] As part of the same rite the candidates then make a Profession of Faith in the Trinity, in order to make explicit their 'faith in the paschal mystery'.[29] The anointing with oil, if it has not been performed already, may be inserted between the Renunciation and the Profession.

There follows the baptism itself, in which the candidates are either immersed three times in the water or have water poured over them three times. This threefold action is linked with the triple name of the Father, of the Son, and of the Holy Spirit. Afterwards several 'explanatory rites' are celebrated. The clothing in a white *baptismal garment* signifies 'the new dignity' the baptized have received. The *candle* presented to each of them shows that they are to 'walk as befits the children of light'.[30]

The three sacraments of baptism, confirmation, and first communion form a single rite of initiation into the body of Christ, which is the Church. If the baptism is celebrated by a priest, he is authorized and normally required to celebrate confirmation immediately, without postponing it until a bishop is available: the conjunction of these two sacraments is said to signify the unity between Easter and Pentecost, which form a single paschal event.[31] The priest or bishop places his

---

27 *RCIA*, 215 [215, 389].
28 *RCIA*, 217 [217].
29 *RCIA*, 203 [30, 211].
30 *RCIA*, 207 [33].
31 *RCIA*, 208 [34].

hand on the candidates' head, and makes the sign of the cross on their forehead with *chrism*, which is perfumed oil. However, if confirmation has for any reason to be postponed, the priest, following a very ancient practice, still signs the candidates' head with oil in a non-sacramental rite. The form of words used indicates its significance: '[God] now anoints you with the chrism of salvation, so that, united with his people, you may remain for ever a member of Christ who is Priest, Prophet, and King.'[32] The Introduction explains that this anointing with chrism is 'a sign of the royal priesthood of the baptized and that they are now numbered in the company of the people of God'.[33] The names Messiah, which comes from the Hebrew, and Christ, which comes from the Greek, both mean 'the anointed one', and recall Jesus' own baptism in the Jordan, which was seen as the equivalent of a messianic anointing.[34] The General Introduction to Christian Initiation indicates the importance of this chrismation as a symbol of the 'sacramental bond of unity linking all who have been signed by it. . . . Because of that unchangeable effect *(given expression in the Latin liturgy by the anointing of the baptised person with chrism in the presence of God's people)*,[35] the rite of baptism is held in the highest honour by all Christians.'[36] Unfortunately, this significant rite, together with its accompanying prayer, is omitted when confirmation follows immediately after baptism, which is normally the case when the *RCIA* is celebrated.

As the culmination of the three sacraments of initiation, the newly baptized, now raised to the ranks of the royal priesthood, fully participate in the eucharist for the first time. By receiving the Body of Christ in holy communion, they complete their entry into the Body of Christ which is the Church.[37]

The sacraments of initiation are followed by a fourth period called *Mystagogy*, which lasts throughout the Easter season up to Pentecost. The name is borrowed from the practice of some places like Jerusalem

---

[32] *RCIA*, 222 [224].

[33] *RCIA*, 207 [33].

[34] 'The word which was proclaimed throughout all Judea, beginning from Galilee after the baptism which John preached: how God anointed Jesus of Nazareth with the Holy Spirit and with power' (Acts 10.37–8).

[35] My italics.

[36] General Introduction n.4. This General Introduction is normally printed before the text of the *RCIA*.

[37] St Paul indicated the link between the eucharist and the Church, both of which he describes as Christ's body: 'The bread which we break, is it not a participation in the body of Christ? Because there is one bread, we who are many are one body, for we all partake of the one bread' (I Cor. 10.16–17).

and Milan in the fourth century, when the rites were so secret and dramatic that it was considered best to celebrate them without any preliminary explanation, and to wait until the week after Easter to teach the newly baptized the meaning of the sacraments they had received. Now, of course, the practice is different: since the candidates will have been taught the meaning of the rites beforehand, mystagogy consists of the experience of full membership of the Church – 'This is a time for the community and the neophytes together to grow in deepening their grasp of the paschal mystery and in making it part of their lives through meditation on the Gospel, sharing in the eucharist, and doing works of charity.'[38] Because this mystagogic experience is essentially that of their new life *within the community*, it is recommended that one of the masses each Sunday of the Easter season should be designated a Mass of the Neophytes, at which the newly baptized are welcomed by their godparents and the people to the sacramental life of the parish.

* * *

What were the sources available to the post-Vatican II commission in its task of restoring the rite of the early Church? The New Testament does not contain clear instructions about the rite, apart from our Lord's command to make disciples of all nations, 'baptizing them in the name of the Father and of the Son and of the Holy Spirit',[39] and Peter's call to the crowd at Pentecost: 'Repent, and be baptized every one of you in the name of Jesus Christ so that your sins may be forgiven; and you will receive the gift of the Holy Spirit.'[40] There are also in Acts several very brief descriptions of baptisms.[41]

The documents from which we derive our knowledge of the early baptismal liturgies are of various kinds.

(1) *Church Orders*, which are collections of regulations for the organization of a Christian community; among these regulations there are generally instructions about the way baptism is to be administered. The earliest of these, the *Didache* (or *Teaching of the Twelve Apostles*),[42] a Syrian compilation which perhaps goes right back

---

[38] *RCIA*, 244 [37].
[39] Matt. 28.19.
[40] Acts 2.38.
[41] E.g. Acts 8.12–17, 8.36–9, 10.44–8.
[42] Throughout the early centuries Church Orders were conventionally given names which suggested they derived from the apostles.

to the first century,[43] contains only the sketchiest directions; but another example, from early in the third century, the *Apostolic Tradition* attributed to Hippolytus of Rome, contains the full text of an elaborate rite.[44] Other important examples are the *Didascalia* (*Teaching of the Twelve Apostles*, third-century Syria), and an enigmatic collection and adaptation of several earlier Church Orders called the *Apostolic Constitutions* (Syria, late fourth century).

(2) *Treatises, sermons and letters* which discuss the meaning of the rites and sometimes contain quotations from the rites themselves. Important examples are Tertullian's *De baptismo* ('on Baptism', North Africa, early third century); Cyprian's letters (from the same region, in the middle of the same century); and the fourth-century baptismal sermons of Cyril of Jerusalem and Ambrose of Milan. Under this heading we can also include the description of the rites in Jerusalem which the Spanish nun Egeria included in the fascinating account of her *Pilgrimage* which she wrote for her community in the 380s.[45]

(3) *Lives of saints*, which, though largely legendary, often included descriptions of baptisms modelled on the way the sacrament was celebrated at the time of writing, such as the *Acts of (Judas) Thomas*, which probably originated in east Syria in the third century.

(4) *Liturgical books*. We have one example from the fourth century, the *Euchologion* (*Prayer-book*) of the Egyptian Sarapion of Thmuis.[46] There are many later examples, such as the sixth(?)-century 'Leonine' Sacramentary, the eighth-century 'Gelasian' Sacramentary, and the *Ordines Romani* (seventh century on).[47]

So meticulously did the post-Vatican II liturgists accomplish their task of 'restoring' former practice, that for almost every detail of the 1972 rite one can point to antecedents attested in these patristic sources.[48] The *Apostolic Tradition* contains almost everything, often in

---

[43] Such is the opinion of J.-P. Audet, *La Didachè* (Paris, 1958).

[44] The provenance, authorship, and reliability of the *Apostolic Tradition* remains the subject of debate among scholars. For a brief account of the debate, see C. Jones, G. Wainwright, E. Yarnold, and P. Bradshaw, *The Study of Liturgy*, 2nd edn (London, 1992), pp. 87–9.

[45] The English reader will enjoy the illustrative material collected in J. Wilkinson, *Egeria's Travels* (London, 1971; rev. edn, Jerusalem and Warminster, 1981).

[46] Some wish to give the *Euchologion* a later date; see Jones, *The Study of Liturgy*, p. 91.

[47] For an account of these liturgical texts see C. Vogel, *Medieval Liturgy: an Introduction to the Sources*, rev. and trans. W. Storey and N. Rasmussen (Washington, DC, 1986).

[48] For a fuller summary of the evidence, see E. J. Yarnold, *The Awe-Inspiring Rites of Initiation*, 2nd edn (Edinburgh, 1994).

surprisingly elaborate form: we can recognize there a Precatechumenate, a process of Acceptance into the Catechumenate, regulations for the Catechumenate itself, an Election, an Exorcism and Scrutiny, rites of Baptism, anointing and first communion, and a brief Mystagogy.[49]

The equivalent of the Precatechumenate is to be found in Augustine's *De catechizandis rudibus* (*On catechizing the unbaptized*). In that work and elsewhere, the saint refers also to the rites for Enrolment into the Catechumenate, namely the tracing of the sign of the cross on the candidates' forehead, the placing of salt in their mouths, and the laying of hands upon their heads.[50] In Augustine's time, indeed, it was not general practice to administer baptism to children born of Christian families; instead they could be admitted at an early age – as was apparently the saint himself[51] – into the catechumenate, which thus became a state of peripheral membership of the Church. In the third century, the *Apostolic Tradition* and Clement of Alexandria indicate three years as the normal length of the catechumenate, during which frequent classes were held.[52] By St Augustine's time, however, the period was prolonged indefinitely, since for various reasons, more worthy or less, baptism was often postponed until the years of youthful passion were over.[53] This was sometimes true even of children of devout Christian parents, like Basil the Great and Ambrose, and even Gregory of Nazianzus, who was the son of a bishop.[54] Instead of classes organized for their needs, catechumens derived their instruction from the ordinary Sunday eucharistic homily, after

---

[49] *Apostolic Tradition*, ed. in B. Botte, *La Tradition apostolique de saint Hippolyte*, LQF 39 (Münster Westfalen, 1963) [= *Hippolyte de Rome: La tradition apostolique, d'après les anciens versions*, ed. B. Botte, SC 11 bis, 2nd edn (Paris, 1984)], cc.15–21. This is how after his description of first communion the author refers to what was later called 'Mystagogy': 'But if it is desirable for anything to be explained, the bishop should speak in private to those who have received baptism' (c.21).

[50] Sign of the cross and salt: *Confessions*, I, xi, 17. Laying on of hands: *De peccatorum meritis et remissione*, II, xxvi, 42 (*PL* 44, col. 176).

[51] *Confessions*, I, xi, 17.

[52] *Apostolic Tradition*, ed. Botte, c.17; Clement of Alexandria, *Stromata*, II, xviii, 95–6: *Clemens Alexandrinus, Zweiter Band: Stromata, Buch I–VI*, ed. O. Stählin, Die Griechische Christliche Schriftsteller der ersten drei Jahrhunderte, 3rd edn, rev. L. Früchter (Berlin, 1960), pp. 164.15–165.14.

[53] Augustine wonders whether the reason for the postponement of his own baptism was the desire to allow him freedom to sin, and quotes the commonly heard remark: 'Leave him alone, let him do it. He is not baptized yet' (*Confessions*, I, xi, 18).

[54] See J. Jeremias, *Infant Baptism in the First Four Centuries* (London, 1960), pp. 88–9.

which they had to leave the assembly, as only the baptized were allowed to be present at the eucharist.[55]

Among the witnesses to the rite of the *Election* the most interesting are Cyril and Egeria, both of whom write in fourth-century Jerusalem. Egeria gives what may have been an eye-witness account of the practice in Jerusalem.[56] Cyril casts light on the less worthy reasons which may have led the candidates to hand in their names – to please a girl-friend or a slave-master – but does not on that account exclude them: 'I make use of the fisherman's bait and admit you. You may have come for the wrong reason, but your good hope will save you. . . . Perhaps you did not know where you were going or that there was a net waiting to catch you. You are in the Church's nets; allow yourself to be caught.'[57] 'Have respect for the place, and be taught by what you see' – words which make sense only if we remember that Cyril was preaching at the very spot where it was believed the Lord had been crucified and had risen again.[58]

During Lent the final preparations for baptism took place; these included exorcisms, the teaching ('*traditio*') and repetition ('*redditio*') of the creed, and sometimes the teaching of the Lord's Prayer.[59] The scrutinies seem to have been observed only in the western Church; the first extant reference to them by this name occurs in the writings of Ambrose.[60]

The rites of initiation themselves, ideally celebrated at the Easter Vigil, are, as one would expect, described in great detail in homilies and church orders. They generally included at least the following elements: an anointing of the whole body with olive oil as a symbol of strength for the struggle against the devil; a renunciation of the devil and a declaration of faith in Christ; an invocation of the Holy Spirit on

[55] Augustine's catechetical sermons and the accompanying rites are examined by W. Harmless, *Augustine and the Catechumenate* (Collegeville, MN, 1995). Harmless identifies twenty-two passages in Augustine's extant sermons in which he expressly addresses the catechumens (pp. 191–2). Cf. M. Dujarier, *A History of the Catechumenate: the First Six Centuries* (New York, 1979).

[56] *Egeria's Travels, Newly Translated with Supporting Documents and Notes*, ed. J. Wilkinson, rev. ed. (Warminster, 1981), xlv.

[57] Cyril, *Procatechesis*, c.5, in *S. Patris nostri Cyrilli Hierosolymorum archiepiscopi Opera quae supersunt omnia*, ed. W. K. Reischl and J. Rupp, 2 vols (Munich, 1848–60), 1, p. 8.

[58] Ibid., 1, p. 6 (c.4).

[59] Many sources refer to these rites. For references see, for example, Yarnold, *Awe-Inspiring Rites*, pp. 9–17; Harmless, *Augustine and the Catechumenate*, ch. 7.

[60] Ambrose, *Explanatio symboli*, 1; included in *Ambroise de Milan: Des sacraments, des mystères, explication du symbole*, ed. B. Botte, SC 25 bis (Paris, 1961), pp. 46–7.

the baptismal water; triple immersion in the name of the Trinity; the clothing of the neophyte in a white robe; one or two anointings with scented oil or chrism, symbolizing a participation in the anointing of the anointed Lord (the Messiah, the Christ); the conferring on the candidate of the gift of the Holy Spirit (the seeds of what came later to be called confirmation are evident here). Some sources allude to the carrying of lights.[61]

We have seen that the modern rite permits baptism by immersion as well as by infusion. For the pouring of water on the candidate's head the traditional small font raised on a pedestal is most serviceable; for immersion however a pool-like font at floor level is required. In the early Church this second design was normal, though archaeologists have been puzzled to find the explanation for the small subsidiary fonts which have often been found beside the large, main font.[62] In the earliest times streams or Jewish ritual baths were probably used. The earliest font which has survived is the rectangular bath in the third-century house-church at Dura Europos on the eastern borders of the Roman Empire. The fourth-century baptistery at Naples, which is one of the earliest extant western examples, consisted of a circular font at floor level, contained in a rectangular chamber; the mosaics in the vault feature a number of motifs which recur later at Ravenna in more sophisticated form.[63] By the end of the fourth century one finds an octagonal building containing a large octagonal font set into the floor. Credit for the design is given to St Ambrose, who used it for the Milanese baptistery which was probably the one in which he baptized St Augustine; the earlier font in which Ambrose himself had been baptized after his dramatic nomination to the see of Milan was also eight-sided, though the octagonal form was not used for the baptistery itself.[64] The octagonal shape was taken to be symbolic, recalling Easter

---

[61] The evidence for these rites is set out in Jones, *The Study of Liturgy*, pp. 134–44; Yarnold, *Awe-Inspiring Rites*, pp. 17–34.

[62] For an overall account of the design of early baptisteries, see J. G. Davies, *The Architectural Setting of Baptism* (London, 1962); S. A. Stauffer, *On Baptismal Fonts: Ancient and Modern*, Alcuin–GROW Liturgical Studies, 29–30 (Nottingham, 1994). On the small subsidiary fonts, cf. Davies, *Architectural Setting*, p. 26.

[63] On the baptistery in Naples, see J. L. Maier, *Le baptistère de Naples et ses mosaïques, étude historique et iconographique*, Paradosis, 19 (Fribourg, 1964).

[64] On the Milanese baptisteries, cf. H. M. Roberti, 'Contributi della ricerca archeologica all'architectura ambrosiana milanese', in G. Lazzati, ed., *Ambrosius Episcopus: atti del Congresso internazionale di studi ambrosiani nel XVI centenario della elevazione di sant'Ambrogio alla cattedra episcopale, Milano, 2–7 dicembre 1974*, 2 vols, Studia patristica Mediolanensia, 6–7 (Milan, 1976), I, pp. 352–9.

Sunday (the eighth day following the Lord's Sabbath); the building, recalling a mausoleum, also symbolized the Christian's sacramental death and resurrection.[65] In Tunisia, where the cruciform pattern was prevalent, some wonderfully ornate fonts have survived.

* * *

When we compare this reconstructed ancient rite with the modern, the dependence of the latter on the former is clear. The liturgical scholarship of the post-Vatican II drafters is plain to see. This last part of the paper, however, offers some critical observations concerning the principles which have guided the adaptation of the ancient rite to the needs of modern Western society.

    1. If the return to the old practices is to be anything other than an exercise in antiquarianism, there needs to be a substantial congruity between the modern situation and that which prevailed in the early Church. As far as the underlying process is concerned, this condition seems to be fulfilled. Now as then the candidates may be expected to experience a threefold movement: they undergo a process of spiritual growth which can be described as one of developing self-knowledge or conversion; they progressively learn the beliefs they are required to profess and the corresponding way of life; they go through an extensive rite of passage akin to a novitiate or an apprenticeship in which step by step they become members of the Church.

    Nevertheless there are other respects in which the modern situation differs markedly from that of the fourth century. First, the *disciplina arcani*, the cloak of secrecy which kept the rites hidden from the uninitiated, and so enabled them to exert a powerful psychological effect, is impossible to re-establish in the age of mass media. Secondly, the sense of coming face to face with supernatural powers, malevolent as well as beneficent, an experience which made the common descriptive term 'awe-inspiring' appropriate in the age of the mystery religions, is unlikely to be present in many western congregations in our own more materialistic age.[66] Thirdly, and partly as a result of these two factors, our own society, though not totally indifferent to ceremonial, suffers from a blunted sensitivity towards the great natural

---

    [65] According to Ambrose his font (or does he mean baptistery?) was shaped like a tomb: 'Hesterno de fonte disputavimus, cuius species veluti quaedam sepulcri forma est' (*De sacramentis*, III, i, 1, in Botte, *Ambroise de Milan*, pp. 90–1).

    [66] On the use of the liturgy as a means of evoking awe, and on the *Disciplina arcani*, cf. Yarnold, *Awe-Inspiring Rites*, pp. 55–66.

symbols. Water and light, for example, lose much of their symbolic power when they are immediately available at the touch of a switch or the turn of a tap. Moreover there may be other reasons for the modern western decline in what has been called *Liturgiefähigkeit*, liturgical sensitivity: undiscriminating saturation in the mass media, especially TV, the craving for unremitting entertainment, and the low level of tolerance for what is judged 'boring'; the difficulty the ordinary parish liturgist will have in competing with the professional standards of entertainment which people generally now take for granted.[67]

2. Early practice has been taken as a model to such an extent that unfamiliar terms derived from ancient usage – such as 'mystagogy' – have been adopted, or the meaning of familiar expressions, such as 'scrutiny' and 'election', has been changed so as to conform with the vocabulary of the old rites. Consequently the rites suffer from an unnecessary in-built quaintness.

3. The restored *RCIA*, which was designed as a process of initiation for the unbaptized, especially in regions where the Church is a minority group among non-Christian religions, is sometimes adapted to the needs of other classes of people, especially those who have been baptized in other Churches but are wishing to enter the Roman Catholic Church. Moreover, since the running of the cate-chumenate is generally thought to have a beneficial effect on the life of a parish, there is a danger that candidates may be forced inflexibly throughout the full process, even if it may not be the best way of meeting their personal pastoral needs.[68]

4. Finally, the use of elements derived from the practice of the early Church may mask a fundamental change in the way in which the rites are understood. This can be shown by a closer examination of one example, the scrutinies.[69] In the modern rite these observances are intended to promote 'self-searching and repentance' so as to 'complete the conversion of the elect'. In the early Church the purpose was different, though the explanations vary. In the early third-century

---

[67] Some of these factors are examined by Bryan Wilson, *Contemporary Transformations of Religion* (Oxford, 1976).

[68] The criticisms made here under headings 2 and 3 are expressed with characteristic verve by A. M. Greeley, 'Against R. C. I. A.', *America*, 161 (1989), pp. 231–4.

[69] On the interpretation of the patristic rite of scrutiny the key article was written by A. Dondeyne, 'La discipline des scrutins dans l'église latine avant Charlemagne', *Revue d'histoire ecclésiastique*, 28 (1932), pp. 5–33, 751–87. See also H. A. Kelly, *The Devil at Baptism* (Ithaca, NY, and London, 1985).

Roman compilation entitled the *Apostolic Tradition*, the bishop is required to perform a special exorcism – previously lesser ministers have exorcized the candidates every day – 'that he may be certain that [the candidate] is purified. If there is one who is not virtuous or not pure' he is to be 'set apart, because he did not hear the word with faith. For it is impossible for the Strange One to hide for ever.'[70] These words suggest that there are visible signs which show whether the candidate has escaped from the devil's power; in another context a fourth-century bishop, Zeno of Verona, describes with relish some of the indications which betray the evil spirit's continual presence: sudden pallor, contortion of the features, rolling of the eyes, gnashing of the teeth, foaming at the mouth, livid lips, shaking, groans, and tears.[71] It was this inspection of the candidate's reaction to exorcism which in the Latin Church was first given the name of 'scrutiny'. Shortly after Zeno, and not very far away, Ambrose of Milan reminds the candidates that they have undergone the 'mysteries of the scrutinies', at which 'an examination was made in case any impurity remained rooted in anyone's body. Through exorcism a means of sanctifying both body and soul was sought and applied.'[72] In the fifth century St Augustine in Hippo shows the same understanding of the scrutiny: exorcism ('rebukes in the name of the dread Trinity') was pronounced over the candidates as they stood on goatskin, denoting that they were trampling on sin, after which the bishop 'ascertained' (*probavimus*) that they are now 'immune' (*immunes*).[73] Augustine also introduces an additional factor into the process, namely the candidates' scrutiny of their own consciences: 'What we do . . . you are to complete by a scrutiny of your hearts and remorse.'[74] Also in North Africa, Quodvultdeus, a younger contemporary of St Augustine, gives a similar description of the rite: while the candidates stood 'with humble neck . . ., with humble feet' upon sackcloth, 'you were submitted to examination [*examen*], the proud devil was rooted out

---

[70] *Apostolic Tradition*, c.20. This translation is based on B. Botte's reconstruction of the oriental texts: Botte, *La Tradition apostolique*, pp. 42–3; Botte, *Hippolyte de Rome*, p. 78.

[71] Zeno, *Tractatus*, I, ii, 6 (*PL* 11, col. 374): 'Discoloratur per momenta color, figura sua tollitur a natura, in obliquos horrores insani vertuntur orbes oculorum, acies dentium spumosis horrida globis inter labra liventia stridit, intorta omnia passim membra tremore vibrantur, gemit, flet.' My thanks to G. P. Jeanes for this reference.

[72] 'Inquisitum est, ne immunditia in corpore alicuius haereret. Per exorcismum non solum corporis, sed etiam animae quaesita et adhibita est sanctificatio'; *Explanatio symboli*, 1.

[73] Augustine, Sermon 216, 10–11: *PL* 38, col. 1082.

[74] Sermon 216, 6: *PL* 38, col. 1080.

from you, and the humble, most high Christ was called down on you.'[75] Not long afterwards two Roman documents suggest the connection, which we have already seen in the *Apostolic Tradition*, between the scrutiny and the subject's faith. Leo the Great explains that the candidates 'are to be scrutinized [*scrutandi*] according to the apostolic rule by means of exorcisms'; the 'apostolic rule' may refer to a profession of faith.[76] This interpretation is shared at the end of the fifth century by a Roman deacon called John, who explains to an inquirer: 'Their hearts are scrutinized through faith, to see whether they have fixed the sacred words in their minds since the renunciation of the devil, whether they have acknowledged the future grace of the Redeemer, whether they confess their belief in God the almighty Father'; evidently profession of Trinitarian faith came to be seen as a sign of the expulsion of the Evil One.[77]

Thus in the early Church many signs were looked for in the scrutinies: absence of the physical marks of diabolical possession, the presence of humility and faith; but invariably the examination is performed by the Church. In the modern rite, however, *self*-scrutiny, which figured in only one early source and even there as a secondary effect, has become the principal purpose of the new rite. When there is continuity, there are sound anthropological reasons for retaining a traditional rite such as confirmation, even though it is interpreted in a new way; but when there is no such living tradition, to reintroduce an old practice and give it a new meaning seems to betray a fascination with the past for its own sake. The only justification can be pastoral effectiveness.

Campion Hall, Oxford

---

[75] *De symbolo*, i.1: *PL* 40, col. 637. This sermon, once included among Augustine's works, is now generally attributed to his disciple Quodvultdeus.

[76] Leo, Epistle xvi, 6: *PL* 54, col. 702.

[77] John the Deacon, *Ad Senarium*, 4, in A. Wilmart, ed., *Analecta reginensia: extraits des manuscrits latins de la reine Christine conservés au Vatican*, Studi e Testi, 59 (1933), pp. 170–9.

INDEX

Note: Page references in *italics* indicate illustrations.

Abbiss, John, Rector of St Bartholomew
    Smithfield 321-2, 327
ablution, and ritualism 384, 393
acolyte, and *traditio instrumentorum* 173
actors
    church attitudes towards 90, 91
    clergy as 93-4, 100
Acts of (Judas) Thomas 487
Acts of Uniformity 160, 348, 355
Adelphi Club 298
Ælfric, Abbot of Eynsham 36 n.28, 46
    n.55, 312
African Traditional Religion xxii, 421,
    423, 425, 426, 430
agape, and eucharist 13, 17, 251
Agnus Dei
    in Reformation liturgies 157, 159,
    162-3, 446
    and ritualism 384
Aikman, John 266 n.16, 268, 270, 271
Alberigo, Guiseppe 225
Albert of Buxhoven, *Gesta* 97-8
Albert the Great, St, and ordination 177
Alcuin
    De laudibus Dei 42-3
    and Gregorian Sacramentary 43, 50
    and lay worship 33, 43
    and the mass 312
Alexander, Pierre 167
Alley, William, Bishop of Exeter 192
Allsop, Thomas 375, 379, 381
altar
    and candles 384, 387, 388
    in Carolingian churches 39-40, 53
    and communion table 400-1
    in English medieval churches 39, 75-7
    in English Reformation 162, 164
    in German Reformation 125
    minor altars of York Minster 104-15
Amalarius of Metz 53, 101

Ambler, R. W. xxiii, 384-95
Ambrose, St
    and catechumenate 487, 489, 490, 493
    De institutione virginis 18 n.1, 19, *20*,
    21-2, 26 n.21
    De virginibus 18 n.1, 19, 25 n.12
    and *Passio* of St Agnes 23
    and Song of Songs 18-19, 22
Ambrosian sacramentary 48, 209, 312
Ammon, C. G. 459
anabaptism
    and Haldane 270
    and Müntzer 157
anamnesis, and liturgy 6, 131, 139-41
Anaphora of Addai and Mara 251
Anderson, Benedict 343-4
Anderson, R. Rowand 406
Anglicanism
    and choral revival 309, 315
    and East African Revival 419-31
    and medievalism 301, 305, 314
    in nineteenth-century Wales 408-18
    and 'Prayer Book fundamentalism' of
        Maurice 345-60
    Prayer Book revision xxiii, 355,
        447-63, 464, 477
    and recovery of ancient Christianity
        xxiii, 303, 314
    and Reformation liturgy 151-2
    and ritualism 313, 317, 322, 323-6, 331
    and validity of orders 297, 317
    see also Anglo-Catholicism; Broad
        Church tradition; Church of
        England
Anglo-Catholicism
    and perpetual reservation 448, 453,
        460-1
    and Prayer Book revision 447, 451,
        453, 455, 457, 459-61, 464-5
Annesley, Dr 230

anointing
    at baptism 116, 158, 160, 163, 480
    at ordination 175, 176
    and catechumenate 480, 483
anthropology, and liturgiology 154
anti-clericalism, and Müntzer 156
antiphoners 79, 211
    in rural parishes 44–6, 49, 51
Antonino of Piacenza, S. 214–15, 219–20
Apostolic Constitutions
    and baptism 487
    and Clementine Liturgy 241, 242, 245,
      249
    and episcopal ordination 175
apostolic succession 182–3, 248, 297, 333
Apostolic Tradition see Hippolytus of
    Rome, *Apostolic Tradition*
apses
    in English parish church chancels 65,
      67–77
    in St Bartholomew Smithfield 322,
      323
Aquinas, St Thomas
    and confirmation 163
    and the eucharist 157
    and ordination 177
architecture
    and Gothic revival 305–6, 312, 313
    and liturgy 65–77, 283
    Romanesque 320
    of rural churches 38–9
Armstrong, B. J. 368
Arno of Salzburg 43
Arnold, Thomas, *Principles of Church
    Reform* 356
arts, performing, in medieval church
    89–103
asceticism, in early Church 15
Ascham, Roger 124–5
Athanasian Creed 161, 348, 352–3, 374
Athanasius, St
    Letters to Virgins 18, 21 n.11
    and Song of Songs 18, 23
Augsburg
    and baptism 116, 121
    and changing nature of public worship
      xxiii, 116–27

    and confession 123–4, 126
    Council xxiii, 116–19, 122, 123, 125–7
    and daily prayer 121–2
    Discipline Ordinance 119, 125
    and the eucharist 120–1
    and lay participation in worship
      124–5, 127
    and preaching houses 116, 119, 125,
      126
    and rejection of ceremony and
      imagery 125–6
    and sermons 122–3, 124
Augsburg Confession 118, 126
Augustine of Hippo, St
    De catechizandis rudibus 479 n.4, 488
    De trinitate 84 n.12
    and eucharist 29
    Sermo 52 84 n.12
    Sermon 216 493
    Sermon against Jews, Pagans and Arians
      102
'Autun sacramentary' 56 n.87
Avis, Paul 354 n.30
Aylmer, John, Bishop of London 193–4,
    197

Bagot, Richard, Bishop of Oxford 314
Bakewell (Derbys.), church chancel 74–5
Balbus, *Catholicon* 108
Baldock, Ralph 85
Baldwin, Stanley 459
Balfour, A. J. 325
Ballantine, William 266–8, 272
Balokole *see* East African Revival
Banks, F. A. 279–80
baptism
    and adult catechumenate 480, 484–5,
      486–90
    in Carolingian church 34, 57–60
    and chrism 116, 480
    in Congregationalism 437–8, 445
    and Cranmer 163
    and creed 350
    in the early Church 10, 14 n.38, 486–7
    in East African Revival 422, 429
    and Flood Prayer (Luther) 160, 163
    in German Reformation 121

and Haldane 264, 265, 270–1, 273
of infants 157, 270–1, 351, 429, 437
by lay readers 188, 191
and Luther 160, 163, 178
and Maurice 350, 351, 354, 357
and Müntzer 157–8, 163
and Voysey 380
baptisteria, in rural parishes 44, 49, 59
Baptists
    and development of hymnody 233
    and psalm-singing 232–3
    and sacraments 437
Barberi, Dominic 305
Barham, Lawrence 427, 429
Barnes, Ernest, Bishop of Birmingham
    451, 454, 464
Baronio, Cesare 213
    Annales ecclesiastici 199–200
Barth, Karl 443, 446
Barton, William 233
    Book of Psalms 232, 235
    Choice and Flower of the Old Psalms
    235
    Psalms and Hymns 232
Barton-on-Humber (Lincs.), church
    chancel 70, 75
Basil of Caesarea, Liturgy 241, 242, 243,
    245, 249
Basle
    and auricular confession 124
    and frequency of communion 143
    and Luther's 'September Bible' 146
    and preaching 133, 134
    and Reformed liturgy 129
Bates, William 230
Baumstark, Anton, *Liturgie comparée* 3–4
Bavaria, and monastic churches 36
Baxter, Richard
    and hymns 234
    and psalm-singing 230, 231, 233
Becket, St Thomas 80, 85 n.16, 95
Bede
    Commentary on Mark 33
    Homiliae in Evangelia 81, 83, 84 n.13
    and the mass 312
    Vita Cuthberti 63–4, 108
belfries, Carolingian 40

The Believer's Magazine (Brethren
    magazine) 282–3, 286
Bell, G. K. A. 452
bell-towers, Carolingian 40
Bellarmine, St Robert 213, 215
Benedict of Aniane, and Gregorian
    sacramentary 47, 50, 59–60
Benson, Edward White, Archbishop of
    Canterbury 362, 364–6, 394
Bentham, Thomas, Bishop of Coventry
    and Lichfield 196
Beresford Hope, J. A. 323
Berne, and preaching 134
Bible
    in daily office 207
    in English Congregationalism 434–7
    historicity xxiii–xxiv
    literal interpretation 262, 270, 272–3
    and origins of Eucharist xxiv
    in Swiss Reformation 129, 146–7
    Zurich 131
    see also New Testament; Old
    Testament
Bibliotheca patrum 243
Bickerstaffe, William 228
Bingham, Joseph, *Origines Ecclesiasticae*
    243, 252
Birkat ha-mazon 6, 11
Birkenhead, F. E. Smith, 1st Earl of 462
Biscop, Benedict 313, 318
Bishop, Edmund 43 n.46
bishops
    and anointing 176
    and Cisalpinism 291–2, 295
    and imposition of Gospel book 175,
    181–2
    and imposition of hands 173–4, 175,
    180, 181
    and lay election 248
    and lay readers 190–2
    and restoration of English hierarchy
    297–8, 300, 302
    and *traditio instrumentorum* 176, 181–2,
    183
Blair, J. 32 n.7
Blomfield, Charles James, Bishop of
    London 362, 365

Bloxam, J. R. 314–15
'Bobbio Missal' 48 n.64, 50, 54 n.81
Bodley, G. F. 371
Bogue, David 266
Bolton, Brenda xxiii, 89–103
Book of Common Order 179, 403
Book of Common Prayer (1662) 329
  in East Africa 420–2, 429
  and eastward celebration of the
    eucharist 369–70
  and 'fundamentalism' of Maurice xxiv,
    345–60
  as national liturgy 351–2
  revision of 1927–9 xxiii, 447–63, 464,
    477
  and Scottish Non-jurors 241–2, 245,
    254, 255
  and Voysey's Revised Prayer Book
    378–83
  see also Prayer Book, of 1549
A Book of Public Worship 444, 445
Borland, Andrew 286
Borromeo, S. Carlo 222
Bossuet, Jacques Bénigne 333, 338
Bossy, John 204, 225
Boutflower, C. H., Bishop of
  Southampton 471
Bouyer, L. 201
Bowes, John 277–8
Boyse, Joseph
  Family Hymns 235–6
  Sacramental Hymns 234–5
Bradley, Ian 309
Bradshaw, Paul F. xxiv, 1–17
Brady, Nicholas, New Version of the Psalms
  of David 232
breaking of bread, among Scottish Open
  Brethren 275, 276, 278–88
Brenz, Johannes, Sermons 148
Brethren movement see Open Brethren
Brett, Thomas, A Collection of the Principal
  Liturgies . . . of the Holy Eucharist . . .
  242–4, 249
breviaries
  English 79
  local 209, 212–17, 219–20, 336
  and Orders 209 n.27, 210

and Reformation liturgies 156–7, 340
Roman 201, 202–3, 205–7, 215–18,
  224, 226, 314
and 'sample week' xxiii, 78–88
structure 210–12
Tridentine 207, 209–12, 217–19
Breviarium pianum 207, 209–12, 217–19
Breviarium sanctae crucis 206–7, 211, 341
Breviary of Halberstad 156
Bridgeman, William 457–8
A Brief Discourse of the Troubles begun at
  Frankfort 197
Brigg (Lincs.), and ritualism 392–3
Brightman, F. E., The English Rite 152,
  154, 250
The British Weekly 435–6, 438
Brittany, liturgy and community 60–1
Broad Church tradition 346–7, 356,
  447
  and Athanasian Creed 374
  and Voysey 374–6, 383
Broadhead, Philip xxiii, 116–27
Brook, V. J. K. 190 n.25
Browning, Thomas 235
Bucer, Martin
  and Augsburg reforms 118, 120, 126
  De ordinatione legitima 178–9
  and English Reformation 167
  and eucharistic liturgy 160, 255
  and reformed Ordinal 161
Bugenhagen, Johann 166
Bull, George, Judicium ecclesiasticae
  catholicae trium primorum saeculorum
  . . . 243
Bullinger, Heinrich
  and Cranmer 167
  and eucharist 140, 143
  and Zurich 144
Bullough, Donald xxiii, 29–64, 114
Burgess, Daniel 230
  Psalms, Hymns and Spiritual Songs 234
burial
  and lay access to liturgy 55–7, 61
  by lay reader 192
  and Voysey's Revised Prayer Book 381
Bury, Samuel 234
Byrhtferth, Vita sancti Oswaldi 62

Cadle, Penelope J. xxiii, 361–73
Cadoux, C. J. 444
Cajetan, Thomas de Vio 177 n.15
Caldwell, John R. 279, 283–4, 286
Calenzio, 199 n.2
Calfhill, James 197
Calvin, John
  and Cranmer 167
  and the eucharist 286, 434, 438–9
  and ordination 178, 179
Calvinism, and Congregationalism 432,
  433–4, 436, 437–8, 441–5
Cambridge University see Camden
  Society
Camden Society 301, 305, 322, 388–9
Campbell, John 270
Campi, Pietro Maria 200, 213–14,
  215–16
  *Apologia dell'innocente e sancta vita del
  glorioso pontifice Gregorio il decimo*
  216, 220
  Dell'historia ecclesiastica di Piacenza
  222–3
  *Insignium gestorum S. Antonini martiris
  Placentiae tutelaris* 220 n.50
  Vita di Margarita da cantiga 220
  Vita di S. Antonino martire 219–20
  Vita di S. Corrado eremita 216, 220
  Vita di S. Franca Vitalta 220
  Vita di S. Raimondo Palmerio 220
cancelli see chancels
candles, altar, and ritualism 384, 387, 388
Canterbury Cathedral
  chancel 73–4
  and Erasmus 104
Canterbury diocese
  and lay readers 187
  and minster parishes 32
Capitularia regum Francorum 36
Caraffa, Gian Pietro (later Pope Paul IV)
  210
Cardwell, Edward 191
Carleton, Kenneth xxii, 172–84
Carlisle Cathedral 361
Carlyle, Thomas 353
Carnebull, Henry, Archdeacon of York
  106, 107

Carolingian church
  and baptism 34, 57–60
  and burial practices 55–7, 61
  capitularies 44, 51, 53, 62
  and chant-settings 51
  and lay role in worship xxiii, 29–64
  and liturgical reform 47, 49–50, 52, 54,
    58–9, 62
  and papacy 338–9, 344
  rural churches 30–4, 36–41, 43–50
  urban churches 30, 41–3
Carpenter, Edward 465
Carter, H. C. 441
Cassander, Georg 203 n.11
catacombs, and historic continuity of
  Catholic Church 295, 301, 302–3,
    311
catechumenate, adult 478–94
  acceptance into 481, 488
  baptism, confirmation and first
    communion 480, 483–90, 494
  in Carolingian church 58
  Catechumen Mass 135–6, 486
  Election/Enrollment 482, 488–9, 492
  Evangelization and Precatechumenate
    480–1, 488
  Mystagogy 485–6, 488, 492
  Purification and Enlightenment 482–3
cathedrals
  as complexes 41
  and daily office 78
  and Henrician Reformation 105
  and lay worship 30, 41, 42–3, 54, 105
  and liturgical books 50
  and liturgical drama 93, 99, 102
  and liturgical settings 51
  and traditional piety 104–15
  see also London, St Paul's Cathedral;
    Winchester Cathedral; York
    Minster
Catholic Apostolic Church 397, 407
Catholicism *see* Anglo-Catholicism;
  Roman Catholicism
Cave, Sydney 443
Cecil, Lord Hugh 459, 462
Cecil, Robert, 3rd Marquess of Salisbury
  370

Cecil, William, 1st Baron Burghley, and
    lay readers 189
Cecil, William, Bishop of Exeter 451
Celtic Church
    and ordination 175 n.6, 176
    and Welsh language 415–16
Chadwick, Owen 362
chalice, mixed 244, 245–7, 253–4, 313,
    326, 337, 384, 393
    in early Church 14–15, 17
Chambers, William Frederick 386–7,
    392
Champ, Judith xxii, 289–319
chancels
    in Carolingian churches 38–40, 53
    in early English churches xxiii, 38–9,
    65–77
chantries
    civic 110
    dissolution 110, 113, 114, 185
    and intercessory prayer 104, 114
    of York Minster 105–14
chants
    'Gregorian' 51, 289
    in rural parishes 51–2, 54–5
Charlemagne
    and liturgical unity 339, 340, 344
    and priests and laity 36
Charles V, Holy Roman Emperor 127
Chartier, Ives 51 n.72
Cheyney, Richard, Bishop of Gloucester
    191
Chicago-Lambeth Quadrilateral 357
Chinnichi, J. P. 292, 293
choir
    Anglican 309, 315, 322–3
    in Church in Wales 412–13
    in Dissenting worship 238
    Roman Catholic 308, 309
    in St Paul's Cathedral 362, 366–9
chrismation see anointing
The Christian World 433, 435–7
Christmas
    liturgical celebrations 42, 402, 411,
    412–13, 429
    and liturgical drama 92–3, 95–6, 99,
    102

Chrodegang of Metz 41, 42
Church, early
    and baptism 10, 14 n.38, 486–7
    and Catholic continuity 200, 202, 207,
    215, 222, 296, 300, 302–3, 333,
    337–8
    and diversity 12
    and the eucharist xxiv, 1–17, 249–53
    and Open Brethren worship 283
    and Protestant continuity xxi, 129,
    261–74, 300, 303, 314, 333, 444
    and scrutinies 492–3
Church Assembly 449–51, 456, 460–1,
    463, 465
Church Association 372, 392–4, 466,
    468
Church of England
    and church music 309, 315
    and church and state 384, 449–50, 452,
    454, 456, 456–60, 461–3, 464, 477
    as comprehensive 356–7, 360, 383,
    450, 477
    and the eucharist 316–17, 439, 459
    and inclusivity of liturgy 349–50,
    352–6, 360, 430
    and Lay Readers xxiii, 185–98
    and liturgical diversity 462–3
    and liturgical revival 315–17, 345–6
    and medievalism and Romanism
    315–17, 322
    as national church 351, 352, 353–5,
    356–8, 360
    and royal authority 183
    and Thirty-Nine Articles xxiv, 353–4,
    375
    and Voysey xxiv, 375–6, 378–9, 383
    see also Anglicanism; Anglo-
    Catholicism; Book of Common
    Prayer; Ordinal; Prayer Book, 1552;
    ritualism
Church, Bartholomew (Elizabethan
    reader) 192 nn.35,38, 195
Church, J. E. 423, 427, 429
Church, Richard William, Dean of St
    Paul's 369, 372
Church of Scotland see Presbyterianism
Church Society 466

churches
  masonry 39, 67–77
  'station' 41
  timber 39–40, 67
churches, Carolingian
  and lay religious experience 29–64
  monastic 35–6, 39, 46–7, 51, 61
  rural 31–4, 36–41, 43–61
  urban 30, 41–3
churches, English
  and celebration of Holy Communion
  38
  chancels xxiii, 38–9, 65–77
Churches of God 280
churching of women, by lay readers 192
Ciconiolano, *Directorium divini Officii* 211
  n.31
Cisalpinism 290–4, 300
Clapham, Alfred 65–7, 77
Clarke, Henry 327
Clement VIII, Pope, Pontifical 183–4
Clement of Alexandria
  and catechumenate 488
  and eucharistic practice 14, 245–7
Clementine Liturgy, and Rattray 241,
  242, 245, 249
Clementine Vulgate 209
clergy
  as actors 93–4, 96, 100
  book ownership 108
  canonical rights 295, 298–300, 390–1
  cathedral 365–6
  and celibacy 96, 116
  and chant-settings 51–2
  chantry 105–15, 185
  and liturgical books 43–9, 50
  and monastic churches 36
  and role of the laity 52–3, 390, 394
  rural 31–2, 33–4, 36–8, 43–4, 47–9,
  50–1, 59
  university education 195, 197
  and Zwingli 140, 142–3, 148
  see also ordination; priesthood; vicars
  choral
Clifford, John, *Sound Words* 236
Clofesho, council (747)
  and chant-settings 52 n.73

and the eucharist 33, 34
Cobb, William 466–8, 470–1
Cockayn, George 230
Cole, Robert 187
Colenso, John William 346 n.3
collectars 79, 82–3
  in rural parishes 45–6
A Collection of Divine Hymns 233–4
Collier, Jeremy 242, 255
community and liturgy 204–5
  in Augsburg 117–22, 126–7
  in Carolingian churches 60–1
  and language 130–1, 344
  and unity 341, 343–4
  in Zurich 128–31, 135–7, 139–42
Compilatio tertia 98, 100, 103
compline
  in medieval liturgies 85
  in Reformation liturgies 161
computus, in rural parishes 44
Confessing Church 443
Confessio fidei 53
confession
  in African Traditional Religion 423
  in Church of England 448
  in East African Revival xxii, 420–4, 430
  in German Reformation 123–4, 126
  in Swiss Reformation 133, 134, 140
  and Voysey 378
confirmation
  and Aquinas 163
  in Carolingian church 59–60
  and catechumenate 480, 483–5, 490,
  494
  and Voysey 382
The Congregational Quarterly 437, 439
Congregationalism
  and Blackheath Group 433, 436, 440
  and catholicity 432, 435, 441, 443–4
  Church Order Group 444
  and organization of services 230
  and preaching 434–7, 439, 442–3,
  444–6
  and reformation of worship xxiii,
  432–46
  and sacraments 437–40, 444–6
  see also Dissent; Independents

Connolly, R. H. 8
conservatism, liturgical xxi, xxii
consignatio (confirmation) 59–60
Constance, Council (1414-18) 209
context, and liturgical texts 2–3, 30
continuity
  of Catholicism with early Church
    200–2, 207, 215, 222, 291, 296, 300,
    302–3, 311, 317, 333, 337–8
  of Catholicism with medieval past
    291, 293–314, 318, 333, 338
  of Protestants with early Church xxi,
    129, 261–74, 300, 303, 314, 333
  of Protestants with medieval past xxi,
    129, 135, 150, 315–17, 322
Convocation of Canterbury and York
  and Elizabethan lay readers 190–2
  and Revised Prayer Book 450–1
Cooper, James 402, 406, 407
Copleston, Edward, Bishop of Llandaff
  and Dean of St Paul's 366
Coward, J. H. 364–5, 373
Cox, Jeffrey 410 n.6, 411 n.9
Cox, Richard, Bishop of Ely 189
Cradock, Samuel, *Knowledge and Practice*
  236–7
Cragoe, Matthew 412
Craik, Henry 277
Cramer, Peter 30, 58 n.92, 59
Cranmer, Thomas
  and baptism 163
  Catechism 183
  and church music 55, 164
  and daily office 79, 160, 161–2
  and the eucharist 151, 160–1, 162–3,
    167–8, 242, 255
  and international Protestant liturgy
    167–8, 171
  and Litany of 1544 160
  and liturgical continuity xxii, 151–4,
    158, 160–1
  and Luther 160
  and national liturgy 166
  and popular religion 160
  and vestments 162, 164, 168
  see also Book of Common Prayer
Crawford, Alexander 399–404

creed
  in Carolingian church 34–5, 59
  in catechumenate 479, 483, 489
  in Church of Scotland 396
  in Congregationalism 440
  and Cranmer 162
  and Luther 159
  and Maurice 350, 357
  and Müntzer 158
  and Rattray 257–8
  and Voysey 374, 378, 383
  and Zwingli 136
  see also Athanasian Creed
Creighton, Mandell, Bishop of London
  and Carlisle Cathedral 361
  and St Bartholomew Smithfield 327–9,
    331–2
  and St Paul's Cathedral 373
Crichton, James 295, 315, 317
Croft, William, *Musica sacra* 238
Cross, F. L. 2, 250
Crossley-Holland, Peter 413 n.22
Cuming, J. G. 152–3, 161, 167, 345, 346
  n.2
Cumnor (Oxon.), church chancel 70, 74
Cuthbert, St, and eucharist 63–4
Cuvier, Georges 4
Cyprian
  and baptism 487
  and eucharistic practice 14, 245–7,
    252–4
  Letter 63 253–4
Cyril of Jerusalem, St
  and baptism 487
  Mystagogical Catecheses 16, 243, 248,
    254
  Procatechesis 489
  and Rattray 241, 248–52, 255

Daldy, Alfred E., Archdeacon of
  Winchester 468–70
Dale, H. Montagu 456
Danby, Sir Christopher 111
dance, and liturgy 89
Darwell Stone, 451, 460–1
Darwin, Charles 4
Davidson, Carol F. xxiii, 65–77

Davidson, Randall Thomas, Archbishop
of Canterbury
and Revised Prayer Book 450–8, 462
and ritualism 325
Davies, Horton 432, 442
Davies, Maurice 377–8, 383
Davies, Wendy 60
Davis, Natalie 204
Davis, Richard, *Hymns* 234, 235
Day, John 185
Daykin, T. E. xxiii, 464–77
De lapsu virginis consecratae 25 n.12
deacons
and lay readers 188, 191
and liturgical drama 93
ordination 174, 180, 183
Deedes, Gordon Frederick 387
Demetrias, consecration 20, 21
Derrida, Jacques 154
Deus castorum corporum (prayer) 21
devotio moderna 149
Dickens, A. G. 104, 165
Dickson, Neil xxii, 275–88
Didache
and baptism 486–7
and eucharist 1, 8–9, 11–13, 251
Didascalia Apostolorum 11, 487
discipline
in apostolic worship 267, 268, 272, 273
in East African Revival 421–2
in German Reformation 119–20, 125
in Presbyterianism 259
disestablishment, and Revised Prayer
Book 454, 460, 461–3
Dissent, English
and Act of Uniformity 355
and Church of England 356
and congregational organization
229–30
and hymnody xxiii, 227–39
and the sacraments 439
see also Congregationalism;
Independents; Presbyterianism
Ditchfield, Simon xxiii, 199–226
Dix, Gregory, *The Shape of the Liturgy* 5, 8,
13–14, 151, 153–4, 250–1
Dixon, Dudley 455

drama, liturgical, and Innocent III xxiii,
89–103
Duchesne, Louis 8
Dudley, Martin xxiii, 320–32
Duffy, Eamon
and Cranmer's liturgy 152–4, 164
and traditional piety 104, 152, 153,
205, 213 n.35
Dunnico, Herbert 459
Duns Scotus, and *traditio instrumentorum*
176
Durandus, William, pontifical 23, 25 n.12

Earle, Thomas (Elizabethan reader) 195,
198
East African Revival xxii, 419–31
and confession 420–4, 430
and conventions 427–9
and hymn-singing 420–1, 424–7
and sacraments 429–30
Easter
in Church in Wales 409, 411, 412, 418
in Congregationalism 435
in East African Revival 429
and liturgical drama 93, 99–101, 102
in Presbyterianism 402
'Echternach Sacramentary' 56
Edward VI of England, Royal Injunctions
of 1547 185, 186
'Egbert of York', Penitential 44, 46 n.55
Egeria, *Pilgrimage* 487, 489
Einsiedeln monastery, and Jud 145
elders
and Haldane 263, 268–9
and Scotch Baptists 265–6
Elizabeth I of England
and lay readers 189–90
Royal Injunctions of 1559 186
Ellard, Gerald 50
Eller, treasure 40
Ellison, Susanna 375
England
Catholic Revival 295
and liturgical drama 102
ordination rites xxii, 172–84
and *panis benedictus* 62, 152
parish church chancels xxiii, 65–77

England (*cont.*):
  restoration of Catholic hierarchy
    297–8, 300, 302
  Romanist and medievalist Catholicism
    289–319
  see also Anglicanism; Church of
    England; Cisalpinism
English Church Union 317, 324, 386–7,
  388, 455, 457, 477
English language, and Church in Wales
  413–17
Episcopalians (Scotland)
  and apostolic liturgy 240–1
  and Apostolic Succession 248
  and eucharistic liturgies 256, 260
  and Liturgy of 1718 242, 244, 255
  and Non-jurors 241–8
  and Presbyterianism 396
  and reservation of the sacrament 450
  see also Rattray, Thomas
Erasmus, Desiderius
  and Canterbury Cathedral 104
  and early Church 129
  and Jud 145–6, 148, 150
  Paraphrases 146
Escomb, St John, church architecture
  38–9
Estonia, Christianization 97–8, 103
eucharist
  bipartite structure 6, 7
  in Church of England 316–17, 439,
    459
  and communion in both kinds 116,
    162, 290
  and comparative liturgiology 4–5
  in Congregationalism 437–8
  continuity of practice 1–2, 8, 17, 151,
    337–8
  and Cranmer 151, 160–1, 162–3,
    167–8, 242
  diversity of meanings 15–17
  diversity of practice 1–3, 7–15,
    249–54
  in the early Church xxiv, 1–17,
    249–53
  eastward celebration 76, 338, 369–70,
    384, 388, 393–4
  elevation of the elements 326, 385
  frequency
    in Carolingian churches 33
    in Church of Scotland 396, 398,
      402–4, 406
    in Church in Wales 409, 411–12
    in Congregationalism 438
    and Haldane 264, 267
    in Reformation churches 143
    and ritualism 388
  in German Reformation 120–1
  and hymn-singing 233–5
  Invocation of the Holy Spirit 244,
    249–50, 252
  and Jud 147–50
  and Maurice 357
  in monastic churches 36
  in Müntzer 157, 163, 164
  and Non-jurors 241–2, 244–5, 247–8,
    250
  and oblation of elements 244, 249–50,
    252
  and parish communion movement
    347
  and preaching 136–8, 143, 159–60
  and priestly ordination 176, 183
  in rural parishes 32–3, 36–8, 61–3
  as sacrifice 15–16, 162, 177, 312
  and table prayers 7, 8, 11
  in thought of Dix 5–6, 13–14, 151
  tripartite pattern 6, 7
  unitary structure 7, 10–12, 15
  and use of bread and wine 12–15, 253
  and Voysey 379
  westward celebration 75–6, 338, 369
  and Zwingli 132–43, 150, 167, 286,
    438
  see also breaking of bread; chalice,
    mixed; intercession; kyries; Last
    Supper; Lord's Supper; mass;
    Rattray, Thomas; real presence;
    Sanctus; Usages; water
Eugenius IV, Pope, *Decretum pro Armenis*
  177
eulogiae 62, 63 n.108
Eustace, John Chetwode, *A Classical Tour
  through Italy* 289–92, 294, 308, 317
Eustochium, and St Jerome 18

evangelicalism
  and Congregationalism 432–3, 434,
    436–7, 441–3, 446
  in Oxford University 375
  and Prayer Book revision 447, 451–5,
    457, 461
  and reform of German worship
    116–27
  and Thirty-Nine Articles 349
Evennett, H. Outram 225
evensong
  in Church in Wales 409–10, 412,
    417
  in Cranmer's liturgy 152, 161, 162
Ewan, Isaac 280, 284
Ewing, Greville
  An Attempt towards a Statement of the
    Doctrine of Scripture . . . 268
  and Ballantine 268, 270
  Facts and Documents . . . 266 n.15
Excerptiones Egberti 38
Exclusive Brethren 276, 280
Exhortatio ad plebem christianam 59
exhortation, mutual 264, 267–70, 273,
    276–9, 420
exorcism
  and adult catechumenate 479, 482,
    483, 488, 489, 493–4
  and baptism 158, 163
exorcist, and traditio instrumentorum 173
Exponi nobis (papal brief) 210

Faber, Frederick William 315
Fabricius, Johann Albert 243–4
Fagius, Paul 167
Falconer, John (Non-juring bishop) 244
Farner, Oscar 145
fast days, Presbyterian 230, 402–3
Feast of Fools 91, 93, 100
fellowship, liturgy of, in East African
    revival xxii, 419–31
Fenwick, John 347
Ferrero, Guido, Cardinal-Bishop of
    Vercelli 217–18
Ferrey, Benjamin 322
festivals, celebration 401–2, 406, 444
Février, P.-A. 56 n.87

First Book of Discipline 179
Flacius Illyricus, Matthias 203
Fleming, J. R. 399
Flint, Valerie 57
Florence, Council (1439) 177
Florus of Lyons, Expositio missae 53
Folco Scotti, S. 216
fonts 37, 490–1
form criticism, and liturgy 154
Formulae Senonenses 34
Forster, Johann (Augsburg preacher) 118,
    120–1, 124, 125–6
Forsyth, P. T. 436, 437, 441
Fortunatus, Salve festa dies 55
France
  and church and state 333–5, 336
  and liturgical drama 93–4
  and Tridentine liturgy 203, 340, 342
  and Ultramontanism see Guéranger,
    Prosper
  see also Gallicanism
Francia see Carolingian church
Frankenhausen, battle (1523) 168
Franklin, Benjamin 320
Franz, 170
Freising charters 37
Frere, Walter Howard, Bishop of Truro
    315, 316, 460, 464
Gallia cristiana 223
Gallicanism
  and liturgy 50, 163, 175, 242, 243, 249,
    336, 339
  and Roman Breviary 203
  see also Cisalpinism
Garatola, Daniele 213, 214–15
Garbett, Cyril, Archbishop of York
  as Bishop of Winchester 464, 466–77
  and Revised Prayer Book 453, 459
Gardiner, Stephen, Bishop of Winchester
    162
Gardiner, William, Music and Friends 228,
    234, 237–8
Garvie, A. E. 456
Gavanti, B., Thesaurus sacrorum rituum . . .
    203
Geetz, Clifford 343

Gelasian Sacramentary
  and baptism 487
  and consecration of virgins 21, 26 n.21
  in rural parishes 44–5, 47, 49, 50
Gellone Sacramentary 54
Gelston, Anthony 162
General Baptists, and psalm-singing 232
Gentilcore, David 204, 205
German language
  and medieval worship 33–4
  in Reformation liturgies 129, 146,
    158–60, 165–6
German Reformation 116–27
  and images 126
  see also Augsburg; Bucer, Martin;
    Luther, Martin; Zwingli, Huldrych;
    Zwinglianism
Ghaerbald of Liège, capitula 36, 38, 44
Gibbings, Richard 411
Gilbert of Hoyland 312
Gildas, Liber Querulus 175 n.6
gilds, and chantries 109, 110
Gilley, Sheridan 346
Giraudo, Cesare 6
Gladstone, William Ewart 370, 374, 375,
    415
Glas, John 266, 276
Glasites 265–6, 277–9
Gloria
  in eucharist 159, 162–3, 167
  in Voysey's services 378
Goar, Jacques, Euchologium sive rituale
    graecorum 243
Goertz, Hans-Jurgen 156
Goodman, A. W. 471, 472, 474–5
Goodwin, Harvey, Dean of Ely 361
Gordon, Bruce xxii, 128–50
Goss, John (organist of St Paul's) 368
Gothics see Romanism
gradales, in rural parishes 45, 51
Grant, J. W. 432, 433–4, 436, 437
Gratian 100–1
Gray, Donald 347, 356 n.38
Gregorian Sacramentary 41
  Aniane Supplement 47, 50, 56–7 n.88,
    59–60
  Hucusque Supplement 43, 50

in rural parishes 44–5, 47, 49, 50
Gregory I 'the Great', Pope
  and church music 289, 304, 308
  Homilia XL 45 n.52
  and Innocent III 101
  Liber responsalis 22–3, 24–8
  and Roman liturgy 81, 338
Gregory VII, Pope, and church and state
    334, 339, 340
Gregory IX, Pope, Decretals 95
Gregory XIII, Pope, and calendar of saints
    215
Gregory XVI, Pope
  and French Church 335
  and Polish Catholics 334
Gregory, Robert 363–73
  A Plea in Behalf of Small Parishes 363–4
  The Position of the Priest . . . 369
Grindal, Edmund, Bishop of London, and
    lay readers 188 n.14, 189–90, 194,
    196–8
Guéranger, Prosper Louis
  Institutions liturgiques 337–44
  and medieval Catholicism xxii, 203,
    335–44
  and restoration of monasticism 336–7
Guest, Edmund, Bishop of Rochester 192
Gy, P.-M. 59

Hadrianum 47, 50, 59
Haggenmüller, R. 44 n.51
hagiography
  and baptism 487
  in daily office 206–8, 210–11, 214–18,
    220
Haigh, Mervyn, Bishop of Winchester
    465
Haito of Basel 43–4, 46 nn.55,57, 53
Haldane, Alexander 272–3
Haldane, James Alexander 261 n.2,
    262–4, 266–70
  and Ballantine 266–7, 272
  and baptism 264, 265, 270–1, 273
  and biblical literalism 270, 272–3
  and the Lord's Supper 264–5
  and mutual exhortation 264, 267–9,
    273

The Obligation of Christian Churches to Observe the Lord's Supper . . . 264–5, 273

Observations on the association of believers 274 n.39

and 'social worship' 277

Social Worship and Ordinances observed by the first Christians 263, 265, 271

Haldane, Robert 261 n.2, 267, 271

Hale, William 363, 364

Halifax, E. F. L. Wood, 1st Earl of 457

Hall, Stuart xi, 240–60

Handbuch der Kirchengeschichte 200–1

Hardman, John 309

Hariulf, *Chronicon Centulense* 47 n.58, 54 n.81

Harnack, Adolf von 14–15

Harper, John 50 n.67

Harrison, Michael 234

Hart, Charlotte 325

Hart, G. W. 315, 316

harvest festivals 409–11, 412, 418

Hastings, Adrian 439

Hatchett, Marion J. 163

Hausmann, Nicholas 153

Häussling, A. A. 42

Hawkes, Peter (Elizabethan reader) 195–6

Headlam, A. C., Bishop of Gloucester 464

Headlam, Stewart 347

Hebert, Gabriel 347

Heimann, Mary 293–4, 297, 305, 318

Heitz, C. 54 n.81

Henry VIII of England, and Reformation 104–5, 113–15, 166, 186, 320

Henry, Matthew, *Family-Hymns* . . . 236

Henry, Nathalie xxiii, 18–28

Henson, Herbert Hensley, Bishop of Durham 461–2

Heros and the Magi (liturgical drama) 99–100

Hickes, George 242, 252

High Churchmanship
in Congregationalism 436, 437–8, 443
in Presbyterianism 397, 406

Hildegar of Meaux 62 n.105, 63 n.108

Hill, Thomas 375

Hinchliff, Peter 359 n.52

Hincmar of Rheims
capitula 38 n.32
Collectio de ecclesiis et capellis 38, 59–60, 62 n.105
and Florus of Lyons 53
and liturgical books 44

Hinde, H. W. 453–4

Hippolytus of Rome, *Apostolic Tradition*
and baptism 487–8
and consecration of virgins 19
and the eucharist 10, 13, 251
and exorcism 493–4
and ordination rites 173–4

Historiae, in daily office 78–9, 83–4

history
and Maurice 350–1, 355, 358–60
and Reformation liturgics 128–9
and Tridentine worship xxiii, 199–226
and worship xxi–xxii, xxiii–xiv

Hixon, John (cantarist of York Minster) 107, 108

Hodgson, Leonard, Dean of Winchester 473

Hogarth, William 320

Hogg, Sir Douglas 459

Hohler, Christopher 50

holiness movement 287

Holland, Henry Scott 347, 372, 410–11

Holy Innocents' Day, and liturgical drama 93, 95, 100

homiliaries, in rural parishes 44–6

Hook, Walter Farquar 392

Hooper, John, Bishop of Gloucester 181

Hopkins, John, *Whole Book of Psalmes* 230–2

How Rachel weeps for her Children (liturgical drama) 99–100

Howe, William Walsham, Bishop of Bedford 322

Hrabanus Maurus of Mainz, and baptism 58

Hugh de Nonant 102

Hugh of St Victor 108

Hughes, Anselm 84 n.11

Hughes, Joshua, Bishop of St Asaph 415

humanism
  and liturgical scholarship 200
  and Reformation 129, 132, 135, 141
Huxtable, John 444, 445, 446
hymnody
  Carolingian 55
  Congregational 441-2, 444, 446
  Dissenting xxiii, 227-39, 264
  in East African Revival 420-1, 424-7
  in German Reformation 124, 159-60
  and instrumental music 237-8
  and medieval breviaries 80, 82, 211-12
  in Presbyterianism 227-8, 230, 234,
    237, 396
  for private use 235-6
  and Voysey 381-2
Hypocrisy Detected . . . 261-2

iconoclasm, and Reformation 126, 128,
  164
images
  and German Reformation 126
  and Swiss Reformation 141-2, 149
imitatio Romae 41-2
imitation of Christ, in Swiss Reformation
  147-50
imposition of hands
  in confirmation 382
  and consecration of virgins 19
  in ordination 172, 174, 175, 177-80,
    383
Independents
  and hymn-singing 227-8, 232-3,
    234-5, 237, 238
  Scottish, and New Testament patterns
    xxii, 261-74
  see also Congregationalism; Tabernacle
    Connexion
Index of Prohibited Books 207
Inge, William Ralph 458
initiation see baptism; catechumenate;
  confirmation
Innocent III, Pope
  and church and state 334
  Cum decorem 95, 98-9
    glosses 99-101, 103
  De Miseria Humane Conditionis 97

and liturgical drama xxiii, 91-2, 93,
  94-103
Inskip, Sir Thomas 452, 457, 459
Institutio Angilberti Centulensi 54 n.81
instruction, and liturgy 119, 122-3,
  135-6, 210, 214, 396
intercession
  in eucharist 15-16, 163, 167, 170,
    259-60
  see also chantries
Iremonger, F. A. 465
Irenaeus, and eucharistic practice 13, 14,
  245-7, 253-4
Irvine, Christopher 347 n.7
Irving, Edward 274, 277
Irwin, Joyce 169-70
Italy
  cathedrals 41
  and liturgical diversity 213-19
  liturgical history 200, 202, 219-24
  monastic churches 36
  rural churches 39

Jackson, John, Bishop of London 369-70
Jacobilli, Lodovico 200
  Nocera nell'Umbria e sua diocesi . . .
    221-2
  Vite de'Santi e Beati dell'Umbria . . .
    221
James of Joigny (Pamelius) 203 n.11
James, St, Liturgy, and Rattray xxii, 241,
  242, 243-4, 245, 248-9, 252, 254-5,
  259
Jaspers, R. C. D. 346
Jenkins, Daniel 441, 443-4, 445
Jenkins, W. J. 392
Jenny, Markus 143
Jerome, St
  Letter 22 18, 25 n.12
  Letter 130 19, 20, 21-2
  on St Matthew 45 n.52
  and Song of Songs 18-21
Jerusalem Liturgy
  and catechumenate 489
  and Rattray 241, 248-54, 255-6
Jesse of Amiens 58 n.92
Jobson, Sir Francis 195

John Chrysostom, St, Liturgy 241, 242, 243, 249, 252
John de Beleth, *Summa de Ecclesiasticis Officiis* 92–3
John the Deacon, *Ad Senarium* 494
John of Fécamp, *Confessio fidei* 53
John of Hildersheim 155
John of Lubeck 155
Johnson, John 249, 252
Johnson, Maxwell 12
Jones, Ieuan Gwynedd 416
Jones, J. D. 443
Joye, George 161
Joynson-Hicks, Sir William 452, 457–8, 461
Jud, Leo
  baptism liturgy 132, 146
  and Bible translations 146–7
  catechetical literature 139, 147
  and eucharist 147, 148–50
  and the laity 144–5
  and Pauline epistles 145–6
  The Suffering of Christ According to the Holy Evangelists 148–50
  and Surgant 133
  and Zwingli 129, 144, 145, 150
Judaism
  and liturgical scholarship 2
  and origin of eucharistic prayers 6, 7, 11, 15
Jungmann, J. A. 8, 201, 203
Justin Martyr, *First Apology*, and Eucharist 11, 15, 243, 245

Kabaza, Zeb 419–20, 429
Kamen, Henry 204–5, 209
Kantz, Kaspar 155
Karlstadt, Andreas 155
Karney, A. B. L., Bishop of Southampton 473–5, 476
Kaye, John, Bishop of Lincoln 363–4, 389
Keach, Benjamin 233
Keller (German preacher) 121, 126
Kelly, J. 18 n.3
Kelly, Thomas 276
Kempe, Charles E. 406

Kempis, Thomas à, *The Imitation of Christ* 149, 442
Kennedy, W. M. 191
Kensit, John 331
Kensit, John Alfred 453
Keswick spirituality 420, 425, 428, 430
Kidd, B. J. 460
Kietlicz, Henry, Archbishop of Gniezno 95–6
Kigozi, Blasio 427, 429
Kilpeck (Herefs.), church chancel 65, 66, 67, 71–2
King, Edward, Bishop of Lincoln, and ritualism 384–5, 391, 393–5
Kinniburgh, Robert 266 n.16, 273
Kinuka, Yosiya 427
Kirchenordnung of 1537 116, 121, 122, 124
Kirk, Robert 229–30, 232
kiss, apostolic 261–2, 265, 273, 337
Klauser, Theodor 201, 203
kneeling, Presbyterian objection to 404
Knight, Frances xxiii, 408–18
Knox, John
  and liturgy 256, 403
  and ordination 179
Kopling, A. 53
kyries
  at burials 56
  at eucharist 55, 157, 159, 162–3

laity
  and baptism 57–60
  and burial practices 55–7, 61
  and chant-settings 51–2, 54–5
  and clergy 96, 390–1, 393–4
  in East African Revival 420
  and the eucharist 32–3, 36–8, 61–4, 76, 152, 202, 205, 411
  and German Reformation 124–5, 126–7, 168–70
  and innovation 398–400
  as lay readers 185–98
  and literacy 52
  and liturgical drama 89, 93
  and monastic churches 35–6
  as patrons 187
  and preaching 134

laity (cont.):
and relics 64
and ritualism 390–1, 393–5, 453,
468–9
role in Carolingian worship xxiii,
29–64
and rural churches 31–5, 37–9
and Swiss Reformation 134, 135, 148
and traditional piety 104–5
Lamennais, Hugues-Félicité de 335, 336
Lanfranc, Archbishop of Canterbury 312
Lang, Cosmo Gordon, Archbishop of
Canterbury 329–30, 451–2, 462
Langton, Stephen, Archbishop of
Canterbury 312
language, and liturgy 130–1, 413–17
Lasko, John à 167, 179
Last Supper
as institution of Eucharist 6–7, 12–13,
253–4
and Rattray's liturgy 245, 247
in Zwingli's liturgy 140–3
Latin
and Carolingian reforms 52
and Reformation liturgies 126, 146,
158–9, 166
lauds
in medieval liturgies 85, 87
in Reformation liturgies 156, 160, 161
Laurentius Hispanus, *Apparatus glossarum
in Compilatio tertia* 100–1, 103
Law, in Reformed theology 135
lay readers
admission 187–9
and Convocation 190–2
in Elizabethan Church xxiii, 185–98
ordination as priest 195–6, 198
ordination as reader 187
schoolteachers as 194 n.41, 197
social background 194–6, 197–8
suspension 190–4
lectionaries 211
in rural parishes 44–6, 48
lector
and lay reader 187, 188–9
and *traditio instrumentorum* 173
Lee, Robert 399, 405

Leicester, and early hymn-singing 227–8,
234, 237–8
Leishman, Thomas 399, 400–4
Lemarignier, Jean 35
Lenwood, Frank 433
Leo I ('the Great'), Pope
and Leonine Sacramentary 19
and scrutinies 494
Leo XIII, Pope, and Anglican orders 183
Leofric of Exeter, and daily office 80
Leofric Psalter, and 'sample week' 80–1,
86, 87
Leonine Sacramentary
and baptism 487
and consecration of virgins 19–22, *20*
Lévi-Strauss, Claude 4
Liber responsalis
Office of virgins 22–3, 24–8
*Responsoria de assumptione sanctae
Mariae* 24 nn.1,3,5,7, 26 n.17, 27
nn.33,34
Liber Viventium Fabariensis 48 n.62
liberalism
in Congregationalism 433–4
and Voysey 376
see also Cisalpinism
Liddon, Henry Parry 352, 367–8, 369–70,
372
Lidgett, Scott 456
Lietzmann, Hans 2, 15
Lightfoot, Joseph Barber 372
Limoges, St Martial, and liturgical drama
100, 101, 102
Lincolnshire
and anti-Catholicism 385–6, 390
and ritualism 384–95
Society for the Encouragement of
Ecclesiastical Antiquities 389
Lingard, John
*The Antiquities of the Anglo Saxon
Church* 292, 308
and Cisalpinism 292–4
History of England 293
*Manual of Prayers for Sundays and
Holydays* 292–3, 297
and medievalism 296, 297–8, 301,
310–11, 314

and Pugin 310–11
and Rock 297–8, 309–10, 317–18
and Romanism 300
Linton (Hereford), church chancel 65, 68,
  71–2
literacy, lay 52
Liturgical Movement 347
liturgiology
  comparative 4–5, 200
  and Maurice 349–50, 359
  and methodology 2, 154–5, 202,
    203–4, 251–2, 491–4
  and restoration of apostolic worship
    240–60, 337–8
liturgy
  and architecture 65–77
  and baptism 57–60
  and burial 55–7
  and Carolingian reform 47, 49–50, 52,
    53, 58–9, 62
  and change 199–226, 249–52, 336
  church context 30–1
  and community see community
  didactic role 119, 122–3, 135–6, 210,
    214, 396
  and drama xxiii, 89–103
  dynamic model 205
  evangelical 116–27
  and lay participation 124–5
  and liturgical books 43–51, 54, 78–88
  as living literature 3
  and music 30, 51–2, 54–5
  as narrative 130–1
  organic model 4
  and philology 2–3
  and Reformation see Reformation
  and restoration 479, 486–94
  in rural churches 43–4
  scriptural model 261–74
  and source criticism 154
  and structural similarities 5–6
  and unity 167, 336–44, 349–50, 352–6,
    357–8, 359–60
  see also continuity; language;
    medievalism; Romanism
Livonia, Christianization 97–8, 103
Lloyd, Charles 349

Lloyd George, David 460
Lockhart, George 248
London
  St Bartholomew Smithfield
    congregation 326–30
    first restoration 322
    Lady Chapel 320, 322, 323, 331–2
    and liturgical reform xxiii, 320–32
    and medievalism 322
    and ritualism accusations 322,
      323–6
    second restoration 323, 327–30
  St Paul's Cathedral
    and choir 362, 366–9
    and clergy 365–6
    decoration 370–1
    and liturgical reform xxiii, 361–73
    medieval psalter 85–6
    and reredos 371–2
    and ritualism 369–70
  Stranger Churches 167
Lord's Prayer
  in catechumenate 479, 483, 489
  in Church of Scotland 396
  in Reformation liturgies 132–3, 139,
    158–60, 161, 162–3
  in vernacular 34
  in Voysey's Revised Prayer Book 380
Lord's Supper
  and Congregationalism 438–9
  in Haldane's liturgy 264–5
  and hymn-singing 233–5
  in Presbyterianism 264, 267, 400–1
  and Scotch Baptists 266
  see also breaking of bread
Louis I the Pious, West Frankish
  Emperor 35, 36, 39
Lovegrove, Deryck xxii, 261–74
Lovell Cocks, H. F. 441, 443
Lowe, E. A. 48 n.64
Lucca diocese, and rural churches 31
Luke's Gospel, and Last Supper 13
Lunette of Mentorella 102
Luther, Martin
  and baptism 160, 163, 178
  Concerning the Order of Pubic Worship
    153

Luther, Martin (*cont.*):
  and daily office 158–9
  Deutsche Messe 158, 159–60, 165–6
  and eucharist 120–1, 159–60, 162, 163,
    165–6
  Formula Missae 158, 159, 166
  Germanica Theologica 165
  and Jud 145
  and liturgical conservatism xxii, 118,
    153–4, 155, 157, 162–3, 164–6
  and ministry 178
  and Müntzer 156, 165, 168, 171
  and national liturgy 165–6, 171
  and preaching 159–60
  Taufbuchlein 158
  and vernacular Bible 146–7
Lutheranism
  and Cranmer 153
  in Reformation Augsburg 117–18,
    121, 124, 126

Mabillon, J., *De liturgia gallicana* 203–4,
    243, 249
MacCulloch, Diarmaid 164, 166, 168
McGowan, Andrew 13–15
Machin, Ian xxiii, 447–63
McKitterick, Rosamund 49 nn.65, 66
McLean, Archibald 266
Macleod, John 397–400, 402–7
Macrae, John 400
Magdeburg Agenda 160
Magdeburg Centuriators 58 n.93, 203
Mainz, Council (813) 58 n.92
The Manger (liturgical drama) 99–100
Manning, B. L. 434–5, 437–41, 443,
    445–6
Marcellina (sister of St Ambrose) 19
Marin, Louis 29
Marini, Leonardo 208
Mark, St, Liturgy 7, 241, 249
Maronite liturgy 241, 244, 245, 249
marriage, and Voysey 380–1
Marriott, Charles 349
Marsh, John 444, 445
Martène, E., *De antiquis Ecclesiae ritibus*
    203
martyrologies, in rural parishes 45
Martyrologium romanum 215

Maskell, William, *The Ancient Liturgy of
    the Church of England* 313, 315–16
mass
  Catechumen 135–6, 486
  chantry 105–6, 109
  and Cranmer 160, 162–3
  and Luther 120–1, 159–60, 162, 163,
    165–6
  and medieval secrecy 52–3, 76, 157
  and Müntzer 157, 159, 162, 163,
    164
  ordination 174–5, 176
  and popular piety 205
  and Rattray 249
  and Rock 311–13
  stational 41, 95
  Tridentine 202
  and Zwingli 132–42
  see also eucharist; transubstantiation
Mateos, Juan 154
matins
  in Church in Wales 409, 417
  and liturgical drama 100
  in medieval office 78, 80–6, 87–8
  in Reformation liturgies 152, 156–7,
    158–9, 161
  in Tridentine liturgies 202, 206, 208
  and Voysey 378, 380
Matthews, Walter Robert, Dean of St
    Paul's 369
Maurice, F. D.
  and Anglican liturgy 345–6, 348–59
  and Athanasian Creed 348, 352–3
  and baptism 350, 351, 354, 357
  The Church a Family 346 n.3, 351
  *Dialogues between a Clergyman and a
    Layman* 346 n.3
  and ecclesiology 348–50, 356–60
  The Faith of the Liturgy 346 n.3
  The Kingdom of Christ 348, 357–9
  The Prayer Book Considered . . . 346 n.3,
    348–50, 352
  and 'Prayer Book fundamentalism'
    xxiv, 345–60
  Sermons on the Sabbath-Day 359
  and 'State' services 352
  Subscription no Bondage 353

and Thirty-Nine Articles 348–9,
353–4
*Thoughts on the Rule of Conscientious
Subscription* 354
The Worship of the Church 346 n.3
*The Worship of God and Fellowship
among Men* 346 n.3
Mazza, Enrico 6, 12
Mead, Matthew 232–3
medievalism
and Church of England 315–17, 320,
322
and English Catholicism 291, 293–314,
318, 333–5
and Guéranger xxii, 335–44
Melanchthon, Philip 156
and Cranmer 167
mendicants
and development of the breviary 211
and missionary theatre 98
Methodism, and Sacramental Fellowship
438
Methodius of Olympus, St
and Song of Songs 18, 23
Symposium 18, 26 n.21
Mexico, Christianization 98
Meyrick, Roland, Bishop of Bangor 187,
190
Micklem, Nathaniel 433, 434–9, 440–6
*Congregationalism and the Church
Catholic* 432
Prayers and Praises 441, 444
Micklem, Romilly 442, 444
Micron, Marten 167
Mildmay, Walter 320
Milman, Henry Hart 370
Milner, John, Vicar Apostolic of the
Midlands 290–1
ministry
in Open Brethren 281–3
in Reformed Churches 142–3, 161,
172–3, 177–80, 181, 183
see also clergy; ordination; priesthood
Minkwitz, Hans von 165
Missal of 1570 209, 242, 336, 340
Missale Francorum, and consecration of
virgins 21

missals, in rural parishes 43–5
mission, and liturgical drama xxiii,
89–103
Mitchell, Rosslyn 457, 458, 460
monasteries
Dissolution 108, 320
and lay burials 57, 61
and lay worship 35–6, 39, 42, 54, 61
and liturgical books 46–7, 49 n.65, 50,
211
and liturgical drama 93, 99
and liturgical settings 51
in post-Revolutionary France 336–7
Montecassino, and liturgical drama 99,
101
Montgomeryshire, and nineteenth-
century Anglicanism 408–18
Mordek, Hubert 48
Morelli, Giorgio 223 n.62
Moretti, I. 39–40 n.37
Morgan, Campbell 434
Morgan, William 418
Morris, J. N. xxiv, 345–60
Moussoulens sacramentary 48 n.63, 50
Mozarabic rite 153, 163, 209, 242, 243,
339
Mozley, Thomas 375
Mukasa, Nasanairi 427
Müller, George 277
Mullins (archdeacon of London) 190, 198
Müntzer, Thomas 120
anti-clericalism 156
and baptism 157–8, 163
and eschatology 170–1
and eucharist 157, 159, 162, 163–4
execution 168
and liturgical reform xxii, 155, 156,
168–71
and Luther 156, 165, 168, 171
and preaching 156
Sermon to the Princes 168
and traditional piety 164
Murray, Douglas M. xxiii, 396–407
Musculus (German preacher) 120, 123
music
in Anglican worship 309, 315, 412–13,
418

music (*cont.*):
in Carolingian church 30, 51–2, 54–5
and Catholic liturgy 89, 283, 289, 307,
308
and Dissenting hymnody 237–8
and Reformation liturgy 164–5
and Voysey 377

nationalism
and Reformation in Germany 165–6,
168, 171
and Romanticism 301
nationality and liturgy 350–1, 353–5,
356–8, 360
Neale, John Mason 345
The Needed Truth (Brethren magazine)
279
Neri, St Philip 199
New Testament, as model for worship
xxiv, 261–74, 283
new year, celebrations 93, 411, 418
Newman, F. W., *Theism* 379
Newman, John Henry 203, 226, 305, 315,
349
Tract XC 354
Nicholetts, Charles, *The Devil's Champion
foil'd* 235 n.23
Nicholls, William, *Defensio* 237
Nockles, Peter 314, 315–16
nocturns *see* matins
Noel, Conrad 347
Non-jurors
and eastern Churches 241–2, 244
and eucharistic Usages 241–2, 244–5,
248, 250
and Liturgy of 1718 242, 244, 255
and patristic research 241, 245–7
and Rattray 240, 242, 244–5, 248
Nonconformism
and revised Prayer Book 454, 455–6,
461
see also Congregationalism; Dissent;
Independents; Open Brethren;
Presbyterianism; Scotch Baptists
Northcote, James Spencer 303
Notker the Stammerer of St Gall 101
Nsibambi, Simeon 427
nuns, initiation xxiii, 18–28

Nussdorfer, Laurie 225

Oath of Supremacy 186
Odo de Sully, Constitutions 94
Oecolampadius, Johannes 129
office, daily
and Cranmer 79, 160, 161–2
and English cathedrals 361–2
and hagiography 206–8, 210–11,
214–18, 220
and Luther 158–9, 162, 166
and Maurice 348–9, 350–1
and Müntzer 156–7, 162, 170
and reformed liturgy 155, 206–12
and 'Sample Week' xxiii, 78–88
see also breviaries
Officium Pastorum (liturgical drama) 100
Old Testament
and liturgical drama 97–8, 102–3
typological interpretation 280, 287–8
Ollivant, Alfred, Bishop of Bangor 415
Ommanney, G. C. 451
Open Brethren
and breaking of bread xxii, 275–88
and cerebralism 284, 285–8
and mutual exhortation 276–9
and sectarianism 280–1
and separatism 284–5, 286–7
and spontaneous worship 275–7,
278–80, 288
and supernaturalism 276, 283, 284–6,
288
oratories, rural 31, 37, 47
Orchard, W. E. 435
orders, minor
at Reformation 185–6
and lay readership 187
see also acolyte; exorcist; lector; ostarius
Ordinal
English 161, 178, 179, 180–3
Scottish 179
ordination
by anointing of hands 175
by imposition of hands 172, 174, 175,
177–80, 383
as lay reader 187
in the early Church 173–4

and Reformation 172–3, 177–81, 298
and Roman Catholicism 172, 173, 177
to minor orders 173–4, 183, 187
by *traditio instrumentorum* xxii, 172–84,
383
and Voysey 382–3
ordines, in Carolingian rural parishes
48–9, 50, 54
Ordo XI 58
Ordo ad representandum Herodem
(liturgical drama) 100
Ordo baptismi adultorum per gradus
catechumenatus dispositi 479–80
Ordo prophetarum (prophet plays) 97–8,
102–3
Ordo Romanus 55, 135, 139, 487
organs
in Anglican worship 322, 323, 413
in Dissenting worship 238, 396, 398,
405, 442
in Roman Catholic worship 289
Osiander, Andreas 167
Osmund, St, *Treatise of the Divine Office*
312
ostarius, and *traditio instrumentorum* 173
Oswald of York and Worcester, St 62
Ouseley, Sir Frederick 413
Owen, John 435, 436, 441
Oxford Movement
influence 322, 386, 388, 447
and Romanticism 314
Oxford University
and evangelicalism 375
and Tractarianism 388

Paleotti, Gabriele, Bishop of Bologna
218–19 n.48
Palmer, Samuel (printer) 320
Palmer, William 345
Panckridge, William, Rector of St
Bartholomew Smithfield 321,
322–5, 329, 331, 332
papacy
and Carolingian church 338–9, 344
and church and state 334–5, 336, 344
and Cisalpine movement 290, 291–2,
294, 299

and liturgical diversity 205–8, 215–19,
225, 336
and liturgical drama 91–2, 93, 94–103
and liturgical unity 338–40
Papias, and eucharistic practice 13
Paris, Council (1213) 94
Paris diocese, and rural churches 31
parish
Carolingian 31–2, 40, 43–51
and lay readership 186–9, 194–6
in Reformation Augsburg 116, 119–20
and ritualism 384–95
and traditional piety 104
Parker, Matthew, Archbishop of
Canterbury
consecration 182
and lay readers 187, 188–90, 194,
196–7
Parker, William 385
Parkhurst, John, Bishop of Norwich 188
Parliament, and Church of England
449–50, 454, 456–63, 477
Parsons, D. 54 n.81, 76
Particular Baptists, and psalm-singing
232
Paschasius Radbertus, *De corpore et*
sanguine domini 53–4
Passio of St Agnes 23, 25 n.14, 27 n.23
patronage
clerical 391, 393
lay 187, 391
reform 394
Paul IV, Pope 210, 217
Paul V, Pope 225
Paul, St
and Jud 145–6
and Last Supper 13, 253–4
and the liturgy 91
Pearce, Ernest, Bishop of Worcester 451
Pearson, J. L. 322
Peel, Albert 433, 435, 438–9, 442–3, 446
Peirce, James, *Vindicæ* 237
Pelletier, A.-M. 19 n.5
penance, in Rattray's liturgy 259
penitentials, in rural parishes 44–5, 48–9
Pentecostalism, and Open Brethren 285
Pentlow (Essex), church chancel 67, 70

Perrott, Thomas (precentor of York Minster) 106, 107
Peter of Capua 94
Peter the Chanter 93
Peter of Corbeil 94
Peter Martyr 167
Petrus Beneventanus, *Compilatio tertia* 98, 100, 103
Pfaff, R. W. xxiii, 78–88
Philimore, Sir Robert 185
Phillips De Lisle, Ambrose 299, 303, 304–5, 306, 308, 313, 314
  On Church Musick 308
Phillips, Frederick Parr 322, 324–5, 332
Phillips, William 321
philology, and liturgical scholarship 2–3
Piacenza, and local devotion 213–16, 219–20, 222–3
Pickering, Henry 279, 288
Piédagnel, Auguste 250
piety, medieval
  clerical 106–7
  lay 104–5, 116, 205, 226
  and Reformation liturgies 150, 152, 153, 164–5
'Pirie Act' 399–401
Pirie, W. R. 399, 405
Pittenweem Manuscript, and Rattray 246, 256–8
Pius IV, Pope, and revised Breviary 205–6, 208, 210, 217
Pius V, Pope, and revised Breviary 207, 217, 336
plainchant
  and Church of England 309
  in Reformation liturgies 156, 164–5, 168
  in Roman Catholic liturgy 289–90, 291, 304, 308–9
Platonism, English, and Maurice 357–8
Play of the Prophets (liturgical drama) 97–8, 102–3
Plummer, Charles 33
pluralism
  and cathedral clergy 356
  and lay readers 187–8
plygain 412 n.14, 413

Poland
  and church and state 334
  and missionary drama 93–4, 95–6, 99
Pole, Reginald 177 n.15
Polebrook (Northants.), church chancel 65, 69, 71–2, 75
Pollock, Bertram, Bishop of Norwich 451
Pontifical (of 1596) 209
Port-Royal convent, eucharistic doctrines 29
Portiforium Oswaldi see Wulstan Portiforium
Poullain, Valerand 167
Prayer Book
  of 1549 152–4, 160–1, 163, 164, 167, 180, 186, 242, 244, 255
  of 1552 152, 161–3, 164, 166, 167–8, 180, 182
  see also Book of Common Prayer
prayer for the dead 16, 160, 244, 259–60, 406, 448, 452–3
preaching
  in English Congregationalism 434–7, 439, 442–6
  in German Reformation 116, 122–3, 124, 156, 159
  and lay readers 188
  and preaching stools 138
  in Swiss Reformation 132–4, 136–7, 143, 145
preaching houses, in Reformation Augsburg 116
presbyter, and laying on of hands 173–4
Presbyterianism
  and baptism 270
  and discipline 259
  and hymn-singing 227–8, 230, 234, 237, 396
  influence on Open Brethren xxii, 278
  and liturgical revival 396–407, 444
  and the Lord's Supper 264, 267
  and ordination 179–80
  and recovery of ancient Christianity xxiii, 396–407
  and Scottish Independents xxii, 262, 265–7, 271–4
Price, E. J. 437, 443

Price, Mary 232–3
priesthood
  and anointing of hands 175
  and imposition of hands 174–5, 180
  and liturgical drama 93
  and Reformation 172–3
  sacrificial nature 175, 177, 181, 183
  and *traditio instrumentorum* 175, 177,
    180–1, 183
priests *see* clergy; ordination
prime
  and medieval liturgies 85, 87
  and Reformation liturgies 161
primers, vernacular 161–2
processions
  in Carolingian church 41–2, 54–5
  and liturgical drama 94
  in medieval parishes 152
  of the sacrament 449
Prodi, Paolo 225
Pronaus, in Switzerland 133–4, 135–6
Protestantism
  and changes in Augsburg xxiii, 116–27
  and continuity with early Church xxi,
    129, 261–74, 300, 303, 314, 333, 444
  and continuity with medieval past 129,
    135, 150
  and international liturgy 167–8, 171
  and lay readership 185–7
  and ordination 177
  and ritualism 393–4
  and Scripture in worship xxi, xxii
  see also Reformation
psalms
  in daily office 78, 80–2, 85, 87, 206–7,
    211–12
  in Dissenting services 229–30, 236, 264
  metrical paraphrases 227, 230–3, 235,
    238–9
  in Presbyterian worship 267
  in Reformation liturgies 124, 158–9,
    161–2
  in Roman Catholic worship 289, 293
  in Voysey's Prayer Book 379
Pugin, Augustus Welby
  and English medievalism 294, 295,
    297, 299–300, 303, 305–10, 315, 317

  and Lingard 310–11
  and liturgy 307–8
  and Lord Shrewsbury 303–4
  and music 307, 308–9
  Principles of Gothic Architecture 295
  and Rock 295, 306, 308, 309–11, 313,
    317–18
  and Romanism 305–7
  *Treatise on Chancel Screens and Rood
    Lofts* 310
Pullen, Robert 312
Pupper, Johann, *Fragmenta* 165
Purchas Judgement 369–70
Pusey, Edward Bouverie 349, 352
Puseyism, accusations 386

Quadripartitus 38 n.33
Quakers
  and Congregationalism 435
  and Open Brethren 277, 285
Quem quaeritis (liturgical drama) 100
Quiñones, Francisco de, and liturgical
  reform 160, 206–8, 210, 211, 341
Quod a nobis (papal bull) 209, 211, 216,
  218
Quodvultdeus, *De symbolo* 493–4

Radulf of Bourges 46 n.57
Raedts, Peter xxii, 333–44
Rahere, Prior 320, 321, 322
Ramsden, Omar 331
Randall, Ian M. xxiii, 432–46
Rasmussen, Neils 213
Ratcliff, E. C. 251, 253
Ratold of Trier 51, 56, 58
Rattray, Thomas
  *The Ancient Liturgy of the Church of
    Jerusalem* 240, 242, 243–6, 248–50,
    252–4, 259
  and apostolic liturgy xxi, xxii,
    240–60
  as Bishop of Brechin 248
  and celebration of 1994 256, 258–9
  influence 241, 259–60
  and Non-jurors 240, 242, 244–5, 248
  *Office for the Sacrifice of the Holy
    Eucharist* 249, 254–6

Rattray, Thomas (*cont.*):
  patristic sources 241, 243–50, 252–3, 260
  and Pittenweem Manuscript 246, 256–8
  subscribers 240–1
real presence 120, 147
  and Church of England 447–8
  and Congregationalism 439
  and Cranmer 162, 167
  and Presbyterianism 400–1
recollection, and liturgy 6, 131, 139–41
Recusants, English 296
redaction criticism, and liturgy 154
Redon Cartulary 60–1
Reformation
  Catholic 225
    see also Trent, Council
  and eucharistic liturgy 151–4, 160–3
  in Germany 116–27
  Henrician 104–5, 113–15, 166, 186
  liturgical continuity and change 151–71, 340
  and ministry 172–3, 177–80, 181, 183
  in Switzerland 128–50
Regensberg, and liturgical drama 96–7, 99
Regino of Prüm
  De harmonica institutione 51
  Libri duo de synodalibus causis et disciplinis ecclesiasticis 56
Regio, Paolo, *Vite de'sette santi potettori di Napoli* 220
Regula Benedicti see Rule of St Benedict
Regularis concordia 55 n.85
relics, and laity 64
religion, popular, and Cranmer's reforms 160
Renaudot, Eusèbe, *Liturgiarum orientalium collectio* 243, 244, 249
Rennie, Ian S. 277, 285
reservation of the sacrament
  at Winchester Cathedral 465–77
  continuous 447–8, 460, 466, 469–76
  occasional 448, 450, 469–71
  and Revised Prayer Book 449–55, 457–61, 463, 465, 473, 477
  in Rock 313

Responsoria de assumptione sanctae Mariae (Liber responsalis) 24 nn.1,3,5,7, 26 n.17, 27 nn.33,34
responsories, in daily office 79, 80, 84, 85–6
revelation, and tradition 182
Revivalism
  East Africa xxii, 419–31
  Gothic 297–300, 303–10
  and Open Brethren 278–9
Rich, Richard 320
Richards, Richard 414
Ricoeur, Paul 154
Righetti, Mario 209 n.28
Ritchie, John 282–3, 284, 286
Rite of Christian Initiation of Adults (RCIA) 480–94
Ritual (of 1614) 209
Ritual Commission (1870) 352–3
ritualism
  Anglican 313, 317
    at St Bartholomew Smithfield 322, 323–6, 331
    at St Paul's Cathedral 369–70
    at Winchester Cathedral xxiii, 465–77
    in nineteenth-century Lincolnshire 384–95
    and Prayer Book revision of 1928–9 447–63
    and university background 388–9
  and Open Brethren 280, 283, 286
  Presbyterian 396–407
  and real presence 447
  Royal Commission (1904) 325–6
Rivenhall (Essex), church chancel 67, 70, 70, 72, 74, 76
Robert de Courçon 93–4
Roblin, M. 31–2 n.6
Rock, Daniel
  and architecture 313
  and catacombs 295, 302–3, 311
  The Church of Our Fathers 296–7, 302, 307, 309, 310–13, 315–16, 318–19
  Hierurgia 297, 301, 302, 310, 311–12
  and Lingard 297–8, 309–10, 318
  and the mass 311–13, 316

and medieval Catholicism xxii, 293–9,
300, 301–2, 311–15, 317–18
and Pugin 295, 306, 308, 309–11, 313,
317–18
and restoration of Catholic hierarchy
297–8, 300, 302
and Romanism 300, 304
Textile Fabrics 302
Rodwell, W. J. 76
Rogers, David 296
Rogers, John 185–6, 187
role reversal, and Feast of Fools 93
Roman Catholicism
and adult catechumenate 478–94
and anti-Catholicism 385–6, 390, 447
and church and state 333–5, 336, 342,
344
and German Reformation 117–18, 119
and minor orders 173–4, 183, 185
and ordination 172, 173, 177, 182–3
and restoration of English hierarchy
295, 297–8, 300, 302
and Tridentine worship xxiii, 199–226
see also Breviaries; Cisalpinism;
continuity; medievalism;
Romanism; Ultramontanism;
Vatican Council, Second
Roman Pontifical, and consecration of
virgins 21, 23
Romanism
and English Catholicism 291, 293–4,
297–300, 304–7, 315, 318
see also Ultramontanism
Romano-German Pontifical, and
consecration of virgins 21, 23
Romanticism
Catholic 297–301, 303, 306, 314, 338
literary 301, 333
and Open Brethren worship 285, 287
and the Oxford Movement 314
rood screens, and English medievalism
299, 306–7, 310–11
Rordorf, Willy 8
Rose, Hugh 349
Ross, Alexander (Non-juring bishop) 244
Rotherham, Thomas, Archbishop of
York 105

Rouen, Council (1214) 94
Routley, Erik 444
Royal Commission on the Church of
England and the Other Religious
Bodies in Wales and Monmouth
(1910) 408, 414–15
Royal Commission on Ecclesiastical
Discipline (1906) 325–6, 448–9
Royal Injunctions
1547 185, 186
1559 186, 190–2
Ruanda Mission, and revivalism 419–20,
422, 426, 428
rubricism, of Tridentine liturgy 201
Rudolf of Bourges 38, 60, 63 n.109
Rule of St Benedict 63 n.109, 78, 84, 337
Rupp, Gordon 155, 158, 171

Sabean, David 204
sacrament
in Congregationalism 434–5, 437–40,
444–6
in East African Revival 429–30
matter and form 172 n.1
in Voysey 379–81, 383
see also baptism; eucharist; Lord's
Supper; mass
sacramentaries
Frankish Gelasian 47, 49
in rural parishes 43–4, 46–50
see also Ambrosian Sacramentary;
Gelasian Sacramentary; Gregorian
Sacramentary
Sacramentarium Fuldense 58 n.92
'sacramentary of Bergamo' 48 n.62
Sacramentary of Gallone 40 n.40
Sacramentary of Sarapion 12, 487
Sacred Congregation of Rites and
Ceremonies 213–14, 216–17, 219,
479
Sacred Heart of Jesus, devotion to 291
sacrifice
eucharist as 15–16, 162, 177, 312
and priestly office 175, 177, 181, 183
and redemption 426
St Albans Abbey, breviary (MS Royal 2
A.x) 87–8

St Bartholomew the Great, Smithfield *see* London, St Bartholomew Smithfield

St Paul's Cathedral *see* London, St Paul's Cathedral

saints

cult 64, 152, 160, 164

and local devotions 213–18, 219–23, 226

and Roman calendar 82–3, 87–8, 207–9, 211, 215

in Tridentine liturgies 202, 205–8, 210–14, 217–18

'Sample Week', in medieval divine office xxiii, 78–88

Sanctorale 82–3, 87

Sanctus, in eucharist 6, 159, 162–3, 250–1, 379

Sande, A. van de 334 n.2

Sandeman, Robert 266

Sandon, Dudley Ryder, Viscount 390

Sandwith, William, Rector of St Bartholomew Smithfield 325, 329–31

Sandys, Edwin, Bishop of London 193, 196

Sarapion of Thmuis, *Euchologion* 12, 487

Sarum rite 79, 84

and Anglicanism 314, 316

and Cranmer 153, 163

and Rock 311, 312, 314

Savage, Rector of St Bartholomew Smithfield 331–2

Savage, Thomas, Archbishop of York 106–7

Savory, Sir Borradaile, Rector of St Bartholomew Smithfield 321, 324–30, 331, 332

Savoy Declaration 438

Schmid, J. 217 n.43

Scotch Baptists 265, 271, 277–8 n.17, 278–9

Scoto-Catholics 397

Scott, Guy H. Guillum 468

Scott, Sir Gilbert 322

Scottish Church Society 397

Scottish Prayer Book

1637 255, 256, 257–8

1929 259–60

Scottish Psalter 232

Scribner, R. W. 164, 204, 205

Scripture, and worship xxi, xxii

scrutinies, pre-baptismal 57–9, 482–3, 488, 489, 492–4

Second Book of Discipline 179

secrecy, and the canon of the mass 52–3, 76, 157

sectarianism, and Open Brethren 280–1

Selbie, W. B. 432–3, 439, 440, 454

Selborne, William Waldegrave Palmer, 2nd Earl of 469–70, 473

Sell, A. P. F. 436

Selwyn, Edward Gordon, Dean of Winchester 465–6, 468–77

Sens diocese, and rural church 34

sermon *see* preaching

Sewell, Samuel 230

Sheils, W. J. xxiii, 104–15

Short, John 443

Shrewsbury, John Talbot, 16th Earl of 295, 298–9, 301, 303–5, 307, 309–10, 318

Sidgwick, Henry 360

Siena diocese, and rural churches 33–4

sign of the cross

and continuity with the early Church 293, 313

and ritualism 326, 384, 387, 393

Sigonio, Carlo 218–19 n.48

silence

in adult catechumenate 483

in Open Brethren worship 277, 284

Simon, Sir John 459, 460

simplicity, and apostolic worship 283, 285, 340

Simpson, Carnegie 456

Simpson, Hubert 440

Sinclair, William, Archdeacon of London 330

Siricius, Pope, and consecration of virgins 21

Sirleto, Guglielmo 217–18

Slesser, Sir Henry 459

Smith, A. Stanley 422

Smith, Pearsall 287
Smith, Sydney 366
Society of Friends *see* Quakers
song, and liturgy 89
Song of Songs
  and consecration of virgins 18–22
  in *Liber responsalis* 22–3, 24–8
  old Latin version 22, 24–5 n.7
source criticism, and liturgy 154
Sparrow Simpson, W. 451
Spencer, George Ignatius 299, 303, 305
Spens, Will 465
Spinckes, Nathaniel 242
Spinks, Bryan D. xxii, 151–71, 347
Sprott, G. W. 407
Spurr, F. C. 442
Stainer, Sir John (organist of St Paul's)
  368–9, 412
Stanley, Arthur P. , Dean of St Paul's 352,
  354, 374
Steetley (Derbys.), church chancel 71–2
Stephen II, Pope 339
Stephen, Leslie 383
Sternhold, Thomas, *Whole Book of Psalmes*
  230–2
Stewart, Alexander 284
Stewart, Isaiah 285–6
Stewart, Robert 405
Stopani, R. 39–40 n.37
Strasbourg Papyrus 7–8, 12 n.32, 16
Street, G. E. 322
Strype, John 187, 191, 194, 195
Stuart, C. E. 429
subdeacon
  and Feast of Fools 93
  and *traditio instrumentorum* 174
Surgant, Johann Ulrich, *Manuale*
  curatorum 133–4, 135
Swan, David 400
Sweden, and traditional piety 164
Switzerland, and Reformation in Zurich
  128–50
Sykes, Stephen 356 n.39
Sylvester, Matthew 233
symbols
  and eucharist 29, 152
  and initiation 491–2

in Presbyterian churches 398, 400–1,
  404, 405–6

Tabernacle Connexion 261–73
Taft, Robert 154
Taio of Saragossa, *Liber sententiarum* 81,
  86
Tait, A. C. 374
Talbot, E. S., Bishop 452
Talbot, John *see* Shrewsbury, John Talbot,
  16th Earl of
Talley, Thomas 6, 7
Tate, Nahum, *New Version of the Psalms of*
  David 232
Tauler, Johann 156
Taylor, A. J. P. 447
Taylor, H. M. & J. 67, 70
Taylor, Isaac 355
Taylor, Jeremy, and Anglican liturgy
  151–2
Tellini, Gianfranco 256
Temple, Frederick, Bishop of London
  and Archbishop of Canterbury 366,
  371–2, 448
Temple, William, Bishop of Manchester
  459
Temporale 83, 87, 88
Ten Commandments
  in Cranmer's liturgy 163, 167
  Reformed version 126, 147
Tertullian, *De baptismo* 487
Thacker, Alan 33
Theatine Order 210
Theistic Church, of Voysey 377–8
Theodore, Penitential 56 n.87
Theodore of Canterbury 316, 318
Theodulf of Orleans
  capitulare 36–7, 53, 63 n.109
  Gloria laus et honor tibi sit 55
  and pre-baptismal scrutinies 58 n.92
Thetford (Norfolk), church chancel 67,
  76
Thiene, S. Gaetano da 210
Thirlwall, Connop 374, 415
Thirty-Nine Articles
  and Maurice xxiv, 348–9, 353–4
  and Voysey 375

Thomas of Chobham 93–4
Thompson, A. Hamilton 65–7, 77
Thomson, William, Archbishop of York 376
Throckmorton, Sir Robert 301–2
Tiraboschi, Girolamo 200, 224 n.63
Todd, James 444, 445
Toledo, Council (633) 176
Toleration Act of 1689 227, 229
Tourist's Church Guide 326, 387–8, 389, 391
Tractarianism
    and liturgical revival 314, 315–16
    and Prayer Book 349
    and ritualism 387, 388, 391–2
Tracts for the Times 349
traditio instrumentorum
    in England xxii, 172–84
    and episcopal consecration 176, 181–2
    and minor orders 173–4, 183
    and priestly ordination 175, 176–7
    in Scotland 179–80
tradition, and revelation 182
traditionalism, and Tridentine liturgy 201
transubstantiation
    and ordination 177
    and Port-Royal 29
    and real presence 448
    and Revised Prayer Book 458, 460
    and Rock 312, 316
    and Zwingli 132, 135
Trent, Council
    and extent of Catholic reformation 225–6
    and liturgical history 199–226
    and liturgical reform 205–10, 213, 340
    and local diversity 209, 213–19, 222–4
    and ordination 174, 182–3
    and rigidity 205
    and rubricism 201
    and united Protestant statement of faith 167
    and universalism 201, 203, 213, 217, 223–4
    see also Roman Catholicism

Trexler, Richard C. 98
Tridentine worship see Trent, Council
Trier diocese, and rural churches 31
tripudia 93–4
Turner, Garth xxiii–xxiv, 374–83

Ughelli, Ferdinando, Italia sacra 200, 223–4
Ultramontanism
    in England 291–2, 293–4, 300, 315, 318
    in France 334, 335
    see also Guéranger, Prosper
Unitarianism
    and Maurice 345, 357–8
    and Voysey 376, 383
United Reformed Church 446
Urban VIII, Pope 225
Usages, eucharistic 241–2, 244–5, 248, 250, 259
Usher, Brett xxiii, 185–98

Valier, Agostino, Bishop of Verona 218
Valla, Lorenzo, Annotationes 145
Van Mildert, William 314
Vatican Council, Second
    Constitution on the Liturgy 478
    Decree on Missionary Activity 478–9
Vaughan, William Gwynne 408–10, 416
velatio, and consecration of virgins 18–28
Vermigli, Peter Martyr 167
vernaculars
    and Carolingian reforms 34–5, 52, 59
    and Reformation 129, 146–50, 156, 159–60, 164–5
    and Roman Catholic liturgy 290
vespers
    in medieval liturgy 83–5, 87–8
    in Reformation liturgies 123, 126, 156, 158–9, 160, 161
vestments
    in Carolingian churches 45
    and Cranmer 162, 164, 168
    in Lincolnshire 385, 387, 388, 393
    and Luther 164, 168
    in medieval York Minster 105, 109, 113

and Müntzer 164
and Pugin 307, 310
and Rock 310, 312, 318
in St Bartholomew Smithfield 326
and Zwingli 137
'Vetus Gallica' 48
Veuillot, Louis 342–3
vicars choral
of St Paul's Cathedral, London 368
of York Minster 105, 106, 107–8,
111–13
Vincentius Hispanus, glosses on
Compilatio tertia 100, 103
Virgin Mary, devotion to 160
virginity
and office for virgin saints 22–3, 24–8
and Song of Songs 18–23
virgins, consecration 19–23
Visitatio sepulchri (liturgical drama) 100
Visitation of the Sick, in Cranmer's
liturgy 152, 164
visitations
diocesan 188–9, 192–4, 196, 329
and Henrician Reformation 105, 107,
108–10, 113–15
Royal 186–7
Voragine, Jacobus de, *Golden Legend*
108
Voysey, Charles xxiii–xxiv, 374–83
and baptism 380
and burial service 381
and Church of England 375–6, 378–9,
383
and confirmation 382
and hymns 381–2
Inaugural Discourse 376–7
and marriage 380–1
and ordination 382–3
Revised Prayer Book 378–83
and Theistic Church 377–8

Wager, William (Elizabethan reader) 190,
198
wakes, and Carolingian church 56
Walahfrid Strabo 38 n.30
Wales
and church and chapel 412

and nineteenth-century Anglicanism
408–18
and Nonconformity 416
Walker, J. H. 400, 404
Walker, John 276
Wallace, Robert 401
Walpole, Horace, *Castle of Otranto* 301
Walsh, Stephen 459
Walsh, Thomas, Vicar Apostolic of the
Midlands 298
Walsh, Walter 317
Wandel, Lee Palmer 141–2
Ward, W. G. 315, 354
Warren, Max 419
water, in eucharistic cup 14–15, 244,
245–7, 253–4, 313
Watts, Enoch 238–9
Watts, Isaac 227–8, 441
Hymns and Spiritual Songs 238–9
The Psalms of David 231–2, 234
Webb, Aston 322, 323, 325, 331–2
Webb, E. A. 322, 323 n.7, 332
Welsh language
and Church in Wales 412, 413–18
and Nonconformity 415–16
Wesley, John 320, 438
West Francia
and monastic churches 35–6
and rural churches 38
West, Frederick 4
West, John Rowland 393
West, Thomas (Elizabethan reader) 192
n.3
Westminster Abbey, chancel 73
Westminster Confession 267, 401, 404
Whale, John S. 434, 436, 438–9, 441,
443–4
Wharram Percy (E. Yorks.), church
chancel 67, 70
Whitehouse, Alec 443
Whitelock, Dorothy 62
Widdrington, Percy 347
Wied, Hermann von, Archbishop of
Cologne 160, 166, 168
Wigley, Thomas 433
Wilberforce, Samuel, Bishop of Oxford
349, 362

Wilcox, Thomas 198
Wild, Emma M. xxii, 419–31
Wilfrid of Hexham, St 313, 318
Wilks, Michael xi
William de Seignelay 94
Williams, A. P. T. 471
Williams, Isaac 364
Willigis of Mainz 39
Winchester Cathedral, and reserved
    sacrament xxiii, 465–77
windows (church), east 74–5, 77
Wiseman, Cardinal Nicholas, and
    English Romanism 294, 298–9, 303,
    306–7, 318
The Witness (Brethren magazine) 279, 281
Wittenbach, Thomas 145
Wittenberg Concord 118
Wittering (Northants.), church chancel
    65, 66
women
    and access to eucharist 63
    in Open Brethren worship 284
Woods, Theodore, Bishop of Winchester
    465–8, 473
worship, as historical xxi–xxii, xxiii–xiv
    see also liturgy; sacrament
Wotherspoon, Henry J. 397
Wright, Roger 52
Wulfstan of Winchester, Life of St
    Æthelwold 62–3
Wulfstan of York 34
Wulstan Portiforium 80, 82–5, 86, 87
Wulstan of Worcester, and daily office
    80, 82, 85 n.16
Wykes, David L. xxiii, 227–39

Yarnold, Edward xxii, 85 n.16, 478–94
Yates, Nigel 314, 316, 317, 448 n.4
York, St William's College 106, 107–8,
    112, 113
York diocese, and rural churches 34

York Minster
    inventories 105, 109–10, 113–14
    and lay access to liturgy 62
    medieval liturgy 42–3, 79
    sixteenth-century minor altars xxiii,
        104–15
Young, David 358
Young, Thomas, Archbishop of York 188

Zeno of Verona 493
Zurich
    and confession 124, 133
    Council 132, 134, 144
    and frequency of communion 143–4
    and iconoclasm 128
    and liturgical reform xxii, 128–50
    and preaching 131, 133–4
    and Ten Commandments 126, 147
    and Zwingli 129–34, 137–8, 141,
        143–4, 145
Zwingli, Huldrych
    An Apology for the Canon of the Mass
        133
    and the clergy 140, 142–3, 148
    De canone missae epichiresis 132
    De vera et falsa religione 135
    death 129–30, 144
    and the laity 135
    and liturgical reform xxii, 128–50
    and preaching 132–4, 136–8, 143
    and recollection 131
    and sacraments 117, 120, 131–43, 150,
        167, 286, 438
Zwingliana 130
Zwinglianism
    and Book of Common Prayer 242
    in Germany 117–18, 120–1
    in Switzerland 129–31

Compiled by Meg Davies (Registered Indexer,
Society of Indexers)